# THE ROUGH GUIDE TO
# BOLIVIA

D1343051

C016563202

ROUGH
GUIDES

This fifth edition
Daniel Jaco

# Contents

OPPOSITE DANCER, FIESTA DE LA VIRGEN DE LA CANDELARIA, COPACABANA **PREVIOUS PAGE** IGLESIA DE LA MERCED, POTOSÍ

# Introduction to
# Bolivia

With soaring Andean peaks and dense Amazonian rainforests, otherworldly salt flats and lush savanna, Bolivia is home to an extraordinarily diverse range of landscapes. The country offers scores of breathtaking attractions, including vast inland lakes, beautifully preserved colonial towns, towering volcanoes, blisteringly hot deserts, mysterious ruins and wildlife-rich national parks, yet it remains remarkably little explored. Landlocked in the remote heart of the continent, Bolivia is too often overlooked, but those who do venture here often find it to be one of South America's most captivating destinations.

The country's cultural diversity and ethnic make-up are as varied as its landscapes. Three centuries of colonial rule have left their mark on the nation's language, religion and architecture, but this is little more than a veneer overlaying **indigenous cultural traditions** that stretch back long before the arrival of the Spanish (and, indeed, the Incas). Though superficially Catholic, many Bolivians are equally at home making offerings to Pachamama (Mother Earth), dancing with the devil at Carnaval or blessing cars with libations of alcohol. While Spanish is the language of government and business, the streets buzz with the cadences of Aymara, Quechua and scores of other **indigenous languages**. Bolivia is dominated by the **Andes**, which march through the west of the country in two parallel chains; between them stretch the barren, windswept expanses of the **Altiplano**. Reached via a series of lush valleys, the country's lowlands range from dense Amazonian rainforest to vast plains of dry thornbrush and scrub. These **geographical extremes** are fascinating to explore and support an extraordinary diversity of **flora and fauna**, from condors to pink freshwater dolphins, hummingbirds to anacondas – Parque Nacional Madidi, for example, has over 860 species of bird, more than the US and Canada combined.

While it spans an area the size of France and Spain combined, Bolivia is home to only around eleven million people, who are concentrated in a handful of cities founded by the **Spanish**. Some of these, most notably Potosí and Sucre, were once among the most important settlements in the Americas (and, in the case of the former, the world), but are

**ABOVE** SALAR DE UYUNI **RIGHT** QUINOA FIELD, SAN JUAN

now half-forgotten, lingering in the memory of past glories and graced by some of the continent's finest colonial architecture. Others, like La Paz and neighbouring El Alto, Cochabamba and particularly Santa Cruz, have grown enormously in recent years, and are now bustling **commercial centres**. The economy is driven by agribusiness and huge oil, gas and mineral reserves, which provide both opportunities for development and serious environmental challenges, particularly for the country's vast **wilderness areas**, which have hitherto survived in near-pristine condition.

Despite its many attractions, and associations with the likes of Che Guevara (who was killed in La Higuera in 1967) and Butch Cassidy and the Sundance Kid, Bolivia remains one of South America's least visited countries. Some blame Queen Victoria, who after a diplomatic spat is reputed to have crossed the country off the map, declaring, "Bolivia does not exist". Among those who have heard a little about Bolivia, meanwhile, **cocaine trafficking** and **political turbulence** remain the dominant images. Although there is some truth in these clichés, travellers will find that the country – one of the **safest** and **least expensive** in South America – has so much more to offer. And as much of the country is still well off the tourist trail, travelling in Bolivia gives you a real sense of breaking new ground.

# Where to go

Most visitors spend a few days in the fascinating city of **La Paz**, Bolivia's de facto capital, which combines a dramatic high-altitude setting with a compelling blend of traditional indigenous and modern urban cultures. La Paz is also close to magical **Lake Titicaca**,

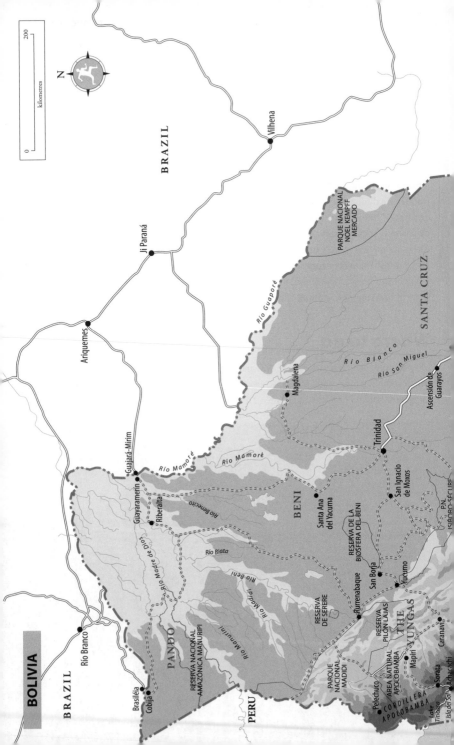

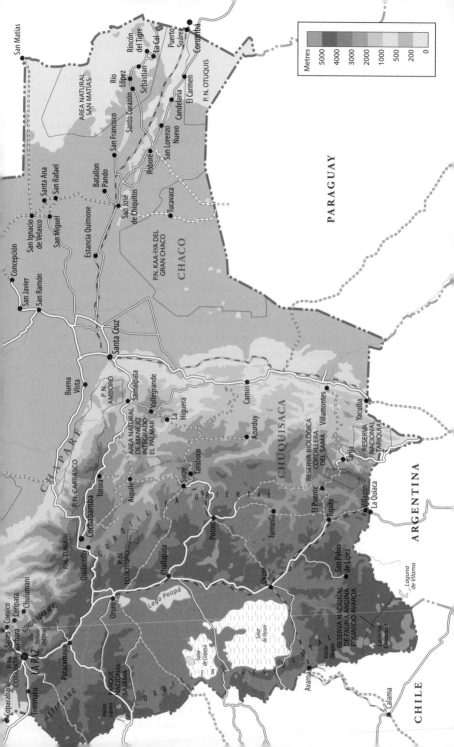

the massive azure lake that straddles the Peruvian border, and is a good base for exploring the magnificent **Cordillera Real**.

Just north of La Paz the Andes plunge into the Amazon basin through the lush valleys of the **Yungas**. The Yungas towns of **Coroico** and **Chulumani** are perfect places to relax, while Coroico also makes a good spot to break the overland journey from La Paz to the Bolivian **Amazon**. The best base for visiting the Amazon is **Rurrenabaque**, close to the near-pristine rainforests of **Parque Nacional Madidi** and the wildlife-rich **Río Yacuma**. More adventurous travellers can head east across the wild savannas of the Llanos de Moxos via the **Reserva de la Bíosfera del Beni** to the regional capital **Trinidad**, the start of exciting trips north along the Río Mamoré towards Brazil or south towards Cochabamba.

South of La Paz, the bleak **southern Altiplano** – stretching between the eastern and western chains of the Andes – is home to some of Bolivia's foremost attractions. The dour mining city of **Oruro** springs to life during its Carnaval, one of South America's most enjoyable fiestas, and the legendary silver-mining city of **Potosí** offers a treasure-trove of colonial architecture and the opportunity to visit the Cerro Rico mines.

Further south, Uyuni is the jumping-off point for expeditions into the astonishing landscapes of the **Salar de Uyuni** and the **Reserva de Fauna Andina Eduardo Avaroa**, a remote region of high-altitude deserts and half-frozen, mineral-stained lakes, populated by flamingos. Further south lie the cactus-strewn badlands and canyons around **Tupiza** and the isolated but welcoming city of **Tarija**.

To the north of Potosí, Bolivia's official capital, **Sucre**, boasts fine colonial architecture, but the city is very different in character: charming and refined, it is set in a warm Andean valley in the midst of a region noted for its textiles. Further north, the modern city of **Cochabamba** has less obvious appeal, but offers a spring-like climate and a friendly welcome. Not far from here are the rainforests and coca fields of the **Chapare region**, but for most travellers Cochabamba is just somewhere to break the journey between La Paz and **Santa Cruz**, the country's eastern capital and a brash, modern and lively tropical metropolis. Beyond a lively nightlife scene, the city has few attractions itself, but is a good base for exploring the **eastern lowlands**, including the rainforests of **Parque Nacional Amboró** and the idyllic town of **Samaipata**. Scattered across the lowlands east of Santa Cruz, the immaculately restored **Jesuit missions of Chiquitos** provide one of Bolivia's most unusual attractions, while a train line heads east to the Brazilian border and the wildlife-rich wetlands of the **Pantanal**.

**FACT FILE**

• Named after Simón Bolívar, Bolivia won its **independence** in 1825, after nearly three centuries as a Spanish colony.

• The country's **population** is around eleven million.

• Bolivia has 36 official **languages**, though only three – Spanish, Quechua and Aymara – are still widely spoken.

• In 2001 the **highest football match** in the world was played on the top of the 6542m Sajama volcano.

• Since independence, Bolivia has lost almost half its territory, including its Pacific coast, which was captured by Chile in 1879. Despite being **landlocked**, the country still has a navy.

# When to go

Generally speaking, climate varies much more as a result of altitude and topography than it does between different seasons. Nevertheless, there are clear-cut seasonal differences. **Winter** (*invierno*) runs between May and October: this is the **dry season**, and in many ways the best time to visit, though it's also the high season for tourism, so some prices will be higher and attractions busier. In the **highlands** it's noticeably colder at night, particularly in June and July. The days are slightly shorter, but usually sunny, and the skies crystal clear, making this the best time of year for trekking and climbing. Winter is also the best time for visiting the hot and humid **lowlands**, when temperatures are generally slightly (but pleasantly) lower, although the dry season is less pronounced and rain remains a possibility all year round. A few times a year, usually between July and August, the country is swept by **cold fronts** coming up from Patagonia, known as *surazos*, which can send temperatures plunging even in the Amazon. Towards the end of the dry season in late August and September, farmers set fire to cleared forest areas across much of Bolivia, which can obscure views and cause respiratory problems.

**Summer** (*verano*) is the **rainy season**, which runs roughly from November to March and is much more pronounced in the lowlands; in the Amazon, road transport becomes pretty much impossible, as huge areas are flooded and everything turns to mud – though, conversely, river transport becomes more frequent. Heat, humidity and mosquitoes are also much worse. In the highlands, particularly the Altiplano, it rains much less and travel is not as restricted, though delays and road closures still occur, while trekking trails get muddier and clouds often obscure views, particularly in the high mountains, where route-finding can become impossible. Despite this, the rainy season is also a very beautiful time in the Andes, as the parched Altiplano and mountainsides are briefly transformed into lush grassland and wild flowers proliferate.

## AVERAGE MONTHLY TEMPERATURES AND RAINFALL

|  | Jan | Feb | Mar | Apr | May | Jun | Jul | Aug | Sep | Oct | Nov | Dec |
|---|---|---|---|---|---|---|---|---|---|---|---|---|
| **LA PAZ** | | | | | | | | | | | | |
| Max (°C/°F) | 17/63 | 17/63 | 18/64 | 18/64 | 18/64 | 17/63 | 17/63 | 17/63 | 18/64 | 19/66 | 19/66 | 18/64 |
| Min (°C/°F) | 6/43 | 6/43 | 6/43 | 4/39 | 3/37 | 1/34 | 1/34 | 2/36 | 3/37 | 4/39 | 6/43 | 6/43 |
| Rainfall (mm) | 114 | 107 | 66 | 33 | 13 | 8 | 10 | 13 | 28 | 41 | 48 | 94 |
| **SANTA CRUZ** | | | | | | | | | | | | |
| Max (°C/°F) | 34/93 | 25/77 | 28/82 | 33/91 | 30/86 | 31/88 | 19/66 | 32/90 | 31/88 | 27/81 | 27/81 | 28/82 |
| Min (°C/°F) | 24/75 | 23/73 | 25/77 | 24/75 | 19/66 | 23/73 | 16/61 | 20/68 | 23/73 | 20/68 | 17/63 | 23/73 |
| Rainfall (mm) | 282 | 180 | 89 | 78 | 136 | 1 | 16 | 16 | 1 | 65 | 296 | 203 |
| **SUCRE** | | | | | | | | | | | | |
| Max (°C/°F) | 18/64 | 22/72 | 19/66 | 19/66 | 20/68 | 17/63 | 20/68 | 25/77 | 25/77 | 23/73 | 23/73 | 14/57 |
| Min (°C/°F) | 11/52 | 12/45 | 8/46 | 8/46 | 5/41 | 5/41 | 3/37 | 4/39 | 7/45 | 10/50 | 7/45 | 11/52 |
| Rainfall (mm) | 238 | 91 | 86 | 32 | 0 | 0 | 0 | 5 | 8 | 68 | 34 | 175 |

# Author picks

Rough Guides' authors covered every corner of Bolivia to research this new edition, from the enchanting Isla del Sol to the awesome expanses of the Salar de Uyuni. Beyond the major sights, here are their personal picks.

**Sacred drink of the Incas** No visit to Bolivia is complete without a glass or two of thick, tart and mildly alcoholic *chicha* – the Cochabamba Valley (p.218) is particularly famous for it.

**Most extreme experience** Once a source of fabled wealth, the Cerro Rico mines (p.162) now offer a chance to see first hand the almost medieval working conditions that miners still endure.

**Most spectacular flight** The scenic La Paz–Rurrenabaque route (p.276) whisks you from snowcapped mountains to the verdant Amazon.

**Eye-popping architecture** El Alto (p.70) is home to one of South America's most distinctive architectural movements. The "Neo-Andean" style is most evident in the city's many *cholets*, gaudy mansions that look like they've come from another planet.

**Dinosaur stampede** A cement works on the outskirts of Sucre is the unlikely home for the world's largest collection – some five thousand strong – of dinosaur footprints (p.201).

**Killer views** The vistas of La Paz that open up as you crest the rim of the Altiplano and begin to descend into the city will take your breath away (p.52).

**Best culinary experience** Opened by the co-founder of Denmark's multi-award-winning *Noma*, *Gustu* in La Paz (p.84) transposes the Nordic seasonal and sustainable philosophy onto Bolivia, with delicious results.

> Our author recommendations don't end here. We've flagged up our favourite places – a perfectly sited hotel, an atmospheric café, a special restaurant – throughout the Guide, highlighted with the ★ symbol.

**FROM TOP** *CHICHA; CHOLET, EL ALTO*

# 18

# things not to miss

It's not possible to see everything that Bolivia has to offer in one trip – and we don't suggest you try. What follows, in no particular order, is a selective taste of the country's highlights: outstanding scenery, lively festivals, ancient sites and colonial architecture. All highlights are colour-coded by chapter and have a page reference to take you straight into the Guide, where you can find out more.

1

### 1 PARQUE NACIONAL MADIDI
Page 274
Covering nearly nineteen thousand square kilometres, this park is home to some of the most diverse plant and animal life in South America.

### 2 SALAR DE UYUNI
Page 169
A vast, perfectly flat expanse of dazzling white surrounded by high mountain peaks, the Salar de Uyuni is the world's biggest salt lake and, perhaps, Bolivia's most extraordinary attraction.

### 3 TIWANAKU
Page 90
One of the cradles of Andean civilization, and once the centre of a massive empire, Tiwanaku is among South America's most intriguing archeological sites.

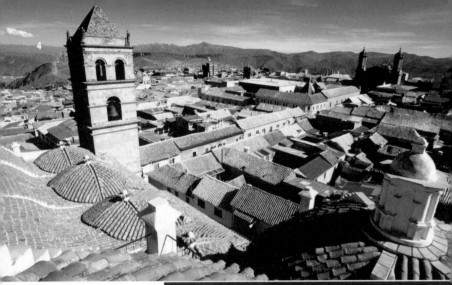

### 4 POTOSÍ

The highest city in the world, the legendary silver-mining centre of Potosí boasts some of the finest Spanish colonial architecture on the continent.

### 5 PINK RIVER DOLPHINS

Frolicking pink freshwater dolphins are a fairly common sight in the rivers of the Bolivian Amazon. You can even swim alongside them.

### 6 FOLK MUSIC AND DANCE

Far more than just panpipes, Bolivian folk music and dance is as vibrant and varied as the country itself.

### 7 ORURO CARNAVAL

One of South America's most colourful fiestas, during which thousands of costumed dancers parade through the streets and revellers indulge in heavy drinking and indiscriminate water fighting.

### 8 LA PAZ

Nestled in a deep canyon at an altitude of over 3500m, Bolivia's de facto capital is the highest in the world, and a fascinating melting pot of modern urban and traditional Aymara cultures.

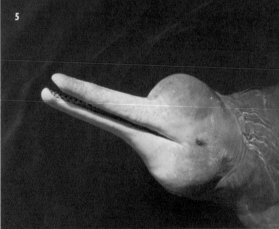

### 14 ANDEAN TEXTILES
Page 87

The traditional weavings of indigenous highland communities are among the finest expressions of Andean culture.

### 15 THE JESUIT MISSIONS OF CHIQUITOS
Page 251

The Jesuit mission churches offer a splash of incongruous splendour and historical intrigue in the wilderness.

### 16 ISLA DEL SOL
Page 109

Isla del Sol is the spiritual centre of the Andean world, revered as the place where the sun and moon were created.

### 17 SUCRE
Page 190

Known as the White City, Bolivia's capital is a jewel of colonial architecture and a lively university city that combines serene dignity with a provincial charm.

### 18 MOUNTAIN CLIMBING
Page 35

With six peaks over 6000m Bolivia is a paradise for experienced mountaineers. Novices can arrange a guided climb up 6090m Huayna Potosí.

# Itineraries

The following itineraries feature a mix of popular and off-the-beaten-path attractions, taking you right across the country, from Inca trails through Andean scenery to boat trips down wildlife-rich Amazonian waterways. Given the distances involved, you may not be able to complete the full lists. But even doing a partial itinerary – or mixing and matching elements from different ones – will give you a wonderful insight into Bolivia's stunning diversity.

## THE GRAND TOUR

This four- to five-week trip takes in dramatic Andean landscapes, colonial cities and former Jesuit missions, colourful fiestas, ancient sites and Amazonian rainforests.

**❶ La Paz** The world's highest de facto capital city is also one of its most compelling, a riot of indigenous colour, vertiginous markets and street protests. **See p.52**

**❷ Tiwanaku** Though a mere fraction of this iconic pre-Columbian, pre-Inca city has been excavated, its mysterious, monumental slabs of sandstone are a must-see. **See p.90**

**❸ Lake Titicaca** A vast, striking blue expanse standing at 3810m, the lake is dotted with sacred islands and surrounded by snowcapped mountains. **See p.100**

**❹ Salar de Uyuni and the Reserva de Fauna Andina Eduardo Avaroa** Best visited together, the world's largest salt lake and this stunning high-altitude reserve have a desolate, otherworldly beauty. **See p.168 & p.172**

**❺ Potosí** The highest city on earth has a tragic history, stunningly preserved colonial architecture and a legendary silver mine. **See p.150**

**❻ Sucre** Bolivia's most appealing city has a welcoming atmosphere, elegant whitewashed buildings, leafy plazas, and a year-round spring-like climate. **See p.190**

**❼ The Jesuit missions of Chiquitos** These Jesuit-founded towns in remote eastern Bolivia boast a series of stunning churches and a fascinating history. **See p.251**

**❽ Rurrenabaque and the Amazon** Perfectly sited on the Río Beni, buzzing Rurrenabaque has the biodiverse wonders of the Amazon on its doorstep. **See p.272**

## NATURE AND WILDLIFE

For travellers who want to explore the country's stunning natural diversity, this three-and-a-half-week tour takes in the country's key national parks and protected areas.

**❶ Yungas, Cordillera Real and Cordillera Apolobamba** This Andean region is home to several excellent treks along pre-Columbian trails. **See p.125, p.120 & p.116**

**❷ Salar de Uyuni and Reserva de Fauna Andina Eduardo Avaroa** Blindingly white lakes of salt, volcanic peaks and colonies of flamingos are just a few of the attractions at these two protected areas. **See p.168 & p.172**

**❸ Cordillera de Chichas** A stark landscape of cactus-strewn badlands and canyons, evocative of the Wild West. **See p.177**

**❹ Parque Nacional Amboró** This park is home to over 830 different species of bird – the highest number of any protected area in the world – including the cock-of-the-rock. **See p.240**

**⑤ Parque Nacional Madidi** Perhaps Bolivia's most famous national park, Madidi is readily accessible and amazingly biodiverse –the flora and fauna includes pink river dolphins. **See p.274**

## INDIGENOUS CULTURE AND SPANISH COLONIALISM

This two-week tour allows you to explore Bolivia's cultural, artistic and musical diversity, as well as its distinct Spanish colonial heritage.

**❶ Mercado de Hechicería, La Paz** The outlandish Witches' Market offers a fascinating window onto the arcane world of Aymara folk medicine, with a bizarre array of wares. **See p.66**

**❷ Peña** A late-night showcase for traditional Andean music, performed on instruments such as charango, zampoña and quena, *peñas* have long been a La Paz institution. **See p.85**

**❸ El Alto** Perched above La Paz, and growing at a prodigious rate, the "Aymara capital of the world" features colourful markets and striking architecture. **See p.70**

**❹ Tiwanaku** The ancient ruins of Tiwanaku offer a tantalizing insight into the mysterious civilization that once had its centre in today's Aymara heartlands. **See p.90**

**❺ Isla del Sol and Isla de la Luna, Lake Titicaca** These sacred islands, considered the birthplace of the sun and the moon, were once among the most important religious sites in the Andean world. **See p.109 & p.115**

**❻ Casa Real de la Moneda, Potosí** The country's former royal mint, now its finest museum, has an outstanding collection of colonial religious art. **See p.154**

**❼ Sucre** An evocative cluster of churches, monasteries and mansions, as well as a fascinating museum showcasing indigenous textiles. **See p.190**

**❽ San Ignacio de Moxos** This Amazonian former mission town has as rich a musical heritage as it does a religious one, with an archive of antique scores and a thriving Baroque music school. **See p.282**

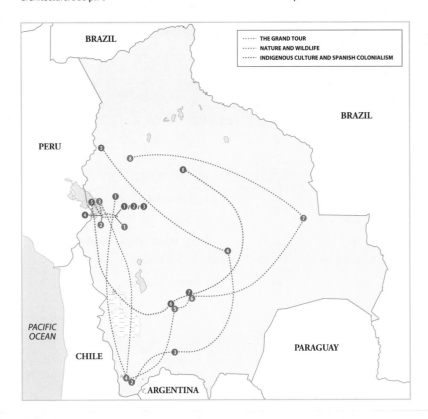

BUS HEADING TOWARDS SORATA

# Basics

# Getting there

There are relatively few flights to Bolivia. At present, the only direct services to the country from outside Latin America are from Washington and Miami in the US, and Madrid in Spain. Failing that, you can fly via Latin American hubs such as Lima, Bogotá, Panama or Santiago. The main international airports in Bolivia are at La Paz and Santa Cruz. You can also travel into Bolivia overland from neighbouring countries.

Air fares to Bolivia are quite high, reflecting the lack of competition. Prices vary with the season, high season being from July to August and during Christmas and Easter; fares drop slightly in the shoulder seasons (May–June & Sept–Oct) and drop further during low season (Jan–April & Nov–late Dec).

## Flights from the US and Canada

From the US, there are direct flights from Miami daily with American Airlines (🌐 aa.com) to La Paz, and four times weekly with Bolivian airline Boliviana de Aviación (🌐 boa.bo) to Santa Cruz and Cochabamba. The Colombian airline Avianca currently has a direct daily flight from Washington DC to La Paz with a stop (but no change of plane) at Bogotá. From other parts of the US and Canada, you'll need to change places at Miami, Bogotá, Lima or Panama. Fares typically start at around US$550–580 from Miami to La Paz or Santa Cruz in low season, rising to US$580–920 in high season. From New York, expect to pay around US$650/US$850 in low/high season, about US$100 more than that from Los Angeles, and from Toronto around Can$1050/Can$1250.

## Flights from the UK and Ireland

There are no direct flights from the UK or Ireland to Bolivia. The most direct route from London to La Paz is **via Miami** with British Airways (🌐 britishairways.com) and American Airlines (🌐 aa.com), but the cheapest routes often involve two changes of plane – typically at Madrid and Lima. Another option is with Air Europa (🌐 aireuropa.com), which offers connections from various British airports via Madrid to Santa Cruz. Fares from Britain to Bolivia start at around £650 in low season, rising to over £1000 in high season. From Ireland expect to pay upwards of €800/€1280 in low/high season.

## Flights from Australia, New Zealand and South Africa

The fastest way to reach Bolivia **from Australia** is with Aerolineas Argentinas (🌐 aerolineas.com) from Sydney or Melbourne to Santa Cruz via Buenos Aires (La Paz is not currently available on this route, unless you fly on to it from Santa Cruz). Longer but usually cheaper routes include Qantas (🌐 qantas.com) in combination with LATAM (🌐 latam.com) via Santiago (this may also involve a change at Lima), Qantas in combination with Avianca via Santiago and Bogotá, or American Airlines (🌐 aa.com) via California (LA or San Francisco) and Miami. Prices start at around Aus$3100 in low season, rising to around Aus$3550 in high season.

**From New Zealand**, your most direct routes are with LATAM to La Paz via Santiago or with Aerolineas Argentinas to Santa Cruz via Buenos Aires. Longer but potentially cheaper routings include Qantas and LATAM via Sydney and Santiago, or American Airlines via Los Angeles and Miami. Tickets start at around NZ$2200 year-round.

The obvious way to Bolivia **from South Africa** is via São Paulo, either with LATAM, or with a combination of SAA (🌐 flysaa.com) with the Bolivian airline Boliviana de Aviación (🌐 boa.bo). Prices start at around ZAR13,507 in low season, ZAR17,200 in high season.

# Travelling overland from neighbouring countries

You can enter Bolivia **by land** on regular bus or train services from all five of the countries with which it shares a border – **Peru**, **Brazil**, **Chile**, **Argentina** and **Paraguay** – so it is easy to include in a wider South American trip.

## Crossing the Peruvian border

The most widely used route – and the easiest – is from **Puno** in Peru on the west shore of Lake Titicaca, via the **Kasani** border crossing near Copacabana, or **Desaguadero**, south of the lake (see p.106); both crossings are an easy bus ride (around 4hr) away from La Paz. One easy way to travel between Peru and Bolivia is with Peru Hop and Bolivia Hop (@boliviahop.com), a hop-on hop-off bus service covering several cities in Peru and also Copacabana and La Paz, with a range of tickets available depending on what route you want to take.

## Crossing the Brazilian border

From Brazil, the main entrance point is at **Quijarro** (see p.263), in the far east of Bolivia close to the Brazilian city of **Corumbá**, which is the main base for visiting the Pantanal region and also well connected to the rest of the country. From Quijarro you can travel to **Santa Cruz** by train (see p.263). There's another minor land crossing from Brazil in the far east of Bolivia at **San Matías**, a day's bus journey from the town of San Ignacio in Chiquitania (see p.251). You can also enter Bolivia from Brazil at several points along the northern border in Amazonia, most notably from **Brasiléia to Cobija** (see p.298) and **Guajará-Mirim to Guayaramerín** (see p.295).

## Crossing the Chilean border

From Chile there are three main routes, all of them passing through spectacular Andean scenery. You can travel to La Paz by bus from Arica on the Pacific Coast via the border crossing of **Tambo Quemado** (see p.142); take the train from **Calama** in Chile to **Uyuni** via Avaroa (see p.167); or cross the border at **Laguna Verde** in the far south of the Reserva Eduardo Avaroa on a jeep tour organized from the Chilean town of **San Pedro de Atacama**, a route which will bring you to Uyuni (see p.167).

## Crossing the Argentine border

From Argentina there are two straightforward crossings: from **La Quiaca** in Argentina to Villazón in the southern Altiplano (see p.177), from where there are road and rail connections north to Tupiza, Uyuni and Oruro; and from **Pocitos** in Argentina to Yacuiba in the Chaco (see p.265), from where you can travel by road and rail north to Santa Cruz or by road west to Tarija. There's also a minor crossing at **Bermejo**, south of Tarija (see p.182).

## Crossing the Paraguayan border

You can enter Bolivia on an arduous bus journey from Asunción in the south of Paraguay to Santa Cruz (roughly 1000km/26–28hr), but buses may not run in the rainy season (Nov–May) if the road is flooded.

## AGENTS AND OPERATORS

**Adventure Life** US ☎ 800 344 6118, UK ☎ 0808 134 9943, @ adventure-life.com. Independent firm offering tailor-made tours, or off-the-shelf packages including a seven-day "ancient cultures" tour (from US$1250) or a ten-day "Bolivia backroads" tour (from US$3095).

**Explore Bolivia** US ☎ 303 545 5278, @ explorebolivia.com. Bolivia specialists offering custom-made tours with an emphasis on activity and nature trips, and getting off the beaten track.

**HighLives** UK ☎ 020 8144 2629, @ highlives.co.uk. UK-based travel agency offering a range of Bolivia tours, including a thirteen-day trip (from £2995) that takes in La Paz, Potosí, the Salar de Uyuni and Lake Titicaca, and a seven-day "Gourmet Tour" (from £3000), which includes visits to vineyards, quinoa plantations and top restaurants.

**Journey Latin America** UK ☎ 020 8747 8315; @ journeylatinamerica.co.uk. Top UK Latin America specialists, offering flights and packages in Bolivia.

**North South Travel** UK ☎ 01245 608291, @ northsouthtravel .co.uk. Friendly, competitive travel agency whose profits support projects in the developing world, especially the promotion of sustainable tourism.

**Soliman Travel** UK ☎ 020 7708 1516. Travel agent specializing in Latin America (largely for London's Latin American community).

**South America Ecotravel** US & Canada ☎ 1 888 553 0103, @ southamericaecotravel.com. North American sister company to America Tours (see p.76), allowing you to book their tours from the US or Canada.

**STA Travel** UK ☎ 0333 321 0099, @ statravel.co.uk; US ☎ 1 800 781 4040, @ statravel.com; Australia ☎ 134 782, @ statravel .com.au; New Zealand ☎ 0800 474400, @ statravel.co.nz; South Africa ☎ 0861 781781, @ statravel.co.za. Independent travel specialists, offering good discounts for students and under-26s.

**Trailfinders** UK ☎ 020 7368 1200, Ireland ☎ 01 677 7888, @ trailfinders.com. One of the best-informed and most efficient agents for independent travellers.

**Travel Cuts** Canada ☎ 1 800 667 2887, @ travelcuts.com. Canadian youth and student travel firm.

**TravelLocal** UK ☎ 0117 325 7898, @ travellocal.com. Reliable UK-based agency offers easy-to-book fixed-itinerary and tailor-made tours throughout Bolivia through local operators.

**USIT** Ireland ☎ 01 602 1906, @ usit.ie. Ireland's main student and youth travel specialists.

# Getting around

**Bolivia's topography, size and basic infra-structure means that getting around is often a challenge. Much of the road network is unpaved, and most main roads are in a poor condition; road safety records, needless to say, are pretty lamentable. However, travelling through the country's varied and stunning landscapes is also one of the most enjoyable aspects of a visit to Bolivia, and the pleasure of many places lies as much in the getting there as in the destination itself.**

Most Bolivians travel by **bus**, as these go pretty much everywhere and are extremely good value. When there are no buses, they often travel on **camiones** (lorries), which are slower, much less comfortable and only slightly cheaper, but often go to places no other transport reaches. The much-reduced **train** network covers only a small fraction of the country, but offers a generally more comfortable and sedate (though not necessarily faster or more reliable) service. In parts of the Amazon lowlands **river boats** are still the main means of getting around.

Though few Bolivians can afford it, **air travel** is a great way of saving a day or two of arduous cross-country travel, and most of the major cities are served by regular internal flights. The approximate journey times and frequencies of all services are given in each chapter, but these should be treated with a hefty pinch of salt: the idea of a fixed timetable would strike most Bolivians as rather ridiculous. Buying or renting a **car or motorbike** is a possibility, but given the state of the roads in many areas and the long distances between towns, it's an adventurous way to travel and doesn't guarantee you'll reach your destination any faster.

## By bus

Bolivia's **buses** (also known as *flotas*) are run by a variety of private companies and ply all the main routes in the country, moving passengers at low cost over great distances despite often appalling road conditions.

Cities and larger towns have **bus terminals** – known as *terminales terrestres* or *terminales de buses* – from which buses to most (but often not all) destinations leave. Departing passengers usually have to pay a few bolivianos for the use of the terminal.

The terminals often have some kind of **information office**, but even so the number of different companies operating the same route can make it difficult at times to work out departure times and frequencies. Taxi drivers usually have a good grasp of the timing of buses to different destinations and where they depart from. For less frequently used routes it's worth buying a **ticket** in advance, but there's no need on busier routes. Buses on many longer-distance routes travel only at night so Bolivian travellers can visit other cities without paying for accommodation.

The major long-distance intercity routes are served by more modern and comfortable buses, often equipped with reclining seats and TVs. Some routes are also served by comparatively luxurious overnight **sleeper-buses** (*bus-camas*), which have extra legroom and seats that recline horizontally. These cost about fifty percent more, but are well worth it.

Most buses, however, are much older and in poor condition. **Breakdowns** are frequent, but fortunately many drivers are masters of mechanical improvisation. Other than sleeper-buses and some smarter long-distance services, Bolivian buses stop anywhere for anyone, even if they're only travelling a few kilometres, until every available crack of space has been filled.

Because of the poor condition of most roads and many vehicles, you should always be prepared for major **delays, breakdowns and accidents**; in the rainy season, buses can arrive days rather than hours late. Most buses stop for regular meal breaks, and food and drink sellers offer their wares at the roadside at every opportunity, but it's worth carrying some food and drink with you. When travelling in the highlands or overnight, you should have **warm clothing** and a blanket or sleeping bag to hand, as it can get bitterly cold, and heated buses are virtually unheard of. If you can, avoid sitting at the back of the bus, as on bumpy roads this is where you'll get bounced around the most.

## By plane

**Flying** in Bolivia is a good way of avoiding exhausting overland journeys and saving time; it's also relatively inexpensive, with a La Paz–Santa Cruz flight costing around Bs550 (US$80). Many flights offer splendid bird's-eye views of the high Andes or the endless green expanse of the Amazon. **La Paz**, **Santa Cruz**, **Sucre** and **Cochabamba** are all connected by daily flights, and there are also frequent services to **Tarija**, **Trinidad** and a number of remote towns in the **Amazon** and the **Eastern Lowlands**.

There's an incredible degree of flux in the Bolivian airline sector, with new carriers frequently popping

## KEEP YOUR BAG SAFE

Unless it's small enough to keep with you inside the bus, your **luggage** will be put on the roof, at the back or in a locked compartment underneath the vehicle. This is generally fairly safe, but it's still worth keeping an eye out at each stop to make sure your bag isn't carried off, whether by accident or design.

With better-organized companies you may be given a **ticket** with which to reclaim your luggage at the end of the journey. Some travellers like to chain their bags to the roof, and you shouldn't be shy about climbing up to check yours if you're feeling nervous about its security. Even if it's under a tarpaulin on the roof or in a **luggage compartment**, it's a good idea to lock and cover your luggage with a **nylon sack** (which you can pick up in any market) to protect it from the elements and the prying fingers of other travellers.

up and old operators going out of business. The main carrier is currently the **state-owned Boliviana de Aviación** (Ⓦ boa.bo). Another operator, **Amazonas** (Ⓦ amaszonas.com), operates flights from La Paz and Santa Cruz to destinations across the country, including Uyuni, Sucre, Cochabamba and Rurrenabaque. The Bolivian air force also operates passenger services under its commercial arm, **Transportes Aereo Militar** (TAM; Ⓦ tam.bo). TAM is often somewhat cheaper than the other airlines, and flies to some out-of-the-way places not served by the others, as well as between most of the main cities.

Busier routes should be booked several days in advance and **reconfirmed** a couple of days before departure, as overbooking is not uncommon. Flights are often cancelled or delayed, and sometimes even leave earlier than scheduled, especially in the Amazon, where the weather can be a problem.

Some particularly remote regions, particularly in the Amazon region, are also served by **light aircraft**, such as five-seater Cessnas, which are an expensive but exciting way to travel.

It should be noted that **safety records** for Bolivian airlines are variable to say the least; The now-defunct airline Aerocon, for example, had fatal crashes in 2011 and 2013, and Bolivian charter airline LaMia crashed in Colombia in 2016, killing most of the squad of Brazil's Chapecoense football club.

## By taxi, moto-taxi, minibus and micro

**Taxis** can be found at any time in most towns and offer a cheap and generally safe way to get around. In Bolivia, anyone can turn their car into a taxi just by sticking a sign in the window, and many people in cities work as part-time taxi drivers to supplement their incomes. There are also **radio-taxis**, which are marked as such and can be called by phone; they tend to cost a little more and, in theory at least, are a safer way to travel.

**Fares** tend to be fixed in each city or town, though there's a tendency to overcharge foreigners, so it's best to agree a price before you set off. Often, fares are charged per passenger rather than for the vehicle as a whole, and it's not unusual to share a taxi with strangers heading in the same general direction. You can also hire taxis by the day; with a little bargaining this can actually be an inexpensive way of seeing a lot in a short time, particularly if there are a few of you.

**Moto-taxis** are motorcycles used as taxis, and are most frequently found in remote cities and towns in the lowlands. In cities like Trinidad, they're by far the most common form of transport. Travelling this way is cheap, fast and only slightly frightening.

**Minibuses** are privately owned vehicles that run all over the country's main cities and have almost completely replaced larger buses as the main form of urban public transport. Trips cost a couple of bolivianos, and they run with great frequency along fixed routes, with their major destinations written on placards on the windscreen and shouted out by the driver's assistant. With extra seats fitted in their already small interiors, they're pretty cramped; if you need extra legroom, try to sit in the front seat next to the driver. Large estate cars – referred to as **trufis** or **colectivos** – are sometimes used in place of minibuses.

Confusingly, what Bolivians call **micros** are actually bigger than minibuses: they're usually older, brightly coloured vehicles and chug along numbered routes; journeys usually cost Bs1.50–3.50.

## By goods truck

The heavy-goods **trucks** (*camiones*) are the other mainstay of Bolivian land transport, and sometimes the only option in remote or little-visited regions. Most carry passengers to supplement their income from carrying goods. Trucks are, however, more uncomfortable, slower and generally more dangerous than buses, and stop more frequently. Still, travelling by truck is a real Bolivian experience; passengers usually sit in the cab alongside the driver, or on the back.

The best place to find a truck is around any town's market areas or at the police checkpoints (*trancas*) at the edge of town; most also stop for passengers who flag them down at the side of the road. This is the closest you'll get to **hitching** in Bolivia, and you will always be expected to pay something for the ride; private cars are few and far between outside towns and rarely pick up hitchers, and in any case hitching a lift in them is risky. For shorter journeys in remote areas, smaller pick-ups, known as **camionetas**, also carry passengers.

## By train

Once a proud symbol of the country's tin-fuelled march to modernity, Bolivia's **railway** network, like the mining industry that spawned it, is now a shadow of its former self. The **Ferrocarril Andino** (or Occidental) (Ⓦwww.fca.com.bo) runs passenger trains from Oruro south across the Altiplano via Uyuni and Tupiza to Villazón on the Argentine border, through magnificent scenery. The company also runs a slow if picturesque service between Sucre and Potosí.

The **Ferrocarril Oriental** (Ⓦwww.fo.com.bo) has two lines from Santa Cruz: one east to the Brazilian border at Quijarro; the other south to Yacuiba in the Chaco on the Argentine border. The former is known as the "Train of Death", not because it's dangerous but because it's such a boring ride.

## By boat

Although Bolivia is a landlocked country, there are still several regions – particularly Lake Titicaca and the Amazon – where water is still the best way of getting around. Several high-end tour agencies run **hydrofoil** and **catamaran** cruises on Lake Titicaca, and smaller passenger launches run between Copacabana and the Isla del Sol.

River boats were for a long time the only means of transport in the Bolivian **Amazon**, but their use has declined rapidly with the expansion of the road network in the region. There are still plenty of river trips you can make, though, and travelling by boat is the ideal way to experience the rainforest. There are two main forms of river transport. **Dugout canoes** powered by outboard motors are the only real way to get deep enough into the jungle to see the wildlife. Tour agencies use these to take groups into protected areas like the Parque Nacional Madidi and irregular passenger services operate along some rivers. Alternatively, you can hire a canoe and its boatman for a few days – this means searching around the riverbank and negotiating, and the high fuel consumption of outboard motors means it won't be cheap.

The second (and much more economical) form of river transport are the larger **cargo boats** that ply the two main water routes not yet supplanted by roads: the **Río Mamoré**, between Trinidad and Guayaramerín on the Brazilian frontier, and the **Río Ichilo**, between Trinidad and Puerto Villarroel in the Chapare. Though generally far from comfortable, these slow-moving vessels allow passengers to hitch hammocks above the deck for a small fee and are a great way to see the Amazon if you're not in a hurry.

## By car

If you're short on time or want to get to some really out-of-the-way destinations, **renting a car** (or **motorbike**) is a possibility, but few travellers ever do. It's usually easier and not much more expensive to hire a taxi to drive you around for a day or longer.

Outside towns, most roads are unpaved and in very poor condition, so **four-wheel drive** (4WD) is essential. **Petrol** (gasoline) stations are few and far between and breakdown services even scarcer, so you should fill your tank whenever you can, carry extra fuel, and take food, drink and warm clothing in case you get stuck. Always carry your passport, driving licence and the vehicle's registration documents, as **police checks** are frequent, and any infringement will usually result in an on-the-spot fine, whether official or not. Small **tolls** are also charged on most roads. Speed limits are irregularly posted, but the speed is usually dictated by the state of the road. Most Bolivians regularly ignore traffic lights and don't indicate when turning, and some drive at night without lights. Vehicles drive on the right, though this rule is obviated on some mountain roads when the vehicle going uphill drives on the right and has priority.

You'll find car rental companies in all the major cities. Rental **costs** vary, starting at around US\$50 per day, or about double that for a 4WD; the Bolivian company Barbol (Ⓦrentacarinbolivia.com) tends to be cheaper than the international franchises. You'll need to be over 25, and leave a major credit card or large cash deposit as security; most rental agencies can arrange insurance, though you should read the small print carefully first.

In several lowland towns, such as Trinidad, Guayaramerín and Riberalta, it's also possible to rent **mopeds** and **motorbikes**, generally leaving your passport as a deposit – a good way of heading off into the back country for a day.

## ROAD DISTANCE CHART

|  | Cochabamba | La Paz | Oruro | Potosí | Rurrenabaque | Santa Cruz | Sucre | Tarija | Trinidad | Uyuni |
|---|---|---|---|---|---|---|---|---|---|---|
| Cochabamba | x | 383 | 210 | 520 | 809 | 473 | 366 | 888 | 985 | 739 |
| La Paz | 383 | x | 229 | 539 | 426 | 858 | 701 | 907 | 602 | 552 |
| Oruro | 210 | 229 | x | 310 | 736 | 683 | 472 | 678 | 812 | 323 |
| Potosí | 520 | 539 | 310 | x | 1046 | 774 | 162 | 368 | 1112 | 200 |
| Rurrenabaque | 809 | 426 | 736 | 1046 | x | 930 | 1208 | 1414 | 380 | 1059 |
| Santa Cruz | 473 | 858 | 683 | 774 | 930 | x | 612 | 703 | 550 | 1212 |
| Sucre | 366 | 701 | 472 | 162 | 1208 | 612 | x | 530 | 1162 | 362 |
| Tarija | 888 | 907 | 678 | 368 | 1414 | 703 | 530 | x | 1253 | 625 |
| Trinidad | 985 | 602 | 812 | 1112 | 380 | 550 | 1162 | 1253 | x | 1135 |
| Uyuni | 739 | 552 | 323 | 200 | 1059 | 1212 | 362 | 625 | 1135 | x |

## By bicycle

Outside La Paz, **bicycles** are rarely available to rent, and those that are aren't usually suitable for extended riding. For proper touring, you'll need to bring your own bike from home; airlines are usually happy to carry them if they're packed in bike boxes with the pedals removed. Given the state of the roads, a mountain bike is better than a conventional touring bike. Bring a comprehensive toolkit and a selection of essential spare parts.

The roads of the Bolivian Andes are ideal for **down-hill mountain biking**, and the country is home to some of the world's best downhill rides. Several agencies in La Paz lead guided mountain-bike trips (see p.76), and biking "the world's most dangerous road", in Coroico, is a popular activity (see p.127).

Cyclists should be aware of Bolivia's poor road safety record, however; in early 2014, a British tourist died in a collision in the southern Altiplano.

## By organized tour

Although relatively expensive, **organized tours** offer a quick and effortless way to see some of Bolivia's popular attractions; they're also a good way of visiting remote sites that are otherwise difficult to reach. In addition, many adventure tour companies both in Bolivia and abroad offer excellent and increasingly exciting itineraries, ranging from mountain climbing, trekking, mountain biking and wildlife safaris to less strenuous city tours and countryside excursions. Tours tend to cost around US$80–150 per person per day, depending on the nature of the trip, the degree of comfort and the number of people going along.

Most **tour agencies** are based in La Paz (see p.76), where you can arrange almost any trip in the country, but for the more popular wilderness excursions it's easier and cheaper to arrange things with local operators: in Uyuni for the Salar de Uyuni and Reserva Eduardo Avaroa, for example, and in Rurrenabaque for the Pampas del Yacuma and Parque Nacional Madidi. Relevant agencies are listed in the Guide under each destination.

# Accommodation

**Accommodation in Bolivia is generally very good value, though standards in all price brackets are variable. In the larger cities you'll find a broad range of places to stay, including top-end hotels charging well over Bs1000 (US$150) a night. In smaller towns, however, there's not much choice, particularly in the mid- and upper price ranges, though there are usually plenty of decent budget places.**

Room rates generally represent excellent value for money. In areas popular with tourists, rates rise slightly during the **high season** (July–Aug) and prices in any town can double or treble during a major fiesta. In addition, room rates in resort towns popular with Bolivians increase at the weekend. These are also the only circumstances in which **reserving** a room in advance is really necessary. Prices also vary by region: accommodation in big cities tends to cost more (notably in Santa Cruz), whereas smaller towns that see a lot of budget travellers – Coroico, Copacabana, Rurrenabaque – tend to have a good range of inexpensive places to stay.

Accommodation names – hotel, hostal, residencial and alojamiento – mean relatively little in Bolivia. Virtually all high-end accommodation will call itself a **hotel**, but then many basic places do so as well. Smaller and cheaper hotels – also known as **hostales**, **alojamientos** or **residenciales** – tend to offer basic rooms with shared bathrooms only, but they still vary widely in price, cleanliness and comfort. **Cabañas** are self-contained cabins or bungalows, sometimes with their own kitchenettes, usually found away from big cities. Note that a **motel** is not an inexpensive roadside hotel, but a place where couples go to have sex, while a **pension** is a cheap place to eat, rather than somewhere to stay.

## Hotels

There's no standard or widely used **rating system** for hotels, so other than the information given in this book, the only way to tell whether a place is suitable or not is to have a look around. It's usually worth asking to see a few different rooms rather than just accepting the first you're offered. There's usually some flexibility in all price ranges, so a little haggling is always worth a try, especially when the hotel seems fairly empty, or if you're in a group: the phrase "Tiene un cuarto más barato?" ("Do you have a cheaper room?") is useful. The least expensive places often charge per person, but otherwise **single rooms** tend to cost as much as or only slightly less than double rooms. Rooms with a double bed (cama matrimonial) usually cost less than those with two beds.

---

**ADDRESSES**

**Addresses** are usually written with just the street name (and often only the surname if the street is named after a person), followed by the number – for example, "Paredes 704" rather than "704 Calle Max Paredes". Often, however, numbers are not used, and the nearest intersection is given instead – for example, "Illampu con Comercio". Note also that the first floor, as in Britain, is the floor above ground.

---

Even in the coldest highland cities **heating** is generally only found in the more expensive hotels. In the lowlands, heat rather than cold is often a problem. All but the most basic rooms are equipped with a fan, and many places offer the option of air-conditioning. In the lowlands, you should also check whether the windows of your room are screened against mosquitoes or if the bed is equipped with a net.

All but the most basic places have **hot water**, but the reliability and effectiveness of water-heating systems varies considerably. Many hotels have a **strong box** where you can lock up your valuables – though you should count cash carefully before handing it in, and ask for a receipt. Many places will also store **luggage** for you, often free of charge.

## Hostels and homestays

The number of **hostels** in Bolivia is slowly increasing, and many of them are affiliated with Hostelling International (⦿ hihostels.com).

---

**ACCOMMODATION PRICES**

Unless otherwise indicated, the accommodation prices in this book are based on the price of the hotel/hostel's cheapest **double room in high season**, and includes breakfast, wi-fi and any taxes. For hostels we quote the price for a dorm bed, and the per person price for camping. Some (mainly upmarket) establishments fix their prices in dollars, in which case we quote their price in dollars, followed by the approximate boliviano equivalent. At cheaper hotels, single rooms are quite often available, sometimes for just half the price of a double, though usually more.

The **cheapest** hotels tend to be found around bus terminals. At their most basic they offer nothing more than bare, box-like rooms with a bed and shared bathroom, and can be far from clean, though for around Bs100–200 you should expect a clean and reasonably comfortable double room. Many budget places offer a choice between private and shared bathroom, and may also include breakfast in their rates, though this is not universal.

**Mid-range** accommodation (generally Bs200 and upwards for a double room) should offer greater comfort, pleasant decor, reliable hot water, towels and soap and extras like TVs. For Bs350–700 (US$50–100) or so you'll find some very pleasant hotels indeed, though you'll need to choose carefully – more expensive doesn't necessarily mean better. At the **top end** of the scale (above Bs700/US$100) there are some beautiful old colonial mansions which have been converted into delightful hotels, as well as more staid modern places aimed primarily at business travellers.

However, relatively few have dorms or traditional hostel facilities like communal kitchens, offering instead simple and inexpensive rooms, normally with a choice of either shared or private bathroom.

**Homestays** are gradually becoming more popular, and both Homestay.com (Ⓦhomestay .com) and Airbnb (Ⓦairbnb.com) have several good-value places on offer across the country.

## Camping

Few travellers bother **camping** in Bolivia, unless they're exploring the country's wilderness areas. Outside cities and towns, however, you can camp almost everywhere, usually for free. Be aware, though, that in the highlands it gets extremely cold at night, while in the lowlands, mosquitoes can be a real problem if your tent isn't screened. In the rainforest, a hammock combined with a fitted mosquito net and a tarpaulin to keep off the rain allows you to camp out pretty much anywhere.

When looking for a **place to camp**, it's usually okay to set up your tent in fields beyond the outskirts of settlements, but you should ask permission from the nearest house first. In wilderness areas where there's no one around to ask, you can camp freely. On the more popular trekking routes you may be asked for a small fee (a few dollars) or two by local villagers. Though **attacks** on trekkers are rare, you're obviously vulnerable if camping out alone: it's best to camp with at least one other person, and women shouldn't camp unless accompanied by men.

In some **national parks** and other protected wilderness areas you'll find rustic shelters – *albergues* or *refugios* – where you can stay for a small fee, often in the *campamentos* used by the park guards. Rudimentary cooking facilities and running water are usually available.

Specialist **camping equipment** is sold in a few shops, mainly in La Paz and Santa Cruz, so it's best to bring equipment from home. Shops on Calle Illampu in La Paz sell camping stoves and gas canisters, as well as weatherproof clothes and even tents. In Copacabana and Cochabamba, The Spitting Llama also sells and rents out some camping gear.

# Food and drink

**Bolivia is not really renowned for its cuisine, but options are improving all the time, and in some of the bigger cities you can find some very accomplished restaurants. Moreover, in most places it's easy to get a decent and filling meal, and there are some interesting national and local specialities. The style of food varies considerably between Bolivia's three main geographical regions: the Altiplano, the highland valleys and the tropical lowlands. Though the differences are fading, each region has comidas típicas (traditional dishes), which include some of the highlights of Bolivian cuisine.**

## Restaurants

All larger towns in Bolivia have a fair selection of **restaurants** (spelt the same way as in English, without the extra "e" at the end used in most Spanish-speaking countries). Almost all offer a set lunch, or **almuerzo**, consisting of a substantial soup (*sopa*) and a main course (*segundo*), usually made up of rice, potatoes, some form of meat or chicken, and a little bit of salad. Sometimes all this will be preceded by a small savoury appetizer and followed by a sweet dessert. Coffee, teas or a soft drink may also be included. Typically costing around Bs15–30, these set lunches are usually filling and good value for money. Many restaurants also offer a similarly economical set dinner (**cena**) in the evening. In addition, most have a range of à la carte main dishes (*platos extras*) available throughout the day – these are usually substantial meat dishes like steak, and rarely cost more than Bs70–100. In smaller towns the choice is much more limited, and sometimes the simple set *almuerzo* and *cena* may be the only meal on offer.

Ordinary restaurants rarely offer much in the way of **vegetarian food**; in out-of-the-way places, vegetarians may find themselves eating rather a lot of egg-based dishes. The situation changes a great deal in popular travellers' haunts, where international food is more and more common, and salads and vegetarian dishes are widely available. Although as a landlocked country Bolivia is obviously not the place to come for seafood, **fish** features regularly on menus. Lake Titicaca produces an abundant harvest of succulent *trucha* (trout) and *pejerrey* (kingfish), while native fish are abundant in the rivers of the lowlands: the tastiest is the juicy white fish known as *surubí*.

Most cities have at least one **Chinese restaurant** (or *chifa*), and **pizzerias** are also fairly widespread. Also reliable are Bolivia's cheap spit-roast **chicken restaurants** known as *pollos spiedo*, *pollos broaster* or *pollos a la brasa*.

Few restaurants open much before 8am for **breakfast** (*desayuno*) – Bolivians tend either to make do with a hot drink and a bread roll or, if they want something more substantial, to head to the market for soup or rice and meat. In touristy places, though, you'll find continental and North American breakfasts, along with fruit juices and travellers' favourites such as banana pancakes.

In smarter restaurants, you may find yourself paying Bs80–100 for a main course, but for this you should expect a pretty good meal, and even in the best restaurants in La Paz or Santa Cruz few dishes cost more than Bs130. **Tipping** is not generally expected, but is always welcome. No additional tax is charged on meals, but there is often a cover charge in restaurants with live music performances, known as **peñas**.

## Markets

Wherever you are in Bolivia, the cheapest place to eat is invariably the **market**. Here you'll find rows of stalls selling juices, soups, snacks and meals that can satisfy most appetites for Bs10–15. Markets, which open for business much earlier than most restaurants and cafés, are also often the best places to try out regional specialities. From around 6am you can find stalls selling coffee and tea with bread, sandwiches and pastries, and – more popular with the locals – *api*, a hot, sweet, thick maize drink flavoured with cloves and cinnamon and served with deep-fried pancakes known as *buñuelos*. Markets are also the place to go to stock up for a trek, a **picnic**, or if you just feel the urge to prepare your own food.

The standard of **hygiene** at market stalls is often not the highest, however, and you should probably avoid eating at them until your stomach has adjusted to local bacteria. In general, food cooked in front of your eyes is probably safe; food that's been left sitting around for a while may not be.

## Snacks

The most popular snack throughout Bolivia is the **salteña**, a pasty filled with a spicy, juicy stew of meat or chicken with chopped vegetables, olives and hard-boiled egg. Named after the city of Salta in Argentina, *salteñas* are sold from street stalls and eaten in the mid-morning accompanied by a cold drink and a spoonful or two of chilli sauce if desired. The best *salteñas* are found in Sucre, where they're also sold in specialist cafés called *salteñerias*, which open only in the mid-morning and serve nothing else. *Salteñas potosinas*, made in Potosí, are less juicy (making them easier to eat in the mines) and are more likely to be meat-free.

Similar to *salteñas*, but deep-fried and with a higher potato content, are **tucumanas**, also named after a city (Tucumán) in Argentina. Also commonly available are **empanadas**, simpler pasties filled with meat, chicken or cheese and either baked or fried. Another snack typical of Santa Cruz is the **cuñape**, a tasty pastry made from cheese and cassava flour. Familiar international snacks are also common in Bolivia, including **hamburgers** (*hamburguesas*) and **hot dogs** (*choripan*).

## Comida típica

In the **Altiplano**, traditional Aymara cuisine is dominated by the **potato**, often served alongside rice as one of two or three different carbohydrates on the same plate. The Andes are the original home of the potato, and over two hundred different varieties are grown in Bolivia. As well as being boiled, baked, mashed and fried, they are also freeze-dried using ancient techniques involving repeated exposure to sunshine and frost. Known as *chuño* and *tunta*, these dehydrated potatoes have an unusual texture and a distinctive, nutty flavour that takes some getting used to. They're often boiled and served instead of (or as well as) fresh potatoes, but they're best appreciated in the many different **soups** that are a feature of Altiplano cuisine. These are thick, hearty affairs laden with potatoes, vegetables and whatever meat is to hand – one of the most widely available is *chairo*, typical of La Paz. Another standard soup ingredient is **quinoa**, a native Andean grain that has a distinctively nutty flavour and a remarkably high nutritional value.

> ### 5 PLACES TO EAT LIKE THE LOCALS
> **Mercado Lanza** La Paz. See p.82
> **Tucumanas El Prado** La Paz. See p.82
> **El Patio** Sucre. See p.205
> **Casa de Campo** Cochabamba. See p.216
> **El Aljibe** Santa Cruz. See p.238

The most common meat in the Altiplano is **mutton**, closely followed by llama, which is lean and tasty. Llama meat is often eaten in a dried form known as *charque* (the origin of the English word jerky). Other Altiplano mainstays include *sajta*, a spicy dish of chicken cooked with dried yellow chilli, potatoes, *tunta*, onions and parsley; and the *plato paceño*, a mixed plate of cheese, potatoes, broad beans and maize, usually with meat, which is typical of La Paz. If you like your food with a kick, all these dishes can be doused in **llajua** – a hot sauce made from tomatoes, locoto chilli peppers and herbs.

The *comida típica* of the **valley regions** around Sucre, Cochabamba and Tarija shares many ingredients with the traditional cuisines of the Altiplano, but combines them with a wider range of fresh fruit and vegetables and tends to be spicier. Maize features strongly, either ground into a flour and used as the basis for thick soups known as *laguas*, or boiled on the cob and served with fresh white cheese – a classic combination known as *choclo con queso*. Meat and chicken are often cooked in spicy sauces known as *picantes*. Pork also features strongly: deliciously deep fried as *chicharrón*, roasted as *lechón* or made into *chorizos chuquisaceños* (spicy sausages originating from Sucre). A popular valley mainstay served throughout Bolivia is *pique a lo macho*, a massive plate of chopped beef and sausage, potatoes (or chips), onions, tomatoes and chillies.

In the **tropical lowlands** of the Amazon and Santa Cruz, **plantain** and **cassava** (*yuca*) generally take the place of potatoes alongside rice as the mainstay sources of carbohydrate. One classic breakfast staple is *masaco*: mashed plantain or cassava mixed with shredded *charque* and fried. The lowlands are cattle-ranching regions, so good-quality, relatively inexpensive **beef** features strongly. This is usually barbecued or fried as steak, or cooked on skewers in massive kebabs (*pacumutus*). Another classic lowland dish is *locro de gallina*, a rich chicken soup. **Game** or bushmeat is also common in the lowlands: *jochi* (agouti), *tatú* (armadillo), *saino* (peccary) and *venado* (venison) all frequently appear on menus, though for conservation reasons it's better not to eat them.

# Drinks

Known as **refrescos**, fizzy drinks are found all over Bolivia, including international brands like Coca-Cola and a wide range of nationally produced beverages. Malta is a malt-flavoured soda much like those found in the Caribbean and West Africa. Bottled processed **fruit juice** from the Cochabamba region, sold under the name "*Jugos del Valle*", is a good alternative to soda pops. The word *refresco* also covers home-made fruit-based drinks served from street stalls, such as **mocochinchi**, made from dried peaches with sugar and cinnamon. **Mineral water**, both sparkling (*agua mineral con gas*) and still (*sin gas*), is fairly widely available, as is less expensive purified water labelled "Naturagua" – a good thing, as it's best not to drink the tap water. Make sure the seals on all bottles are intact when you buy them.

The delicious variety of tropical fruits grown in Bolivia is available as **juices** (*jugos*) from market stalls, and freshly squeezed orange and grapefruit juice is also sold on the streets from handcarts. **Tea** (*té*) and **coffee** (*café*) are available almost everywhere, though the latter is rarely prepared to the strength favoured by most Europeans, and sometimes comes with sugar already added – a shame, as Bolivia produces some excellent coffee. **Café con leche** is a big glass of hot milk flavoured with coffee. Many Bolivians prefer herbal teas, known as **mates**; *mate de coca* is the best known. **Hot chocolate** is usually very good too.

## Alcoholic drinks

Locally produced **alcoholic drinks** are widely available, and drinking is a serious pastime. Drinking with locals can be great fun, but shouldn't be entered into lightly, as slipping away after a couple is easier said than done. Remember, too, that until you become acclimatized, high altitude magnifies both the effects of alcohol and the resulting hangover.

**Beer** (*cerveza*) is available in shops, restaurants and bars almost everywhere, and Bolivians consume it in large quantities, especially at fiestas. All the major cities have their own breweries, producing German lager-style beers of reasonable quality with a strength of around five percent. Most beer still comes in returnable bottles, though cans are becoming more widespread. Paceña and Huari are the big industrial brands. Taquiña from Cochabamba is also good, while Potosina, from Potosí, has a stronger malt flavour. On some beer labels you'll see the word **tropicalizada** – this means it has been produced in the highlands but is more highly pressurized for consumption at lower altitudes where the air pressure is higher: if opened at altitude it will spray all over the place. More expensive **imported beers** are available only in larger cities, but a number of independent firms and **microbreweries** are now producing quality beers in Bolivia itself, of which Saya in La Paz and Prost in Santa Cruz are the most widely available.

## COCA: SACRED LEAF OF THE ANDES

Nothing is more emblematic of Bolivia than **coca**, the controversial leaf that has been cultivated for thousands of years in the Andean foothills. To ordinary Bolivians, coca is at once a useful stimulant to combat hunger and tiredness, a medicine for altitude sickness and a key religious and cultural sacrament with magical powers used in rituals and offerings. To the outside world, however, it is infamous as the raw material for the manufacture of **cocaine** (as well as, reputedly, still a key ingredient of Coca-Cola).

Thousands of farmers depend on coca for their livelihoods, and President Evo Morales – who remains head of the biggest coca-growing union – has repeatedly stressed that the leaf is an intrinsic part of indigenous Andean culture. Although Morales has promised a policy of "zero cocaine but not zero coca", Bolivia remains the world's third-largest producer of the drug, and cocaine use within the country has risen dramatically in recent years. In 2011 the country renounced a UN anti-drug convention because it classified the coca leaf as an illegal drug. But in 2013, after a successful bout of international lobbying, Bolivia was readmitted to the convention, gaining a special dispensation that recognized that the chewing of coca leaves was legal in the country.

Although not widely consumed, Bolivia also produces a growing variety of **wines** (*vinos*). Production is centred in the Tarija valley, home to the highest vineyards in the world, and quality is improving all the time – the best labels are Concepción, Kohlberg and Aranjuez. Imported wines from Chile and Argentina are also widely available and often cheaper, as they're frequently smuggled across the border to avoid tax and duty.

When Bolivians really want to get drunk they turn to spirits, in particular a white grape brandy called **singani**, produced in the Tarija valley. The more expensive high-grade *singanis* are very good, but most are pretty rough. It's usually drunk mixed with Sprite or Seven-Up, a fast-acting combination known as **Chufflay**. Those who can't afford *singani* (which includes most campesinos and miners) turn to virtually pure industrial **alcohol potable**, sold in large metal cans. Consumed at rural fiestas and used to make offerings to mountain spirits and other supernatural beings, this is fearsome stuff, and you drink it at your peril.

### CHICHA COCHABAMBINA

No visit to the Cochabamba is complete without a taste of **chicha Cochabambina**, a thick, mildly alcoholic beer made of fermented maize which is available throughout the region wherever you see a white flag or bunch of flowers raised on a pole outside a house. Considered sacred by the Incas, its tart, yeasty flavour is definitely an acquired taste, and it can play havoc with the digestion.

# Fiestas

**Bolivia enjoys a huge number of national, regional and local fiestas. These are taken very seriously, often involving lengthy preparations and substantial expense; the largest feature thousands of costumed dancers, massed brass bands and plenty of food and drink. You should definitely try to catch a fiesta at some point during your visit, as they are among the most vibrant and colourful spectacles Bolivia has to offer, and at the heart of the country's culture.**

Most national fiestas mark famous events in Bolivia's post-conquest history and the standard festivals of the **Catholic Church**, but many of the latter coincide with far older **indigenous celebrations** related to the sun, stars and agricultural cycle. Carnaval time (late Feb or early March) is marked by fiestas and celebrations throughout the country (the most famous being in Oruro), and involves copious eating and drinking, and indiscriminate water-fighting.

In addition to the major national and regional celebrations, almost every town and village has its own annual **local fiesta** (some have several), usually to honour a patron saint. These celebrations can be much more fun to visit than major events in larger towns and cities, and often stretch out over a whole week, with religious processions, masked and costumed folkloric dances, traditional music and eating and drinking. In indigenous communities these fiestas are often important ritual events associated with religious beliefs and agricultural cycles – it's believed that if they're not celebrated with due extravagance, the Catholic saints or mountain gods (or both) may be displeased, and the fortunes of the community will suffer as a result. Fiestas also play an important role in maintaining social cohesion, and are usually financed under a system known as *prestes*, whereby wealthier members of the community spend large amounts of money on food, drink and musicians, gaining enhanced status and respect in return.

The occasional visitor will usually be warmly welcomed to local fiestas, but these are often fairly private affairs, and crowds of camera-wielding tourists may provoke a hostile reaction – **sensitivity** is the key.

## MAJOR FIESTAS AND PUBLIC HOLIDAYS

### JANUARY–APRIL

**New Year's Day** January 1. Public holiday.

**Reyes Magos** January 6. The arrival of the biblical Three Kings is celebrated with processions in various towns in the Beni.

**Plurinational State Foundation Day** January 22. **Public holiday.**

**Feria de Alasitas** January 24; La Paz. Large areas of the city are taken over by market stalls selling miniature items used as offerings to Ekeko, the household god of abundance (see box, p.57).

**Fiesta de la Virgen de la Candelaria** February 2. Celebrated particularly in Copacabana (see box, p.105).

**Oruro Revolution Day** February 10. Public holiday in Oruro department (see p.145).

**Carnaval** February/March. Celebrated throughout the country on the last days before Lent (the Monday and Shrove Tuesday are public holidays). The Oruro Carnaval (see box, p.143) is the most famous, but Santa Cruz (see p.239) and Tarija (see box, p.184) also stage massive fiestas.

**Pujllay** March 12. Thousands of indigenous revellers descend on the town of Tarabuco, near Sucre, to celebrate a local victory over Spanish troops during the Independence War (see box, p.208).

**Semana Santa** (Easter) March/April. Celebrated with religious processions throughout Bolivia. Good Friday is a public holiday.

**Anniversary of the Battle of La Tablada** April 15. Public holiday in Tarija department (see p.180).

### MAY–AUGUST

**Labour Day** May 1. Public holiday.

**Día de la Cruz** May 3. Tinku ritual combats (see box, p.164) are staged in some communities in the northern Potosí region.

**Anniversary of Primer Grito Libertario de America** May 25. Public holiday in Chuquisaca department (see box, p.193).

**Santísima Trinidad** (Trinity Sunday) May/June (8th Sun after Easter). Major religious fiesta in Trinidad (see p.285).

**Corpus Christi** May/June (Thursday after Trinity Sunday). Public holiday. La Paz stages the Señor del Gran Poder (see box, p.57), its biggest and most colourful folkloric dance parade.

**Aymara New Year** June 21. The winter solstice and Aymara New Year (public holiday) are celebrated with overnight vigils and religious ceremonies at Tiwanaku (see box. p.91), Copacabana (see box. p.105), Samaipata (see p.245) and other ancient sites throughout the country.

**San Juan** (Feast of St John the Baptist) June 24. Christian version of the winter solstice and Aymara New Year, marked with bonfires and fireworks around Bolivia.

**Virgen del Carmen** July 16. Processions and dances in honour of the Virgen del Carmen, the patron saint of many towns and villages across Bolivia. Public holiday in La Paz department.

**Fiesta Patronal** July 31. San Ignacio de Moxos hosts the largest and most colourful saint's day festival in the Bolivian Amazon (see box, p.281).

**Independence Day** August 6. Public holiday. Parades and parties throughout the country.

**Virgen de Urkupiña** August 15. Pilgrims descend on the market town of Quillacollo, just outside Cochabamba, for the region's biggest religious fiesta (see box p.220).

**San Bartolomé** (also known as Ch'utillos) August 24. Potosí's biggest annual fiesta (see box. p.153), a three-day celebration with pre-Christian roots, marked by folkloric dances and religious processions.

### SEPTEMBER–DECEMBER

**Anniversary of 1810 uprising** September 14. Public holiday in Cochabamba department (see p.209).

**Anniversary of 1810 Grito Libertario** September 24. Public holiday in Santa Cruz (see p.235), and Pando department (anniversary of its creation in 1938).

**All Saints and Day of the Dead** November 1–2. Public holiday. Remembrance parties are held in cemeteries throughout the highlands, with the decorated skulls of dead relatives often on display.

**Anniversary of 1810 uprising** November 10. Public holiday in Potosí department (see p.163).

**Public holiday, Beni department** November 18. Anniversary of the department's creation in 1842.

**Christmas Day** December 25. **Public holiday.** Christmas (Navidad) is celebrated throughout the country, and there are particularly colourful festivities in San Ignacio de Moxos and Tarija.

# Outdoor activities

**Dominated by dramatic Andean scenery and home to some of South America's most pristine wilderness areas, Bolivia should be one of the world's top destinations for outdoor enthusiasts. As yet, though, its enormous potential is only starting to be tapped – which for many travellers will only add to its appeal.**

For climbers, trekkers and mountain bikers, Bolivia's possibilities are virtually limitless. The best season for all these activities is between May and September, during the **southern-hemisphere winter** (the most pleasant and reliable weather is between June and August). During the **rainy season** between December and March or April, rain turns paths and roads to mud, and streams to impassable torrents, while cloud covers the high passes and blocks many of the best views.

# Trekking

Whether you want to stroll for half a day or take a hardcore hike for two weeks over high passes and down into remote Amazonian valleys, Bolivia is a paradise for **trekking**. The most popular trekking region is the **Cordillera Real**, which is blessed with spectacular high Andean scenery and is easily accessible from La Paz. The mountains here are crisscrossed by paths and mule trains used by local people that make excellent trekking routes – the best of these are ancient stone-paved highways built by the Incas and earlier Andean societies. Starting near La Paz, three of Bolivia's most popular treks – the **Choro** (see p.130), **Takesi** (see p.132) and **Yunga Cruz** (see p.133) – follow these Inca trails across the Cordillera Real. Another good base for exploring the Cordillera Real is the town of **Sorata** (see box p.124), where many good trekking routes begin. **Isla del Sol** and the shores of **Lake Titicaca** are also excellent for hiking, combining awesome scenery with gentle gradients. People looking for more seclusion should head for the remote and beautiful **Cordillera Apolobamba**.

## Equipment and guides

You should always be **well equipped** when walking, even if it's just a half-day hike. Weather can change quickly in the mountains and it gets very cold at night. You'll need strong hiking boots; warm layers; a waterproof top layer; a hat and gloves; an adequate first-aid kit; a water bottle and water purifiers; sunscreen, a sun hat and sunglasses. For **camping** out you'll need a decent tent; a sleeping bag that keeps you warm in temperatures as low as -5°C; an insulated sleeping mat; and a cooking stove (ideally a multi-fuel stove).

The easiest way to go trekking is on an **organized trip**, which takes all the hassle out of route-finding and means you don't need to supply your own equipment. You'll also have all your meals cooked for you and transport to and from trailheads arranged. If you pay a little more, you can have your gear carried for you by a **porter** or pack animal. Trekking this way costs around Bs200–400 per person per day.

---

**TOP 5 TREKS**

**Choro** See p.130
**Takesi** See p.132
**Condoriri Massif** See p.122
**Trans-Apolobamba** See p.120
**Inca trail** See p.187

---

Things are cheaper if you have all your own equipment, organize the logistics yourself, and just hire a **guide** (around Bs200–250 a day). In rural towns and villages you can usually find local campesinos who know all the trails and will act as a guide for a relatively small fee (on treks of more than one day you'll also need to provide them with food and possibly a tent). If you're hiring **pack animals** (such as mules, donkeys or llamas), then the mule handlers double up as guides. As well as making sure you don't get lost, a local guide can help avoid any possible misunderstandings with the communities you pass through – it's also a good way to ensure local people see a little economic benefit from tourism.

If you plan to go trekking over longer distances without a guide, you should be competent at route-finding and map-reading, carry a **compass** and GPS, and equip yourself with the relevant topographical **maps**, where available. Most areas are covered by 1:50,000-scale maps produced by the Bolivian military, which you can buy in La Paz (see p.88) or download for free from ⓦ www.igmbolivia.gob.bo. You can also find trekking maps at ⓦ wikiloc.com, where you can download a handy map phone app, which you need only GPS (not phone network) coverage to use. Really, though, it's much better to trek with a guide. Getting lost in remote mountain or forested regions is easy and can be very dangerous, and rescue services are pretty much nonexistent. In addition, you should always let someone in town know your plans before you head off on a long walk. It's especially important **not to trek alone** – if you sprain an ankle, it could be the last anyone ever sees of you. In case of emergency, the best people to call are Socorro Andino Boliviano (☎7158 1118 or ☎7197 1147, ⓦ facebook.com/sabagmtb).

# Climbing

With hundreds of peaks over 5000m and a dozen over 6000m, Bolivia has plenty of types of **mountain climbing**, and many new routes still to explore. As with trekking, the most popular region is the dramatic **Cordillera Real**, which is blessed with numerous high peaks, easy access from La Paz and fairly stable weather conditions during the dry season. In addition, the volcanic peaks of the **Cordillera Occidental**, particularly Sajama (see box, p.141), offer some excellent climbs, while the more remote **Cordillera Apolobamba** and **Cordillera Quimsa Cruz** also boast a wealth of possibilities. Several of the higher peaks are well within the reach of climbers with only limited experience, while **Huayna Potosí** (6090m), in the Cordillera Real, is one of the few 6000m-plus peaks in South America that can be climbed by people with no mountaineering experience at all. The leading book on climbing in Bolivia, though two decades old, is still Yossi Brain's *Bolivia: A Climbing Guide* (Mountaineers Books, 1999).

Though some **equipment** is available for rent in La Paz, you should really bring your own equipment from home if you're planning on doing any serious independent climbing. You should also take care to acclimatize properly and be aware of the dangers of altitude sickness (see p.38) and extreme cold. Agencies in La Paz such as Climbing South America (see p.76) offer guided ascents of the most popular peaks: check carefully that the equipment is reliable and the guide is qualified (the Asociación de Guías de Montaña y Trekking de Bolivia list all qualified guides on their website at Ⓦ agmtb.org). If in doubt, go with a more reputable and expensive agency.

## Mountain biking

Bolivia is home to some of the finest **mountain bike** routes in the world, and travelling by bike is one of the best ways to experience the Andes. Numerous tour companies in La Paz (see p.76) have set up **downhill mountain biking** trips. These involve being driven up to a high pass, put on a bike, and then riding downhill at your own pace, accompanied by a guide and followed by a support vehicle. This is not an activity where you should try to save money by going with a cheap operator – look for a company with experienced guides, well-maintained and high-quality bikes and adequate safety equipment; Gravity Assisted Mountain Biking (see p.77) has the best reputation.

Easily the most popular route is down the road from **La Paz to Coroico** in the Yungas (see box p.127), a stunning 3500m descent which many travellers rate as one of the highlights of South America, never mind Bolivia. You don't need any previous mountain-biking experience to do this ride, which is easy to organize as a day-trip from La Paz. Other popular routes include **Chacaltaya** (see p.90) to La Paz, and down the **Zongo valley** into the Yungas from Chacaltaya, while hard-core mountain bikers can try their luck on the **Takesi Trail** (see p.132). As with trekking and climbing, though, the possibilities are pretty much endless, especially if you have your own bike.

For advice on new routes or mountain biking in general, contact Gravity Assisted Mountain Biking in La Paz (see p.77), who can also help organize specialist guided tours.

## Rafting and kayaking

The many rivers rushing down from the Andes into the Upper Amazon valleys offer massive potential for **kayaking** and **white-water rafting**, though these activities are not as developed as they could be. The most easily accessible and popular river is the **Río Coroico**, in the Yungas, which offers rapids from grade II to IV (and sometimes higher) and is accessible on day-trips from Coroico. The most challenging trip is down the **Río Tuichi**, which runs from the high Andes down into the rainforest of the Parque Nacional Madidi (see p.274).

# National parks and reserves

**Bolivia's system of protected areas currently covers around fifteen percent of the country. These national parks (parques nacionales), national reserves (reservas nacionales) and "natural areas" (areas naturales de manejo integrado) encompass the full range of terrains and ecosystems in Bolivia, from the tropical forests of the Amazon lowlands to the frozen peaks and high-altitude Andean deserts. They include many of Bolivia's most outstanding scenic attractions, but their principal aim is to protect native flora and fauna, and there are relatively few facilities for tourism. Though in some parks you can find basic accommodation, in general visiting these areas involves a wilderness expedition, which is usually possible only with the help of a tour operator.**

The country's national parks and reserves are administered by the **Servicio Nacional de Areas Protegidas** (SERNAP), which has a head office in La Paz (Ⓣ 02 2426272, Ⓦ sernap.gob.bo), though it offers little in the way of practical information. In cases where you need **permission** to visit a park or reserve, you can do so in the local or regional SERNAP offices. Details about permission and entrance fees for individual parks and reserves are given in the Guide. Protected areas range in size from the vast 34,411-square-kilometre **Parque Nacional Kaa-Iya del Gran Chaco**, the largest in South America, to the relatively small 164-square-kilometre **Parque Nacional Torotoro**.

Many of Bolivia's protected areas were established only relatively recently in response to pressure and incentives from international conservation groups. Some, including the **Parque Nacional Madidi**, were set up through **debt-for-nature swaps**, whereby international groups bought up large amounts of the country's international debt at discounted rates, then cancelled the debts in return for Bolivia agreeing to establish protected areas and invest money in their conservation. **Parque Nacional Noel Kempff Mercado** was expanded as part of a pioneer **carbon-trading scheme**, under which US energy corporations finance the protection of forest areas in Bolivia in return for being allowed to claim credits for the carbon dioxide the forests absorb from the atmosphere when meeting their own emissions targets.

Despite such schemes, many national parks and other protected areas are under intense pressure from **landless peasants**, mostly migrants from the highlands looking for new areas of forest to clear and cultivate. Small teams of park guards with almost no resources struggle to protect thousands of square kilometres of wilderness from incursions by hunters, logging and mining companies, cattle ranchers and peasant colonizers, who are often better organized, financed and equipped. In addition, though many Bolivians are aware of the enormous value of their remaining wilderness areas and support conservation measures, there is also widespread opposition to the **national parks system**. Peasant federations in particular view the protected areas as a form of imperialism whereby natural resources that are rightfully theirs are handed over to international conservation groups intent, they believe, on stealing Bolivia's biodiversity and patenting any scientifically valuable species discovered.

# Health

**Bolivia is one of the poorest countries in Latin America, with a limited public health system. Generally speaking, the larger the city or town, the better the medical care is likely to be. In La Paz and Santa Cruz, English-speaking doctors trained overseas are fairly easy to find. Standards decrease rapidly the further you go from the cities, and in rural areas medical facilities are poor to nonexistent. If you have a choice, private hospitals and clinics are better staffed and equipped than public ones. Make sure you have adequate health insurance**

**before you leave home, as costs can mount rapidly, and remember to obtain itemized receipts of your treatment so that you can recover your costs.**

You'll find **pharmacies** (*farmacias*) in most Bolivian towns; in larger places they operate a rota system, with at least one staying open 24 hours a day. These sell a wide range of familiar drugs and medicines without prescription (many, for example, sell the morning-after pill), so for minor ailments you can usually buy what you need over the counter. For any serious illness, you should go to a doctor or hospital; these are detailed throughout the Guide in the relevant city directory. Many Bolivians are too poor to afford modern medical attention, and most make frequent recourse to traditional **herbalists**, known as *curanderos* – the most famous are the Kallawayas from the Cordillera Apolobamba (see box p.118). In addition, the market of every town has a section selling curative plants, herbs and charms for the most common ailments.

Although Bolivia is home to some very unpleasant **tropical diseases**, you shouldn't get too paranoid about contracting them: most are rare and pose more of a threat to poor locals with limited access to healthcare and clean water. Most serious illnesses can be avoided if you take the necessary precautions and make sure you have the right **vaccinations** before you go.

If you're planning a long trip it's worth consulting your doctor before you leave, as well as having a **dental check-up**. Take an adequate supply of any prescription medicines you normally use and, if you wear glasses or contact lenses, carry a spare pair and a copy of your prescription.

It's currently recommended that visitors to Bolivia have **immunizations** for hepatitis A, typhoid and yellow fever. Advice can change, however, so check with your doctor or a travel clinic at least two months before travelling so that there's time to have any courses of injections you might need. You should also make sure your polio and tetanus vaccinations and boosters are up to date. In the case of **yellow fever**, make sure you get an international vaccination certificate, as you may have to show it when entering or leaving the country, especially by land.

## Water and food

Though the **tap water** in some cities and towns is chlorinated, it's best to avoid drinking it entirely while in Bolivia. **Bottled water**, both mineral and purified, is sold throughout the country, though rarely consumed by Bolivians themselves: check the seals on all bottles are intact, as refilling is not unknown. Soft drinks, tea and coffee are also perfectly safe to drink, and more widely available.

There are several ways of **purifying water** while travelling, whether your source is tap water or a spring or stream. Boiling water for at least ten minutes is effective, though at high altitude water boils at below 100°C, so you should let it boil for twice as long. Chemical purification with **iodine** (*yodo*) tablets or tincture (available in camping shops at home and at pharmacies in Bolivia) is easier, and generally effective, though not all microbes are eliminated and the resulting taste leaves much to be desired (although you can buy neutralizing powder that improves the taste somewhat, and a squeeze of lemon is also effective). Note that pregnant women, babies and people with thyroid complaints shouldn't use iodine. Portable **water filters** give the most complete treatment, but are fiddly, expensive and relatively heavy to carry.

Almost any kind of **food** served in any kind of restaurant can make you sick – even if the food is clean, the waiters' hands may not be – but you can reduce your chances of contracting a stomach bug by avoiding certain things. Be wary of anything bought from street stalls, and avoid salads, unpasteurized milk and cheese, undercooked or reheated fish or chicken and anything that's been left lying around where flies can get at it.

### Diarrhoea and dysentery

However careful you are, the chances are that sooner or later you'll suffer a bout of **diarrhoea**, sometimes accompanied by vomiting and stomach cramps. This is usually caused by contaminated food or water, and there's not much you can do about it except drink plenty of liquid (but not alcohol or caffeine). Herbal teas like coca and camomile (*manzanilla*) can help with stomach cramps, and you should also replace **salts** either by taking oral rehydration salts or by mixing a teaspoon of salt and eight of sugar in a litre of purified water. "Blocking" drugs like loperamide (Imodium, Lomotil, etc) are useful if you have to keep travelling when suffering from diarrhoea, but they only alleviate the symptoms temporarily and can actually make things worse if you have dysentery. Once you're holding down liquid, eat bland food like rice, soup and crackers, but avoid spicy, fatty and fried food, dairy products, raw fruit and alcohol until you've recovered.

You should seek **medical advice** if your diarrhoea contains blood; if it's accompanied by a high fever (over 39°C); if abdominal pain becomes constant; or if the symptoms continue for more than five days. If your diarrhoea contains blood or mucus, the cause may be amoebic dysentery, bacterial dysentery or giardia. With a fever, it could be caused by **bacterial dysentery**, which may clear up without treatment. If it doesn't, a course of antibiotics such as ciprofloxacin, tetracycline or ampicillin (consider taking a course of one of these with you if you're going off the beaten track for a while) should do the trick, though they will reduce your natural resistance to future bouts.

Similar symptoms to bacterial dysentery persisting or recurring over a period of weeks could indicate **amoebic dysentery**, which can have serious long-term effects such as liver damage. This can be treated with a course of metronidazole (Flagyl) or tinidazole (Fasigyn), antibiotics that should not be taken with alcohol. Sudden, watery and bad-smelling diarrhoea, accompanied by rotten-egg belches and flatulence, is probably giardia, which is also treated with metronidazole or tinidazole. You should only take these drugs without consultation if there's no possibility of seeing a doctor. The only sure way to tell what is causing your diarrhoea is to have a stool test, which can be arranged by doctors in most towns.

## The sun

The sun can be strong in Bolivia, and serious **sunburn** and **sunstroke** are real risks. This is particularly true at high altitudes (where the temperature is not that hot but the thin air amplifies the harm done by ultraviolet rays), or when travelling by boat on rivers or lakes (where cool breezes disguise the effects of the sun as it is reflected off the water). Exposure to the sun can also increase your chances of developing skin cancer. Long sleeves and trousers protect your skin from the sun and reduce fluid loss, and you should use a wide-brimmed hat, decent sunglasses to protect your eyes and a high-factor sunscreen (fifteen or above) on all exposed skin. Sunblock and suntan lotion are available in pharmacies in the main cities, but they're generally expensive, so it's better to bring a supply with you from home. Sunscreen lip-balm is also worth using. Drink plenty of liquid, particularly if you're exercising, to prevent **dehydration**, and consider adding extra salt to your food to compensate for the effects of excessive sweating.

## Altitude sickness

**Altitude sickness** – known as **soroche** in Bolivia – is a serious and potentially life-threatening illness caused by reduced atmospheric pressure and correspondingly lower oxygen levels at high altitudes. It can affect anyone who normally lives at low altitude and ascends **above 2500m**, which means much of Bolivia, including most major cities. You're most likely to be affected if you **fly into La Paz** from near sea level – the airport is at over 4000m, and almost everyone feels at least a touch of breathlessness (see box, p.56).

Mild symptoms can include headache, insomnia, breathlessness, nausea, dizziness, loss of appetite, tiredness, rapid heartbeat and vomiting. The best way to avoid this is to ascend slowly, if at all possible, and allow yourself time to acclimatize. Avoiding alcohol and physical exertion and drinking plenty of liquid also help. Bolivians swear by **coca tea** (*mate de coca*) as a remedy, and this is available throughout the country; the prescription drug acetazolamide (Diamox) can also help with acclimatization. Normal advice is to ascend no more than 300m a day once over 3000m, so far as possible.

The symptoms of serious altitude sickness, also known as **acute mountain sickness**, are usually experienced only over 4000m. In this condition, fluid can build up in the lungs or brain, causing high-altitude pulmonary or cerebral oedema; left untreated, severely affected sufferers can lapse into unconsciousness and die within hours. Symptoms include loss of balance, confusion, intense headache, difficulty breathing and coughing up frothy, bloodstained sputum. Prompt and rapid descent is the only treatment, and you should seek immediate medical help.

## Malaria and other insect-borne diseases

**Malaria** is fairly common in lowland regions of Bolivia, particularly the Amazon, and you should take anti-malaria tablets if you'll be going anywhere below 2500m – the altitude limit of the mosquito that spreads the disease (though it's uncommon over 1500m). Consult your doctor several weeks before you leave home to see which treatment is most suitable for you. Chloroquine (Avloclor or Nivaquine) or proguanil (Paludrine) are usually recommended for risk areas in the west of the country. Atovaquone/proguanil (Malarone), doxycycline or mefloquine (Larium) is usually recommended for the Amazon basin; note that some people suffer bad side effects from mefloquine, so, if you haven't used it before, get medical advice before taking it. Whichever anti-malarial you take, it is vital to complete the full course of treatment. Malaria symptoms include fever, joint pains, loss of appetite and vomiting; if you suspect

you've caught the disease, see a doctor and get a blood test.

**Dengue fever**, **zika virus** and **yellow fever** also exist in Bolivia, and are also spread by **mosquitoes** (day-biting ones this time), and the best way to avoid malaria and all of these is not to get bitten in the first place. Try to wear long sleeves, trousers and socks, and sleep in a screened room or under mosquito netting, preferably treated with a repellent chemical. It's also a good idea to put repellent on your skin: make sure it has at least 35 percent DEET or PMD. It's best to bring this with you from home, as it's hard to come by, expensive and usually of poor quality in Bolivia.

Another insect-borne danger is American trypanosomiasis, or **Chagas' disease**. This is spread by the bite of the *vinchuca*, also known as the assassin bug, a small flying insect found mainly in thatched roofs and adobe walls in rural areas of the Cochabamba, Chuquisaca and Tarija departments up to elevations of about 3000m. The disease is fatal, though usually only after a number of years, and in some rural areas up to ninety percent of the human population is thought to be infected. The bite is usually painful and infection can be detected by a blood test; though the disease does respond to some drug treatments, the best defence is to try to avoid being bitten – if you do have to sleep under a thatched roof in affected regions, use a mosquito net.

**Leishmaniasis** is a gruesome protozoan disease spread by the bite of the sandfly, common throughout the Bolivian lowlands. The bites enlarge and ulcerate, causing large lesions that over months or years can spread to other parts of the body and eat the cartilage around the nose and mouth. Treatment involves a course of injections, available in some Bolivian hospitals; the only prevention is to avoid getting bitten. Less serious but still unpleasant is the **human botfly**, or *boro*, which lays its eggs on damp clothes or on the proboscis of a mosquito, which then transfers them to human flesh. When the eggs hatch, the larvae burrow under the skin, producing a painful lump as they grow. To remove them, cover with oil or Vaseline to cut off the air supply, then squeeze the larvae out.

## Other health issues

Bolivia is home to a wide range of **venomous snakes** (*viboras*), some of which can be lethal. Most are more concerned with getting away from you than attacking, and, even if they do strike, they may not inject any venom. Wearing boots, watching where you step and put your hands, and making a lot of noise when walking through vegetation all reduce the chances of getting bitten. In the event of a snakebite, keep the victim still and get medical help as quickly as possible. If possible, kill the snake for identification. **Stings and bites** from other creatures such as spiders and scorpions are uncommon but can be very painful or even fatal. It's a good idea to shake out your shoes and clothes before putting them on, and to check your bedclothes and under lavatory seats.

**Rabies** exists in Bolivia and people die from it. If you're spending time in remote areas or in contact with animals, it's worth having the vaccine, though all it does is buy you extra time to seek medical treatment. If you get bitten by a dog, vampire bat or other wild animal, thoroughly clean the wound with soap and water followed by alcohol or iodine and seek urgent medical attention. The only treatment is a series of injections in the stomach, which must be administered as soon as possible; these are available in most Bolivian hospitals.

### MEDICAL RESOURCES FOR TRAVELLERS

**Canadian Society for International Health** Canada ☎ 1 613 241 5785, ⓦ csih.org. Extensive list of travel health centres.
**CDC** US ☎ 1 800 232 4636, TTY 1 888 232 6348, ⓦ cdc.gov/travel. Official US government travel health site.
**fitfortravel** UK ⓦ fitfortravel.nhs.uk. NHS travel health website.
**Hospital for Tropical Diseases Travel Clinic** UK ⓦ www.thehtd .org/TravelClinic.aspx.
**International Society for Travel Medicine** US ☎ 1 404 373 8282, ⓦ istm.org. Has a full list of travel health clinics.
**MASTA (Medical Advisory Service for Travellers Abroad)** UK ☎ 0330 100 4200, ⓦ www.masta-travel-health.com.
**The Travel Doctor** Australia ☎ 1300 658 844, ⓦ traveldoctor .com.au. Lists travel clinics in Australia and New Zealand.
**Tropical Medical Bureau** Ireland ☎ 1850 487 674, ⓦ tmb.ie.

# Crime and personal safety

**Despite being among the poorest countries in the region, Bolivia has lower levels of theft and violent crime than neighbouring Peru and Brazil, though in recent years levels have risen. This is to the dismay of most ordinary Bolivians, who are shocked and outraged by stories of theft or assault, and in general the threat of crime is no greater in Bolivian cities than in North America or Europe.**

The difference is that whereas back home you blend in and can spot potential danger signs much more easily, in Bolivia you stand out like a sore thumb – an extremely wealthy sore thumb, moreover, at least in the eyes of most Bolivians. There's no need to be paranoid, though: the vast majority of crime against tourists is **opportunistic theft**, and violence is rare. By using common sense, keeping alert and taking some simple precautions, you can greatly reduce the chances of becoming a victim and help ensure you join the vast majority of foreign visitors who visit the country without experiencing any trouble at all.

## Theft

**Petty theft** is the most common crime that tourists face, and more often than not it's simply the result of carelessness. If you really don't want to lose something, don't bring it with you in the first place: wearing jewellery or expensive watches is asking for trouble.

### Precautions

It's important to make sure you have adequate **travel insurance** (see p.44), and check what the insurance company's requirements are in the event that you need to make a claim – almost all will need a police report of any theft. To reduce the problems after a potential theft, make a careful note of airline ticket numbers, hotline phone numbers if you need to cancel a credit card, travellers' cheque numbers (always keep the receipt separately) and insurance details; in addition, copy the important pages of your **passport** and **travel documents** (or scan them and save them on a USB stick or email them to yourself) and keep all these details separate from your valuables. You should also keep an emergency stash of **cash** hidden somewhere about your person. If you're staying in Bolivia for a while, consider registering with your embassy: this can save lots of time if you have to replace a lost or stolen passport.

Always carry your valuables – passport, money, travellers' cheques, credit cards, airline tickets – out of sight and under your clothing next to your skin; and keep them on you at all times. **Money belts** are good for this, but you can also get secure holders that hang under your shirt or from a loop on your belt under your trousers; a false pocket sewn inside your clothing, a leg pouch or a belt with a secret zip for cash are even more difficult for thieves to find. It's also a good idea to keep your petty cash separate from your main stash of valuables, so your hidden money belt is not revealed every time you spend a few bolivianos.

Better hotels will have a **safe** (*caja fuerte*) at reception where you can deposit your valuables if you trust the staff – this is usually safe, though it's better to leave stuff in a tamper-proof holder or a signed and sealed envelope, get an itemized receipt for what you leave, and count cash carefully before and after. Never leave cameras or other valuables lying around in your hotel room, and be cautious if sharing a room with people you don't know well – other travellers can be thieves too. Officially, you're supposed to carry your **passport** with you at all times, but if asked by the police for ID it's usually sufficient to show them a photocopy of your passport and explain that the original is in your hotel.

You are at your most vulnerable, and have the most to lose, when you're on the move or arriving in a new town and have all your luggage with you. **Bus stations** are a favourite hunting ground of thieves the world over, and Bolivia is no exception: try not to arrive after dark, keep a close eye and hand on your bags, and consider taking a taxi from the bus terminal to your hotel as a security precaution. As well as transport terminals, markets, city centres, fiestas and other crowded public places where tourists congregate are favoured by pickpockets and thieves. If you're carrying a daypack or small bag, keep it in front of you where you can see it to avoid having it slashed; when you stop and sit down, loop a strap around your leg to make it more difficult for someone to grab.

## Violent crime

**Mugging, violent robbery and assaults** are much less common, but do occur, usually at night, so try to avoid having to walk down empty streets in the early hours, particularly on your own. ATMs are an obvious target for robbers, so don't use them at night, if possible. If the robbers are armed, it's better not to resist.

Some travellers have been targeted for what's known as **express kidnapping**. This involves armed men, sometimes disguised as police, entering the taxi or minibus the victims are travelling in (usually with the complicity of the driver) and taking them to a secret location where they are forced to reveal their ATM credit card PIN and are held for several days while the account is drained. In two instances

the kidnapped travellers were murdered; most of the gang responsible were later arrested. Most cases occurred on the La Paz–Copacabana route; as such, it's best to stick to larger buses with plenty of other travellers on board when travelling on that route, and to be particularly careful when arriving after dark in the cemetery district of La Paz.

Though usually safer than walking, **taxis** carry an element of risk. If travelling alone, don't sit in the front seat, lock passenger doors to stop people jumping in beside you, and be wary of cabs driving away with your bags – if your luggage is in the boot, wait for the driver to get out first. Radio taxis called by phone are safer than unmarked cabs, and you can always refuse to share a cab with strangers if it makes you uncomfortable.

Robbery and attacks are rare (though not unknown) in more **rural areas**, though campsites are sometimes targeted on some of the more popular trekking routes – keep all your possessions inside your tent at night, avoid camping near villages where possible, and always get local advice before setting off.

## Scams

As well as opportunistic thefts, there are several **scams** used by teams of professional thieves that you should be aware of. One classic technique is distraction: your bag or clothing is mysteriously sprayed with mustard or the like, a friendly passer-by points this out and helps you clean it – while their accomplice picks your pocket or makes off with your coat or bag.

Another involves something valuable – cash, a credit card – being dropped at your feet. A passer-by spots it and asks you to check your wallet to see if it is yours, or offers to share it with you. The story ends with your own money disappearing by sleight of hand, or you being accused of theft, so walk away as quickly as possible and ignore anything dropped at your feet.

A third scam, usually used at **bus terminals**, involves thieves posing as plain-clothes police officers, complete with fake documents, asking to see your money to check for counterfeit notes or something similar. Often, an accomplice (usually a taxi driver) will already have engaged you in conversation and will vouch for this being normal procedure. It isn't. If approached by people claiming to be **undercover police**, don't get in a car with them or show them your documents or valuables, and insist on the presence of a uniformed officer – you can call one yourself on ☎110.

## The police

With any luck, most of your contact with the police will be at **frontiers and road checkpoints**. Sometimes, particularly near borders and in remote regions, you may have to register with them, so carry your **passport** with you at all times (though a photocopy may be enough if you're not travelling far). Generally the police rarely trouble tourists, but in any dealings with them it's important to be polite and respectful, as they can make problems for you if you're not. Anyone claiming to be an **undercover policeman** is probably a thief or confidence trickster (see p.41); don't get in a car with them or show them your documents or valuables, and insist on the presence of a **uniformed officer**.

If you are the victim of theft, you'll probably need to go to the police to make a report (*denuncia*) and get a **written report** for insurance purposes – this is rarely a problem, though it may take some time. In La Paz you should go to the **tourist police** (see p.89) or call them (24hr toll-free ☎800 140081 or ☎800 140071) if you are the victim of any crime.

Occasionally, the police may visit hostels with sniffer dogs and may even search your bags. If they do, watch and ideally get a witness to watch with you. Possessing a small amount of marijuana or cocaine for personal use (the exact quantity is not defined) will not result in a prison sentence although you may be arrested and interrogated. Any amount deemed to be enough for trafficking will lead to a jail sentence: a fair number of foreigners languish in Bolivian jails on drugs charges, and many wait a long time before they come to trial. You may be offered an opportunity to **"pay your fine now"**, which is obviously preferable to jail, but tread carefully, as bribing public officials is obviously a criminal offence.

## Political demonstrations

**Political unrest** is a constant in Bolivia, and demonstrations are a regular event in La Paz and the other major cities. Though usually peaceful and interesting to watch, these sometimes turn violent, so keep your distance and make sure you can get out of the area fast if things turn nasty.

**Road blockades** are also a feature of Bolivian political life, particularly in the Altiplano, where radical Aymara peasants often block the roads between La Paz and Peru. Generally, this is an inconvenience that travellers have to put up with, and you should follow events in the media if you're worried you may get cut off. If you get caught up in the blockades, keep your head down and get out of the area, and don't try running the blockades unless you really have to. Tempers can run high, with blockade-breaking buses sometimes getting stoned or torched.

## The Chapare

The election of the coca-growers' leader, Evo Morales, as president in 2006 did much to defuse the sometimes **violent confrontation** between the security forces and peasants in the **Chapare** in Cochabamba department, Bolivia's main cocaine-producing region. But away from the towns on the main road from Cochabamba to Santa Cruz this is still a dangerous area and you should be wary of going off the beaten track hereabouts, as you may be mistaken for a drug trafficker or undercover drug-enforcement agent.

# Culture and etiquette

**Particularly in the highlands, Bolivia is quite a formal country, and old-fashioned values of politeness and courtesy are still widespread. It's normal to greet everyone you talk to with a formal "good morning/afternoon/evening" ("*buenos dias, buenas tardes/noches*") before starting conversation; indeed, failure to do so can be taken as rude. In smaller towns and villages, you'll find even strangers exchange greetings as they pass on the street. "Please" ("*por favor*") and "thank you" ("*gracias*") are also very important. Bolivians in positions of authority expect to be treated with due respect, and can make things difficult for you if you fail to show it. Generally, it's best to call people *señor* or *señora*, especially if they are older than you, and to use a formal title such as doctor or mayor when addressing someone who has one.**

Many Bolivians are generous, but apt to take offence if you don't accept what they have offered you, particularly when it comes to food and drink. As for **alcohol**, escaping a drinking session after just one or two is difficult to achieve – it can be better to just slip away rather than announce that you've had enough.

**Race** is a very sensitive issue in Bolivia, both politically and on a day-to-day basis. Indigenous people should never be referred to as *Indios* (Indians) as this is considered racist and deeply offensive. *Indigena* is much better, but most refer to themselves by their specific ethnic or linguistic group – Aymaras, Quechuas, and so on. **Religion** – both Christian and indigenous – is also a serious matter, and you should always ask permission before intruding on ceremonies, and act with due respect and sensitivity inside churches and at fiestas or ritual events. Similarly, always ask permission before taking anyone's **photo**, as some Bolivians find this offensive, or expect to be paid.

Attitudes to what constitutes **appropriate clothing** vary sharply between the highlands and the tropical lowlands. Bolivians everywhere are used to foreigners wearing shorts, but in the conservative highlands it's not the done thing to show off too much flesh. In remote villages in particular this can cause real offence. In the hot and humid lowlands, on the other hand, it's acceptable to strip down to a bare minimum of shorts and sleeveless vest. Santa Cruz is particularly liberal in this respect.

The **sexism and machismo** characteristic of Latin America is arguably less prevalent in Bolivia than in many other countries, but it can still present an annoyance for foreign women, particularly those travelling alone or accompanied only by other women. Generally speaking, everyday sexual harassment is less of a problem in high-altitude cities like La Paz, where indigenous cultures predominate, and worse in lower, warmer cities like **Santa Cruz**, where Latino culture has more of a hold. Harassment usually takes the form of whistling and lewd catcalling in the street: most Bolivian women just walk on and ignore this, and you'll probably find it easiest to do likewise.

Many women find this problem increases in February and March in the run-up to **Carnaval**, when the usually good-natured custom of water fighting is used by some men as an excuse to harass women with water bombs. **Sexual assault** and rape are not common in Bolivia, but there have been a number of incidents reported by female travellers. It's best to exercise at least the same degree of caution as you would at home.

Most Bolivians do not have a very liberal attitude to **homosexuality**: though legal, it is frowned upon and kept under wraps. Though LGBT travellers are unlikely to suffer any direct abuse, it's best to be discreet and avoid public displays of affection. Larger cities have a handful of gay bars, but these tend to be fairly clandestine to avoid harassment.

# Travel essentials

## Costs

Bolivia is **one of the least expensive** countries in South America, and considerably cheaper than neighbouring Chile, Brazil and Argentina. Imported goods are expensive, but food, accommodation and transport are all relatively cheap, and travellers on a tight budget should be able to get around on Bs200/US$30/£25/€28 per day, staying in basic hotels and eating set meals in local restaurants. For about Bs400/US$60/£50/€55 per day you can enjoy more comfortable hotels and good food, take taxis when necessary and go on the occasional guided tour. Spend more than Bs700/US$100/£85/€95 per day and you can have a very comfortable trip.

Things are a bit more expensive in larger cities, especially **Santa Cruz**, and in isolated regions where goods have to be brought in over long distances. Goods and services aimed specifically at foreign tourists tend to be more expensive (flights to/from Uyuni, for example), and there is sometimes a tendency to slightly overcharge foreigners – if in doubt, always agree a price in advance before accepting a service. Prices in shops and restaurants tend to be fixed, but there is some room for **bargaining** in markets, when looking for a hotel room or buying a bus ticket – try asking for a reduction (*rebaja*). There's a limit to this, though. Bolivians don't generally enjoy bargaining for its own sake, and there are few sights more ridiculous than a wealthy gringo haggling vociferously for a tiny discount on an already inexpensive item being sold by a very poor market trader.

## Disabled travellers

Very little provision is made in Bolivia for people with disabilities. Public transport, hotels and public places such as museums are seldom equipped with ramps, widened doorways or disabled toilets, and pavements, where they exist at all, are often narrow and covered with dangerous potholes and other obstructions.

## Electricity

The electricity supply in most of Bolivia is 220V/50Hz; in La Paz, however, 110V and 220V supplies both exist, sometimes in the same house, so check before plugging in equipment. Plugs are two-pronged with round pins, but US-style flat-pinned plugs can also usually be used.

## Entry requirements

Most visitors to Bolivia do not need a visa, although the situation does change periodically, so check before travelling. **US citizens** do require a visa (currently US$160, payable in dollars or bolivianos); this is valid for ten years, allows multiple entries and up to ninety days per year, and is generally available on entry, where it must be paid for in cash, and they may possibly want (and sometimes keep) documents such as a passport-size photo, photocopy of passport, copies and printed proof of an onward flight and a hotel booking. But you never know what they'll say at a border, especially if entering by land, so it's always better if possible to get your visa in advance from a Bolivian embassy or consulate. Citizens of South Africa also need a visa (prices fluctuate, but currently around US$100 or ZAR1350); these are generally available on entry, but again it's better to get one in advance if you can.

On arrival, all travellers are issued with a **tourist card** (*tarjeta de turismo*) valid for up to ninety days' stay for citizens of most EU countries, and up to thirty days for citizens of Australia, Canada and New Zealand; your passport will also be stamped. Make sure you ask for the full ninety days if you need it and are eligible, as border officials sometimes give only thirty days, particularly at remote border crossings. A thirty-day tourist card/visa can be extended to ninety days at the **migraciónes** (immigration offices) in La Paz, Santa Cruz and other major cities; the price fluctuates but is currently around Bs550.

Border officials may ask for evidence that you have enough money to support yourself during your stay, so be prepared to show a credit card or a wad of travellers' cheques; keep cash out of sight, as officials have been known to angle for bribes. Tourist cards, as well as entry and exit stamps, are **free of charge**.

If you are coming from any country considered a risk area for yellow fever (including Argentina, Brazil, Colombia, Ecuador, Paraguay and Peru), or if you intend to travel to any part of Bolivia below 2500m in altitude, including Santa Cruz or anywhere in the Amazon, you may need to show on entry a **yellow fever vaccination certificate** at least ten days old, or an exemption certificate (for example if you are pregnant), and you may also need to show one if leaving for a high-risk country. In practice you may not be asked for it, but bring one anyway.

If you lose your tourist card, go to a *migración* office to get a new one before you try to leave the country – this involves a lengthy bureaucratic procedure, so it's best not to lose your card in the first place. If you overstay, you'll be charged a **small fine**

---

> ### BOLIVIAN EMBASSIES AND CONSULATES
>
> A full list can be found at ⓦwww .cancilleria.gob.bo (click on "Bolivia en el Exterior").
> **Australia** Suite 602, level 6, 90 Pitt St, Sydney, NSW 2000 ☎02 9247 4235, ⓦbolivia.org.au.
> **Canada** Suite 416, 130 Albert St, Ottawa, ON K1P 5G4 ☎1 613 236 5730, ⓦemboliviacanada.com.
> **South Africa** 1 Erlswold Way, Saxonwold 2129, Johannesburg ☎011 646 1408, ⓔseabeco@tiscali.co.za.
> **UK** 106 Eaton Square, London, SW1W 9AD ☎020 7235 4248, ⓦbolivianembassy.co.uk.
> **USA** Suite 200C, 1825 Connecticut Ave NW, Washington, DC 20009 ☎1 202 232 4827, ⓦboliviawdc.org; Suite 110, 2401 Fountain View Drive, Houston, TX 77057 ☎1 832 916 4200; Suite 1065, 3701 Wilshire Blvd, Los Angeles, CA 90010 ☎1 213 388 0475; Suite 240, Doral Corporate Center, 3750 NW 87th Ave, Doral, FL 33178 ☎1 786 536 9326; Suite 1004, 211 E 43rd St, New York, NY 10017 ☎1 212 687 0530.

---

for each extra day, payable at a *migración* before you try to leave the country. If you're leaving Bolivia by a particularly remote border crossing, you may need to get an exit stamp **in advance** from the *migración* in the nearest major town. **Under-18s** travelling to Bolivia without their parents need written parental consent authorized by a Bolivian embassy.

Officially you must carry your **passport** with you at all times in Bolivia, but within towns in practice you can carry a photocopy of the main page and your tourist card and entry stamps.

## Insurance

It's essential to take out an insurance policy before travelling to cover against theft, loss, illness or injury. A **typical policy** usually provides cover for the loss of baggage, tickets and – up to a certain limit – cash or cheques, as well as cancellation or curtailment of your journey. Most exclude **dangerous sports** unless an extra premium is paid: in Bolivia this can mean white-water rafting, trekking and mountain-eering, though probably not kayaking or jeep safaris.

Many policies can be tailored to exclude coverage you don't need – for example, sickness and accident benefits can often be excluded or included at will. With **medical coverage**, check whether benefits will be paid as treatment proceeds or only after you return home, and whether there is a 24-hour medical emergency number. When securing **baggage cover**, make sure that the per-article limit – typically under £500 – will cover your most valuable possession. If you need to make a claim, you should keep receipts for medicines and medical treatment; if you have things stolen, you'll need an official statement (*denuncia*) from the police.

## The internet

**Internet cafés** are most common where there are large student populations, and tend to charge about Bs2–5 an hour, or sometimes more in remote areas where competition is thin on the ground. Connections usually aren't very fast, especially outside the main cities.

A few (but not most) internet cafés also offer net phone or **Skype**, allowing you to make calls via the internet for the same price as surfing the net – by far the cheapest way of calling home.

Most hotels, and increasing numbers of cafés, restaurants and bars in the more touristy areas offer free **wi-fi**.

## Laundry

In cities and larger towns you'll find **laundries** (*lavanderías*) offering a machine wash for around Bs10–20 per kilo. Top-end hotels have laundry services, and smaller hotels should know someone who'll wash your clothes. Some budget hotels have facilities for washing your own clothes.

## LGBT travellers

Bolivia is quite conservative but it isn't actively homophobic. Single-sex marriage is not allowed, and polls indicate that around two-thirds of the population are opposed to it, but gay sex is legal for both men and women, and discrimination on grounds of sexuality is banned by law, although that does not, of course, mean that it doesn't occur. A 2016 reform allows transsexuals to change their gender on identity documents. Don't expect to find a big gay scene in Bolivia, however: gay bars and clubs are extremely thin on the ground, even in La Paz, where we are aware of only one (see p.85). Lesbians may have more luck making contacts via feminist groups such as Mujeres Creando (Ⓦmujerescreando.org), who have a congenial hangout in La Paz (see p.83), and there's a Lesbianas de Bolivia website at Ⓦlesbianas_estadea.tripod.com.

## Living and working in Bolivia

Official requirements to gain **residency** in Bolivia are complicated and time-consuming, so most travellers who want to stay in the country for longer periods do so informally, leaving Bolivia every ninety days to come back in on a new tourist card.

There are several options available to people looking to work or study in Bolivia. Several cities have **language schools** where you can study Spanish, Quechua or Aymara, and those with initiative and enthusiasm shouldn't have much trouble finding **voluntary work** with one of the many NGOs operating in Bolivia. **Paid work** is trickier to come by, and getting formal permission to work even more so, but opportunities do exist, particularly for those with valuable skills to offer.

### Studying Spanish

Bolivia is a good place to **study Spanish**. Bolivian pronunciation is slow and clear, making the language easier to pick up, and tuition costs are lower than in neighbouring countries. Spending one or several weeks on an intensive course is a good way of immersing yourself in Bolivian culture and getting to know a particular city in more detail, and can provide a good reason for living in Bolivia for a while without being a tourist.

La Paz, Sucre and Cochabamba are the most popular places for studying Spanish – **language schools** are detailed in our Directory section for each of these cities in the Guide (see p.89, p.206 & p.217). You'll also find individual Spanish language teachers offering their services on a one-to-one basis in these cities and in smaller towns around Bolivia. These can be very good, though it's worth trying a lesson or two before you commit to a long course with a particular teacher. More adventurous linguists can also study **Quechua** (in Cochabamba) or **Aymara** (in La Paz).

### Volunteering

Most opportunities for volunteering in Bolivia require you to pay for your own food and accommodation and to stay for at least a month. Unless you're willing to pay the (often high) fees charged by agencies that match volunteers with charities, the best way to find volunteering work is by **word of mouth**. Ask around in cities like La Paz, Sucre and Cochabamba and you're likely to find something worthwhile if you're prepared to work for free, especially if you have useful skills to offer. Also try contacting **local NGOs** – and international ones working in Bolivia – directly. You'll need a reasonable level of **Spanish** if you want to do any kind of volunteer work with local communities. A useful website with information on free and low-cost volunteering opportunities is ⓦvolunteersouth america.net.

One place that does take volunteers on a regular basis is the **Parque Machia** animal refuge in Villa Tunari in the Chapare region, east of Cochabamba (see p.225). Volunteers do everything from maintaining trails and looking after rescued animals to cleaning toilets and showing school children around the park. Conservation-centred tour operator **Madidi Travel**, on Calle Comercio in Rurrenabaque or c/o *Posada de la Abuela Obdulia* in La Paz (☎03 8922153 or ☎02 2318313, ⓦmadidi-travel.com), also welcomes volunteers to help out with both its Rurrenabaque office and private rainforest reserve; jungle-based volunteers get room and board. **Up Close Bolivia** (ⓦupclosebolivia.org), associated with Colibri Camping (see p.81), offers volunteering opportunities near La Paz, and in Coroico (see p.129) you may be able to volunteer with the Senda Verde Animal Refuge (ⓦsendaverde.com).

### Paid work

Unless you have arranged something in advance with an international company or non-government organization, your chances of finding paid work in Bolivia are slim. The best bet is **teaching English** in La Paz, Cochabamba or Santa Cruz, though pay is low unless you get work with the British Council or a similar international agency, best arranged in advance. Obviously, work as a teacher is easier to find if you have a formal TEFL/CELTA qualification. Even if you do find paid employment, getting a work permit is a costly and drawn-out bureaucratic nightmare – contact *migración* in La Paz or any major city for details.

## Mail

There's constant talk of shutting down **post offices** (ⓦcorreosbolivia.com), but so far that hasn't happened, although offices in small towns do seem gradually to be disappearing. Letters and postcards sent by airmail (*por avión*) take one to two weeks to Europe and North America, longer to the rest of the world. Letters cost Bs23 to Britain or Europe, Bs20 to North America, Bs26 to Australasia or South Africa; postcards cost less (Bs14–18). For a small extra charge, you can send letters **certified** (*certificado*), which is more reliable, but even then it's not a good idea to send anything you can't afford to lose.

**Parcels** up to 2kg can be airmailed from major post offices; this costs about Bs100–120 per kilo to Europe and about half that to North America; the contents must be checked by a customs officer in a post office before being sealed. There's no point sending anything from small town post offices, as you'll almost certainly reach the nearest city or large town before your letter or package does. To send anything important or urgent internationally, it's worth splashing out and using an internationally recognized **courier service**: FedEx and DHL have offices in major cities.

If you wish to **receive mail** in Bolivia, you can do so through the **poste restante** (general delivery) service available in most post offices – it's best to use those in major towns or cities. Have mail sent to "Lista de Correos, Correo Central, the town concerned, Bolivia", and make sure your surname is written in capitals and as obviously as possible, as your post will be filed under whatever the clerk thinks your surname is; if you suspect something sent to you has gone astray, ask them to check under your first name too. Mail is usually held for about three months, and you'll need your passport to collect it.

## Maps

No two maps of Bolivia are identical, and none is absolutely accurate. Most errors are in the mapping of **dirt roads and tracks**. Some maps mark them incorrectly as proper roads; some miss them out altogether. And some show roads quite clearly in areas where they have never existed except in the dreams of planners.

It's worth buying a good map of Bolivia from a **specialist map outlet** in your home country before you go, as they can be difficult to find in Bolivia itself. The best **general map** of Bolivia is published by the German firm Reise Know-How (1:3,000,000); alternatives include those published by National Geographic (1:1,415,000) and by the Argentine firm deDios (1:1,250,000).

If you're planning to do any **trekking** or **climbing** in the Cordillera Real, you should try to get hold of Liam O'Brien's *A New Map of the Cordillera Real de Los Andes*, which is an excellent map of that range (if you can't get it at home, bookshops in Bolivia sometimes still have copies of it). The Bolivian Instituto Geográfico Militar, or IGM, produces maps at a scale of 1:50,000 and 1:250,000 that cover about three-quarters of the country and are useful for trekkers or anyone planning to explore more remote areas; they can be bought from the Instituto Geográfico Militar in La Paz (see p.88), or downloaded from their website (W igmbolivia.gob .bo). You can also find maps at W wikiloc.com, where you can download a handy map phone app, which requires only GPS (not phone network) coverage.

## The media

### Newspapers and magazines

In La Paz, the main quality **dailies** are *La Prensa* (W laprensa.com.bo), which has good foreign coverage, the politically conservative *El Diario* (W eldiario.net), and the less reliable *La Razón* (W la-razon.com). The main provincial cities have their own newspapers, with a strong regional perspective, the best of which are *Los Tiempos* from Cochabamba (W lostiempos.com) and *El Deber* from Santa Cruz (W eldeber.com.bo). Foreign newspapers and magazines are not commonly available, but you may find *Time*, *Newsweek* and *The Economist* at upmarket hotels in La Paz and Santa Cruz. There is also an English-language cultural magazine, the *Bolivian Express*, which is available for free in a few bars and hotels, and also online (W bolivianexpress .org).

### Radio

Radio is the most democratic of Bolivia's media, and the only one that adequately reflects the country's cultural diversity, with many of the country's hundreds of different stations broadcasting in **indigenous languages**. The leading national news radio station is Radio Fides (W radiofides.com), owned by the Catholic Church and broadcast on different FM frequencies in all the major cities. There's also a feminist station, Radio Deseo, at 103.3FM and W radiodeseo.com. For a full rundown of Bolivian radio stations, see W emisorasbolivianas.com.

### Television

Bolivians watch a huge amount of television, most of it pretty trashy. Typically, people turn it on and then ignore it, leaving it to drone away in the background. Hotels often have cable TV, with scores of channels that often include CNN and BBC World and other English-language options.

## Money

The Bolivian currency is the **peso boliviano** (Bs), referred to as both the peso and (more commonly) the **boliviano**. Thanks to the flux in the Bolivian economy the boliviano remains vulnerable to volatility, and some businesses in Bolivia effectively operate in US dollars (given throughout the Guide as $). Many tour operators and mid-range/top-end hotels quote their prices in US dollars rather than bolivianos, accepting payment in either currency. Otherwise, it's usual to pay for everything in bolivianos – indeed, most places won't accept anything else.

**Notes** come in denominations of 200, 100, 50, 20 and 10 bolivianos; coins in denominations of 1 and 2 bolivianos (these look very similar), 5 bolivianos, and 10, 20 and 50 centavos. At time of writing the exchange rates were roughly: £1 = Bs8.40; US$1 = Bs6.75; €1 = Bs7.20.

### Credit cards and cash

The best way to carry money in Bolivia is to have both plastic and cash dollars, so that if one lets you down you can turn to another. The easiest way to access funds is using plastic. **ATM**s are widespread; from those attached to bank branches you can take out US dollars as well as bolivianos. The cash limit varies from bank to bank, as does the commission and transaction fee. Banco Mercantil de Santa Cruz, Bisa and BNB tend to be the best ones to use. Credit and debit cards are mainly only used in expensive shops and restaurants, and in some hotels and tour agencies. Visa is the most widely accepted, followed by Mastercard; American Express cards are rarely used. Because plastic is so little used, especially outside of big cities, it's a good idea to carry plenty of **cash** when you head to rural areas, although most towns have ATMs, and US dollars can be changed into bolivianos at banks and by money changers almost everywhere in the country.

**Small change** is often in short supply in Bolivia and people may be reluctant to accept larger-denomination notes, so it's best to break them at every opportunity – in big shops, hotels and bus company offices. You should also be wary of forged notes – dollars and bolivianos – particularly if changing money with street money changers.

## Opening hours

Shops, businesses and public offices in Bolivia generally open Monday to Saturday from around 8.30am or 9.30am. They mostly close for a **long lunch break** between about noon and 2pm (even longer in some regions), and then open again until around 5.30pm to 7pm. Some offices, however, have adopted a newer system, known as *hora corrida*, whereby they work straight though from 8.30am to 4pm without closing for lunch.

**Banks'** opening hours are generally Monday to Friday from 8.30am to noon and 2.30pm to 5pm, and on Saturdays in the morning. **Public museums** usually open on Sundays for at least half the day, and close instead on Mondays. All these times are approximate, though: Bolivians aren't noted for their punctuality, and public offices in particular often open later and close earlier than they are supposed to; conversely, private businesses, particularly those connected with tourism, often work longer hours and open on Sundays. If you're arranging to meet a Bolivian, make it somewhere you don't mind waiting

around, as they're unlikely to turn up on time. Note that during **public holidays** – of which there are both national and regional ones – and **local fiestas** (see p.33), pretty much everything closes down.

## Phones

Bolivia's phone system is fairly efficient. The Bolivian national telephone company, **ENTEL**, has offices in all cities and most towns where you can make local, national and international calls. Smaller offices of Punto ENTEL or Punto Cotel are even more widespread. Local calls are very cheap, and long-distance or international calls are usually quite moderately priced. Internet cafés generally don't have facilities for using VOIP services such as Skype. Many shops and kiosks have phones from which you can make short local calls for a small fee.

### Mobile phones

Mobile (cell) phone coverage is generally good in large towns and cities and improving in rural areas. If you want to use one while in Bolivia, the easiest option is to bring your own phone from home and buy a Bolivian **SIM card** ("chip") from one of the several mobile network operators – such as Viva, Tigo or ENTEL – which you can then top up with credit. Annoyingly, foreigners can only – officially at least – buy SIM cards from bigger branches of the mobile companies, which tend to be in the larger towns or cities; take your passport. If you have a mobile but not a local SIM card and want to call a Bolivian mobile, note that most Bolivian cell phone users are on Whatsapp.

---

## TELEPHONE CODES AND USEFUL NUMBERS

### INTERNATIONAL CALLS

|  | From Bolivia | To Bolivia |
|---|---|---|
| **UK** | ☎00 44 | ☎00 591 |
| **Ireland** | ☎00 353 | ☎00 591 |
| **US and Canada** | ☎00 1 | ☎011 591 |
| **Australia** | ☎00 61 | ☎0011 591 |
| **New Zealand** | ☎00 64 | ☎00 591 |
| **South Africa** | ☎00 27 | ☎09 591 |

### REGIONAL AREA CODES

La Paz, Oruro and Potosí ☎02, Chuquisaca and Tarija ☎04, Beni, Pando and Santa Cruz ☎03. Calling from abroad, after dialling 591, you then omit the initial zero.

### USEFUL NUMBERS

Police emergency ☎110
Fire brigade ☎119

Operator ☎101
Directory enquiries ☎104

## Photography

The light in Bolivia is very bright, particularly at **high altitudes**, so the best times to take photos in the highlands are early morning and late afternoon, when the sunlight is not too harsh. Under the **forest canopy** in the lowlands, on the other hand, light is poor, so you need a longer exposure. Taking photos of people without permission can offend, particularly in rural areas. It's best to ask politely ("*Puedo sacar una fotito?*" – "Can I take a little photo?"); most people react favourably to this approach, though some may refuse or ask for a small fee.

## Time

Bolivia is on GMT–4. It's an hour ahead of US Eastern Standard Time (the same as Eastern Daylight Time).

## Tourist information

Bolivia has no national tourist offices. Although you can sometimes get limited information from some of the country's embassies, you'll probably find that **tour companies** who run trips to Bolivia are a better bet.

Most major Bolivian cities have a **regional tourism office**, either run by the city municipality or by the departmental prefecture. Some are fairly helpful, handing out free leaflets and doing their best to answer questions (though rarely in English). Others offer a much more limited service, though you should at least be able to get a plan of the city from them. Local Bolivian **tour operators** are generally a good source of information, and many are happy to answer queries, often in English, though obviously their main aim is to sell you one of their tours. The best source of information is often **word of mouth** from fellow travellers.

## Travelling with children

Because of the extremes of climate, travelling with children can be a challenge in Bolivia, but certainly not an insuperable one. Most Bolivians are very family-orientated and will give children a warm welcome. Less warm at times is the **weather**: winter can get fiendishly cold at high altitude, and the **altitude** itself can be hard on kids, so gradual adjustment is the key, and you should always keep a close eye out for symptoms of altitude sickness. Despite the cold, the sun can also be a danger, so make sure your kids are well protected with hats and sunscreen. In case of **diarrhoea** – a much more serious threat to children's health than it is for adults – it's also a good idea to carry bottled water and sachets of oral rehydration salts (*sales de rehidratación*), which you can buy at many but not all Bolivian pharmacies. Children also, of course, need to be aware of the dangers of playing with animals such as dogs or cats, especially stray ones. In the jungle, on the other hand, they should enjoy animal spotting, and llamas are pretty approachable too, although they aren't big on being petted as such. One or two hotels, such as *Hostal La Cúpula* in Copacabana (see p.108), keep semi-tame animals. Most hotels will let children stay in your room for not very much or nothing at all (depending on their age). On public transport, children usually pay if occupying their own seat. Generally speaking, if travelling with kids, you should take it easy, always give them time to adjust to the climate and altitude, and where possible use private transport (taxis, chartered minibuses, private tours) that will let you stop whenever you need a break – for a family of, say, four, booking a private tour will not cost much more than joining a group.

# La Paz

LA PAZ AND MOUNT ILLIMANI

**1**

# La Paz

Few cities in the world have as spectacular a setting as La Paz. Glimpsed for the first time as your bus or taxi crawls over the lip of the narrow canyon in which the city sits hunched, it's a sight that will leave your lungs gasping for breath – quite literally, since La Paz sits at over 3500m above sea level. Set amid a hollow gouged into the Altiplano, the city is a scene of stunning contrasts: a central cluster of church spires and office blocks lies dwarfed by the magnificent icebound peak of Mount Illimani rising imperiously to the southeast, while on either side, the steep valley slopes are smothered by the ramshackle red-brick homes of the city's poorer inhabitants, clinging precariously to even the harshest gradients.

With a population of some 800,000 people (getting on for two million in its urban area), La Paz is the political and commercial hub of Bolivia and the capital in all but name (technically, that honour belongs to Sucre). Though protected to some extent from the tides of globalization by its isolation and singular cultural make-up, La Paz feels very much part of the twenty-first century, its manic bustle and offbeat, cosmopolitan charm luring travellers back time and again.

Founded as a centre of Spanish power in the Andes, La Paz has always had a dual identity, with two very distinct societies – the indigenous and the European – coexisting in the same geographical space. International banks, fast-food chains and government offices rub shoulders with vibrant street markets selling all manner of ritual paraphernalia for appeasing the spirits and mountain gods that still play a central role in the lives of the indigenous **Aymaras**. The Aymaras, in fact, make up not only the majority of the city's population, but also that of the neighbouring city of **El Alto**, La Paz's militant, red-brick alter ego, which continues to outstrip it in terms of population, and often media coverage.

La Paz's geography makes it a difficult place to get lost in: from most parts of town, just head downhill and you'll eventually hit the city's main commercial thoroughfare, the broad avenue known as the **Prado**, a popular thoroughfare for strolling and socializing. The street runs along the course of La Paz's river, the **Río Choqueyapu**, now entombed in concrete beneath it. Halfway along the Prado, **Plaza San Francisco** is at the very centre of town. To its east is the **Casco Viejo**, the main administrative district, dominated by banks and ministries, and also home to most of the city's museums and surviving colonial churches. On the other side is the main tourist zone, around **Calle Sagárnaga**. South of the centre lies the pleasant middle-class suburb of **Sopocachi**, an area inhabited predominantly by the descendants of Europeans. Many of the city's wealthiest residents likewise now live in the suburbs that have sprung up down the valley in the **Zona Sur**, about 5km from the city centre.

TIWANAKU

# Highlights

**1 Calle Jaén** The best-preserved colonial street in La Paz is lined with elegant Spanish-style mansions, several intriguing museums, an authentic *peña* and an art gallery. **See p.61**

**2 Iglesia de San Francisco** The city's most beautiful colonial church. **See p.64**

**3 Mercado de Hechicería** This most colourful and compelling of La Paz's innumerable street markets sells all manner of Aymara ritual paraphernalia and herbal cures. **See p.66**

**4 Mi Teleférico** La Paz's new cable-car system offers a scintillating (and cheap) ride over the rim of the Altiplano. **See p.75**

**5 Mercado Lanza** The most adventurous and entertaining eating experience in the city, a giant complex crammed with home-style Aymara food stalls. **See p.82**

**6 Gustu restaurant** Splurge on a visit to this culinary pioneer, brainchild of the co-founder of Denmark's lauded *Noma*. **See p.84**

**7 Tiwanaku** Just an hour away from La Paz, the ancient ruined city of Tiwanaku is one of the most monumental and intriguing archeological sites in South America. **See p.90**

**HIGHLIGHTS ARE MARKED ON THE MAPS ON P.54, P.58 & P.80**

**1**

Horrendous congestion and belching pollution notwithstanding, most visitors find that La Paz's compelling street life and tremendous cultural energy warrant spending at least a few days here, even if conventional tourist attractions are limited to a scattering of **colonial palaces**, **plazas** and **churches** in the centre of town. The city's **museums**, while perhaps not fully doing justice to Bolivia's fascinating history and culture, likewise deserve at least a day or two's browsing.

## Brief history

La Ciudad de Nuestra Señora de la Paz – "**The City of Our Lady of Peace**" – was founded on October 20, 1548 by Spanish conquistador Alonso de Mendoza, on the orders of Viceroy Pedro de la Gasca. The foundation of La Paz was to commemorate the end of almost ten years of bitter civil war between rival Spanish factions fighting over the combined territories of Alto and Bajo Peru – Gasca had ended the war with a judicious blend of amnesty and force, executing rebel leader Gonzalo Pizarro in April 1548. Sited in the **Chukiyapu** (or Choqueyapu) valley, the city developed an economy based on commerce rather than mining.

### The seventeenth and eighteenth centuries

The merchants of La Paz grew rich through the trade in **coca** from the Yungas to the mines of Potosí, and the city also prospered as a waystation on the route between the mines and the coast, and between Lima and Buenos Aires. By 1665 some five hundred

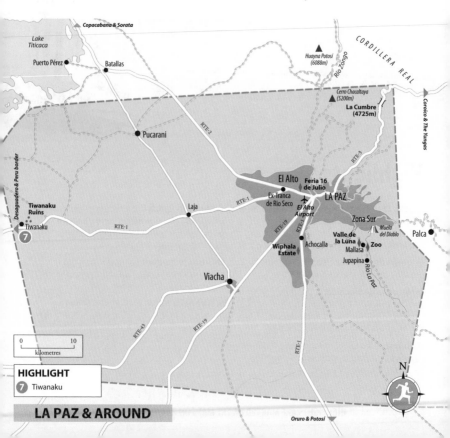

**HIGHLIGHT**

**7** Tiwanaku

**LA PAZ & AROUND**

1

Spaniards were living in La Paz, with a much larger indigenous population housed on the other side of the fledgling city across the **Río Choqueyapu**. In 1781 an indigenous army led by **Tupac Katari** twice laid siege to La Paz (see p.306), though the city survived and held out until it was relieved by the army sent from **Buenos Aires** that finally crushed the rebellion.

### Independence

By the time Bolivia's independence from Spain was finally secured in 1825 (see p.307), La Paz was the biggest city in the country, with a population of forty thousand. Though **Sucre** remained the capital, La Paz was increasingly the focus of the new republic's turbulent political life. In 1899 the growing rivalry between the two cities was resolved in a short but bloody **civil war** that left La Paz as the seat of government, home to the president and the congress, and the capital in all but name.

### The twentieth century

The first half of the twentieth century saw La Paz's population grow to over three hundred thousand. In 1952 La Paz was the scene of the fierce street fighting that ushered in the **revolution** led by the MNR, or Movimiento Nacionalista Revolucionario (see p.312). The sweeping changes that followed further fuelled the city's growth as the Aymara population of the Altiplano, released from servitude by the Agrarian reform (see p.313), migrated en masse to the metropolis. This migration from the countryside changed the character of La Paz profoundly, quadrupling its population and transforming it into a predominantly Aymara city, albeit still ruled by a wealthy European-descended minority.

### Into the twenty-first century

While this ethnic and geographical gulf is hardly without precedent in Latin America, age-old tensions reached a boiling point in the first decade of the new century, with violent civil disturbances toppling a series of neo-liberal presidents. La Paz continued to be the focus for national demonstrations: plans to export natural gas via a Chilean pipeline prompted the first "**gas war**" in 2003 (see p.318). Further unrest over the unresolved gas issue erupted in May and June 2005 with hundreds of thousands of indigenous protestors massing in La Paz, effectively cutting off the city and effecting the resignation of then-president **Carlos Mesa**.

The **mayor** of La Paz between 2000 and 2010 was human-rights lawyer **Juan del Granado**, founder of the progressive **Movimiento Sin Miedo** (MSM; Movement Without Fear) and a nominal ally of President Evo Morales (see below). Granado, who rose to prominence after prosecuting former dictator General Tejada in the 1980s and early 1990s, was credited with tackling corruption in the city government, as well as initiating a spate of major infrastructure projects – his tenure is widely regarded as one of the most successful in Bolivian history.

### The reign of Evo Morales

With the 2005 election of Bolivia's first indigenous president, **Evo Morales**, the Aymaras finally achieved real political power and the traditional campesinos-versus-the-state ferment was superseded, to some extent, by a wider geopolitical cultural spat between the radical Altiplano and the conservative lowlands. Still, **demonstrations** by discontented miners, pensioners, fuel protestors and indeed anyone at all who feels hard done by have continued, underlying the fact that La Paz, in its strategic relation to El Alto and the Highland Aymara communities, remains a vital crucible for popular protest.

In 2010 the MSM once again dominated municipal elections, with candidate **Luis Revilla** duly elected mayor of La Paz. However, the alliance between the MSM and

1

### ALTITUDE SICKNESS

The main problem you're likely to face when you arrive in La Paz is the **altitude**: the city centre stands at over 3500m above sea level, and the airport in El Alto is even higher, at 4061m. If you're flying in or arriving by bus from lower elevations you may suffer from **altitude sickness**, known locally as **soroche**, a debilitating and potentially dangerous condition caused by the reduced oxygen levels found at high elevations. Mild **symptoms** can include breathlessness and tiredness, sometimes accompanied by rapid heartbeat, nausea, dizziness, headache, insomnia and loss of appetite. For most people these fade within a couple of days as the body adjusts to the rarefied air. On arrival at high altitude you should take things very slowly and get straight to a hotel where you can leave your luggage and rest; avoid alcohol and drink plenty of water.

In its more serious forms, altitude sickness can be dangerous and even life-threatening. **Acute mountain sickness** (AMS), usually experienced only over 4000m, requires immediate medical help – the best place for this is the High Altitude Pathology Institute, Clinica IPPA, Av Copacabana Prolongación 55 (T 02 2245394, W altitudeclinic.com).

For more on *soroche* and AMS, see Basics (p.38).

Evo's **Movimiento al Socialismo** (Movement for Socialism; MaS) became strained, and Juan del Granado ran against Evo in the 2014 presidential election, though he gained few votes. Evo's party suffered big setbacks in the 2015 municipal elections however, losing not only in La Paz – where Luis Revilla was re-elected on a Soberanía y Libertad (Sovereignty and Freedom, SoL) ticket – but even in El Alto, formerly a staunch MaS stronghold, which fell to centre-right candidate Soledad Chapetón, known locally as "La Sole". These divisions have not stopped the central government gracing La Paz with a new and excellent cable-car system (see box, p.75), which when completed will serve La Paz as other cities are served by a metro.

# Casco Viejo

The well-ordered streets of the colonial city centre or **Casco Viejo** contain the grandest buildings in La Paz, as well as the best museums and key government buildings. Laid out on the slopes on the eastern side of the Prado, this is where the Spanish founded their administrative centre in the sixteenth century. Today, the central **Plaza Murillo** remains home to both the parliament building and the presidential palace. Many colonial buildings in the area are in a poor state of repair; the exceptions are concentrated around the Plaza Murillo and nearby **Calle Jaén**, both of which are also home to several museums.

## Plaza Murillo and around

Though it remains the epicentre of Bolivia's political life, **Plaza Murillo** – the main square of the colonial city centre – has an endearingly provincial feel, busy with people feeding pigeons and eating ice cream, and filled with smartly dressed families on weekends. On the south side of the plaza stand two great symbols of political and spiritual power in Bolivia, the **Catedral** and the **Palacio de Gobernio**. The square is named after the independence martyr **Pedro Domingo Murillo**, hanged here in 1810 after leading a failed rebellion against the colonial authorities, one of several bloody scenes the square has witnessed during Bolivia's turbulent political past. A grand statue of Murillo now stands at the centre of the plaza. On the southwest side of the plaza facing the cathedral stands a bust of former president **Gualberto Villarroel**, who as recently as 1946 was thrown to his death from a balcony of the Palacio de Gobierno by a mob and then hung from a lamppost.

**1**

## Catedral Metropolitana
Comercio and Socabaya (on Plaza Murillo) • Mon–Fri 9am–noon & 3–7pm, Sat & Sun 8am–noon • Free

With its twin bell towers and imposing but rather plain Neoclassical facade, the **Catedral Metropolitana Nuestra Señora de La Paz** is remarkable more for the time it took to complete than for its aesthetic value. Work started in 1835, but the cathedral was only opened in 1925, the interior wasn't finished until 1932, and the two towers were inaugurated in 1989 during the visit of Pope John Paul II. The cool, vaulted interior is relatively unadorned, in contrast to La Paz's many Baroque churches; its most unusual feature is a stained-glass window depicting former presidents Mariscal Andrés de Santa Cruz and General José de Ballivián and their families receiving blessings from on high, a surprisingly explicit expression of the historic conflation in Bolivia of Church, military and state.

## Palacio de Gobierno
Comercio and Ayacucho (on Plaza Murillo) • Closed to the public

Next door to the cathedral stands the elegant Neoclassical presidential palace, the **Palacio de Gobierno**, its ceremonial guards in red nineteenth-century uniforms from

---

### FESTIVE LA PAZ

Aside from the usual celebrations of Carnaval, Semana Santa (Easter week), Christmas and the New Year, La Paz has three big festivals of its own that are well worth seeing if you manage to coincide with them.

#### FERIA DE ALASITAS: THE FESTIVAL OF ABUNDANCE

The **Feria de Alasitas**, held in the last week of January, is one of Bolivia's most unusual fiestas. Large areas of the city are taken over by market stalls selling all manner of miniature items. At the centre of the festivities is a diminutive figure of a mustachioed man with rosy cheeks and a broad smile, dressed in a tiny suit and hat and laden with foodstuffs and material possessions. This is the **Ekeko**, the household god of abundance. A common sight in Paceño homes, the Ekeko is a demanding god who must be kept happy with regular supplies of alcohol, cigarettes and **miniature gifts**. In return, he watches over the household, ensuring happiness and prosperity and returning in kind any gift he receives. At the fair each year, people buy objects they desire in miniature to give to the Ekeko, thereby ensuring that the real thing will be theirs before the year is out. Originally, gifts to the Ekeko would have been farm animals and foodstuffs, but nowadays miniature cars, houses, electrical goods, wads of dollar bills and even airline tickets and university degrees are generally preferred.

#### FIESTA DEL GRAN PODER

**La Fiesta del Gran Poder** is a dramatic religious fiesta held during late May or early June in homage to a miraculous image of Christ known as **Nuestro Señor del Gran Poder** (Our Lord of Great Power). The origins of the Gran Poder are surprisingly recent. It started in 1974 as a local celebration among Aymara migrants in the market district, but has now grown into an enormous festival that takes over the centre of the city and is enjoyed by Paceños of all classes. Tens of thousands of costumed dancers from over a hundred different folkloric fraternities take part in the **entrada** – the procession that marks the start of the fiesta – parading through the centre of La Paz to the cacophonous accompaniment of massed brass bands. The dances performed during the *entrada* represent Aymara and **Catholic traditions** from all over the department of La Paz and further afield.

#### ENTRADA FOLKLÓRICA UNIVERSITARIA

On the last Saturday in June, students at the University of San Andrés perform in the **Entrada Folklórica Universitaria** – a parade of dancing and costume through the city centre, featuring brass bands and a huge selection of traditional dances from different parts of the country continuing long into the night. Parts of the Prado and Avenida Camacho are closed to traffic for the event, with viewing stands set up to watch the parade.

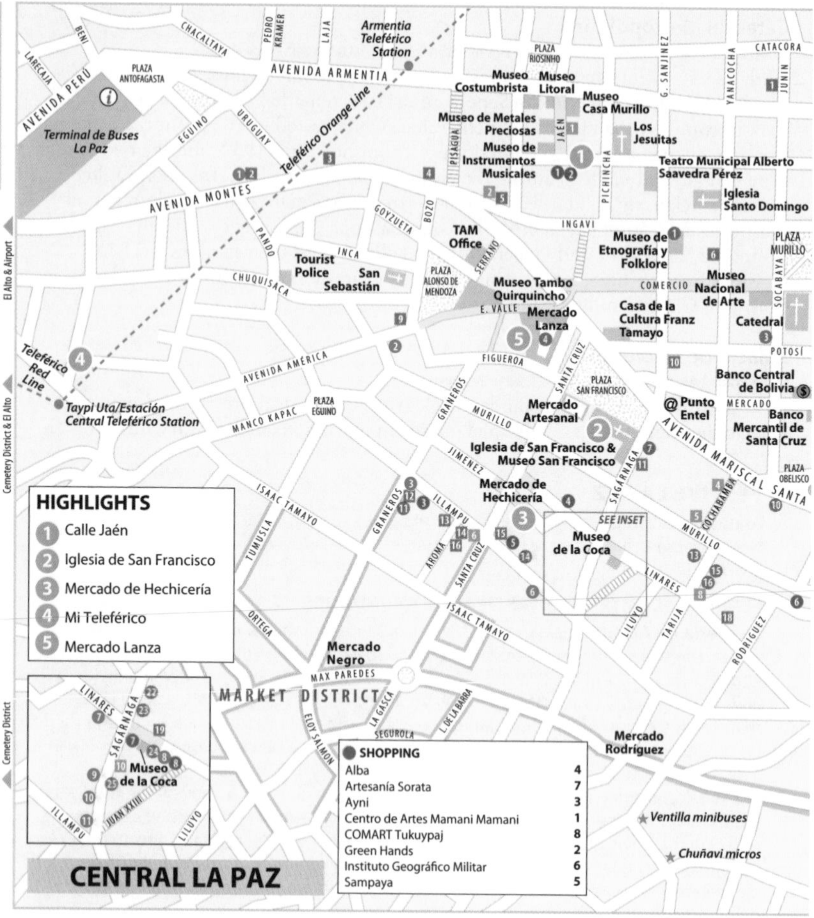

**1**

**HIGHLIGHTS**

1 Calle Jaén
2 Iglesia de San Francisco
3 Mercado de Hechicería
4 Mi Teleférico
5 Mercado Lanza

**CENTRAL LA PAZ**

**SHOPPING**

| | |
|---|---|
| Alba | 4 |
| Artesanía Sorata | 7 |
| Ayni | 3 |
| Centro de Artes Mamani Mamani | 1 |
| COMART Tukuypaj | 8 |
| Green Hands | 2 |
| Instituto Geográfico Militar | 6 |
| Sampaya | 5 |

the War of the Pacific discreetly backed up by military policemen with more modern weapons. As the day-to-day office of the president, the palace isn't open to the public, though Evo Morales has suggested it could be turned into a museum in the future. Completed in 1852, the palace is known as the **Palacio Quemado** – the "Burnt Palace" – after being damaged by fire in 1875 during one of Bolivia's more violent revolutionary episodes.

## Palacio Legislativo

Ayacucho (east side of Plaza Murillo) • Visitors' Gallery open to the public for select debates; passport required

The Neoclassical **Palacio Legislativo** is the seat of the Bolivian parliament, built in the style of a grand French palace in 1905. It stands on the site previously occupied by the Jesuit headquarters until their expulsion from the Spanish Empire in 1767. Inside are the two branches of the national legislature, the Cámara de Diputados (chamber of deputies) and the Cámara de Senadores (senate). Even this building hasn't been immune to the worst effects of Bolivia's tumultuous political climate, with a miner infamously blowing himself up inside in 2004, in protest at the lack of retirement provision.

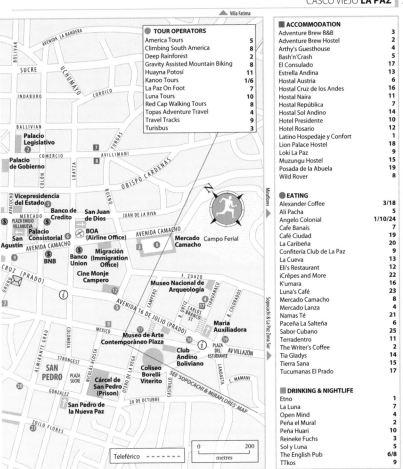

● **TOUR OPERATORS**

| | |
|---|---|
| America Tours | 5 |
| Climbing South America | 8 |
| Deep Rainforest | 2 |
| Gravity Assisted Mountain Biking | 8 |
| Huayna Potosí | 11 |
| Kanoo Tours | 1/6 |
| La Paz On Foot | 7 |
| Luna Tours | 10 |
| Red Cap Walking Tours | 8 |
| Topas Adventure Travel | 4 |
| Travel Tracks | 9 |
| Turisbus | 3 |

■ **ACCOMMODATION**

| | |
|---|---|
| Adventure Brew B&B | 3 |
| Adventure Brew Hostel | 2 |
| Arthy's Guesthouse | 4 |
| Bash'n'Crash | 5 |
| El Consulado | 17 |
| Estrella Andina | 13 |
| Hostal Austria | 6 |
| Hostal Cruz de los Andes | 16 |
| Hostal Naira | 11 |
| Hostal República | 7 |
| Hostal Sol Andino | 14 |
| Hotel Presidente | 10 |
| Hotel Rosario | 12 |
| Latino Hospedaje y Confort | 1 |
| Lion Palace Hostel | 18 |
| Loki La Paz | 9 |
| Muzungu Hostel | 15 |
| Posada de la Abuela | 19 |
| Wild Rover | 8 |

● **EATING**

| | |
|---|---|
| Alexander Coffee | 3/18 |
| Ali Pacha | 5 |
| Angelo Colonial | 1/10/24 |
| Cafe Banaís | 7 |
| Café Ciudad | 19 |
| La Caribeña | 20 |
| Confitería Club de La Paz | 9 |
| La Cueva | 13 |
| Eli's Restaurant | 12 |
| iCrêpes and More | 22 |
| K'umara | 16 |
| Luna's Café | 23 |
| Mercado Camacho | 8 |
| Mercado Lanza | 4 |
| Namas Té | 21 |
| Paceña La Salteña | 6 |
| Sabor Cubano | 25 |
| Terradentro | 11 |
| The Writer's Coffee | 2 |
| Tia Gladys | 14 |
| Tierra Sana | 15 |
| Tucumanas El Prado | 17 |

■ **DRINKING & NIGHTLIFE**

| | |
|---|---|
| Etno | 1 |
| La Luna | 7 |
| Open Mind | 4 |
| Peña el Mural | 2 |
| Peña Huari | 10 |
| Reineke Fuchs | 3 |
| Sol y Luna | 5 |
| The English Pub | 6/8 |
| TTkos | 9 |

## Museo Nacional de Arte

Comercio 485, at Socabaya (on the southwest corner of Plaza Murillo) • Tues–Fri 9.30am–12.30pm & 3–7pm, Sat 10am–5.30pm, Sun 10am–1.30pm • Bs20 • ☎ 02 2408600, ⓦ facebook.com/museonacionaldeartebolivia

It would be difficult to think of a more magnificent setting for Bolivia's premier art gallery, the **Museo Nacional de Arte**, than the colonial palace in which it is housed – one of La Paz's finest surviving examples. Built for Don Francisco Tadeo Díez de Medina, once the city's mayor, the palace was completed in 1775, when La Paz was at the peak of its colonial prosperity, and is a pre-eminent example of Baroque architecture, with a grand portico opening onto a central patio overlooked by three floors of arched walkways, all elaborately carved from pink granite in a Rococo style with stylized shells, flowers and feathers. The museum itself is well worth visiting for its comprehensive collection of works by major Bolivian painters.

### Colonial art

The emphasis of the museum's art collection is firmly on colonial religious art. Among the highlights are several works by **Melchor Pérez de Holguín** (1660–1732), the great master of Andean colonial painting, and a magnificent eighteenth-century picture by an

**1**

anonymous La Paz artist of an Archangel Arquebusero, an iconic image of an angel carrying a primitive firearm, which neatly encapsulates the spiritual and military contradictions of the Spanish conquest. Perhaps the most fascinating of the museum's colonial works, however, is the small, anonymous canvas, *Virgin Mountain* (1720), donated by Madrid's Reina Sofía gallery, and based on a design attributed to indigenous Bolivian sculptor **Francisco Tito Yupanqui** (1550–1616). The piece, one of the finest extant examples of mestizo-Baroque, depicts Potosí's Cerro Rico with the Virgin Mary inlaid ghost-like at its summit, flanked by the Pillars of Hercules and looming over tiny, stick-like representations of Inca Huayna Capac (see p.303) and Diego Huallpa. Dense in allegory and syncretism, it conflates the purity of the Virgin with the purity of Cerro Rico's silver and Pachamama – the Andean earth goddess herself.

### Modern art

The museum boasts a whole room dedicated to the elegant torsos of Bolivian sculptor **Marina Núñez del Prado** (1910–95), yet the most compelling among the museum's modern pieces are arguably the works of **Cecilio Gúzman de Rojas** (1899–1950), a leading figure in the Indigenismo movement of the early twentieth century. His stylized depictions of the Andean feminine face are hugely compelling, strong and almost cat-like in their grace and power. His most striking work is probably the wall-sized *Mujeres Andinas*, an aquiline huddle of women under a blazing sky alive with animist spirits.

## Iglesia de Santo Domingo

Yanacocha and Ingavi • Mon–Sat 8am–noon & 3.30–6pm, Sun 8am–noon • Free

One block northwest of Plaza Murillo, the **Iglesia de Santo Domingo** was established in 1609, though the fabulous stone-carved facade you see today dates from 1760. The simple, all-white interior was remodelled in Neoclassical style in the nineteenth century. Note the small shrine to **San Judas Tadeo** left of the entrance, which is especially popular with the Aymaras.

## Museo Nacional de Etnografía y Folklore

Ingavi 916, at Gerardo Sanjinez • Mon–Fri 9am–12.30pm & 3–7pm, Sat 9am–4.30pm, Sun 9am–noon • Bs20 • ☎ 02 2406642, Ⓦ musef.org.bo

The small but rewarding **Museo Nacional de Etnografía y Folklore** on Calle Ingavi is housed in a seventeenth-century mansion built for the Marques de Villaverde, whose coat of arms looks down on the central patio from an exquisite mestizo-Baroque portico, complete with floral designs, parrots and feline figures. The mansion's street facade boasts the only surviving example of the elegant carved wooden balconies that were common in colonial La Paz, and there's a branch of the *Angelo Colonial* restaurant chain attached (see p.82).

In addition to temporary exhibits, the museum includes several permanent galleries, including a section on the history of **Andean ceramics**, with a hoard of largely anthropomorphic pieces from the Chimú, Chancay and Tiwanaku cultures, as well as strange ritual *muñecas* (dolls), Inca *kerus* (ceremonial wooden cups) and some lovely colonial painted vases. The Sala Plumas is dedicated to **Arte Plumario**, or feather art. Conferring honour and respect on their wearers and serving as a kind of spiritual cleanser and conduit, the feathers on display here are much more than simply cast-off plumage: the brilliant designs of the Moxos plains are clearly reflections of the tropical sun, while the Altiplano incarnations are conspicuous for their height; the Cabezade Phusipia headdress resembles a veritable flower garden in the sky.

If these aren't surreal enough for you, the darkened **Sala Mascaras** should suffice, a by turns grotesque, outrageous, hilarious and never less than fascinating combination of familiar masks and the more obscure, including a Nazca death mask, lesser seen Chaco carnival masks and the sinister *Aaqui Aaqui* from Charazani, a malformed doctor/lawyer parody.

The real highlight, however, has to be the museum's exhaustive **Sala Tejidos**, or textile room, going way back into the pre-Columbian era with tattered fragments from the Chimú, Tiwanaku, Paracas, Nazca, Chancay and Inca cultures, much of it – in stark contrast to the more familiar linear patterns favoured from the colonial era onwards – featuring geometric designs and zoomorphic figures. Note that labelling is in Spanish only throughout the museum.

# Calle Jaén

Three blocks northwest of Plaza Murillo lies the enchanting **Calle Jaén** ("ha-en") the best-preserved colonial street in La Paz and home to no fewer than five **museums**. A narrow cobbled street lined with whitewashed houses adorned with elegant wooden balconies, red-tiled roofs and carved stone doorways opening onto quiet courtyards, Calle Jaén could almost be in a small town in Andalusia or Extremadura, so strong is the Spanish influence.

### Museo Costumbrista Juan de Vargas

At the top of Jaén; the entrance is around the corner on Av Armentia (Plaza Riosinho) • Tues–Fri 9.30am–12.30pm & 3–7pm, Sat & Sun 9am–1pm • Bs20; includes entry to Museo del Litoral Boliviano, Museo de Metales Preciosos and Museo Casa de Murillo • ☎ 02 2280758

Named after the first mayor of La Paz, the **Museo Costumbrista Juan de Vargas** is an illuminating cultural and history museum, though little is labelled in English. Exhibits include a room dedicated to the city's iconic *cholas paceñas* (see box, p.62), folk art, and a collection of **elaborate costumes** and **grotesque masks**, including the monstrous Danzante mask, whose wearer used to be expected to dance until he literally dropped dead, thereby ensuring a drought- and disease-free year for his community.

There is also a series of richly detailed **ceramic dioramas** of historical scenes, ranging from the founding of La Paz and the city's *tambos* (see p.67), to the execution of Murillo and a disturbing re-imagining of captured rebel leader Túpac Katari about to be torn apart by four horses in 1781.

### Museo del Litoral Boliviano

Jaén 789 • Tues–Fri 9.30am–12.30pm & 3–7pm, Sat & Sun 9am–1pm • Bs20, tickets sold only at the Museo Costumbrista Juan de Vargas; includes entry to Museo de Metales Preciosos, Museo Casa de Murillo and Museo Costumbrista Juan de Vargas • ☎ 02 2280758

The **Museo del Litoral Boliviano** is dedicated to one of Bolivia's national obsessions: the loss of its coastline to Chile during the nineteenth-century War of the Pacific (see p.309). Unless you share that obsession and read Spanish, however, you are unlikely to learn much from the introductory video and displays of old uniforms, weapons, photos of the lost ports and maps justifying Bolivia's claim to the coast.

### Museo de Metales Preciosos

Jaén 777 • Tues–Fri 9.30am–12.30pm & 3–7pm, Sat & Sun 9am–1pm • Bs20, tickets sold only at the Museo Costumbrista Juan de Vargas; includes entry to Museo del Litoral Boliviano, Museo Casa de Murillo and Museo Costumbrista Juan de Vargas • ☎ 02 2280758

Next door to the Museo del Litoral (in the former home of revolutionary Apolinar Jaén), the highlight of the **Museo de Metales Preciosos** is its small but impressive hoard of Inca and Tiwanaku gold and silver ornaments, housed in a giant steel vault. The delicate skill evident in the work – everything from gold-encrusted stone pipes and thimble-like cups to gold-disc-embroidered ponchos and funerary masks – makes it obvious why these indigenous artisans were so quickly enrolled into producing religious artwork by the Spanish. The **Tesoro de San Sebastian**, discovered in an excavated tomb in 1916 near Cochabamba, is especially rich, but the core of the collection once belonged to Fritz Buck, a German jeweller who migrated to Bolivia and was fascinated by Tiwanaku. But for some desperate last-minute negotiations, it would all have gone to the West German government after Buck's death in 1961.

**1**

### THE CHOLA PACEÑA AND HER BOWLER HAT

One of the most striking images in La Paz is that of the ubiquitous **cholas paceñas**, the Aymara and mestiza women dressed in voluminous skirts and bowler hats, who dominate much of the day-to-day business in the city's endless markets. The word *chola* (*cholo* for men) was originally a derogatory term used to refer to indigenous women who moved to the city and adopted the lifestyle of urban mestizos, but now refers more to women who were born in La Paz (*paceñas*) and are proud of their urban indigenous identity.

The distinctive dress of the *chola* is derived from seventeenth-century Spanish costumes, which indigenous women were obliged to copy under colonial rule. The crucial element of the outfit is the **pollera**, a layered skirt made from lengths of material up to 5m long, which are wrapped around the waist and reinforced with numerous petticoats to emphasize the width of the wearer's hips. These skirts can make women appear almost as wide as they are tall, and represent a glorious celebration of a very distinct ideal of female beauty. The *pollera* is worn in combination with knee-high boots, an elaborate lacy blouse, a shawl wrapped around the shoulders and a **felt bowler** or derby hat.

The origins of this millinery fashion are somewhat mysterious. Some say the bowler hat was adopted from those worn by gringo mining and railway engineers, others that the trend was started by a businessman as recently as the 1920s, who erroneously imported a job lot of bowler hats from Europe intended for rail workers – as they were the wrong colour, he struck on the idea of marketing them as women's headgear. However, Bolivians tend to point to Spanish regulations instituted after the rebellion of 1781 as the basis for native women being forced to wear "Western" dresses like the *pollera*, and that the bowler hat fashion evolved naturally from this.

The *chola* costume was originally confined to the wealthier mestiza women of La Paz, but has since become widespread among Aymara migrants in the city and across the Altiplano. The acceptability of the *chola* as one of the central icons of La Paz and an expression of pride in indigenous culture was confirmed in 1989, when **Remedios Loza** became the first woman to take a seat in the Bolivian Congress dressed in full *chola* regalia. In the decades since, not least since Evo Morales came to power in 2005, the colourfully attired *chola* has become almost as familiar a political fixture as the traditional drab-suited gent.

Other rooms display prehistoric artefacts and pottery, more elaborate ceramics made by pre-Inca civilizations and a collection of Inca weapons, masks, *tumis* (knives) and *topos* (clothes pins).

### Museo Casa de Murillo

Jaén 790 • Tues–Fri 9.30am–12.30pm & 3–7pm, Sat & Sun 9am–1pm • Bs20, tickets sold only at the Museo Costumbrista Juan de Vargas; includes entry to Museo del Litoral Boliviano, Museo de Metales Preciosos and Museo Costumbrista Juan de Vargas • ☎ 02 2280758

Inside the sumptuous mansion which was once the home of Pedro Domingo Murillo (see p.56), the **Museo Casa de Murillo** contains several rooms dressed up in colonial style, with religious art, antique furniture, ceremonial *keru* cups and portraits of former presidents. There's also a typical **oratorio** (chapel), obscure artefacts used in indigenous "witchcraft" and miniatures portraying the Aymara **Alasitas** festival (see box, p.57). Murillo lived in the house from 1803 to 1809 – the last meeting of his fellow conspirators took place here on July 15, 1809. The event is commemorated in the **Sala de la Conspiracion**, a sombre space with an old wooden table from the period and portraits, and another room dedicated to the various images created of Murillo and the other rebels.

### Museo de Instrumentos Folkloricos

Jaén 711 • Mon–Sat 9.30am–1.30pm & 4.30–6.30pm, Sun 10am–6.30pm • Bs5 • ☎ 02 2408177

Set around yet another pretty colonial courtyard on Jaén, the delightful **Museo de Instrumentos Folkloricos** is home to an astonishing variety of handmade musical instruments from all over Bolivia, some of which you can play with in-house lessons at competitive rates (Bs150 for a 12hr course in charango, *guitarra*, *zampoña* or quena;

enquire at reception). A labyrinth of rooms kicks off with a collection of pre-Columbian pipes, nose flutes, wood and stone *oscarinas* and music-related ceramics. This is followed by a plethora of the **stringed instruments** – guitars, violins, mandolins and charangos – which were introduced by the Spanish, and eagerly seized upon by an indigenous population who quickly combined these two elements to create the distinctive Andean music of today.

Most interesting, however, are the **percussion and wind rooms**, cramming in maracas, bells and shells, toucan beaks, strange little leather trumpets and wonderful palm-leaf *bajones* from San Ignacio de Moxos. Further chambers feature an array of Bolivian-invented instruments (many of them created by the museum's famous, charango-playing founder, Ernesto Cavour) including a chamber-pot *tambor*, a saxophone-like quena and a five-necked charango. A collection of old concert posters, articles, scores and vinyl completes the tour.

The museum's small theatre, the **Teatro del Charango**, is dedicated to the charango and traditional Bolivian music. Shows usually start at 7pm on Saturdays and cost Bs20, and feature a number of performers playing different instruments that you'll have seen in the museum.

## Plaza Emilio Villanueva

Essentially a widened section of Calle Mercado, **Plaza Emilio Villanueva** was once the civic and financial heart of La Paz, and still hums with wheelers and dealers. The plaza is dominated by the **Palacio Consistorial de la Paz**, the grand wedding-cake municipal building completed in 1925 by revolutionary Bolivian architect Emilio Villanueva – it still houses the offices of the city government. Next door is the **Templo de San Agustín**, and opposite, the **Vicepresidencia del Estado**, the grand *belle époque* home of Bolivia's vice president, built in 1911 for Banco de la Nación. On the other side of the square, the Brutalist **Banco Central de Bolivia** faces the rather prettier **Banco Mercantil de Santa Cruz**. You can admire most of these buildings from the outside only.

### Templo de San Agustín

Mercado, on Plaza Emilio Villanueva • Mon–Fri 7.30am–noon & 3–8pm, Sat & Sun 8am–noon • Free

Dating back to 1668 but remodelled several times in the nineteenth century, the **Templo de San Agustín** is the elegant religious component of Plaza Emilio Villanueva, its grand facade and dome showing a subtle Moorish influence. Inside, the main focus for worshippers is the three small but popular shrines near the entrance: the Señor de Mayo (first on the left), Señor de los Milagros (second on the right) and the revered Bolivian apparition of Mary from Quillacollo, the Virgen de Urkupiña (first on the right). You'll see votive plaques (*plaquetas*) smothering the surrounding walls around the shrines, though the practice was banned in 2009 and devotees are now encouraged to donate money to charity instead.

# Plaza San Francisco and the market district

At the north end of the Prado and the western boundary of the Casco Viejo, **Plaza San Francisco** was the traditional gateway to the Aymara neighbourhoods of La Paz, which climb up the slopes of the valley to the west. Founded in the colonial era as the *parroquias de Indios* – the Indian parishes – these neighbourhoods were where the Aymara population from the surrounding countryside was encouraged to settle, living around churches built as part of the effort to convert them to Christianity; less idealistically, this separate indigenous quarter was also designed as a pool of cheap labour, neatly separated from the Spanish city by the Río Choqueyapu. Today the area retains an Aymara identity thanks to the market stalls that jostle for space with

**1**

minivans on its narrow and steep streets, but it's best known for the concentration of tour agents, hostels and travellers' cafés along **Sagárnaga** and **Linares**. The main sight is the lovely **Iglesia de San Francisco**.

# Plaza San Francisco

With frenetic traffic running past it, the **Plaza San Francisco** lacks the charm of the city's other major plazas, and is no longer a major Aymara centre. It is, however, an important bus stop and a focus for tour groups thanks to the looming Iglesia de San Francisco that dominates the plaza. **Protests** and demonstrations do still take place here, but are generally small-scale and mostly colourful pieces of political theatre. For cheap, home-cooked Aymara and Bolivian food, check out **Mercado Lanza** at the plaza's northern end (see p.82); the market also has a large and photogenic fresh flowers section.

## Iglesia de San Francisco

Plaza San Francisco • Daily 6.30am–noon & 3.30–8pm • Free

The **Iglesia de San Francisco** is the prettiest colonial church in La Paz. The first incarnation was built around 1549 as the headquarters of the Franciscans' campaign to Christianize Alto Peru, but the original structure collapsed under a heavy snowfall early in the seventeenth century. Most of what you see today was built between 1743 and 1784, financed by donations from mine owners. The richly decorated facade (completed in 1790) is a flamboyant example of the mestizo-Baroque style, showing clear indigenous influence, with carved anthropomorphic figures reminiscent of pre-Columbian sculpture as well as more common birds and intertwined floral designs. Above the main door is a statue of St Francis himself, facing towards the old city with his arms held aloft.

Inside, the walls of the church are lined with extravagantly carved altarpieces where abundant gold leaf and smiling angels frame gruesome depictions of the Crucifixion or images of individual saints that are the principal objects of veneration for those who come here to pray; San Judas Tadeo, the patron saint of the poor and miserable, is particularly popular among indigenous supplicants. To really experience the enormity of the place from on high (and to access the bell tower) it's well worth paying for a ticket to the excellent Museo San Francisco (see below).

## Museo San Francisco

Plaza San Francisco 501 • Mon–Sat 9am–6pm • Bs20 • ☎ 02 2318472, ⓦ facebook.com/MuseoSanFrancisco

Torched in the uprising of Túpac Katari in 1781 (see p.306), and subsequently used as, variously, a customs office, a barracks and a school, the cloisters and choir of the Iglesia de San Francisco now comprise the **Museo San Francisco**. A sometimes unfocused yet always interesting exhibition of religious art, furniture, old photos and documents, the museum offers a revealing window into the lives of the Franciscans who once lived, ate, prayed and slept here, as well as giving the unmissable opportunity to explore the less frequently visited extremities of the Iglesia de San Francisco itself.

### Coro (the choir)

The main route through the museum begins upstairs in Iglesia de San Francisco's **Coro** or choir (the loft at the upper eastern end of the nave). Much more compelling than the cedar-wood stalls or the exhibits themselves (old vestments, antique chalices, reliquaries and the like) is the perspective of the church from the choir's edge. You'll also get thrillingly close to the interior of the domes themselves and their magnificently worked stone.

Two tiny narrow stone staircases lead up from here to the **roof**. You can wander beneath the behemoths in the **bell tower**, with the weathered pantiles of the domes spread out below and a monk's-eye view of La Paz in its chaotic entirety.

**FROM TOP** PLAZA MURILLO (P.56); LUCHA LIBRE DE CHOLITAS (P.71) >

**1**

The cloisters

Most of the museum galleries lie around two pretty cloisters. The two-storey **Claustro Mayor**, built 1894–97, is a large, quiet space crammed with lush gardens, enclosed by rooms containing the bodega (wine cellar replete with giant wood barrels) and several rooms of religious art and murals. The upper storey of the narrower eighteenth-century **Claustro Antiguo** contains more religious art of the Collao and Potosí schools (with special rooms dedicated to images of St Francis and *Cristo Redentor*, Christ the Redeemer), as well as a poignant reproduction of the monk's cell inhabited by **Juan de Dios Delgado**, a friar who was also one of the 1809 revolutionaries.

## Calle Sagárnaga

To the south of Plaza San Francisco lies **Calle Sagárnaga**, La Paz's main tourist street (along with **Linares**, which bisects it), crammed with budget hotels, tour agencies, restaurants, handicraft shops and stalls. Often dubbed "Gringo Alley", the street has always catered to travellers: in the colonial era, it was where wayfarers en route between Potosí and the Peruvian coast would be put up, and several buildings that are today occupied by hotels were built in the eighteenth century for that very purpose.

## Mercado de Hechicería

Linares and Jiménez, off Santa Cruz • Daily, hours vary – stalls open as early as 6am and close as late as 8pm in summer

The **Mercado de Hechicería**, or Witches' Market, is the generic name given to a handful of stalls clustered on Linares and Jiménez, leading off Santa Cruz, that cater to **herbal medicine** and **Aymara mysticism**. Most stalls sell the same stuff, and, though intriguing, you'll need to speak (in Spanish) to the stallholders to make sense of it all. The stalls are all heavily laden with a colourful cornucopia of ritual and medicinal items, ranging from herbal cures for minor ailments like rheumatism or stomach pain, to incense, coloured sweets, protective talismans and, the most ghoulish for foreign visitors, **dried llama foetuses** (these are miscarried or stillborn baby llamas – no animals are killed simply to provide a foetus). These items are combined in packages known as *mesas* or *pagos* and are then burned or buried as offerings to placate the various tutelary spirits and magical beings that are believed to hold sway over all aspects of daily life. There's no clear border between the medicinal and magical here: the *Yatiris* and *Kallawayas* – **indigenous traditional healers** – who are the market's main customers adopt a holistic approach in which a herbal cure for a specific symptom is usually combined with magical efforts to address the imbalances in the supernatural world that may be responsible for the ailment.

---

### THE LUSTRABOTAS OF LA PAZ

Wandering around La Paz, you'll inevitably come across the initially unnerving sight of young men crouching along the side of the street, their faces hidden by thick balaclavas and baseball caps. Don't worry – these are not terrorists but some of the city's 3500 "**lustrabotas**", or shoeshine boys. Given the street pollution and low rates (around Bs5 per shine), it's a pretty miserable job, and the masks have become one of the more contentious issues in La Paz. Being a *lustrabota* is heavily stigmatized, and the shoeshine boys hide their faces for fear of prejudice and discrimination – some are thought to be poor college students trying to pay their way, while others are orphans or teenagers. Substance abuse remains a problem ("clefa" or glue-sniffing being the drug of choice). Mayor Luis Revilla formalized the profession in 2011, arguing that it is a proper, dignified job, but – as you'll see – it's going to be a while before the masks come off.

## Museo de la Coca

Linares 906 • Daily 10am–7pm • Bs13 • ☎ 02 2311998, ⓦ cocamuseum.com

Tucked away inside an atmospheric little courtyard a block south of Sagárnaga, the tiny **Museo de la Coca** provides an exhaustive examination of everything coca – the small green leaf that is both the central religious and cultural sacrament of the Andes and the raw material for the manufacture of cocaine. A series of display boards covered in photos and explanations in Spanish (pick up a booklet at the entrance with English translations) gives a good overview of the history, chemistry, cultivation and uses of this most controversial of plants. Its mystical significance in the Andes is explained, as well as the psychology behind cocaine addiction and the nutritional value of coca, which contains several vitamins and minerals. The café upstairs offers an approximation of the original **Coca-Cola**, which began life in 1886 using unrefined coca; that practice changed in 1903, and today the company uses a cocaine-free coca leaf extract, mainly sourced from Peru.

## The market district

Around Max Paredes • Daily, hours vary – stalls open as early as 6am and close as late as 8pm, with some food stalls open later

As you climb Santa Cruz west of Illampu, tiny market stalls and street merchants begin to occupy the narrow pavements, often precariously close to the fume-belching traffic. This informal **market district** is where La Paz's **Aymara majority** conduct their daily business, a vast open-air bazaar sprawling over some thirty city blocks (mostly shared with traffic), where anything and everything is bought and sold. The market area goes by many names – locals tend to refer to specific streets where certain products are sold – but is generally known as **Mercado Negro** around Max Paredes and Graneros (shoes and clothing), and **Huyustus** (or just "Uyustus"), further west around the street of the same name (clothing, bedding, toys, shoes and musical instruments). To the south, where Paredes meets Rodríguez, the fresh fruit and food section is usually known as **Mercado Rodríguez. Miamicito** or Little Miami is for linen and women's clothing, while **Calle Eloy Salmón** is the place to go for bikes and electronic goods.

Street after street is lined with stalls piled high with all manner of goods: sacks of sweet-smelling coca leaf and great mounds of brightly coloured tropical fruit from the Yungas; enormous heaps of potatoes from the Altiplano; piles of smelly, silver-scaled fish from Lake Titicaca; stacks of stereos and televisions smuggled across the border; endless racks laden with the latest imitation designer clothes (for bowler hats, go to Paredes and Sagárnaga). Behind almost every stall sits or stands an Aymara woman in a bowler hat, calling out her wares or counting out small change from the deep pockets of her apron, often with a baby strapped to her back or sleeping in a bundle nearby.

Though cheap and plentiful, the quality of the goods is not high, and it's not really a place to come looking for souvenirs. Like most markets, it's also a favourite haunt of thieves and pickpockets, and the area is best avoided after dark.

## Museo Tambo Quirquincho

Evaristo Valle (Plaza Alonso de Mendoza) • Tues–Fri 9am–12.30pm & 3–7pm, Sat & Sun 9am–1pm • Bs8 • ☎ 02 2390969

An imperious statue of the founder of La Paz graces laidback Plaza Alonso de Mendoza, on the southern side of which sits the **Museo Tambo Quirquincho**. The museum is ostensibly a showcase for Bolivian contemporary art (five galleries are permanent, the rest temporary), but more interesting is its setting inside one of the largest examples of an eighteenth-century *tambo*, a compound that served during the colonial era both as accommodation and marketplace for rural Aymaras. The ornate mestizo-Baroque arches around the main courtyard were recovered from the ruins of the Convento de la Concepción on Calle Genaro Sanjinés, after it was torn down to make way for a cinema in the 1980s.

**1**

# Prado South and around

In the Prado's southern reaches, a kilometre or so south of Plaza San Francisco, it officially becomes Avenida 16 de Julio and passes between the suburb of **San Pedro** to the east and the more modern neighbourhood of **Miraflores** further to the west, before coming to an abrupt end at chaotic **Plaza del Estudiante** (featuring a giant equestrian

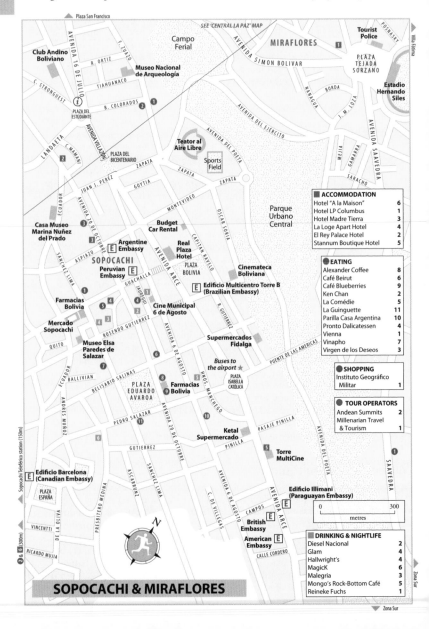

**ACCOMMODATION**

| | |
|---|---|
| Hotel "A la Maison" | 6 |
| Hotel LP Columbus | 1 |
| Hotel Madre Tierra | 3 |
| La Loge Apart Hotel | 4 |
| El Rey Palace Hotel | 2 |
| Stannum Boutique Hotel | 5 |

**EATING**

| | |
|---|---|
| Alexander Coffee | 8 |
| Café Beirut | 6 |
| Café Blueberries | 9 |
| Ken Chan | 2 |
| La Comédie | 5 |
| La Guinguette | 11 |
| Parilla Casa Argentina | 10 |
| Pronto Dalicatessen | 4 |
| Vienna | 1 |
| Vinapho | 7 |
| Virgen de los Deseos | 3 |

**SHOPPING**

| | |
|---|---|
| Instituto Geográfico Militar | 1 |

**TOUR OPERATORS**

| | |
|---|---|
| Andean Summits | 2 |
| Millenarian Travel & Tourism | 1 |

**DRINKING & NIGHTLIFE**

| | |
|---|---|
| Diesel Nacional | 2 |
| Glam | 4 |
| Hallwright's | 4 |
| MagicK | 6 |
| Malegria | 3 |
| Mongo's Rock-Bottom Café | 5 |
| Reineke Fuchs | 1 |

**SOPOCACHI & MIRAFLORES**

1

statue of **General Antonio José de Sucre**). Directly south lies the middle-class suburb of **Sopocachi**, the city's most pleasant residential area, centring around the parallel avenues 6 de Agosto and 20 de Octubre; the suburb is home to many of La Paz's higher-end restaurants and nightlife spots.

## Museo Nacional de Arqueología

Tiwanaku 93 at Federico Zuazo • Tues–Fri 8.30am–12.30pm, Sat & Sun 9am–1pm • Bs14 • ☎ 02 2311621

Housed in the **Palacio Tiwanaku**, built for archeologist Arturo Posnansky in 1916, the **Museo Nacional de Arqueología** is a short but very sweet exhibition of Bolivian archeology. Most explanations are in Spanish, but audio-tours in English should be available by 2018. Early items include a couple of beautiful **stone palettes** dating from 800–200 BC, one featuring a serpent with geometric shapes, the other a "Yaya-Mama" face surrounded by bendy arrows and little animals. A room dedicated to the **Tiwanaku culture** (400–1000 AD) holds the most impressive pieces, including an incense burner in the form of a puma, a llama jug that pours through the tail, and some macabre elongated skulls, one of which has been trepanned. There's also a superb jar in the form of a grim-faced man with plugs in his lip and ears. Following these, the **Inca** artefacts (1430–1535) are a lot less exciting. The exhibition rounds off with some pieces from the lowlands spanning the period 800 BC to 1650 AD.

## Museo de Arte Contemporáneo Plaza

Av 16 de Julio (Prado) 1698 • Daily 10am–7pm • Bs15; photo permit Bs20 • ☎ 02 2335905

The **Museo de Arte Contemporáneo Plaza** showcases home-grown and international talent, but it's the building itself that really steals the show: a gorgeous pale-blue Art Nouveau mansion that originally served as a club for Lebanese expats, it boasts Middle Eastern stained-glass windows and Gustave Eiffel iron staircases. Balletic bronzes by American sculptor Richard Hallier dot the museum, whose **ground floor** hosts temporary exhibitions. On the **middle floor**, where you get the full glory of the Arabic stained glass, don't miss Cochabamba-born sculptor Hans Hoffman's striking *Pelea de Gallos* ("Cockfight"), made of old bolts. Paintings include several Che Guevara images (one made of dominoes), Remy Daza Rojas's firelit *Nocturno* and Zenon Sansute's sensitively erotic *Flores de la Importación*, with Sansute himself in the background. The **top floor** features another Zenon Sansute painting, *Secreto Amor* ("Secret Love"), in which a sleeping girl dreams of her lover, as well as – slightly incongruously – two sculptures by Frederic Remington, a nineteenth-century artist of the old American West.

## Plaza Sucre

Two blocks southwest of the Prado along Colombia

**Plaza Sucre** (also known as Plaza San Pedro) lies at the centre of **San Pedro**, one of the city's oldest suburbs. On the face of it, the square is peaceful enough, home to shoe shiners and snack sellers, and with well-tended gardens surrounding another statue of Bolivia's first president, the Venezuelan **General Antonio José de Sucre**. Yet looming over the plaza's southeastern edge are the pockmarked adobe walls of **San Pedro Prison** (see box, p.70), where protests often see the teargas flying as police battle with disgruntled prisoners. The prison – and in fact the whole San Pedro area – is best avoided entirely come nightfall.

The other main attraction on the square is the **Templo de San Pedro de la Nueva Paz**, a church favoured by the Aymaras, with a wonderful Baroque stone facade dating from 1790, and an ornate *retablo* inside.

1

### SAN PEDRO PRISON

On the southeast side of Plaza Sucre rises the formidable bulk of **San Pedro Prison** (Cárcel de San Pedro): critically overcrowded (there are around 1500 inmates), structurally precarious and rife with tuberculosis, the prison is increasingly a scene of desperate protest.

Inside lies a self-governed microcosm of Bolivian society, with **shops**, **restaurants** and **billiard halls**; prisoners with money can live quite well here. Comfortable cells in the nicer areas change hands for thousands of dollars, and many inmates have cell phones and satellite televisions. Like the city on the other side of the walls, the prison is divided into rich and poor neighbourhoods, with the most luxurious area (known as "La Posta") reserved for big-time drug traffickers, white-collar criminals and corrupt politicians: the most high-profile resident in recent years has been the ex-Prefect of Pando, **Leopoldo Fernández**, who was released from remand in 2013, before getting a fifteen-year sentence in 2017 (see box p.297). Those without any income, however, sleep in the corridors and struggle to survive on the meagre official rations. **Family visitors** come and go regularly, and some children live inside with their fathers; when the riots erupt, it's the families who are often caught in the midst of it.

For years the prison was one of Bolivia's most infamous tourist "attractions", as inmates gave tours of the place to foreigners, including the chance to sample its high-grade cocaine; eventually this became so blatant (complete with videos on YouTube) that the authorities were forced to clamp down, and prison tours are no longer on the tourist itinerary. Life in the prison was documented in Rusty Young's *Marching Powder* (2003), which tells the story of drug smuggler and British inmate Thomas McFadden, who did time here between 1996 and 2000 and is credited with starting tours of the institution.

# El Alto

On the rim of the Altiplano overlooking La Paz, **El Alto** is populated largely by Aymara migrants from the surrounding high plains. When it was recognized as a municipality in 1986, El Alto instantly became the fourth-biggest, poorest and fastest-growing city in Bolivia. With a population larger than La Paz's – rapidly approaching one million (sixty percent under 25 years old) – the place resembles a vast, impoverished yet dynamic suburb, full of tin-roofed adobe shacks, half-finished red-brick buildings and industrial warehouses.

Most tourists just pass through El Alto on the way into or out of La Paz, whether by plane or by bus, or come here to watch the Fighting Cholitas (see box, opposite), but El Alto is worth a second look, especially now that it can be accessed so easily by La Paz's cable-car system, the **Teleférico** (see box, p.75). The panorama of La Paz from the rim of the Altiplano is spectacular: there's a **mirador** (viewpoint) just below the toll booths, where only vehicles heading down towards La Paz can stop, but the Teleférico, whose red line passes almost directly overhead, offers better views still. At the road junction near the *mirador*, local sculptor Felix Durán's impressive giant scrap metal **statue of Che Guevara** greets arriving motorists.

Twice a week, the streets north of Avenida Juan Pablo II (which leads west from the junction near the *mirador*) are taken over by the **Feria 16 de Julio** (Thurs & Sun 6am–7pm), the world's biggest flea market, dealing in new and used clothes, groceries, furniture, and pretty much anything else that can be sold from a street stall. A visit here can be combined with the Fighting Cholitas show, which takes place on the same days. The market is a favourite spot for pickpockets, so leave your wallet behind.

El Alto's other big attraction is its **cholets**, colourful mansions in a gaudy, vibrant style known as "Neo-Andean", typically with shops on the ground floor, party venues on the first and sometimes second, and a family home on the floors above that; *cholets* are scattered around town, so not easy to see on foot, but Turisbus (see p.77) offers a tour of them, or you could find a cab driver who knows them and ask to be driven round to a few.

At the southern end of El Alto, the **Wiphala estate** in El Mercedario consists of seven 12-storey apartment blocks decorated with multicoloured murals by Roberto Mamani Mamani; the apartments themselves were rather shoddily built and have failed to attract many tenants, but the murals are huge and impressive for all that.

## ARRIVAL AND DEPARTURE                                                                    LA PAZ

As the de facto capital of Bolivia it's no surprise that La Paz is the country's major transport hub, and many travellers use it as a base to which they return to collect or drop off luggage and equipment and rest up between forays into the country's many different geographical and climatic regions. Arriving here by **bus** or **plane** is a relatively painless experience: traffic problems notwithstanding, the city's small size makes it fairly easy to find your way around and there are inexpensive taxis and still cheaper public transport, though the latter isn't always easy to travel on with big bags.

### BY PLANE

Given the great distances involved and the generally poor condition of the country's roads, the best way to travel into or out of La Paz is by plane – indeed, during the wet season this is sometimes the only way to reach certain destinations. International, and pretty much all domestic, flights arrive at and depart from El Alto airport on the rim of the Altiplano, about 10km away from – and almost 500m above – central La Paz. At over 4000m above sea level, this is the highest international airport in the world, and it can feel as if planes have to climb rather than descend when they come in to land. Basics has more information on international flight routes (see p.23).

### INFORMATION

The airport's rather limited facilities include ATMs and a bureau to change foreign currency (though not at the best rates). There's also a café and a few restaurants, plus newsstands and souvenir shops.

### TO/FROM CENTRAL LA PAZ

**By taxi** The easiest way into the centre from here is by airport taxi (30min; Bs70–80); don't accept lifts in any car not marked with the "airport taxi" label. The rate will depend on where your hotel is, but fix the amount before you depart – there are no meters.

**By minibus** Alternatively, an airport shuttle minibus runs down into the city along the length of the Prado to Plaza Isabella La Católica in Sopocachi (Mon–Sat every 10–20min 6am–6.30pm, Sun every 30min; Bs4 including baggage). If you're heading out to the airport, wait on the Prado and flag down one of the special minibuses marked "Aeropuerto".

### DOMESTIC AIRLINES

Boliviana de Aviación (Camacho 1413; ☎02 2117993, ⓦboa.bo) offer the biggest choice of flights to most destinations. Budget airline Ecojet (Torre Zafiro, suite 5, Av Ballivian 322 between Calles 9 and 10 in Calacoto, Zona Sur; ☎901 105055, ⓦecojet.bo) usually offers lower prices. Amaszonas (Torre Multicine, Av Arce 2631, Sopocachi; ☎901 105500, ⓦwww.amaszonas.com) is your best bet for Rurrenabaque. The military airline TAM (Av Montes and Serrano 734; ☎02 268 1111, ⓦtam.bo) runs flights to smaller, more remote airports as well as to the major ones. You can buy tickets for all these airlines from their own offices or, for a small commission, through any travel agent. The following list includes all direct flights, though airlines also sell tickets to destinations with one or more plane changes (for Oruro or Postosí, for example, you'd have to change at Cochabamba).

Destinations Cobija (1–3 daily; 1hr; BoA, Ecojet, TAM); Cochabamba (13–18 daily; 35min; BoA, Ecojet, TAM);

---

### THE FIGHTING CHOLITAS

*Cholas paceñas* wrestling? El Alto is probably the last place you'd expect to find Mexican-style wrestling, yet – as ever – Bolivia turns your expectations upside down, quite literally, as bowler-hatted *cholitas* aim flying pigtailed kicks at each other and at a motley array of male and female masked baddies, while a mixed local/gringo crowd laps it up. Shows involving the "**Fighting Cholitas**" (part of the Titanes del Ring group) take place at the Multifuncional de la Ceja, Av Naciones Unidas, every Thursday and Sunday between 4pm and 7pm. Agencies in La Paz (see p.76) typically arrange all-inclusive **tours** including transport and tickets for Bs90; these usually depart La Paz around 3.45pm, and your fee normally includes popcorn and seats in the "VIP" area. Be warned that a typical visit lasts three to four hours, and that everything's in Spanish (there's commentary throughout and the local crowd really gets into the action); it can be cold in the arena, so bring a sweater. It's also possible to get there under your own steam: take a minibus headed for Ceja from San Francisco church or along the Prado, and get off just 150m after the toll booths; tickets are Bs50 on the door.

**1**

## STREET CRIME

Travellers arriving at the **main bus terminal** are occasionally targeted by thieves posing as plain-clothes police officers, complete with fake documents. With so many real policemen around, this is becoming rare, but it pays to be on the lookout. One popular scam involves them asking to inspect your money for counterfeit notes, or your bags for drugs, then robbing you (they often work in tandem with someone pretending to be a tourist, who will befriend you before they approach and vouch for the legitimacy of their request). If approached by people claiming to be **undercover police**, don't get in a car with them or show them your documents or valuables, and insist on the presence of an olive-green **uniformed officer** – you can call one yourself on ☎110.

Scams often involve **taxis**; travellers and even ordinary Paceños have been assaulted, kidnapped (while the perpetrators empty their bank account at the nearest ATM), and occasionally even killed by rogue taxi and bus drivers, though the situation has improved in recent years. If you have a phone, take and send off a photo of the licence plate of any vehicle you travel in, or at least make a note of it, and never share a cab with strangers. Never accept **food** or drink from anyone you don't know in case it is drugged. See p.75 for further info on taxi security.

Guayaramerin (1 weekly; 40min; TAM); Puerto Suárez (15–21 daily; 1hr; BoA, Amazonas); Rurrenabaque (4–6 daily; 40min; Amazonas, TAM); Santa Cruz (11–20 daily; 1hr; BoA, Amazonas, TAM); Sucre (2 daily; 40–50min; BoA, TAM); Tarija (1–2 daily; 1hr 5min; BoA, TAM); Trinidad (1 daily; 50min; BoA); Uyuni (4–5 daily; 50min; Amazonas, BoA).

### BY TAXI

**Long-distance taxis** For trips outside the city, Taxi Diplomático (☎02 2224343) offers a 24hr long-distance taxi service; you can usually pick one up outside the *Real Plaza* hotel on Av Arce in Sopocachi, though almost every major hotel will have links with a taxi company that offers similar services and rates. Travel is safe, convenient and comfortable (drivers will stop along the route for food, toilets, photos etc), but rates are expensive and are usually quoted in US dollars: it's $120 (Bs815) one way to Copacabana, for example, about the same as a day-trip with a tour agency. Other one-way rates are as follows: Cochabamba $350 (Bs2380); Coroico $120 (Bs815); Desaguadero (Peru border) $80 (Bs545); Oruro $150 (Bs1020); and Sorata $250 (Bs1700). Taxis will run to Tiwanaku for $80 (Bs545) return, and will wait as long as you like.

### BY BUS

There are three spots in the city where buses arrive at and depart from: the Terminal de Buses La Paz (central bus station), the cemetery district and Villa Fátima.

#### TERMINAL DE BUSES LA PAZ

Most international and long-distance inter-departmental buses use the Terminal de Buses La Paz on Plaza Antofagasta, about 1km northeast of Plaza San Francisco.

From the terminal, it's a short taxi ride (Bs15) via dedicated Terminal Taxis (☎02 2281919), or a 20min walk down Uruguay then Av Montes to the main accommodation areas in the city centre. You can also wave down any minibus heading in that direction (easier on Av Armentia). Security and services in the terminal have improved in recent years, with plenty of police, cheap snack bars, luggage storage, a post office, a pharmacy, ATM, telephones and an excellent information office (Mon–Fri 6am–1pm & 2–9pm, Sat & Sun 7am–noon; ☎02 2285858). Departing passengers have to pay Bs2.50 to use the terminal – tickets are sold from the kiosk marked "Boletería" in the centre of the station. Each company has its own ticket office, though most routes are similar: Cochabamba, Oruro, Potosí, Santa Cruz and Sucre are the most frequently served. You can also get direct buses to Lima (Bs500), Cusco (Bs220), Arica (Bs200) and even Buenos Aires (US$150–200/Bs1020–1360; 48hr) and São Paulo (US$150/Bs1020; 48hr), though these journeys are not for those of a queasy disposition.

**To Copacabana** In addition to ordinary services to Copacabana, run by firms such as Manco Kapac, there are "tourist buses" (typically older minibuses) run by companies including Milton Tours (Calle Illampu at Calderón 1123; ☎02 2368003, ⓦhotelmiltonbolivia.com) and Titicaca Bolivia (Illampu 773 and kiosk #16 in the terminal; ☎02 2462655, ⓦtiticacabolivia.com); both offer hotel pick-ups from 7am (Titicaca Bolivia also call at the terminal at 8am). Don't forget your passport as you may need to show it en route.

**To Puno/Cusco** Titicaca Transportes Internacional buses to Copacabana (see above) continue to Puno, and they also have a 2pm bus that continues to Cusco. Buses to Puno via Desaguadero (run by Trans Salvador at kiosk #19 and Internacional Continente at kiosk #24) are around 2hr

**1**

faster (taking 6hr) than those going via Copacabana.

**To Uyuni** The most deluxe service is with Todo Turismo (Suite 6, 2nd floor, Edificio Paola, 102 Av Uruguay; ☎02 2119418, ⓦ todoturismo.bo), departing at 9pm daily from the street in front of the bus station, with a meal service, and sleepers on some buses, semi-sleepers on others; tickets are Bs250 or Bs300 depending on which bus it is. Cheaper firms include Bus Belgrano (kiosk #43; ☎02 228 1159), whose semi-sleeper service (Bs90) leaves the terminal at 9pm. Both services should arrive in Uyuni at around 6am.

**To Tarija** Platinum buses (kiosk #28-B in the terminal; ☎02 2284261) depart at 7pm daily except Saturday, arriving at 8am the following day; tickets cost Bs175 for a semi-sleeper seat, or Bs265 for a sleeper. Other services are cheaper but less comfortable.

Destinations Arica, Chile (4 daily; 9hr); Cochabamba (roughly hourly; 7–8hr); Copacabana (6 daily; 3–4hr); Cusco, Peru (1 daily; 15hr); Lima, Peru (2 daily; 32hr); Oruro (1–3 hourly; 3hr 30min); Potosí (roughly hourly; 9–11hr); Puno, Peru (4 daily; 6–8hr); Santa Cruz (10 daily, leaving afternoons only; 16–18hr); Sucre (3 daily; 14hr); Tarija (17 daily; 16hr); Uyuni (5 daily; 9–12hr).

**CEMETERY DISTRICT**

Buses, shared taxis, minibuses and micros to the Lake Titicaca region, Charazani, Copacabana, Sorata and Tiwanaku, arrive and depart from various offices in the streets around the cemetery district on the west side of the city, starting around 6am. Plenty of minibuses and micros (marked *Cementerio*) ply the route between the city centre and the cemetery, but the easiest way to get here is by Teleférico; it's just one stop on the red line (Línea Roja) from Estación Central/Taypi Uta to Cementerio/Ajayuni. The departure points are strung out along Av Kollasuyo (Av América) east from Plaza Tomás Katari, which is opposite the cemetery entrance, a 10min walk from the Teleférico station.

**To Charazani** Buses to Charazani in the Cordillera Apolobamba leave from Reyes Cardona 732, three blocks east of Plaza Tomás Katari (and across Av Kollasuyo).

**To Copacabana** Buses and micros to Copacabana (Bs20) leave from different offices on Plaza Tomás Katari. Don't forget your passport as you may need to show it when crossing the Estrecho de Tiquina (see p.106). If you want to continue into Peru, it's very easy to do so from Copacabana, where there are frequent cross-border minibuses (see p.106).

**To Desaguadero** Shared taxis (Bs30) and minibuses (Bs15–20) leave from José Maria Asín, a block east of Plaza Tomás Katari.

**To Sorata** Minibuses to Sorata leave from Manuel Bustillos 675, two blocks east of Plaza Tomás Katari.

**To Tiwanaku** Minibuses (Bs15) leave from just behind Plaza Tomás Katari, at Jose M Aliaga 678.

Destinations Charazani (1 daily; 9hr); Copacabana (every 30min; 3hr 30min); Desaguadero (depart when full; 2hr 30min); Sorata (depart when full; 4hr 30min); Tiwanaku (depart when full; 1hr 30min).

**VILLA FÁTIMA**

Buses and minibuses for Coroico and Chulumani in the Yungas, plus one Rurrenabaque bus, arrive at and depart from Terminal Puente Minasa in Villa Fátima, 2km from the centre in the northeast of the city. Buses for Rurrenabaque, Guayaramerín and Riberalta in the Beni and Cobija in the Pando depart from offices around the intersection of Av de las Américas and Virgen del Carmel, five blocks below the terminal. Flota Yungueña, whose office is a block below Virgen del Carmel, at the intersection of Av de las Américas and Yanacachi (☎02 2212344, ⓦ facebook.com/FlotaYunguena), has the best reputation for services to Rurrenabaque, Guayaramerín, Riberalta and Cobija. For long-haul routes to the Beni and Pando, it's worth booking a ticket in advance. To get here from the city centre, take a minibus or micro displaying "Villa Fátima", or (if you want to go to the Terminal Puente Minasa) "Terminal" or "Terminal Minasa", from San Francisco or heading east on Camacho.

Destinations Chulumani (7 daily buses plus minibuses; 4hr–4hr 30min); Cobija (1–2 daily; 48hr); Coroico (minibuses and minivans leaving when full; 2hr–2hr 40min); Guayaramerín (2 daily; 32hr); Riberalta (2 daily; 30–40hr); Rurrenabaque (5 daily; 20hr).

**EL ALTO**

Buses to Pelechuco (4 weekly; 13hr) depart from the interprovincial bus station at Ex-Tranca de Río Seco in El Alto. To get there, catch a minibus from the Prado to La Ceja, and then another one to the terminal; alternatively, take the Teleférico red line (Línea Roja) from Taypi Uta/Estación Central to Jach'a Qhathu/16 de Julio and then the blue line (Línea Azul) to Rio Seco/Waña Jawira.

**BY TRAIN**

Though trains no longer run to La Paz itself, there is a tourist train from El Alto to Tiwanaku and Guaqui on Lake Titicaca, which runs on the second Sunday of each month. The train departs El Alto (Calle 8, 3 blocks from Av 6 de Marzo) at 8am, then stops in Tiwanaku (10.35am–12.35pm) and Guaqui (1.20–4pm) before heading back to El Alto, arriving around 6.20pm. Tickets cost $80 (Bs545) for business class (*clase ejecutiva*) or $20 (Bs135) for normal class (*clase normal*) – the main difference being that normal class is not heated – and can be bought at travel agents, and possibly – if they ever get their website to work properly – online (☎02 2184555, ⓦ www.fca.com.bo). Note that, to get a place, this service usually needs to be booked well in advance (three months if possible).

## GETTING AROUND

**1**

You'll probably spend most of your time in the city centre, which is compact and easily **walkable** – it takes less than 30min to get from one end of the Prado to the other on foot, and the traffic is so congested that walking is often the quickest way to get around, though at this altitude the steeper streets can be pretty exhausting to climb. That said, **taxis** are plentiful and relatively good value, and the city's **public transport** network, though slow and hopelessly chaotic, is very cheap. The city is currently developing a more integrated mass transit system dubbed "La Paz Bus", which includes the new Teleférico (see box, below) and the new "PumaKatari" buses, though for now this is primarily targeted at commuters.

### BY TAXI

To reduce your chances of being robbed, assaulted or worse, it's advisable to only ever take a radio taxi: they're marked as such, usually with a telephone number painted on the side. When you enter the cab, the driver is obliged by law to call their office and inform them of your destination; drivers also often – but not always – have photo ID on display. They charge a flat rate of Bs15–20 for anywhere in the city centre regardless of the number of passengers, which makes them good value for more than one person. Bear in mind that radio taxis are obliged to provide an exclusive service, and are not allowed to pick up other passengers en route; protest vehemently if they try to do so. Fares increase for longer journeys, especially if they involve a steep climb which consumes more fuel; a taxi to the Zona Sur should cost about Bs20–25. It's also a good idea to come equipped with a pocketful of small change as drivers rarely have any.

### BY MINIBUS

Privately owned minivans – known as minibuses – run along all the city's main thoroughfares and are one of the main causes of the ever-worsening traffic congestion. They're also pretty cramped, and usually entail a lot of getting out and in to accommodate your fellow passengers, a move you'll quickly master with the grace of a ballerina should you spend any amount of time in them. Destinations are written on signs inside the windscreen and bellowed incessantly by the driver's assistants, who hang from the open doors in the hope of coaxing just one more passenger into the already packed vehicle. The minibuses you'll most likely want to use are those that run up and down the Prado between the Terminal de Buses La Paz and Plaza San Francisco in the north and Av 6 de Agosto in Sopocachi, to the south. To go anywhere else in the city, it's usually enough to wait by any major intersection until you hear the name of your destination shouted out; alternatively, ask a driver's assistant where to catch the relevant bus. Fares are usually fixed at Bs2 for journeys in the city centre, and Bs2.60 for trips to the Zona Sur; fares increase to Bs2.20 and Bs2.80 respectively after 9pm.

### BY MICRO/PUMAKATARI

Bigger than minibuses but confusingly known as "micros", the other common form of transport in the city are older, brightly coloured minibuses that chug along numbered routes and usually cost Bs1–2. The new "PumaKatari" is a more conventional, modern city bus service with six routes that mainly serve the suburbs (see ⓦlapazbus.bo for further information).

### BY TRUFI

The city's other main form of transport is trufis – large estate cars that are used as collective taxis and follow fixed routes, mostly between Plaza del Estudiante and the wealthy suburbs of the Zona Sur (Bs3–3.50). They're designated by route numbers and, like minibuses, have their principal destinations written on a sign inside the

## MI TELEFÉRICO – LA PAZ BY CABLE CAR

In 2014 the commute between El Alto and La Paz became a lot more serene with the opening of an Austrian-built cable car, the **Teleférico**, part of an ambitious scheme that will eventually see a whole system of cable cars serving the city like a metro network. At the time of writing only four lines were up and running, but the Teleférico is expanding fast, and Paceños already refer affectionately to their *gondolas voladoras* ("flying gondolas"). Each cabin seats up to ten passengers, and services depart every twelve seconds, seventeen hours a day (Mon–Sat 6am–11pm, Sun 7am–9pm).

Though not billed as a tourist attraction, the **red line** (Línea Roja) which runs from Taypi Uta/Estación Central (at the old train station on Avenida Maco Capac) to Jach'a Qhathu/16 de Julio (on Avenida Panorámica Norte in El Alto), gives a scintillating ride across the rim of the Altiplano for only Bs3, and is worth taking just for the view. At present, Taypi Uta/Estación Central is the most central Teleférico station in La Paz, but the **orange line** (Línea Naranja), due to be open by the time this book is published, will link this to a station at Armentia, near the bus terminal, and there will eventually be stations at San José (behind the central post office) and Prado (pretty much opposite the post office). See ⓦwww.miteleferico.bo for the latest information.

**1**

windscreen. In common with minibuses, they charge extra if your luggage fills a space that might otherwise be occupied by another passenger.

### CAR RENTAL

Though driving in the city itself is not a good idea, there are plenty of car rental firms in La Paz for trips further afield.

Local firm Barbol at Av Héroes 777 (km 7) opposite El Alto airport (☎ 02 2820675, ⊚ barbolsrl.com) are usually less costly than the international franchises, which include Budget (⊚ budget.bo) at Capitán Ravelo 2130 (opposite the *Camino Real Hotel*; ☎ 02 2911925) and at the airport (☎ 7655 5509), and Europcar (⊚ europcar.com.bo) at Av Camacho 1574 (☎ 02 2202933) and at the airport (☎ 7720 5118).

## INFORMATION AND TOURS

### TOURIST INFORMATION

Both of the offices listed below are extremely friendly and helpful, and usually have someone on hand who speaks English. There is also a very helpful kiosk in the bus terminal (see p.72), and a handy website at ⊚ turismolapaz.com.

**Municipal tourist office** Plaza del Estudiante ☎ 02 2371044; map p.58. Has information on La Paz and the surrounding area, including free city maps of the city and flyers for several tour agencies, but not much on destinations further afield. Mon–Fri 8.30am–noon & 2.30–7pm.

**InfoTur** On the Prado at Av Mariscal Santa Cruz 1400, at Colombia ☎ 02 2651255, ⊚ facebook.com/lapazmaravillosa; map p.58. Offers city maps, and is better informed on destinations outside of La Paz than the municipal tourist office. Mon–Fri 9am–7pm, Sat & Sun 9am–1pm.

### TOUR OPERATORS

**America Tours** Ground floor, suite 9, Edificio Avenida, Av 16 de Julio 1490 ☎ 02 2374204, ⊚ america-ecotours .com; map p.58. Veteran operators with a track record in conservation and sustainable tourism; they're the main

booking agent for *Chalalán Albergue Ecológico* (see p.277) in Parque Nacional Madidi, and are a good place to book internal flights, as well as trips to the Pampas del Yacuma, Sajama and the Salar de Uyuni. Mon–Fri 9am–5.30pm, plus Sat April–Oct 10.30am–12.30pm.

**Andean Summits** Edificio Luisa, Muñoz Cornejo 1009 and Sotomayor, Sopocachi ☎ 02 2422106, ⊚ andeansummits.com; map p.68. Professional and much respected upmarket adventure tour operator with an excellent reputation that runs "off the beaten track" mountaineering and trekking expeditions throughout Bolivia, led by experienced and highly qualified English-speaking guides. Call before visiting. Mon–Fri 9am–6pm.

**Climbing South America** Upper floor, Linares 940 ☎ 02 2971543, ⊚ climbingsouthamerica.com; map p.58. Run by affable Australian Jeff Sandifort, this professional and dedicated company offers trips to all the Bolivian peaks, as well as those further afield such as Aconcagua in Argentina, along with pioneering two-week treks from the Cordillera Apolobamba to Rurrenabaque. Mon–Fri 9am–12.30pm & 2.30–6.30pm, Sat 10am–2.30pm.

**Deep Rainforest** Ground floor, Edificio Casablanca, Av América 121 ☎ 02 2150385, ⊚ deep-rainforest.com;

---

## TOURS FROM LA PAZ

La Paz is home to a plethora of **tour operators** offering everything from half- or one-day tours around the city to expeditions in remote parts of the country lasting several weeks; the number and variety – especially on calles **Sagárnaga**, **Illampu** and around – is mind-boggling, but a fair number of them are not officially registered. While this doesn't matter so much with the day-trips offered by almost every company, you should take greater care when considering a **mountain biking** trip down the "world's most dangerous road" to Coroico or any of the longer **mountaineering expeditions** and treks in the Cordillera Real.

### PRICES AND GUIDES

**City tours**, usually combined with the Valle de la Luna and Muela del Diablo, plus Tiwanaku or Chacaltaya, start at around Bs350/$50 per person. The **mountain biking** trip to Coroico costs around Bs850/$125. With an average-sized group of four to six people and an accredited guide, prices for **climbing tours** start at around Bs1000/$150 per person per day – this usually includes food and accommodation, but be sure to check. Whatever you do, don't buy tours from pirate operators approaching you in the street, and if you do buy a more expensive climbing tour, make sure the name of the guide is on your receipt; you can then check their credentials on the **guide association website** ⊚ agmtb.org. Cheaper companies may send a couple of *aspirantes* (part-qualified guides) alongside a fully qualified one, while the worst operators might send you out with a young, inexperienced guide; avoid the latter at all costs – people can and do die.

map p.58. The original boat-to-Rurrenabaque operator, and an attractive alternative to flying if you have the time and cash. The boat tours last four days and three nights ($308/Bs2115), starting with a bus ride to Guanay, from where you take the 230km/two-and-a-half-day river trip to Rurrenabaque. They also offer a "no noise" rafting alternative, slightly more expensive at six days and five nights ($352/Bs2415). Mon–Sat 10am–2pm & 3–7pm.

**Gravity Assisted Mountain Biking** Upper floor, Linares 940 ☎02 2310218, ⓦwww.gravitybolivia .com; map p.58. The original, and still widely regarded as the best, downhill mountain bike operator in Bolivia, with a sterling safety record, high-spec equipment and highly experienced and trained guides who are certified in rope rescue and first aid. As well as the media-saturated Death Road jaunt – which finishes at the gorgeous La Senda Verde animal refuge (see p.129) – they offer a selection of half-day rides, a five- to six-day combined bike ride and boat trip to Rurrenabaque (from $795/Bs5565 per person in a group of four, more in a smaller group, less in a larger one) and, for the experienced, hardcore single-track expeditions around both Sorata and La Paz. Mon–Fri 9am–7pm, Sat 10am–3pm.

**Huayna Potosí Travel Agency** Sagárnaga 398 ☎02 2317324, ⓦhuayna-potosi.com; map p.58. Friendly and long-established family firm run by the inimitable Dr Hugo Berrios, specializing in climbing and trekking expeditions in the Cordillera Real. While most operators use the public *refugios*, Hugo accommodates expedition members in several of his own privately owned ones, including one up at 5400m. He also offers ice-climbing courses at beginner, intermediate and advanced levels. Mon–Sat 9.30am–6.30pm.

**Kanoo Tours** Illampu 832, map p.58; Av Montes 503 (inside Adventure Brew Hostel), map p.58; ☎02 2460003, ⓦkanootours.com. This English-owned place has established itself as one of the principal backpacker-oriented agencies in La Paz, selling all the usual tours including the Salar de Uyuni, mountain biking to Coroico, pampas trekking, etc. Illampu office Mon–Fri 10am–6.30pm; Adventure Brew Hostel office Mon–Fri 10am–6pm, Sat 10am–5pm.

**La Paz On Foot** Linares 882-B ☎7154 3918, ⓦlapazonfoot.com; map p.58. Conservation-minded, culturally orientated company with strong community links and an academically astute staff numbering biologists, archeologists, anthropologists and ecologists. Alongside city tours, their impressive portfolio includes trips to the Lake Titicaca village of Santiago de Okola, an organic Yungas coffee farm and butterfly sanctuary, and treks in the Apolobamba range. Call before visiting.

**Luna Tours** Sagárnaga 380 ☎02 2310940, ⓦlunatourstravel.com; map p.58. The most high-profile of the Coroico mountain biking newcomers, with a

café (see p.81) and a separate office. They're wholly Bolivian owned, use Bolivian guides (all with at least eight years' experience) and bikes are apparently equipped with the best parts available in the world. Mon–Sat 10am–8pm.

**Millenarian Travel & Tourism** Sánchez Lima 2193, Sopocachi ☎02 2414753, ⓦboliviamilenaria.com; map p.68. A reliable, well-established agency offering a wide selection of mid-range and top-end tours across Bolivia. The company is particularly good for trips to the Salar de Uyuni and the Reserva Eduardo Avaroa. It also has a number of themed tours, including ones that focus on arts and crafts, culture and mysticism, and archeology. Mon–Fri 9am–5pm, Sat 10am–1pm.

**Motorcycle Tours Bolivia** Av Florida 609, Mallasa ☎02 2745572, ⓦmotorcycletoursbolivia.com. Bolivia's premier motorbike tour agency, with a sizeable fleet of machines and a choice of either guided trips (Salar de Uyuni, Tiwanaku, etc) or a self-determined itinerary; they'll supply a support vehicle. Mon–Sat 9am–5pm.

**Red Cap Walking Tours** c/o Gravity Assisted Mountain Biking, upper floor, Linares 940 ☎7628 5738, ⓦredcapwalkingtours.com; map p.58. This company runs half-day city walking tours, departing every day at 11am and 2pm from Plaza Sucre (Bs20); just turn up and look for the guide wearing their red cap and T-shirt. They also offer food and drinking tours and visits to El Alto. Mon–Fri 9am–7pm, Sat 10am–3pm.

**Topas Adventure Travel Bolivia** Carlos Bravo 299, at Tiwanaku (inside El Consulado hotel) ☎02 2111082 or ☎7308 8333, ⓦtopas.bo; map p.58. Running since 1973, this veteran operator has knowledgeable and enthusiastic English-speaking staff and guides specializing in the Cordillera Apolobamba and the Choro and Takesi trails; they also offer treks in Sajama and the Condoriri massif. Mon–Fri 8.30am–4.30pm, Sat 8.30am–noon.

**Travel Tracks** Sagárnaga 366 ☎02 2004513, ⓦtravel-tracks.com; map p.58. Run by Dutch expat Aly Bakker and Bolivian-American Gardiel Monteverde, this recommended operator specializes in two-/three-day trips to the mountain of Huayna Potosí with a hands-on approach and certified guides (one guide per two climbers). They also organize Choro and Takesi trail treks. Mon–Fri 10.30am–7pm, Sat & Sun 11am–7pm.

**Turisbus** C 10 #501, Calacoto, Zona Sur, map p.80; Av Illampu 704 (inside Hotel Rosario), map p.58; ☎02 2798786, ⓦturisbus.com. Upmarket agency offering a variety of tours, including wildlife and city tours, a half-day tour (US$43/Bs295 per person in a group of four) of El Alto's *cholets* (see p.70) and a trip to Lake Titicaca's Isla del Sol and Isla de la Luna (from US$139/Bs940 for two days/one night). Mon–Fri 9am–12.30pm & 3–8pm, Sat 9am–12.30pm.

**1**

## ACCOMMODATION

There's been an explosion in the La Paz accommodation scene in recent years, even if prices have likewise risen steeply and there now seems to be a dearth of rooms at the lower mid-range price. **Budget** accommodation – typically around Bs50 in a dorm – tends to be spartan and chilly; ask for a room that gets some sunlight, as this makes a big temperature difference. **Heating** is only available in the top-range hotels, and though most places have 24hr **hot water**, it's worth checking that it's not just lukewarm. Prices quoted below include **breakfast** unless otherwise stated.

### CITY CENTRE

The bulk of the city's gringo-oriented budget accommodation is split between the busy market district west of Plaza San Francisco and the more sedate colonial centre to the east, where you'll find most of the best budget options and a few crumbling colonial bargains. Bear in mind the steep gradients of the city's streets: what looks like a short walk back to your hotel on the map can in fact be an exhausting climb, particularly if you haven't yet adjusted to the altitude.

### BUDGET

**Adventure Brew B&B** Av Montes 533 ☎02 2461614, ⓦtheadventurebrewhostel.com; map p.58. Sister property to the hostel 50m down the road (see below), but quieter and more sedate, with comfortable private en-suite rooms (as well as four- and eight-bed dorms), a roof restaurant for the buffet breakfast, and a free Saya beer included in the room rate (the B&B was originally the Saya brewery and shares the same owner). Doubles ~~Bs220~~, dorms ~~Bs80~~

★**Adventure Brew Hostel** Av Montes 503 ☎02 2915896, ⓦtheadventurebrewhostel.com; map p.58. Popular hostel with a range of dorms, one free beer every day, an underground bar with pool table, a DVD lounge, top-floor restaurant and terrace with amazing views, Friday barbecues, and good food. Staff are incredibly friendly and the hostel is very popular so it's best to book online in advance, although they can usually find a bed. Wi-fi gets weaker as you go up the building, but plans are afoot to remedy this. Dorms ~~Bs52~~

**Arthy's Guesthouse** Av Montes 693 ☎02 2281439, ⓦarthyshouse.tripod.com; map p.58. A cheap hotel rather than a hostel (there are no dorms), this welcoming, pot-planted retreat offers carpeted rooms with bedside lamps, a TV room and a communal kitchen. It's a bit worn round the edges, but in a comfortable kind of way; there's a midnight curfew, and breakfast is Bs10 extra. ~~Bs90~~

**Bash'n'Crash** Ingavi 681 ☎02 2280934; map p.58. This self-styled party hostel (the name says it all, really) is rough and ready, rather raucous, but very cheap and lots of fun. Accommodation consists largely of dorm beds, with a few private rooms, while the communal areas have enough bonhomie to take the chill off the coldest La Paz nights. There's a kitchen for self-caterers, plus a ping-pong room and a TV area. Residents get free entry to *El Mural peña* downstairs (see p.85). Dorms ~~Bs35~~, doubles ~~Bs115~~

**Estrella Andina** Illampu 716 ☎02 2456421,

ⓔestrellaandina@hotmail.es; map p.58. Bright, fun and very friendly, this place has a roof terrace with views of Mount Illimani and features Andean naïf murals filling every centimetre of plaster, with walls – and even doors – cannily painted as picture-book windows to lend an impression of space; garish, but it almost works. The rooms themselves are en suite, clean and just as colourful. ~~Bs300~~

**Hostal Austria** Yanacocha 531, on the left at the top of the stairs ☎02 2408540, ⓔhotelaustria58@hotmail.com; map p.58. In a colonial building with lofty ceilings and a warren of wood and glass corridors, this place oozes history, though is somewhat ramshackle. All bathrooms are shared, the gas-powered showers sometimes need some help, and some rooms don't have outside windows (although these are quieter). There's a TV room and a kitchen, but breakfast isn't included. Dorms ~~Bs42~~, doubles ~~Bs98~~

**Hostal Cruz de los Andes** Aroma 216 ☎02 2451401, ⓔcruzdelosandes@hotmail.com; map p.58. Part of the *Estrella Andina* empire (see above), this budget branch has the requisite indigenous art and similarly furnished rooms (slightly smaller than in the *Estrella Andina*, and with a slightly smaller breakfast), as well as an elegant wrought-iron stairwell and a sociable pool room. ~~Bs220~~

**Hostal República** Comercio 1455 ☎02 2202742, ⓦhostalrepublica.com; map p.58. The former home of Bolivian president Jose M. Pando, this renovated pile is set around two cobbled courtyards. The downstairs rooms are fairly poky and noisy, but the upper rooms are brighter, and there's also a modern five-person villa with a secluded garden and chairs at the back. Best of all, they sell hot water bottles (Bs30) which you can fill with hot water from the café. Rooms with private bathroom cost Bs60 more. ~~Bs190~~

**Hostal Sol Andino** Aroma 6 ☎02 2456421, ⓔsolandinohostal@gmail.com; map p.58. If the bright primary colours and Andean fantasy-scapes of *Estrella Andina* (see above) take your fancy, but the price doesn't, *Hostal Sol Andino*, just round the corner on Aroma, might be the answer. It's basically an extension of *Andina* with similar decor and furnishings, slightly smaller rooms and no lift, for a cheaper price. ~~Bs240~~

**Latino Hospedaje y Confort** Junín 857 ☎02 2285463, ⓦresidenciallatino.com; map p.58. This veteran colonial place has a wealth of clean, pastel-painted rooms (some with private bathroom; extra Bs60) facing onto a bright enclosed courtyard. The whole place feels incredibly spacious, with a black-and-orange colour scheme and faux-colonial lamps throughout. ~~Bs200~~

1

**Lion Palace Hostel** Linares 1017 ☎02 2900454, ⓦlionpalacehotel.com; map p.58. This budget hotel is a mini riot of Neoclassical-pillared, mock-colonial kitsch complete with plaster lion heads. Some of the paintwork's a bit scuffed but the rooms are comfortable and quite spacious, with parquet floors, and pretty decent value in all. Bs160

**Loki La Paz** Av América 120 ☎02 2457300, ⓦlokihostel.com; map p.58. The La Paz branch of this Peru-based party hostel chain is large, efficient and well run. The ground floor (shared with the Banco Ecofutura) was once the home of Spanish conquistador Alonzo de Mendoza, but the upper floors are super-modern, with at least one bathroom to every dorm, and one dorm reserved for women. There's a seventh-floor bar with great views, a TV room, a smoking room, and pool and ping-pong tables. Loki also own the former *Hotel Viena*, a wonderful dandy-pink, red-velvet-draped townhouse on Loayza, which they're planning to open as a more sedate branch with mainly private rooms. Dorms Bs62, doubles Bs205

**Muzungu Hostel** Illampu and Santa Cruz 441 ☎02 2451640, ⓦmuzunguhostel.com; map p.58. A small, quiet (as opposed to party) hostel, with large, spacious dorms (beds rather than bunks) and double rooms; if staying in the latter, it's worth paying Bs20 more to get one with a private bathroom. The painted concrete floors make the rooms feel hard, bare and a little bit industrial, but otherwise there are all the facilities you need, as well as friendly staff and a top-floor bar and breakfast area with great city views. Dorms Bs40, doubles Bs140

**Wild Rover** Comercio 1476 ☎02 2116903, ⓦwildroverhostels.com; map p.58. La Paz's other big gringo party hostel, very clean and safe, centred on a yellow-painted courtyard and an in-house bar which, in line with the hostel's (admittedly subtle) Irish theme, keeps the Guinness flowing till well into the wee hours. They claim they have "the comfiest beds in South America"; given the firm emphasis on living large, however, chances are you won't spend much time in them. Guests can sometimes work for their board. Dorms Bs59, doubles Bs198

### MID-RANGE/UPMARKET

★ **El Consulado** Carlos Bravo 299 ☎02 2117706, ⓦhotel-elconsulado.com; map p.58. The majordomo of the city's historical conversions, this boutique hotel near the Prado – the one-time Consulate of Panama – has a limited number of rooms, stylishly faithful to the original decor and fittings. Period wallpaper and chequered tiles, antique baths and feather duvets impart a sense of luxury you won't find elsewhere. There's also *artesanía* for sale, a gourmet breakfast and the highly respected Topas Adventure Travel (see p.77) in the basement. $79 (Bs538)

**Hostal Naira** Sagárnaga 161 ☎02 2355645, ⓦhostalnaira.com; map p.58. In a 200-year-old building with high, corniced ceilings, the *Naira*'s rooms are as elegant and spotlessly clean as any in La Paz, making beguiling use of light and glass, all set around a capacious colonial courtyard. The rooms at the back are the oldest and quietest, but the street-front rooms have wonderful period shutters and gorgeous tiled balconies, and rooms on the top floor get extra light in return for a higher climb. $66 (Bs450)

**Hotel Presidente** Potosí 920 ☎02 2406666, ⓦhotelpresidente.com.bo; map p.58. Ricky Martin once bedded down here, and the place is still frequented by visiting Latin American singers and celebs. Decor-wise, it's in a 1970s time warp, especially the lobby, but the rooms are warm and comfortable, if a little retro, and there's also a pool, a sauna and two restaurants, including one on the 16th floor with great views in all directions. Bs1120

**Hotel Rosario** Av Illampu 704 ☎02 2451658, ⓦhotelrosario.com/la-paz; map p.58. The *Rosario*'s warren of elegant heated rooms and eccentric little corridors surrounds a series of cobbled, pot-planted courtyards. A fair-trade shop (see p.87), the excellent *Terradentro* restaurant (see p.83), a copious buffet breakfast and a great, sun-soaked rooftop café round out the experience. They're also about to open a sister hotel in the Zona Sur, for those who prefer a leafier and lower-altitude location. $83 (Bs565)

**Posada de la Abuela Obdulia** Linares 947 ☎02 2332285, ⓦhostalposadaabuela.com; map p.58. Housed in a tastefully restored 1908 mansion, rooms are furnished in fresh pine and wrought iron and built around a pretty courtyard. Front-facing rooms 202–205 are especially inviting, with balconies looking onto Calle Linares below, and the glowing recommendations in the guest book speak for themselves. They usually offer discounts to guests staying three nights or more. $49 (Bs335)

### MIRAFLORES AND SOPOCACHI

Many of La Paz's more luxurious hotels are to be found in the prosperous suburb of Sopocachi, home to most of the city's more fashionable bars and restaurants, and a pleasant place to stroll around in the evening. There are also a couple of places to stay in San Pedro and Miraflores, relatively less frenzied suburbs on either side of the main thoroughfare.

**Hotel "A la Maison"** Pasaje Muñoz Cornejo 15 (off Muñoz Cornejo between Vincentti and Ricardo Mujia), Sopocachi ☎02 2413704, ⓦwww.alamaison-lapaz.com; map p.68. Cloistered within a cul-de-sac and almost entirely anonymous (no sign), this old house has a handful of spotlessly clean, spacious apartments, accessed by a beautifully tiled stairwell and idiosyncratically decorated with rustic furniture, hemp curtains, abstract art and faded French novels. Staff are low-key yet amenable, and the simple kitchens are supplied with butter, jam, fruit juice and fresh bread every morning. $60 (Bs408)

**Hotel LP Columbus** Av Illimani 1990, Miraflores ⊕02 2242444, ⊕lphoteles.com; map p.68. Though it's slightly out of the way, this is a great-value mid-range option with the feel and facilities of a posher hotel (albeit no pool or sauna). The bright rooms offer business-like comfort and functionality, firm beds, and a choice of seven different types of pillow. **$74 (Bs504)**

**Hotel Madre Tierra** Av 20 de Octubre 2080, Sopocachi ⊕02 2419910, ⊕hotelmadretierra.com; map p.68. As one of the few hotels in central Sopocachi, this tower block represents fair value for money, with clean, brick-walled rooms, a spacious dining room, pleasant staff and a generally bright, functional ambience. **Bs450**

**La Loge Apart Hotel** Pasaje Medinacelli 2234, Sopocachi ⊕02 2423561, ⊕lacomedie-lapaz.com; map p.68. A very blue stairwell accesses this cluster of chic, self-catering apartments, run by the same people as *La Comédie* restaurant (see p.83). Decor is more polished than the similarly French-owned *Hotel "A la Maison"*, with breakfast bar-style kitchens (supplied with fresh fruit juice, bread and jam), and all rooms come equipped with internet-ready computer. **Bs580**

**El Rey Palace Hotel** Av 20 de Octubre 1947, Sopocachi ⊕02 2418541, ⊕reypalacehotel.com; map p.68. One of the most accommodating top-range options in La Paz, with stained glass, an endearingly plush dining room and big, comfortable rooms with feather duvets and polished dark wood furniture. Staff couldn't be more helpful, and the kitchen is big on quinoa and healthy food in general. **Bs700**

★**Stannum Boutique Hotel** Torre Multicine 12/F, Av Arce, Sopocachi 2631 ⊕02 2148393, ⊕stannumhotels.com; map p.68. This exceptional hotel is the most popular high-end place in La Paz, though it's a bit of a hike from the city centre. Perched on top of the Torre Multicine, a shopping and entertainment complex, it's loaded with quirky, contemporary design and lavish rooms sporting magnificent views of the Andes. The official (rack) rate is steep, but discounts are usually available, especially if you book online. **$200 (Bs1360)**

### ZONA SUR

If you'd rather restrict your appreciation of La Paz's frantic charm to measured doses, or you simply want to minimize the adverse effects of altitude, the Zona Sur is a more oxygenated option. With a spectacular Wild West backdrop, palm-tree-lined boulevards and a climate to match, it feels very much removed from the rest of the city. It's served by Irpawi/Irpavi station on the Teleférico's green line (Línea Verde), with connections to Sopocachi, but not as yet to the city centre.

**Atix** C 16 #8052 (between Julio Patiño and Sánchez Bustamente), Calacoto ⊕02 2776500, ⊕atixhotel.com; map below. A very swanky boutique hotel, beautifully designed, with stylish, modern rooms, a rooftop pool and bar offering great views, a restaurant serving gourmet Bolivian food, and super-attentive staff. Promotional rates often apply, especially if you book online. **$128 (Bs870)**

**Camino Real Suites** Av Ballivián 369, at C 10, Calacoto ⊕02 2792323, ⊕caminoreal.com.bo; map below. A conspicuously modern, sun-glinting skyscraper that looks much taller than its eight floors suggest. Arranged in vertigo-inducing circles with lots of greenery above an imposing black marble reception, it's home to state-of-the-art executive rooms, some with great canyon views. Extras include pool, sauna and entrance to the local golf club. **$198 (Bs1345)**

**1**

**Hotel Calacoto** C 13 #8009, at Sánchez Bustamente, Calacoto ☎02 2774600, ⓦhotelcalacoto.com; map opposite. Hidden away down a leafy, serene side street, this hacienda conversion has dispensed with much of its former quirky charm in favour of more blandly modern decor, though it's still a decent deal for the location and a fraction of the price of its skyscraping neighbours. There's a lush garden and a choice of rooms or self-catering apartments. Doubles Bs610, apartments Bs715

**Hotel Oberland** Av Florida and C 2, Mallasa ☎02 2745040, ⓦh-oberland.com; map opposite. This Swiss-owned complex in the suburb of Mallasa, 5km south of Zona Sur, has an environmental bias, and an "eco spa" with a dome-covered pool maintained at an inviting 35 degrees. The en-suite rooms and three-person apartments are modern-rustic, with beamed ceilings and the occasional brick fireplace, while the well-manicured garden is the scene of regular BBQs. The Valle de la Luna (see p.89) is nearby. Apartments $130 (Bs885), doubles $70 (Bs475)

**Hotel Rosario La Paz Sur** Calle 16 #20 at Sauces and Av Montenegro, Calacoto ☎02 2776286, ⓦhotelrosario.com; map opposite. The bright, new Zona Sur branch of the classy Illampu hotel (see p.79) has spacious rooms, an attractive garden and a good bar-restaurant, plus its own spa. $119 (Bs810)

**CAMPING**

**Colibri Camping** C 4, Jupapina, just beyond Mallasa ☎7629 5658, ⓦcolibricamping.com; map opposite. In a spectacular mountainside location overlooking La Muela del Diablo (see p.90), *Colibri Camping* is run using recycled materials and renewable energy by an extremely welcoming British-Bolivian family. The tranquil site boasts two cabins sleeping up to four, two tepees and several spots to pitch a tent (equipment is available to rent if you don't have your own), plus outdoor kitchen, hot tub and hammocks. There are plenty of activities on offer – hiking, mountain biking and Spanish-language classes – as well as volunteer opportunities through sister organization Up Close Bolivia (ⓦupclosebolivia.org). It's a 30min drive south of La Paz (around Bs70 in a taxi). Camping (per person) Bs50, tepees (for two people) Bs200, cabins (for two people) Bs200

## EATING

La Paz has a wide range of **restaurants**, **cafés** and **street stalls** to suit most tastes and budgets. Few places open for breakfast much before 8am, and Paceños treat lunch as the main meal of the day, eating lightly in the evening. Most restaurants serve **set lunch menus** known as almuerzos (typically noon–2pm), which are generally extremely filling and great value. The least expensive restaurants are hole-in-the-wall places catering to workers and students; these are concentrated in the city's upper reaches, and serve set almuerzos for Bs10–15, as do lunch stalls in Mercado Lanza (see box, p.82). The city also has an increasingly cosmopolitan range of European-style restaurants, especially in **Sopocachi**. Restaurants begin serving dinner at around 7pm. As a general rule, the more gringo-friendly places will open later and fill up later, but it's difficult to find a sit-down meal anywhere after 11pm. La Paz also now has a couple of "third-wave" cafés, where Bolivian-grown **coffee** is carefully brewed to gourmet standards, making them an excellent place to sample the local bean.

### CITY CENTRE

#### CAFÉS

**Alexander Coffee** Potosí 1091 ☎02 2406482; Av 16 de Julio 1832 on the Prado ☎02 312790; ⓦwww .alexander-coffee.com; map p.58. This Western-style mini chain ("the Bolivian Starbucks") offers decent cappuccinos (Bs15) and generous breakfast plates. Daily 8am–10.30pm.

★**Cafe Banaís** Sagárnaga 161 ☎02 2311214; map p.58. Adjacent to *Hostal Naira* (see p.79), this is one of the most reliable and elegant breakfast venues in La Paz (the buffet is Bs38), with smiling staff, hideaway booths, great chocolate milkshakes (Bs18) and mountainous bowls of fruit, yoghurt and muesli (Bs20). Its coca tea (Bs9) crams in more leaves than water, and there's decent espresso, too (from Bs10). Daily 7am–10pm.

**Café Ciudad** Batallón Colorados (Plaza del Estudiante) ☎02 2441827; map p.58. Old-fashioned all-night café that looks older than it is (it opened in 1990). The coffee (Bs5) and food in general isn't that good, but the peerlessly fluffy omelettes (Bs24) are among the best in the city; also on the menu are sandwiches (Bs20–42), pizza, pasta and more ambitious dishes like trout (Bs56–60). There's also an upstairs terrace and an outdoor patio at the back, though the views are mainly of the jam-packed roads. Daily 24hr.

**Confitería Club de La Paz** Av Camacho 1202 ☎02 2312266; map p.58. Though this august café isn't quite as atmospheric as it once was, the coffee is usually good, and the breakfasts (Bs22–30) are cheaper than some of the nearby chains. They also serve beer, and a Bs27 almuerzo. It was supposedly the haunt of Nazi war criminal Klaus Barbie before his 1983 extradition to France, and more happily, of contemporary Bolivian poet Hector Borda. Mon–Fri 8am–midnight, Sat 8am–6.30pm.

**K'umara** Tarija 263 ☎7194 2945; map p.58. This hutch-like hole in the wall on the steps of Tarija is perfect for a light, healthy breakfast. Mix and match your cereal from jars of organic Bolivian cereals such as quinoa and amaranto, with fresh fruit, natural yoghurt and strong coffee; set breakfasts cost Bs25–45, juices Bs10–20. Mon–Sat 9am–10pm.

**Luna's Café** Sagárnaga 289 ☎02 2311568; map p.58. A friendly, engaging and always busy little place, serving set breakfasts (Bs20–30), moderately priced soups, sandwiches,

1

## LA PAZ STREET FOOD

For those whose stomachs have adjusted to basic local food, the cheapest places to eat are the city's **markets**, where you can get entire meals for as little as Bs10. **Street food** is another good low-cost option: the ubiquitous *salteñas* and *tucumanas* – delicious pastries filled with meat or chicken with vegetables – make excellent snacks. If there's a large crowd eating from the same stall you can assume it will be OK.

**Mercado Camacho** At the end of Avenida Camacho; map p.58. This multi-level concrete complex has a *patio de comidas* (food court) on the bottom floor, serving decent fast food (tacos, ribs, burgers, pasta, salad and even paella). The adjoining *anexo*, a favourite haunt of local students, has stalls churning out delicious fresh fruit salads (Bs7–8) and juices (Bs5–6). Food court daily 11am–10.30pm; anexo Mon–Fri 8am–9pm, Sat & Sun 8am–6pm.

**Mercado Lanza** Just north of Plaza San Francisco; map p.58. A huge concrete labyrinth with an astounding range of food stalls on the upper levels, loosely divided into "sectors": *desayuno* (breakfast); *comidas* (lunch); and *jugos* (juices). There's also a fun café/coffeeshop row. The food is usually very good, cooked up by Aymara women and served in heaped plates of stew, plantains and rice. Daily 7am–9pm.

**Tucumanas El Prado** Just off the Prado on México (at the top of the steps up from the Prado); map p.58. This series of street carts is a perennial favourite with hungry Paceños lining up to munch their delicious fried *tucumanas* (Bs6). Daily 8am–1.30pm.

omelettes and creamy-sweet milkshakes amid a handsomely shabby colonial interior. Mains like lasagne (Bs70) and llama steak (Bs80) are a bit pricier. Daily 7.30am–9.30pm.

**The Writer's Coffee** Calle Libreria Gisbert, Comercio 1270 ☎02 2200122, ⓦthewriterscoffee.com; map p.58. Inside a bookshop just off Plaza Murillo, this little café does the third-wave business on Bolivian coffee varieties such as Buena Vista, Circuata or Munaipata, serving them espresso, macchiato, cappuccino or – for you really serious coffee gourmets – from a V60 dripper, with tasty pastries to keep them company. Mon–Fri 8.30am–7.30pm, Sat 9am–12.30pm.

### RESTAURANTS

★**Ali Pacha** Colón 1306 at Potosí ☎02 220 2366, ⓦalipacha.com; map p.58. You'll need to reserve ahead to get a place at this gourmet vegan restaurant, one of the top foodie hotspots in town. You certainly don't need to be vegan to eat here: even confirmed carnivores rave about the amazingly creative veg cuisine. Everything's made from fresh seasonal ingredients, and served up in the form of a three-course (Bs100), five-course (Bs150) or seven-course (Bs200) set meal that varies daily but never disappoints. Tues noon–3pm, Wed–Sat noon–3pm & 7–10pm.

**Angelo Colonial** Av Mariscal Santa Cruz 1066; Linares 922, off Sagárnaga; inside the Museo Nacional de Etnografía; ☎02 2124979, ⓦfacebook.com/angelocolonial; map p.58. The Av Mariscal restaurant is a rare retreat, and as convenient a place as any for that candlelit dinner. Rustic bench seating and a hoard of antiques make for atmosphere in abundance, though the food (llama or trout *a la plancha* Bs70/62) doesn't quite match the fittings. The Linares branch is a smaller affair on the rickety balcony of an atmospheric *tambo*, loaded with antiques, while the branch in

the brick-vaulted cellars of the Museo Nacional de Etnografía (see p.60) is a great choice for breakfast or for an evening drink (it serves alcohol, with coffee from Bs8). Av Mariscal daily 8am–11.30pm; Linares daily 7.30am–11pm; Ethnographic Museum Mon–Sat 9am–10.30pm.

**La Caribeña** Av Gonzalez 1248 ☎7770 0007; map p.58. Arrive here early (before 11.30am-odd) to get the best choice of *salteñas* (pasties) in town – they sell out fast. There's simple chicken or beef, obviously, but if you're early enough they'll also have spicy beef, pork fricassee, barbecue pork, pizza-style (ham, cheese and tomato sauce), and *charque* (dried llama meat). At just Bs7 for a *salteña*, with banana, papaya or strawberry *jugos* on hand to wash them down, you can't really go wrong. Daily from 9.30am until they sell out completely (usually around 1.30pm).

**La Cueva** Tarija 210B, at Murillo ☎02 2147115, ⓦ4cornerslapaz.com; map p.58. Colourful, authentic-feeling Mexican with a sense of humour (check out the Spiderman shrine), super-friendly management and a cosy orange glow. There are *quesadillas* (Bs28–32), chicken enchiladas (Bs40) and even chilli con carne (yes, we know, not really Mexican; Bs40), not to mention a wide range of tequilas, including Jimador, Herradura and Don Julio. Daily noon–midnight.

**Eli's Restaurant** Av 16 de Julio 1491 ☎02 2335566; map p.58. This perennially popular La Paz institution has been cooking up Italian and South American food (spaghetti with meatballs Bs55, "baby beef" aka tenderloin Bs69) since 1942, with an interior reminiscent of an American 1950s diner. The walls are decked with old photos of movie stars, and Che Guevara is said to have worked or at least eaten here in the 1950s. Don't confuse the restaurant with the *Eli's Pizza Express* mini chain, which knocks out basic slices at outlets on the other side of Cine

Monje Campero and across the Prado. Daily 8am–11pm.

**iCrêpes and More** Galeria Chuquiago, Sagárnaga 217 ☏ 6993 0868, ⓦ facebook.com/iCrepesandMore; map p.58. As you might guess from the name, this place serves is crêpes, both sweet and savoury, and very nice they are too. Options include *quattro formaggi* (Bs30), prawn and vegetarian, while for dessert there's nutella or lemon cream crêpes, or a Bolivian crêpe Suzette (flambéed with *singani*; Bs35). Mon–Fri 10am–7pm, Sat 10am–6pm.

**Namas Té** Zoilo Flores 1334, at Almirante Grau ☏ 02 2481401, ⓦ namastebolivia.com; map p.58. Run by Gonz Jove, an artist/sculptor responsible for several of the alfresco murals around La Paz, this colourful bohemian enclave offers the best-value vegetarian (much of it vegan) almuerzos (Bs29) in the city, prepared with healthy doses of quinoa and a flair for traditional adaptations. The fruity desserts are similarly imaginative, and they also do delicious takes on the usual sandwiches, burritos, tacos, etc. Mon–Fri 8.30am–7pm, Sat 8.30am–4pm.

**Paceña La Salteña** Loayza 237 ☏ 02 2202347, ⓦ pacenalasaltena.com; map p.58. A La Paz institution with several branches in the city (this is the most central), where a tasty pasty (meat, chicken or veg) will set you back the princely sum of Bs6. Note that the chopped peppers which come in a little bowl with your *salteñas* and look disarmingly like the sweet variety are in fact locoto chillies. Mon–Fri & Sun 8.30am–2pm, Sat 8.30am–3pm.

**Sabor Cubano** Sagárnaga 357 ☏ 02 2451797, ⓦ bit.ly/ SaborCubano; map p.58. Cheap, tasty and filling food in satisfyingly tattered surroundings, with graffiti-daubed walls and vintage Cuban sounds. Various permutations of rice, beans, avocado and cassava are on offer, as well as standbys like *ropa vieja* (shredded beef, onion, wine and tomato; Bs50) and the obligatory mojitos (Bs25), making this the best lazy evening option on Sagárnaga by far. The Cuban set lunch is just Bs30. Mon–Sat noon–midnight.

**Terradentro** Illampu 704 ☏ 02 2451658, ⓦ hotelrosario .com/la-paz/terradentro; map p.58. This contemporary Bolivian restaurant in *Hotel Rosario* (open for breakfast and dinner only) is one of the best places to sample creative local dishes (and even Bolivian wine) – expect the likes of Lake Titicaca trout with chickpea (*garbanzo*) purée (Bs89), or leg of llama served with jalapeño relish (Bs91). The stylish dining room is decorated with local art and colonial artefacts, but the atmosphere is fairly informal, with a primarily foreign clientele. Daily 7–9.30am & 6.30–9.45pm.

**Tia Gladys** Illampu 809 ☏ 02 2452070; map p.58. A great little budget café-restaurant near the witches' market, handy for a set breakfast (Bs13–30), a plate of pasta (Bs35), or just a coffee and a cake (apple cake Bs10, tiramisu Bs12). Daily 8am–11pm.

**Tierra Sana** Tarija 213, at Murillo ☏ 02 2120101, ⓦ 4cornerslapaz.com; map p.58. This healthy-eating restaurant offers soups, salads and a range of veg meals for

Bs40, and non-veg, mainly chicken-based versions of the same dishes for Bs62, including a Sri Lankan-style coconut curry and a Cameroon-style "African stew" with lentils and plantains, all served in a bright, fresh, self-consciously modern interior. Daily 8am–10pm.

## SOPACACHI

### CAFÉS

**Alexander Coffee** Av 20 de Octubre 2463 (northeast side of Plaza Avaroa), Sopacachi ☏ 02 2431006, ⓦ www.alexander-coffee.com; map p.68. The main Sopacachi branch of this popular café chain (see p.81). Daily 8am–10.30pm.

★ **Café Blueberries** Av 20 de Octubre 2475 (northeast side of Plaza Avaroa), Sopacachi ☏ 02 2433402, ⓦ bit .ly/CafeBlueberries; map p.68. In a city where coffee is king, this is a humble tea-drinker's haven, where you can sip from exquisite pots of Ceylon, Darjeeling and Assam (Bs11–16); don't miss the sweetly astringent ginger brew. The pancakes (Bs62) are delicious, made with nutritious Andean blueberries, and the rich house blueberry yoghurt (Bs18) is unlike anything you'll have tasted. There's also a garden backdrop, and live jazz every Saturday. Mains Bs30–45. Mon–Sat 8.30am–10.30pm, Sun 4–10pm.

**Virgen de los Deseos** 20 de Octubre 2060, Sopacachi ☏ 02 2413764, ⓦ mujerescreando.org; map p.68. Run by the feminist group Mujeres Creando, this is primarily a space for women to hang out in and make contacts, but men are welcome too. Aside from the politics, there's street-art decor, coffee and vegetarian food (almuerzo Bs23), and it's a great place to come if you can speak Spanish and want to learn about the local political scene, although with a left-wing bias, obviously. In the evening they serve beer and it becomes more of a bar. Daily 9am–11pm.

### RESTAURANTS

**Café Beirut** Belisario Salinas 380 ☏ 02 2444486; map p.68. Though this cavernous café-restaurant lacks any Middle Eastern atmosphere and the music – and much of the food – is in fact inexplicably Mexican, they do nonetheless have the tastiest falafel in La Paz (Bs26 for four), not to mention further Lebanese-style *mezze* delights such as stuffed vine leaves (Bs39 for ten) and *kebbi* (fried bulgur wheat balls stuffed with meat; Bs15 each). Mon–Sat 9am–midnight, Sun 9am–10.30pm.

★ **La Comédie** Pasaje Medinacelli 2234 ☏ 02 2423561, ⓦ lacomedie-lapaz.com; map p.68. This indefatigably stylish institution is a favourite meeting place for La Paz's French community. Amid an art and antique-arranged interior, you can watch the chefs whipping up several varieties of duck (Bs55–82) – potted, pâteed and roasted – or lighter snacks such as *La Comédie Salad* (mixed greens, smoked duck breast and trout; Bs45). The chocolate mousse is to *mourir for*

**1**

(Bs35). Needless to say, there's also a cellar of real French wine. Mon–Fri noon–3pm & 7–11pm, Sat 5–11pm.

**La Guinguette** Pedro Salazar 497, on Plaza Avaroa ☎02 2412519; map p.68. A laidback bar-restaurant in the heart of Sopocachi, with a range of wines and aperitifs, a smoking terrace, a weekday almuerzo for Bs35 (Bs40 with coffee and dessert), and an à la carte menu that changes weekly but typically features standards such as trout fillet (Bs55) and burger with brie (Bs50). Mon–Fri noon–3pm & 6–11pm, Sun 6.30–10pm.

**Ken Chan** Batallón Colorados 98 at Federico Suazo ☎02 2442292; map p.68. Attached to the Japanese cultural centre, this restaurant is where La Paz's Japanese-Bolivian community come for a bit of comfort food, and it's where you'll find the best Japanese nosh in town. Treats include a tempura *teishoku* for Bs68 or a big plate of trout sushi for Bs69. Tues–Sun 11.30am–2.30pm & 6–11pm.

**Parilla Casa Argentina** Av 6 de Agosto 2535 ☎02 2310440; map p.68. Claiming "the best meat in the world" (better even than in Argentina itself), this excellent Argentine steak house serves up some serious slabs of beef – including the favourite Argentine cut, *bife chorizo* (top loin, aka sirloin strip; Bs95) – along with alternative options such as *chorizo* sausage or *morcilla*, accompanied by fries and a salad bar. Mon–Sat 11am–10.30pm, Sun 11am–4pm.

**Pronto Dalicatessen** Pasaje Jáuregui 2248 (between 20 de Octubre and 6 de Agosto) ☎02 2441369, ⓦfacebook.com/ProntoDalicatessen; map p.68. This "dalicatessen" (Salvador Dalí images and posters line the walls) is a cosy Italian-Bolivian fusion restaurant, definitely not your standard pizza and pasta joint. The pasta in particular has a decidedly South American twist to it. House specialities include gorgonzola steak (Bs85), "Peruvian" seafood fettuccine (Bs95) and trout ravioli (Bs80). Mon–Sat 6.30–10.30pm.

**Vienna** Federico Zuazo 1905 ☎02 2441660, ⓦrestaurantvienna.com; map p.68. Justly popular Austrian restaurant in an elegant house on the edge of downtown. Highlights of a very large menu include a plate of three different *würste* with *sauerkraut* and potatoes (Bs78), or Viennese goulash with noodles (Bs76). Mon–Fri noon–2pm & 6–10pm, Sun noon–2.30pm.

**Vinapho** Edificio Valentina, Sánchez Lima 2326 (between Belisario Salinas and Rosendo Gutiérrez) ☎02 2424619, ⓦfacebook.com/Vinapho.LP; map p.68. The only Vietnamese restaurant in Bolivia and the best Asian restaurant in town. There's a variety of tasty *pho* soups (from Bs42) followed by main dishes such as squid and shrimp *kung pao* (Bs70), and lunchtime set menus (except Sun) for Bs35. Mon–Sat noon–4pm & 5–10.30pm, Sun noon–3pm.

### ZONA SUR

★**Gustu** C 10 #300 at Av Costanera, Calacoto ☎02 2117491, ⓦrestaurantgustu.com; map p.80. Opened in 2013 by Claus Meyer, co-founder of Denmark's acclaimed *Noma*, *Gustu* is currently the trendsetter in Bolivian cuisine, dedicated to the seasonal ingredients/sustainable farming philosophy of its Nordic role model. There are two tasting menus (Bs410 and Bs530), each with a vegetarian version (Bs360 and Bs470). Otherwise, of course, you can order à la carte: menus change, but on any given day they should have five starters, five main courses (Bs95–130) and five desserts. Ingredients they typically like to use include house-made bacon, wild rabbit, wild cocoa and *chankaka* (a sweet sauce made of unrefined sugar), not to mention llama and trout of course, and fine Bolivian wines. Tues–Sat noon–3pm & 6.30–11pm.

**Roaster** Moreno E-20, San Miguel, Zona Sur ☎02 2795446, ⓦroasterboutique.com; map p.80. If you really care about your coffee, this is the place to come. They started out just growing it, but now they toast it and serve it too, with a choice of roasts, blends and single varieties, all high-grade Bolivian arabica, and all carefully quality-controlled at every stage from the bush to the cup. Daily 7.30am–10.30pm.

## DRINKING AND NIGHTLIFE

Backpackers on a budget tend to stick to the **gringo-friendly** nightlife around Calles Linares, Tarija and Murillo, as well as the in-house hostel bars – *Adventure Brew*'s in particular (see p.78) – though locals with a bit of cash frequent the more sophisticated haunts of **Sopocachi**. The legendary illegal bar Ruta 36, which serves (mediocre and overpriced) cocaine with your (not very good and not very cold) beer and changes its location every couple of months, really does exist, but you'd need to find the right taxi driver, and of course bear in mind the dangers of being found in possession of illegal drugs (see p.42). La Paz's **club** scene isn't the most cutting-edge: Latin pop, rock, salsa, *cumbia* and 1980s music are commonplace, but you can find genuine Latin jazz, salsa, reggae, rock and electronic dance music if you look hard enough. For more traditional entertainment, the folk music venues known as **peñas** put on Andean folk dancing accompanied by traditional Andean music involving drums, charangos, guitars, quenas (notched flutes) and the inevitable *zampoñas* (panpipes).

### CITY CENTRE
**BARS**

**Etno** Jaén 722 ☎02 2280343, ⓦetnocafecultural .blogspot.com; map p.58. The most self-consciously bohemian café-bar in town, tending towards the gothic,

with spooky abstract photography and absinthe cocktails (it's the only place in La Paz serving absinthe). Surprisingly enough, they also whip up arguably the city's best *café con leche*; be sure to taste their Amazonian whisky too. Live music (Wed–Sat from 8pm; Bs15–20 entry) keeps the clientele busy. Mon–Sat 11am–3am.

**La Luna** Oruro 197 at Murillo ☎02 2335523, ⓦfacebook.com/lalunapublapazbolivia; map p.58. Atmospheric, frayed late-night drinking cave where you're almost always guaranteed great music (vintage Latin jazz, Seventies rock, blues, etc), a comfy seat and a friendly welcome. A real tonic if you're suffering from cheesy Latin pop overkill. Tues–Sat 7pm–3am.

**Reineke Fuchs** Av Camacho by Camacho market ☎02 2310744, ⓦfacebook.com/reinekefuchscentro; map p.58. City-centre branch of Sopacachi's German-style brew-pub (see p.86). Daily 6.30pm–1am.

**Sol y Luna** Murillo 999, at Cochabamba ☎02 2115323, ⓦsolyluna-lapaz.com; map p.58. Dutch-owned café-bar serving strong coffee and cold beer in a mellow, stone-walled, candlelit atmosphere, with huge windows perfect for watching La Paz's night-time street life hustle by. It's a great place to try out beers from different Bolivian microbreweries, and is conveniently close to the main accommodation area. Food (in the Bs40–75 bracket) includes Indonesian-style *gado gado*. Don't miss the annual riot of orange wigs that is the "Oranje bal" (around April 30). Daily 9am–1am.

**The English Pub** Linares 189 at Tarija, map p.58; Illampu 740, map p.58; ☎02 2334717, ⓦfacebook .com/pg/englishpub.lp. Well, the ale isn't English but the pints are imperial (0.57 litres) and the beer is decent enough (Bs26 for a pint of Saya) at this city-centre bar with two branches. The pub grub includes such gourmet delights as fish and chips (Bs60), bangers and mash (Bs55) and veg curry (Bs45). With European and Premier League footie on the telly, what more could you ask? Daily 9am–1am.

### CLUBS

**Open Mind** Cochabamba 100 ☎7675 5474, ⓦfacebook.com/omc.openmindclub; map p.58. La Paz doesn't really have much of a gay scene, and in fact this small nightclub is pretty much it, but although (at present) it's only open on Saturday nights, it has everything you need for a good night out: a dancefloor, guest DJs, good music, a friendly atmosphere, and everybody of either gender is welcome. Cover charge Bs20. Sat 10pm–4am.

★**TTkos** Mexico 1555 ☎7011 5660, ⓦbit.ly/ TTkosLaPaz; map p.58. Hot, dark, sweaty and often packed subterranean bolt hole with a jumping local crowd losing themselves in some of the best live music, DJs and club nights in La Paz, notably reggae night (Tues). Bolivian bands Matamba and Chuquiago Reggae often perform here. Try the legendary fruity cocktail dubbed "Tutuma", a blend of papaya, *singani* and other "secret" but potent ingredients. Look for the battered door topped with an oversized miner's helmet (next to *Pan American Hotel*); you may have to knock a few times to get in. Cover charge is usually Bs15–30. Wed–Sat 10pm–4am.

---

**TOP 5 LIVE MUSIC VENUES**

**Casa de la Cultura Franz Tamayo/ Teatro Modesta Sanginés** See p.86

**La Luna** See above

**Malegria** See p.86

**Teatro Municipal Alberto Saavedra Pérez** See p.87

**TTkos** See below

---

### PEÑAS

**Peña El Mural** Ingavi 681 ☎07 0119458; map p.58. Way off the regular *peña* tourist trail, this earthy, devilishly painted, mirror-balled venue is conveniently located below the *Bash'n'Crash* hostel (see p.78), whose residents get in free. Charges are Bs10–15. Once the charangos and open fire die down, the disco starts up. Fri & Sat 8pm–3am (shows usually 11.30pm & 1.30am).

**Peña Huari** Sagárnaga 339 ☎02 2316225; map p.58. The longest-established and most touristy *peña* in town – hence the Bs105 cover charge – tends to divide opinion. It delivers a reasonably authentic folk music show (2hr 30min), combined with pricey, traditional Altiplano food, including a list of llama dishes well into double figures. It is, however, very conveniently located and starts earlier than most of its competitors. Shows daily 8pm.

### SOPACACHI
### BARS

**Diesel Nacional** Av 20 de Octubre 2271, between Rosendo Gutiérrez and Fernando Guachalla ☎02 2423477; map p.68. Steampunk bar with recycled metal and wood furniture, old Curtiss aircraft engines (circa 1948) dangling from the ceiling, a futuristic log brazier burning away in the centre (it tends to reek, however, so unless you're feeling the chill, sit elsewhere) and – delightfully incongruously – a drinks menu peppered with wry quotes from the likes of W.C. Fields and Compton Mackenzi (cocktails from Bs30). Mon–Sat 7pm–3am.

★**Hallwright's** Av Sánchez Lima 2235 ☎6702 4250, ⓦfacebook.com/hallwrightsbar; map p.68. This is primarily a wine bar, offering a congenial and knowledgeable introduction to Bolivian wine (which is a lot better than you might imagine). You can munch on a decent selection of tapas including cheeses and cold cuts (even alpaca salami and llama chorizo on occasion), with the friendly staff offering advice on what to order. No smoking, and cash only. Mon–Sat 5pm–midnight.

**MagicK** Presbítero Medina 2526 ☎02 2910625, ⓦcafemagick.com; map p.68. This place calls itself a "cultural café", and it does indeed serve coffee (and vegetarian food), but it's also a bar, with great beer and

**1**

cocktails, not to mention regular music nights, when there's a Bs20 cover charge and DJs spin dance sounds till past midnight. On the third Saturday of the month, they open early (10am) for a big Bs50 brunch. Tues–Sat 4–11pm.

**Mongo's Rock-Bottom Café** Hermanos Manchego 2444 ☏ 02 2440714; map p.68. This bar is the granddaddy of La Paz's gringo hang-outs, though there seem to be more locals than gringos here these days. There's live music most nights followed by a DJ, but even before that it's a good place for an atmospheric early to mid-evening drink, although the food isn't great. The most popular night is Tuesday, which is salsa night. Daily 6pm–3.30am.

**Reineke Fuchs** Pasaje Jáuregui 2241 ☏ 02 2442979, ⓦ reinekefuchs.com; map p.68. You won't go hungry or thirsty in this sophisticated German-style bar, where they serve up hearty Teutonic grub (goulash Bs82, bratwurst Bs79) and – along with local and imported lagers – their own delicious German-style beer (Bs33), which comes in three varieties: lager, pils and dunkel. Daily 6.30pm–1am.

**CLUBS**

**Glam** Av Sánchez Lima 2237 ☏ 7061 6000, ⓦ bit.ly /GlamLaPaz; map p.68. One of the city's most popular nightclubs, with a wide range of sounds – everything from salsa and bossa nova to retro rock, funk, house and techno. Saturday is the main night for electronic dance music, Fridays (in principle, salsa night) tend to be more soulful, but that isn't a hard-and-fast rule. Cover charge Bs20–25. Thurs–Sat 8pm–3am.

**Malegria** Pasaje Medinacelli 2282 ☏ 02 2423700; map p.68. Tribal-themed nightclub with ethnic masks, stone walls and a middling music policy that runs between ska, Mexican and Argentine rock, and the usual generic stuff. The real reason to come here is the live Thursday-night Afro-Bolivian music (aka "Saya"), a veritable orgy of rhythm and colour. Thurs–Sat 10pm–3am.

**ZONA SUR**

**Reineke Fuchs** Av Montenegro at Calle 18, San Miguel ☏ 02 2772103, ⓦ reinekefuchs.com; map p.80. Zona Sur branch of Sopocachi's German-style brew-pub (see above). Daily 6.30pm–1am.

## ENTERTAINMENT

Thanks to a vibrant student population and growing cultural scene (and more people with money to spend on it), appreciation of the **performing arts** in La Paz is growing, and there are a few places where you can catch theatre, classical music concerts, ballet and even opera. **Film** is popular, and though the emphasis tends to be on Hollywood action blockbusters (almost always in English with Spanish subtitles), La Paz, surprisingly perhaps, has some excellent **art-house cinemas**. You can pick up *Jiwaki*, a free, pocket-sized monthly guide to public museums, galleries, cinema and theatre, at the artier cafés and bars, or check out the culture section of the Metro La Paz blog at ⓦ lapaz.metro-blog.com.

**THEATRES AND CINEMAS**

**Casa de la Cultura Franz Tamayo/Teatro Modesta Sanginés** Av Mariscal Santa Cruz, opposite Plaza San Francisco ☏ 02 2406816, ⓦ bit.ly/CasadelaCulturaLaPaz; map p.58. Hosts a wide range of cultural events including theatre, folk music, art exhibitions and film screenings. Most performances are, incredibly, free.

**Cine Monje Campero** Av 16 de Julio 1495 ☏ 02 2333332, ⓦ monjecampero.com.bo; map p.58. Garishly painted Art Deco landmark from 1938, showing

standard Hollywood fare. Most tickets Bs35–45.

**Cine Municipal 6 de Agosto** Av 6 de Agosto 2284, Sopocachi ☏ 02 2440709; map p.68. Cultural films and concerts at low rates (the concerts are usually Bs50, the films less and sometimes even free). The foyer is decorated with old movie projectors, and has a café where you can hang out with a snack, a coffee or a juice. Daily 3–11pm.

**Cinemateca Boliviana** Oscar Soria 110, at Rosendo Gutiérrez, Sopocachi ☏ 02 2444090, ⓦ cinemateca boliviana.net; map p.68. The best cinema in Bolivia, with a

### THANK GOD IT'S (BACHELOR) FRIDAY

La Paz is fairly quiet on weekday evenings, but explodes into life on **Friday nights** – known as *viernes de solteros* (bachelor Fridays) – when much of the city's male population goes out drinking. In the city centre – above all the market district along Max Paredes and Avenida Buenos Aires – there are countless rough-and-ready **whiskerías** and **karaoke bars** where hard-drinking, almost exclusively male crowds gather to drown their sorrows in beer and *chufflay*, a lethal mix of *singani* and lemonade, while playing *cacho*, a popular dice game, or singing along to the latest Latin pop songs. Going out to these bars is certainly an authentic Bolivian experience if you're male, but as a foreigner you should expect to attract some attention and be prepared to drink until you drop – refusing an invitation from a fellow drinker is considered rude. If you're female on the other hand, such places are best avoided.

tastefully presented selection of Bolivian, Latin American and European releases past and present (as well as the odd Hollywood classic), and a fine upstairs café. Tickets Bs10–30.
**Multicine** Av Arce 2631, Sopocachi ☎ 02 2112463, Ⓦ www.multicine.com.bo; map p.68. US-style multi-screen complex in Sopocachi, showing the latest digitally enhanced animations and big-budget remakes. Tickets cost Bs40–45 (3D Bs50–55), except on Wed when they are Bs20 (Bs25).

**Teatro Municipal Alberto Saavedra Pérez** Genaro Sanjinés and Indaburo ☎ 02 2406183; map p.58. Elegant Neoclassical building that is now the city's premier venue for theatre, folk, world and classical music, opera and ballet. Programmes have included Brecht's *Threepenny Opera*, a tribute to the late Mercedes Sosa, and top artists such as Bajofondo Tango Club collaborator Adriana Varela.

## SHOPPING

Given that the city can at times feel like one massive marketplace, it should come as no surprise that La Paz is a good place to go **shopping**. You'll find a wider range of **artesanía** (handicrafts) here than anywhere else in Bolivia, with goods from all over the country, which means you don't have to lug souvenirs back with you from Sucre or Potosí. Most of what's on sale is good quality, too, and prices aren't much higher than at the point of manufacture.

### ARTESANÍA

The best places to shop for handicrafts and other souvenirs are Calle Sagárnaga, Calle Linares and the surrounding streets, where you'll find dozens of shops and stalls. Many of the different magic charms, bracelets and carved stone figures sold in the Mercado de Hechicería (see p.66) also make inexpensive souvenirs and outlandish gifts for people back home. Note that most of the fossils sold on the street are fake.
**Prices** The cost (though not necessarily the quality) of crafts is generally lower on the street stalls than in the shops and it's worth shopping around and comparing prices before you buy. There's room for a certain amount of bargaining, but don't expect prices to come down too much; haggling with someone far poorer than you over a dollar or two will make you look foolish and mean-spirited.
**Textiles and clothing** Some of the best offerings are the traditional textiles from all over the highlands, including beautiful handmade ponchos, woven belts, blankets and women's shawls that make very nice wall hangings. Be warned, though, that a well-made poncho with an intricate design can cost well over Bs700. For a more moderately priced and practical souvenir, you can't beat the llama and alpaca wool jumpers, socks and hats. You can pick up a hat for just Bs30 and a warm sweater for as little as Bs100 on the street stalls, though you can pay several times that for a finely made and professionally designed one in some of the shops.
**Leather and jewellery** Leather items are pretty good value – especially the hard-wearing and stylish belts and bags decorated with strips of traditional weaving. Silver jewellery is also abundant and very good value, though the silver content of the stuff sold on the streets isn't always as high as vendors claim it is.
**Musical instruments** There are several good musical instrument shops on Linares near the junction with Santa Cruz where you can pick up some beautiful handmade guitars, charangos and other stringed instruments, as well

as cheaper quena flutes and *zampoñas* (panpipes), which make excellent gifts.

### ARTESANÍA SHOPS
**Alba** Linares 818 ☎ 02 2305113, Ⓦ facebook.com/charangosalbabolivia; map p.58. Jhonny Sarmiento Alba's traditional instrument store is worth a visit even if you don't intend to buy one of his beautifully handmade charangos (Jhonny hails from Aiquile, a town near Cochabamba, known for its traditional charango making). It's a trove of guitars, drums, pipes, mandolins and the brightly covered cases that carry them. Mon–Sat 9am–7pm.
**Ayni** Illampu 704 (by Hotel Rosario) ☎ 02 2457487, Ⓦ aynibolivia.com; map p.58. For almost a decade Ayni has flown the flag for fair trade *artesanía* in La Paz, and is now a member of the World Fair Trade Organization. Look out for the "orange art" – souvenirs made of oven-dried orange peel. Mon–Fri 9am–8pm, Sat 9am–noon.
**COMART Tukuypaj** Linares 958 ☎ 02 2312686, Ⓦ comart-tukuypaj.com; map p.58. This non-profit organization sells the wares of 37 workshops of Bolivian artisans and craftspeople (mostly Aymaras, Quechuas, Guarani and Mollo), everything from fashionable shawls, jackets and tops for women, to model llamas and boats made of bulrushes, straw pots, llama skin bags, wool hats and embroidered purses. Mon–Fri 10am–1pm & 2–7pm, Sat 10am–1pm & 2–5pm.
**Green Hands** Indaburo 710 (at Jaén) ☎ 7156 7306, Ⓦ greenhandsbolivia.com; map p.58. Bolivian ethnic and ecological handicrafts, mostly from tribes in the Chaco lowlands and Amazon regions (the Ayoreos, Guaranies, Guarayos and Chiquitanos). Lovely woodcarvings, wicker pots, ceramics and pots made of plant fibres. Mon–Fri 9am–noon & 3.30–6.30pm, Sat 9am–1pm.

### ART
**Centro de Artes Mamani Mamani** Indaburo 710 (at Jaén) ☎ 02 2906294, map p.58; Moreno 1248, Zona Sur

**1**

☎ 02 2796908, map p.80; ⊚ mamani.com. Gallery and showroom for the colourful works of local artist Roberto Mamani Mamani, available as originals, prints, greetings cards and postcards. It's also a free exhibition of his work, so you're welcome to pop in and look with no obligation or intention to buy. Mon–Sat 9am–5pm.

## CLOTHES

**Artesanía Sorata** Sagárnaga 303, at Linares ☎ 02 2454728, ⊚ artesaniasorata.com; map p.58. Specializing in high-quality, handmade alpaca garments since 1978, this company was operating on fair-trade principles well before the concept became commonplace, and currently runs various volunteer-run community programmes. Daily 10am–7pm.

**Liliana Castellanos** Av Montenegro 810, San Miguel, Zona Sur ☎ 02 2124535, ⊚ lilianacastellanos.com; map p.80. Haute-couture designer clothing made from alpaca and baby alpaca wool (sometimes taken just from the neck and breast, where the hair is longer and softer). Most of the clothes here are for women, but they have a range for men too, and they do formal wear as well as casual. Mon–Fri 10am–1pm & 3.30–7.30pm, Sat 10.30am–1pm & 3.30–6.30pm.

**Walisuma** Claudio Aliaga 1231, San Miguel, Zona Sur ☎ 02 2145704, ⊚ facebook.com/pg/walisuma.org; map p.80. Chic and innovative clothes and accessories,

made with natural dyes and materials, and based on traditional designs – a world away from the tourist tat in the city centre. You'll find llama leather handbags, men's and women's alpaca wool jackets, and baby alpaca scarfs, all staunchly Bolivian but cracklingly modern. Mon–Fri 10am–1.30pm & 2.30–8pm, Sat 10.30am–1.30pm & 2.30–7pm.

## MAPS AND OUTDOOR EQUIPMENT

**Instituto Geográfico Militar** Calle Juan XXIII 100, map p.58; Saavedra 2303, Miraflores, map p.68; ☎ 02 2229786, ⊚ www.igmbolivia.gob.bo. You can buy 1:50,000 and 1:250,000 topographical maps for most of Bolivia (some areas are yet to be surveyed), but often only as photocopies, for Bs35–50; you'll need your passport for identification. Alternatively, you can download the maps for free from their website. The city-centre office may direct you to the branch in Miraflores if they don't have maps available. Mon–Fri 8.30am–12.30pm & 2.30–6.30pm.

**Sampaya** Illampu 803 ☎ 02 2000004; map p.58. Camping equipment of all varieties, from tents, sleeping bags and sleeping mats to compasses, camping stoves, boots, jackets and thermals. This is about the biggest outdoor equipment store on Illampu, but there are several others within spitting distance to compare prices and quality before buying. Daily 10am–8pm.

## DIRECTORY

**Banks and exchange** There are plenty of ATMs in the centre of town, and in Sopocachi and the Zona Sur. There's a BNB on Av Camacho at Colón, and a Banco Mercantil Santa Cruz at Av Camacho 1448, with other branches around town. Money changers are concentrated on the stretch of the Prado opposite the post office.

**Dentist** Claudia Suárez Blancourt, Av Arce and Pasaje Cordero, Edificio el Escorial, 1st Floor, Office No.105 ☎ 02 2433019. English spoken.

**Doctor** Clinica del Sur, Av Hernando Siles 3539, at C 7, Obrajes, Zona Sur, 2881 (☎ 02 2784003, ⊚ clinicadelsur .com.bo), has a 24hr emergency facility and is used by most embassy staff. Try Clinica CEMES, Av 6 de Agosto 2881 (☎ 02 2430350), for less serious ailments. On arrival in La Paz, you need to be aware of altitude sickness (see box, p.56).

**Embassies and consulates** Argentina, Aspiazu 497 ☎ 02 2417737, ⊚ ebolv.cancilleria.gov.ar; Australia, Moreno 1091, San Miguel, Zona Sur ☎ 7061 0626, ⊜ cristinafernandezm@gmail.com (consulate only; see embassy in Lima for full range of services, ⊚ peru.embassy. gov.au); Brazil, Ground Floor, Torre B, Edificio Multicentro, Av Arce at Rosendo Gutiérrez, Sopocachi ☎ 02 2166400, ⊚ lapaz.itamaraty.gov.br; Canada, 2nd Floor, Edificio Barcelona, Victor Sanjinés 2678, Plaza España, Sopocachi ☎ 02 2415141, ⊜ lapaz@international.gc.ca; Chile, C 14

#8024, Calacoto, Zona Sur ☎ 02 2797331, ⊚ chile.gob.cl/ la-paz; Ecuador, C 14 #8136, Calacoto, Zona Sur ☎ 02 2115869, ⊚ bolivia.embajada.gob.ec; Ireland, Pasaje Gandarillas 2667 at Macario Pinilla, San Pedro ☎ 02 2413949, ⊜ consulbolivia@gmail.com (honorary consulate only; see embassy in Buenos Aires for full range of services, ⊚ dfa.ie/argentina); New Zealand covered by embassy in Santiago, Chile ☎ 0056 2 2616 3000, ⊜ embajada @nzembassy.cl; Paraguay, 1st Floor, Edificio Illimani II, Av 6 de Agosto 2512, Sopocachi ☎ 02 2433176, ⊜ embapar@ acelerate.com; Peru, Fernando Guachalla 300, Sopocachi ☎ 02 2441250, ⊚ embaperubolivia.com; South Africa covered by embassy in Lima, Peru ☎ 00511 612 4848, ⊜ general.peru@dirco.gov.za; UK, Av Arce 2732, Sopocachi ☎ 02 2433424, ⊚ gov.uk/government/world/bolivia; US, Av Arce 2780, Sopocachi ☎ 02 2168000, ⊚ bolivia. usembassy.gov.

**Emergencies** Ambulance ☎ 118, police ☎ 110 (for tourist police, see opposite).

**Immigration** Oficina de Migración, Av Camacho 1480 ☎ 02 2110960 (Mon–Fri 7am–3pm). For visa extensions, bring a photocopy of your passport ID page, Bolivian entry stamp and tourist card, and the original documents.

**Internet** There are many internet cafés in central La Paz, including Punto Entel opposite Sagárnaga (Mon–Fri

8am–10pm, Sat 9am–10pm, Sun 9am–9pm) and more on the section of the Prado opposite the post office; they generally charge Bs2–3/hr. Punto Cotel branches, dotted around the centre, usually have an internet terminal section.

**Language schools** Reputable schools offering Spanish lessons include: Instituto Exclusivo, 1st Floor, 20 de Octubre 2315, Sopocachi (☎02 242 1072, ⌨instituto-exclusivo. com), Pico Verde, 2nd Floor, Sagárnaga 363 (☎02 2713528, ⌨pico-verde.com), and the Spanish Language Institute, C 14 and Av Aviador 180, Achumani, Zona Sur (☎02 2796074, ⌨spanbol.com). If you're feeling linguistically adventurous, Instituto de Lengua y Cultura Aymara (ILCA), Casilla 2681 (☎02 2419650, ⌨ilcanet.org), also offers Aymara and Quechua classes.

**Laundry** Most hotels have a laundry service, and there are plenty of *lavanderías* around town, charging Bs8–10/kg. Try Lavandería Maya, Sagárnaga 339, inside the same gallery as *Hostal Maya Inn* (Mon–Sat 9am–7.30pm), or the friendly Fines, Ilampu 853 (Mon–Sat 8.30am–8pm).

**Pharmacies** Farmacias Bolivia (⌨facebook.com/ FarmaciasBolivia) has branches all over town, including a 24hr branch at Av 16 de Julio 1473, by the Monje Campero cinema (☎02 2331838).

**Police** The tourist police are at Edificio Olimpia, Plaza Tejada Sorzano, opposite the stadium in Miraflores (24hr; ☎02 2225016, toll-free ☎800 140081); also downtown on Pando at Chuquisaca (☎02 2462111, toll-free ☎800 140071), and in the bus terminal.

**Post office** Correo Central, Av Mariscal Santa Cruz 1228, at Oruro (Mon–Fri 8am–7.30pm, Sat 8am–5pm, Sun 8–11am). There's also an endearing little office in the far corner of the *Angelo Colonial* courtyard, Linares 922 (in principle daily 9am–4pm but often closed for no apparent reason).

**Telephones** One of the cheapest places to make international calls is Punto Entel on the Prado opposite Sagárnaga (Mon–Fri 8am–10pm, Sat 9am–10pm, Sun 9am–9pm), which charges Bs1/min to international landlines, Bs3/min to mobiles.

# Around La Paz

Just south of the city the barren, moon-like landscapes of the **Valle de la Luna** and the **Muela del Diablo**, near the suburbs of **Mallasa** and **Calacoto** respectively, make for energetic day-trips if you want a little taste of the kind of dramatic mountain scenery that awaits you elsewhere in Bolivia; a gentler half-day can be had at Mallasa's zoo.

To the north of La Paz, the spectacular high Andean scenery of the Cordillera Real can be easily reached on a day-trip to **Chacaltaya**, even if the famous glacier and high-altitude skiing are now increasingly distant memories. Further east towards the Peruvian border lies the mysterious ruined city of **Tiwanaku**, Bolivia's most impressive archeological site.

## Mallasa

From Calacoto, the southernmost suburb of the Zona Sur in La Paz, a road follows the course of the Río Choqueyapu about 5km southeast towards the suburb of **MALLASA**, in the surrounding environs of which you'll find both the **Valle de la Luna** and the **municipal zoo**.

### Valle de la Luna

Daily 8am–5pm • Bs15 • Take a micro showing "Mallasa" from the Prado or Calle Mexico (Bs2.80–3), and get off at the roundabout with the small obelisk, shortly after the road passes through two tunnels

The stretch of eerie, cactus-strewn badlands around Mallasa is known as the **Valle de la Luna**. Scarred by deep canyons and strange formations of clay and rock carved by seasonal rains into pinnacles resembling church organ pipes, the valley is a popular excursion from the city and, at less than 3500m, makes a pleasant area for a half-day walk, though if you're travelling in the Bolivian highlands for any length of time, you may find the scenery here rather tame by comparison. There's now an entry charge (as well as an *artesanía* shop and a subterranean information centre illuminating the valley's geology), payable at the kiosk on the left, on the road that switches back to the right from the roundabout; look out for the flags of the adjacent golf course, predictably dubbed the world's highest.

### Zoo Municipal Vesty Pakos

Av Florida • Daily 10am–6pm (last ticket sold 5pm) • Bs10 (Bs5 for children 5–12; free for under-5s) • ☎ 02 2745992, ⓦ facebook.com/zoolapaz • Take a micro showing "Zoológico" from the Prado or Calle Mexico, or from the Valle de la Luna (the same place you got off); it's 1km further to the centre of Mallasa

Located at the end of the main road that runs through Mallasa and set in ample parkland shaded by eucalyptus groves, the city zoo is a great place to escape La Paz's concrete jungle, even if the stressed-looking big cats look like they'd rather be in a real one. The larger birds likewise look pretty miserable, though most of the animals have fairly spacious enclosures and overall it's a good place to familiarize yourself with Bolivian wildlife, including the rare Andean spectacled bear, pumas, jaguars, llamas, vicuñas and all manner of birds, some of them endangered.

## La Muela del Diablo

Take micro #207 or #288 from the Plaza del Estudiante in La Paz to the village of Pedregal, a couple of kilometres beyond Zona Sur. From Pedregal, it's an hour's steep uphill walk to the foot of the Muela – the trail starts behind the cemetery and is easy to follow

Set amid more badlands beyond the Zona Sur, the volcanic outcrop known as **La Muela del Diablo** – the Devil's Molar – makes a good half-day trip out of the city. The jagged rock formation is impressive rather than spectacular, especially if you've already travelled elsewhere in the high Andes, but the views back across the desert-like landscape towards La Paz are a dramatic reminder of just what an inhospitable and unlikely place this was to build a major city. You can climb the Muela, though this is not advisable without experience and some basic equipment. A further trail leads around the back of the peak, down and across the Río Choqueyapu via a hanging bridge and up to the city zoo (see above), a good half-day's hike in itself. Be sure to take sunscreen and plenty of water.

## Chacaltaya

There's no public transport to Chacaltaya, though many tour agencies in La Paz (see p.76) run trips for around Bs80, sometimes combined with the Valle de la Luna (see p.89)

About 40km north of La Paz, **Chacaltaya** was, until 2009, Bolivia's only developed ski slope and, at over 5000m above sea level, the highest in the world. The glacier has now melted completely, however, and with it the ski industry. For many observers, its demise remains one of the starkest examples of global warming in the Americas, and a portent of diminishing water supplies across the Andes. It's nevertheless still worth visiting for the magnificent scenery, even if you first need to be altitude acclimatized (and even then bring plenty of warm clothing, sunscreen and sunglasses). From up here the massive icebound peak of Illimani seems close enough to touch, while La Paz and El Alto, far below in the Altiplano, look minuscule by comparison. You can also see the crystalline waters of Lake Titicaca to the west, with the mountains of Peru rising behind, and on clear days the volcanic cone of Sajama, Bolivia's highest mountain, is visible far across the Altiplano to the southwest. If you make the short climb up the peak of **Mount Chacaltaya** (5395m) behind the ski refuge, the views open up further – a truly breathtaking panorama.

## Tiwanaku

Av Manco Kapac, Tiahuanacu • Daily 9am–5pm (last entry 4pm) • Bs100, guides Bs130/2hr in Spanish, or Bs150/2hr in English

On the Altiplano, 72km west of La Paz and 3872m above sea level, the ruined city of **TIWANAKU** is one of the most intriguing archeological sites in South America. Founded around 1500 BC, Tiwanaku became the capital of a massive empire that lasted almost a thousand years, developing into a sophisticated urban

## THE SACRED GEOGRAPHY OF TIWANAKU AND THE AYMARA NEW YEAR

For all its political and economic power, Tiwanaku's transcendental importance was undoubtedly **religious**. The first Spanish chroniclers to visit were told its name was "Taipicala", after the stone at the centre, where it was believed the universe was created and whence humans first set forth to colonize the world. The Incas consciously sought to associate themselves with its spiritual legitimacy, claiming their own dynasty had been brought into existence at nearby Lake Titicaca.

The US anthropologist Johan Reinhard has sought to explain the spiritual importance of Tiwanaku in terms of **sacred geography**, a system of beliefs related to mountain worship and fertility cults, still prevalent in the Andes today. The high mountain peaks are considered powerful deities, known as *achachilas* in Aymara, who control meteorological phenomena and the fertility of crops and animals.

The most spectacular manifestation of these beliefs is during the **Aymara New Year** on the June winter solstice, when hundreds of *yatiris* (traditional priests) from all over the region (as well as a sizeable contingent of gringos) congregate at Tiwanaku to watch the sun rise and celebrate with music, dancing, elaborate rituals and copious quantities of coca and alcohol. **Evo Morales** even sealed his election victory with a crowning ceremony here.

In terms of sacred geography, Tiwanaku's position could not be more propitious, set close to **Lake Titicaca** with a view east to **Illimani**, the most important **mountain god** in the Altiplano, and aligned with **Illampu** and **Sajama**, the second and third most important peaks. Though it can't be proved, it seems likely that the builders of Tiwanaku chose the site with these concepts in mind, even though it meant they had to transport stones weighing hundreds of tonnes from across the lake.

centre that at its peak was home to some fifty thousand people, with pyramids and opulent palaces painted in bright colours and inlaid with gold. The city was in many ways the cradle of Andean civilization, with enormous cultural impact throughout the region, providing the fundamental inspiration for the better-known Inca empire.

Though the city originally covered several square kilometres, only a fraction of the site has been excavated. The **main ruins** can easily be visited in half a day, and occupy a fairly small area which was once the ceremonial centre of the city, a jumble of tumbled pyramids and ruined palaces and temples made from megalithic stone blocks. The only other major site that has been excavated is **Puma Punku**, a second pyramid complex just to the southwest. A couple of **museums** by the entrance house many of the smaller archeological finds.

Official site **tour guides** operate out of an office next to the ticket counter (*boleteria*), and really do make a huge difference – there are very few signs or explanations on the site itself and it's easy to miss important objects. The same guides can also lead you around the museums, where the labelling is in Spanish only. English-speaking guides cost a bit more than Spanish-speaking ones, but also tend to be more experienced in the job.

### Brief history

The Tiwanaku civilization was first established around 1500 BC, with an economy based on **potato cultivation** and **llama herding** – it is thought that the shores of Lake Titicaca were much closer at that time. By 100 BC it had become an important urban centre, and an organized state with distinct classes of priests, warriors, artisans and aristocrats is thought to have emerged. Beginning around 400 AD – the so-called "Classic Period" – this state eventually controlled the whole Titicaca basin – an area of some 57,000 square kilometres extending out from the lake between Bolivia's Cordillera Real and Peru and Chile's Cordillera Occidental – and had begun extending its influence.

**1**

700–1000 AD

From around 700 AD Tiwanaku expanded rapidly to dominate an area comprising much of modern Bolivia, southern Peru, northeast Argentina and northern Chile. The key to this expansion was a remarkable agricultural system of raised fields, known as **sukakullo** (see box, below), which revolutionized food production along the shores of Lake Titicaca and freed vast amounts of labour for the construction of monumental temples and palaces. It also allowed trade with other societies, though as their power grew, direct control of other regions through conquest or colonization probably came to replace this. Tiwanaku's influence thus spread to encompass a vast area, crisscrossed with paved roads along which caravans of hundreds of llamas carried all kinds of produce to the centre of the empire.

Decline and abandonment

Some time after 1000 AD, Tiwanaku fell into a rapid and irreversible **decline**. The fields were abandoned, the population dispersed and, within a period of about fifty years, the empire disappeared, most likely due to **climate change**. Scientists studying ice cores from Andean glaciers have discovered that from about 1000 AD the region suffered a long-term decline in rainfall. Though the imperial storehouses could no doubt withstand a few lean years, this searing **drought** lasted for decades, even centuries. Unable to feed the hungry masses, Tiwanaku's civilization had collapsed by 1200 AD.

The colonial era to the twentieth century

Most of the **destruction** of the remains of Tiwanaku occurred relatively recently. When the Spanish first came here in the sixteenth century many of the buildings were still standing, but the presence of gold meant that they quickly set about tearing them down. Licences to loot the site were handed out by the Spanish Crown in the same way as for mining, and many of the great stones were dragged away to build churches and houses. Still more were destroyed with **dynamite** at the beginning of the twentieth century to provide gravel for the foundations of the railway that passes nearby, while early **archeological excavations** varied little in nature from the looting of the Spaniards, stripping the site of its most beautiful statues to adorn the museums of Europe and the US. Restoration and haphazard

---

## SUKAKULLOS

The most impressive achievement of the Tiwanaku civilization was undoubtedly the intensification of agriculture along the shores of Lake Titicaca using a system of raised fields known in Aymara as **sukakullo**. This system enabled the inhabitants of Tiwanaku to overcome the problems of drought, floods, frost and soil exhaustion. The Altiplano, the plain surrounding the ruins – which today provides a marginal living for just over seven thousand campesinos – was 1500 years ago producing harvests big enough to feed over one hundred thousand people.

The platforms stand over 1m high, with planting surfaces up to 200m long and 15m wide, and each is carefully structured, with a base of stones followed by a layer of clay to prevent **salination** by the slightly brackish waters of Lake Titicaca. Above this is a layer of gravel, followed by one of sandy soil and finally a coating of rich, organic topsoil. The raised fields run in parallel lines, with **water-filled ditches** running between them, providing irrigation during the dry season and preventing flooding when the level of the lake rose. By storing the heat of the sun during the day and releasing it at night, the water in the ditches also protected crops from frost, extending the growing season considerably. Whereas present-day farmers produce about one tonne of potatoes per acre, research suggests that the *sukakullo* produced astonishing yields of up to eight tonnes per acre. Experimental projects are now under way to help local **campesinos** reintroduce these techniques.

reconstruction began in the 1960s, but after years of neglect and deterioration due to dampness, moss and lichen, the Bolivian government appealed to **UNESCO** for financial help (the site was declared a World Heritage Site in 2000), and decided to initiate criminal proceedings against officials in charge of early restorations. Sadly, the site remains in a relatively precarious state, with erosion and damage to the remaining ruins ongoing, and little agreement among the authorities about how to proceed, other than roping off the key monuments.

## Museo Cerámica

On the main road just outside the historic ruin itself, the **Museo Cerámica** houses the huge cache of tools, pottery and ceramics found on-site, the main means used to distinguish between the different eras in Tiwanaku civilization. The earliest **stone tools** have been dated at 20,000 years old, challenging the consensus that humans only arrived in the Americas 15,000 years ago. There are also animal bone tools used later at Tiwanaku and moulds for casting bronze.

The earliest pottery, from between about 1000 and 300 BC – a period traditionally known as the Village Stage or Tiwanaku I – consists mainly of simple but well-made pots, decorated with geometric incisions and designs (including puma and bird motifs) painted in red, white and yellow on a chestnut-brown background. Ceramics from the period known as the Urban Stage – Tiwanaku II, from about the first century AD – show a clear advance in quality and design, with finely made pots richly painted with multiple colours and highly burnished. Through the periods III to IV, up to the end of the first millennium AD, the pots, jars and carved heads become ever more elaborate and iconographically distinctive. The **Inca** pottery found here, though dating to a later period, is clearly less accomplished.

Pieces to look out for include little heads and **figurines**, one of which looks very Chinese, supporting claims of pre-Columbian visits by Chinese explorers; another, more dubiously, is said to be African. Nearby, a collection of **ceramic whistles** includes one in the form of a house – a valuable depiction of what the roofs looked like at Tiwanaku. In a cabinet round the corner, the "**Llama man**" is a rare bronze/ceramic composite carving of a ring-shaped llama creature with a human head holding the decapitated head of an enemy; in the same cabinet, a ceramic **seahorse** accompanies the remains of a real one, from a time when Lake Titicaca was much more saline and supported a community of the creatures.

## Museo Lítico

Behind the Museo Cerámica, the minimalistic **Museo Lítico** has two main galleries, each with a side room. The first gallery houses the 7.3m-high **Bennett Monolith**, unearthed by archeologist Wendell C. Bennett in 1932 in the Templete Semi-Subterráneo. The sandstone monolith was displayed in Miraflores in La Paz for many years before finally being returned to Tiwanaku in 2002 (a replica now stands in Miraflores). In the adjoining room, a round offering stone is inscribed with what must be writing, as yet undeciphered.

Across the courtyard, a second gallery displays smaller monoliths, plus a big andesite head, evidently from a much larger piece, its huge eyes round from use of psychedelic snuff. In the adjoining chamber, representations of **Chacha Puma** (a feline god with a human body) include a beautiful piece carved from hard black basalt around 700 AD.

## Akapana

As you enter the ruins themselves, the big mound on your right is **Akapana**, a great earth pyramid with seven terraced platforms faced with stone constructed in stages over many centuries. This was the biggest structure in the complex, measuring about 200m by 190m, and some 18m tall, and is thought to have been the city's most important

**1**

religious centre, constructed as an imitation of a sacred mountain. From the west it now looks more like a hill than a man-made feature; archeologists originally believed it had been built around a natural hill. You can still make out the tiers, and some of the huge stone blocks have been uncovered on the east side, many of them carved with a step motif characteristic of Tiwanaku.

On the top, you can still see where a giant pool in the shape of an Andean cross was located. Like much of the site, this is thought to have had religious and astronomical significance, with the arms of the cross lining up with the Southern Cross constellation at each solstice. Other scattered monuments up here include an original andesite gateway, now flat on the ground, and a row of six magnetic standing stones on the east side – try holding a compass or GPS device up to them and watch the directions flip. Just below the pyramid summit on the north side are the foundations of small rooms thought to have been used by priests – notice the double-wall insulation.

## Templete Semi-Subterráneo

Next to Akapana, to the north, the **Templete Semi-Subterráneo** – the Semi-Subterranean Temple – is a sunken rectangular patio about 2m deep whose walls are studded with 177 carved limestone heads, which jut out like keystones. These are thought to represent the gods of different ethnic groups conquered and absorbed into the expanding empire – they may even have been idols taken from these peoples and held as symbolic hostages to represent their submission to the supremacy of Tiwanaku. This is the oldest temple discovered so far, dating back to at least 250 BC. In the centre the sandstone **Kontiki** or "**Beard**" **Monolith**, richly adorned with zoomorphic carvings, was moved here from another location.

## Kalasasaya

The larger complex next to the Templete Semi-Subterráneo is **Kalasasaya**, a walled temple compound that's thought to have been the sacred centre of Tiwanaku, where the ruling god-emperors were buried. The stone walls of the complex are among the most impressive masonry still standing at the site, made with colossal megaliths weighing up to 150 tonnes interspersed with smaller blocks, and with carved stone drains that may also have been related to the ritual importance of water. The compound's re-erected monoliths, alas, have suffered some of the most visible climatic damage in recent times. The intriguing **Monolith Fraile** in the southwest corner was carved from a single piece of two-tone sandstone, while the **Monolith Ponce** in the northeast corner is an ornately carved piece of andesite. A nearby mud altar is still used for Aymara ceremonies (see box, p.90). On the east side of the compound, a massive doorway is astronomically aligned so that the sun appears in its centre at the spring and autumn equinoxes.

### Puerta del Sol

Set into Kalasasaya's northeastern corner is the iconic **Puerta del Sol** – the Gateway of the Sun – an elaborately decorated portico carved from a single block of andesite weighing ten tonnes that has sadly been broken, probably when it was moved here from its original location in the centre. The **central figure** above the doorway is the best-known image of Tiwanaku, probably the supreme creator god known to the Aymaras as Thunupa and to the Incas as Viracocha. The 24 rays emanating from his head have led some to think of him as a sun god, but there's not much evidence to suggest such a cult existed before the Incas: it's more likely that they're just a stylized representation of hair. From his arms hang severed heads, probably trophies of war. These are no mere metaphors: sixteen headless bodies were found during excavations in the Akapana pyramid. Like much Tiwanaku art, the style is strikingly similar to that of the Mayans of Mexico, strongly suggesting some kind of contact between this region and theirs.

## Putini

Just west of Kalasasaya, ongoing excavations have revealed the remains of another extensive complex, known as **Putini**, which was probably a burial area. Several enormous stones cut with holes big enough to accommodate human bodies led early twentieth-century investigators, no doubt influenced by their contemporaries' fascination with Egyptology, to call it the "Palace of the Sarcophagi".

## Puma Punku

Set apart from the main complex, 1km to the southwest, are the ruins of another major pyramid, **Puma Punku** – the Gateway of the Puma. Similar in style and function to Akapana, though slightly smaller, this three-tiered pyramid is believed to have been built around 700 AD. The skill and exactitude with which the massive stone blocks were carved is deeply impressive, particularly in a society without iron tools.

### ARRIVAL AND DEPARTURE                                                      TIWANAKU

**By minibus** Minibuses to Tiwanaku depart from Jose M Aliaga 678 (by Plaza Tomás Katari) in the cemetery district in La Paz, and more reliably from the Rio Seco terminal in El Alto (every 30min; 1hr 30min; Bs25–30); on the way back they leave from the square in Tiwanaku town, just under 1km walk away down Av Ferrocarril, though you can usually flag them down as they pass the entrance to the ruins.

**Tour operators** Most tour agencies in La Paz (see p.76) run full- or half-day trips to the site for Bs100–140/person plus entry and lunch.

**By taxi** Most radio taxi operators (especially the ones that serve major hotels) offer trips to Tiwanaku for around $80 or Bs550 (for two people; groups of three to four people will pay a little more) – the prices are usually quoted in US dollars but they'll accept either currency. You can stay at the site as long as you like, and the driver will usually stop on the way if you want to take photos of the mountains and La Paz from the rim of El Alto.

**By train** A tourist train runs between El Alto, Tiwanaku, and Guaqui on Lake Titicaca, and back again, on the second Sunday of every month (see p.74), but it doesn't give you much time at Tiwanaku (2hr), and it needs to be booked well in advance.

### ACCOMMODATION AND EATING

**Hotel Akapana** Av Manco Kapac 20 ☎02 2895104, ⓦhotelakapana.com. You can't miss the incongruous, quasi-temple-like exterior of this hotel, just across from the site entrance. Rooms are spacious, with parquet floors and en-suite bathrooms, and there's also a small library and garden, a decent restaurant and a scenic terrace complete with astronomical telescope. On some Thursdays purification ceremonies are held. Tasty home-cooked dinners cost Bs35–40/person. No wi-fi. Rates double for Aymara New Year (21 June). $\underline{Bs180}$

**Taypi Uta Eco Restaurant** By the archway on the way into Tiwanaku, 500m south of Puma Punku ☎7358 2846, ⓦfacebook.com/pg/taypiutaecorestaurant. This quirky restaurant serves up decent buffet lunches of llama, trout, chicken, beef or omelette, and houses a small private museum of finds unearthed during its construction. Daily 11.30am–2.30pm; closed May–July.

# Lake Titicaca, the cordilleras and the Yungas

ISLA DEL SOL, LAKE TITICACA

# Lake Titicaca, the cordilleras and the Yungas

Encompassing a wide variety of landscapes – including subtropical valleys, expansive plains and soaring Andean peaks – the captivating high-altitude region surrounding La Paz can seem like a microcosm of the country as a whole, and is sometimes known as "Little Bolivia" because of it. Its focal point is the mesmerizing, shimmering blue of Lake Titicaca, held sacred by the Incas and venerated to this day by local indigenous communities. The nearby Cordillera Real, Cordillera Apolobamba and the Yungas forests are dotted with tranquil towns, many with balmy temperatures and stunning views, which make them perfect places to relax or to escape the chill of the Altiplano. There are also innumerable options for exploring the diverse countryside on hiking, mountain biking or climbing excursions. Moreover, with regular transport links to both La Paz and across the border to Peru, the area is easy to access and incorporate into a wider trip.

Lying some 75km northwest of La Paz, **Lake Titicaca** is a vast, high-altitude lake. Straddling the border with Peru, it dominates the northern section of the Altiplano, the rolling, 3800m-high plateau that stretches between the eastern and western chains of the Andes – the cordilleras Oriental and Occidental – as they march south through Bolivia. The best base from which to explore the Bolivian side of the lake is **Copacabana**, which is home to the country's most revered religious image, and is also the jumping-off point for boat trips to **Isla del Sol** and **Isla de la Luna**, two idyllic islands dotted with Inca ruins.

Further north, on the Peruvian border, the isolated **Cordillera Apolobamba** (also part of the Cordillera Oriental) offers tantalizing trekking and climbing opportunities in a far more remote setting. South of here and just east of Lake Titicaca is the **Cordillera Real**, the highest and most spectacular section of the Cordillera Oriental within Bolivia. Stretching some 160km along the edge of the Altiplano, from **Mount Illimani** (6439m), southeast of La Paz, to the **Illampu massif** (6368m), which towers over the eastern side of Lake Titicaca, the Cordillera Real can easily be explored from La Paz or the town of **Sorata**, at the northwestern end of the range.

The **Yungas'** rugged, forest-covered mountains, rivers and warm, fertile valleys offer a stark contrast to the nearby Cordillera and arid Altiplano. With a new highway

MOUNTAIN VIEW FROM COROICO

# Highlights

**❶ Copacabana** Beautifully located on the shores of Lake Titicaca, this backpacker hub is also a major pilgrimage centre, and home to the Virgen de Copacabana, Bolivia's most revered religious image. **See p.102**

**❷ Isla del Sol** The spiritual centre of the Andean world, set amid the deep blue waters of Lake Titicaca and dotted with ancient ruins and traditional Aymara communities. **See p.109**

**❸ Cordillera Apolobamba** This remote and beautiful mountain range offers some of the best trekking in Bolivia, and is also home to the mysterious Kallawaya medicine men. **See p.116**

**❹ Coroico** Scenically located in the lush subtropical valleys of the Yungas, this enchanting resort town offers the perfect antidote to the cold of the nearby Altiplano. **See p.126**

**❺ World's most dangerous road** Descending over 3500m in a day, the mountain bike trip from La Paz down to Coroico is one of the planet's most scintillating rides. **See p.127**

**❻ La Senda Verde Animal Refuge & Eco Lodge** This sanctuary for rescued monkeys, parrots and assorted Andean animals is also a magical place to stay. **See p.129**

**❼ Inca trails** Running from the high Andes down into the Yungas, Bolivia's three "Inca" trails – the Choro, Takesi and Yunga Cruz – are among the most awe-inspiring trekking routes in the country. **See p.130, p.132 & p.133**

**HIGHLIGHTS ARE MARKED ON THE MAP ON P.100**

inaugurated in 2006, the old hair-raising route down to the Yungas from La Paz – dubbed the **most dangerous road in the world** – is now largely the domain of mountain bikers. The most popular Yungas destination is **Coroico**, a resort town set amid beautiful scenery. Within easy striking distance of Coroico are the diverse ecosystems of **Parque Nacional Cotapata**, through which the rewarding **Choro Trail** passes. The **Takesi Trail**, which also follows a pre-Hispanic paved path, is one of the most popular treks in the region. **Chulumani**, a peaceful town, is less touristy than Coroico but boasts equally commanding views.

# Lake Titicaca

An immense, sapphire-blue lake sitting astride the border with Peru at the northern end of the Altiplano, **LAKE TITICACA** is one of the classic images of South America, and few scenes are more evocative of the country than the sight of a poncho-clad fisherman paddling across its azure waters against the backdrop of snowcapped mountains. Set at an altitude of 3810m, and measuring 190km by 80km, it's by far the biggest high-altitude body of water in the world – the remnant of an ancient inland sea formed as the Andes were thrust up from the ocean floor. The surrounding area is the heartland of the **Aymara** people, whose language and culture have survived centuries of domination.

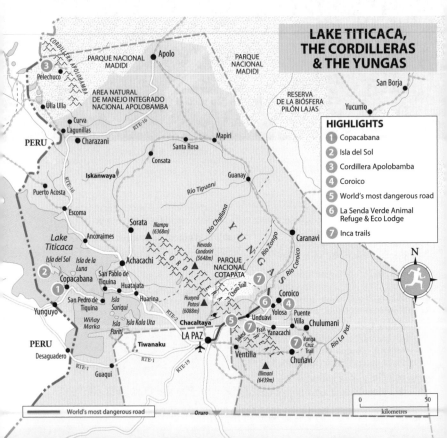

**LAKE TITICACA, THE CORDILLERAS & THE YUNGAS**

**HIGHLIGHTS**

1. Copacabana
2. Isla del Sol
3. Cordillera Apolobamba
4. Coroico
5. World's most dangerous road
6. La Senda Verde Animal Refuge & Eco Lodge
7. Inca trails

The lake itself is rich in fish (especially **trout**), and the water it contains stores the heat of the sun and then releases it overnight, raising average temperatures around its shores. Lake Titicaca is fed by a number of rivers that carry rainfall down from the Cordillera Real and across the Altiplano, though none of its waters ever reaches the sea, and almost ninety percent of the lake's water loss is through evaporation (the rest is drained by its only outlet, the Río Desaguadero). The water level in the lake fluctuates sharply with slight variations in rainfall; since 2000 levels have fallen to historic lows.

Titicaca has always played a major role in Andean religious conceptions. As the biggest body of water in this arid region, it's considered a powerful female deity that controls climate and rainfall, and the Incas believed the creator god Viracocha rose from its waters, calling forth the sun and moon to light up the world. The Incas also claimed their own ancestors came into being here, and the remains of their shrines and temples can be seen on **Isla del Sol** and nearby **Isla de la Luna**, whose serene beauty and tranquillity is a highlight of any visit to the lake. Nor did Lake Titicaca lose its religious importance with the advent of Christianity: Bolivia's most important Catholic shrine is in **Copacabana**, the lakeside town closest to Isla del Sol.

## Huatajata and the islands of Wiñay Marka

Around 75km northwest of La Paz lies **HUATAJATA**, a lakeside village popular with Paceños, who come here to eat fresh trout, drink cold beer and enjoy the views from the numerous restaurants on the shoreline. Huatajata is on the smaller section of Lake Titicaca, known as **Wiñay Marka** or Lago Menor, which is joined to the main body of the lake by the Estrecho de Tiquina (Tiquina Strait). Many of the restaurants in Huatajata operate **boat trips** to the nearby **islands**: motorboat hire (with boatman) costs around Bs400; a sailboat costs less but takes considerably longer.

### Isla Suriqui

About 45 minutes by motorboat from Huatajata, **Isla Suriqui** is home to a small fishing community that still uses traditional boats made from the totora reeds that grow all around the lake. In 1970 the boatmakers of Suriqui helped Norwegian explorer Thor Heyerdahl design and build the *Ra II*, a large reed boat in which he sailed from Africa to the Caribbean in an attempt to prove transatlantic travel was possible using ancient technology. Partly as a result of this, Isla Suriqui is now rather over-touristed, but you can still get a glimpse of a lifestyle that has changed little in centuries.

---

### LUXURY TOURS OF LAKE TITICACA

Several La Paz agencies offer **luxury tours** of Lake Titicaca that connect the Peruvian side with the Bolivian (or vice versa), with transport to the main Bolivian islands in comfortable, high-speeds boats and transfers between Puno (Peru) and Copacabana (Bolivia) by bus. Note that it's very rare to find a tour that operates a boat direct between Puno and Copacabana. Trips with both Transturin and Crillon Tours cost from around $260 (Bs1750) per person per day ranging to over $370 (Bs2500) per person (in a double room) for an overnight tour; the price includes accommodation, food and transport.

**Crillon Tours** Av Camacho 1223, La Paz ☎ 02 2337533, ⓦ titicaca.com. Runs "international" day tours that include bus transfer from La Paz, fast hydrofoils from Huatajata to Isla del Sol and Isla de la Luna, before docking at Copacabana and continuing by bus to Puno, Peru. Overnight tours (2–3 days) also offer accommodation at the classy *Inca Utama Hotel and Spa* in Huatajata and the exclusive *Posada del Inca Ecolodge* on Isla del Sol.

**Transturin** Calle 6 no. 100, Achumani, La Paz ☎ 02 2422222, ⓦ transturin.com. Runs sightseeing tours to Copacabana and Isla del Sol in luxurious catamarans from its dock at Chúa, a few kilometres west of Huatajata. The boat ends up at Copacabana, where a bus travels across the border to Puno. Overnight tours entail spending the night in comfy cabins on board the catamaran.

### Isla Pariti

Just to the south of Isla Suriqui, the smaller **Isla Pariti**, home to another small Aymara fishing community, was an important ceremonial destination during the Tiwanaku era. A cache of beautiful ceramics dating back to this period was discovered here in 2004, and many of the items are displayed at the island's **Museo de Pariti** (Bs20).

### Isla Kala Uta

Close to Isla Pariti and connected to the mainland by a narrow spit when the level of the lake is low, **Isla Kala Uta** has a series of stone tombs (*chullpas*) built by the Aymara-speaking tribes who dominated this area before the Inca conquest.

---

**ARRIVAL AND DEPARTURE** HUATAJATA

**By bus** All buses heading to Copacabana (see p.105) pass through Huatajata. You should be able to flag one down if you're moving on.

## Copacabana and around

The small town and backpacker hang-out of **COPACABANA** overlooks the deep blue waters of Lake Titicaca, some 155km from La Paz and just 9km from the Peruvian border. Located on the Copacabana peninsula – connected to the rest of Bolivia by ferry across the Estrecho de Tiquina – it's the main stepping-off point for the Isla del Sol and Isla de la Luna, Titicaca's two sacred islands. It's also the most important Catholic pilgrimage site in the country, being home to Bolivia's most revered image, the **Virgen de Copacabana**.

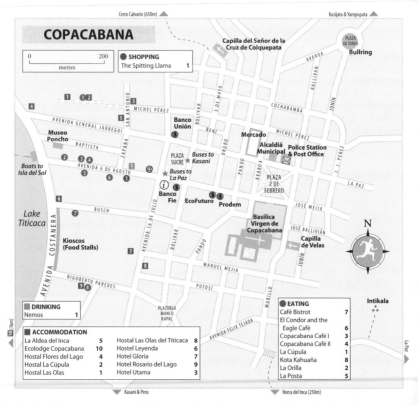

Though its location between two hills is pretty and the lake views are gorgeous, the town itself is not especially attractive – don't expect a tranquil Aymara village. Like most of the larger settlements in this part of Bolivia, Copacabana is a fast-expanding, ramshackle collection of red breeze-block houses (most of them look half-finished), with a growing litter problem and an uncomfortably large population of feral dogs (other than begging for scraps, these generally leave people alone, but certainly don't add to the ambience). The main drag, **Avenida 6 de Agosto**, is pleasant enough and where most travellers spend time, lined with cafés, bars, *cambios*, tour agents and hippie street entertainers – if you've been travelling in rural Bolivia or Peru for a while, you'll probably find it quite touristy, though development, as it is, is fairly low-key.

## The waterfront

Avenida Costanera runs along Copacabana's **waterfront**, a scrappy beach much loved by the local dogs, and lined, rather incongruously, with pedal boats. The views are magnificent however, and this is where ferries depart to Isla del Sol (see p.114). Between Paredes and Busch there are numerous, almost identical food *kioskos* serving cheap beer and fried trout (see p.108). The more famous Copacabana beach in Rio is actually named after this one.

## Museo del Poncho

Baptista (aka Tito Yupanqui) 42 • Mon–Sat 10.30am–5pm, Sun 10am–3pm • Bs15 • Ⓦ museodelponcho.org

Copacabana's small but enlightening **Museo del Poncho** is tucked away down Baptista, just off the waterfront (the street is officially "Calle Tito Yupanqui"), and houses a remarkable collection of Andean ponchos. The permanent exhibit charts each stage of the weaving process, as well as the history of the male poncho, with colourful examples from different regions in Bolivia. You'll soon be spotting the difference between an *unku* and a *ch'umpi* like a pro. Note that the posted hours are nominal; the museum is often closed for lunch and for whole days if staff is short.

## Basílica de Nuestra Señora de Copacabana

Plaza 2 de Febrero • Daily 7am–8pm; museum opens within these times for groups of six or more • Free; museum Bs10

Copacabana's imposing **Basílica de Nuestra Señora de Copacabana** looks out over Plaza 2 de Febrero and dominates the town like a grand Baroque palace. Known as the "Moorish Cathedral", it shows slight *mudéjar* influences, with whitewashed stone walls and domes decorated with deep blue *azulejo* tiles. Originally built between 1589 and 1669 by the Augustinian order (and funded partly by looted gold and silver offerings from local pre-Christian shrines) to house the miraculous Virgen de Copacabana, it has since been extensively modified.

Between the plaza and the basilica is a broad walled **courtyard** with a minor chapel at each corner – a layout very similar to that of pre-conquest indigenous ceremonial centres. Inside the bright vaulted interior of the cathedral itself the main focus is the massive gold retablo (altarpiece), with a less venerated image of the Virgin in the centre. The door to the left of the altar leads to a staircase and a small chapel (*camarín*) housing the **Virgen de Copacabana** herself. A slight 120cm-high wooden image with an Andean face (and brown skin), the Virgin wears lavish robes embroidered with gold and silver thread, and is crowned with a golden halo; at her feet is a wide silver crescent moon – a traditional Andean symbol of female divinity. Encased in glass, the statue is never removed: locals believe this could trigger catastrophic floods (you can see the replica used in festivals in a special room behind the altar). Note that this section is often closed (the shrine was robbed in 2013, and the statue stripped of its gold and silver adornments; all have now been replaced). Also behind the altar is the modern **Capilla de las Advocaciones**, containing images of major saints.

The small **Museo Virgen de Copacabana** inside the compound has a collection of colonial religious art and sculpture, but is only open to groups of six or more. To the

**2**

---

### THE LADY OF THE LAKE

The speed with which the **Virgen de Copacabana** emerged as the most revered religious image in the Altiplano after the Spanish conquest suggests that her cult was a continuation of previous, pre-Christian religious traditions associated with Lake Titicaca. Immediately after the conquest the **Inca temples** around the lake were looted by Spanish treasure-seekers, and their shrines and idols destroyed. These included, at Copacabana, a large female idol with a fish's tail – probably a representation of the lake as a goddess. The town was refounded in 1573 as the parish of Santa Ana de Copacabana, but a series of devastating early frosts swiftly ensued, convincing locals of the need for a new supernatural protector. Santa Ana was abandoned and the town rededicated in honour of the **Virgen de la Candelaria**, one of the most popular representations of the Virgin Mary during the Spanish conquest of the Americas.

A locally born man, **Francisco Inca Yupanqui**, grandson of the Inca Huayna Capac (himself the father of Atahualpa, whose capture by the Spanish led to the fall of the Inca empire), began fashioning an image of the Virgin. After his first crude efforts were rejected by the Spanish priests he went to Potosí to study sculpture, eventually returning in 1583 with the figure that graces the church today, the **Virgen de Copacabana**, who was immediately credited with a series of miracles. The town quickly became the most important Catholic pilgrimage destination in the southern Andes, and after independence, the Virgin was also proclaimed the patron saint of Bolivia. The Virgin's feast days are celebrated on February 2 and August 5.

---

east of the basilica (just outside the compound) is the **Capilla de Velas**, a modern side chapel where supplicants come to light candles – visit on Sunday to see huge banks of candles and messages in wax.

### Plaza 2 de Febrero

Outside the basilica, leafy **Plaza 2 de Febrero** is often occupied by cars, buses and trucks decorated with colourful streamers and rosettes. These are blessed with holy water by a priest and doused liberally in beer and liquor in frequent rituals (generally daily around 10am and 2pm on Sundays) known as **ch'alla**, which aim to ensure their future safety. At fiesta times, pilgrims bring models of desirable objects to be blessed, in the belief that doing so ensures that the real thing will be theirs within a year – a modern version of traditional requests for sufficient rain, bountiful harvests or successful fishing.

### Horca del Inca

Cerro Sancollani • Daily 9am–6pm • Bs10 • Walk south to the end of Calle Murillo, then follow the dirt path uphill

High on Cerro Sancollani, the hill rising above Copacabana to the south, stands the **Horca del Inca** or Pachataka, a gnarled stone structure formed by two vertical crags of rock, their bases buried in the ground and topped by a stone lintel, creating a gateway. The name means "Gallows of the Incas", but this structure was almost certainly used by Inca astronomer-priests to observe the sun, since a small hole carved in another rock crag about 20m to the northeast casts a well-defined point of light onto the centre of the lintel on the morning of June 22, the date of the winter solstice and Aymara New Year. It's a little underwhelming (and blighted by graffiti), but the views are magnificent.

### Intikala

Av Felix Tejada, Defensores del Chaco, opposite the church 200m east of Calle Murillo • Daily 9am–6pm • Bs5 (but often free if the ticket office is closed)

A collection of thirteen large boulders carved with niches, steps, channels and abstract designs, just a fifteen-minute walk southeast of Plaza Sucre, **Intikala** means "Seat of the Sun" in Aymara, and it's likely this site was a religious shrine used for astronomical observations. The biggest boulder (dubbed the "Trono del Inka"), is carved with a groove shaped like a serpent, which was probably used to channel offerings of *chicha* (maize beer) or sacrificial blood – it's believed throughout the Andes that large rocks like these are the home of powerful spirits. Along with the Horca del Inca, Intikala hosts a small gathering of Aymara *yatiris* (traditional priests) to celebrate the winter solstice on the night of June 21–22. This site is especially neglected; litter and graffiti despoil the area.

## Cerro Calvario

The trail begins beside the Capilla del Señor de la Cruz de Colquepata, at the north end of Bolívar • Free

The hill rising steeply above the north of town, **Cerro Calvario**, is an intriguing religious site that provides by far the most dizzying views in the region – on a clear day you'll feel like it's the top of the Andes. Be warned, however: it's a short (less than a kilometre) but very steep half-hour ascent to 3973m, and the thin air can make the climb much longer than it looks from the bottom. The route is marked by fourteen Stations of the Cross, the **Via Crucis** (built in the 1950s), with a break before the really steep bit at the **Mirador Sagrado Corazón de Jesús**. The summit itself is topped by a larger cross and several smaller shrines, as well as ramshackle stone altars where pilgrims light candles, burn offerings and pour alcoholic libations to ensure their prayers are heard. The whole town, most of the lake, Isla del Sol and the surrounding mountains are visible from here. The hill is popular with pilgrims throughout the year, but particularly during Easter, when thousands accompany the Virgen de Copacabana as she is carried up here in a candlelit procession. Sadly, the path up is strewn with litter, and graffiti adorns rocks and even some of the crosses.

## Kusijata

3km northeast of Copacabana • Opening hours are very irregular: there's usually someone here at the weekend, but otherwise you may need to ask around nearby houses for the key • Bs10 • A return taxi costs around Bs30; alternatively, on foot, follow Calle Junín past the bullring, then cut across the football pitch; the track climbs towards a eucalyptus grove on the hillside (30–40min)

**Kusijata** is a small network of well-made Inca agricultural terraces and stone irrigation canals, one of which feeds a pool known as the **Baño del Inca** – possibly a ritual bath. There's also the rather dilapidated **Museo Arqueológico Regional** in an old colonial mansion with a small collection of local Inca ceramics and a dusty Inca mummy. Even if you can't get into the museum, the pleasant walk out along the lakeside makes the trip worthwhile.

### ARRIVAL AND DEPARTURE                                    COPACABANA

**To La Paz** Buses and *combis* (minibuses) to La Paz (4hr) depart from Plaza Sucre, the last at around 6.30pm. The *combis* and most buses (roughly every 30min) run to La Paz's cemetery district (see p.74), but some services will take you to the main Terminal de Buses (see p.72), and these tend to be better. From La Paz, there are several types of tourist and regular buses (see p.72 & p.74).

**Crossing the Estrecho de Tiquina** The only connection between the Copacabana peninsula and the rest of Bolivia is by ferry across the Estrecho de Tiquina between the villages of San Pablo de Tiquina and San Pedro de Tiquina, 40km from Copacabana. Barges (daily

---

### FIESTAS IN COPACABANA

Copacabana's main religious fiestas are the **Fiesta de la Virgen de la Candelaria** (Feb 2) and the **Coronación de la Virgen de Copacabana** (Aug 5), which attract thousands of pilgrims from across Bolivia and southern Peru. The Virgin's statue is paraded around town accompanied by brass bands and dance troupes, and several days of festivities culminate in bullfights in the ring on the town's northern outskirts. **Semana Santa** (Easter) is more solemn. Many pilgrims walk to Copacabana from as far away as La Paz in penance, and thousands more take part in a candlelit nocturnal procession up Cerro Calvario, where they pray for the forgiveness of their sins and for success in the coming years. There's also a more local festival, the **Fiesta de Colquepata** on 3 May, when residents of a nearby village come into town to pay their own homage to the Virgin, again with brass bands, costumes and dancing. Far more mysterious, distinctly non-Christian ceremonies are staged on the night of June 21 to celebrate the winter solstice and **Aymara New Year**, when small crowds led by traditional Aymara religious leaders gather to perform ceremonies at the Horca del Inca and Intikala, two ancient shrines on the outskirts of town.

**2**

## CROSSING THE PERUVIAN BORDER

The Peruvian border is just 9km away from Copacabana, at **Kasani**. You can also cross into Peru at **Desaguadero** on Lake Titicaca's southern side, which has regular transport from La Paz.

### KASANI

**Minibuses** (minivans) run from Plaza Sucre in Copacabana to **Kasani** (every 30min or so; 15min; Bs4); you can also take shared taxis for Bs5 (three people minimum). At Kasani, get your exit stamp at passport control (daily 8.30am–7.30pm) and then walk across the border. On the Peruvian side, micros and taxis wait to take passengers to the town of **Yunguyo** (10min), from where regular buses head to Puno and on to Cusco and Arequipa; there are places to stay if you arrive too late to move on. Alternatively, catch one of the more convenient **tourist buses** from Copacabana to Puno (3hr) which depart daily at 9am, 1.30pm and 6.30pm, or Titicaca Tours' 6.30pm service direct to Cusco (12hr); tickets are available from travel agencies in Copacabana.

### DESAGUADERO

**Desaguadero** is served by **trufis** (shared taxis) and **minibuses** (2hr 30min) from La Paz, which leave when full from Calle José Maria Asín, a block east of Plaza Tomás Katari in the cemetery district (see p.74). Get your exit stamp at the frontier from passport control (daily 8.30am–8.30pm), then walk across the bridge and get an entry stamp at the Peruvian *migración*. The scruffy Peruvian border town of Desaguadero has basic accommodation, but it's better to move on immediately by bus or trufi to Puno (roughly every 30min; 3–4hr). There are also **direct buses** to Puno via Desaguadero from La Paz's main terminal (4 daily; 6–8hr); you disembark at the border to go through immigration, so make sure you remember which bus is yours so you can re-board it on the other side.

5am–9pm) chug across continually, charging Bs40–50 for vehicles, Bs2 for individuals. Bus and minibus passengers must disembark, pay the fee, and cross separately; they may also be checked here by immigration officials, so don't forget your passport.

**To Sorata** The road to Sorata branches off from the La Paz–Copacabana road at Huarina, but minibuses coming through from La Paz to Sorata are likely to be full, especially at weekends and holidays, in which case they will not pick up passengers. Your safest option is to get a vehicle to the Cemetery District in La Paz and change there.

**To Peru** See box, above.

### INFORMATION AND TOURS

**Tourist information** There's a rudimentary tourist information office on Plaza Sucre (Mon–Fri 8am–noon & 2–6pm, Sat 8am–2pm).

**Tour agencies** Copacabana's tour agencies are concentrated around Plaza Sucre; they all sell tours, as well as tickets for the boats to Isla de Sol (see p.114) and for tourist buses to La Paz, Puno and Cusco, but there's no particular advantage to buying tickets from agencies rather than directly from the bus and boat companies.

### ACCOMMODATION

Copacabana has an enormous number of places to stay. Most are simple *alojamientos* and *residenciales* catering for pilgrims, but there are some decent mid-range and top-end **hotels** aimed at tourists. Rooms fill up fast, and prices double or triple during the main fiestas. Backpacker **hostels** are generally not very good, but La Paz's *Adventure Brew Hostel* (see p.78) is planning to open a branch here. Most places provide wi-fi but signals are patchy.

**La Aldea del Inca** San Antonio 2 ☎ 02 8622452, ⓦ aldeadelinca.com; map p.102. Off a steep and unpromisingly rubbish-strewn street, this hotel has been designed to look like a traditional Inca village. The en-suite rooms though are refreshingly modern with bright furnishings, solar-powered showers and TV/DVD players. There's a cobbled courtyard, and a garden overlooking the lake, plus a coffee shop and laundry service. **Bs320**

**Ecolodge Copacabana** Av Costanera ☎ 02 8622500, ⓦ ecocopacabana.com; map p.102. A kilometre from the town centre along the beach, this peaceful lodge has adobe cabins (sleeping up to three people) with thatched roofs, solar heating and private bathrooms. There are also a couple of suites with kitchenettes (sleeping up to five people) – plus a restaurant and pleasant gardens. Cash only. **Bs180**

**FROM TOP** COPACABANA CATHEDRAL (P.103); REED BOAT ON LAKE TITICACA >

**2**

**Hostal Flores Del Lago** Jáuregui (at the end) ☎02 8622117, ✉floresdellago@hotmail.com; map p.102. Overlooking the ferry dock, this budget option is OK if you just want somewhere to crash while passing through. The rooms are quite large and very yellow, all with bathrooms and some with lake views, and there's a pleasant terrace. Breakfast not included. Bs120

★**Hostal La Cúpula** Michel Pérez 1–3 ☎02 8622029, ⓦhotelcupula.com; map p.102. A delightful European-owned neo-Moorish-style hotel perched on a hillside with superlative views. Whitewashed arches lend an Andalusian air of seclusion that extends to the bamboo-furnished rooms (with heaters, comfy beds and shared or private bathrooms) and the hammock-slung gardens (with alpacas). There's a kitchen, laundry service, TV lounge, library, book exchange and a superb restaurant (see opposite). Staff are extremely helpful and well informed, and there are nice touches like hot water bottles. Breakfast not included. $39 (Bs265)

**Hostal Las Olas** Michel Pérez (at the end) ☎02 8622112, ⓦhostallasolas.com; map p.102. Just beyond La Cúpula, and under the same management, this wonderful lodge has a handful of sumptuous suites featuring stained-glass windows, pine floors and eucalyptus wood stairs – and beautiful views. There's also a hot tub, log fire, hammocks and friendly service. No breakfast. $49 (Bs335)

**Hostal Las Olas del Titicaca** Av 16 de Julio ☎02 8622205, ✉olasdeltiticaca_@hotmail.com; map p.102. Not to be confused with its posher namesake (see above), this is probably the best of Copacabana's bargain-basement traveller haunts, in a central location with spacious and clean en-suite doubles and hot water. Breakfast (Bs15) not included. Dorms Bs30, doubles Bs120

**Hostel Leyenda** Av Costanera and Busch; map p.102. A unique mix of faux-colonial extravagance and elaborate neo-native trimmings, this eye-catching hotel has an enviable beachfront position and a certain quirky charm, but has recently changed owners and may now undergo a change of style (and quite probably of price). Contact details not available at time of going to press.

**Hotel Gloria** Av 16 de Julio ☎02 8622094, ⓦhotelgloria.com.bo; map p.102. This grand hotel has comfortable if overpriced and dated en-suite rooms overlooking the lake. Its bay-windowed dining room, however, is the most elegant in town, with breathtaking views. There's also a games room (billiards, table football and ping pong), acres of garden and topiary animals out front. It's worth asking for a room with a lake view (the price is the same). Bs540

★**Hotel Rosario del Lago** Rigoberto Paredes ☎02 8622141, ⓦgruporosario.com; map p.102. Plush sister hotel to its namesake in La Paz, set near the waterfront in a modern colonial-style building. All of the spacious en-suite rooms have excellent lake views, heaters, safes, TVs and stylish bed covers and cushions; the spiral staircase-accessed, beam-ceilinged suite ($168/Bs1145) is well worth a splurge. Service is unfailingly polite, and there's a renowned restaurant (see opposite), luxurious terrace and small craft store. $109 (Bs740)

**Hotel Utama** Michel Pérez 60, at San Antonio ☎02 8622013, ⓦutamahotel.com; map p.102. Despite the unpromising brick exterior, this is a friendly and comfortable place, as the international flag-filled lobby testifies. Rooms come with chintzy bedspreads and murals and armchairs. You pay Bs30 more for a lake view, or Bs80 more for room #208, a corner room with the best views of all. Bs210

## EATING

Most restaurants offer delicious Titicaca **trout** (*trucha*), and more rarely *pejerrey* (silverside fish), which you can also get in the form of ceviche around Plaza 2 de Febrero in the mornings. The **market** just off Plaza 2 de Febrero on Calle La Paz is a good place for cheap meals, and there are also numerous simple **foodstalls** on the waterfront (most open daily 10am–7pm) serving fresh fried trout (Bs25) and other local favourites. Boatmen at the harbour offer round trips (from 10am, last departure 6pm; Bs45–50) to the **Isla Flotante**, a raft by a trout cage where they'll fish out a trout for you and cook it straight away – fresher than that you won't get.

**Café Bistrot** Busch at Av Costanera ☎7151 8310; map p.102. Backpacker favourite, mostly due to the (usually) charming Bolivian owner Fatima (who speaks French, English and Spanish) and is a fount of local information. Her tasty Bolivian-international fusion menu features decent espresso, seasonal fresh fruit juices, plenty of veggie dishes and Thai curry – there's even Marmite and Vegemite for hardcore fans. Chilled-out music completes the experience. Mains Bs60–90. Daily 7.30am–2.30pm & 5.30–9.30pm.

**El Condor and the Eagle Café** Av 6 de Agosto (in Hostal Residencial Paris) ⓦfacebook.com /elcondorandtheeaglecafe; map p.102. A great vegetarian breakfast café (owned by an Irishman and his Bolivian wife) serving excellent organic coffee, hot chocolate and proper Irish tea (all Bs12–18), home-made dishes like baked beans on soda bread, and cakes and muffins. There are books for sale, and a useful compendium of travellers' tips to flick through. Mon–Fri 7am–1.30pm.

**Copacabana Café I & II** Av 6 de Agosto ☎02 8622531; map p.102. These two sister cafés lie close to one another on the main drag, both offering huge menus and rustic decor of wooden tables and chairs. They make a relaxing place for a coffee, tea (Bs8–12) or a Paceña beer (Bs25), and *Café II* has a great, sunny terrace. Food options range from sandwiches, salads and burgers to trout (Bs50) and llama steaks (Bs60). The fresh juices range from Bs17–20, while the ubiquitous lemon pie is Bs20. Daily 7am–9.30pm.

★**La Cúpula** Michel Pérez 1–3 (inside Hostal La Cúpula) ☎02 8622029, ⍟hotelcupula.com; map p.102. This luminous domed dining room overlooking the lake has probably the best food in town, with good breakfasts (Bs27–34), creative main courses, including numerous vegetarian options and superlative *trucha* (Bs44–50), and tempting desserts. The highlights, however, are the decadent fondues (from Bs90). Try to reserve in advance for dinner. Daily 7.30am–3pm (Tues closes 10am) & 6–9.30pm.

★**Kota Kahuaña** Rigoberto Paredes (inside Hotel Rosario del Lago) ☎02 8622141, ⍟gruporosario.com; map p.102. Huge windows with superb views are the backdrop for some of Copacabana's most adventurous cuisine. Highlights include trout meunière (Bs79) and llama with mustard sauce (Bs81). Daily 7–9.30am, noon–2.30pm & 6.30–9.30pm.

**La Orilla** Av 6 de Agosto ☎02 8622267; map p.102. Perennially popular restaurant, usually packed full by 6pm. *Orilla* tends to divide opinion despite the hype, and it really depends on your expectations: it's not bad if you've been on the road for a while, but don't expect international standards of haute cuisine – overall the food is a bit hit and miss. The pizzas are usually solid choices (Bs45–73), and the stuffed trout is good (Bs58). Mon–Sat 5–10.30pm (last order 9.30pm).

**La Posta** Av 6 de Agosto ☎6818 0949; map p.102. Partly Argentine-owned with a vague tango theme and sometimes a Carlos Gardel soundtrack, this joint is usually crammed with Argentine travellers, especially if there's a football match on TV. The pizzas (from Bs35) are the town's best, but remember, this is rural Bolivia. Daily 7am–11pm.

## DRINKING

**Nemos** Av 6 de Agosto at Zapana; map p.102. This popular Anglo-Bolivian-run bar is a cool, low-lit space, with great sounds (live music most night) and a good choice of beers and cocktails, coffees and hot chocolates. Daily 5–11.30pm.

## SHOPPING

**The Spitting Llama** Av 6 de Agosto (half a block down from Plaza Sucre) ☎02 2599073, ⍟bit.ly/SpittingLlama; map p.102. This shop sells, exchanges and loans books, and also rents out travel and camping equipment. It also stores luggage (Bs3/day/item) and recycles plastic bottles and used batteries.

## DIRECTORY

**Banks and exchange** Three ATMs in town accept international cards (EcoFuturo on Av 6 de Agosto, Banco Fie on Plaza Sucre and, with higher charges, Banco Unión on Plaza Sucre), and Prodem on Av 6 de Agosto will pay out cash against plastic over the counter. *Cambios* along Av 6 de Agosto change dollars, euros and soles. Note that you get better rates changing soles to bolivianos or vice versa here and at the border than you will elsewhere in Peru or Bolivia.

**Internet** Several internet cafés line Av 6 de Agosto towards the docks, including Nayra Puma (daily 10am–10pm; Bs6/hr).

**Post office** Copacabana post office is on Plaza 2 de Febrero, located within the police station next to the Alcaldía (City Hall): it's officially open Tues–Sat 9am–noon and 2.30–6pm, Sun 9am–2pm, but often closed anyway; if you're heading to La Paz you're better off posting letters when you get there.

# Isla del Sol

Just off the northern tip of the Copacabana peninsula, about 12km northwest of Copacabana town, **ISLA DEL SOL** (Island of the Sun) is a world apart from the mainland, a beautifully preserved slice of old Bolivia. In the sixteenth century the island, 9km long by 6km wide at its broadest point, was one of the most important religious sites in the Andean world, revered as the place where the sun and moon were created and the Inca dynasty was born, and covered with shrines and temples that attracted thousands of pilgrims. After the Spanish conquest the island was looted, and the cut stones from its temples plundered to build churches on the mainland. But five centuries later it's still easy to see why it was (and still is) considered sacred. Surrounded by the azure Lake Titicaca, with the imperious peaks of the Cordillera Real rising above the shore on the mainland to the east, it's a place of great natural beauty and tranquillity.

**2**

## HIKING TO ISLA DEL SOL

Instead of taking a boat directly from Copacabana to Isla del Sol (see p.114), you can follow the trail formerly used by **Inca pilgrims** by hiking to the tip of the Copacabana peninsula at the village of **Yampupata**, the closest mainland point to the island, and then take a boat from there. The walk to Yampupata from Copacabana takes about five hours, following a very pleasant 17km trail along the shores of Lake Titicaca (see map, below).

### COPACABANA TO TITICACHI

Follow Calle Junín out of town to the bullring, then continue along the lakeside road round the shore to the north. The flat, marshy land beside the lake is worked using the ancient system of raised fields called *sukakullos* (see box, p.110), which use the warmth of water taken from the lake to protect crops from frost and boost production. After about an hour the road climbs into the hills overlooking the lake; after another hour you'll see a grotto-like cave on the hillside to your left, aka Gruta de Lourdes; now occupied by a statue of the Virgin, it was doubtless also a pre-Christian shrine. The road then climbs gently to a pass before descending, reaching the lakeside hamlet of **Titicachi**, which stands on a horseshoe bay, after about 45 minutes.

### SICUANI TO YAMPUPATA

Another half-hour's walk along the shore brings you to the village of **Sicuani**, where you can spend the night and get a basic meal at the simple *Hostal Inca Thaki* (no phone; rooms around Bs100). The owner, Señor Hilario Quispe, sometimes takes visitors out onto the lake or to Isla del Sol in a totora reed boat or zippier motorboat for around Bs120; he is also a mine of local information. From Sicuani it's another hour or so to the village of **Yampupata**, where you should be able to find a rowing boat or motorboat (Bs50–70 one way) to take you across to **Yumani** (see p.113) on Isla del Sol, or to the Isla de la Luna (Bs200 for motorboats).

Isla del Sol is the largest of the forty or so islands in Lake Titicaca and home to several thousand Aymara campesinos. The three main settlements, **Yumani**, **Challa** and **Challapampa**, are all on the east coast. Scattered with enigmatic ancient ruins and populated by traditional Aymara communities, the island is an enticing place to spend some time hiking and contemplating the jaw-dropping scenery; it's blissfully free of traffic and the litter that plagues Copacabana. Most visitors hike along the spectacular ridge from Challa to Yumani – you can do this on a day-trip or, much more comfortably, stay the night and depart Yumani the following day.

## ISLA DEL SOL & ISLA DE LA LUNA

## Challapampa

The island's northernmost settlement, **CHALLAPAMPA** was founded by the Incas as a service centre for the nearby ceremonial complexes. Set on a narrow spit of land between two large bays on the east coast of the island, the village has a small museum, and several places to stay and eat. At the dock you'll find public toilets (Bs2), and a couple of stalls selling sandwiches, water and snacks, while a short walk from the village lie several fascinating **Inca sites**. Note that local guides (free) meet the boats from Copacabana and try to shepherd day-trip visitors around these Inca sites at a healthy pace (worried they will miss the boat back) – you'll learn a lot (if you speak Spanish or someone translates), but this can also be a little restrictive, and you are not obliged to join them.

### Museo del Oro

On the beachside of the village • Daily 9am–noon & 2–5pm • Bs15; includes entry to Kasapata, Titikala and La Chincana; keep hold of the ticket, as there are a couple of checkpoints

The tiny, single-room **Museo del Oro** has artefacts found both on the island and at sites off the coast, where offerings were dropped into the water – tales of lost underwater cities persist to this day. The collection includes bronze idols, primarily Tiwanaku

### ISLA DEL SOL AND THE INCAS

The remains of ritual offerings found by archeologists show that Isla del Sol was an important local religious shrine long before the arrival of the Incas. When the island came under Tiwanaku control around 500 AD, larger ritual complexes were built and pilgrimages to the island began. Under **Inca rule**, though, the island was transformed into a pan-Andean pilgrimage destination visited annually by thousands of people from across the empire. The Incas believed the creator god **Viracocha** rose from the waters of Lake Titicaca and called forth the sun and moon from a rock on the island. They also claimed the founding fathers of their own dynasty – **Manco Capac** and **Mama Ocllo** – were brought into being here by Viracocha before travelling north to establish the city of Cusco and spread civilization throughout the Andes. In fact, it's very unlikely the Incas originated on the shores of the lake. This dynastic myth was probably an attempt to add legitimacy to the Inca regime by associating them with Lake Titicaca and the birthplace of the sun – from which the Inca rulers claimed to be directly descended – as well as providing a link with the pre-existing Tiwanaku civilization that was based on the shores of the lake.

After conquering the region in the mid-fifteenth century, the Incas invested heavily in building roads, agricultural terraces, shrines and temples on Isla del Sol, and establishing the town of **Copacabana** as a stop-off point for pilgrims. The entire Copacabana peninsula, as well as the sacred islands, was cleared of its indigenous Lupaqa and Colla population and turned into a **restricted sacred area**, its original populace being replaced by loyal settlers from elsewhere in the empire, who maintained the places of worship, attended to the needs of the astronomer priests and visiting pilgrims, and cultivated maize for use in elaborate religious rituals. A **wall** was built across the neck of the peninsula at Yunguyo, with gates where guards controlled access to Copacabana (nearly five centuries later the **peninsula** is still separated from the rest of the mainland by the border between Peru and Bolivia, which follows almost exactly the same line). Pilgrims entering Copacabana would abstain from salt, meat and chilli and spend several days praying at the complex of shrines here before walking round to the tip of the peninsula at Yampupata, from where they would cross over the water to Isla del Sol.

Part of the island's religious importance was no doubt related to the fertility of its fields. Insulated by the waters of the lake, Isla del Sol enjoys slightly higher average temperatures than the mainland, as a result of which its terraced slopes produce more and better maize than anywhere else in the region. **Maize** was a sacred crop for the Incas anyway, but that grown on Isla del Sol was especially important. Though most was used to make *chicha* (maize beer) for use in rituals on the island, grains of maize from the Isla del Sol were distributed across the **Inca empire**, carried by returning pilgrims who believed that a single grain placed in their stores would ensure bountiful harvests for evermore.

pottery (400–1100 AD), and miniature human and llama figures delicately carved from spondylus shells. Note that even if you don't go into the museum, you'll need to buy a ticket here to continue on to the island's Inca ruins.

### Kasapata

Daily 9am–5pm • Admission covered by Museo de Oro ticket (Bs15) (see p.111)

From Challapampa it's a forty-minute walk northwest along a steep but easy-to-follow path to a cluster of Inca sights and ruins, beginning with **Kasapata**. The path leads around the beach from the museum, and up past clumps of wild thyme, small farms and fields of broad beans, squealing pigs and llamas. Halfway up there's a checkpoint where you must show the entry ticket purchased at the Museo del Oro. **Kasapata** was probably an Inca village, but what you can see today was likely a *tambo* (waystation) for pilgrims. It's mostly rubble now, but to the left of the path a large building still stands with five characteristically Inca trapezoidal doorways, while to the north is a large carved stone block (**Piedra Sagrada**) that probably had ritual importance.

### Roca Sagrada (Titikala)

Daily 9am–5pm • Admission covered by Museo del Oro ticket (Bs15) (see p.111)

A short walk along the path beyond Kasapata is the main Inca sanctuary (1400–1532), marked by the remnants of a low wall and the **Roca Sagrada** or **Titikala**, a huge slab of sandstone on the right. On the way the path crosses a bare rock marked by two depressions shaped like **giant footprints** – dubbed the "Huellas del Thunupa" ("Footprints of Thunupa") or **Pisadas del Sol** ("Footprints of the Sun").

The sacred rock is where the Incas believed the sun or the Inca creator god Viracocha rose at the beginning of the world, though there's little in the appearance of this large outcrop of weather-beaten pink sandstone to suggest what an important religious site it once was. The first section is supposed to resemble the face of Viracocha, while the second section is supposed to look like a puma head. Small shrines lie all along the rock, and guides will tell you to touch the stone to "feel its energy".

During Inca times gold, silver, coca, shells, birds' feathers and sacrificial animals (and the occasional human) were brought here as offerings to the **sun god**, Inti, while the rock itself would have been covered in fine cloth and silver and gold plates; in the open space on its southern side was a large stone basin where sacred libations of *chicha* were poured and an **altar** where sacrifices were made.

The rock was the focal point of a ceremonial complex staffed by hundreds of priests and servants, and at certain times of year thousands of pilgrims, including the Inca himself, would come here to take part in elaborate rituals involving music, dance and sacrifices. Most pilgrims would not even be allowed near the rock, but worshipped from outside the sanctuary wall; those who entered the inner sanctum did so only after passing through a series of doorways where they would undergo **cleansing rituals**. Opposite the rock, the **Mesa Ceremonial** (ceremonial table), made from a massive cut stone slab, has been assembled with stones from other ruined buildings as a place for re-enactments.

### La Chincana

Daily 9am–5pm • Admission covered by Museo del Oro ticket (Bs15) (see p.111)

About 200m beyond Titikala to the northwest is a rambling complex of ruined buildings looking out west across the lake to the Peruvian shore. Known as **La Chincana** (The Labyrinth), this series of interlinked rooms, plazas and passageways with numerous trapezoidal niches and doorways is thought to have been both the storehouse for sacred maize grown on the island and the living quarters for the *mamaconas*, the so-called "Virgins of the Sun", women specially chosen for their beauty and purity who attended the shrine, making *chicha* and weaving cloth for use in rituals. If you have the energy, it's worth walking ten to fifteen minutes up to Cerro Tikani (3936m) at the far northern tip of Isla del Sol for panoramic views.

### Ruta Sagrada de la Eternidad del Sol (Willka Thaki)

From La Chincana you can return to Challapampa for the boats or to link up with the coastal trail (see below) leading south to Yumani, or you can take the much more scenic **Ruta Sagrada de la Eternidad del Sol (Willka Thaki)**, paved for most of the way to resemble an old Inca road. The trail runs along the central ridge of the island, with spectacular views throughout its 7km length (allow 3hr–4hr 30min). About halfway along there's a checkpoint where you pay a Bs15 fee, and towards the end the trail cuts through shady thickets of eucalyptus trees (it's otherwise completely open to the elements). The path does go and up a down a bit, and though the rises are mostly gentle, it can be a strenuous hike if you've just arrived in Bolivia (the path runs just below 4000m). There are a few snack stalls along the way, but bring plenty of water and sunscreen. Just before **Yumani** you'll pass through another checkpoint to pay the Bs10 village entry fee.

**2**

### The coastal trail

The **coastal trail** between Challapampa and Yumani is a slightly easier route than the Ruta Sagrada de la Eternidad, running at a lower altitude through small farms and villages. The main attraction on the way is the small village of Challa.

#### Challa

Village admission Bs15, including the museum

About an hour south of Challapampa on the coastal path you reach **Playa Challa**, a picturesque beach on a wide bay, and the *Qhumphuri hostal* and restaurant (see p.114). South of here, the path climbs over a headland to the main square of the village of **CHALLA** (where you will probably be sold your village admission ticket) before dropping down to a southern bay. The small **Museo Arqueológico** near the waterfront on the southern bay has a collection of intriguing dance costumes, masks and musical instruments, but is often closed (if you want to see it, ask the person who sells you the village admission ticket).

### Yumani

Village admission Bs10, including Escalera del Inca and Pilko Kaina

Straggling up the slope from the small harbour, **YUMANI** is the island's largest village and home to most of its accommodation. Note that if you arrive by boat (as opposed to by trail from the north part of the island), the climb up to the accommodation on the ridge (200m up) is a very steep, breathless hike. Yumani's only sight is the **Escalera del Inca** (222 steps), a stairway running steeply for 60m up from the dock through a natural amphitheatre covered by some of the island's finest Inca agricultural terracing, irrigated by bubbling stone canals. The canals are fed by the **Fuente del Inca** (or Fuente de las Tres Aguas) at the top of the staircase, a three-spouted spring believed to have magic powers: drink from all three, the locals say, and you'll gain knowledge of the Spanish, Quechua and Aymara languages. Also at the top of the main trail lies the modest **Iglesia de San Antonio**, the village church. The public toilets at the docks are Bs2.

#### Pilko Kaina

Daily 9am–5pm • Yumani admission ticket (Bs10) includes site admission

A short walk from Yumani, around the coast to the south along a path raised on an Inca stone platform, brings you to **Pilko Kaina** (Temple of the Sun), the island's best-preserved Inca site. Set on a cliff about 20m above the lake, the main structure is a large and fairly well-preserved two-storey stone building with classic Inca trapezoidal doorways facing east across the lake to the Isla de la Luna and the mountain peaks beyond – its original function remains obscure. Pilgrims travelling to the Titikala from the mainland would have passed through here after landing at the far southern tip of the island.

## ARRIVAL AND DEPARTURE — ISLA DEL SOL

You can visit Isla del Sol on a half- or full-day trip from **Copacabana**, but it's really worth spending at least a night on the island if you can. Boats call at the settlement of **Yumani**, where most of the hotels are located, and the village of **Challapampa** at the northern end of the island. It is also possible to hike to **Yampupata** at the tip of the Copacabana peninsula and then take a boat from there (see box, p.110).

### BY BOAT

Boats leave from the waterfront in Copacabana at around 8.30am and 1.30pm, calling at "Parte Norte" (Challapampa; Bs25 there, Bs30 for the return leg) via "Parte Sur" (Yumani; Bs20 there, Bs25 for the return leg), though this sometimes depends on demand, returning to Copacabana from Challapampa at 8.30am, 10.30am and 1.30pm, and from Yumani at 10.30am and 4pm. If you are not staying the night, you can get a boat to Challapampa, hike across the island and head back from Yumani (round trip Bs35) – highly recommended, but you'll need to watch the time. If you're staying, you can mix and match any leg of these routes, paying one-way rates as you go. Note that it is very rare for any boat to leave Yumani after

4pm, so you'll have to hire a private boat if you get stuck (see below).

**Boat operators** Plenty of agencies sell tickets for the two main boat companies, Andes Amazonia and Turismo Comunitario (aka Titicaca Isla del Sol); the former tends to be a bit quicker. A couple of smaller operators also run services. Unless things are really busy, you can usually just turn up in the morning and buy a ticket at the dock.

**Private boat hire** If you want to halve the journey time and escape the crowds (the boats can be disturbingly crowded) there's the option of private boat hire; shop around in Copacabana, and agree the itinerary beforehand. Between Yumani and Copacabana expect to pay Bs600–700 (Bs800–900 for Challapampa).

### GETTING AROUND

**On foot** The best way to see the island is to walk its length from Challapampa in the north to Yumani in the south – (see p.113). There are no vehicles on the island, so the only other way of getting around is by boat (see above).

### ACCOMMODATION AND EATING

#### CHALLAPAMPA

The beach area in Challapampa boasts a few basic restaurants with inexpensive almuerzos. You can camp on the north beach.

**Hostal Cultural Pachamama** Just off the north beach, beyond the museum ☎ 7190 0272. A friendly place, overlooking the beach, with claustrophobic (but en-suite) ground-floor rooms and more spacious ones upstairs, mostly with shared bathrooms. There's solar-powered hot water, but no wi-fi and no breakfast. **Bs60**

**Hostal Inca Uta** In a courtyard close to the dock ☎ 7353 4990. This stone-walled *hostal* boasts the relative luxury of en-suite rooms, though it remains very basic and, as everywhere on the island, the wi-fi comes and goes. No breakfast. **Bs80**

#### CHALLA

**Hostal Qhumphuri** Playa Challa ☎ 7152 1188. This friendly, family-run lodge on a hillside overlooking Playa Challa (the beach on the north side of the village) has reasonable en-suite rooms and a campfire on the terrace in the evenings. The restaurant also serves decent though simple meals. **Bs80**

#### YUMANI

The village's tightly packed thatched houses (and hotels) are arranged in a labyrinthine street plan that's difficult to find your way around, particularly after dark (bring a light).

Most of Yumani's hotels and *hostals* have in-house restaurants serving pizza, pasta and trout; prices are higher than in Copacabana.

★**Ecolodge La Estancia** On a hilltop 1.2km north of town ☎ 02 2442727, ⬥ecolodge-laketiticaca.com. These delightful adobe-thatched-roof en-suite cottages are arranged on terraces and connected by cobbled paths, with rustic wood furniture, bright bathrooms and spectacular views across the lake to the Andes. Water is brought up by donkey and llama each day, and heated by solar power – showers are hot, but guests are asked to stick to 5min. Rooms are heated by a Trombe wall (a small annexe covered with a plastic roof), but it can still get cold in winter. Rates include a tasty dinner on arrival (usually featuring trout), and breakfast the following morning. It's a good idea to book in advance. **$180 (Bs1225)**

**Hostal Inti Wayra** In view of the church ☎ 7194 2015. A decent budget choice with sizeable, balconied rooms (with shared and private bathrooms) and excellent east-facing lake views. Those of a spiritual bent can avail themselves of the meditation room, and there's also a decent restaurant, although breakfast is not included in the room rate. **Bs140**

**Hostal Puerta del Sol** At the top of the main street, on the left-hand side ☎ 7195 5181. The mustard-coloured *Puerta del Sol* has plain, clean rooms and fantastic views from its terrace. Breakfast, served in a rustic little dining room, is included if you take an en-suite room (Bs240), but not if you take a room with shared bathroom. **Bs100**

**Hotel Imperio del Sol** Near the church on the left-hand side of the steps ☎ 7359 1952, ⓦ imperiodelsolhotel .com. This modern peach-coloured *hostal* has great views and clean, though still pretty basic and somewhat overpriced, rooms (those with a private bathroom cost twice as much), plus a restaurant. Wi-fi in reception area only, and no hot water most of the day. <u>$40 (Bs270)</u>

**Inti Kala** Right at the top of town ☎ 7194 4013, ⓔ javierintikala@hotmail.com. A handsome stone and wood construction with huge windows, winding balconies and a spacious terrace with incredible views, the *Inti Kala* has some of the most stylish private bathrooms on the island. They'll even come and pick you up from Copacabana. <u>Bs180</u>

**Palla Khasa** 500m before Yumani (if coming from the north) ☎ 7321 1585, ⓔ palla-khasa@hotmail.com. In a quiet spot, this lovely hotel managed by the affable Vanessa has cosy yellow-walled rooms with rugs and stunning views; some also have private bathrooms (Bs200 extra) with solar-heated water. There are also newer cabins, all with those amazing sunset views, plus a good restaurant (sample the trout). <u>$50 (Bs360)</u>

**Las Velas** Turn right just before the steps down to the dock and follow the signs to the eucalyptus woods ☎ 7123 5616. Run by a former chef at a top Bolivian resort, *The Candle* (it really is lit by candles, no electricity; bring a light, and some warm clothes) has a similar menu to the other restaurants in Yumani, but significantly higher standards; note, though, that food takes 90min–2hr to arrive after ordering. Try the vegetable pizza or trout in wine sauce. Mains around Bs50–70. Mon–Sat noon–2.30pm & 6–10pm.

# Isla de la Luna

About 8km west of Isla del Sol, the far smaller **ISLA DE LA LUNA** (Island of the Moon) was another important Inca religious site. Known as Coati ("Queen Island"), it was associated with the moon, considered the female counterpart of the sun, and a powerful deity in her own right. Many pilgrims would continue here after their visit to the sanctuary on Isla del Sol. Made up of a single ridge 3km long and just over 1km across at its widest point, the island has limited agricultural land and is home to a small community. For much of the twentieth century it was used as a political prison.

### Iñak Uyu

Daily 8am–6pm • Bs10

Isla de la Luna's main site – and one of Bolivia's best-preserved Inca complexes – is a temple on the east coast known as **Iñak Uyu**. The "Court of Women" was probably a temple dedicated to the moon and staffed entirely by women. It takes about an hour to reach by boat from Yumani on Isla del Sol; from the beach a series of broad Inca agricultural terraces leads up to the temple complex, stone buildings facing inwards

---

**THE SECRETS OF THE STARS**

Anyone who sees the night sky from the Altiplano can't fail to be impressed by the bright canopy of the southern sky. It's no surprise that the Incas were fascinated by the stars, using their comparatively **advanced astronomical understanding** to forecast agricultural cycles and future climatic events. What is surprising, however, is that five centuries later their astronomical knowledge is still being used by Quechua and Aymara campesinos in both Peru and Bolivia. In June of each year the campesinos observe the **Pleiades** – a group of stars sacred to the Incas. If the multi-star cluster appears bright and clear in the pre-dawn sky, they anticipate early, abundant rains and a bountiful potato harvest. If the stars appear dim, however, they expect a poor harvest and delay planting to reduce the adverse effects of late and meagre rains. This practice was considered just a superstitious peasant tradition until 1999, when a team of US anthropologists and astronomers discovered that using this method the campesinos were accurately forecasting the arrival of **El Niño**, a periodic change in Pacific Ocean currents that occurs every two to seven years, triggering changes in global weather patterns, including drought in the Andes. The scientists found that in El Niño years, high-altitude clouds form, which are invisible to the naked eye but which are sufficient to decrease the brightness of the stars. Thus, by using a traditional folk technique, Andean campesinos accurately predict the onset of El Niño, a capability modern science only achieved right at the end of the twentieth century.

from three sides onto a broad central plaza. The facades of the buildings contain eleven massive external niches over 4m high and 1.5m deep, still covered in mud stucco, and decorated with smaller niches with a stepped diamond motif more characteristic of the Tiwanaku Inca architectural style – the Inca builders may have incorporated this design to please local sensibilities. Colonial-era materials including finely made textiles have been found buried here, suggesting that ritual offerings were still being made long after the fall of the Incas.

**2**

### ARRIVAL AND DEPARTURE                                                    ISLA DE LA LUNA

**By boat** Boats from Copacabana to Isla del Sol (see p.114) sometimes call at Isla de la Luna if there's enough demand. Otherwise, you can charter a private boat from Copacabana (see p.114), Yampupata (see box, p.110) or Yumani on Isla del Sol (around Bs400).

### ACCOMMODATION AND EATING

**Lodges** Although far fewer (and more basic) than the accommodation options on Isla del Sol, there is a handful of simple, locally run lodges dotted throughout the island; a double room costs around Bs100.
**Shops** There are a few shops to buy food, though you should bring some with you too.

# The Cordillera Apolobamba

North of Lake Titicaca, flush with the Peruvian border, is the **Cordillera Apolobamba**, the remote northern extension of the Cordillera Oriental. The splendour of the high mountain scenery in this isolated range equals or even exceeds that of the Cordillera Real, and the environment is more pristine. The region is protected by the **Area Natural de Manejo Integrado Nacional Apolobamba**, which covers nearly five hundred square kilometres. The range is still rich in wildlife only rarely seen elsewhere: condors, caracaras and other big birds are frequently spotted; pumas and spectacled bears still roam the most isolated regions; and large herds of vicuña can be seen from the road which crosses the plain of **Ulla Ulla**, a high plateau that runs along the western side of the range.

   Tourist infrastructure is virtually nonexistent in this isolated region, but for the adventurous the Cordillera Apolobamba offers perhaps Bolivia's best high-mountain trekking. The only real towns are **Charazani** and **Pelechuco**, both of which can be reached by tough but spectacular bus journeys from La Paz. Between the two runs the fabulous four- or five-day **Trans-Apolobamba Trek**.

## Charazani

Perched at about 3250m on the side of a deep valley and about 260km by road from La Paz, **CHARAZANI** is the market centre for the Kallawaya communities (see box, p.118), and the nearest town to the Trans-Apolobamba Trek; the southern trailhead at Curva is a four-hour walk away. Charazani itself dates back to colonial times, but the steep valley slopes all around are sculpted into pre-Hispanic terraces. A few crumbling colonial houses still survive, but most of the town's buildings are cheap, modern constructions. A couple of *pensiones* on the plaza serve simple meals.

### Aguas Termales de la Putina
Daily 7am–9pm • Bs10

About ten minutes' walk east of town along the road to Curva and then down a steep path to the valley floor are the **Aguas Termales de la Putina**, natural hot springs channelled into an open-air concrete swimming pool that offer an excellent way to soothe tired muscles after a long trek. These hot springs are allegedly the inspiration behind the perennially popular Bolivian "k'antu"-style folk song *Agüita de Phutiña*.

## ARRIVAL AND DEPARTURE CHARAZANI

**By bus** Transportes Trans-Altiplano buses from La Paz (1 daily; 9hr; Bs30) depart around 6–6.30am from Reyes Cardona 732 in the cemetery district; they return from the main plaza in Charazani at around 6pm.

## ACCOMMODATION

**Hotel Akhamani** A block south of the plaza ☎7201 0646. The best place to stay in town; the clean rooms have shared bathrooms and there is a small private en-suite apartment with its own kitchen. Staff can help organize mules and guides for the trek to Pelechuco. Bs100

**2**

# Lagunillas

Most hikers begin the Trans-Apolobamba Trek at **LAGUNILLAS**, a modern village beside a tranquil lake 310km from La Paz and a short walk from Curva, where the main trail begins. Usually busy with ducks, *huallata* geese and other wildfowl, the lake is actually artificial, having been built as a reservoir to feed a series of pools nearby which are used to prepare freeze-dried potatoes known as *tunta*. The rangers at the *albergue* (see below) can help find guides and mules to take you on the Trans-Apolobamba Trek, and you should register with them before proceeding further into the mountains. Ask around here and you should be able to arrange a consultation with a **Kallawaya medicine man** (see box, p.118).

## ARRIVAL AND DEPARTURE LAGUNILLAS

**By bus** Transportes Trans-Altiplano buses from La Paz to Lagunillas (1 daily; 9hr; Bs25) depart around 6am from Reyes Cardona 732 in the cemetery district; from Lagunillas it's a 1km walk up to Curva and the main trail.

## ACCOMMODATION

**Albergue Lagunillas** ☎02 2413432 (in La Paz), ⓦsernap.gob.bo. The protected areas agency SERNAP operates a community-run *albergue* for trekkers here, with warm dormitories, solar-heated showers and a kitchen, though no restaurant; you can also camp beside the lake. Check in advance to see if it is open. Dorms Bs25

# Curva

Sitting at 3780m, **CURVA** is the centre of Kallawaya culture (see box, p.118) and the starting or ending point of the **Trans-Apolobamba Trek** (see p.120). Even if you're not planning to trek to Pelechuco, the walk up from Charazani to Curva is very rewarding: the valley is beautiful, its steep sides sculpted by ancient terraces, and the path takes you through several Kallawaya farming villages.

Perched on a narrow ridge above the valley, with the snows of **Akhamani**, the sacred mountain of the Kallawayas, rising above, Curva itself is a deeply traditional community and the effective capital of Kallawaya culture. With its thatched stone houses and cobbled streets, the village is very picturesque, but people here are quite wary of outsiders, and if you're staying the night you're better off in Lagunillas.

## ARRIVAL AND DEPARTURE CURVA

**On foot** You can walk up to Curva from Charazani in about 4hr, following the footpath that starts near the hot springs and cuts across the valley floor, before climbing up the other side to Curva (the road itself contours round and takes much longer to walk). From Lagunillas it's just a 15min walk to Curva.

# The Ulla Ulla plateau

From the junction where the side road to Charazani branches off, the road running north along the Peruvian frontier towards Pelechuco (see p.118) climbs onto the **Ulla Ulla plateau**, which runs along the western side of the Cordillera Apolobamba and is traversed by the **Trans-Apolobamba Trek** (see p.120). Covering some two thousand

**2**

## THE KALLAWAYAS: MEDICINE MEN OF THE ANDES

The Cordillera Apolobamba is home to Bolivia's smallest and most mysterious ethnic group: the **Kallawayas**. Inhabiting half a dozen villages in the Upper Charazani Valley, the Kallawayas are a secretive caste of traditional **herbal medicine practitioners**, thought to number just a few hundred, who are famous throughout the Andes for their healing powers – even more so since UNESCO declared their "Andean cosmovision" (ie the totality of their belief system, encompassing every aspect of life) a "Masterpiece of the Oral and Intangible Heritage of Humanity" in 2003. The enormous **ecological diversity** of the Cordillera Apolobamba means the Kallawayas have a vast natural pharmacy of plants to draw on, while the region's proximity to the tropical lowlands has also given them access to the vast medicinal resources of **Amazonian shamanism**. Individual Kallawayas may know the medical properties of over nine hundred different plant species, a knowledge that is passed from father to son. Some historical sources credit the Kallawayas with being the first to use the dried bark of the cinchona tree, the source of **quinine**, to prevent and cure malaria; taken to Europe by the Jesuits, quinine remains to this day the basis for most treatments of the disease. More recently, scientists have studied chemicals derived from herbs used by the Kallawayas as possible treatments for **HIV**.

Most Kallawayas are also powerful **ritual specialists**, combining their skills as herbalists with the supposed ability to predict the future and diagnose illness by reading coca leaves. Although the main language spoken in their communities is Quechua, the Kallawaya medicine men famously speak a secret tongue known as **Machaj Juyay**, which is used only in healing rituals and other ceremonies. Some researchers believe Machaj Juyay is related to the secret language spoken in private by the **Inca ruling elite**. Certainly, the earliest post-conquest chroniclers linked the Kallawayas to the Incas. One wrote that the Kallawayas were brought to Cusco to act as herbalists and carry out important religious ceremonies and divination rituals for the Inca rulers; another claimed they had been charged with carrying the litter of the Inca himself. Other evidence suggests that the Kallawayas date back far into **Andean prehistory**: in 1970 archeologists uncovered a skeleton in the Charazani valley which had been buried with recognizable Kallawaya paraphernalia – this was carbon-dated to between 800 and 1000 BC, two thousand years before the rise of the Inca Empire.

These days the Kallawayas no longer wander as far and wide as they used to, and their numbers are thought to be dwindling, as fewer sons acquire their fathers' knowledge. However, a growing number are now resident in **La Paz**, where their skills remain in high demand.

square kilometres at an average altitude of 4300m, Ulla Ulla's broad expanse of green pasture and marshland is set against a dramatic backdrop of snowcapped peaks.

The plateau has been a protected area since 1972, and its once highly endangered vicuña population now falls within the **Área Natural de Manejo Integrado Nacional Apolobamba**. The vicuña population has made an astonishing recovery, and just driving across the plateau you'll see dozens of the animals, plus many hundreds of alpacas and llamas, as well as a wide variety of birds including flamingos, ibises and *huallata* geese. Signs of human habitation, by contrast, are few and far between. The biggest settlement is **Ulla Ulla village**, though it has no facilities of any kind. If you want to spend the night here and explore areas away from the road you'll need to camp.

## Pelechuco

Beyond Ulla Ulla the road climbs up from the plateau and over a 4860m pass between glittering glacial peaks before dropping down to the town of **PELECHUCO**, set in a deep valley that is often shrouded in cloud. This is the end of the road for vehicles but the starting (or ending) point of the **Trans-Apolobamba Trek** (see p.120). Pelechuco was founded by the Spanish in 1560 as a gold-mining outpost, and limited mining activity continues, though the town now serves mainly as a market centre.

**2**

**By bus** Trans Norte buses to Pelechuco (and Agua Blanca, just beyond it) from La Paz (13hr; Bs70) depart at 6am most days from the inter-provincial bus station at Ex-Tranca de Río

Seco on the outskirts of El Alto (served by the Teleférico blue line), which is also where you need to buy your ticket, two days ahead if possible; they return from the centre of town.

**Hotel Apolobamba** On the central plaza; ☎7195 3252. This basic but friendly hotel has a handful of clean rooms, some with private bathrooms (Bs40 extra); rooms at

the back are more comfortable. There are simple meals available, and the owner can help you find mules and guides. No wi-fi. <u>Bs80</u>

## The Trans-Apolobamba Trek

The tough four- or five-day **Trans-Apolobamba Trek** between Pelechuco and Curva takes you through the heart of the Cordillera Apolobamba and some of the most magnificent high-Andean scenery in Bolivia. The trek climbs across dizzying high passes and drops down through lush glacial valleys, passing a scattering of small villages – including **Ilo-Ilo** and the alpaca-herding hamlet of **Jatun Pampa** – as well as the abandoned mining village of **Viscachani**, and a collection of ancient (presumably Inca) ruined buildings at **Incachani**. It also passes through the homeland of the Kallawayas (see box, p.118), and around the peak of their sacred mountain, Akhamani. Crossing several high passes, including one over 5100m, this is a hard trek, and shouldn't really be attempted without a guide; alternatively, you can arrange to do the trek with a tour operator in La Paz (see below). There are no reliable maps of the region, and even if you have good directions it's easy to get lost, particularly if you're over 4000m up and the clouds close in.

**Route** You can walk the trek either from Pelechuco south to Curva or vice versa, though it's best to start in Pelechuco, where guides and mules are easier to arrange, and finish in Curva, close to Charazani, from where transport out is much more reliable – end your trek in Pelechuco and you could wait several days for the next bus.

**Food and equipment** You can buy basic foodstuffs in Pelechuco and Charazani, but you'll need to bring all other

equipment and supplies with you from La Paz.

**Guides and mules** Guides and mules (around Bs120/day, plus the same again for a muleteer) can be organized in Curva (through the rangers at Lagunillas), Pelechuco and Charazani.

**Tours** America Tours (see p.76) and Climbing South America (see p.76) are among the La Paz firms offering this trek as a package.

## The Pacha Trek

An interesting alternative to the Trans-Apolobamba Trek is the **Pacha Trek**, a four-day trek organized by local communities that visits remote Apolobamban settlements and offers an insight into traditional life. Millenarian Travel in La Paz (see p.77) are among firms who may be able to organize a trek on this trail if you can get a group together for it. Unfortunately, a lot of this trail has been ruined by mining works.

# The Cordillera Real

Stretching for about 160km along the northeastern edge of the Altiplano, the **Cordillera Real** (Royal Range) is the loftiest and most dramatic section of the Cordillera Oriental in Bolivia. With six peaks over 6000m high and many more over 5000m, it forms a jagged wall of soaring, ice-bound peaks that separates the Altiplano from the Amazon basin. Easily accessible from La Paz, the **mountains** are perfect for climbing and **trekking**. Populated by isolated Aymara communities, the cordillera is a largely pristine natural environment: the Andean condor is still a common sight, and other birds like

### TREKKING IN THE CORDILLERA REAL

Many of the best and most popular treks start close to La Paz, including the three so-called "Inca trails" which cross the cordillera, connecting the Altiplano with the warm, forested valleys of the Yungas (see p.125). Two of these ancient paved routes – the **Choro Trail** (see p.130) and the **Takesi Trail** (see p.132) – are relatively easy to follow without a guide, although it's still safer to hire one; the third, the **Yunga Cruz Trail** (see p.133), is more difficult. You can do all three of these treks, as well as treks in the magnificent **Condoriri Massif** (see box, p.122) and many other routes, with adventure tour agencies in La Paz (see p.76).

The other major base for trekking is the town of **Sorata**, nestled in a valley at the north end of the range at the foot of the mighty Illampu massif. From here, numerous trekking routes (see box, p.124) take you high up among the glacial peaks, while others plunge down into the remote forested valleys of the Yungas. Hiring guides and equipment in Sorata is cheaper than going with a La Paz tour operator.

**Maps and equipment** Unless you're going on a fully organized trek such as with an agency in La Paz (see p.76), you'll need all your own camping equipment. The books *Trekking in Bolivia: a Traveller's Guide*, by Yossi Brain, and *Peru and Bolivia: Backpacking and Trekking*, by Hilary Bradt, both have detailed descriptions of many of the trekking routes. Most of the routes are also covered in the excellent *Cordillera Real Recreation Map*, published in the US by O'Brien Cartographics, while the Instituto Geográfico Militar in La Paz (see p.88) sells larger-scale maps covering some of the routes.

**Guides and mules** Especially in the more remote areas, you should not go trekking in these mountains alone, as the consequences of a minor fall or a twisted ankle can quickly prove disastrous; it's much better to go with a local guide. Getting lost is easy and can be very dangerous – rescue services are pretty much nonexistent. Hiring a guide is a good way to ensure local people benefit economically from tourism, and in addition they can help avoid any possible misunderstandings with the communities you pass through. You may also want to hire a mule to carry your pack, either for your entire trip or for that first gruelling ascent to a high pass.

eagles, caracaras and hawks are also frequently seen; though rarely spotted, pumas still prowl the upper reaches, while the elusive Andean spectacled bear roams the high **cloudforest** that fringes the mountains' upper eastern slopes.

# Sorata

Some 55km north of Achacachi, enclosed in a deep, fertile valley at the foot of the mighty 6400m Illampu massif, **SORATA** has an idyllic setting, though the settlement itself is a typically scruffy Bolivian rural town – don't expect some picturesque oasis. Hemmed in by steep mountain slopes and often shrouded in cloud, the surrounding area has a Shangri-la feel – early Spanish explorers even compared the valley to the Garden of Eden. At an altitude of 2695m, it is significantly warmer than La Paz, but is still cool at night compared to the Yungas. Though there's little to do in the town itself, it's a good base for hikes in the surrounding countryside. The heart of town is the ample **Plaza General Enrique Peñaranda**, shaded by massive palm trees and with good views of Mount Illampu.

### ARRIVAL AND DEPARTURE                    SORATA

**By bus** Minibuses from the cemetery district in La Paz, operated by Trans Unificada Sorata at Manuel Bustillos 675, off Av Kollasuyo (☎02 2381693; daily 4am–6pm; leaving every 30min or when full; 4hr 30min; Bs20), drop you in the central Plaza Enrique Peñaranda. Going back to La Paz, minibuses leave from 14 de Septiembre, 300m south of Plaza Enrique Peñaranda, but note that some terminate in El Alto; Trans Unificada Sorata's are the only ones which serve La Paz's cemetery district. The only way to reach Copacabana without going via La Paz is to take a La Paz-bound vehicle, change at Huarina, and hope that a Copacabana-bound bus or *combi* will stop for you (which they should do if they have space); for Coroico you'll have to go via La Paz.

## CLIMBING IN THE CORDILLERA REAL

With so many high peaks, the Cordillera Real is obviously an excellent place for **mountain climbing**. While serious climbers should bring all their own equipment from home, inexperienced climbers can also scale some of these high peaks with help from specialist **tour agencies** in La Paz; reputable companies (see p.76) offering some or all of the climbs listed below include Andean Summits, Climbing South America, Huayna Potosí, Topas Adventure Travel and Travel Tracks. For **guides**, and to check the credentials of those offering their services, visit the website of the Asociación de Guías de Montaña y Trekking de Bolivia at ⓦ agmtb.org.

To avoid the risk of severe **altitude sickness**, which can potentially be fatal (see p.38), you should not try to climb mountains over 6000m in a single day. In case of serious trouble, the people to contact are **Socorro Andino Boliviano mountain rescue** (☎7158 1118, ⓦ facebook.com/SocorroAndinoBoliviano).

Popular climbing destinations in the Cordillera Real include:

### THE CONDORIRI MASSIF (MACIZO DEL CONDORIRI)

With thirteen peaks over 5000m, the magnificent **Condoriri Massif** is popular for both climbing and high-altitude trekking. The most iconic of its peaks, **Nevado Condoriri** (5648m), looks like the head of a condor rising out of two flanks that resemble outstretched wings. An easier climb is **Cerro Áustria** (5320m), which needs no specialist equipment and can even be done as a day-trip from La Paz, though normally you would take a two- or three-day trip.

### HUAYNA POTOSÍ

This 6090m-high **Huayna Potosí** near La Paz is one of the few peaks in South America over 6000m that can be climbed by people with no mountaineering experience. Agencies will take you up it for around $200 (Bs1450), usually over three days, though you should check carefully that the guide they provide is qualified and experienced and the equipment is adequate – if in doubt, go with a more reputable and expensive agency.

### ILLIMANI

The 6439m-high **Illimani** is one of Bolivia's classic climbs, an iconic peak with outstanding views, but you need at least some climbing experience to attempt it. It's quite physically demanding, and there isn't much infrastructure here so you need to come well equipped. Mules will carry your equipment up to the base camp. Illimani is offered as a four-day expedition from La Paz (around $600/Bs4000 per person per day; minimum four people).

### INFORMATION AND TOURS

**Tourist information** Sorata has no formal tourist office. The Asociación de Guías de Turismo Sorata at Sucre 302 (☎7883 8808; often closed) and the manager of *Residencial Sorata* (see opposite) are experts on the region. The *Casa Reggae* bar (see p.125) also dispenses tourist information.
**Tour agencies** Although based in La Paz at Linares 940,

Gravity Assisted Mountain (☎02 2310218, ⓦ www .gravitybolivia.com) offers mountain-biking trips in the countryside surrounding Sorata, including an amazing six-day combined bike and raft expedition to Rurrenabaque (from $795/Bs5565 per person in a group of four, more in a smaller group, less in a larger one).

### ACCOMMODATION

★**Altai Oasis** Thirty minutes from town on foot via the road to the Gruta ☎7151 9856, ⓦ www.altaioasis .com; map opposite. Johny Resnikowski and wife Roxana have constructed a series of imaginative cabins, rooms and dorms among the wild anis, pine and eucalyptus on the folds of the riverbank, a 30min (steep) hike from town, though guests have access to a short cut which takes about half as long. Accommodation includes a tree-house-like hideaway and a conical yurt-like construction, as well as more humble abodes, all conceived with real love and dedication. There are also camping spots, a dorm, a pool and a great restaurant

(see opposite). Dorms B̲s̲8̲4̲, doubles B̲s̲2̲5̲0̲, three-person cabin B̲s̲8̲0̲0̲, camping (per person) B̲s̲3̲0̲
**Hostal Las Piedras** Villa Elisa, C 2, below the football field on the short cut to the Gruta ☎7191 6341, ✉ soratalaspiedras@yahoo.com; map opposite. *Las Piedras* offers spotless rooms named after precious stones and styled with a creative dedication and attention to detail rare at budget level; all have great views and some have private bathrooms (Bs70 more). Breakfasts (an additional Bs35) are great, and may in season include home-made bread, yoghurt and marmalade from the *Café*

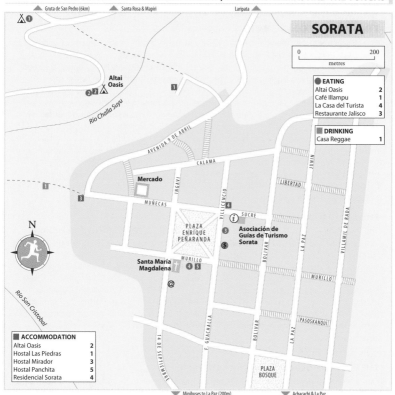

**SORATA**

| ● EATING | |
| --- | --- |
| Altai Oasis | 2 |
| Café Illampu | 1 |
| La Casa del Turista | 4 |
| Restaurante Jalisco | 3 |

| ■ DRINKING | |
| --- | --- |
| Casa Reggae | 1 |

| ■ ACCOMMODATION | |
| --- | --- |
| Altai Oasis | 2 |
| Hostal Las Piedras | 1 |
| Hostal Mirador | 3 |
| Hostal Panchita | 5 |
| Residencial Sorata | 4 |

*Illampu* (see below). Good dinners are also available, but no wi-fi. **Bs100**

**Hostal Mirador** Muñecas 400 (two blocks west of the plaza) ☎7350 5453, ⬤bit.ly/HostalMIrador; map above. Perched on the edge of a steep valley, the *Mirador* lives up to its name ("viewpoint"), with the best views in town, from its terrace at any rate. There's a shared kitchen, cosy rooms (available with private bathrooms for Bs80 more) and an easy-going vibe. No wi-fi; breakfast not included. Dorms **Bs25**, doubles **Bs60**

**Hostal Panchita** Plaza Enrique Peñaranda ☎02 2134242; map above. A friendly place on the main square, with simple rooms set around a small courtyard; those at

the front have small balconies overlooking the plaza (room 10 is the best). There's also a TV lounge at the front. On the downside, hot water can be sporadic and breakfast isn't included. **Bs70**

**Residencial Sorata** Plaza Enrique Peñaranda ☎02 2136672; map above. Set in the rambling, 1830s Casa Gunther (once home to a family of powerful German rubber merchants), this hotel has a warren of ancient, dusky rooms with looming ceilings and metre-thick walls, and a couple of cobbled courtyards. The older rooms have more charm, but the anonymous newer en-suite ones (Bs50 more expensive) are more comfortable. There's a kitchen that you can use, but breakfast isn't included and there's no wi-fi. **Bs50**

## EATING

Restaurant **opening times** are erratic: many places close on Tuesdays and some have shorter hours (or even close altogether) during the November–March rainy season.

**Altai Oasis** ☎7151 9856, ⬤altaioasis.com; map above. You can dine to the peal of wind chimes and distant rattle of campsite bongos on *Altai*'s idyllic outdoor deck. It's one of Sorata's best places to eat, with Eastern European dishes like goulash and borscht, vast T-bone steaks,

numerous veggie options and a wide range of breakfast choices. Look out for the log-carved board games. Mains Bs30–80. Daily except Mon 8am–7.30pm.

**Café Illampu** On the road to the Gruta San Pedro, a 15–20min walk from town ☎7322 7761; map above.

**2**

## TREKKING FROM SORATA

As well as numerous half- and one-day hikes immediately around town – the most popular of which is to the Gruta de San Pedro (see below) – some excellent longer treks start near Sorata. These take you through remote traditional communities and high Andean scenery, up among the glacial peaks of Mount Illampu or across the spine of the cordillera and down into the steamy tropical valleys of the Yungas.

La Paz tour operators (see p.76) can organize treks. Alternatively, most local guides, porters and mule handlers in Sorata align themselves with the **Asociación de Guías de Turismo Sorata**, whose office is opposite *Residencial Sorata*, just off the plaza on Calle Sucre (see p.122). In principle, they can arrange guides for about Bs200 a day plus food and mules, which can carry up to 20kg and cost roughly Bs120 a day plus food for the handler. They also have a limited amount of camping equipment for rent.

Most local guides know the routes up to the main base camps for climbing Illampu, though they're not qualified climbing guides; if you want a climbing guide you should hire one through a climbing agency in La Paz.

### THE GRUTA DE SAN PEDRO

The hike (4–6hr return trip) down the San Cristóbal valley to the **Gruta de San Pedro**, a large cave about 6km away (taxis charge Bs35 return), is one of the best short hikes around Sorata. Follow Avenida 9 de Abril out of town past the football pitch, then take the left turn, signposted to the *gruta*, about fifteen minutes outside town, which leads you along the opposite side of the valley (alternatively, cut straight across the valley from town). The road continues down the narrow ravine of the Río San Cristóbal, with good views of Illampu looming above. After about 5km you'll reach the small village of **San Pedro**; the Gruta de San Pedro is just above the road on the right, about 1km further on. The cave (daily 9am–5pm) is long, narrow and about 12m high, with plenty of bats – you can go about 150m inside before you reach an underground lake. A guardian will turn on the lights in the cave in return for the admission fee (Bs20).

### THE LAGUNAS GLACIER AND CHILLATA TREK

One of the most popular high-altitude treks from Sorata is the four-day **Lagunas Glacier and Chillata Trek**. This takes you high up the western side of the Illampu massif to two lakes set at over 5000m.

### THE ILLAMPU CIRCUIT

A longer, tougher and even more spectacular trek is the **Illampu Circuit** (6–7 days), which takes you round the Illampu massif past isolated settlements and over several passes between 4500m and 5045m, the highest of which, Abra Calzada, affords incredible views over Lake Titicaca. However, there have been violent robberies near Laguna San Francisco, towards the end of the circuit; many agencies have stopped operating the route: check the latest security situation before heading off, and always use knowledgeable local guides.

### THE MAPIRI TRAIL

One of two long treks down into the tropical valleys of the Yungas, the **Mapiri Trail** (7–8 days) is a tough descent to the mining town of Mapiri, from where you can continue by motorized canoe and road to Coroico or down to Rurrenabaque. Built in the nineteenth century as a route for bringing quinine up from the Amazon lowlands, the trail runs through a beautiful and remote region of forest-covered mountains. It is frequently overgrown, so a machete is needed; water is also scarce along much of the route.

### THE CAMINO DE ORO

The **Camino de Oro** (Goldminers' Trail; 5–7 days) dates back to pre-Columbian times. It connects the Altiplano with the alluvial goldfields of the Yungas, and impressive remnants of Inca stonework can still be seen along its length, though the lower stretches pass through areas badly deforested by mining activity. The trail emerges at the gold-mining camps along the Río Tipuani, from where transport is available downriver to Guanay.

## ISKANWAYA

Older and more extensive but less well-preserved than Peru's Machu Picchu, the ancient site of **Iskanwaya**, a twenty-minute drive above the remote village of Aucapata on the River Llica, north of Sorata, was built during the Mollo culture (one of the successors of Tiwanaku) some time between 1145 and 1425. The site has a museum and there are camping facilities nearby, as well as basic *alojamientos* in Aucapata. Because it is so remote, the site receives very few visitors. Climbing South America (see p.76) offer it as part of a four-day 4WD excursion from La Paz.

This Swiss-run café and bakery, on the mountainside looking back across to Sorata, is known for its tasty and wholesome breads, jams, yoghurts (Bs8) and muesli (Bs20). Mid-March to Dec daily except Tues 9am–6pm.

**La Casa del Turista** Plaza Enrique Peñaranda ☎7326 6320, ⓦbit.ly/LaCasadelTurista; map p.123. This place calls itself a pizzeria, but it's best to skip the pizzas and pastas and plump for one of the more interesting Mexican options: there are well-prepared tacos, enchiladas, quesadillas and nachos. The *pique de*

*macho* (diced beef and fried potatoes in a spicy sauce) is also pretty good. The restaurant itself is cluttered with paintings, wall hangings and reed boats, and has a surprisingly well-stocked bar. Mains Bs25–50. Daily 11am–10pm.

**Restaurante Jalisco** Plaza Enrique Peñaranda ☎7151 5801; map p.123. This simple restaurant boasts a rather varied menu of Mexican and Italian food (pasta Bs29–37), as well as more traditional dishes. The enchiladas are surprisingly tasty (Bs29). Daily 8am–10pm.

### DRINKING

**Casa Reggae** Just down the hill from Hostal El Mirador; map p.123. A rather rustic outdoor bar (doubling as a backpackers' inn), serving juices, wines

and caipirinhas in the evening, with reggae music and a chilled out, hippyish feel. Daily 7pm–midnight or later.

### DIRECTORY

**Banks and exchange** There's no ATM in Sorata, but Prodem, Plaza Enrique Peñaranda 136 (Mon 12.30–4.30pm, Tues–Fri 8.30am–4pm, Sat 8am–3pm), changes US dollars and gives cash advances against a credit (but not debit) card for a five-percent commission fee. For all these services, bring your passport.

**Internet** Slow access (Bs12/hr) is available at a few small shops just off Plaza Enrique Peñaranda on 14 de Septiembre (Bs6/hr). Connections tend to be faster in the mornings.

**Laundry** *Residencial Sorata* (see p.123) charges Bs15/kg.

**Post office** There's no longer a post office in Sorata, so if you have anything to send, hold on to it till you get to La Paz.

# The Yungas

East of La Paz, the Cordillera Real drops precipitously into the Amazon lowlands, plunging through the **Yungas**, a region of rugged, forest-covered mountains and deep subtropical valleys. Blessed with fertile soils and watered by plentiful rains, the warm valleys of the Yungas produce abundant crops of coffee, tropical fruit and coca for the markets of La Paz and the rest of the Altiplano; indeed, long before the Spanish conquest the peoples of the Andes maintained agricultural colonies here to supply the Altiplano with coca and other subtropical products. Several of the sturdy stone roads that originally transported the leaves – and linked the Yungas outposts to the main population centres – today provide some of the most scenic, challenging hiking in the region.

Even if you don't hike, the journey down to the Yungas from the Altiplano is truly spectacular. The original road from **La Paz to Coroico** is widely considered the **most dangerous in the world**, hugging the forest-covered mountain slopes as it winds above fearsome precipices. It's also among the most scenic and dramatic, and – since the opening of a bypass – frequented predominantly by mountain bikers.

Three of the well-built stone roads that linked the agricultural outposts of the Yungas to the main population centres before the Spanish conquest, the so-called "Inca" trails – the **Takesi**, **Choro** and **Yunga Cruz** – make excellent multi-day hikes. The most frequently visited Yungas town is the idyllic resort of **Coroico**, set amid spectacular scenery and tropical vegetation. From Coroico, the road continues north towards Rurrenabaque and the Bolivian Amazon (covered in Chapter 6). The quiet town of **Chulumani** is less frequently visited than Coroico, but has similarly good views, while midway between Coroico and La Paz, **Parque Nacional Cotapata** is one of the few areas where the natural Yungas vegetation is still well preserved.

## Coroico

Rightly considered one of the most enchanting spots in the Yungas, the peaceful little town of **COROICO** is perched on a steep mountain slope with panoramic views across the forest-covered Andean foothills to the icy peaks of the Cordillera Real beyond. At an altitude of 1760m, it enjoys a warm and pleasantly humid climate, and this, combined with the dazzling scenery, good facilities, easy walks (see box, p.130) and refreshing swimming, makes it the perfect place to relax and recuperate – especially if you've spent the day cycling the "Death Road" (see box, opposite).

Coroico gets very busy at weekends and during Bolivian public holidays, when it's transformed by large numbers of Paceños on vacation; if you want to relax in peace, visit during the week, though note that many cafés and restaurants close on Tuesdays. The mosquitoes and especially **sandflies** in the countryside around here can be ferocious year-round: cover up, bring plenty of repellent and, if possible, tuck your trousers into your socks when hiking.

### ARRIVAL AND DEPARTURE                                                    COROICO

**By bus** Minibuses (2hr 40min; Bs20) and smaller but faster minivans (2hr; Bs30) leave when full from Terminal Puente Minasa in La Paz's Villa Fátima district. They may drop you in Coroico's Plaza Principal (Plaza García Lanza), but to go back to La Paz, you'll need to go to the bus station southwest of the main square on Av Manning (last departure around 6pm). To go to Chulumani from Coroico, you can try changing at Unduavi, where the roads to the

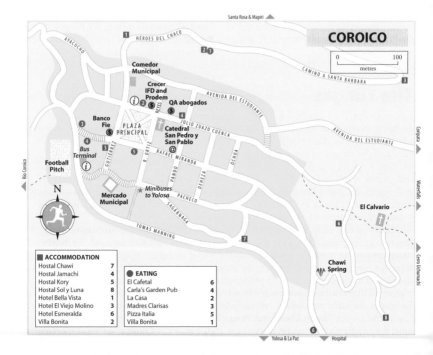

## THE WORLD'S MOST DANGEROUS ROAD

Few highways have as intimidating a reputation as the original road linking La Paz with Coroico in the North Yungas. A rough, narrow track chiselled out of near-vertical mountainsides that descends more than 3500m over a distance of just 64km, it's still widely referred to as the **world's most dangerous road** (aka "the Death Road"), a title bestowed on it by the Inter-American Development Bank. Statistically, the sobriquet is difficult to dispute: before a new **multi-million-dollar bypass** around the most perilous stretch opened in 2006, dozens of vehicles went off the road each year, and with vertical drops of up to 1000m over the edge, annual fatalities reached into the hundreds.

Following the route in its entirety from Unduavi, the first 40km are the most perilous and spectacular of the entire route. At times the road is only 3m wide, looming over deep precipices. To make matters worse, the road is often swathed in **cloud**, and in places waterfalls crash down onto its surface.

The 106km bypass follows a route that looms high over the old road on the opposite side of the valley and which tunnels intermittently through the mountainside. While some of the concrete and supporting rods have fallen prey to the elements, it's still a huge improvement – at least space- and safety-wise – over the old route. It has also slashed the journey time from La Paz to Coroico to about two hours by minibus or minivan; the old road took about four and a half hours.

From Villa Fátima in La Paz, the road to the Yungas climbs northeast to **La Cumbre**, a 4800m pass over the Cordillera Real. From here it descends to the hamlet of **Unduavi**, where the road forks, one branch descending southeast towards Chulumani in the South Yungas (see p.134), the other heading down northeast towards Coroico and the Amazon lowlands. The *nueva carretera* (new road) initially follows the original northeast fork before splitting off and climbing high above it, following a similar trajectory along the spine of the mountains before descending to join the original road north of **Yolosa**, a hamlet set at about 1200m, about 85km from La Paz. Here, a newly cobbled side road climbs up to Coroico, 10km away, while the main road continues 74km north to Caranavi and beyond to Rurrenabaque.

### CYCLING DOWN

What the statistics don't tell you is that the old route – and to a certain extent the bypass as well – is among the most awe-inspiring and scenic roads in the world. Starting amid the ice-bound peaks of the Cordillera Real, it plunges down through the clouds into the humid valleys of the Yungas, winding along deep, narrow gorges clad with dense cloudforest.

So spectacular is the descent that travelling the old Yungas road by **mountain bike** is one of Bolivia's most popular tourist attractions, an exhilarating five- to six-hour ride that's easy to organize with tour companies in La Paz – Gravity Assisted Mountain Biking has one of the best reputations (see p.77). Most trips end at La Senda Verde (see box, p.129), and a chance to ride the zip line (see box, p.128).

The re-routing of most traffic to the bypass means – in theory, at least – cycling the route is now **safer** than it's ever been, especially if you go with a reputable tour company with good guides and well-maintained bikes. Though virtually anyone that can ride a bike can make the trip, the road is not entirely without risk, and people have been hurt and several even killed during the descent in the past, forced off the edge by traffic.

north and south Yungas divide, but through vehicles are likely to be full (buses should stop for you, but you may have to stand); your safest bet is to go back to La Paz. Buses for most other destinations stop at Yolosa, connected with Coroico by regular minibus (Bs5, or Bs7 if you've got heavy baggage; 15min), which stop in Coroico just above the Mercado Municipal on Sagárnaga. Buses for Rurrenabaque (a journey of at least 15hr) stop at Yolosa mid-afternoon on their way through from La Paz; to get a seat you'll need to

book in the morning (or the day before) with Tunki Tours in the bus terminal or at the tourist office on Plaza Principal; you'll need to get a minibus down to Yolosa to join the bus. **By boat** It is possible to reach Rurrenabaque by river from Coroico, although most of the regular trips go from Guanay instead (reachable by shared taxi, changing at Caranavi). If you can get a group together, however, Deep Rainforest in La Paz (see p.76) can organize a trip.

## COROICO'S FIESTA

Around October 20 each year, Coroico celebrates its biggest annual **fiesta** with several days of drinking, processions and costumed dances. The fiesta commemorates the day in 1811 when the statue of the Virgin in the church – brought here from Barcelona in 1680, when Coroico was founded – supposedly summoned a ghost army to drive off a force of indigenous rebels who were besieging the town.

**2**

### INFORMATION AND TOURS

**Tourist information** There is a tourist office staffed by local guides on Plaza Principal (daily 9am–1pm & 4–8pm; ☎7306 3696). The bus station also has a tourist office (daily 8am–noon & 2–6pm, but sometimes closed even within those hours).

**Tours** The guides at the Plaza Principal tourist office offer a range of activities including hikes up nearby Cerro Uchamachi and down to the Río Vagantes in the valley below, and excursions to Afro-Yungueño villages (see box, p.135) like Tocaña and Mururata (usually Bs400/day for a group of up to four, including transport). It's also possible in the dry season (May–Oct) to go rafting, kayaking and inner-tubing near Coroico – ask at the tourist office for details, but note that some firms will not cover these activities because unpredictable water levels can make them potentially dangerous.

### ACCOMMODATION

Coroico has an impressive range of places to stay, aimed primarily at visitors from La Paz. At weekends and on **public holidays** (especially in the high season) everywhere gets very full and prices go up, so it's worth booking in advance. Even if you're on a tight budget, it's worth spending a little more to stay somewhere with a **swimming pool**.

**Hostal Chawi** Just off the road to La Paz ☎7355 5644, ⓦhostalchawi.com; map p.126. The friendliest and cosiest budget option in town. Basic but comfy rooms, with dorms or private doubles with hot showers. Dizzying views, lush gardens, wonderful Bolivian hospitality and amazing home-cooked food and home-grown coffee add to the experience. It sometimes closes up during the week if there are no customers. Dorms Bs70, doubles Bs180

**Hostal Jamachi** Suazo Cuenca at Pando ☎7623 7004, ⓦfabasfm@hotmail.com; map p.126. This small place just a block from the main square is the best of the ultra-budget options: central, cheap and basic, with shared bathrooms, no breakfast, and wi-fi 7am–11pm only; they lock up around 10pm, but you can ring the doorbell to get in. Bs70

**Hostal Kory** Pasaje Adalid Linares 3501 (entrance in Gutiérrez) ☎7156 4050; map p.126. A good-value choice with a good-sized pool (open to non-guests for Bs25), incredible views and airy rooms, some en-suite (Bs240), with lino-tiled floors and chintzy bedspreads. Breakfast not included; wi-fi in attached restaurant only. Bs160

★**Hostal Sol y Luna** Just under 1.5km outside town uphill on Julio Zuazo Cuenca, beyond the Hotel Esmeralda ☎7156 1626, ⓦsolyluna-bolivia.com; map p.126. One of the most charming hideaways in Bolivia, *Sol y Luna* has a collection of delightful rustic cabins scattered among extensive forest gardens, as well as simpler rooms in the main building, all with a wonderful feeling of being immersed in a peaceful, natural environment. There's also camping and a restaurant, pool, hot tub and scenic viewpoints. A taxi from town costs about Bs20–25. Wi-fi in the main building only, and breakfast not included. Camping (per person) Bs50, cabins Bs360, doubles Bs160

**Hotel Bella Vista** Héroes del Chaco (two blocks north of Plaza Principal) ☎02 2136059, ⓔcoroicohotelbellavista @hotmail.com; map p.126. This stylish, Bolivian-owned place has faux-colonial decor, towering ceilings and a contemporary twist. Each room (most of them en-suite, costing Bs70 more) comes with TV and inspirational views, and there's also a rooftop *mirador*. Bs180

**Hotel El Viejo Molino** 1km from town on the road to Caranavi ☎02 2430020, ⓦhotelviejomolino.com; map p.126. On the far northeastern fringe of town, the perfectly perched "Old Mill" (a former coffee estate with a water-mill) has an air of exclusivity. Although some rooms are slightly musty, they're very comfortable and the hotel also has a lovely large pool, sauna and small gym, and

### ZZIP THE FLYING FOX

Zip lines have made it to Bolivia, with this incarnation a 1555m-long beast in three sections, swooping 200m over the forest canopy at speeds of over 85km/hr. **Zzip the Flying Fox** (ⓣ02 2313849, ⓦziplinebolivia.com), a Kiwi-Bolivian-run outfit, is located in Yolosa, 10km from Coroico, and most organized "Death Road" trips (see box, p.127) include a stop here as an optional extra. It's open daily 9am to 11am and 1pm to 5pm. Rides are around Bs220.

## YUNGAS ANIMAL REFUGE

If you're cycling down the "Death Road" you'll most likely end up at **La Senda Verde Animal Refuge & Eco Lodge** (☎ 7472 2825, ⓦ sendaverde.com), situated 7km outside of Coroico, half a kilometre south of Yolosa (Coroico–Yolosa minibuses will drop you off on the way; a taxi from Coroico will charge about Bs40). Set in a gorgeous valley next to a river that you can swim in, this sanctuary provides a home for animals rescued by illegal traffickers; numerous (very cheeky) monkeys, colourful toucans and parrots, ocelots and even Aruma bears. The reserve has **tours** daily at 10am, 11am, noon and 3pm (standard 45min tour Bs100, or Bs130 if you want to see the Aruma bears; no shorts, short skirts or children under 10), but it's possible to **stay the night** – highly recommended – and also to **volunteer** (Bs1365 per week including meals; two weeks minimum). There are sprawling, lush grounds to wander around, pretty views and a restaurant that serves up home-made pasta and salads (buffet Bs65). Accommodation is in two- to five-person cabins, which are dotted around the grounds. Prices include breakfast and a tour. Double cabins are Bs440, with more basic huts Bs320 and the treehouse Bs380.

**2**

restaurant (lunch Bs80, dinner Bs75), not to mention great views and wooded surrounds. Bs520
**Hotel Esmeralda** Julio Zuazo Cuenca 725 (400m above Plaza Principal) ☎ 02 2136017, ⓦ hotelesmeraldacoroico .com; map p.126. This large hotel has great views, an attractive garden and pool, and a reasonable restaurant. There's a wide range of rooms, the best of which have private bathrooms and balconies with stunning vistas. There's also table football, wi-fi in the reception area, and a book exchange. Dorms Bs120, doubles Bs240
**Villa Bonita** Héroes del Chaco (100m past Hotel Bella Vista on the road to Caranavi) ☎ 7191 8298, ⓔ villa_ bonita05@yahoo.com; map p.126. Amid the laidback, familial environs of their raspberry-coloured home and leafy garden – site, too, of a great café (see p.130) – friendly Bolivian-Swiss couple Ninfa and Gianni Pedetti have three lovely cabins and a double room. Ninfa offers free yoga and dance classes on Wed mornings. Double Bs120, cabins Bs160

### EATING

A number of small restaurants offer cheap almuerzos and also cenas, and there are good-value food stalls in the **Mercado Municipal** on Sagárnaga, a block south of Plaza Principal; there's also a cheap **Comedor Municipal** and assorted nocturnal food stalls on Héroes del Chaco, just north of Plaza Principal. At weekends in the high season, many of the restaurants double up as bars.

**El Cafetal** Miranda (near the hospital, 15min walk up from Plaza Principal) ☎ 7193 3979, ⓦ elcafetal.coroico .info; map p.126. Great-value French-run hotel restaurant with panoramic views and delicious food, including llama goulash (Bs50), trout lasagne (Bs63), steak in Roquefort sauce (Bs55), crêpes, soufflés and curries. All that's missing is the French wine, although Tarija supplies a fine substitute. Daily except Tues 8am–8pm.
**Carla's Garden Pub** Pasaje Adalid Linares (50m down the steps beyond Hostal Kory) ☎ 7207 5620; map p.126. Carla van Zetten's relaxed joint with views down the valley does good, simple food and a fine range of beers. It's also home to the *Back-Stube Pasteleria Alemana*, a German-style bakery offering excellent home-made cakes and pastries. Wed–Fri 4–10pm or later, Sat & Sun noon–10pm or later (a light at the top of the stairs tells you if it's still open).
**La Casa** North side of Plaza Principal ☎ 7328 1035; map p.126. Akin to a continental sitting room, complete with cuckoo clock and cheesy European jigsaw scenes, this German/Bolivian-run restaurant serves authentic fondues for a minimum of two people (Bs50 each), as well as dishes

like raclette (Bs50) and goulash (Bs40). Daily 6.30–10.30pm.
**Madres Clarisas** Pasaje Adalid Linares, diagonally opposite *Carla's Garden Pub*; map p.126. The nuns at this convent sell home-made cakes, biscuits and wine; just ring the bell to be let in. Daily 8am–8pm.
**Pizza Italia** South side of Plaza Principal; map p.126. A decent tourist restaurant on the main square, where you can get a variety of pizzas (Bs38–86, depending on size and toppings), and vegetarian (but not vegan) dishes such as gnocchi in blue cheese sauce (Bs40) or a Spanish omelette (Bs30). Daily 8am–11pm.
★**Villa Bonita** Héroes del Chaco; map p.126. This idyllic vegetarian garden café has just a handful of chairs, delightful service and a concise menu with wonderful breakfasts, pastas (Bs35 with walnut or pesto), salads, sandwiches and pancakes. The highlights, however, are the mouthwatering home-made ice creams and sorbets (Bs6/scoop) flavoured with local ingredients like *hierbabuena* (spearmint), lavender and passion fruit: the sundaes should not be missed. Wed–Sun 9am–5pm.

**2**

## HIKES AROUND COROICO

Coroico is surrounded by lush subtropical hills and valleys that offer numerous possibilities for hiking. Although you can do some hikes on your own, it is often safer and easier to go with a guide; they are available from the tourist information office on Plaza Principal (see p.128).

### TO CERRO UCHUMACHI

The hike up **Cerro Uchumachi**, the hill rising above Coroico, takes about two hours there and back. To reach the summit, continue uphill beyond the *Hotel Esmeralda* along a path marked by the Stations of the Cross, which leads to the El Calvario chapel. From here a path climbs to the summit, marked by three wooden crosses; there are excellent views. Although incidents of robbery and rape on the Uchumachi hike have not been reported recently, travellers – and in particular women – are still advised not to go on this hike alone.

### TO PUENTE MURURATA

A difficult to follow but rewarding hike follows the path that heads down into the valley to the **Río Coroico** from beside the football pitch. After about an hour's walk downhill the path hits the main road to Caranavi; turn right and you'll soon reach **Puente Mururata**, a bridge over the stream of the same name, upstream of which there are some pools where you can swim. From the other side of Puente Mururata a path climbs to the left of the road to the peaceful Afro-Yungueño village (see box, p.135) of **Tocaña**, about a twenty-minute walk away.

### THE KORI HUAYKU TRAIL

This trail (around 8–9hr return) starts from Coroico Viejo, near the settlement of Yolosa. Guides can take you through coca fields to the Kori Río Huayku, from where you follow an old Inca trail. There are opportunities to swim and spot monkeys and other wildlife.

---

### DIRECTORY

**Banks and exchange** Banco Fie has an ATM on Plaza Principal, Banco Unión just off it. The Prodem ATM on Plaza Principal doesn't take foreign cards, but you can get cash with your card over the counter inside. Crecer IFD on Plaza Principal will change dollars; QA abogados on Zuazo Cuenca will change dollars and euros.

**Hospital** A 10min walk southeast of town along Pacheco (just past *El Cafetal*).

**Internet** Try Internet Coroico on Rafael Miranda (daily 8am–9pm; Bs4/hr).

**Language lessons** The amiable Siria Leon Domínguez (☎7195 5431, ⓦfacebook.com/siria.leondominguez) offers private Spanish lessons (Bs45/hr).

**Laundry** Launderers opposite the hospital will wash items by hand, usually for around Bs2 per item.

**Post office** There is no longer a post office in town.

## Parque Nacional Cotapata

Around 20km north of La Paz, some four hundred square kilometres of the north face of the Cordillera Real are protected by **PARQUE NACIONAL COTAPATA** (otherwise known as Parque Nacional y Área Natural de Manejo Integrado Cotapata). Ranging in elevation from 1000m to 6000m, Cotapata encompasses many of the astonishing range of different ecosystems and climatic zones formed as the Andes plunge down into the valleys of the upper Amazon Basin. Within a remarkably short distance high mountain peaks, snowfields and *puna* grasslands give way to dense cloudforest, which in turn blends into the humid montane forest that covers the lower slopes of the Andes in a thick green blanket. The **cloudforest** – also known as the *ceja de selva* or "jungle's eyebrows" – is particularly striking, made up of low, gnarled trees and home to many unique bird species, and elusive pumas and spectacled bears.

### The Choro Trail

The only way to experience Cotapata properly is by hiking through the park along the pre-Hispanic **Choro Trail**, although the first part of the hike has been spoiled in recent years by mining works and road building, and is now not as scenic as it once was. Running mainly downhill (quite steeply on the first section – to the extent that it can hurt your knees and you may want to bring walking poles), the 58km trail is easy to follow and can be walked in three to four days. If you have your own camping equipment, a compass and (ideally) a map, it's relatively simple to do without a guide.

### La Cumbre to Chukura

The trail starts near **La Cumbre** (4725m), the high pass 22km north of La Paz. From the lakes just before La Cumbre, head north-northwest to another pass, **Abra Chukura** (4860m), which is marked by a stone cairn (*apacheta*). This 45-minute walk is the only part of the route that is difficult to follow – if in doubt, stick to the rough track winding up to the pass. From the *apacheta*, a well-paved stone path plunges down the left side of the deep valley of the Río Phajchiri, passing the ruins of an Inca waystation, or *tambo*, after an hour or so. After two to three hours you'll reach the small village of **Chukura** (3600m), where there is a local toll of Bs20.

### Chukura to Challapampa and Chairo

Below Chukura the cloudforest begins, the vegetation gradually thickening as you descend. After another hour you reach **Challapampa** (2825m), a small village with a shop and a camping spot by the stream. Three hours down the valley, at the village of **Choro** (2200m), the path crosses over the Río Chukura on a bridge and climbs east along the right-hand side of a deep, densely forested valley – the track is still largely paved and is supported by a well-preserved stone platform in places. Note that robberies have occurred in this area. The next available water and camping spot is another two hours or so away where a stream crosses the path; about three hours beyond that you reach **Casa Sandillani** (2050m). From here it's another two hours down the valley to the end of the trail at the village of **Chairo**.

## ARRIVAL AND DEPARTURE                              PARQUE NACIONAL COTAPATA

**By bus** To reach the Choro Trail, take any bus heading to the Yungas from Terminal Puente Minasa in Villa Fátima in La Paz (see p.74) and get off at La Cumbre. Once you reach Chairo, it's about 16km to Yolosa (see box, p.127). There's regular transport from here on to Coroico (another 7km), and back to La Paz. If you're lucky you'll find a *camioneta*

from Chairo to Yolosa, though it's more likely you'll either have to walk or hire a taxi to take you there (about Bs280).
**By tour** Most trekking agencies in La Paz (see p.76) run tours along the Choro Trail, which include transport. A four-day/three-night trek with America Tours, for example, costs from $350 (Bs2400) per person in a group of four.

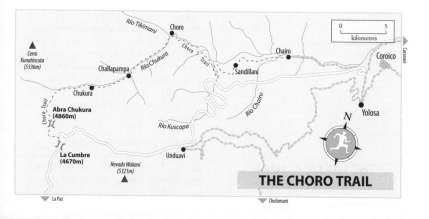

**THE CHORO TRAIL**

**ACCOMMODATION AND EATING**

There is a shop selling soft drinks, beer and food in **Challapampa**. There's a good camping spot by the stream here, though locals will expect you to pay a small fee (around Bs20/person). There's also a campsite a further three hours down the valley, just before the village of **Choro** (also Bs20), and the next one after that is two hours beyond Choro, where a stream crosses the path. You can also camp at **Casa Sandillani**, where there's a small shop. Finally, there's camping and supplies in **Chairo**.

## The Takesi Trail

One of Bolivia's best and most popular treks, the two-day **Takesi Trail** is a fantastic 45km hike starting near La Paz that crosses the Cordillera Real and plunges down into the steamy forested valleys of the Yungas, emerging at the village of **Yanacachi**, west of Chulumani on the road from La Paz. Though it's also known as the Camino del Inca (the Inca Trail), the Takesi existed long before the Incas arrived in the area, and was probably built by the Tiwanaku culture. Whatever the origins, the trail is one of the finest remaining **pre-Columbian** paved roads in Bolivia, and passes through an amazing variety of scenery. Relatively easy to follow and not too strenuous, it's suitable for less experienced trekkers, although note that robberies have occurred on this route, so it's best not to go alone. Most people complete the trail in two or three days depending on their pace. Agencies such as America Tours (see p.76) can organize the trek for you, and arrange mules.

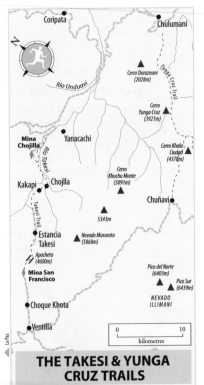

**THE TAKESI & YUNGA CRUZ TRAILS**

### Ventilla to Estancia Takesi

From **Ventilla**, a small village at an altitude of 3200m some 20km east of La Paz, turn left off the main road and follow the clearly signposted track that winds up the Río Palca valley northeast to the village of **Choque Khota**, ninety minutes away. Follow the track uphill for another ninety minutes to the **Mina San Francisco**, where the actual trail begins. From here the path winds steeply uphill, with fine pre-Columbian paving soon evident. After ninety minutes or so you reach the highest point on the trail, a 4600m pass marked by a stone *apacheta* from where there are fantastic views of the looming glacial peak of Mururata (5868m) to the east. The trail continues about ninety minutes northeast down a broad valley, through llama pastures to the herding hamlet of **Estancia Takesi**, passing an abundance of good camping spots along the way. Typically it should take around 6–8 hours to get from Ventilla to Estancia Takesi.

### Estancia Takesi to Yanacachi

Below Estancia Takesi, the path crosses the Río Takesi onto its right bank and gets steadily warmer as the trail drops below 3000m. After two to three hours

## ACHACHILAS AND APUS

To locals, the high mountain peaks are more than just breathtaking natural phenomena. Known as **achachilas** in Aymara and **apus** in Quechua, they're also considered living beings inhabited by powerful spirits. As controllers of weather and the source of vital irrigation water, these mountain gods must be appeased with constant offerings and worship, since if angered they're liable to send hailstorms, frost or drought to destroy crops. At almost every high pass you'll see stone cairns known as **apachetas**. As well as marking the pass on the horizon to make it easier for travellers to find, these *apachetas* are also shrines to the mountain gods. Travellers carry stones up to the pass to add to the *apacheta*, thereby securing the goodwill of the *achachilas* and leaving the burden of their worries behind. Offerings of coca and alcohol are also made at these shrines, which vary in size and form from jumbled heaps of rocks to neatly built piles topped by a cross, depending on the importance of the route and the relative power and visibility of the nearby peaks.

**2**

it reaches the village of **Kakapi**. Continue uphill for half an hour from Kakapi to the small and friendly settlement of **Chojila**. You then descend for 45 minutes until you reach a concrete bridge, marking the end of the old Inca trail. Cross the Río Takesi and turn to the right; after a while, you'll reach an aqueduct, which leads straight to a road (be careful if following the aqueduct in the dark as there are holes in the concrete slabs underfoot). Follow the road around the bend, and take the left, uphill fork to the sulphur mining camp known as **Mina Chojlla**. Unless you get a lift from a passing vehicle, you'll have to follow the road for another two hours to get to the tranquil village of **Yanacachi**, just off the La Paz–Chulumani road. Typically it should take around 6–8 hours to get from Estancia Takesi to Yanacachi.

### ARRIVAL AND DEPARTURE                                    THE TAKESI TRAIL

**By minibus** Several minibuses a day leave for Ventilla from the corner of Luis Lara and Rodriguez in La Paz, two blocks above Illampu (7am–noon; 3hr; Bs25); they return at similar times. Alternatively, you can walk to the main road in about an hour, and then flag down buses (hourly) travelling in either direction between Chulumani and La Paz.

**By taxi** A taxi from La Paz (for 1–3 passengers) costs around Bs430 to Choque Khota or Bs650 to Yanacachi.
**By tour** Trekking agencies in La Paz, including America Tours, Huayna Potosí, Topas Adventure Travel Bolivia and Travel Tracks (see p.76), run tours along the Takesi Trail. A four-day/three-night trek with America Tours, for example, costs from $220 (Bs1500) per person in a group of four.

### ACCOMMODATION AND EATING

Yanacachi has several basic *alojamientos* and places to eat. Basic meals and food supplies are available in the main villages, though it's advisable to carry at least some of your own supplies.

# The Yunga Cruz Trail

Connecting Chuñavi, at the foot of the mighty Mount Illimani, with Chulumani in the Yungas (see p.134), the **Yunga Cruz Trail** (see map, opposite) is at once the toughest, most scenic and most pristine of the three Inca trails that link the Altiplano with the tropical valleys. Instead of following a river, like most Bolivian trails, the path leads along the spine of a giant ridge nearly all the way, giving trekkers a spectacular view of the dramatic landscape. En route it passes the 4378m **Cerro Khala Ciudad** (Stone City Mountain), where condors nest amid its soaring towers. Water is scarce and the weather unpredictable, with heavy rain a possibility even during the dry season: you'll need to carry at least two one-litre water bottles per person and take waterproof clothing. No mules are available in the region, so if you're don't want to carry stuff yourself you'll need to hire porters. Route-finding is fairly difficult and stretches of the trail may be overgrown (with a machete needed); moreover, parts of the trail have been severely disrupted by heavy mining activity, so tours nowadays have to take various diversions to avoid those parts. For these reasons the trail is very difficult to follow independently and the best way to do it is with an organized tour. The trail traditionally starts in **Chuñavi**, a small village on the northeast slopes of Mount Illimani, six hours by road from La Paz, but organized tours nowadays generally start the trek elsewhere.

**By micro** A micro to Chuñavi (5hr) leaves most days at around 7am from the corner of Luis Lara and Boquerón in the Mercado Rodriguez neighbourhood (three blocks above Illampu). See the Chulumani section (see below) for information on the return journey.

**By tour** Andean Summits (see p.76) are one of the few tour agencies currently offering this trek, and they will need a bit of notice to organize it.

# Chulumani

From Unduavi on the road from La Paz to the Yungas, a side road heads east towards the provincial capital of **CHULUMANI**, providing a dramatic ride as it plunges down from the high Andes into the lush vegetation of the Yungas. Chulumani is far less touristy than Coroico, though its setting – at an elevation of 1640m, on a steep hillside overlooking a broad river valley – is equally scenic. With its palm-shaded plaza and steep, dusty, narrow cobbled streets, lined with scruffy houses with red-tiled roofs, Chulumani – whose name is from the Aymara for "where pumas drink water" – is a typical Yungas town, and makes a perfect base for exploring the surrounding countryside. In the 1950s, it was notorious as a hideout for fugitive Nazi war criminals, including Klaus Barbie, the "Butcher of Lyon", who reputedly once sold fruit juices on the plaza.

**By bus** Minibuses from La Paz's Terminal Puente Minasa in Villa Fátima arrive at the *tranca* (police post) on Av Junín, 500m north of Plaza Libertad, and depart from the same place (daily 4am–8pm; depart when full; 4hr–4hr 30min; Bs30).

**Tourist information** The best source of information is Javier Sarabia, owner of the *Country House* (see below), who can advise on hikes from Chulumani; he also runs guided excursions and camping trips, and can arrange bicycle and motorbike rental.

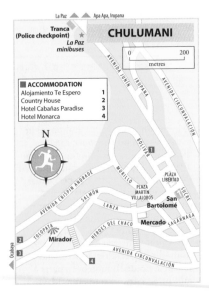

La Paz — Apa Apa, Irupana

**Tranca (Police checkpoint)**
*La Paz minibuses*

**CHULUMANI**

0 — 200
metres

■ **ACCOMMODATION**
Alojamiento Te Espero — 1
Country House — 2
Hotel Cabañas Paradise — 3
Hotel Monarca — 4

N

AVENIDA JUNÍN
IRUPANA
AVENIDA CIRCUNVALACIÓN
BOLÍVAR
MURILLO
PLAZA LIBERTAD
SUCRE
PLAZA MARTÍN VILLALOBOS
San Bartolomé
AVENIDA CRISPÍN ANDRADE
SALMÓN
LANZA
Mercado SAGÁRNAGA
TOLOPATA
Mirador
HÉROES DEL CHACO
AVENIDA CIRCUNVALACIÓN
Ocabaya

## ACCOMMODATION

**Alojamiento Te Espero** Bolívar, two blocks north of Plaza Libertad ☎ 02 2136369; map opposite. The best of a trio of very simple hotels in the centre of town. Bathroom facilities are shared and there's no wi-fi or breakfast, but it's clean and decent enough, and you certainly can't complain about the price. Bs60

★**Country House** Tolopata 13, 1km southeast of town beyond the *mirador* ☎ 7322 9014, ⊛ countryhousebolivia.com; map opposite. This bohemian guesthouse is Chulumani's best option by far, with quirky but very homely rooms set around an eccentric garden with a springwater swimming pool. Walls and shelves are crammed with old wine bottles, magazines, books, art, textiles, insect specimens and random newspaper articles. Helpful English-speaking owner Javier Sarabia is a mine of information and can organize excursions. The tasty breakfast and dinner costs Bs50 extra per meal. Bs200

**Hotel Cabañas Paradise** Tolopata 10 ☎ 7755 6871, ⊛ bit.ly/HotelCabanasParadise; map opposite. Quite a comfy option, featuring rooms with shared-bath or private bathroom, as well as a large lush garden and an outdoor

## AFRO-BOLIVIANOS

Isolated in a handful of villages in the Yungas valleys is perhaps Bolivia's most forgotten ethnic group: the **Afro-Bolivianos**. Numbering about 25,000 today, the Afro-Bolivianos are descendants of African slaves brought to the Andes by the Spanish during the colonial era to work in the Potosí mines. When silver-mining declined they were moved to the Yungas to work on coca and other plantations – their higher natural **resistance to malaria** meant they were more resilient workers than Aymara migrants from the Altiplano. Though slavery was officially abolished with **independence from Spain** in 1825, Bolivia's black population remained in bondage to landowners until the early 1950s. Most subsequently remained in the Yungas to cultivate coca, fruit and coffee.

The Afro-Bolivianos have been heavily influenced by their indigenous neighbours: most speak Aymara as well as Spanish, and many Afro-Bolivian women dress in the bowler hats and *pollera* skirts favoured by the Aymaras. But they also maintain a distinctive cultural identity. The most powerful reminder of their African roots is found in their **music and dance**, such as the intricate and compelling drum-driven rhythms of musical styles like the *saya*. Incorporated into dances like the *Morenada*, seen at the Oruro Carnaval and fiestas throughout the Andes, these rhythms are also reminders of the cultural influence this small group has had on mainstream Bolivian society, despite a tendency by the authorities to ignore their existence.

2

pool, around 800m from the main plaza. It's a little bit run-down, but easy-going and a good standby if the neighbouring *Country House* is full. There's also a restaurant (12.30–8pm) serving trout, pizza and, if ordered in advance, paella. No wi-fi. **$10 (Bs70)**

**Hotel Monarca** Below the town on Av Circumvalación ☏ 7673 6121, ⓦ bit.ly/HotelMonarca; map opposite. Although the front gate is evocative of Alcatraz, this dated holiday-camp-style hotel is friendly enough. The parquet-floored, net-curtained chalets are en suite, have fans and look out onto a huge pool that's seen better days. There's also a bar and a decent restaurant. **Bs240**

### EATING

The selection of places to eat in Chulumani is disappointing, and the better places are usually open only at weekends. There is a decent **restaurant** in *Cabañas Paradise* and another in the *Monarca*, though finding them open is another matter; even if you're a guest, it will usually require some notice. **Stalls** around the market (currently under reconstruction) and around Plaza Libertad offer simple meals, and there are breakfast stalls in Plaza Martín Villalobos, two blocks west of Plaza Libertad.

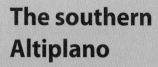

# The southern Altiplano

EL ÁRBOL DE PIEDRA

# The southern Altiplano

South of La Paz, the southern Altiplano – the high plateau between the eastern and western chains of the Andes – stretches 800km to the Chilean and Argentine borders. It was formed millions of years ago by sediments washed down from the mountains into the deep valley between the cordilleras Oriental and Occidental as they were pushed up from the seabed. Set at an average altitude of around 3700m, this starkly beautiful, barren landscape has arid steppes stretching to the horizon, where snowcapped mountains shimmer under deep-blue skies. With scant rainfall and infertile soils it supports only a sparse rural population. Since the Spanish conquest, the Altiplano's prime importance has lain in its rich mineral deposits; its silver deposits have largely run out, but tin and lithium remain.

**3**

The unavoidable transport nexus of the region is the tin-mining city of **Oruro**, 230km south of La Paz. West of Oruro, a chain of snowcapped volcanic peaks – the Cordillera Occidental – marks the border with Chile and the edge of the Altiplano. One of these peaks, **Volcán Sajama**, is Bolivia's tallest mountain and centre of a national park.

Some 310km southeast of Oruro is the legendary silver-mining city of **Potosí**, marooned at 4100m above sea level. From **Uyuni**, 323km south of Oruro, you can venture into the dazzling white **Salar de Uyuni**, the world's biggest salt lake and one of Bolivia's best-known attractions. Beyond the Salar in far southwestern Bolivia is the **Reserva de Fauna Andina Eduardo Avaroa**, a remote region of high-altitude deserts, surreal rock formations, volcanic peaks and mineral-stained lakes that supports great populations of flamingos and vicuñas. Southeast of Uyuni the Altiplano changes character. The town of **Tupiza** is surrounded by the arid red mountains and cactus-strewn badlands of the **Cordillera de Chichas**. Different again is **Tarija**, in the far south, a welcoming city in a fertile valley known as the Andalusia of Bolivia.

The whole region is bitterly **cold** at night, particularly from May to July. Even during the day temperatures can fall sharply, though you'll also need to protect yourself from the fierce, high-altitude sunshine.

**GETTING AROUND**  **THE SOUTHERN ALTIPLANO**

**By road/train** Travel around the region is painfully slow, given that most roads south of Oruro are unpaved; the trains which run between Oruro and Villazón on the Argentine border offer a faster and more comfortable alternative.

RESERVA DE FAUNA ANDINA EDUARDO AVAROA

# Highlights

**❶ Oruro Carnaval** One of South America's liveliest and most colourful fiestas, the Oruro Carnaval features thousands of dancers in extravagant devil costumes. **See p.143**

**❷ Casa Real de la Moneda** The monumental former royal mint in Potosí houses Bolivia's best museum and numerous stunning examples of colonial religious art. **See p.154**

**❸ Potosí's churches** The highest city in the world boasts exceptional Spanish colonial-era architecture and some of the most outstanding churches in the Americas. **See p.157**

**❹ Cerro Rico** A journey into the labyrinthine Cerro Rico mines offers the chance to witness working conditions of incredible harshness, as

well as the bizarre customs and beliefs that help the miners survive them. **See p.162**

**❺ Salar de Uyuni** Perhaps Bolivia's most extraordinary landscape, featuring the world's biggest salt lake – a vast expanse of dazzling white surrounded by mountains. **See p.168**

**❻ Reserva de Fauna Andina Eduardo Avaroa** This remote and spectacular region of icebound volcanic peaks and mineral-stained lakes is home to a surprising array of wildlife, including flamingos and vicuñas. **See p.172**

**❼ Tarija** Enjoy wine from the world's highest vineyards in the self-styled "Andalusia of Bolivia", a charming colonial city in a warm Andean valley. **See p.178**

**HIGHLIGHTS ARE MARKED ON THE MAP ON P.140**

# Parque Nacional Sajama and around

Southwest of La Paz, the road to Chile passes through some of the Altiplano's starkest scenery, a desert plain virtually devoid of vegetation presided over by the perfect snowcapped cone of **Volcán Sajama**. At 6542m, Sajama is Bolivia's highest mountain, and the first in a chain of icebound volcanic peaks known as the Cordillera Occidental that

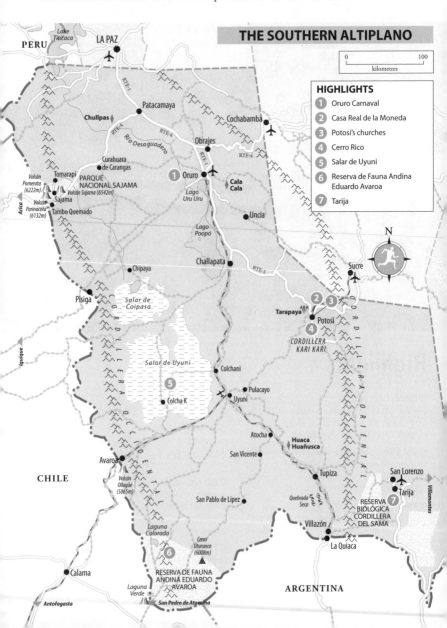

**THE SOUTHERN ALTIPLANO**

0             100
kilometres

**HIGHLIGHTS**

1. Oruro Carnaval
2. Casa Real de la Moneda
3. Potosí's churches
4. Cerro Rico
5. Salar de Uyuni
6. Reserva de Fauna Andina Eduardo Avaroa
7. Tarija

---

### SCALING SAJAMA'S PEAKS

**Mountain climbing** is only allowed between April and October, when the ice on the mountain is sufficiently frozen. To climb Sajama or any of the surrounding peaks, check in at the Centro de Interpretación de Alta Montaña in Sajama village. They can help arrange guides, mules and porters, but you'll need to bring your own equipment and supplies. **Volcán Parinacota**, to the west of the park on the Chilean border, is also a technically simple climb and, as you can drive to the base camp, is particularly popular with climbers eager to conquer a 6000m peak.

---

straddle the Chilean border and mark the edge of the Altiplano – although Sajama stands alone, separated from the rest of the range. Sajama is also the centre of Bolivia's oldest national park, the **PARQUE NACIONAL SAJAMA**, established in 1939 to protect the local population of **vicuñas**, a wild relative of the llama that had been hunted to the verge of extinction for its wool. The animals have since made a dramatic recovery, and large herds can be found grazing 25km or so north of the village at the area known as Patoca.

The park covers roughly one thousand square kilometres, encompassing the entire mountain and a large area of the surrounding desert, where pumas, Andean deer and rheas are also found – though rarely seen. Sajama's slopes also support the world's highest forest, a patch of **queñua** trees that survive up to 5200m. The records don't stop there: in 2001 the highest football match in the world was played in the crater at the top of Sajama.

Most visitors are **climbers**, drawn by the chance to ascend a peak of over 6000m that requires relatively little technical expertise. However, the mountain's lower slopes make for excellent **hiking**, and there are bubbling geysers and hot springs to be explored in the plain below. West of the park on the Chilean border, the two volcanic peaks of **Parinacota** (6132m) and **Pomerata** (6222m) provide a stunning backdrop. Known as the *payachatas* ("twins"), and considered the female consorts of Sajama, these mountains can also be scaled.

## Curahuara de Carangas

Church: Mon–Fri and every other Sat & Sun 8.30am–6pm (if closed in those hours, knock on the door of the parish office next door) • Bs30
• To visit Curahuara de Carangas you will need either your own transport, or to charter a taxi from Patacamaya or Sajama village; some Sajama tours also include a stop-off at the village

En route to the national park, around 49km from Patacamaya, the road to Sajama passes a group of *chullpas* (ancient tombs), which are worth checking out if you're able to stop here. After another 46km, you come to the turn-off for **CURAHUARA DE CARANGAS**, a village 4km off the main road. In the main square is a lovely old **church** dating from the beginning of the seventeenth century, whose walls and ceiling are still decorated with their original **frescoes**, beautifully preserved, and well worth stopping off to see.

### ACCOMMODATION                                 CURAHUARA DE CARANGAS

**Hostal Kory Wara** Curahuara de Carangas ☎ 7197 5356, ✉ hkorywara@hotmail.com. A sweet little place on the road into the village, where the welcome is warm and the rooms are done out in earth colours, each with a bathroom and hot water. There's an old *chullpa* directly opposite the side entrance. No wi-fi. Bs100

## Sajama

The national park's main centre is the village of **SAJAMA** at the foot of the volcano. Here you can find food, accommodation, guides, jeep rental and information. The routes to attractions close to the village are marked with signposts and are reasonably easy to follow. One of the best hikes (3–4hr each way) is up to the **Sajama base camp**, a well-marked trek that offers fantastic views. The **highest forest in the world** is about thirty minutes' walk up from Sajama village, though it's not overly impressive.

### The geyser field

The **geyser field** roughly 8km west of the village in the foothills of the *payachatas* is a good excursion. An easy walk (around 1hr 30min) along a well-defined trail, the geyser field is made up of 87 different pools of boiling water. The mixture of mineral salts and algae that thrive in the warm waters creates bizarre colours, including blood reds, shiny greens and sulphurous yellows. On no account should you bathe in any of the geysers, as temperatures can change rapidly.

### Aguas termales

4km north of the village • Daily 8am–6pm • Bs30

If you fancy a soak, there are some **aguas termales** (hot springs) about 4km north of the village, along an easy-to-follow trail. The natural hot water is fed into an open-air pool, making it a fantastic place to ease your aching limbs while enjoying the scenery.

## ARRIVAL AND INFORMATION                                                SAJAMA

**By guided tour** By far the easiest way to visit the park is on a tour from La Paz with an operator (see p.76) such as America Tours, Kanoo, Millenarian Travel or Topas. A variety of tours is available: Kanoo for example offer a two-day tour (from $217/Bs1480 per person) which includes the Curahuara de Carangas, a two-hour hike and a visit to the geyser field; their three-day tour (from $263/Bs1800 per person) throws in a visit to the hot springs, while their four-day tour (from $540/Bs3675 per person) includes climbing Mt Sorata.

**By bus** From the town of Patacamaya, a few kilometres off the La Paz–Oruro highway (reached by *surubi* minibus from Ceja terminal at the entrance to El Alto – served by minibuses along the Prado showing "Ceja" – or by micro from Oruro or Cochabamba) there's a single daily micro to Sajama village, operated by Sindicato Trans Sajama, leaving at 1pm (Mon–Sat) from *Capitol Restaurant* in the

middle of town, or at 1.30pm (Sun) from the marketplace six blocks west. Buses from La Paz to Arica in Chile (from the Terminal de Buses La Paz; 4 daily) also stop in Patacamaya, or can drop you at the Sajama turn-off, 12km from the village. You can call ahead to the *Hostal Sajama* or to ☎7408 3873 or ☎7372 2394 to arrange for a vehicle to pick you up and bring you to the village (Bs80), but a lot of people just walk (2hr 30min–3hr).

**Park entrance fee** Buy your park entry ticket (Bs100) at the office on the way into Sajama (1km from the turn-off, 11km from Sajama itself; daily 9.30am–6pm). Keep your ticket with you in the park as you may need to show it.

**Park transport and guides** Most of the hotels and lodgings in Sajama can arrange transport and trekking guides (around Bs550/day) to places within the park.

## ACCOMMODATION AND EATING

Several places in Sajama, including most of the lodgings, serve simple and inexpensive breakfasts and set meals, though it's best to order a few hours in advance. There are a few **shops** selling basic foodstuffs.

**Albergue Tomarapi** Tomarapi village, 12km from Sajama village ☎7247 2785, ⓦecotomarapi.com. This community-run place has basic though clean rooms with wooden floors in thatched bungalows with heaters, private bathrooms and hot water. Staff can organize trekking guides and excursions. No wi-fi. Price includes full board. **Bs550**

**Hostal Sajama** Sajama village ☎7150 9158, ⓔeliseosajama@hotmail.com. There are lots of lodgings in Sajama, with prices as low as Bs30 per person, but this is the best and most comfortable, with cute little thatched huts, neat and fresh, with wooden floors, attached bathrooms and hot water. No wi-fi. Call ahead to arrange transport from the Sajama turn-off. **Bs200**

### CROSSING THE CHILEAN BORDER VIA TAMBO QUEMADO

Crossing into Chile is straightforward: the Chilean border is 9km west of the turn-off to Sajama at **Tambo Quemado**. There's a *migración* where you get your exit stamp and a couple of restaurants. If you're coming **from La Paz**, the bus will take you all the way through to Arica on Chile's Pacific coast, though you may want to stop off at the Parque Nacional Lauca, which encompasses similar scenery to the Parque Nacional Sajama. To get to Chile **from Sajama** is a lot harder: you'll need to get to the turn-off 12km from the village and flag down a La Paz–Arica bus, of which there are only four a day; you can board them more reliably at Patacamaya (see above).

# Oruro

Huddled on the bleak Altiplano some 230km south of La Paz, **ORURO** was Bolivia's economic powerhouse for much of the twentieth century, centre of the country's richest **tin-mining** region. Mines established in the nearby mountains in the late nineteenth century turned Oruro into a thriving industrial city. After the fall of world tin prices in 1985, however, Oruro's fortunes plummeted, and though it's still the biggest city in the Altiplano after La Paz and El Alto, years of economic decline have turned it into a shadow of its former self. Although a few buildings dating from Oruro's heyday still survive, the city is dominated by the unappealing, functional architecture you'd expect to find in a mining town at the wrong end of half a century of decline. Situated 3709m above sea level and swept by bitter Altiplano winds, Oruro is a cold and rather sombre place. This dour demeanour is deceptive, however, as every year Oruro explodes into life when it celebrates its **Carnaval** (see box, below).

## Brief history

Originally named the Villa Imperial de Don Felipe de Austria in honour of the reigning Spanish king, Felipe III, Oruro was **founded** on November 1, 1606, a decade after the discovery of rich **silver** deposits in the nearby Cerro Pie de Gallo. Though its mines never rivalled Potosí's, Oruro grew quickly, and by the 1670s was the second-biggest city in Alto Peru, with a population of about eighty thousand.

Oruro was the biggest Spanish city to be captured in the **Great Rebellion** of 1780–81 (p.305), when its mestizos and criollos joined the indigenous uprising, massacring the Spanish-born population. The alliance didn't last long: the rebel army raised from the *ayllus* of the surrounding Altiplano soon turned on the criollos, looting and burning

## DANCING WITH THE DEVIL: THE ORURO CARNAVAL

A moveable feast celebrated in late February or early March, the **Oruro Carnaval** is Bolivia's most spectacular fiesta. During the week-long party thousands of costumed dancers parade through Oruro in a vibrant and bizarre celebration of the sacred and profane that combines Christian beliefs with Andean folklore – as well as heavy drinking and chaotic water-fighting.

On the first Sunday of November the Santuario del Socavón church hosts a special Mass, and rehearsals are then held every subsequent Sunday until Carnaval itself. The Carnaval's main event is the **Entrada** on the Saturday before Ash Wednesday, a massive procession of costumed dancers accompanied by brass bands. The parade is led by floats festooned with offerings for the Virgen del Socavón (see p.146), in whose honour the Carnaval is held. Behind them comes the Carnaval's central feature, the **Diablada** (Dance of the Devils), led by two dancers representing Lucifer and St Michael, followed by hundreds of devil dancers, and massed brass bands.

On the one hand, the Diablada is a morality play in which the Archangel Michael triumphs over the Devil of Christian belief. But it also celebrates the devil as an incarnation of **Huari**, the pre-Columbian god of the underworld – closely related to El Tío (see box, p.163) – who owns the mineral wealth of the mines and is a patron of the miners dancing in his honour.

Behind the Diablada follow other costumed dance troupes, each with its own folk history and mythology. The dancing and drinking continues into Sunday morning, and the procession also continues on Sunday. On Monday, the troupes conduct their **despedida fiestas**, saying their farewells until the following year. Finally, on Ash Wednesday, with the carnival over, townsfolk visit a series of rocks on the outskirts of Oruro to make **offerings** to what are claimed to be the petrified remains of the fearsome beasts defeated by the Virgin to save the town.

### CARNAVAL PRACTICALITIES

The main procession route is lined with benches that are rented out (Bs155–250/day) by the shop or house in front of which they stand or the tourist offices. Gringos are popular targets for foam and water-bomb attacks, so be prepared to get soaked – and to strike back.

**3**

3

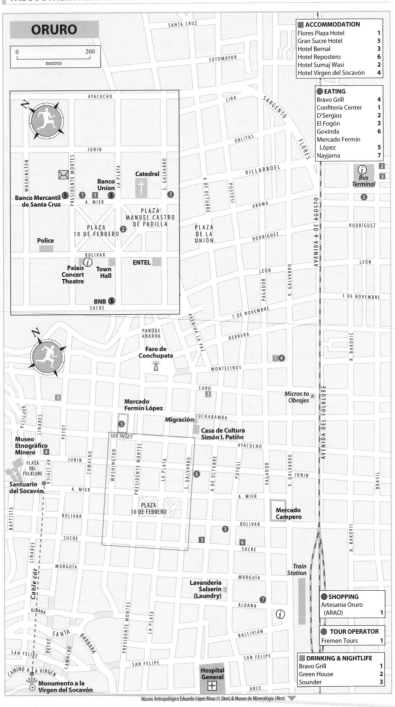

**ORURO**

0 _____ 200
metres

Museo Antropológico Eduardo López Rivas (1.5km) & Museo de Mineralógia (4km) ▼

their houses and killing their leader, Sebastián Pagador, before meeting the same fate themselves at the hands of the royalist army when it retook the city.

Oruro changed hands several times during the **Independence War** (1809–24), and its economy was severely disrupted. The city gradually recovered as silver production grew again, aided by foreign capital, improved industrial technology and the completion of a railway linking Oruro with the Pacific coast in 1892. The railway meant Oruro was perfectly placed to exploit the growing world demand for **tin**, which was found in great abundance in the surrounding mountains.

The three entrepreneurs who controlled most of Oruro's **mines** – Aramayo, Hochschild and Patiño – came to dominate national politics, but their treatment of the miners sowed the seeds of their downfall. The FSTMB mineworkers' union, which emerged in Oruro, played a key role in the 1952 revolution that led to nationalization of the mines. However, when the price of tin crashed in 1985, the mining industry collapsed, and with it went the power of the miners' union and Oruro's economic fortunes; most of the mines were closed and thousands lost their jobs. Although some (mainly gold and tin) mines have opened since, Oruro has never really recovered.

**3**

## Plaza 10 de Febrero

In the city centre, **Plaza 10 de Febrero** is named after the date on which the people of Oruro joined the Great Rebellion of 1781 (now a public holiday in the province). It has a statue of Aniceto Arce, the president who oversaw the construction of the vital first railway link between Oruro and the coast in 1892. A few buildings here hint at past prosperity, most notably the **town hall** on the southeast corner, the **Palais Concert Theatre** a few doors along and the grandiose **post office** a block north on Avenida Presidente Montes.

## Casa de Cultura Simón I. Patiño

Northwest of Plaza 10 de Febrero on Soria Galvarro • Guided tours Mon–Fri hourly 9am–noon & 3–6pm, Sat 9am–3pm • Bs8 • ☎ 02 5254015

The **Casa de Cultura Simón I. Patiño** is the city's best reminder of the great wealth the Oruro mines once produced. This elegant Neoclassical palace was built as a townhouse for the eponymous tin baron (see box, p.146) in the early years of the twentieth century, though by the time it was completed he no longer lived in Bolivia. Many rooms have been maintained in their original state: the astonishingly opulent living quarters, complete with Venetian crystal chandeliers, Louis XV furniture and Persian carpets, are set around a beautifully tiled, glass-roofed central patio.

## Faro de Conchupata

Entrance at La Plata and Montecinos • No fixed opening times • Free

Three blocks up Soria Galvarro from the Casa Cultura, a left turn takes you up a steep hill to the **Faro de Conchupata**, a lighthouse monument built to commemorate the first raising of the current Bolivian national flag, which took place on this site in 1851. The lighthouse serves no practical purpose but – municipal budget permitting – still lights up every evening. There are good views from its base.

## Avenida La Paz

Most of the city's Carnaval costumes and masks are made in workshops on **Avenida La Paz**, which runs northwards parallel to Soria Galvarro, and it's worth strolling along the street to have a look at the beautiful craftsmanship. As well as being very expensive, most of the masks are too bulky and delicate to make good souvenirs, though some shops sell affordable pocket-sized copies.

**3**

---

## THE KING OF TIN: SIMÓN PATIÑO

Few individuals played a greater role in shaping modern Bolivia than tin baron **Simón Patiño**, who rose from humble mestizo origins to become one of the world's richest men, popularly known as the "Rockefeller of the Andes" and the "King of Tin". Born in 1860 to a poor family in the Cochabamba valley, Patiño moved to Oruro in 1894 to work in a mining supply store. A year later he bought his first share in the nearby **La Salvadora mine**, and in 1897 bought out his partner to control what turned out to be one of the biggest deposits of **high-grade tin** in the world. Legend has it that at first he and his wife Albina dug out the precious ore with their own hands, carried it downhill in wheelbarrows and then across country by llama train. But in 1900 Patiño struck one of the richest veins of ore ever found in Bolivia, which was to make his fortune.

By 1905, La Salvadora was the **country's most productive mine**, operated by foreign technicians with high-tech equipment. Patiño used the wealth it generated to buy up the surrounding mines and link them to the main railway line to the coast. Within fifteen years he controlled **about half of Bolivia's tin output**, was the country's most important private banker, and enjoyed an income far greater than the government, which he effectively controlled. This wealth came at the expense of the thousands of miners he employed, who suffered low pay, appalling working conditions and **severe oppression**.

Patiño also expanded his empire internationally, buying up mining interests and foundries in Asia, Africa, Germany, the USA and Britain. This corporation controlled the entire production process for about a quarter of the world's tin and played an important role in **setting international prices**. By the early 1920s his fortune was estimated at **$100 million**, making him one of the five richest men in the world. Despite this, Patiño never really overcame the prejudices of Bolivia's white elite, and from 1924 onwards he lived permanently abroad. In 1925 he moved his corporate base to the USA, but spent most of his time in London, Paris and the French Riviera. Rumoured to have Nazi sympathies, he was said to have helped finance Franco's victory in the Spanish Civil War. He died in Buenos Aires in 1947 and thus never lived to see the nationalization of his Bolivian mine holdings.

---

## Santuario del Socavón

Five blocks west of the Plaza 10 de Febrero at the foot of the Pie de Gallo mountain • Daily 7am–6pm • Free

The **Santuario del Socavón** (Sanctuary of the Mineshaft) is home to the image of the Virgen del Socavón, the patron saint of miners, in whose honour the Carnaval celebrations are staged. The sanctuary was first built around 1781 to shelter the image, and later expanded and rebuilt. It's now a rather haphazard construction, with a modern concrete shell, a stone nineteenth-century bell tower, and an elegant older portico. Inside, the high, arched ceiling is painted with bright **frescoes** of the Virgen del Socavón defending Oruro from various supernatural menaces.

Painstakingly restored, the main **image of the Virgen del Socavón**, painted on an adobe wall behind the altar, depicts the Virgin Mary in a blue robe being crowned by two cherubs. It is said to have appeared miraculously in the late eighteenth century in the abandoned mineshaft over which the church is built. The mineshaft was used as a hideout by **Chiru-Chiru**, a bandit with a reputation for stealing from the rich and giving to the poor. As he lay mortally wounded in the mine after a shoot-out with the authorities, Chiru-Chiru repented before a vision of the Virgin; after his death, her image was discovered painted on the wall beside his body. His deathbed scene is depicted in one of the church's stained-glass windows.

At the time of research, a **cable car** was under construction linking the **Plaza del Folklore** – a broad, paved square directly in front of the Santuario del Socavón, where the climax of the Carnaval procession takes place – to the **Monumento a la Virgen del Socavón**, a giant statue of the Virgin on a hill west of town, which has great panoramic views over Oruro.

### Museo Etnográfico Minero

Underneath the Santuario del Socavón • Daily 9–11.30am & 3.15–5.30pm • Bs10 • ☎ 02 5277860

The abandoned mineshaft beneath the Santuario del Socavón houses the **Museo**

**Etnográfico Minero**, which looks at the history of mining from the miners' perspective. Guided tours (in Spanish) take you into the mine via a flight of steps at the back of the church. On your way down, you'll see a life-sized statue of Chiru-Chiru. At the bottom of the shaft the mine gallery is lined with an interesting collection of **mining equipment**. At one end of the shaft stand two statues of **El Tío**, the devil-like figure worshipped by Bolivian miners (see box, p.163). A section upstairs is filled with Carnaval paraphernalia.

## Museo Antropológico Eduardo López Rivas

On Av España in the city's southern outskirts • Mon–Fri 10am–6pm • Bs5 • ☏ 02 5274020 • A long walk (eight blocks south from the station to Lizárraga, then eleven blocks west), short taxi ride (Bs10–15), or micro (Zona Sur, Zoológico) heading south from Plaza 10 de Febrero

The **Museo Antropológico Eduardo López Rivas** has an extensive collection of artefacts, ranging from ancient stone axes and arrowheads to Carnaval masks and costumes. Sadly, though, most of the displays are poorly explained, with little background information. Many exhibits are from the **Aymara** or **Colla** kingdoms that dominated the Altiplano between the fall of Tiwanaku and the Inca conquest of the region in the fifteenth century. Another section of the museum is dedicated to the **Chipayas** and the **Urus** (see p.150).

## Museo de Mineralogía

A few kilometres southwest of the city on Calle Universidad • Mon–Fri 8.30am–noon & 2.30–5.30pm • Bs10 • ☏ 02 5261250 • Take a taxi (Bs10–15) or any micro marked "Ciudad Universitaria" from outside the train station

The **Museo de Mineralogía** has one of South America's biggest collections of minerals – about four thousand pieces. Of most interest to those with a specialist interest in geology or mineralogy, the bewildering variety of shapes and colours is still impressive.

### ARRIVAL AND DEPARTURE ORURO

**By plane** BoA (ⓦ boa.bo) fly from Oruro airport, around 3.5km east of the city centre (Bs20–30 by taxi), to Cochabamba (1–2 daily; 30min) and Santa Cruz (5 weekly; 50min).

**By train** Oruro is at the centre of what's left of Bolivia's railway network. Trains (ⓦ www.fca.com.bo) south to Villazón via Uyuni and Tupiza depart from the train station, just east of the centre at Av Galvarro and Aldana. The *Expreso del Sur* (departs Tues & Fri, returns Thurs & Sun) is quicker and more comfortable than the cheaper *Wara Wara del Sur* (departs Wed & Sun, returns Tues & Fri).

Destinations Tupiza (4 weekly; 12hr 30min–13hr 35min); Uyuni (4 weekly; 6hr 50min–7hr 20min); Villazón (4 weekly; 15hr 35min–17hr 5min).

**By bus** All buses heading south or west from La Paz pass through Oruro. Buses between Tarija and La Paz will drop you off on Av Ejército on the eastern outskirts of the city. Most other long-distance buses pull in at the Terminal Terrestre, ten blocks northeast of the centre on Villarroel; a taxi into town should cost Bs10–15, or take any micro heading south along Av 6 de Agosto.

Destinations Cochabamba (6–7 daily; 5–8hr); Iquique, Chile (17 daily; 8hr); La Paz (1–3 hourly; 3hr 30min); Potosí (roughly hourly; 5hr); Santa Cruz (1 daily; 12–14hr; or via Cochabamba); Sucre (2 daily; 10–12hr); Uyuni (12 overnight buses; 7–9hr).

### INFORMATION AND TOURS

#### TOURIST INFORMATION

There's a tourist information kiosk just outside the bus station (Mon–Fri 9am–noon & 2.30–6.30pm; ☏ 02 5287774), another opposite the train station (opens to meet train arrivals) and a third in the Palais Concert Theatre on Plaza 10 de Febrero (Mon–Fri 9am–noon & 2.30–6.30pm; ☏ 02 5250144), but the official opening hours should be taken with a pinch of salt.

#### TOUR OPERATORS

**Charlie Tours** Av Tomas Barron 555, between calles 9 and 10 in Barrio Miraflores, north of the centre ☏ 02 5240666, ⓔ charlietours@yahoo.com. Specializes in tours of the region, including visits to mines, to ancient cave paintings at Cala Cala (see p.149) and to local indigenous communities, but also runs trips further afield, including to Parque Nacional Sajama (see p.140).

**Fremen Tours** Suite 18, 1st floor, Edificio Pinto, Bolívar 513 ☏ 02 5281054, ⓦ bit.ly/FremenTours; map p.144. The local branch of the well-regarded Cochabamba tour firm (see p.213).

3

**3**

## ACCOMMODATION

There's a decent range of places to stay, though everything fills up during **Carnaval** (in late Feb or early March), when prices go up by as much as five times, and most places only rent rooms for a minimum of three nights. It's best to book well in advance, though even if you arrive the day before you should be able to find a place to sleep in a **private home** – ask at one of the tourist offices.

**Flores Plaza Hotel** Adolfo Mier 735 ☎ 02 5252561, ⓦ floresplazahotel.com; map p.144. This modern hotel overlooking the main plaza couldn't be more central. The rooms are clean and functional: all are en suite and have TVs; those at the top also have great views. **Bs450**

**Gran Sucre Hotel** Sucre 519 ☎ 02 5276800, ⓔ hotelsucreoruro@hotmail.com; map p.144. There's bags of character at this old hotel which harks back to Oruro's heyday, with elegant wood-panelled corridors and a glass-roofed ballroom (where breakfast is now served). The slightly overpriced rooms are cosy with floral furnishings, private bathrooms, TVs and phones. **Bs360**

**Hotel Bernal** Av Brasil 701 at Aroma ☎ 02 5279468; map p.144. Rooms at this place opposite the bus station are dilapidated but decent value, with abundant hot water in the private or shared bathrooms; the quieter rooms are at the back. **Bs120**

**Hotel Repostero** Sucre 370 ☎ 02 5258001; map p.144.

Decent mid-range hotel in a once elegant nineteenth-century building. The classier upstairs rooms (Bs250) overlook a sunny courtyard, and have comfortable beds, private bathrooms and TVs; there are also some less comfortable economy rooms on the ground floor. **Bs200**

**Hotel Sumaj Wasi** Av Brasil 232 at Aroma ☎ 02 5276737, ⓦ hotelessamaywasi.com; map p.144. Handily located just opposite the bus terminal, this good-value, mid-range option has clean and comfortable en-suite rooms with TVs. Road noise can be an issue, however. **Bs270**

**Hotel Virgen del Socavón** Junín 1179 ☎ 02 5282184, ⓔ hotelvirgendelsocavon@hotmail.com; map p.144. This excellent hotel is situated across the street from the Plaza del Folklore, making it a perfect base for Carnaval. There is a strong Christian theme to the modern decor, including a crucifix above the bed, which may surprise some guests. There's also a sauna. **Bs420**

## EATING

Most restaurants don't open until mid-morning (and are closed on Sun), but early breakfasts can be had at the **Mercado Campero**. On Friday and Saturday nights restaurants and bars stay open late. A local speciality is **rostro asado** (roasted sheep's head), sold at night (around 10.30pm–2am, especially Friday and Saturday) from street stalls on Avenida 6 de Octubre between Montecinos and Junín; restaurants tend to serve more conventional roast lamb dishes like *mecheado* and *brazuelo*.

**Bravo Grill** Montecinos between Pagador and Velasco Galvarro ☎ 02 5280980; map p.144. The speciality at this rather meaty restaurant is steak stuffed with cheese and ham (Bs65), or you can hedge your bets with a triple grill combo of chicken breast, pork chop and prawns (Bs80); the Bs22 lunchtime set menu is a bargain. Mon & Tues noon–3pm, Wed–Sat noon–3pm & 5–11pm, Sun 11am–3pm.

**Confitería Center** Plaza 10 de Febrero; map p.144. This mellow café-bar right on the main square attracts an older crowd with decent coffee, juices and sandwiches (Bs9–13), plus a few meat dishes (Bs50), giving way to beers and spirits (if you ask for them) in the evening. Daily 8am–midnight.

**D'Sergios** Plaza 10 de Febrero ☎ 02 5253820; map p.144. In a prime spot opposite the main square, this appealing, if slightly shambolic, restaurant has local artworks on the walls and specializes in pizzas (Bs60–80) and ice-cream sundaes (Bs18–25). Mon–Sat 9am–1.30pm & 3.30pm–midnight.

**El Fogón** San Felipe and Brasil ☎ 02 5279456, ⓦ bit.ly/ElFogonOruro; map p.144. A convenient restaurant near the bus terminal, specializing in pork dishes (mains Bs60–90) such as *lechón* (roast pork) and *chicharrón* (deep-fried pork), and *charque* (dried llama meat, similar to jerky), all

accompanied by *wa'tya* (potatoes cooked in a traditional earth oven). Daily 7am–10pm.

**Govinda** Junín 533 ☎ 02 5255205; map p.144. This low-priced Hare Krishna-run vegetarian restaurant (no meat, fish, eggs, onions or garlic) isn't vegan – they use dairy products – but vegan versions of most things are available, and it's a great place for a healthy snack. There are soya burgers (Bs8), samosas (Bs7), pasta and freshly blended fruit *licuados* made with a choice of water, milk, soya milk or yoghurt. Mon–Sat noon–2pm & 4–10pm.

**Mercado Fermín López** Ayacucho 856 (with other entrances on Cochabamba and Washington); map p.144. This is the city's most central market. Stalls on the west side (off Washington) serve breakfast from 5am until around 11am, but the main eating section is the *Comedor Popular* right in the middle, where lunch stalls start serving around 11am, and you can eat heartily for Bs10 or less. Some food stalls stay open until closing time, but most wind up around 2pm. For dessert, try the red cinnamon sorbet (Bs5 a cup), served at two stalls (10am–6pm) by the market's northeastern entrance, on Cochabamba. Daily 5am–8pm.

**Nayjama** Pagador 1880 at Aldana ☎ 02 5277699; map p.144. One of Oruro's best restaurants, serving vast portions of tasty dishes (mains Bs50–150) like roast lamb, fresh *pejerry* (kingfish) and *surubí* (catfish), and a mixed grill known as "*El Intendente*" after the visiting government official who devised it. And if you're not too squeamish, they also have *criadillos* (bull's testicles; Bs75). Mon–Sat 11.30am–9pm, Sun 11.30am–3pm.

### DRINKING AND NIGHTLIFE

**Bravo Grill** Montecinos between Pagador and Velasco Galvaro ☎02 5280980; map p.144. Popular disco bar and karaoke club underneath the *Bravo Grill* restaurant and run by the same management. Wed–Sun 9am–3am.

**Green House** Caro 511 (between 6 de Octubre and Soria Galvarro) ☎6182 4094; map p.144. A dark and decidedly underground-style café with a club at the back playing techno, house and electronica. Free entry Thurs & Fri, Bs20 Sat. Thurs 7pm–3am, Fri & Sat 7pm–sunrise.

**Sounder** Petot 1140 at Cochabamba ☎02 5255915, ⓦfacebook.com/complejosounder; map p.144. Oruro's most popular disco (it claims to be the biggest in Bolivia) plays jolly music to a jolly crowd into the wee hours. Not exactly cutting-edge, but fun. Thurs–Sat 10pm–4am, Sun 11am–3pm & 10pm–4am.

### SHOPPING

**Artesania Oruro (ARAO)** Soria Galvarro 5999 ☎02 5250331, ⓦartesaniasoruro.com; map p.144. This fair-trade outlet for rural craft workers in the region has a decent selection of the usual crafts: sweaters, scarves, hats and gloves, plus keyrings, earrings, little figurines and felt slippers. Mon–Fri 9am–12.30pm & 3–7.30pm, Sat 10.30am–5.30pm.

### DIRECTORY

**Banks and exchange** Banks with ATMs include BNB at Plata 6160 at Sucre, and Banco Mercantil de Santa Cruz on Adolfo Mier at Presidente Montes (in the northwest corner of Plaza 10 de Febrero). There's a money changer in the bus station, but their rates aren't great.

**Hospital** Hospital General, San Felipe between 6 de Octubre and Potosí (☎02 5275405).

**Internet** There are innumerable cybercafés in Oruro, especially in the streets around the Plaza 10 de Febrero. There's a free wi-fi zone outside ENTEL in the southeast corner of Plaza Manuel Castro de Padilla.

**Laundry** Numerous, including Lavandería Salcerín, Potosí 6324.

**Post office** Half a block north of Plaza 10 de Febrero on Presidente Montes.

# Around Oruro

There is a handful of worthwhile excursions around Oruro. If you're in need of some relaxation, head to the **thermal baths** at **Obrajes**, 25km away. **Cala Cala** is the site of ancient rock paintings, while **Lago Uru Uru** is home to hundreds of flamingos during the rainy season.

## Obrajes hot springs

About 25km northeast of Oruro in Obrajes • Daily 7am–6pm • Bs15 • Micros (every 30min or so; around 30min) head to Obrajes from the corner of Av 6 de Agosto and Caro

The **hot springs** (*aguas termales*) at Obrajes are a good place to soak away the chill of the Altiplano. The thermal baths are fed by hot springs with reputedly curative powers, and there are also more expensive private baths for rent, as well as places to buy drinks and snacks, and an overpriced restaurant.

## Cala Cala

26km southeast of Oruro • No fixed hours • Bs20 • A taxi will cost around Bs120 for the round trip with waiting time

The archeological site of **Cala Cala** (whose name means "rock rock" in Aymara) is home to a group of 2500-year-old rock paintings of llamas, other animals and human figures, in red, white and black. The paintings, on a rock face under an overhang and accessed via a wooden walkway, lie 2km beyond the village of Cala Cala, where you'll need to find the

**3**

---

### THE UNIQUE CHIPAYA COMMUNITY

About 180km southwest of Oruro, the remote village of Chipaya is home to the **Chipayas**, an ethnic group culturally and linguistically distinct from both the Aymaras and Quechuas. Now confined to a small territory in this desolate region, the Chipayas are thought to have descended from the **Urus** (see p.150). Driven into the unforgiving environment of this remote corner of the Altiplano over several centuries under population pressure from the Aymaras, the Chipayas eke out a marginal living by growing quinoa, fishing and catching aquatic birds. Despite their desperate poverty, they have maintained their unique language, culture and religious beliefs, and many of the village's buildings are still distinctive **circular huts** with doors made from cactus and roofs thatched with aquatic reeds. If you're interested in seeing something of Chipaya daily life, contact **Charlie Tours** in Oruro (see p.147).

---

caretaker to go and see them. There's no public transport, so unless you go with an operator such as Charlie Tours (see p.147), you'll need to have your own vehicle or charter a taxi.

## Lago Uru Uru and the Chilean border

Roughly 12km southeast of Oruro, **Lago Uru Uru** is a shallow, brackish lake fed by the Río Desaguadero, which drains the overflow from Lake Titicaca to the north. During the rainy season (between January and March, or later if it has been a wet year) you may see hundreds of flamingos here. The marshy fringes of the lake have long been home to small communities of **Urus**, the oldest ethnic group of the Altiplano. South of Lago Uru Uru, on the way to the market centre and road junction of Challapata, you pass the shallow, brackish waters of **Lago Poopó**, Bolivia's second-largest lake. Flamingos are sometimes spotted here, though mining pollution has greatly reduced their numbers.

From the north side of Lago Uru Uru a rough road heads southwest towards the **Chilean border** at Pisiga, 228km from Oruro, though relatively few travellers use this route. It cuts across the northern fringes of the lake along a colonial-era raised causeway, the **Puente Español**, a thirty-minute drive from Oruro. From the start of the causeway, a short walk around the lakeshore to the northwest takes you to **Chusaqueri**, a virtually abandoned farming hamlet overlooked by about a dozen **chullpas** (pre-Columbian tombs). These 2m-high adobe structures sit on solid stone platforms, with narrow doorways and roofs tiled with flat stones.

# Potosí

*I am rich Potosí, treasure of the world, king of the mountains, envy of kings.*

Legend on Potosí's coat of arms

On a desolate, windswept plain amid barren mountains at almost 4100m above sea level, **POTOSÍ** is the highest city in the world, and at once the most fascinating and tragic place in Bolivia. It owes its existence to **Cerro Rico** (Rich Mountain), which rises imperiously above the city to the south. Cerro Rico was the richest source of silver the world had ever seen: its mines turned Potosí into the most valuable jewel in the Spanish emperors' crown, and one of the world's wealthiest and largest cities. In the early seventeenth century its population was 160,000, far bigger than Madrid, and equal in size to London. The expression "*eso vale un Potosí*" ("this is worth a Potosí") was used in colloquial Spanish to describe anything priceless. However, this wealth was achieved at the expense of the lives of millions of indigenous forced labourers and African slaves.

Today, Potosí, a UNESCO World Heritage Site, is a treasure-trove of **colonial art and architecture**; it has more than two thousand colonial buildings, many of which have been restored. The colonial royal mint is the city's most outstanding monument, but there are also hundreds of townhouses and mansions, complete with red-tiled roofs and

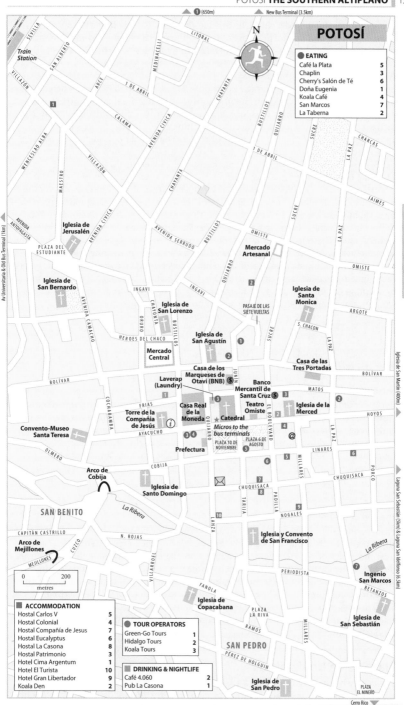

**EATING**

| | |
|---|---|
| Café la Plata | 5 |
| Chaplin | 3 |
| Cherry's Salón de Té | 6 |
| Doña Eugenia | 1 |
| Koala Café | 4 |
| San Marcos | 7 |
| La Taberna | 2 |

**ACCOMMODATION**

| | |
|---|---|
| Hostal Carlos V | 5 |
| Hostal Colonial | 4 |
| Hostal Compañía de Jesus | 7 |
| Hostal Eucalyptus | 6 |
| Hostal La Casona | 8 |
| Hostal Patrimonio | 3 |
| Hotel Cima Argentum | 1 |
| Hotel El Turista | 10 |
| Hotel Gran Libertador | 9 |
| Koala Den | 2 |

**TOUR OPERATORS**

| | |
|---|---|
| Green-Go Tours | 1 |
| Hidalgo Tours | 2 |
| Koala Tours | 3 |

**DRINKING & NIGHTLIFE**

| | |
|---|---|
| Café 4.060 | 2 |
| Pub La Casona | 1 |

decorative balconies, and a clutch of striking churches. Potosí's **tragic history** weighs heavily though, and is evident in the sense of sadness that seems to haunt its narrow streets and the appalling conditions still endured by miners at Cerro Rico.

### A brief history of silver in Potosí

Legend has it the **Incas** were on the point of mining Cerro Rico in 1462 when a supernatural voice warned them that the gods were saving the silver for others who would come from afar. Inca Huayna Capac subsequently declared the mountain sacrosanct, naming it *Ppotojsi* (Quechua for "thunder" or "burst"). The silver was apparently rediscovered in 1545 by llama herder **Diego Huallpa**. Caught after dark on Cerro Rico, he started a fire to keep warm, and a trickle of molten silver ran out from the blaze. News of this reached the Spaniards, and a **silver rush** was soon under way. Over the next twenty years Potosí became the richest source of silver in the world.

Surface deposits with high ore contents were easily extracted and processed, but as these ran out, and shaft mining developed, the purity of the ore declined and production costs rose. Labour also became increasingly scarce, thanks to the appalling conditions in the mines. These problems were tackled by **Viceroy Francisco de Toledo**, who arrived in Potosí in 1572 and orchestrated the construction of a massive system of dams, artificial lakes and aqueducts to power the water wheels that crushed the ore for processing. He also introduced the new amalgam process for refining silver using mercury, established the first royal mint and regulated property rights. Most importantly, he tackled the labour shortage by adapting the Inca system of mandatory labour service, the **mita**, providing an annual workforce of about 13,500 *mitayos* at almost no cost to the mine owners.

These reforms greatly boosted silver production, and Potosí boomed for almost a century. By the beginning of the seventeenth century Potosí's population was 160,000 and the city boasted dozens of magnificent **churches**, as well as theatres, gambling-houses, brothels and dancehalls. The silver also had a global impact, funding Spain's wars and fuelling economic growth throughout Europe.

#### The human cost

For the **indigenous workers** and **imported African slaves** who produced this wealth, the consequences were catastrophic. Staying deep underground for up to a week at a time and forced to meet ever more outrageous quotas, they died at a terrible rate; outside, the **mercury** used in processing the silver posed an equal threat to workers in the foundries. One sixteenth-century writer described the mines as a ravening beast that swallowed men alive. Estimates of the total number who died over three centuries of colonial mining in Potosí run as high as nine million, making the mines a central factor in the demographic collapse that swept the Andes under Spanish rule.

#### The end of the boom

From about 1650, silver production – and Potosí – entered a century-long decline. The city remained rich enough to be hotly disputed during the **Independence War**, but by the time independence was won, in 1825, its population was just nine thousand. From the end of the nineteenth century the city came to rely increasingly on mining **tin**, another metal abundant in Cerro Rico, but previously ignored. In 1985, however, the price of tin collapsed and the state-owned mines closed down or were privatized. Though cooperative miners continue to scrape a living by working Cerro Rico's tired old veins for tin and other metals, Potosí never recovered from the decline of silver production, much less the tin crash.

## Plaza 10 de Noviembre

The centre of the city is the **Plaza 10 de Noviembre**, a pleasant square shaded by trees, with a fountain and a mini Statue of Liberty, erected in 1926 to celebrate

### FIESTAS IN POTOSÍ

Potosí is known as the "*ciudad de los costumbres*" ("the city of customs") because of the importance its inhabitants attach to traditional religious rituals and celebrations, which combine Catholic and traditional Andean beliefs.

**The Circumcision of Christ** (Jan 1). Procession and folkloric dances in the San Benito neighbourhood.

**Día de los Compadres** (Feb, two weeks before Carnaval). Miners carry the crosses (*Tata Ckacchas*) that stand at the entrances to the mines down from Cerro Rico accompanied by brass bands, dancers and dynamite explosions.

**Carnaval** (Feb/March). Celebrated with water fights and costumed dances, and also the occasion for *ch'alla* – the blessing of cars, buildings and other property with ritual libations of alcohol, streamers and llama or sheep blood.

**San Juan de Dios** (March 8). Procession of the image of San Juan de Dios which is kept in San Lorenzo de Carangas, accompanied by folkloric dances.

**Semana Santa** (April). Easter is marked by a series of Masses and processions, and a special meal of seven meat-free dishes.

**Pentecostés** (May or June). Llama sacrifices – accompanied by eating, drinking, coca-chewing, music and dance – are performed in the mines on the seventh Sun after Easter in honour of Pachamama, the earth goddess.

**San Bartolomé** or **Ch'utillos** (Aug 24–26). Potosí's biggest fiesta centres on the re-enactment of an ancient legend by unmarried young men (Ch'utillos) mounted on horseback and dressed in their finest traditional costumes. Accompanied by dancers and musicians, the Ch'utillos ride to the Cueva del Diablo (Devil's Cave) near La Puerta village, where an evil spirit was reputedly exorcized by priests using a San Bartolomé statue.

**Señor de la Vera Cruz** (Sept 14). Procession celebrating Potosí's patron saint, whose statue is housed in the Iglesia de San Francisco.

the *grito libertario* ("cry of freedom") of **November 10, 1810**, when the citizens of Potosí rose up in support of independence, imprisoning the local governor. Spanish troops put down the Potosí rebellion, although this prevented them from reconquering insurgent Argentina. The date remains a public holiday in the province.

The square was formerly surrounded by the city's principal church, the *cabildo* (town hall) and the first royal mint, though sadly none of these has survived. On its north side, the site of the original church is now occupied by the Neoclassical **cathedral** (see below). The site of the *cabildo* is now occupied by the departmental **Prefectura**, a nineteenth-century administrative building whose simple carved stone portico is all that remains of the colonial town hall; the site of the first royal mint is occupied by the late nineteenth-century **Palacio de Justicia**.

### Catedral
Plaza 10 de Noviembre (entrance at the back at Matos 26) • Mon–Sat 9am–noon & 2.30–6pm • Bs20

Completed in 1836, the Neoclassical **Catedral** houses striking wooden images of Christ carved in the sixteenth century by renowned sculptor Gaspar de la Cueva, who was responsible for many of the city's other religious statues. Keep an eye out for the Masonic imagery on the altarpiece, and make sure you climb the bell tower, from which there are stupendous views.

## Plaza 6 de Agosto

On its eastern side, Plaza 10 de Noviembre adjoins another open space, the **Plaza 6 de Agosto**. At its centre is a column commemorating the 1824 Battle of Ayacucho, which secured Bolivian independence. On the north side is the **Teatro Omiste**, a former church, hospital and convent completed in 1753, with a recessed mestizo-Baroque facade; it was converted into a theatre in 1850. The bustling pedestrianized **El Boulevard** runs along the east side of the plaza.

# Casa Real de la Moneda

Ayacucho, just west of the Plaza 10 de Noviembre • Guided tours (90min) Mon–Sat 9am–noon (last tour 10.30am) & 2.30–6pm (last tour 4.30pm), Sun 9am–noon (last tour 10.30am) • Tours Bs40, camera Bs20, video Bs40 • ⊕ casanacionaldemoneda.org.bo

The unmissable **Casa Real de la Moneda** (Royal Mint) is one of South America's most outstanding examples of colonial civil architecture and home to Bolivia's best museum. The vast, eclectic collection includes the original machinery used in the minting process; some of Bolivia's finest colonial religious art; militaria; archeological artefacts; and a huge collection of coins. Visits are by **guided tour** only: these start soon after the morning and afternoon opening times, in Spanish, English or French depending on demand. It can be very cold inside the complex, so wear something warm.

Constructed between 1759 and 1773 for over a million *pesos de oro* to replace the earlier royal mint, La Moneda is a formidable construction, built as part of a concerted effort by the Spanish crown to reform the economic and financial machinery of the empire and increase its revenues. Along with Lima and Mexico City, Potosí was one of three cities in Spanish America authorized to produce **coins**. Occupying an entire city block, La Moneda is enclosed by 1m-thick stone walls with only a few barred windows, giving it the appearance of a fortress. Inside is a two-storey complex of about two hundred rooms off five internal courtyards. As well as housing the **heavy machinery** needed to produce coins, La Moneda also housed troops, workers, slaves and the royal officials responsible for ensuring the Spanish crown got its ten-percent cut of Cerro Rico's silver. A vital nerve centre of Spanish imperial power, it also served as a **prison**, treasury, and stronghold in times of strife.

## The entrance and courtyard

The main Calle Ayacucho entrance is an ornate Baroque portal with double doors 4m high: the coat of arms above them bears the lion and castle of the Spanish kingdoms of Castille and Léon, and the door knockers are in the form of the double-headed eagle of the Habsburg dynasty. Overlooking the first interior courtyard is a large plaster mask of a smiling face crowned by a garland of leaves and grapes. Known as **El Mascarón**, this caricature has become one of Potosí's best-known symbols, though neither its origin nor meaning is clear. The most likely story is that it was made by Eugenio Mulón, a Frenchman working in the mint in the mid-nineteenth century – it's variously thought to represent Bacchus (the Roman god of plenty), Diego Huallpa (the llama herder who discovered Cerro Rico's silver), a parody of either President Belzu or of the mint's director, or a veiled caricature of avarice. It's also been suggested that the mysterious mask was created during the Independence War to cover a royal coat of arms in mockery of Spanish rule.

## Colonial religious art

The guided tour typically begins with three rooms full of **colonial paintings**. Those in the first room include portraits of kings and mine owners, and a series depicting the victories of the Spanish emperor, Carlos V. The next room is dedicated to paintings of the Virgin Mary in the mestizo-Baroque style, in all of which her dress gives her a triangular shape. This is explained by the first of them, the **Virgen del Cerro**, which shows her in the triangular form of Cerro Rico, fusing the Catholic Mother of God with Pachamama, the Andean earth goddess. From the heavens above the Virgin-mountain, the Father, Son and Holy Ghost reach down to place a crown on her head. In the sky, either side of the Virgin, are the sun and the moon, central figures in Inca religion. The mountain itself is richly detailed: between the Virgin's hands, Diego Huallpa sits by the fire that first revealed the existence of silver; elsewhere on the mountain, miners are at work, a lordly Spaniard arrives, preceded by a priest on horseback, and at the foot of the mountain stands the Inca Huayna Capac, his presence a subtle reminder, perhaps, of the people to whom these lands once belonged.

The third room is filled with paintings by **Melchor Pérez de Holguín**, perhaps the finest exponent of the Andean Baroque style. Known as *La Brocha de Oro* – the Golden Brush – Holguín was the outstanding painter of the Potosí School. His religious paintings found their way into all the major churches and convents of the city, but those here form the single biggest collection of his work, and include a series of portraits of the Evangelists produced shortly before his death around 1730.

### Coins and minting machinery

The next part of the tour takes you to the **Numismatic Room**, filled with coins minted in Potosí. The earliest silver coins – known as *macuquinas* – were crudely made using hammers and primitive die stamps. Later coins, produced with more advanced machinery, have regular, milled edges (to stop people clipping them), and clearer detail.

Next door are the massive wooden **laminadoras**, or rolling mills, used to roll out silver ingots gradually thinner and thinner to produce sheets roughly 2mm thick, from which the coins were punched. These huge, intricate and perfectly preserved machines, made of Spanish oak, shipped to Buenos Aires, and hauled overland from there, are the only examples of Spanish engineering of their type and era still in existence. Downstairs, you can see how the rolling mills were powered: by mules, whose life expectancy in the thin air and harsh conditions was a matter of months.

### The smelting rooms

The tour continues in the **smelting rooms**, where the silver was melted down before rolling – one of these rooms has been preserved, complete with furnaces and crucibles. Other smelting rooms now house a haphazard collection of carved altarpieces from some of Potosí's churches, plus other displays including a collection of arms and uniforms, archeological and geological finds, and silverwork. Finally, you get to see how steam and then electricity transformed the minting process. Coins were still made in the Casa Real until 1951.

## La Torre de la Compañia de Jesús

Ayacucho; access is via the stairs inside the Infotur office • Officially Mon–Fri 9am–noon & 2–6pm, though sometimes closes early • Bs10

A block west along Calle Ayacucho from the Casa Real de la Moneda stands the bell tower of **La Torre de la Compañia de Jesús**, which is all that remains of a Jesuit church originally founded in 1581. Completed in 1707, the grandiose tower is one of Bolivia's finest eighteenth-century religious monuments and a sublime example of the mestizo-Baroque style. Climb to the top of the tower for panoramic **views** of the city.

## Convento-Museo Santa Teresa

At the western end of Ayacucho • Guided tours (90min) Mon–Sat 9am–12.30pm (last entry 11am) & 2.30–6pm (last entry 4.30pm), Sun 3–6pm (last entry 4.30pm) • Tours Bs30, camera Bs15 • ☎ 02 6223847

The **Convento-Museo Santa Teresa** is a beautiful colonial church and convent worth visiting both for its fine collection of colonial religious painting and sculpture, and for a somewhat disturbing insight into the bizarre lifestyle of nuns in the colonial era. Visits are by guided tour only. Built between 1686 and 1691 by the order of Carmelitas Descalzadas, the convent thrived on donations from rich mine owners, and once sprawled over several city blocks. It's now greatly reduced in size, and much of what is left has been converted into the museum, though some areas are still reserved for the small surviving community of nuns – after the tour you can buy some of their delicious home-made sweets.

During the **colonial era**, young women who entered the convent as nuns renounced the material world in order to dedicate themselves to matters spiritual. These women were mostly drawn from the families of wealthy Spanish aristocrats and mine owners, who paid handsomely in return. Once inside, girls submitted to a rigid regime of prayer, work and abstinence.

The convent's simple but elegant pink stone **facade** is the oldest example of mestizo-Baroque architecture in Potosí, dating back to 1691. Inside is a peaceful complex of courtyards, gardens and cloisters, and an exhaustive collection of colonial religious art. There are more than two hundred beautifully preserved **paintings**, including outstanding works by Melchor Pérez de Holguín and Gaspar Miguel de Berrio. The convent **church** also features a lavish carved wooden Baroque retable, along with a beautiful panelled wooden roof painted in *mudéjar* style.

## Arco de Cobija

Heading south from the Convento-Museo Santa Teresa and following the street down and round to the left brings you to the **Arco de Cobija** on Calle Cobija, a colonial stone gateway that once marked the entrance to the Spanish city centre from the Indian parishes to the south. Unlike the Spanish side of the city, the Indian parishes have a much more disordered layout, with narrow, cobbled streets winding between crumbling colonial and nineteenth-century houses.

## Iglesia de Santo Domingo

Cobija • Open for Mass • Free

Unexceptional by Potosí's standards, the **Iglesia de Santo Domingo** dates back to 1620, but was extensively remodelled in the nineteenth century in Neoclassical style. It's rarely open to the public, but if you manage to get in before or after the Sunday-morning service, check out the carved wooden statue of the Virgen del Rosario, which was brought over from Spain in the sixteenth century and used as a model by Inca Yupanqui when he carved the Virgen de Copacabana in 1582 (see box, p.104).

---

### DOUBLE MEANINGS: THE CHURCHES OF POTOSÍ

With beautifully carved porticos and interiors dripping with gold leaf, Potosí's churches are among the finest examples of the **mestizo-Baroque style**, in which Christian European and pre-Christian Andean symbolism are combined. The churches were built partly as a straightforward expression of religious faith, but gratitude for the wealth of Potosí also played a role: whereas Catholic churches almost always face west, those of Potosí look south towards Cerro Rico. They were also part of a determined effort to **convert** the indigenous population: with hundreds of thousands of indigenous people from different ethnic groups spending time in the city as workers under the **mita** system, Potosí offered a perfect opportunity for inculcating the Catholic faith. As well as the many churches and convents built for their own use, the Spaniards built fourteen parish churches for exclusive use by the indigenous *mitayos*.

In time, Christianity gained widespread acceptance among the indigenous population, at least on the surface. But as responsibility for building and decorating Potosí's churches passed to indigenous and mestizo craftsmen and artists, a very distinct religious vision began to emerge. From the second half of the sixteenth century the religious art and architecture of Potosí began to incorporate more and more **indigenous religious motifs** in a style that became known as mestizo-Baroque. The sun, moon and stars – central objects in traditional Andean religion – appear alongside images of Christ and the saints, with the Virgin Mary represented in **triangular form** like a mountain, clearly conflated with the Andean earth goddess Pachamama.

These developments did not pass unnoticed by the Spanish authorities, but allowing a little Andean religious imagery into the decoration of churches may have seemed a small price to pay for getting the indigenous population to accept Christianity, albeit superficially. Despite their beauty, however, these churches were the product of **slave labour**, and they could scarcely conceal the contradiction between the avowed Christian beliefs of the Spanish mine owners who funded them and the brutal reality of the mining regime these same men controlled. It was said that though God ruled in Potosí's 34 churches, the Devil laughed in his six thousand mines.

## Calle Chuquisaca

On and around **Calle Chuquisaca**, a block south of Plaza 10 de Noviembre, are some of Potosí's best-preserved and most luxurious **colonial townhouses**, their carved stone doorways decorated with the coats of arms of the Spanish noblemen who owned them. Many are painted in pastel shades – such as pale blue or lemon yellow – or the rich ochre colour made with natural pigments from the red earth of Cerro Rico.

## Iglesia y Convento de San Francisco

Tarija • Guided tours (40min) Mon–Fri 9.30am, 11am, 3pm, 4pm & 5pm, Sat 9.30am & 11am • Bs15 • ☎ 02 6222539

A couple of blocks south of Chuquisaca is the **Iglesia y Convento de San Francisco**, once a church and convent and now a museum, worth visiting for the views from its roof, as well as for its collection of colonial religious art. The original church, the first to be built in Potosí, was created when the Franciscan monastery was founded in 1547, but demolished in 1707 and replaced by the bulky structure you see today.

The main point of interest inside is the reputedly miraculous statue of the **Señor de la Vera Cruz**, the patron saint of Potosí, which stands behind the altar. According to legend, this statue of a crucified Christ appeared in front of the church one morning in 1550 and was adopted by the Franciscans. Christ's beard is made of real human hair and is said to need regular trimming, while the cross is also reputed to grow a little each year – some believe the world will end when it reaches the floor of the church. Among the paintings on display are two big canvases by Holguín, one a luridly detailed Day of Judgement. The climb up onto the roof of the church is well worth it for the panoramic **views**. You can also visit the **crypts**, where the skulls of the monks and wealthy citizens interred here lie in heaps.

## Iglesia de la Merced

Hoyos • Guided tours (30–45min) Mon–Fri 8am– noon & 2.30–6pm, Sat 9am–noon • Bs15

A block east of Plaza 6 de Agosto, along Calle Hoyos, stands the attractive **Iglesia de la Merced**, completed in 1687 alongside a Mercedarian monastery dating back to 1555. It has a two-level carved stone facade featuring the coat of arms of the Mercedarian order, and there are great views from the rooftop mirador.

## Iglesia de San Martín

Hoyos • Open for Mass • Free

The **Iglesia de San Martín** is an adobe church with a simple stone portico and a beautiful interior. It was built in 1592 as the parish church for *mita* labourers from the Lupaca tribe. Inside, the walls are covered in paintings, including individual portraits of all the archangels; behind the altar stands a fabulous wooden retable.

## Along Calle Bolívar

Two blocks north of Plaza 10 de Noviembre, **Calle Bolívar** is a narrow street bustling with commercial activity, which runs past the **Mercado Central**. A short walk east of the market is the **Casa de las Tres Portadas**, an eighteenth-century colonial house with wooden balconies and three highly ornate doorways decorated with varied designs including the sun and moon, angels, floral patterns and gargoyle-like faces.

On the corner of Bolívar and Junín, the colonial mansion now occupied by the Banco Nacional de Bolivia (open to the public) is the **Casa de los Marqueses de Otavi**; its strikingly carved mestizo-Baroque stone facade – unusual in a non-religious building – features two lions with near-human faces holding aloft a coat of arms, flanked by the sun and moon. Heading south down Junín, then right again, you'll reach the narrow, twisting, dead-end alley known as **El Pasaje de las Siete Vueltas** ("Seven-turn Passage"), the only remnant in the Spanish city centre of the disorderly street plan that existed before Viceroy Toledo ordered it to be relaid.

Back on Bolívar, at Quijarro, the seventeenth-century **Iglesia de San Agustín** (open for Mass; free) was the church used by Potosí's substantial Basque community in the colonial era. Only the simple but elegant Renaissance portico survives from the original structure, and the bare interior is rarely open.

## Iglesia de San Lorenzo de Carangas

Bustillos and Heroes del Chaco • Open for Mass • Free

Behind the Mercado Central stands the spectacular **Iglesia de San Lorenzo de Carangas**, whose splendid carved stone portal is perhaps the defining example of the mestizo-Baroque architectural style in Potosí. One of Potosí's oldest churches, it was built in the mid-sixteenth century and initially called La Anunciación and used only by the Spanish. The church was renamed a few decades later when it became the parish church for *mitayos* belonging to the Carangas tribe.

The richly decorated **doorway** was created in the eighteenth century, when the church was thoroughly remodelled. It features fantastically intricate floral patterns intertwined with twisting grape-laden vines and angels' faces, while the inner arch on either side of the door is supported by bizarre carved figures of bare-breasted women. Stranger still are the mermaids who strum guitars above the doorway: they are thought to represent creatures who figure in legends of the powerful mountain god Thunupa.

## Iglesia de San Bernardo

On the south side of the Plaza del Estudiante • Open for Mass • Free

From the Mercado Central, Calle Oruro runs northwest to the university and the Plaza del Estudiante, which is flanked by two colonial churches. The bulky **Iglesia de San Bernardo** was built from uncut stone blocks and completed in 1731. It now houses the workshops used in the ongoing restoration of Potosí's historic buildings, and though it's not officially open to the public, you can usually have a peep inside.

## Iglesia de Jerusalén

On the north side of the Plaza del Estudiante • Mon–Fri 8am–noon & 2.30–6.30pm, Sat 8am–noon • Free

The small, late seventeenth-century **Iglesia de Jerusalén** has been converted into a museum featuring yet more colonial religious art. Highlights include an extravagant mestizo-Baroque retable covered in gold leaf, and an ornate carved pulpit decorated with tiny pictures painted on bronze by Melchor Peréz de Holguín. The most unusual painting is a portrait of **Francisco de Aguirre**, a wealthy mine owner who turned his back on worldly goods to become a priest, and is now buried in the walls of the church.

### ARRIVAL AND DEPARTURE                              POTOSÍ

**By plane** Capitán Nicolas Rojas Airport, 5km northwest of town, has a morning BoA flight to Cochabamba (35min). Sucre airport (see p.202) is easily accessible by bus, train or taxi.

**By train** There are trains to Sucre (departing Tues, Thurs & Sat 8am, returning Mon, Wed & Fri; 6hr) from the station at avenidas Sevilla and Villazón, 1.5km northwest of the city centre; it's a pleasant trip, but much slower than by road.

**By bus** It's worth arriving or leaving during daylight for the local scenery. The new bus station is on Av Banderas, near the Centro Recreasional Los Pinos (micro E, F, J or #150 from Plaza

10 de Noviembre). All services depart from here apart from the Uyuni buses, which still use the old terminal ("ex-terminal") on Av Universitario, on the way out of town towards Oruro (micro N or #150 from Plaza 10 de Noviembre). A taxi into the centre from either terminal costs Bs10–15.

Destinations La Paz (roughly hourly; 9–11hr); Oruro (roughly hourly; 5hr); Sucre (roughly every 30min; 3hr); Tarija (9 daily, mostly at night; 8hr), Uyuni (6–7 daily; 5hr).

**By taxi** Collective taxis for Sucre (2hr 30min) depart from the old bus terminal as soon as they have at least four passengers; to save a wait, organize through your hotel.

## INFORMATION AND TOURS

### TOURIST INFORMATION

The fairly helpful Infotur office (Mon–Fri 8am–noon & 2.30–6.30pm; ☎02 6231021) is in the modern mirrored building through the arch of Torre de la Compañía on Calle Ayacucho.

### TOUR OPERATORS

Most tour operators offer half-day trips to the Cerro Rico mines (see p.160) and city tours. Some also organize hikes in the Cordillera Kari Kari (see p.163). You can arrange Salar de Uyuni tours here too.

**Green-Go Tours** Junín 15–17 ☎02 6231362, ✉ greengotours@hotmail.com; map p.151. Popular agency (with attached café) specializing in tours of Cerro Rico.
**Hidalgo Tours** La Paz 1113 at Matos ☎02 6225186, ⊛ salardeuyuni.net; map p.151. High-end operator offering mine, city and Salar trips.
**Koala Tours** Ayacucho 5 ☎02 6222092, ⊛ koalabolivia .com.bo; map p.151. Experienced, reliable operator with English-speaking mine guides. They also run hiking trips around the Kari Kari lakes, mountain biking and Macha *Tinku* tours (see box, p.164).

## ACCOMMODATION

Night-time temperatures often dip below zero, so the main consideration when choosing where to stay is **warmth**. Most of the smarter places have heating; if your hotel does not, try at least to find a room that gets some sun during the day, and ask for extra **blankets**. It's worth booking in advance if you want to stay in one of the mid- or top-end hotels, especially between June and August. If you prefer to stay outside the city and at a lower altitude, try *Hostal Museo Cayara* (see p.164).

**Hostal Carlos V** Linares 42 ☎02 6231010; map p.151. Charming hotel offering cosy, tasteful rooms with shared facilities, and more spacious ones (for Bs240) with private bathrooms, flatscreen TVs and huge beds. There's a communal kitchen, a TV/DVD lounge and laundry service, but wi-fi in public areas only. Bs160
★**Hostal Colonial** Hoyos 8 ☎02 6224265, ⊛ hostalcolonialpotosi.com.bo; map p.151. Beautifully restored Spanish-era mansion with a centrally heated modern interior and compact, well-furnished rooms set around a couple of peaceful, tiled courtyards with fountains and cacti. Bs480
**Hostal Compañía de Jesus** Chuquisaca 445 ☎02 6223173, ⊛ hostalcompania.galeon.com; map p.151. Right in the centre of town, this economical hotel has a range of clean rooms (shared or private bathrooms) and a welcoming atmosphere. The wi-fi is rather iffy, and the rooms can get a bit chilly (there's no heating), but the beds are warm and the showers hot. Bs90
**Hostal Eucalyptus** Linares 88A ☎7240 1884, ⊛ koalabolivia.com.bo; map p.151. Run by the Koala Tours agency (see above), this popular hostel has spacious en-suite rooms, a TV room, kitchen and a same-day laundry service. There are great views from the roof terrace, where you can order beers via an intercom which come up on a hand-cranked dumb waiter. Bs230
**Hostal La Casona** Chuquisaca 460 ☎02 6230523, ⊛ hotelpotosi.com; map p.151. A good choice for anyone on a tight budget, this place has a dorm as well as private rooms (with either shared or en-suite bathrooms – the latter have flatscreen TVs too). There's a sociable buzz, and facilities include a TV and DVD room, laundry service and book exchange. Dorms Bs40, doubles Bs100

**Hostal Patrimonio** Matos 62 ☎02 6222659, ✉ hp .potosi@gmail.com; map p.151. In a good location just a block away from the main square, this pleasant hotel is bright and airy but still cosy. It's also very clean – even the TV remotes are pre-sanitized. The quietest rooms are at the back. Bs522
**Hotel Cima Argentum** Villazon 239 ☎02 6229538, ⊛ hca-potosi.com; map p.151. A 15min (uphill) walk from the centre, this smart hotel has a sunny central atrium presided over by an eye-catching copper eagle. The rooms are very comfortable, if not the most stylish: each one has radiators, a fridge, TV, safe and modern bathroom; quieter ones are at the back. Bs420
**Hotel El Turista** Lanza 19 ☎02 6222492, ✉ hotelturista10nov@hotmail.com; map p.151. This friendly old hotel has an orange exterior, 1960s-era leather sofas and flights of rickety stairs. The rooms are slightly musty but comfortable and come with private bath, heaters and TVs. For excellent views of Cerro Rico, ask for room 33 or 34 at the top of the building. Bs240
**Hotel Gran Libertador** Millares 58 ☎02 6227877, ⊛ hotelgranlibertador.com; map p.151. A modern hotel with central heating and bright rooms, just slightly chintzy, but in a nice way, with private baths, flatscreen TVs and phones. Bs480
**Koala Den** Junin 56 ☎02 6226467, ⊛ koalabolivia .com.bo; map p.151. Under the same management as *Hostal Eucalyptus*, this friendly hostel on a quaint street has clean dorms and private rooms, central heating, hot showers, a TV/DVD lounge, book exchange, laundry service, bike rental and a nearby annexe with pool and ping-pong tables. Dorms Bs50, doubles Bs150

## EATING

Potosí has a growing variety of places to eat, with more and more cafés and restaurants offering vegetarian food and travellers' favourites. Don't miss out, however, on the tasty **local cuisine**, particularly the thick, warming soups and meat dishes cooked in spicy sauces. The **Mercado Central** on Calle Bolívar is the best place to eat if you're on a **budget**, with coffee, pastries and *apí* – a hot thick maize drink flavoured with cloves and cinnamon – served up from early in the morning.

**Café La Plata** Plaza 10 de Noviembre ☎02 6226085; map p.151. This café-bar overlooks the plaza and has good coffees (Bs10–24), cakes and pastries for the daytime, as well as beer (Bs20–24) and wine in the evening. There's a rack of magazines and numerous board games to keep you occupied. Service, however, can be a little bit snooty. Mon–Sat 9am–10pm.

**Chaplin** Matos 10 at Quijarro ☎7616 4944; map p.151. Bustling place attracting a young local crowd (and particularly students) with a wide range of inexpensive snacks, including burgers, veg burgers and tacos (all Bs12), plus juices and decent coffee. Mon–Sat 7.30am–noon & 6–10pm.

**Cherry's Salón de Té** Padilla 8 ☎02 6226753; map p.151. Appealing tearoom with orange walls, faux wrought-iron furnishings and plastic flowers. The economical menu features breakfasts (Bs18–25), coffee (Bs5–15) and cakes (Bs4–10), as well as burgers (Bs13–17) and a few more substantial meals. Daily 8am–10pm.

**Doña Eugenia** Santa Cruz at Hermanos Ortega ☎02 6262247; map p.151. This inexpensive restaurant on the outskirts of the city is just about the only place that serves regional speciality *k'ala phurka* (Bs18), a thick, spicy maize soup served in earthenware bowls into which a hot stone is plunged just before serving, so it stays piping hot and bubbles

like a volcano as you eat it. 9am–1pm; closed Wed & Thurs.

★**Koala Café** Ayacucho 5 ☎02 6228050; map p.151. Mellow traveller café opposite the Casa Real de la Moneda serving a mix of local and international dishes, and good breakfasts; if you're hungry, try the three-course set lunch/dinner (Bs40 veg, Bs45 with meat). Daily 8am–9pm.

**San Marcos** La Paz 1565 ☎02 6226717; map p.151. Housed in an old colonial-era silver foundry, this excellent restaurant features glass tables mounted on restored pieces of nineteenth-century industrial machinery and an inventive menu featuring llama carpaccio, ceviche and garlic prawns (mains from around Bs40). You can have a look round the old foundry while you're here: the building still features the nineteenth-century furnaces used to cook the mineral ore, and the raised stone canal that carried water from the mountains above the city – the water was used to power the huge water wheel and heavy stone hammers that crushed the ore for processing. Mon–Sat noon–3pm & 6.30–10.30pm, Sun noon–3pm.

**La Taberna** Junín 12 ☎02 6230123; map p.151. Swish restaurant decked out with French posters, wine racks and antique typewriters, open for breakfast, lunch and supper. Dishes include a pretty good llama steak. Daily 8am–10pm.

## DRINKING

**Café 4.060** Hoyos 1 ☎02 6222623; map p.151. This contemporary café-bar has a slick, low-lit interior and an array of drinks: the coffee (Bs10–35) is organic and has been grown at an altitude exceeding 4060m in the Yungas, and there's a lengthy cocktail, wine and beer list. The food (Bs20–80) is good quality, but a little pricey. Mon–Sat 4–11.30pm.

★**Pub La Casona** Frias 41 ☎02 6222954; map p.151. The liveliest nightspot in town, housed in an eighteenth-century mansion whose inside walls are decorated with contemporary graffiti. The atmosphere is friendly, with ice-cold beer (from Bs22) and good food (mains Bs25–50) including excellent trout. Live music on Friday nights. Mon–Sat 6pm–12.30am.

## SHOPPING

Unsurprisingly, Potosí is home to a fair number of **silversmiths**, though they tend to produce traditional religious ornaments and household items rather than fashionable jewellery. There are several silverwork shops on Bolívar and Sucre, but be careful when buying silver from street stalls as purity is often low. A wide variety of beautiful **textiles** (*tejidos*), hand-woven by different indigenous groups in the region, can also be picked up from shops along Sucre and in the Mercado Artesanal at Sucre and Omiste; the most famous weaving communities include Potolo, Chayanta and Calcha. The Mercado Artesanal also sells a good range of hand-crafted **musical instruments**.

## DIRECTORY

**Banks and exchange** Banks with ATMs include Banco Mercantil de Santa Cruz on Padilla and Matos, and BNB on Junín at Bolívar (Casa de los Marqueses de Otavi). There are a couple of money changers at the rear of the central market, on Heroes del Chaco.

**Internet** There are plenty of cybercafés, including Pueblitos Net, 18-B Millares (daily 8am–10pm; Bs2/hr).

**Laundry** Lavarap, Quijjaro and Matos (Bs10/kg).

**Post office** Correo Central, a block south of Plaza 10 de Noviembre on Lanza and Chuquisaca.

# Around Potosí

There are several worthwhile excursions from Potosí, most notably to the **mines** of Cerro Rico. Immediately southeast of the city, the **Cordillera Kari Kari** is a good place for hiking amid the lakes that provided water for the silver-processing *ingenios* (smelters). To the northwest, the natural **hot springs** at Tarapaya are a calming place to relax.

## Cerro Rico

*There are those who, having entered only out of curiosity to see that horrible labyrinth, have come out totally robbed of colour, grinding their teeth and unable to pronounce a word; they have not known even how to ponder it nor make reference to the horrors that are in there.*

Bartolomé Arzans de Orsua, Historia de la Villa Imperial de Potosí, 1703

Immediately south of Potosí the near-perfect cone of **Cerro Rico** (Sumaj Orko in Quechua) rises above the city, its slopes stained startling hues of red and yellow by centuries of mining waste, and pockmarked with the entrances to thousands of mines. For many travellers a visit to one of the mines is a highlight of their trip to Potosí, an amazing and disturbing journey into the bowels of the earth. No less fascinating are the customs, rituals and beliefs that sustain the Quechua-speaking miners.

Most of the miners are reworking old silver mines for tin, lead and other less valuable metals, so the entrances to the shafts tend to be lined with stone facing dating back to the **colonial era**. As you descend deeper, though, the passageways become narrower and less well made. The miners work in shift teams who divide the profits of what they

---

### CERRO RICO TOURS

Several agencies run regular **tours** to the mines (see p.160). These last half a day and cost around Bs130 per person, though some companies charge less, particularly outside the June to September high season. Most guides are former miners and know what they're talking about, though few speak more than limited English. Groups should be no bigger than eight, and you should be provided with rubber boots, a mining jacket or overalls, safety helmet and headlamp; it's worth bringing along some water and a handkerchief to cover your mouth.

Be warned, though, that this is an unpleasant and highly **dangerous** environment, where safety precautions are largely left to supernatural forces. The mines are dirty, wet, muddy and very **claustrophobic**. The air is fetid with dust and gases, including arsenic, and the chances of being hit by falling rocks or a speeding mine trolley are real. Many of the tunnels are narrow and have low ceilings, and temperatures can reach over 40°C, so walking and crawling through the mines would be exhausting even if the entrances weren't situated at over **4000m above sea level**. From every group, one or two usually head for the exit within ten minutes of entering the mine – if you don't like it, your guide will lead you out.

Once inside, tours generally involve walking, crawling and clambering through often dirty and narrow tunnels deep underground for two or three hours – you should be reasonably fit and altitude-acclimatized; don't visit if you have heart or respiratory difficulties or are claustrophobic. Some people also question the ethics of making a tourist attraction of a workplace where conditions are so appalling. That said, however, most people who do visit the mines find the experience one of the most unforgettable in Bolivia.

Tours of the mines begin with a visit to the **miners' market** around Plaza El Calvario, where you can buy coca, dynamite, black-tobacco cigarettes, pure cane alcohol and fizzy drinks – take a selection of these as **gifts** for the miners you'll be visiting. Thousands of miners still work in Cerro Rico (around 15 percent of Potosí's male population have mining-related jobs), including a high proportion of children, divided between a number of different mining cooperatives. The most commonly visited mines include Candelaria, Santa Rita, Santa Rosita and Rosario.

Avoid tour agencies that offer travellers the opportunity to throw (lit) dynamite around or provide a dynamite demonstration – as well as being dangerous, this also damages the already unstable ground surrounding Cerro Rico (see opposite).

## SYMPATHY FOR THE DEVIL: EL TÍO

In every mine, usually in an alcove just beyond the point from which the last ray of sunlight can be seen, you'll find a statue of a sinister horned and bearded figure complete with erect phallus and leering smile. Known as **El Tío** (the Uncle) this demonic character is considered to be the king of the underworld, to whom sacrifices must be made and homage paid if miners are to stay safe and find rich deposits. El Tío is given regular **libations** of alcohol and offerings of coca and lit cigarettes, particularly on Fridays. At certain times of the year, **blood sacrifices** are also made to El Tío, with llamas being slaughtered outside the mine entrance to assuage a thirst for blood that might otherwise be satisfied only by the death of a miner. Though El Tío is clearly related to **pre-Columbian mountain deities** and is never referred to as the Devil by name, there's little doubt that he owes much to **Christian belief**. When the first *mitayos* heard Spanish priests describe heaven and hell, they can only have concluded that the mines were hell itself. If that was so, then they were working in the Devil's domain, and it was to him that they had to look for succour. To this day most miners are Christians when above ground, taking part in fiestas and worshipping Christ and the Virgin. But once inside the mines, it is to the owner of the minerals and the king of the underworld that they pray.

**3**

extract on an equal basis, though some of those working in the mines – particularly the children – are paid a fixed daily wage as employees. The miners are generally proud of their work, and are usually happy to talk about their lives with visitors. Many of the miners previously worked in large **state-run mines**; others are campesinos who come to work in the mines for short periods on a seasonal basis. Few earn more than a marginal living, though the dream of striking lucky sustains many in their labour. **Life expectancy** in the mines is generally short, with many miners falling victim to the deadly lung disease **silicosis**. Cave-ins and other accidents claim the lives of many others.

Few miners eat when they are underground, relying for sustenance instead on coca leaves, harsh black-tobacco cigarettes and the occasional swig of neat cane alcohol. Today, as in the colonial era, **coca** is considered an essential requirement without which work in the mines would be impossible. Miners spend a good hour chewing coca before entering the shaft to begin work, and all agree that it helps them endure the heat, exhaustion and backbreaking labour. Coca, tobacco and alcohol are also taken in as offerings to **El Tío** – the supernatural being who is believed to own the mine's silver and other metals (see box, above).

The future of Cerro Rico is unclear. Riddled with almost five hundred years' worth of tunnels and numerous sinkholes (one in 2011 was around 50m wide), the mountain is increasingly unstable and even, some say, on the verge of collapse. Although stabilization measures have been put in place, many experts believe they are insufficient.

## Cordillera Kari Kari

5km southeast of central Potosí • To reach the lakes by foot, walk up to Plaza Sucre along Calle Chuquisaca, then follow the road to the southeast that turns into a track leading up into the mountains; alternatively, visit with one of Potosí's travel agencies (see p.160)

The **Cordillera Kari Kari** is home to a network of artificial lakes, dams, aqueducts and dykes that Viceroy Toledo ordered to be built in the late sixteenth century to ensure a supply of water to the foundries in Potosí. By contemporary standards, the artificial lakes represented a monumental feat of construction, employing twenty thousand indigenous forced labourers and taking almost a century to complete. During peak silver production there were 32 lakes, but only a few now survive to supply the city's water. In 1625 the retaining wall supporting Laguna San Sebastián burst, killing thousands of people.

Set amid arid red-brown mountains, the lakes are easily reached from the city and make a good place for **hiking**, albeit at altitudes of up to 5000m. If you're planning to stay overnight you'll need your own food and camping gear, and you'll have to be prepared for subzero temperatures. Alternatively, you can go on an organized trip (see

**3**

---

### TINKU: RITUAL COMBAT IN THE ANDES

The **Tinku** is a form of ritual hand-to-hand combat that still takes place on certain feast days in some small rural towns in the northern areas of Potosí department. During the *Tinku*, young men from two rival communities (*ayllus*) take turns to engage in bloody one-on-one **fist fights** in the midst of a drunken and raucous fiesta. The young fighters wear **leather helmets** modelled on those worn by the Spanish conquistadors, and leather breastplates for protection. They bind their fists with woven belts, sometimes adding a stone in the palm of their hand to add extra force to their blows.

The **two- or three-day fiestas** start with the arrival of the young men from their home villages, marching and playing long panpipes known as *suqusu*. The clashes take place in a charged atmosphere of music, dancing and drunkenness. Local people and sometimes the police oversee proceedings, but as the fiesta goes on things often escalate beyond their control, with pitched battles between rival *ayllus*, and it's rare for a year to go by without someone being killed. **Bloodshed** is perhaps the most important part of the ritual: as well as serving as a warlike rite of passage for young men, the *Tinku* acts as a **fertility rite** during which blood must be shed on both sides to satisfy the earth goddess, **Pachamama**, and ensure a bountiful harvest. The *Tinku* is also an important way of reaffirming indigenous cultural identity, and can help defuse all too real conflicts between communities that can otherwise erupt into more serious violence. **Unmarried young women** also sometimes fight in the *Tinku*, though their aim is usually to pull hair and rip clothes rather than draw blood.

The best-known *Tinku* takes place in the community of **Macha**, 120km north of Potosí, in the first week of May, but there are several others in small villages in the region at other times of the year – including Torotoro (see p.222). Several **tour companies** in Potosí (see p.160) take groups along each year. Be warned, though, that these violent and alcoholic spectacles often get out of hand and it's easy for an outsider to unwittingly provoke trouble. If you do visit, go with a Bolivian guide who knows the area, stay clear of the crowds, don't take photographs without permission and generally exercise maximum cultural sensitivity.

---

p.160). The first lake, about 5km from the city centre, is **Laguna San Sebastián**, which is supported by a massive retaining wall, built by hand in the sixteenth century. From here you can head across the ridge to the northeast to **Laguna San Idelfonso**, about 1.5km away, or continue south along the remains of an abandoned aqueduct towards lagunas **Pisco Cocha** and **Chalaviri**. Keep sight of Cerro Rico and you shouldn't have any problems finding your way back to Potosí.

## Tarapaya hot springs

25km northwest of Potosí • No fixed opening times • Bs5 • Take a micro to Tarapaya (roughly every half-hour from Av Universitaria) and ask to be dropped off just after the bridge before Tarapaya, from where it's a 10min walk up the track that climbs to the left; alternatively, a taxi costs around Bs70 each way

The *aguas termales* (hot springs) at **Tarapaya**, 25km northwest of Potosí, can be visited as a half-day trip. Known as **El Ojo del Inca** ("The Eye of the Inca"), the natural hot springs bubble up into a perfectly circular pool about 50m in diameter and are believed to have curative powers. As with all hot springs, you should check the temperature before jumping in. Locals also strongly advise against swimming out into the centre of the pool, where they say occasional whirlpools can suck unwary bathers to their doom.

### ACCOMMODATION
**AROUND POTOSÍ**

**Hostal Museo Cayara** Cayara village, 20km west of Potosí ☎6740 9024, ⓦhotelmuseocayara.com. This beautiful colonial-era hacienda (the oldest in South America) is a relaxing and atmospheric place to stay. Rooms come with attractive features like high ceilings and wooden beams, as well as attached bathrooms and heaters. There's also a chapel, a 6000-book library, and a wonderful museum with exhibits ranging from a 500-year-old suit of armour to Stone Age axe heads. A taxi from the city centre costs around Bs70. **$110 (Bs750)**

# Uyuni

Set on the bleak southern Altiplano 212km southwest of Potosí, the town of **UYUNI** is mostly of interest as a jumping-off point for journeys into the beautiful and remote landscapes of the surrounding region. Founded in 1889 at the junction of the railways that enter Bolivia from Chile and Argentina, it was in its heyday Bolivia's main gateway to the outside world, a symbol of modernity and industrial progress. Today, by contrast, it's rather shabby, and at 3668m above sea level, with no shelter from the wind, it can get bitterly cold, especially at night. Given the decline in the fortunes of Bolivia's railways, it's surprising Uyuni hasn't become a ghost town like many of the mining settlements whose ore exports once passed through it. That it hasn't is due to the ever-growing number of travellers who come here to visit the spectacular scenery of the Salar de Uyuni and the Reserva de Fauna Andina Eduardo Avaroa (see p.168).

The effective centre of town is the nineteenth-century **clock tower** at the intersection of Arce and Potosí. The **municipal museum**, close by on Avenida Arce, has been demolished but is due to be rebuilt, its main exhibits being ancient skulls and mummies. **Street stall**s along Potosí sell woollen jumpers, hats, gloves, socks and ponchos; the Thursday market is a particularly good hunting ground.

**3**

## Museo Ferrocarril

Tomás Frías, behind the railway station • Mon–Fri 8.30am–noon & 2.30–6pm • Bs10

Billed as the biggest rail museum in South America, Uyuni's **Museo Ferrocarril** is essentially a big shed built to protect and exhibit a collection of old locomotives, train cars and engineering bogeys which had been sitting on the sidings at the station for years. Elsewhere in town, there are more rail-related machines on display along the central

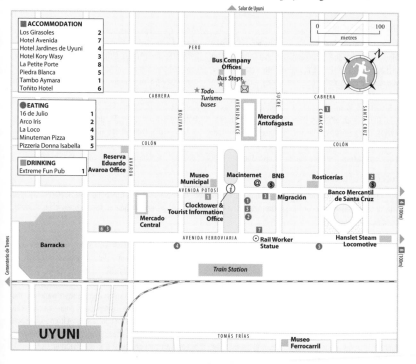

reservation of Avenida Ferroviaria, including (between Santa Cruz and Colombia) a **steam locomotive** made by Hanslet Engine Co of Leeds, Yorkshire, in 1912. There's also a great **statue** of a rail worker, poised dramatically, spanner in hand, between Arce and Sucre.

## Cementerio de Trenes

A 20min walk west of town down Av Ferroviaria and along the railway line

Just west of town is the **Cementerio de Trenes** (Train Cemetery). Set on the desolate fringe of the Salar, with good views back towards the town, this graveyard of rusting steam locomotives, passenger carriages and freight wagons that used to carry ore from long-abandoned mines is a sombre monument to the past glory of the age of steam and steel.

### ARRIVAL AND DEPARTURE                                        UYUNI

**By plane** There's a small airport 1km north of Uyuni; a taxi to/from town costs around Bs10. Amazonas and BoA fly to/from La Paz (4–5 daily; 50min).

**By train** Trains (ⓦ www.fca.com.bo) south to Villazón via Tupiza and north to Oruro depart from the train station on Av Ferroviaria, in the town centre. The *Expreso del Sur* is quicker and more comfortable than the cheaper *Wara Wara del Sur*. Note that the passenger service to Avaroa on the Chilean border no longer runs, but there are buses (see box, opposite). Destinations Oruro (4 weekly; 7hr 5min–7hr 25min); Tupiza (4 weekly; 5hr 20min–5hr 45min); Villazón (4 weekly; 8hr 25min–9hr 15min).

**By bus** Buses from Potosí, Oruro and Tupiza pull up in front of the various bus company offices (an area optimistically described as "the terminal"), three blocks north of the train station along Av Arce. Todo Turismo (ⓣ 02 6933337, ⓦ todoturismo.bo), at Cabrera 208, has easily the most comfortable services to La Paz (around 10hr) via Oruro; its buses have heaters and a meal service, but cost significantly more than the competition. The journey to Tupiza is scenic but rough, and you may have to change buses midway at the town of Atocha; quicker and more comfortable jeeps sometimes run for the second part of the journey. Destinations Calama, Chile (1–2 daily; 10hr); La Paz (5 daily, usually departing around 8pm; 10–12hr); Oruro (6–7 daily; 5hr); Potosí (hourly; 4hr); Tupiza (3 daily; 7hr).

### INFORMATION

**Tourist information** There is a tourist office (officially Mon–Fri 8am–noon & 2.30–6pm, though it's often empty) in the clock tower on Potosí, though it's only worth visiting if you want to complain about a tour agency – tourist police officers share the same office. The Reserva Eduardo Avaroa (Mon–Fri 8.30am–12.30pm & 2.30–6.30pm; ⓣ 02 6932400) has an office on Colón near the junction with Avaroa. Tour agencies can be a good source of information, though obviously their main aim is to sell you a trip.

**Tour operators** There are dozens of operators in Uyuni offering very similar tours of the Salar de Uyuni and Reserva Eduardo Avaroa. Although you'll pay less for a tour booked here than one arranged in La Paz (see p.76) or Tupiza (see p.176), bear in mind that few local operators are entirely satisfactory and a lot of them are real cowboys (see box, p.171). Uyuni also has branch offices of La Paz's Motorcycle Tours (see p.77; Uruguay 529 at Santa Cruz; ⓣ 7877 3787), Potosí-based Hidalgo Tours (see p.160; in the *Hotel Jardines de Uyuni*) and Tupiza Tours (see p.176; Loa between Alonzo and Calvimontes; ⓣ 6516 4704).

### ACCOMMODATION

Although the majority of Uyuni's hotels are aimed at backpackers, there are several smarter options. Most places stay open late for **train passengers** arriving in the middle of the night. Hotels fill up between June and September, when it's worth booking in advance.

**Los Girasoles** Santa Cruz 155 ⓣ 02 6933323, ⓔ girasoleshotel@hotmail.com; map p.165. "The Sunflowers" is a comfortable mid-range choice featuring pleasant rooms with private bathrooms, heaters, TVs and plenty of space. Laundry service and bike rental are available. **Bs500**

**Hotel Avenida** Av Ferroviaria 11 ⓣ 02 6932078; map p.165. The best budget option in town, with clean, functional rooms (some en suite), diagonally opposite the train station. No breakfast; wi-fi mainly in the lobby area, although you may pick up a signal in your room. **Bs90**

**Hotel Jardines de Uyuni** Potosí 113 ⓣ 02 6932989, reservations ⓣ 02 6225186, ⓦ hotelesrusticosjardines .com; map p.165. This smart hotel, a short walk from the centre, has attractive communal areas slung with hammocks, a small indoor pool, a very welcome sauna and a restaurant. The rooms have windows facing inward only, but are very comfortable and all have heating. **Bs727**

## ROUTES FROM UYUNI INTO CHILE

There are two ways of crossing into Chile from Uyuni. The most direct is to take a bus to **Calama** (1–2 daily; 10hr including border formalities) via the Bolivian border post of **Avaroa**. A more popular route into Chile is at the border post 7km from Laguna Verde (see p.173) in the far south of the **Reserva Eduardo Avaroa**. Most agencies will drop you off here at the end of their tour on request, but check that it's included in the cost of your tour, and let the tour company you're travelling with know before leaving Uyuni, so that they can arrange onward transport for the 35km to San Pedro de Atacama, which will otherwise be hard to come by. Whichever route you choose, you should be able to get an **exit stamp** at the border, but it's advisable, just in case, to get one in advance at the *migración* office in Uyuni, on Potosí between Arce and Sucre.

**Hotel Kory Wasy** Potosí 304 ☏02 6932670, ✉kory_wasi@hotmail.com; map p.165. Compact but bare en-suite rooms set around a plastic-roofed central hallway. Some rooms are a bit gloomy, so ask to see a few before making your choice. Breakfast not included. Bs150

★**La Petite Porte** Av Ferroviaria 742 ☏02 6933597, ⊕hotel-lapetiteporte-uyuni.com; map p.165. This delightful B&B, a 10min walk east of the train station, has just four super-stylish rooms with wooden floors, central heating and private bathrooms. Service is excellent. Advance reservations a must. $100 (Bs680)

**Piedra Blanca** Arce 27 ☏7222 3274, ⊕piedrablancabackpackers.hostel.com; map p.165. Central budget option, with basic shared-bath rooms around a courtyard set back from the street. Guests can use the kitchen,

and the showers are nice and hot. Wi-fi in public areas only and a bit iffy even then. Dorms Bs75, doubles Bs210

**Tambo Aymara** Camacho ☏02 6932227, ⊕hoteltamboaymara.com; map p.165. This appealing, mid-range option with friendly staff, a short walk from the central clock tower, offers bright and spacious rooms with heaters, TVs, easy chairs and private bathrooms. Wi-fi is mainly in the lobby area, although you may pick up a signal in your room. Bs500

**Toñito Hotel** Av Ferroviaria 60 ☏02 6933186, ⊕tonitouyuni.com; map p.165. Well-run hotel set around two communal lounges, with heated rooms, solar-powered hot water and a book exchange. An excellent breakfast is included at the attached *Minuteman Pizza* (see below). Wi-fi in public areas only. Bs500

### EATING

**Tourist restaurants** are centred on pedestrianized Plaza Arce, the majority offering mediocre and slightly overpriced gringo-oriented fare. Stalls in the **Mercado Central** on Potosí open at 6am and are inexpensive, though hygiene isn't always a top priority. In the evenings, a row of *rosticerías* on Av Potosí between Sucre and Camacho serve roasted llama, chicken or sausages, with rice, fries and salad, for around Bs20 a go.

**16 de Julio** Plaza Arce; map p.165. This glass-fronted restaurant remains a good choice for its hearty Bolivian staples such as beef and llama steaks (Bs55), *silpancho* (thin breaded steak; Bs55) and an array of omelettes. Coca beer is available too. Daily 9am–10pm.

**Arco Iris** Arce 53 ☏02 6933177; map p.165. This central restaurant has decent pizza (portions Bs23–30, individual pizzas Bs38–45) and pasta (Bs35–50), a cosy ambience and good background music. Despite the slow service, it's popular with travellers, particularly in the evenings. Mon–Sat 3–10pm.

★**La Loco** Av Ferroviaria 13 ☏02 6933105; map p.165. This rustic restaurant-bar by the station has a railway theme and a French touch, with dishes including llama in blue cheese sauce (Bs45) and chocolate crêpes (Bs18). It does breakfasts

too. Happy hour is 7–8pm. Mon–Sat 7am–1am.

★**Minuteman Pizza** Toñito Hotel, Av Ferroviaria 60 ☏02 6933186, ⊕tonitouyuni.com; map p.165. This American-Bolivian-run pizzeria serves a superb buffet breakfast (Bs50), and the pizzas (from Bs55), sandwiches and desserts keep up the high standards in the evening. If you drop off your old sunglasses here, *Minuteman* will donate them to salt workers in the Salar. Daily 8–10am & 5–9pm.

**Pizzeria Donna Isabella** Av Ferroviaria opposite the end of Camacho ☏7375 9824; map p.165. Bright, modern restaurant whose thin(ish)-crust pizzas (Bs60–90) are surprisingly good, especially as they're made with quinoa flour; each one is enough for two people. Daily 6–10pm.

### DRINKING

**Extreme Fun Pub** Av Potosí ☏7573 4008; map p.165. Although it doesn't live up to its name, this backpacker bar has an extensive range of drinks (cocktails Bs40–80; happy hour 2–7pm for beer, 7–9pm for cocktails), decent food, a

booming soundtrack and numerous drinking games, records of which are posted up on the walls alongside photos of the naked backsides of past visitors. You'll either love it or hate it. Daily 2pm–1am.

**3**

### DIRECTORY

**Banks and exchange** There are numerous ATMs, and a handful of money changers on Potosí around the junction with Arce.

**Internet** Mac Internet (daily 9am–10pm; Bs5/hr) on Potosí is one of the better cybercafés.

# The Salar de Uyuni and the far southwest

Covering some nine thousand square kilometres of the Altiplano west of Uyuni, the **Salar de Uyuni** is the world's biggest salt lake, and one of Bolivia's – and South America's – most extraordinary attractions. Most people visit the Salar on a tour (see box, p.171) that continues southward to take in the equally dramatic **Reserva de Fauna Andina Eduardo Avaroa**, a high-altitude wildlife reserve covering the most southwestern corner of Bolivia, taking in en route a series of incredible landscapes and jaw-droppingly scenic **lakes**, several of which host large populations of **flamingos**.

Even compared to the rest of the Altiplano, the Salar de Uyuni (and the Reserva Eduardo Avaroa) can get extremely cold. Though by day the sun can take **temperatures** as high as 30°C, the high altitude and reflective surface of the Salar mean that little heat is retained, so night temperatures can drop below -25°C, and as far as -40°C when the **wind-chill factor** is included – one of the widest day-night temperature fluctuations anywhere in the world. Consider taking a sleeping bag to supplement the bedding provided in the refuges, a warm hat, gloves, a windproof jacket and several layers of clothing including a fleece or woollen jumper and, ideally, thermal underwear (or even

---

## THE ORIGINS OF THE SALAR DE UYUNI

The Salar de Uyuni occupies what was once the deepest part of an enormous lake, known as **Lago Tauca**, which covered the southern Altiplano until 12,000 years ago. Reaching depths of up to 70m, Lago Tauca existed for a thousand years and covered the area now occupied by Lago Poopó, the Salar de Coipasa and the Salar de Uyuni – and was itself the successor to an earlier lake, Lago Minchín. The Salar was formed when the last waters of Lago Tauca evaporated, leaving behind salt that had been leached into the lake from the surrounding mountains, where it had been deposited millions of years ago before the Andes were formed, when what is now Bolivia was beneath the ocean.

According to studies, the **salt** extends to depths of up to 120m, packed in layers sandwiched between sedimentary deposits. In the dry season, the surface of the Salar, up to a depth of 10–20cm, becomes extremely hard and dry. Beneath this crust, though, the salt remains saturated with water. As the top layer dries, it contracts, forming cracks which draw the underlying salt water up by capillary action, thereby forming the strange polygonal lines of raised salt that cover the Salar in the dry season. As well as salt, the Salar is also home to the world's largest deposit of **lithium** (a mineral used in mobile phones, laptops and tablets, electric cars and many other devices). The Bolivian government has started **extraction projects** – and international mining conglomerates would dearly like to do so too – but there are fears that mining could have disastrous consequences for the fragile ecosystems surrounding the Salar.

### LEGENDS OF THE SALAR

For the campesinos living on the shores of the lake, explanations of the Salar's origin are rather different. Legend has it that the mountain goddess **Yana Pollera** – the nearest peak to Uyuni – was amorously involved with both Thunupa, the volcano on the north shore of the Salar, and a second volcano named Q'osqo. When she gave birth to a child, the two male volcanoes fought bitterly over who was the father. Worried for the child's safety, Yana Pollera sent it far away to the west. Then, concerned that her child would not survive alone, she flooded the plain between them with her milk so it could feed. Eventually the milk turned to salt, and the lake – traditionally known as the **Salar de Thunupa** – came into being.

a hot water bottle). You should also take sunblock and sunglasses to counter the fierce glare – snow blindness is a real possibility here.

## Salar de Uyuni

The **Salar de Uyuni** is not a lake in the conventional sense: though below the surface it is largely saturated by water, its uppermost layer consists of a thick, hard **crust of salt**, easily

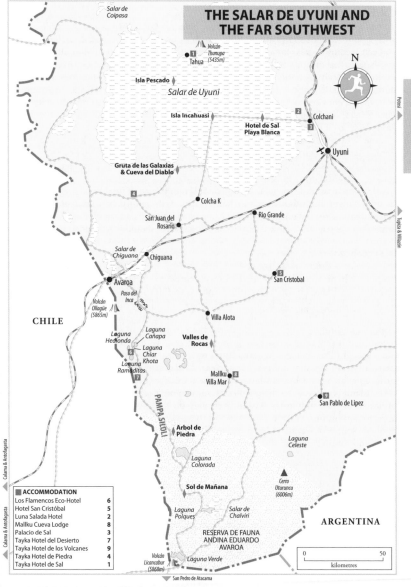

**THE SALAR DE UYUNI AND THE FAR SOUTHWEST**

| ACCOMMODATION | |
|---|---|
| Los Flamencos Eco-Hotel | 6 |
| Hotel San Cristóbal | 5 |
| Luna Salada Hotel | 2 |
| Mallku Cueva Lodge | 8 |
| Palacio de Sal | 3 |
| Tayka Hotel del Desierto | 7 |
| Tayka Hotel de los Volcanes | 9 |
| Tayka Hotel de Piedra | 4 |
| Tayka Hotel de Sal | 1 |

capable of supporting the weight of a car. Driving across this perfectly flat white expanse, with unbroken chains of snowcapped mountains lining the far horizon, it's easy to believe you're on another planet, so harsh and **inhospitable** is the terrain. When dry, the dazzling salt surface shines with such intense whiteness that it appears to be ice or snow, while by night the entire landscape is illuminated by the eerie white glow of moonlight reflected in the salt. When it's covered in water after rain (Dec–April), the Salar is turned into an enormous mirror that reflects the surrounding mountain peaks and the sky so perfectly that at times the horizon disappears and the mountains appear like islands floating in the sky.

## Colchani

Tours (see box, opposite) generally enter the Salar via **COLCHANI**, a salt-processing village on its eastern shores about 20km north of Uyuni. Here, at small **salt factories**, you can see how locals extract salt, scraping it off the ground into small mounds, which are then carried off for processing. Until relatively recently, communities like Colchani exploited the salt primarily to exchange with other indigenous communities. Every year dozens of pack llamas would set off, carrying salt as far away as Tarija, and returning with maize, coca and other goods. There's a small museum of salt sculptures (daily 10am–4pm; free) and another with explanations about salt and llamas (daily 7am–3pm; Bs5; pick up the English explanation at the entrance).

Some budget travellers, to avoid the cost of a full tour, come to Colchani by bus (any service between Uyuni and Oruro), sleep in a basic lodging here, and set out into the Salar on foot. It's certainly possible to do this, but you're obviously restricted by walking distance; don't forget to carry enough water.

A short drive west of Colchani is **Hotel de Sal Playa Blanca**: it used to be possible to spend the night, but this has been curtailed due to well-founded environmental concerns regarding the serious damage operating a hotel had on the Salar; travellers are advised to boycott the hotel, which now claims to be a "museum", should their tour stop at it.

## Isla Incahuasi

Entry Bs30, payable at an office at the base of the island

From Colchani, tours head 60km or so west across the Salar to **Isla Incahuasi**, one of several small islands in the Salar, called Inca Wasi ("Inca House") in Quechua. From its peak, a short sharp climb up on a well-marked trail, the views across the immense white expanse of the Salar are unforgettable. To the north is a series of snowcapped peaks, including the imperious Thunupa, the extinct volcano that is considered the region's most powerful *achachila*, or mountain god. To the west you can just make out a straight line like an old agricultural terrace running along the mountainside that rises from the shore: this is the ancient shoreline of Lago Tauca, 70m above the surface of the Salar. On the island itself, the rocks are covered in **fossilized algae**.

The island is also covered by **giant cacti**, some more than 9m tall and thought to be hundreds of years old; in January and February they produce bright white flowers that attract giant hummingbirds. The trunks of these giant cacti are about the only locally available source of wood, and you can see their distinctively pockmarked timber in doors and roofs all around the Salar.

In the rainy season this part of the Salar is sometimes too deeply flooded to be crossed by car, but during the high season the island gets very busy with tours. Some people therefore head on to **Isla de Pescado**, a fish-shaped island that's less spectacular but correspondingly less crowded (and has no entry fee).

## From the Salar de Uyuni to the Reserva Eduardo Avaroa

There are two routes south over the 160-odd kilometres from the Salar de Uyuni to the Reserva de Fauna Andina Eduardo Avaroa, and you may well go up on one and come back via the other.

## TOURS OF THE SALAR AND THE RESERVA EDUARDO AVAROA

Given their remoteness, really only way to visit the Salar de Uyuni and Reserva Eduardo Avaroa is on an **organized tour**. Even if you have your own 4WD complete with supplies and navigational aids, you should be very cautious; it's very easy to get lost, the hard crust on the surface can occasionally give way under the weight of vehicles and the consequences of a breakdown can be grave. Even with the best-maintained vehicles **mechanical failures** and breakdowns are not uncommon; drivers from different companies do, however, usually help each other out to make sure everyone gets back to Uyuni safely.

### TOUR AGENCIES

Uyuni has dozens of **tour agencies**, all of which run combined trips to the Salar and the reserve. Some run one- or two-day excursions, but if you've come this far it would be crazy not to go for the full circuit. The most popular trip is a **three-day tour** taking in, among other sights, the Salar de Uyuni, Lagunas Colorada and Verde, and the Sol de Mañana geyser.

Choosing an agency can be a bit random: all offer almost **identical tours**, but are prone to the same recurring problems: late departures, dangerous (and sometimes drunk) drivers, insufficient food, inadequate accommodation and vehicle breakdowns. Agencies regularly swap drivers, guides and vehicles, and many travellers find that they booked with one company only to be put on a tour run by another. While the bigger, more expensive **La Paz-based operators** (see p.76) and the **Tupiza-based operators** (see p.176) are generally reliable and have smaller groups, few locally based operators have a blemish-free record, and some have been involved in fatal accidents. The best way to make a decision is by chatting with travellers who have just returned from a tour. You should also visit several companies, ask for written itineraries, check the vehicles and confirm how many other people will be in the jeep with you: six or fewer is preferable; seven or eight can be very uncomfortable. Despite all the hassles and potential pitfalls, however, these tours are well worth the trouble, and almost everyone who goes counts them among their best experiences in Bolivia.

### COSTS

A standard three-day budget tour costs roughly $120–165 (Bs800–1100) per person if booked in Uyuni; tours booked in Tupiza tend to be a bit more expensive (and often last four days); those booked in La Paz or Potosí are more expensive again. A three-day tour with private transport and mid-range accommodation costs $550–660 (Bs3700–4400). You may also get charged more in **peak season** (June–Aug) and when the Salar is partly covered in water during the rainy season (Dec–April), since the salt water damages the vehicles; indeed, parts of the Salar become completely impassable during the rainy season. Be wary of very cheap deals – the savings will be made at your expense. Even if you're travelling alone, you should be able to find a group easily in Uyuni. The cost includes food, accommodation, transport and Spanish-speaking guide (an English-speaking guide costs extra). You also have to pay a Bs150 fee to enter the **Reserva Eduardo Avaroa** (payable at the rangers' office at Laguna Colorada); keep your ticket as you'll need to show it when you leave the reserve. A smaller fee to pay is the Bs30 Isla Incahuasi entry fee (payable at the island).

### ACCOMMODATION AND EATING

On the less expensive trips accommodation is in very basic **huts** or **refuges**. Food is usually little more than adequate, so it's worth taking along some extra supplies. On the more expensive trips, by contrast, there are some very comfortable hotels (see p.173) with equally good restaurants.

### CUSTOMIZE YOUR SALAR TOUR

While the classic three-day trip is very rewarding, there is a lot of scope for creating your own tour. As well as reversing the three-day circuit (which allows you to see the Salar in glorious morning light on the final day) you can add in a connection to **San Pedro de Atacama** in Chile (something that is increasingly popular) or **Tupiza** (see p.174). If you have the time and money, a four-day (or longer) trip gives you more time to explore, the chance to escape other tour groups, and the opportunity to build in extra activities; **volcano climbing** is increasingly popular and several **hikes** are possible. At any rate, you should always make sure that your tour will take in the specific things you want to see.

### The western route

The western route, partly impassable in the rainy season, heads from Isla Incahuasi to Colcha K and on to **San Juan del Rosario**, where there's a fascinating necropolis (Bs15) containing rock tombs and mummies from the Tiwanaku period. You then cross the edge of the smaller **Salar de Chiguana**, over the rail line from Uyuni to the Chilean border, and head south past **Ollagüe** (5865m), Bolivia's only active volcano – you can usually make out thin plumes of smoke rising from just below its peak. In the gorge called **Paso del Inca**, you may be lucky and spot some vizcachas, rabbit-like rodents that have become habituated to tourists here.

The route then passes a series of four brackish, blue-white **lakes** – Cañapa, Hedionda, Ramaditas and Chiar Khota – surrounded by snowy peaks. All four lakes support large colonies of **flamingos** and other water birds like ducks and wallata geese, and you're also likely to see herds of vicuña nearby. You can get closest to the flamingos at Laguna Hedionda. The track then climbs to over 4500m and enters the limits of the reserve at the **Pampa Siloli**, a high-altitude desert of volcanic ash and gravel scattered with rock outcrops sandblasted into surreal shapes by the constant, howling winds. The strangest of these is the **Árbol de Piedra** (Stone Tree), a massive 8m-high boulder balanced on a narrow stem.

### The eastern route

The eastern route down from Uyuni to the Reserva Eduardo Avaroa passes through **San Cristóbal**, a village rebuilt 10km from its original site in 1999 by a Japanese-led consortium who found silver there, which they are now mining, giving new homes and fresh employment to the villagers. The village's colonial church was moved stone by stone to its new location. The other main attraction on this route is the **Valle de Rocas**, with its haunting rock formations.

## Reserva de Fauna Andina Eduardo Avaroa

Bs150; payable at the park office by Laguna Colorada (see box, p.171)

Ranging between 4000m and 6000m in altitude, the starkly beautiful **RESERVA DE FAUNA ANDINA EDUARDO AVAROA** is a 7147-square-kilometre wildlife reserve covering the most southwestern corner of Bolivia. It is usually visited on an organized tour, and unless you have your own transport, that's the only way to do it.

### Laguna Colorada

All tour groups heading south have to buy tickets at the park office by **Laguna Colorada**, the reserve's biggest lake. It owes its bizarre red colour, which changes in intensity during the day, to the natural pigments of the algae that live in its shallow, mineral-laden water. These algae are a rich source of food for **flamingos**, all three species of which nest here in large numbers – the lake is thought to be the world's single biggest nesting site of the rare James flamingo. The fringes of the lake are encrusted with bright white deposits of ice and borax, a mineral used in paint, acid and glass manufacture. There are several basic huts and refuges here, where many tour groups spend the night.

### Sol de Mañana geyser and Laguna Polques

You need to set off before dawn the next morning in subzero temperatures to enjoy the full spectacle of the **Sol de Mañana geyser**. Set at an altitude of 5000m amid boiling pools of mud and sulphur, the geyser's high-pressure jet of steam shoots out from the earth to a great height, but diminishes in power later in the day. After the geyser the trail drops down to **Laguna Polques**, which has a series of **hot springs** on its southern shore. The deliciously warm waters are the perfect antidote to the high-altitude chill.

## Laguna Verde, Laguna Blanca and Volcán Licancabur

Thirty kilometres beyond Laguna Polques is **Laguna Verde**, a striking green lake set at over 4300m in the southeastern-most corner of the reserve. The lake owes its dramatic green hues to the arsenic and other minerals that are suspended in its waters – the colour ranges from turquoise to deep emerald depending on how much the wind stirs up its sediments. Divided by a narrow causeway from Laguna Verde is **Laguna Blanca**, home to more flamingos. Above the lakes rises the perfect snow-covered cone of **Volcán Licancabur**, a 5868m-high dormant volcano straddling the border with Chile. It's possible to climb to its peak, which has a crater lake and ruins of an Inca ceremonial site.

There's a small **refuge** beside the lakes, though most groups press on from here; some travellers return to Uyuni, others cross into Chile (see box, p.167).

### ACCOMMODATION                THE SALAR DE UYUNI AND THE FAR SOUTHWEST

There are some wonderful places to stay around the Salar de Uyuni and the Reserva Eduardo Avaroa, including several hotels made from salt. It is illegal to build on the salt flats themselves, however, which is why *Hotel de Sal Playa Blanca* (see p.170) should be avoided. The hotels are spread out over a wide area, and tend to be pretty expensive, although cheaper, much more basic lodgings can be found in Colchani, Villa Alota (especially in the rainy season, when the western route from Uyuni to the Reserva Eduardo Avaroa is impassable), Laguna Colorada and Laguna Verde.

**3**

**Los Flamencos Eco-Hotel** Laguna Hedionda **☎**02 6933107, **W**hotelesecologicosbolivia.com/los -flamencos.php; map p.169. This hotel is "eco" in the sense that it uses largely solar power and only switches on the generator when it has to (2hr every day), which means wi-fi at night only, and hot water only in the evenings. The rooms are very jolly, brightly coloured and set around a warm communal area, and each room has a little viewing space to watch the flamingos in the laguna. Still, it has to be said, for what you get, the price is a bit steep. **$153 (Bs1035)**

**Hotel San Cristóbal** San Cristóbal **☎**7300 4635; map p.169. Rather more modest than most of the hotels in the region, and more modestly priced too, this simple hostelry nonetheless has all the creature comforts you need: comfy beds, clean rooms and a restaurant, although it doesn't offer the scenic locations that the pricier places do. **Bs220**

**Luna Salada Hotel** 7km northwest of Colchani **☎**02 2770885, **W**lunasaladahotel.com; map p.169. Located 30km from Uyuni and 7km from Colchani, this slick hotel is constructed almost entirely from salt – from the walls to the chairs to the beds – and also boasts central heating and a good restaurant. Wi-fi in communal areas only. **$152 (Bs1030)**

**Mallku Cueva Lodge** Mallku Villa Mar village **☎**02 6932989, **W**mallkucueva.com; map p.169. In the isolated village of Mallku Villa Mar, to the south of Villa Alota, this comfortable option overlooks a stream and has pleasant en-suite rooms with central heating and a certain rustic charm. **Bs950**

**Palacio de Sal** 5km west of Colchani **☎**02 6225186, **W**palaciodesal.com.bo; map p.169. The "Palace of Salt" (the world's first salt hotel) has comfortable en-suite rooms, a restaurant-bar and a games room with pool table and dartboard; the nine-hole golf course was closed at the time of research but may reopen. There's also a spa

with sauna, whirlpool, massages and salt-based treatments. **$175 (Bs1200)**

### THE TAYKA PROJECT

The community-run sustainable-tourism Tayka Project (**☎**02 6932987 or **☎**7202 0069, **W**taykahoteles.com) has four hotels in stunningly remote locations. All have solar power, hot water and restaurants, and staff can organize transport and activities.

**Hotel del Desierto** Ojo de Perdiz; map p.169. A 90min drive from Laguna Colarada and 220km from Uyuni, this beautiful stone-walled lodge is surrounded by spectacular other-worldly terrain – at times it feels as if you're on the surface of Mars. There are great views from the dining room; rooms with a desert view (*vista al desierto*) are a bit more rustic than the comfier rooms (*habitaciones nuevas*) on the other side of the hotel. **$154 (Bs1045)**

**Hotel de los Volcanes** San Pablo de Lipez (150km east of Tupiza); map p.169. The newest Tayka hotel, 230km from Uyuni and 150km from Tupiza, close to the Chilean border, looks out at the dramatic Uturunco volcano. The terracotta-coloured lodge has homely rooms with wooden fixtures and fittings. **$154 (Bs1045)**

**Hotel de Piedra** Southern edge of the Salar de Uyuni; map p.169. The atmospheric "Rock Hotel" is located 170km northeast of the Chilean city of Calama and close to some fascinating rock formations and ancient remains. Although it has been designed to look like a pre-Columbian village, the lodge has modern standards of comfort. **$154 (Bs1045)**

**Hotel de Sal** Just outside the village of Tahua; map p.169. Situated 110km northwest of Uyuni, *Hotel de Sal* sits in the foothills of the Thunupa volcano. Constructed predominantly of salt, the hotel has comfortable rooms with wooden floors, private bathrooms and colourful throws. **$154 (Bs1045)**

# Tupiza

Some 200km southeast of Uyuni, the isolated town of **TUPIZA** nestles in a narrow, fertile valley that cuts through the harsh desert landscape of the Cordillera de Chichas. Sheltered from the bitter winds of the Altiplano by steep jagged mountains, the town enjoys a comparatively warm climate, while its friendly and laidback inhabitants help make it a popular stop for travellers passing through southern Bolivia. The real attraction, though, is the surrounding **dramatic desert scenery**, a landscape of red, eroded rock formations, cactus-strewn mountains and deep canyons, ideal for hiking, mountain biking, horseriding or just touring in a jeep – all of which are easy to arrange in town.

Tupiza was founded in 1535 by the conquistador **Diego de Almagro**. For most of its history the town's economy has been dominated by mining operations in the surrounding mountains. In the late nineteenth and early twentieth centuries it was the base of Carlos Aramayo, one of Bolivia's biggest mining barons, and the mine payrolls were rich enough to attract the attentions of **Butch Cassidy** and the **Sundance Kid** (see box, p.179), who are believed to have died 100km to the northwest. Today,

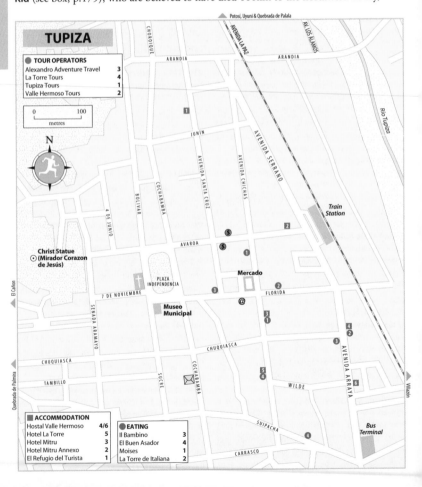

**TUPIZA**

**TOUR OPERATORS**

| | |
|---|---|
| Alexandro Adventure Travel | 3 |
| La Torre Tours | 4 |
| Tupiza Tours | 1 |
| Valle Hermoso Tours | 2 |

**ACCOMMODATION**

| | |
|---|---|
| Hostal Valle Hermoso | 4/6 |
| Hotel La Torre | 5 |
| Hotel Mitru | 3 |
| Hotel Mitru Annexo | 2 |
| El Refugio del Turista | 1 |

**EATING**

| | |
|---|---|
| Il Bambino | 3 |
| El Buen Asador | 4 |
| Moises | 1 |
| La Torre de Italiana | 2 |

the mineral deposits are largely exhausted, and Tupiza's economy depends more on its role as a **market centre** for the surrounding agricultural communities, as well as tourism.

## Plaza de Independencia and around

At the centre of the main square, the **Plaza de Independencia**, stands a statue of José Avelino Aramayo, founder of the once great Tupiza-based mining dynasty. As in most Bolivian mining towns, the late nineteenth- and early twentieth-century civic architecture around the square reflects a past age of prosperity now long gone. The unexceptional Neoclassical church on the west side dates from 1897. There's a **museum** of sorts (Mon–Fri 8am–noon & 2–6pm; Bs10) behind the town hall just south of the plaza on Sucre, which has a limited collection of historic photographs and archeological finds; if you arrive during the official opening times to find it closed (which is actually quite likely), ask in the town hall for someone to let you in.

## Mirador Corazón de Jesús

On the hilltop northwest of the city centre, the **Mirador Corazón de Jesús** has good views over the town's tin rooftops and the narrow valley of the Río Tupiza, and is topped by a **statue of Christ**. To get there, just walk a few minutes west of the plaza along Avaroa, then follow the Stations of the Cross up the hill.

## El Cañon

There is a good walk (2hr return) up **El Cañon**, a deep, narrow canyon lined with spectacularly eroded rock pinnacles. Walk out of town to the west, past the church, and follow the road as it curves round behind the hill with the statue of Christ. From here, turn up the (usually) dry river bed that climbs into the mountains on your left – the canyon gets deeper and narrower as you climb.

### ARRIVAL AND INFORMATION
### TUPIZA

**By train** The train station is three blocks east of the main plaza on Av Serrano. Trains (ⓦ www.fca.com.bo) head south to Villazón and north to Uyuni and Oruro. The *Expreso del Sur* is quicker and more comfortable than the cheaper *Wara Wara del Sur*.
Destinations Oruro (4 weekly; 12hr 45min–14hr 5min); Uyuni (4 weekly; 5hr 25min–6hr 10min); Villazón (4 weekly; 2hr 55min–3hr).

**By bus** The terminal is on Av Araya, three blocks south and two blocks east of Plaza Independencia. The journey to Uyuni is scenic (especially the first hour, through Salo) but rough,

and you may have to change buses midway at the town of Atocha, which is sometimes served by quicker and more comfortable jeeps. All routes out of Tupiza pass through some fairly spectacular landscapes, so try to travel in daylight.
Destinations Tarija (5 daily, departing morning and evening; 6–7hr, sometimes longer in the rainy season); Uyuni (3 daily; 7hr); Villazón (12 daily; 2–3hr).

**Tourist information** There's no formal tourist information office, but the town's tour operators (see box, p.176) can tell you all you need to know, though obviously with a view to selling you some kind of trip.

### ACCOMMODATION

**Hostal Valle Hermoso** Av Pedro Arraya 478 ⓣ 02 6942370, ⓦ vallehermosotours.com; map opposite. Split between a main building and a smaller annexe, the Hostelling International-affiliated *Valle Hermoso* has a range of clean and sunny dorms and private rooms (with either shared or private bathrooms; most also have TVs). There's a book exchange, laundry service, common rooms with TVs, a DVD library and a roof terrace. Wi-fi in the lobby area and some rooms; breakfast not included. Dorms Bs40, doubles Bs100

**Hotel La Torre** Av Chichas 220 ⓣ 02 6942633, ⓦ latorretours-tupiza.com; map opposite. A fine alternative to the bigger operators, with a welcoming, family feel: there are potted plants galore, polished floors and a lovely roof terrace. Most rooms have private bathrooms (Bs160) and TVs, though a couple have shared facilities. Wi-fi mainly in the lobby area. Bs120

★**Hotel Mitru** Av Chichas 187 ⓣ 02 6943001, ⓦ hotelmitru.com; map opposite. Tupiza's top hotel is divided into the older "Garden" and more modern

**3**

## ORGANIZED TOURS FROM TUPIZA

Tupiza's **tour agencies** all offer broadly similar excursions into the desert landscapes around the town in 4WDs (from Bs200–250 for a half day, Bs400 for a full day) or on mountain bike, horseback or foot (from Bs160), as well as trips (from Bs270) to **San Vicente** (see p.178), where Butch Cassidy and the Sundance Kid are thought to have died, and **Huaca Huañusca** (see p.178) where they committed their final robbery (see box, p.179). An increasingly popular excursion is the "triathlon", a day-trip that combines mountain biking, horseriding and a jeep ride.

Tupiza's agencies can also organize trips (around Bs1250/person for a four-day circuit, rising to Bs1600 in high season) to the **Reserva de Fauna Andina Eduardo Avaroa** and the **Salar de Uyuni**, entering the reserve via the remote **Sur Lípez** region, heading north into the Salar and then either dropping you off in Uyuni or returning to Tupiza. This route is arguably more aesthetically pleasing than the traditional circuit leaving from Uyuni – though a rapid ascent to 5000m on the second day can be a bit challenging.

### TOUR OPERATORS

**Alexandro Adventure Travel** Av Pedro Arraya and Chuquisaca ☎6546 9059, ⓦalexandrotours.com; map p.174. The usual tours, plus motorbike and quad-bike rental.

**La Torre Tours** Inside Hotel La Torre ☎02 6942633, ⓦlatorretours-tupiza.com; map p.174. Friendly, professionally run operation, with a range of tailored Salar tours and local excursions, plus trips to Parque Nacional Sajama (see p.140).

**Tupiza Tours** Inside Hotel Mitru ☎02 6943003, ⓦtupizatours.com; map p.174. The oldest and biggest tour operator in Tupiza, this has one of the better reputations for Reserva and Salar tours. They also run a two-day jeep tour following the last steps of Butch and Sundance, and offer an excellent deal of four tours to different areas around Tupiza, one after the other (with a break for lunch) at 8am, 10am, 1pm and 3.30pm, which you can take all at once for Bs200, or over two days for Bs250, with horseback or bicycle add-ons available.

**Valle Hermoso Tours** In the Hostal Valle Hermoso ☎02 6942370, ⓦvallehermosotours.com; map p.174. Offers the same range of excursions as Tupiza Tours, as well as longer horseback camping trips.

"Cactus" sections: rooms in both are comfortable, spacious and not without style; the more expensive ones (Bs280) have private bathrooms, TVs and phones. There's a heated pool, central courtyard, book exchange and laundry service. The same management runs the *Hotel Mitru Annexo* round the corner at Av Avaroa and Chichas, with similar standards and prices, and a more basic facility, *El Refugio del Turista* on Av Santa Cruz, featuring simple rooms with shared bathrooms (Bs100) and no breakfast. $\overline{Bs160}$

## EATING

The cheapest place for food is the upper floor of the **market** at Av Chichas and Florida; try the tasty *tamales* (spicy meat covered with mashed corn and cooked in corn husks). There are also numerous, rather samey, restaurants aimed at foreign travellers. Keep an eye out for local **specialities** like *asado de cordero* (roast lamb) and *cangrejitos* (soft-shelled freshwater crabs).

**Il Bambino** Florida and Av Santa Cruz ☎7033 4542; map p.174. Eating at this first-floor restaurant feels a little like dining in someone's house, and appropriately the food has a homely touch. It's a good-value spot for a hearty lunch or dinner, which is either way a set menu (Bs15). Mon–Sat noon–9pm.

**El Buen Asador** Suipacha 14; map p.174. The best food in town, popular with locals for its filling set almuerzos (Bs13–20), excellent meat dishes (including delicious Argentine-style steaks, such as *bife chorizo* at Bs50), and special lamb roasts at the weekend. There's sometimes even live music. Mon–Sat 10am–9pm, Sun 10am–5pm.

**Moises** Av Chichas 166 ☎7186 6675; map p.174. A popular *churrasquería* (grill, in other words), where the emphasis is on meat. You can get an almuerzo here at midday for Bs18, but the real deal is to come in the evening, when you get meat of your choice (*bife chorizo* steak, pork steak or whatever) with rice, fries and salad for Bs50. Daily noon–10pm.

**La Torre de Italiana** Florida ☎7256 2488; map p.174. As well as decent pizza and pasta (from Bs30), this touristy restaurant has tacos and enchiladas (Bs25–40), tasty Spanish omelettes (Bs30) and a good range of coffee. Daily 8am–10pm.

## DIRECTORY

**Banks and exchange** There are a couple of ATMs on the main plaza, and a couple of *cambios* on Calle Avaroa. *Hotel Mitru* and the *Hostal Valle Hermoso* will change dollars, and the latter will also change euros and Argentine pesos.

**Internet** Punto Viva, 121 Florida, opposite the market.
**Post office** Cochabamba 75, between Chuquiasco and Suipacha.

# Cordillera de Chichas

Around Tupiza stretches the harsh but beautiful **CORDILLERA DE CHICAS**, a striking landscape of cactus-strewn badlands, deep gulches and canyons, and strangely shaped rock formations and pinnacles. The easiest way to see the cordillera is to take a jeep excursion with one of Tupiza's tour companies (see box, opposite), but travelling on foot, bike or horseback offers a much more relaxed way to explore the eerie desert landscapes. Bring plenty of water with you, particularly if travelling on foot, as the sun can be very intense and water is scarce. There are plenty of good spots to camp in the cordillera's secluded valleys, but avoid pitching your tent on river beds in case of flash floods.

## Quebrada de Palala

A few kilometres northwest of Tupiza along the road to Uyuni is the mouth of the **Quebrada de Palala**, a ravine formed by a tributary of the Río Tupiza. The river bed is dry for most of the year, and is used as a highway by vehicles heading to isolated mines

---

### CROSSING THE ARGENTINE BORDER VIA VILLAZÓN

About 92km south of Tupiza, the ramshackle frontier town of **Villazón** is the main **border crossing** between Bolivia and Argentina. Set at an altitude of 3445m, it's a busy little place bustling with cross-border traffic. Most of the people crossing the border here are Bolivian migrants who live and work in Argentina. Unless you get stuck overnight, there's really no reason to linger here; it's better to push straight on into Argentina or to Tupiza or Tarija.

Crossing the border couldn't be easier. From the main square (Plaza 6 de Agosto), walk 500m south along Av República de Argentina, and cross over the Horacio Guzmán Bridge. Make sure you get stamped out by the Bolivians and stamped in by the Argentines; the **offices** are open 6am–10pm Bolivian time (7am–11pm Argentine time). From the Argentine border town of **La Quiaca** there are regular buses to the city of Jujuy, from where there are connections to the rest of the country; beware of touts selling overpriced tickets. Accommodation and food in La Quiaca are better than in Villazón, but cost more. It's best to get rid of your Bolivian pesos before you cross the border.

Arriving in Bolivia from Argentina, it's a 1.5km walk from the border to the train station, around eight blocks north of the main square. Trains (4 weekly; a better option than buses if you can coincide with them; ⊕www.fca.com.bo) head north to Tupiza (2hr 45min–2hr 55min), Uyuni (8hr 20min–9hr 45min) and Oruro (15hr 40min–17hr 40min); the *Expreso del Sur* (Wed & Sat 3.30pm) is quicker and more comfortable than the cheaper *Wara Wara del Sur* (Mon & Thurs 3.30pm). The bus terminal on Av Tumusla, 2km northeast of the town centre, has services to Tarija (5 daily, all but one in the evening; 8hr) and Tupiza (12 daily; 2–3hr). Several cambios in town change dollars and Argentine pesos.

#### ACCOMMODATION AND EATING

There are plenty of **food stalls** around the bus terminal and inside the covered market on the east side of the plaza, and a number of cheap fried-chicken **restaurants** on the way down to the border along Av República de Argentina (Av Internacional).

**Hotel Center** Plaza 6 de Agosto 125 ☎02 5975472. If you get stuck, this is the best place to stay in Villazón, right on the main square. Hot water is only available at specific times, and breakfast is limited, but they take bolivianos, Argentine pesos or dollars. **Bs160**

to the northwest. If you journey 6km or so up the gorge you'll come to a series of red rock formations that have been eroded into massive fins. A few kilometres further on you'll reach a high saddle between two peaks known as **El Sillar**, around which stands a stone forest of tall pinnacles of eroded rock.

## Quebrada de Palmira to the Canyon del Inca

A few kilometres southwest of Tupiza, the **Quebrada de Palmira** is another deep, cactus-strewn ravine gouged out of the red mountains by a seasonal river, with dramatic rock formations on either side. If you walk, ride or drive about 6km along the *quebrada* you'll reach the **Puerta del Diablo** ("Devil's Gate"), a gateway formed by two great vertical slabs. A few kilometres further along is the **Valle de Los Machos**, a stone forest of rock pinnacles eroded into distinctly phallic shapes. The ravine eventually peters out into a narrow canyon with steep blood-red walls, the **Canyon del Inca**.

## Quebrada Seca and La Angostura

Ten kilometres to the south of Tupiza, **Quebrada Seca** is a deep and usually dry ravine with dramatic, eroded rock formations forming a series of spires, pinnacles and even arches, giving the sides of the valley the appearance of a Gothic cathedral.

A few kilometres east of Quebrada Seca, also about 10km south of town, the road and railway to Villazón pass through a narrow defile known as **La Angostura**, where the Río Tupiza has cut a deep gorge through a narrow opening – it's usually included in day-long jeep tours of the region around Tupiza, though it isn't worth making a special journey to see on its own.

## San Vincente

Tupiza's tour agencies run several trips following the trail of the infamous US outlaws, **Butch Cassidy and the Sundance Kid** (see box, opposite). Located some 100km northwest of Tupiza at an altitude of over 4300m, the bleak mining village of **San Vicente**, where Butch and Sundance are believed to have died in a shoot-out, is pretty much abandoned. Apart from the adobe hut where the outlaws made their last stand, the grave in the cemetery where they are thought to have been buried, and a small museum (Bs40), there's little to look at in this virtual ghost town. Note that although the trip takes six to seven hours, you only spend an hour or so at the site.

## Huaca Huañusca

There's very little to see at **HUACA HUAÑUSCA**, the mountain pass about 45km north of Tupiza where Butch and Sundance made their last robbery (see box, opposite). Having said that, quite a few travellers do visit, and it's usually possible to get a group together for a tour within a day or two.

# Tarija

In the far south of the country, hemmed in by the high Altiplano to the west and the cactus-choked hills that drop down into the impenetrable forests of the Chaco to the east, isolated **TARIJA** feels a world away from the rest of Bolivia. Indeed, the country's two biggest cities, La Paz and Santa Cruz, are both around 24 hours away by road. Set in a broad, fertile valley at an altitude of 1924m, Tarija lies at the centre of a rich agricultural region known as the **Andalusia of Bolivia** on account of its sunny climate, vineyard-filled valley and the arid mountain scenery that surrounds it. Indeed, so

## THE LAST DAYS OF BUTCH CASSIDY AND THE SUNDANCE KID

The wilds of Bolivia have always attracted their fair share of renegades and desperadoes, but few have received as much posthumous attention as **Butch Cassidy and the Sundance Kid**. Made famous by the 1969 movie starring Paul Newman and Robert Redford, they belonged to a band of outlaws who robbed banks, trains and mines in the Rocky Mountains in the United States. In 1901, with the golden age of Wild West gunslingers coming to an end, a price on their heads and the Pinkerton Detective Agency (often hired by the US authorities to track down criminals before the FBI was set up) hot on their trail, Butch and Sundance fled by ship to South America.

They settled in **Argentina** under assumed names, living on a ranch in the Cholilla Valley in Patagonia. But the Pinkerton Agency had not given up the hunt, and in 1905 the two outlaws went on the run after their names were linked with a bank robbery in Río Gallegos, in the far south of Argentina. They fled to **Chile**, apparently returning to Argentina to rob another bank, before showing up in **Bolivia** in 1906, where they found work at the Concordia Tin Mine – their duties, ironically, included guarding the payroll. A year later they made a trip to Santa Cruz, and Butch returned determined to start life again as a rancher in the Eastern Lowlands. Perhaps in need of capital to finance their retirement, in 1908 they quit their jobs and returned to their old ways, heading to **Tupiza**, where the wealth of the Aramayo mining company offered a tempting prize. Put off from robbing the town bank by the presence of Bolivian troops, on November 3 Butch and Sundance intercepted a convoy of mules carrying a mine payroll at **Huaca Huañusca** (see opposite), a mountain pass north of Tupiza. Finding only $90,000 rather than the half million they had expected, the outlaws fled south with the loot. With military patrols and posses of angry miners (whose pay had been stolen) scouring the countryside, and the Argentine and Chilean border guards alerted, the bandits stopped at the home of an English friend, mining engineer A.G. Francis.

Warned the authorities were on their trail, Butch and Sundance turned north, heading towards Uyuni. On November 6 they stopped for the night in **San Vicente** (see opposite), a remote mining village about 100km northwest of Tupiza. Unknown to them, however, a four-man military patrol was also spending the night in the village. Informed of the outlaws' presence, they attacked the room where Butch and Sundance were staying. After a brief shoot-out, all went quiet. In the morning, the two bandits were found dead, Butch having apparently shot his wounded partner before turning his gun on himself. The bodies were buried in an **unmarked grave** in the cemetery.

Or were they? In subsequent decades rumours suggested the two dead men were not Butch and Sundance. The two outlaws were reported to have returned to the USA or Argentina, having assumed new identities; one report even had them finally gunned down in Paris. In 1991 forensic anthropologists exhumed a body from the San Vicente cemetery, but were unable to settle the mystery surrounding the outlaws' fate. A good book on the subject is *Digging Up Butch and Sundance* (see p.324).

**3**

striking are the similarities with southern Spain that Luis de Fuentes, the conquistador who founded the city, named the river on whose banks it sits the Guadalquivir, after the river that flows past Seville.

Tarija is famous for its **wine** production, and the valley's rich soils and fecund climate attracted many Andalusian farmers during the colonial period. The peasant culture they brought with them is still evident in the traditional costumes, folkloric dances, religious fiestas, love of food and wine, and languid, sing-song accents of the Tarijeños. Known as **Chapacos**, Tarijeños take considerable pride in their distinct cultural identity; closer culturally to northern Argentina, they think of themselves as a people apart from the rest of Bolivia.

Laid out in a classic grid pattern, Tarija has few obvious sightseeing attractions – its appeal lies more in the easy charm of its citizens and the warm, balmy climate. Although the population has mushroomed to over one hundred thousand, the city remains provincial in the best sense of the word: small enough to get around on foot and culturally self-contained, but open to foreign influences and welcoming to outsiders. Moreover, Tarija's **Carnaval** is one of Bolivia's most enjoyable fiestas.

### Brief history

Tarija was founded on July 4, 1574 as a Spanish frontier outpost on the far southeast edge of Alto Peru to guard against incursions by the indomitable **Chiriguano** tribes of the Chaco. The settlement thrived, exporting wine, cattle and grain to the mines of the Altiplano, but despite its prosperity, Tarija remained on the front line of missionary and military expeditions against the Chiriguanos – only after the final Chiriguano uprising was crushed in 1892 were outlying settlements finally freed from the threat of tribal raiders. The greatest moment in Tarija's history came during the **Independence War** on April 15, 1817, when a combined force of Argentine troops and Chapaco guerrilla riders led by a one-armed rebel named Eustaquio "Moto" Mendez defeated a Spanish army outside the city at the battle of **La Tablada**. After this victory Tarija enjoyed eight years of de facto independence before voting to join the newly proclaimed Republic of Bolivia rather than Argentina in 1825. Although the region has provided two **presidents** in recent decades, it has otherwise managed to avoid much of the upheaval of the past century.

**3**

## Plaza Luis de Fuentes

The focal point of the city is the peaceful, palm-lined **Plaza Luis de Fuentes**, named after the city's founder, whose statue stands on its southern side, dressed in full conquistador armour, flourishing his sword in front of him. Surrounding the plaza are several restaurants and cafés, as well as the governor's palace on the west side and the town hall on the south side.

## Catedral

Campero, a block west of Plaza Luis de Fuentes • Mon–Sat 6.30am–10am & 5–8pm, Sun 6.30am–noon & 5–8.30pm • Free

The dull modern **Catedral**'s main redeeming feature is its bright stained-glass windows, including one depicting local peasants harvesting grapes. It stands on the site once occupied by the Jesuit college, which was founded in 1690 and provided an important base for missionary ventures down into the Chaco, before the order was expelled from the Spanish empire in 1767. Some of the paintings and retablos inside survive from Tarija's parish church, demolished in 1830.

## Iglesia de San Francisco

A block east of Plaza Luis de Fuentes on Madrid • Mon–Sat 6.30am–9am & 6–7.30pm, Sun 6am–noon & 6–8pm • Free

The simple **Iglesia de San Francisco**, founded in 1606, was Tarija's first church. The Franciscan college next door still houses a massive archive of historical documents from several centuries of Franciscan missionary endeavour, and there's also a small collection of colonial religious art inside, but you'll need to persuade one of the priests to show you around.

## Museo Paleontológico

Virginio Lema and Trigo, a block south of the plaza • Mon–Fri 8am–noon & 3–6pm, Sat 9am–noon & 3–6pm • Free

The **Museo Paleontológico** has a fantastic collection of **fossils** from the Tarija valley. Most are of mammals from the Pleistocene era (between a million and 250,000 years ago), many from relatives of species that exist today. Entering the main gallery, you'll see on your left the skeleton of a long-extinct **megatherium** (giant sloth), 5m tall and one of the biggest land mammals ever to exist. Laid out on a table in the middle of the room is the skeleton of a *Cuvieronius tarijensis*, a local extinct relative of the **elephant**, and at the end of the room another one stands proud next to two **glyptodons**, bumptious armour-plated mammals related to the armadillo. The minerals and human artefacts upstairs are less exciting, but there's a curious 35cm **mummy** of unknown age whose teeth show it to have been an adult, perhaps just someone unusually small.

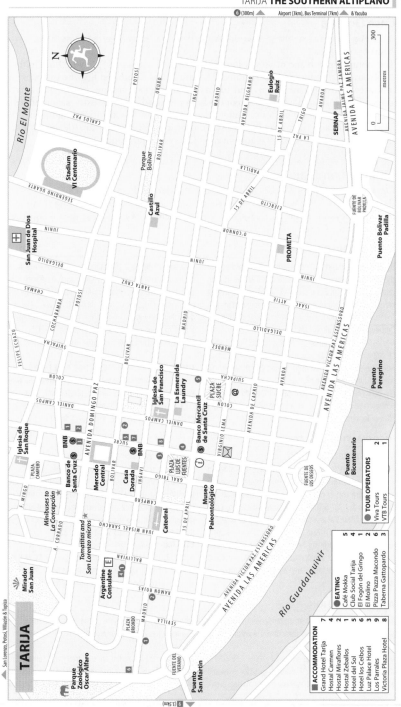

**6** (300m) ▲  Airport (3km), Bus Terminal (7km) ▲ & Yacuba

**3**

N

Río El Monte

Río Guadalquivir

TARIJA

San Lorenzo, Potosí, Villazón & Tupiza

0     300
metres

Stadium VI Centenario

San Juan de Dios Hospital

Parque Bolívar

Castillo Azul

Eulogio Ruiz

SERNAP

PROMETA

Puente Bolívar Padilla

Iglesia de San Roque

Iglesia de San Francisco

La Esmeralda Laundry

Banco Mercantil de Santa Cruz

Banco de Santa Cruz

BNB

BNB

Mercado Central

Casa Dorada

Museo Paleontológico

Catedral

Plaza Campero

Plaza Luis de Fuentes

Plaza Sucre

Minibuses to La Concepción

Tomatitas and San Lorenzo micros

Mirador San Juan

Argentine Consulate

Parque Zoológico Oscar Alfaro

Plaza Uriondo

Plaza San Martín

Puente San Martín

Puente Bicentenario

Puente Peregrino

Fuente de los Deseos

Fuente del Verano

Fuente de Bolívar Padilla

**● TOUR OPERATORS**
Viva Tours ........... 2
VTB Tours ........... 1

**● EATING**
Café Mokka ........................ 5
Club Social Tarija ............... 4
El Fogón del Gringo ........... 1
El Molino ........................... 2
Pizza Pizza Macondo ........ 9
Taberna Gattopardo .......... 3

**■ ACCOMMODATION**
Grand Hotel Tarija ............. 7
Hostal Carmen ................... 4
Hostal Miraflores .............. 2
Hostal Zeballos ................. 1
Hotel del Sol ..................... 5
Hotel los Ceibos ............... 6
Luz Palace Hotel ............... 3
Los Parrales ...................... 9
Victoria Plaza Hotel .......... 8

## Casa Dorada

Ingavi and Trigo • Guided tours (45min) in Spanish only Mon–Fri at 9am, 10am, 11am, 3pm, 4pm & 5pm • Bs5 • ☎ 04 6634201, ⓦ casadelaculturatarija.com

The looming, garish and decidedly kitsch "**Gold House**" dates back to 1903. Built in the Art Nouveau style for local businessman Moisés Navajas Ichazo and his wife Esperanza, it now contains a theatre, library and cultural centre. To look around, you need to join a guided tour. Inside, much of the decor has been preserved: there are extravagant murals and frescoes, crystal lamps in the dining room, and a music room with a grand piano. The **Castillo Azul**, a slightly less extravagant eccentric blue mansion from the same era (and not open to the public), is at Bolívar 644, between Junín and O'Connor.

## Mirador San Juan

On a hilltop northwest of the city centre, the **Mirador San Juan** is a pleasant park shaded by palm trees, with good views across Tarija and the mountains rising above the valley beyond. To get there, walk west along Avenida Domingo Paz then follow the Stations of the Cross up the hill to your right.

### ARRIVAL AND DEPARTURE                                TARIJA

**By plane** The airport (☎ 04 6642399) is 3km southeast of the city centre along Av Jaime Paz Zamora. A taxi into the centre costs Bs20, or Bs8 if you walk out of the airport and catch one on the main road; there are also frequent micros. To return to the airport catch a micro heading east along Av Domingo Paz. Local airport tax is Bs11.
Destinations Cochabamba (1–3 daily; 50min; BoA); La Paz (1 daily; 1hr 5min; BoA); Santa Cruz (1–2 daily; 55min; BoA, Ecojet); Sucre (4 weekly; 35min; BoA); Yacuiba (4 weekly; 20min; Amaszonas).

**By bus** The bus terminal is 7km southeast of the city centre; take a taxi (Bs15), or a micro (Bs1.50) showing "Nueva Terminal" from Av Domingo Paz.

Destinations Bermejo (20 daily; 4hr; plus minibuses from behind the terminal); La Paz (17 daily, generally departing in the late afternoon/early evening; 16hr); Oruro (15 daily, mostly overnight; 12hr); Santa Cruz (6 daily; 14hr); Tupiza (5 daily, departing morning and evening; 6–7hr, sometimes longer in the rainy season); Villamontes (4 daily; 10–12hr; plus minibuses from behind the terminal); Villazón (5 daily; 8hr).

### CROSSING THE ARGENTINE BORDER

The most convenient border crossing into Argentina is at Bermejo (20 daily buses plus minibuses; 4hr), just over 200km south of Tarija. Villazón (see p.177) is only 191km southwest but takes longer to get to (5 daily buses; 8hr).

### INFORMATION AND TOURS

#### TOURIST INFORMATION
There's a tourist information office round the side (in Calle Sucre) of the municipal council building at the southeastern corner of Plaza Luis de Fuentes (Mon–Fri 8am–noon & 2.30–6.30pm, Sat & Sun 8am–noon; ☎ 04 6633581). There's also a tourist information desk at the bus station (Mon–Fri 7am–9pm, Sat & Sun 8am–2pm; ☎ 04 6639415). Both are helpful and give out a good town map, but don't speak much English. Viva Tours and VTB Tours (see below) are also good sources of information.

#### TOUR OPERATORS
**Viva Tours** Bolívar 251 ☎ 04 6638325, ⓦ vivatoursbolivia.com; map p.181. Runs enjoyable tours (from around Bs170 for a half-day tour) of the Tarija valley's vineyards (see p.186) with experienced English-speaking guides, and also takes groups on the Inca Trail in the Reserva Cordillera del Sama (see p.186).
**VTB Tours** Ingavi 784 (inside Hostal Carmen) ☎ 04 6643372, ⓦ vtbtourtarija.com; map p.181. As well as offering similar vineyard and Inca Trail trips to Viva Tours (see above), VTB can also arrange palaeontology tours (see p.185).

### ACCOMMODATION

Tarija has a good range of accommodation, most of it located in the city centre; some of the mid-range hotels are particularly good value. Book ahead if you're visiting during **Carnaval**, when prices rise sharply.

**Grand Hotel Tarija** Sucre 762 ☎ 04 6642893, ⓦ grandhoteltarija.com; map p.181. Aimed predominantly at business travellers, the rooms here aren't as grand as the lobby, but are still pretty well turned-out, with a/c, TV, safe and minibar. There's also a restaurant-bar and a sauna. It's worth paying Bs40 more for a slightly

3

## FIESTAS IN TARIJA

Tarijeños are known throughout Bolivia for their love of music, dance and a good party. Though not as strongly influenced by pre-Christian beliefs as the festivals elsewhere in the Bolivian Andes, fiestas in Tarija are still deeply rooted in the agricultural cycle, as well as the calendar of Catholic saints' days. The distinctive Chapaco **folk music** features strongly at all the fiestas, played on unusual woodwind instruments like the *erque* and *quenilla*. This music is accompanied by poetic and often comic folk songs known as *coplas* – usually sung as duets. The best known of the region's folkloric **dances** is the *chuncho*, in which dancers wear brightly coloured robes, feathered headdresses and masks in ritual portrayal of the Chiriguano tribes of the Chaco.

Tarija's **Carnaval** celebrations in February or March are among the most colourful in Bolivia. On the Thursday before Carnaval, the Dia de Comadres is marked by an exchange of cakes and gifts, and a parade of all the women in the city. Carnaval itself is celebrated with a mass parade of folkloric dances and campesinos in elaborate traditional costumes, and several days of water-fighting, dancing, singing, drinking and eating. The fiesta ends with the ritual burial of the Devil. The end of Carnaval coincides with the **Fiesta de la Uva** (Grape Festival) in La Concepción, 35km south of Tarija, where grape-growers show off their wares amid further celebrations.

On August 15 Tarijeños celebrate the fiesta of the **Virgen de la Asunción** with a mass pilgrimage to the village of Chaguaya, 70km south of the city. Tarija's patron saint is **San Roque**, whose fiesta is celebrated on the first weekend of September with a religious procession accompanied by troupes of *chuncho* dancers.

---

larger room with an outside window. **Bs400**

★**Hostal Carmen** Ingavi 784 ☎04 6643372, ⓦhostalcarmentarija.com; map p.181. This rightly popular hotel has a range of well-decorated en-suite rooms, including some economical ones on the top floor; all have TVs and phones. There are also suites and semi-suites with a kitchenette (Bs400–420). Perks include free filtered water, tea and coffee. This is also the HQ of VTB Tours (see p.182). **Bs290**

**Hostal Miraflores** Sucre 920 ☎04 6643355, ⓔleozurita@yahoo.com; map p.181. Converted colonial house with a sunny central courtyard, efficient staff and a choice between decent rooms with TVs and private bathrooms (Bs80 more) or tiny, spartan rooms without. Wi-fi in lobby area only. No breakfast. **Bs100**

**Hostal Zeballos** Sucre 966 ☎04 6642068; map p.181. Friendly budget *hostal* with a patio overflowing with grapevines and other plants, and a choice of plain, clean rooms with private bathrooms, or simple but still quite spacious ones with shared facilities. No breakfast. **Bs120**

**Hotel del Sol** Sucre 782 ☎04 6665259, ⓦhoteldelsol.com.bo; map p.181. This comfortable city-centre three-star, just across from the central market, is a solid, if unspectacular, mid-range option with modern decor and rooms set around a central atrium. Ask for a room with an outside window if you like more light. **Bs400**

**Hotel los Ceibos** Av Las Américas and Madrid ☎04 6634430, ⓦwww.hotellosceibos.com; map p.181. Luxurious four-star with warm, spacious and well-appointed a/c rooms, each with a private balcony. There's a large swimming pool, as well as a restaurant, bar, sauna, spa and gym. **Bs639**

**Luz Palace Hotel** Sucre 326 ☎04 6635700, ⓦhotelluzpalace.com; map p.181. A lovely, faintly Moorish-style courtyard is the focal point of this reliable business hotel. The en-suite rooms – with minibars, TVs and phones – are bright and comfortable rather than stylish. A bit pricey for what you get, but still a good choice. **Bs300**

**Los Parrales** Urbanización El Carmen de Aranjuez, 3.5km west of Tarija ☎04 6648444, ⓦlosparraleshotel.com; map p.181. This top-end resort, a short drive from the centre, is the most luxurious option in the area, with big en-suite rooms, restaurant, bar, pool, spa and huge jacuzzi. Rack rates are high, but include a spa session, and discounted deals are often available. **Bs1054**

**Victoria Plaza Hotel** Madrid and Sucre ☎04 6642600, ⓦvictoriaplazahoteltarija.com; map p.181. This once-grand hotel overlooking the main plaza is comfortably if creakily old-fashioned, all wooden floors and a whiff of polish. The rooms are sober but well equipped, with a/c, TV and minibar, and there's also a café-bar. **Bs500**

## EATING

Tarija's strong **Argentine** influence is particularly evident in its restaurants; good-quality grilled beef, ideally accompanied by local wine, features strongly. There are also some great spicy-sauced dishes to try, including *ranga-ranga* (tripe with potatoes, onions and yellow chilli), *saice* (meat in a red chilli sauce) or *chancho de pollo* (spicy chicken); a good place to sample these is in the **Mercado Central**. A particular local speciality is *sopa la poderosa*, a rich soup made with a bull's penis – considered, unsurprisingly, to be a powerful aphrodisiac.

**Café Mokka** Plaza Sucre ☎ 04 6650505; map p.181. In a good people-watching spot, this busy café has a lengthy menu featuring more than twenty types of coffee (from Bs9), as well as Argentine-style *submarinos* (hot chocolate; Bs16), cocktails and beer. Food-wise the breakfast and snacks are good, but the mains are a bit overpriced. Mon–Sat 8am–11pm, Sun 4–11pm.

**Club Social Tarija** Plaza Luis de Fuentes ☎ 04 6632473; map p.181. Good-value traditional almuerzos (Bs18–40) and more expensive à la carte options for dinner in a rather staid atmosphere favoured by Tarija's business community and older citizens. Daily 8.30am–11pm.

**El Fogón del Gringo** Madrid 1051 ☎ 04 6643399; map p.181. In culinary terms this is as close as you'll get to Argentina without actually crossing the border. Succulent steaks (Bs70–95) come with access to a well-stocked salad bar, and there's also a fine selection of wines. Mon 7–11pm, Tues–Sat noon–3pm & 7–11pm, Sun noon–3pm.

**El Molino** Madrid 803 at Ramón Rojas ☎ 04 6643659, ⓦ bit.ly/ElMolinoTarija; map p.181. Vegetarian restaurant where lunch (Bs20) consists of soup, salad bar and a choice of two main dishes; alternatively, come back later for just the main dish at Bs17. It's also a good place to pop into in the morning for a refreshing fruit salad (Bs6). Mon–Fri & Sun 10am–3pm, but evening opening is planned in the future.

**Pizza Pazza Macondo** Lazcano 317 ☎ 04 6654020; map p.181. Eccentric art centre open only two evenings a week, for art and music events accompanied by pizza (Bs65). Thurs 8–11pm, Fri 8pm–3am.

★**Taberna Gattopardo** Plaza Luis de Fuentes ☎ 04 6630656; map p.181. Vintage typewriters, radios and rifles, jazz paintings and discreet booths give this stylish restaurant-bar plenty of character. The vast menu includes sandwiches, pizzas, pastas, Mexican-style tacos (Bs54), *filet mignon* (Bs56) and *fondue bourguinonne* (Bs85), plus good coffee. Daily 8am–midnight (last order 11pm).

### DIRECTORY

**Banks and exchange** The Banco Nacional de Bolivia is on Sucre at Ingavi, and Banco Mercantil de Santa Cruz is on Sucre at 15 de Abril. There are ATMs around Plaza Luis de Fuentes, and money changers on Bolívar between Sucre and Daniel Campos.

**Consulate** The Argentine consulate is at Ballivián 669, on the corner of Bolívar (☎ 04 6644273).

**Internet** Try Punto Entel at Lema 144 on Plaza Sucre.

**Laundry** La Esmeralda, Madrid 157 between Campos and Colón.

**Post office** The Correo Central is on Lema and Sucre.

# Around Tarija

There are some worthwhile excursions in the warm and fertile **Tarija valley**, which is notable for its sleepy villages, easy pace of life and beautiful countryside. Just outside Tarija itself are rich **fossil deposits** that attract palaeontologists from all over the world, while further afield you can visit the bodegas and **vineyards** of the world's highest wine-producing region (see box, p.186). Above the Tarija valley to the west, the **Reserva Biológica Cordillera del Sama** has striking high Andean scenery and an Inca trail that makes an excellent hike.

## Tarija valley fossils

About 5km northeast of Tarija • Free • VTB Tours trips Bs170 (3–6 people) or Bs140 (7–10 people); minimum 3 people; arrange in advance

The eroded gulches and badlands around the airport and the gas pipeline on the other side of the main road are a treasure-trove for **fossil** hunters. The sedimentary layers of volcanic ash, clay and sand here are full of well-preserved fossilized bones and teeth from Pleistocene megafauna like the mastodon (Andean elephant) and megatherium (giant sloth), as well as distant ancestors of llamas, horses and other contemporary mammals. You can take a micro or taxi out here, but if you have a particular interest in fossils it's worth hiring a knowledgeable **guide**; VTB Tours (see p.182) run special trips, in which you're allowed to excavate major fossils under supervision before handing them over to the museum.

## Tomatitas

Around 5km north of Tarija • Micros "A" and "B" (every 5–10min; around 15min) leave from the corner of Av Domingo Paz and Juan Misael Saracho in Tarija

Just north of Tarija, the village of **TOMATITAS** is a popular weekend getaway for Tarijeños, who come here to swim in the natural river pools during the warmer, wetter summer

**3**

## TARIJA VALLEY VINEYARDS

The **Tarija valley** and surrounding area is Bolivia's prime wine-producing region. At up to 2000m above sea level, these are the highest **vineyards** in the world. The first **vines** in the region were planted by Franciscan monks, who found the soil and climate of the Tarija valley ideal for producing wine. During the colonial era Tarija produced much of the wine consumed in Potosí, as well as large quantities of **singani**, a fierce, roughly 40% ABV, white-grape marc (distilled from the grape remains left after winemaking, like grappa or eau de vie) that's extremely popular throughout Bolivia. Today, Tarija's expanding wine industry produces well over two million litres of wine a year. Wine consumption within Bolivia is growing, and production techniques in the main bodegas have been modernized, with quality improving all the time. The main obstacle to further increases in production is the influx of contraband wine from Chile and Argentina, which is much cheaper than Bolivian wine, as no duty is paid on it.

### VISITING THE BODEGAS

A visit to one or more of the **bodegas** (wineries) makes an excellent half-day excursion; tour operators in Tarija (see p.182) run trips which allow you to see all the stages of the production process, as well as sample a few glasses at source. The vineyards are at their greenest and most beautiful during the February to March grape harvest. The La Concepción bodega (see below) is the easiest to visit independently – and produces arguably the best wine in Bolivia.

**Aranjuez** On the southern outskirts of the city ☎ 04 664552, 🕸 facebook.com/vinosaranjuez.

**Casa Real** Santa Ana, 15km southeast of Tarija ☎ 04 4645498, 🕸 casa-real.com.

**La Concepción** Valle La Concepción, 27km south of Tarija ☎ 04 4645040, 🕸 laconcepcion.bo. If you telephone the vineyard's office in Tarija in advance to make an appointment, staff are usually happy to show

you around, though visits may not be possible during busy periods of the harvest. Minibuses marked "V" (every 30min or so; 30min) depart from Corrado at Campero in Tarija to the village of Concepción, from where it's about a 20min walk along a track that heads out across a bridge to the right of the main road.

**Kohlberg** Santa Ana, 15km southeast of Tarija ☎ 04 4266170, 🕸 facebook.com/pg/VinosKohlberg.

months from November to April. You can also picnic in the fragrant eucalyptus woods beside the river, or eat in one of the village's many inexpensive **restaurants**, where you can sample traditional local specialities like *chicharrón* (deep-fried pork) and *cangrejitos* (soft-shelled freshwater crabs).

## Museo Moto Méndez, San Lorenzo

San Lorenzo, 15km north of Tarija • Tues–Fri 8am–noon & 3–6pm, Sat & Sun 9am–noon & 3–6pm • Free • Minibuses (every 20min or so; around 25min) leave from the corner of Av Domingo Paz and Juan Misael Saracho in Tarija

Ten kilometres north of Tomatitas, the peaceful farming village of **SAN LORENZO** has many colonial buildings including, on the corner of the plaza, the former home of the one-handed independence guerrilla hero, Eustaquio "Moto" Méndez. The building has been preserved as the shrine-like **Museo Moto Méndez**. The leader of a guerrilla band that played a key role in the Battle of La Tablada, which liberated Tarija from Spanish control in 1817, "Moto" Méndez is considered the consummate ideal of Tarijeño manhood. Inside, the colonial-era house has been left much as it was when he lived there, complete with rustic furniture and agricultural tools.

## Reserva Biológica Cordillera del Sama

Starting about 5km west of Tarija, more than a thousand square kilometres of the Altiplano and the deep valleys that drop down into the Tarija valley are protected by the **RESERVA BIOLÓGICA CORDILLERA DEL SAMA**, which is home to many endangered species including vicuñas, Andean deer, pumas and a wide variety of birds. Established in 1991, the reserve is administered by SERNAP (the Servicio Nacional de Areas Protegidas), which you should contact in advance for permission to visit (see below). Most of the reserve is composed of the high-altitude grasslands (*puna*) of the Cordillera de Sama, which rises above the Tarija valley to an altitude of over 4000m and marks the eastern edge of the Altiplano. The three brackish lakes here – the largest is the **Laguna Tajzara** – are home to many different water birds, including all three Andean species of flamingo.

### The Inca Trail

From a high pass about two hours' walk (or a 4WD journey) due east of Pujzara – a village around two hours' drive from Tarija on the road to Tupiza – a well-preserved **Inca Trail** drops down through spectacular scenery to the village of Los Pinos in the Tarija valley, making for an excellent hike. If you get an early start from Pujazara, at a push you can walk this trail in a day and be back in Tarija the same evening. The trail itself is a good seven- or eight-hour hike, and from its end at the village of Los Pinos it's another 16km – about three hours – along a flat road to the village of San Andrés, where you can get transport back to Tarija. If you have camping equipment, it may be better to break the walk into two days. Alternatively, you can arrange to do the hike with a tour agency in Tarija (see p.182).

The first pass is marked by a large *apacheta* (stone cairn); once you've found it, the rest of the trail is easy to follow without a guide. From the pass, the trail zigzags down to the village of **Calderillas**, about two hours' walk away. From Calderillas, walk southeast for about half an hour to where two rivers meet and enter a narrow gorge. Cross over to the right bank of the river and follow the lower path that runs into the gorge along the riverbank. After about 45 minutes the path climbs to the right and over a ridge, opening up spectacular views of the Tarija valley below – it's also an excellent spot to see condors. The path follows the ridge round and then zigzags down to the east to **Los Pinos**, about two hours' walk away.

**3**

#### ARRIVAL AND INFORMATION

**By bus** The main road from Tarija to Tupiza passes through the reserve close by the lakes: take any Tupiza- or Villazón-bound bus (10 daily) and ask the driver to drop you at the village of Pujzara, about two hours' drive from Tarija. Pujzara is about 2km from Laguna Tajzara. From Los Pinos at the end of the trail, an easy-to-follow road runs 16km to San Andrés, from where there are frequent micros back to Tarija. If you arrive after dark when the last micro has gone, use the public telephone in a shop on the plaza to call a radio taxi from Tarija to come and pick you up (☏04 6647700; Bs100–120).

**By guided tour** Agencies in Tarija can provide a guide and transport to the pass and back to Tarija from Los Pinos; an all-inclusive two-day trip costs around Bs1300 (minimum three people; book three days in advance); alternatively,

#### RESERVA BIOLÓGICA CORDILLERA DEL SAMA

you could arrange transport and a guide (or transport alone) independently for considerably less money, though significantly more hassle. As well as the tour operators listed in the Tarija account (see p.182), you can also arrange tours through the NGO that looks after the reserve, Prometa (☏04 6645865, ⓦprometa.org.bo); their office is in Tarija at Alejandro del Carpio 659 (Mon–Fri 8.30am–12.30pm & 3–7pm).

**Permission to visit** Visiting the Reserva Biológica Cordillera del Sama is free, but permission is needed in advance from SERNAP (☏04 6650605, ⓦfacebook.com/reservadesama) in Tarija; their office is at Av Jaime Paz Zamora 1171 between La Paz and Eulogio Ruiz, opposite the old bus terminal (Mon–Fri 8am–12.30pm & 3–6.30pm).

#### ACCOMMODATION

**Albergue Comunitario de Pujzara** Pujzara, Yunchará ☏7824 2566. Unless you're equipped to camp, this lodge is the only place to stay in the reserve. It has six rooms, hot

water and a kitchen. Meals can be arranged if you contact them a couple of days in advance of your arrival, which you'll need to do to make a booking anyway. **Bs80**

# Sucre, Cochabamba and the central valleys

UNIVERSIDAD DE SAN FRANCISCO XAVIER, SUCRE

# Sucre, Cochabamba and the central valleys

East of the Altiplano, the Andes march gradually down towards the eastern lowlands in a series of rugged north–south mountain ranges, scarred with long narrow valleys formed by rivers draining to the east. Blessed with rich alluvial soils, and midway in climate and altitude between the cold of the Altiplano and the tropical heat of the lowlands, these central valleys have historically been among the most fertile and habitable areas in Bolivia. In the fifteenth century the Incas established substantial agricultural colonies in the region, which formed the easternmost frontier of their empire – to this day the majority of the rural population still speak Quechua, the language the Incas introduced. The Spanish were attracted by the same qualities, and the two main cities they founded, Sucre and Cochabamba, remain the most important in the region, though they could not be more different in character.

**4**

The administrative, political and religious centre of Bolivia during Spanish rule, and still officially the capital, **Sucre** is a masterpiece of immaculately preserved colonial architecture, full of elegant churches, mansions and museums. It's also the market centre for the deeply traditional Quechua-speaking communities of the surrounding mountains, whose fine weavings are sold at the market town of **Tarabuco**.

The charms of **Cochabamba**, on the other hand, are much more prosaic. A bustling trading hub for a rich agricultural hinterland, it has few conventional tourist attractions, and for most travellers is no more than a place to break a journey between La Paz and Santa Cruz in the eastern lowlands. Those who do spend some time here, however, find it to be one of Bolivia's friendliest cities, and the surrounding Cochabamba Valley's mixture of Inca ruins and lively rural market towns is worth exploring as well. It's also the jumping-off point for an adventurous journey south into the remote Northern Potosí province, where **Parque Nacional Torotoro** features labyrinthine limestone caves, deep canyons and waterfalls, dinosaur footprints and ancient ruins.

East of Cochabamba, meanwhile, the main road to Santa Cruz passes through the **Chapare**, a beautiful region of rushing rivers and dense tropical forests, where the last foothills of the Andes plunge into the Amazon basin. The area became notorious as the main source of Bolivia's coca crop, which in turn makes up a significant proportion of the world's cocaine supply.

## Sucre

In a broad highland valley on the Altiplano's eastern edge, about 162km north of Potosí, **SUCRE** is Bolivia's most refined and beautiful city. Known at various times as

# Highlights

**❶ Sucre** Known as the White City, Bolivia's official capital combines delightful colonial-era architecture with the lively atmosphere of a university town. **See opposite**

**❷ Museo de Arte Indígena** Sucre's best museum is dedicated to the remarkable weaving of the indigenous groups from the surrounding region. **See p.198**

**❸ Cal Orko** One of the world's most significant paleontological sites, with a stunning collection of over five thousand dinosaur prints. **See p.201**

**❹ Cochabamba** A friendly, modern city, Cochabamba boasts a year-round sunny climate, some great restaurants and a buzzing nightlife scene. **See p.208**

**❺ La Cancha** Cochabamba's vast covered market is the throbbing heart of the city, and of the Quechua-speaking communities of the surrounding valley. **See p.212**

**❻ Parque Nacional Torotoro** Set amid deep canyons and rushing waterfalls, Bolivia's smallest national park is dotted with dinosaur footprints and pre-Inca ruins. **See p.222**

**HIGHLIGHTS ARE MARKED ON THE MAP ON P.192**

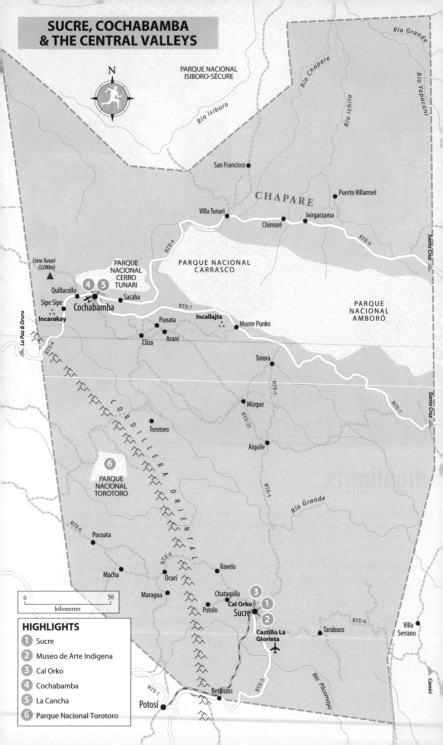

Chuquisaca, Charcas and La Ciudad de la Plata – and thus also as "The City of Four Names" – it has some of the finest colonial architecture in South America, and enjoys a spring-like climate all year round, thanks to its setting at an altitude of 2790m.

The centre of Spanish power in Alto Peru, Sucre was made **capital of Bolivia** after independence, a status it retains today, although all real power has long since passed to La Paz. The city exudes the sense of being frozen in time somewhere back in the late nineteenth century. Although the courtly manners and conservatism of the old aristocratic families who dominate Sucre can seem stuffy, it's nicely tempered by the youthful vitality the city enjoys as home of one of the Americas' oldest universities.

Laid out in a classic grid pattern, the city is an architectural jewel, with splendid churches, monasteries and mansions. The **historic centre**, a UNESCO World Heritage Site, is protected by strict building codes, and as a result most of it has been preserved as it was a century ago. Municipal regulations require all buildings to be whitewashed annually, maintaining the characteristic that earned Sucre another of its many grandiose titles: "La Ciudad Blanca de Las Americas" – "The White City of the Americas". Sucre is also the market centre for a mountainous rural hinterland inhabited by Quechua-speaking indigenous communities renowned for their beautiful **weavings**; their work can be seen at Sucre's stunning **Museo de Arte Indigena**, or on a day-trip to **Tarabuco**, about 60km to the southeast.

## Brief history

Sucre was founded between 1538 and 1540 (the exact date is hotly disputed by Bolivian historians) by the conquistador Pedro de Anzures during the second major Spanish incursion into the Andes south of Lake Titicaca. Initially named **Chuquisaca** (probably a Spanish corruption of the original indigenous name Choquechaca, meaning "Golden Bridge"), it was given the official title **Villa de la Plata** ("City of Silver") after significant quantities of silver were found nearby. The title proved prescient, as the massive silver deposits of Potosí were discovered soon after, and the city quickly emerged as the administrative headquarters for the mines and the centre of Spanish political, religious and military power in the region. In 1559 the **Audiencia de Charcas** – an independent court representing the Spanish crown, with judicial and executive power over an area comprising modern-day Bolivia, Argentina and part of Peru – was established here. The city became home to the first bishopric in Alto Peru in 1552, and in 1624 the **Universidad de San Francisco Xavier** – only the third university in all the Americas – was founded here to train the religious and administrative specialists needed to manage the vast conquered territories.

### The silver boom

The first half of the seventeenth century was La Plata's golden age, as the **wealth** from Potosí's mines funded the construction of lavish churches, monasteries, palaces and administrative buildings. Its power waned with the flow of silver, however, and in 1776 it was made subject to the rule of the new Spanish Virreinato de la Plata in Buenos

**4**

---

### FIESTAS IN SUCRE

Sucre's main religious celebration is the **Fiesta de la Virgen de Guadeloupe**, held annually on September 8 and marked by a procession and folkloric dances. In the second half of September each year the city hosts an **International Cultural Festival**, with performances by local and international theatre and dance groups.

The anniversary of the 1809 "**Primer Grito Libertario de America**", the first declaration of independence in South America, is marked every May 25 with civic and military parades, and is a public holiday throughout the Department of Chuquisaca. The department's most famous annual fiesta, however, is the indigenous celebration of **Pujllay** (see box, p.208) on the third Sunday of March in Tarabuco.

Aires, reverting to the name of Chuquisaca to avoid confusion. The university retained its importance, and became a centre in developing the **liberal ideas** that led to the first qualified declaration of independence from Spain, which was made here on May 25, 1809. Known as the **Primer Grito Libertario de America**, it is commemorated each year (see box, p.193).

### Post independence

After independence in 1825 the city was made the **capital** of the Republic of Bolivia and renamed Sucre in honour of Antonio José de Sucre, the Venezuelan general who completed the defeat of the Spanish at the battle of Ayacucho and served as Bolivia's first president. Its economic importance continued to decline, however, and the seat of both congress and the presidency was moved to La Paz after the 1899 civil war between the two cities. In a very Bolivian compromise, Sucre remained the seat of the supreme court and was allowed to retain the title of official or **constitutional capital**, an honorary position it still holds today.

## Plaza 25 de Mayo

The centre of Sucre is the spacious **Plaza 25 de Mayo**, shaded by tall palms and dotted with benches where locals pass the time of day chatting, reading newspapers, having their shoes cleaned or greeting passing acquaintances. In the middle of the plaza, flanked by bronze lions, stands a statue of **Mariscal Antonio José de Sucre**, the Venezuelan-born South American independence hero and first president of Bolivia whose name the city bears. The plaza is lined with elegant colonial and republican public and religious buildings, all painted an immaculate white that dazzles in the sunshine.

## Casa de la Libertad

Plaza 25 de Mayo • Tues–Sat 9.15–11.45am & 2.45–5.45pm, Sun 9.15–11.15am • Bs15, including guided tour • ☎ 04 6454200

On the northwest side of the plaza is the eye-catching Neoclassical **Casa de la Libertad**. Built in 1888 to replace a colonial *cabildo*, the Casa de la Libertad (then known as the Alcadia Municipal) was where the Bolivian **Act of Independence** was signed on August 6, 1825. The building now houses a small but interesting museum dedicated to the birth of the republic. Inside, the original signed document proclaiming a sovereign and independent state is on display in the assembly hall where the declaration was made; the same hall also housed the Bolivian congress from then until the seat of government was moved to La Paz in 1899. On the walls hang portraits of Sucre and Bolívar – the latter, by the Peruvian painter Gil de Castro, was described by the *Libertador* himself as being the best likeness ever made of him. Beside the Casa de la Libertad stands the simple but well-preserved colonial facade of the original seventeenth-century **Jesuit University**. Guided tours (included in the entry fee) are provided in English, French, Spanish and Quechua.

## La Prefectura

Plaza 25 de Mayo

Around the corner from the Casa de la Libertad on the southwest side of the plaza stands the lavish Neoclassical facade of what was to have been the **presidential palace**, a glorious monument to hubris completed shortly before the seat of the presidency was moved to La Paz; it now houses the **Prefectura de Chuquisaca** (departmental government).

## La Catedral

Plaza 25 de Mayo • Thurs & Sun 9am (for Mass); alternatively, you can visit via the Museo Eclesiastico (see p.196) • Free

Next to the Prefectura stands the **Catedral**, or Basilica Mayor. Built between 1551 and

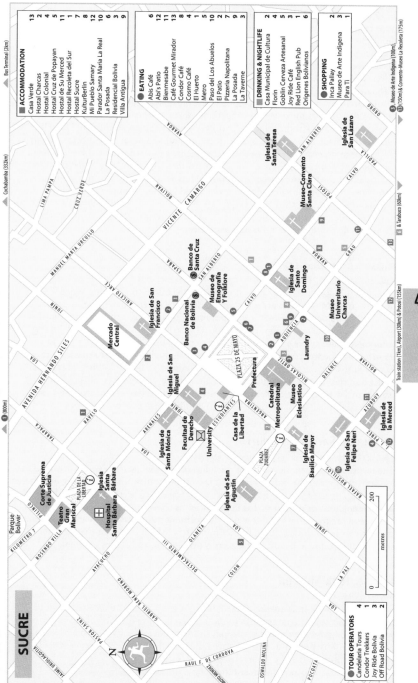

# SUCRE

### ■ ACCOMMODATION

| | |
|---|---|
| Casa Verde | 13 |
| Hostal Charcas | 2 |
| Hostal Colonial | 4 |
| Hostal Cruz de Popayan | 5 |
| Hostal de Su Merced | 11 |
| Hostal Recoleta del Sur | 7 |
| Hostal Sucre | 1 |
| KulturBerlin | 8 |
| Mi Pueblo Samary | 12 |
| Parador Santa Maria La Real | 10 |
| La Posada | 6 |
| Residencial Bolivia | 3 |
| Villa Antigua | 9 |

### ● EATING

| | |
|---|---|
| Abis Café | 6 |
| Abi's Patio | 12 |
| Bienmesabe | 11 |
| Café Gourmet Mirador | 13 |
| Condor Café | 8 |
| Cosmo Café | 4 |
| El Huerto | 5 |
| Metro | 1 |
| Paso del Los Abuelos | 10 |
| El Patio | 2 |
| Pizzeria Napolitana | 7 |
| La Posada | 9 |
| La Taverne | 3 |

### ■ DRINKING & NIGHTLIFE

| | |
|---|---|
| Casa Municipal de Cultura | 2 |
| Florin | 4 |
| Goblin Cerveza Artesanal | 5 |
| Joy Ride Café | 3 |
| Red Lion English Pub | 1 |
| Orígenes Bolivianos | 6 |

### ● SHOPPING

| | |
|---|---|
| Inca Pallay | 2 |
| Museo de Arte Indigena | 3 |
| Para Ti | 1 |

### ● TOUR OPERATORS

| | |
|---|---|
| Candelaria Tours | 4 |
| Condor Trekkers | 1 |
| Joy Ride Bolivia | 3 |
| Off Road Bolivia | 2 |

4

1712 and extensively modified since, it combines various architectural styles. The side door facing the plaza and main door looking onto Calle Ortiz are both highly decorative seventeenth-century stone porticos carved in the distinctive **mestizo-Baroque style**, while the square bell tower with three balconies decorated with statues of the Apostles and Evangelists dates from the late eighteenth century; the clock in the tower, which still keeps perfect time, was made in London in 1772.

The decor in the lavish **Neoclassical interior** dates back to 1826, with soaring pillars painted in immaculate white and piped with gold, extravagant crystal chandeliers and massive silver candlesticks. A side chapel houses the jewel-encrusted image of the **Virgen de Guadeloupe**, the religious patron of Sucre. Painted in 1601 by Fray Diego de Ocaña, the image quickly developed cult status, and wealthy devotees began sticking gold, diamonds, emeralds and pearls to the picture as an expression of faith or in gratitude for wishes granted and miracles performed. These were arranged in a more orderly fashion when the image was laminated in gold in 1734, and though the popular saying that the value of the jewels would be enough to pay off Bolivia's international debt is probably an exaggeration (as well as a veiled critique of the wealth of the Church compared to the poverty of many Bolivians), the glittering opulence of the bejewelled Virgin is astonishing nonetheless.

## Museo Eclesiastico

Entrance beside the cathedral on Calle Ortiz • Mon–Fri 10am–noon & 3–5pm • Bs20

Although it is open for Mass, the best way to see the cathedral – and the Virgin – is as part of a visit to the **Museo Eclesiastico**, which boasts a fine collection of colonial religious art. Visits are by **guided tour** only, so turn up shortly after opening, otherwise you may have to wait a while for the next group to form; tours (in Spanish) last about an hour. Among the paintings on display is a series of portraits of saints by the Cochabamba-born master of the mestizo-Baroque style, Melchor Pérez de Holguín, as well as works in a much more European style by the sixteenth-century Italian-born Jesuit Bernardo Bitti, who studied under Raphael. There's also a substantial hoard of finely crafted silver and gold religious paraphernalia, much of it encrusted with gems, further evidence of the enormous wealth that flowed through Sucre (and the Church) during the silver boom in Potosí.

## Iglesia de San Felipe Neri

Calle Ortiz • Roof: Mon–Fri 2.30–6pm, Sat 9am–6pm • Bs15 • ☏ 04 6454333

The formidable Neoclassical bulk of the **Iglesia de San Felipe Neri**, with its two tall bell towers, was built in the last years of the nineteenth century. This is the only building in the city not painted white – its brick and stone walls have been left bare, as they have been throughout its existence. The church itself is rarely open to the public, but you can often get up on to its roof to enjoy the splendid panoramic views across the city – access is via the adjoining former monastery, which boasts an elegant colonial courtyard surrounded by arched cloisters on two levels, and is now a school.

## Iglesia de la Merced

Perez and Azurduy

The seventeenth-century **Iglesia de la Merced** has an unremarkable exterior, but its interior boasts some extravagant Baroque altarpieces smothered in gold leaf, one of which is thought to be the oldest in Bolivia; the elaborately carved wooden pulpit and altar are also very beautiful. The bell tower, meanwhile, offers stunning views over the city. Unfortunately, the church has been closed for several years for renovation, though hopefully it will reopen in the near future.

## Museo Universitario Charcas

Dalence and Bolívar • Mon–Fri 9am–12.30pm & 2.30–6.30pm, Sat 9.30am–12.30pm • Bs20 • ☎ 04 6456100

Housed in a delightful seventeenth-century mansion, the rambling but worthwhile **Museo Universitario Charcas** is really four museums in one. It combines the university's archeological, anthropological, colonial and modern art collections, all of which are set around a series of colonial patios and surrounded by arched cloisters. Visits are by guided tour (generally in Spanish, though some guides speak a little English) only and last around an hour.

The **modern art** collection is perhaps the least impressive of the four, comprising works by local artists in derivative styles ranging from surrealism and abstract expressionism to socialist realism, all applied to local subjects. The **colonial religious art** collection is much more substantial and includes some very fine works, though the subject matter – Christ, the Virgin, and assorted saints and bishops – is repetitive, to say the least. Highlights include a whole room full of pictures by the mestizo-Baroque master **Melchor Pérez de Holguín** and a finely detailed bird's-eye view of Potosí painted in 1758 by Gaspar Miguel de Berrio. There's also some beautiful colonial furniture on display, including decorative desks richly inlaid or delicately carved with images of flowers and animals. The **anthropology section** is a mishmash of indigenous costumes and artefacts from all over Bolivia: Andean musical instruments; woven vegetable-fibre clothes from the Amazon; lurid *diablada* masks from Oruro. The **archeology section** comprises an extensive collection of artefacts – pottery, tools, weapons, some metalwork, textile fragments – from all the major Andean civilizations.

## Museo-Convento Santa Clara

Calvo and Bolívar • Mon–Fri 2–6pm, Sat 2–5.30pm • Bs15 • ☎ 04 645 2295

The **Museo-Convento Santa Clara** is a still-functioning nunnery with a range of fairly standard colonial religious pictures, most of them painted by anonymous indigenous artists in the seventeenth and eighteenth centuries, as well as some antique furniture and religious vestments; you can also see the church's Neoclassical interior, most notable for its seventeenth-century organ.

## Museo de Arte Indigena

Pasaje Iturricho 314, a 20min uphill walk from Plaza 25 de Mayo • Mon–Fri 9am–12.30pm & 2.30–6pm, Sat 9am–noon & 2.30–6pm • Bs22 • ☎ 04 6453841, Ⓦ asur.org.bo

In an elegant colonial building, the fascinating **Museo de Arte Indigena** is dedicated to the distinctive weavings of two local Quechua-speaking indigenous groups: the **Jalq'as**, who number about 26,000 and live in the mountains west of Sucre, and the **Tarabuceños** (see box, opposite), a more numerous group who live around the town of Tarabuco to the east. The museum is run by an NGO, ASUR (Antropologos del Sur Andino), which works with Jalq'a and Tarabuceño communities to revive traditional weaving designs and techniques that had been dying out. This renaissance of indigenous art has seen both the quality and market value of the weavings of both groups rise dramatically, turning the craft into a source of income for hundreds of desperately poor campesino families.

Expertly laid out, with precise text explanations in Spanish, English, French and German, the museum introduces the different ethnic groups with maps and colour photos, then explains the weaving techniques and describes the different plants used to make natural dyes. There is often a Jalq'a or Tarabuceño woman weaving away in the courtyard as you wander around the museum, so you can see the creative process in action. The **archeological finds** on display demonstrate that many of the wood and bone weaving tools in use today are identical to those used in the Andes more than a thousand years ago, while some beautiful and well-preserved ancient **textile fragments** reveal an astonishing continuity of style, technique and aesthetic stretching back over many centuries. The central attractions, though, are the weavings themselves: brightly coloured, intricately detailed and laden with a complex symbolism, they're works of great creativity that express a distinctively Andean artistic vision. The textiles are displayed in chronological order, revealing the development and changing style over time, and there are also examples of how they are worn in daily dress and in ritual costumes for fiestas. You can buy items in the museum shop.

## Convento-Museo La Recoleta

Plaza Pedro de Anzares, a 20min uphill walk southeast of the main plaza • Mon–Fri 9–11.30am & 2.30–4.30pm, Sat 3–5pm • Bs15 • ℹ 04 6451987

The **Convento-Museo La Recoleta**, a tranquil Franciscan monastery, houses an interesting little museum of colonial religious art and materials related to the missionary work of the Franciscan order in Bolivia. Visits are by guided tour only, so it's best to turn up shortly after the museum opens so that you don't have to wait long for a tour – if you do have to wait, head to the *Café Gourmet Mirador* (see p.205).

Founded in 1538, La Recoleta was for nearly three centuries the headquarters of Franciscan efforts to convert the indigenous peoples of Bolivia. Set around a series of delightful flower-filled colonial patios lined with arched cloisters, the museum is home to a substantial collection of **colonial religious paintings**. More interesting are the items relating to Franciscan missionary efforts, including bows and arrows, feather headdresses and plant-fibre clothing given to the missionaries by the different lowland tribes they contacted, and photographs of early twentieth-century missionaries.

Though it dates back to 1600, the **monastery church** was remodelled in rather anodyne style in the nineteenth century: the one noteworthy feature is the exquisite set of Baroque wooden choir stalls in the upper choir, beautifully carved in 1674 with gruesome images of a massacre of Franciscan missionaries in Nagasaki, Japan. Though it is now back in Franciscan hands, in the early nineteenth century the monastery was briefly requisitioned by the Bolivian authorities and used as a barracks; in the corridor

**4**

---

### JALQ'A AND TARABUCEÑO WEAVINGS

The difference in style between the weavings of the Jalq'as and Tarabuceños could hardly be more dramatic, even though the two groups live only a short distance apart to the west and east of Sucre. **Tarabuceño ponchos** (*unkus*) are woven with bright stripes of orange, black, red, green and gold, while smaller items like the *chuspa* coca bags and *chumpi* waist bands are decorated with finely detailed and usually symmetrical designs depicting scenes from everyday life: wild and domestic animals; trees and crops; people ploughing, harvesting or dancing at fiestas.

The **Jalq'a** designs, on the other hand, are entirely figurative, eschewing symmetry and abstract geometry. Woven into women's shawls known as *aqsus* and almost always only black and red in colour, they depict a kind of primordial chaos filled with strange beasts: animals with elongated bodies and multiple heads or eyes sprouting from their tails; birds with puma heads; toads with wings. The few human figures that do appear seem lost in this forest of supernatural animals. This is the **ukchu pacha**, a mythological underworld of extraordinary and untamed creatures, over which rules the *Sax'ra*, a horned devil-like figure with wings who appears in the centre of some of the weavings, part Andean demon and part god of fertility and abundance. Many of the designs are inspired by dreams, and new themes are constantly being incorporated, and though every piece is unique they all fall within a set of artistic norms that makes them instantly recognizable as Jalq'a.

Examples of both weaving styles are available to buy in a shop attached to the Museo de Arte Indígena, and though they're far from cheap, particularly the Jalq'a items – larger individual pieces can cost well over $110 (Bs800) – the money goes direct to the **indigenous artists** who made them, and the quality is exquisite.

outside the choir a plaque and portrait mark the spot where the Bolivian president Pedro Blanco was murdered during a successful coup in 1829, just five days after taking office. Beside the monastery stands the **Cedro Millenario**, a great, gnarled *cedro* tree over a thousand years old and 5m in diameter.

## Museo de Etnografía y Folklore

España 74 • Mon–Fri 9am–12.30pm & 2.30–7pm, Sat 9.30am–12.30pm • Free • ☎ 04 6455293, Ⓦ musef.org.bo

Popularly known as **Musef**, and housed in the colonial-era former Banco Nacional building, the **Museo de Etnografía y Folklore** showcases Bolivia's cultural diversity through a collection of anthropological and ethnological exhibits, which includes traditional musical instruments, and icons used in rites and ceremonies. The highlight is the stunning display of masks and headdresses, which features numerous elaborate examples from Carnaval celebrations.

## Iglesia de San Francisco

Ravelo and Arce • Mon–Fri 9am–noon & 3–5pm • Bs15 • ☎ 04 6451853

The **Iglesia de San Francisco** was built between 1540 and 1581 to minister to the growing indigenous population of the newly founded city, and remains the most popular church with Sucre's Quechua-speaking population – modern signs on the walls warning against the use of holy water in witchcraft and magic reveal that, centuries later, the priests here still face an uphill struggle against deeply entrenched pre-Christian practices. The entrance to the church is flanked by two square towers, one of which houses the **Campana de la Libertad**, the bell that sounded the call to arms at the start of the pro-independence uprising in 1809. The interior boasts splendid gilded Baroque altarpieces and an elaborate panelled *mudéjar* ceiling.

## Iglesia de San Miguel

Arenales • Open early for Mass (around 7–8am) most mornings • Free

The modest whitewashed Baroque facade of the **Iglesia de San Miguel**, completed in 1621, conceals one of the most lavish church interiors in Sucre, with glorious carved Baroque altarpieces covered in **gold leaf** and an exquisite panelled *mudéjar* ceiling of intricate interlocking geometric shapes.

## Iglesia de Santa Mónica

Arenales and Junín • No fixed opening hours • Free

Founded in 1547, the **Iglesia de Santa Mónica** boasts an extravagant stone portico that is the finest example of the **mestizo-Baroque** style in Sucre, carved with palm trees and floral designs, spiralled columns, and pillars supported by human figures who look like pre-Columbian idols; sadly, the interior is closed to the general public, though occasionally opens for special events.

## Universidad de San Francisco Xavier

Junín, just southwest of the Iglesia Santa Mónica • No fixed opening hours • Free

The **University** (or the Universidad Mayor Real y Pontificia de San Francisco Xavier, to give it its full title) was founded by the Jesuits in 1624, predating Harvard in the US, and was a major seat of learning throughout the colonial period as well as an important centre of liberal thought in the early nineteenth century. Crucial ideas developed here, particularly the so-called *Silogismo altoperuano* – the argument that the loyalty of the colonies was owed to the personage of the king and not to the Spanish government, and that sovereignty therefore reverted to the colonies once King Fernando VII was forced to abdicate by Napoleon – and played a key role in the declaration of independence from Spain in 1809. The university is still central to the city's social, cultural and economic life, and is worth visiting for a look inside the **Facultad de Derecho** at Junín 652, which has the biggest colonial courtyard in Sucre.

## Plaza de la Libertad

Three blocks northwest of Plaza 25 de Mayo on Calle Arenales

The small **Plaza de la Libertad** is lined with palm trees and centred on an obelisk donated by the city of Buenos Aires to commemorate the 1809 Declaration of Independence. On the southwest side stands the elegant Renaissance facade of the **Hospital Santa Bárbara**, built between 1554 and 1563 and still functioning as a health centre. Set back from the northwest side of the square is the grandiose facade of the **Teatro Gran Mariscal**, one of several buildings in this part of town built in French Neoclassical style at the start of the twentieth century.

## Parque Simón Bolívar

Just off Calle Kilometro 7

Kilometro 7 runs from the right-hand side of the Teatro Gran Mariscal to **Parque Simón Bolívar**, a peaceful park neatly laid out in a French style. There's even a model of the Eiffel Tower at its centre, reputedly built by Gustave Eiffel himself – for reasons unknown, it has been painted bright orange. Looking over the park from its south end stands the grandiose **Corte Suprema de Justicia**, completed in 1945 in opulent French Neoclassical style. This is the only branch of government still based in Sucre, and as such the only real justification for the city's continuing status as constitutional capital of Bolivia.

## Cal Orko dinosaur footprints

5km outside Sucre on the Cochabamba road • Parque Cretácico Mon–Fri 9am–5pm, Sat 10am–8pm, Sun 10am–5pm • Bs30 includes guided tour (every 30min); at noon & 1pm these tours take you down into the quarry; cameras Bs5 • ☏ 04 645 7392 • "Dino buses" run to the park from the cathedral (Tues–Fri 11am, noon, 2pm & 3pm, Sat & Sun 9.30am, 11am, noon, 2pm, 3pm & 4.30pm; Bs15 return); alternatively, take micro #4 (30min) from the city centre or a taxi (around Bs50 return with waiting time)

Just outside Sucre, the **Cal Orko** cliff is home to the world's biggest-known collection of **dinosaur footprints**, discovered in 1994 by workers at the city's cement works and limestone quarry. Approximately five thousand prints from at least 150 different types of dinosaur can be seen here, covering an area of around thirty thousand square metres of near-vertical rock face, an astonishing profusion given that the second-biggest known site, in Germany, contains just 240 prints from two types of dinosaur. The prints were laid down between 65 and 85 million years ago on a flat bed of mud or sand covered by shallow water, and were then covered by a protective layer of ash from a **volcanic explosion**. Further layers of ash, silt and other sediments followed, the prints became fossilized, and about 25 million years ago the Andes began to rise, eventually bringing them to where they stand today.

### The footprints

The prints are scattered across a long plane of greyish rock about 100m high and set at an incline of about seventy degrees, and they look at first like pockmarks. Study them for a while, though, and you'll see the clear footprints of many different sizes running in long lines across the surface, and the astonishing fact that you're looking at the trails of animals who lived some seventy million years ago in the Cretaceous period begins to sink in. It's thought the site may have been the scene of a **chase and kill** by predators, who were followed by various scavengers. The largest prints are about 1m in diameter – these are thought to have belonged to an **apatosaurus** (commonly, though erroneously, referred to as a brontosaurus). The longest single track (easily the longest in the world) stretches for over half a kilometre and was laid down by a **baby Tyrannosaurus rex** known to researchers as Johnny Walker. The cement plant is still operating, and new prints are constantly being revealed, but ongoing quarrying and natural erosion threaten to destroy the tracks so far uncovered. The site has been declared a national monument, and in recent years conservation measures have been put in place to try and preserve it. At the time of research, there was talk of the site securing UNESCO World Heritage status.

### Parque Cretácico

Upon arrival you can either gaze upon the tracks through a chain-link gate or pay an additional fee to enter the rather underwhelming **Parque Cretácico**, which has a better-positioned viewing platform. The entrance fee includes a guided tour of the park: twice daily (noon & 1pm) these tours take you down into the quarry itself where you can view the footprints up close, and are well worth doing; the rest of the tours focus on the plaster replicas – you may as well skip these, and head directly to the viewing platform overlooking Cal Orko.

## Castillo La Glorieta

About 6km outside Sucre on the road south to Potosí • Tues–Sun 9am–5pm • Bs20, cameras Bs10 • Take micro #4 from Ravelo and Arce (30min); a taxi costs around Bs50 return with waiting time

The bizarre shell of the **Castillo La Glorieta** is a must for lovers of kitsch. Built over seven years from 1890 as a home for mining baron Francisco Argandoña and his wife, Clotilda, La Glorieta is probably the most ridiculous construction in Bolivia. The extravagant **pink sandstone structure** combines a surreal mishmash of different architectural styles, including a minaret, a Gothic clock tower and a Byzantine onion dome, while life-size stucco horses' heads running the length of the roof add a sublime Dalí-esque touch. The once-lavish interior still boasts elaborate Neoclassical stucco ceilings, Venetian stained glass and fireplaces of pink Veronese marble, as well as portraits of Francisco and Clotilda in full princely regalia meeting Pope Leo XIII, who pronounced them "Principes de la Glorieta" ("Princes of Glorieta") during their visit to Europe in 1898 in recognition for their work looking after orphans. The grounds are now home to a military training school.

### ARRIVAL AND DEPARTURE                                      SUCRE

**By plane** Sucre's new international airport, 30km south of the city, opened in 2016. There are ATMs, cafés/restaurants, chocolate shops, and a small tourist office. The departure tax is Bs11. A taxi to or from the city centre costs Bs50 for one passenger, Bs60 for two or more; alternatively, take a micro (every 30min–1hr; 45min–1hr). The flights below are all direct; for most destinations, there are several more connecting flights.

Destinations Cochabamba (2 daily; 30min); La Paz (1–2 daily; 40min); Santa Cruz (5–6 daily; 30min); Tarija (1 daily; 40min).

**By train** A single-carriage service to Potosí (Mon, Wed & Fri 8am, returning Tues, Thurs & Sat 8am; 6–8hr; ⓦ fca .com.bo) departs from the El Tejar station, 1km south of the centre on the road to Potosí. It's a pleasant journey, but considerably slower than travelling by road.

**By bus** Long-distance buses arrive at and depart from the bus terminal (☎04 6456732), about 2.5km northeast of the city centre on Av Ostria Gutiérrez. From here it's a short taxi ride (around Bs20) into central Sucre, or you can catch Micro A, which runs down to the Mercado Central, a block north of the main Plaza 25 de Mayo. As well as the destinations listed here, when the road is passable, usually only in the dry season, a few buses also head via Camiri to Villamontes (20–25hr) and Yacuiba (21–26hr), an arduous but exceptionally scenic journey down from the Andes into the Chaco lowlands.

Destinations Cochabamba (3 daily, departing early eve; 10–12hr); La Paz (3 daily;14hr); Oruro (2 dailyLa Paz (3 daily; 14hr) [so delete departing early eve; 12–12hr); Potosí (hourly; 3hr) Santa Cruz (5 daily, from late afternoon onwards; 14–16hr; some travel via Samaipata).

**By taxi** *Colectivo* taxis from Potosí will drop you off outside your hotel or anywhere else in the centre of town; heading in the opposite direction, they can be caught from the bus station or organized via your hotel. Regular taxis for journeys around town generally cost around Bs20.

## INFORMATION AND TOURS

### TOURIST INFORMATION
There are several municipal tourist offices: the most useful is at Plaza Zudañez, a brief stroll from the central plaza (Mon–Fri 8.30am–noon & 2.30–6pm; ☎04 643 5240, ⓦdestino.sucre.travel/en); there are also booths at the airport, the bus station, Plaza de la Libertad and Pasaje Iturricha (same hours). There's also a university-run tourist office at – appropriately enough – Estudiantes 49, just off Plaza 25 de Mayo (Mon–Fri 8.30am–12.30pm & 2.30–6.30pm; ☎04 6452283); it is manned by enthusiastic students who sometimes act as guides; the information they provide, though, isn't always as accurate as it could be.

### WEBSITES
Sucre Life (ⓦsucrelife.com) and Soy Sucre (ⓦsoysucre.info) are both useful sources of information on the city.

### TOUR OPERATORS
★**Candelaria Tours** Plaza Cochabamba, at Perez and Azurduy ☎04 6440340, ⓦcandelariatours.com; map p.195. Runs excellent one- and two-day trips to Candelaria village, which has a long-standing textile tradition. It's far less touristy than Tarabuco (see p.207), and you can stay at a delightful hacienda. Volunteering opportunities and numerous other tours are also on offer, including a horse ride to La Glorieta.

**Climb Sucre** ☎7866 9637, ⓔjustmarsden@gmail.com, ⓦclimbsucre.com. Offers beginner, intermediate and advanced climbing tours in the mountains surrounding the city. There's no office, so get in touch by phone or email. If you need a little practice first, try out the indoor climbing wall at *Condor Café* (see p.205).

**Condor Trekkers** Calvo 102 ☎7289 1740, ⓦcondortrekkers.org; map p.195. Non-profit agency specializing in walks and treks (from Bs70) that take in everything from dinosaur footprints to the Tarabuco market, local villages to the Maragua crater, Inca trails to city tours, as well as a trip to visit local organic farms whose produce is used in the agency's café (see p.205).

**Joy Ride Bolivia** Audiencia and Ortíz ☎04 6425544, ⓦjoyridebol.com; map p.195. Dutch-run company next to the *Joy Ride Café*, which organizes mountain biking, hiking, horseriding, climbing, paragliding, quad-biking and motorcycling trips (from around Bs250), as well as city tours and other excursions, including to Tarabuco.

**Off Road Bolivia** Audiencia 44 ☎7033 8123, ⓦoffroadbolivia.com; map p.195. Runs guided quad, ATV (all-terrain vehicle) and motorbike tours through the countryside surrounding Sucre. Half-day trips cost from Bs500, while full-day tours (including to the Maragua crater) cost Bs1180.

## ACCOMMODATION

Sucre has an excellent range of accommodation for all budgets, most of it located in the heart of the old city centre. There are some particularly beautiful places set inside converted **colonial mansions**, which represent very good value in the middle and upper price ranges: if you're on a tight budget but like to splash out every so often, this is the place to do it. All rates include **breakfast** unless stated otherwise.

**Casa Verde** Potosí 374 ☎04 6458291, ⓦcasaverdesucre.com; map p.195. A warm welcome is guaranteed at this guesthouse, which has a wide range of rooms (including a good-value single priced at Bs145), all with private bathrooms. There's a sun-trap patio, a small pool, and a communal kitchen for guests to use. **Bs260**

**Hostal Charcas** Ravelo 62 ☎04 6453972, ⓔhostalcharcas@yahoo.com; map p.195. Accessed via a ridiculously narrow entrance hall, this long-standing budget establishment has clean but rather cramped rooms; those with private bathrooms (Bs130) lack ventilation. Breakfast costs extra. **Bs80**

**Hostal Colonial** Plaza 25 de Mayo 3 ☎04 6440309, ⓦhostalcolonial-bo.com; map p.195. Unbeatable location, right on the plaza, though this place is sadly rather lacking in character. Rooms are adequate, if a bit musty and gloomy, and only the somewhat overpriced suites (nos 117 and 118; Bs511) have views over the plaza. **Bs406**

**Hostal Cruz de Popayan** Loa 881 ☎04 6440889, ⓦhotelsucre.com; map p.195. This popular place is based in a restored seventeenth-century townhouse. Although the rooms are a bit scruffy, most are en suite and come with TVs. There is also an eight-bed dorm. Dorms **Bs45**, doubles **Bs150**

**Hostal de Su Merced** Azurduy 16 ☎04 6442706, ⓦdesumerced.com; map p.195. Immaculately restored eighteenth-century house with a wonderful sun-drenched roof terrace offering panoramic views of the city. Rooms blend classy antique furniture with all the modern comforts you'd expect. The multilingual staff are welcoming and attentive. **Bs550**

**4**

**Hostal Recoleta del Sur** Ravelo 205 ⓣ04 6454789, ⓔmariateresadalenz@gmail.com; map p.195. This reliable mid-range choice has comfortable en-suite rooms with TVs in a converted colonial house with a glass-roofed patio. Despite the name, the hotel is not actually in the Recoleta district, but instead a 10min walk northwest of the main square. Bs180

**Hostal Sucre** Bustillos 113 ⓣ04 6451411, ⓦhostalsucre.com.bo; map p.195. Based in a historic townhouse, this hotel boasts two charming flower-filled courtyards. The dated rooms, sadly, don't quite live up to expectations, but remain a good choice (all have TVs, private bathrooms and twee decor). Those at the back are quieter. Bs280

**KulturBerlin** Avaroa 326 ⓣ04 6466854, ⓦkulturberlin.com; map p.195. Also known as *Hostal Berlin*, an attractive German-run hostel in an old colonial house with six-bed dorms and private rooms set around a courtyard and a lush garden. Facilities include a fine café-bar (open to non-guests), Spanish lessons, cookery classes and much more. Dorms Bs80, doubles Bs230

**Mi Pueblo Samary** Dalence 349 ⓣ04 643 8117, ⓦsamaryhotel.com; map p.195. Attractive boutique hotel in a gorgeous converted colonial-era townhouse that aims to re-create a traditional village vibe, right down to the *chicha* (see p.32) bar. The stylish en suites come with all mod cons, rates include airport transfers and there are plenty of online discounts available. $80 (Bs544)

4

★**Parador Santa Maria La Real** Bolívar 625 ⓣ04 6439592, ⓦparador.com.bo; map p.195. Sucre's best hotel is a joy: a painstakingly renovated colonial building housing elegant rooms and suites for $174 (Bs1183) with period furnishings, arched ceilings and sinks fashioned from old Singer sewing machine stands. A series of underground chambers has been turned into an atmospheric "museum restaurant", and there's a roof terrace, small spa and gym, and a jacuzzi with vistas over the city. $121 (Bs823)

**La Posada** Audiencia 92 ⓣ04 6460101, ⓦhotellaposada.com.bo; map p.195. This swish boutique hotel is just a few steps away from the main square, with beautiful gardens, a superb restaurant (see opposite) and professional service. The en-suite rooms have wood-beamed ceilings, whitewashed walls, tasteful furnishings and swish bathrooms. $80 (Bs544)

**Residencial Bolivia** San Alberto 42 ⓣ04 6454346; map p.195. This long-running *residencial* has spacious rooms with shared or private bathrooms (the latter cost Bs180) and TVs; there are a few duds, though, so ask to be shown a selection first. They are set around a courtyard with plenty of plants and a questionable mauve-and-peach colour scheme. Bs100

**Villa Antigua** Calvo 237 ⓣ04 6443437, ⓦvillaantiguahotel.com; map p.195. This sumptuous colonial mansion is a real treat: the immaculate en suites have wooden floors and high ceilings, and overlook a colonnaded courtyard complete with fountain. There's also a lovely garden, rooftop *mirador* with views over the city, small gym and sauna. $89 (Bs605)

## EATING

Sucre has a good variety of restaurants (a disproportionate number of which are run by Dutch expats) where you can get everything from the spicy local cuisine to authentic international dishes; most offer a good-value two- or three-course set lunch for around Bs40. If you're on a budget, the **Mercado Central**, at the junction of calles Ravelo and Arce, is good for inexpensive meals. Some hotels and hostels also have good restaurants, including *KulturBerlin* (see above).

**Abis Café** Plaza 25 de Mayo ⓣ04 6460222; map p.195. Occupying a prime location overlooking the main square, this appealing café is a great place for a pit stop. The menu features good coffee (Bs9–28), breakfasts, a set lunch (Bs40–50), sandwiches and burgers, and a few light meals, plus home-made ice cream sundaes (Bs15–30). There's a more formal sister restaurant, *Abi's Patio*, at Perez 366 (same opening hours). Mon–Fri 8.30am–10pm, Sat & Sun 8.30am–midnight.

**Bienmesabe** Grau 280 ⓣ7009 0039; map p.195. Delightful Venezuelan joint specializing in *arepas*, hearty cornbread pockets filled with shredded beef, chicken and avocado salad, cheese and black beans, or a variety of other combinations. You can get one, and a fresh juice, for Bs25–30. Mon, Wed & Fri 11.30am–1.30pm & 4.30–8pm, Tues & Thurs 11.30am–2pm.

### SUCRE'S CULINARY DELIGHTS

The **salteñas** (meat-, cheese- or vegetable-filled pasties) in Sucre are rightly considered Bolivia's best, and locals consume them with a passion – they're available from stalls and handcarts throughout the city, and from specialist *salteñerias*, which open only from mid-morning to noon and serve almost nothing else. Another local speciality is **chorizos chuquisaqueños**, spicy pork sausages sold in the market and in restaurants. Sucre is also famous throughout Bolivia for the quality and variety of its **chocolates**, which you'll find on sale at specialist shops on Calle Arenales, just off the plaza; Para Ti at no. 7 is the pick of the bunch.

★**Café Gourmet Mirador** Plaza Anzures ☎04 6452330; map p.195. Grab a deckchair in the lush garden of this outdoor café and enjoy the fantastic views over the city. There are snacks (Bs10–30), great pasta, and treats such as crêpes and tiramisu, along with beers (Bs20–35), wine (glasses from Bs20), fresh juices and excellent iced cappuccinos. Profits help fund a museum and educational project for local children. Daily 9.30am–7.30pm.

**Condor Café** Calvo 102 ☎7343 3392, ⓦcondortrekkers .org; map p.195. Non-profit café-restaurant run by travel agency Condor Trekkers (see p.203). The concise menu features excellent organic Yungas coffee (Bs10–18), breakfast options (Bs9–18) and pastries, snacks and light meals. From Thursday to Saturday evening it offers tapas and two-for-one drinks. There's a patio, plenty of board games and, improbably, a small indoor climbing wall (Bs20). Mon–Sat 8.30am–10pm, Sun noon–8pm.

**Cosmo Café** Plaza 25 de Mayo 58 ☎7342 8898; map p.195. A reliable option at any time of day, with good breakfast combos, mains like ceviche and *feijoada* (a Brazilian stew) for Bs30–70, a strong range of beers and wine and an economical set lunch (Bs39). Daily 8am–11pm.

**El Huerto** Ladislao Cabrera 86 ☎04 6451538, ⓦelhuertorestaurante.net; map p.195. Ask a local for the best restaurant in town, and the chances are they'll direct you here. The menu features excellent meat, chicken and fish dishes (mains Bs67–85) cooked to both traditional Bolivian and international recipes and served in a beautiful garden. It is around 2km north of the city centre, but well worth the taxi fare (around Bs20). Mon, Tues & Sun noon–4pm, Wed–Sat noon–4pm & 7–10pm.

**Metro** Calvo 2 ☎04 6468035, ⓦfacebook.com/ CafeMetroBolivia; map p.195. Diagonally opposite the main square, this high-ceilinged, mural-filled café has a touch of class, with black-and-white-suited waiters and a menu ranging from quesadillas to quiches, stroganoffs to salads (mains around Bs50), plus good coffee. Mon–Sat 8.30am–10pm, Sun 8.30am–6pm.

**Paso del Los Abuelos** Bustillos 216 ☎04 6455173; map p.195. Smarter than average *salteñeria* where Sucre's wealthier citizens go for their mid-morning snacks: at around Bs8 each, the *salteñas* here are relatively expensive, but worth every cent. Mon–Sat 8am–1pm.

★**El Patio** San Alberto 18; map p.195. Widely considered the best *salteñeria* in town, popular with locals and tourists alike. Head to the cashier first and then take your order to the counter, where you may have to elbow your way to the front of the scrum. Once you've got your rich, juicy *salteñas* (from Bs8), grab a seat in the beautiful colonial patio, which is filled with bougainvillea and other flowering plants. Get here early, as they sell out quickly. Daily 8am–1pm.

**Pizzeria Napolitana** Plaza 25 de Mayo 30 ☎04 6451934; map p.195. Sucre's longest-running Italian restaurant, facing the main plaza, serves reasonable pizza (Bs35–100) and pasta, as well as copious *copas* (ice-cream sundaes; try the banana split) and strong coffee. The two-course-and-coffee lunch special costs Bs35. Mon & Wed–Sun 8.30am–10.30pm.

**La Posada** Audiencia 92 ☎04 6460101, ⓦhotellaposada.com.bo; map p.195. Located within the hotel of the same name, this classy restaurant has an attractive courtyard setting, and a menu that is strong on fish and seafood (mains Bs45–80; set lunch Bs40). It's a romantic spot for an early evening drink too (beer from Bs25). Mon–Sat 7am–10.30pm, Sun 7am–3pm.

**La Taverne** Arce 35 ☎04 6455719, ⓦlataverne .com.bo; map p.195. The Alliance Française's restaurant has a mix of French standards, like onion soup and steak in blue cheese sauce, and international dishes from as far away as India and Thailand (mains Bs45–80), all presented with a certain flair. The four-course set lunch (Bs50) is well worth hunting out. There's a quaint little dining room, filled with scores of wine bottles and Gallic knick-knacks, and a tranquil outdoor terrace. Mon–Sat 8.30am–11pm, Sun 7–10.30pm.

## DRINKING AND NIGHTLIFE

Sucre has a lively nightlife scene, thanks in part to its large student presence, and many places stay open until the early hours, especially at weekends. It has a particularly strong range of **bars** and pubs, many of them run by expats. Several places also host performances of **Andean folk music and dance**.

### BARS

**Florin** Bolívar 567 ☎04 6451313, ⓦfacebook.com/ Cafe.Florin; map p.195. This lively Dutch-run place has an authentic pub feel with a huge central bar, prominent photos of the Netherlands' football team, live sport on TV, excellent beer (including from the owner's microbrewery; around Bs25) and a daily happy hour (9.30–10.30pm). The menu also has dishes from all over the world. Mon–Fri noon–2am, Sat 8.30am–2am, Sun 8.30am–midnight.

**Goblin Cerveza Artesanal** Grau 246 ☎7303 5722, ⓦfacebook.com/goblincervezaartesanal; map p.195. This small bar is run by a local microbrewery, and offers everything from amber ales to stouts (from Bs20), plus tasty meat and cheese platters. Live bands often play; at other times rock concerts are screened on the TVs. Thurs–Sat 8pm–2am.

**Joy Ride Café** Ortíz 14 ☎04 6425544, ⓦjoyridebol .com; map p.195. Part of a Dutch-run empire (there's also a travel agency, shop and hostel), this bar-restaurant serves an exhaustive range of dishes (mains Bs35–85), but the drinks (cocktails and shots around Bs30) and atmosphere are the real draw. There are film screenings, salsa classes, pool tables, a heated patio, book exchange, and plenty of special offers (including two-for-one desserts daily 5–7pm). Weekends are particularly rowdy. Mon–Fri 7am–late, Sat & Sun 9am–late.

**Red Lion English Pub** Bolívar 490 ⊙ 7612 6801; map p.195. This British-run joint lives up to expectations, with a good range of draught and bottled beers (from Bs20), fish and chips and a full English breakfast on the menu, and live sport on the TV, as well as a pleasant terrace. Mon–Thurs 5pm–midnight, Fri 5pm–2am, Sat 7pm–2am.

### SHOPPING

**Inca Pallay** Audiencia 97 ⊙ 04 6461936, ⊚ incapallay .org; map p.195. This fair-trade shop offers quality – and rather pricey – products from the Jalq'a and Tarabuceño (see opposite) communities, from textiles to cushions, belts to bags. Mon–Sat 9am–6pm, Sun 9am–4pm.

**Museo de Arte Indigena** Pasaje Iturricho 314 ⊙ 04 6453841, ⊚ asur.org.bo; map p.195. This museum shop has an outstanding range of Jalq'a and Tarabuceño textiles. There is often a weaver working here, so you can also see

### TRADITIONAL MUSIC AND DANCE

**Casa Municipal de Cultura** Argentina ⊙ 04 6435240; map p.195. The Casa Municipal de Cultura often hosts folk music concerts, as well as small exhibitions of local arts and crafts, and other events – pop in or phone up to see what's on. There are free live music performances on Friday evenings (from 7pm).

**Origenes Bolivianos** Azurduy 473 ⊙ 04 6457091, ⊚ espacioculturalorigenes.com; map p.195. If you're after an entertaining folkloric dance and music show (2hr), head to *Origenes Bolivianos*. Most travel agencies sell tickets (Bs150 with a decent dinner). Tues–Thurs 8.30–10.30pm, Fri–Sun 8–10pm.

how they are made. Mon–Fri 9am–12.30pm & 2.30–6pm, Sat 9am–noon & 2.30–6pm.

**Para Ti** Audiencia 68 ⊙ 04 6437901, ⊚ chocolatesparati .net/en; map p.195. Sucre's finest chocolatier has a tempting array of treats, many of them flavoured with Bolivian ingredients like coca, quinoa and Salar de Uyuni salt. There are several branches around Sucre (and, indeed, the country), but this is the pick of the bunch, thanks to the attached tiny café, which has delicious hot chocolates, milkshakes, coffees and liqueurs. Daily 8.30am–8.30pm.

### DIRECTORY

**Banks and exchange** Casas de cambio around the main square change foreign currencies at reasonable rates. There are also plenty of ATMs, including at the Banco de Santa Cruz and Banco Nacional de Bolivia, opposite each other near the corner of San Alberto and España.

**Hospital** Hospital Santa Bárbara, Plaza de la Libertad (⊙ 04 6451900).

**Language schools** Academia Latinoamericana de

Español, Dalence 109 at Ortiz (⊙ 04 6439613, ⊚ latinoschools.com), is the most prominent of the numerous Spanish schools in Sucre. It offers private or group lessons, and can arrange homestays and voluntary placements. There are also branches in Peru and Ecuador.

**Laundry** Lava Yá (Bs12/kg), Audiencia 81, opposite *La Posada*.

**Post office** Correo Central, Junín and Ayacucho.

# Around Sucre

The green hills and pleasant climate surrounding Sucre make this an area well worth setting aside time to explore. Day-trips to the market at **Tarabuco** are popular, as are explorations – on foot, bike or horse – of the dramatic **Cordillera de los Frailes** (see box, below).

---

## THE CORDILLERA DE LOS FRAILES

The eastern section of the **Cordillera de los Frailes**, the mountain range that cuts across Potosí and Chuquisaca departments, is easy to explore from Sucre. Most travel agencies (see p.203) in the city offer hikes, typically lasting one to four days in the region, and often following Inca trails. Highlights include the spectacular **Maragua Crater**, near the village of the same name, the pretty stone chapel at **Chataquila**, the **Garganta del Diablo** waterfall and **Boca del Diablo** cave, the dinosaur footprints and fossils at **Niñu Mayu** and **Mayu**, and the charming Jal'qa villages of **Potolo** and **Quila Quila**. Note that much of these treks are at altitude, so make sure you're fully acclimatized before setting off.

# Tarabuco

One of the most popular excursions from Sucre is to the small rural town of **TARABUCO**, set amid crumpled brown mountains about 60km southeast of the city. The town itself is an unremarkable collection of red-tiled adobe houses and cobbled streets leading to a small plaza with a modern church, but its real claim to fame is its **Sunday market**, which acts as a focus for the indigenous communities of the surrounding mountains, the so-called **Tarabuceños** (see box below), who come to sell the beautiful **weavings** for which they're famous throughout Bolivia. The market is a bit of a tourist trap but it's still principally geared towards the indigenous campesinos of the surrounding region, and the stalls selling weavings and other handicrafts to tourists are far outnumbered by those selling basic supplies such as dried foodstuffs, agricultural tools, sandals made from tyres, coca leaves and pure cane alcohol. If you walk a few blocks away from the centre of town you can still see campesinos engaging in **trueque**, a traditional Andean system of non-monetary trade in which agricultural products from different ecological zones are exchanged according to standard ratios – potatoes for maize, dried llama meat for oranges, and so on.

You can pick up some nice **souvenirs** at the market, though it's best to have some idea of quality and price before you arrive (have a look at things on sale in Sucre). Small items like decorative *chuspa* coca-bags make good mementoes; larger items like ponchos and shawls cost a lot more. Be prepared to bargain, but not too hard: many of the sellers are poor campesinos who may be desperate to sell something so they can buy essential goods to take home to their families. **Photographing people** without permission is considered rude and can provoke an angry reaction: ask first, and be prepared to pay a few bolivianos for the privilege. For a less touristy experience, try one of Candelaria Tours' trips (see p.203) to Candelaria village.

**4**

---

### THE TARABUCEÑOS: MASTER WEAVERS

Though they wear the same traditional costume, speak the same language (Quechua) and share many cultural traditions, strictly speaking it's not correct to refer to the **Tarabuceños** as an ethnic group: the name was simply given by the colonial authorities to all the indigenous communities living around Tarabuco. When the Spanish first arrived, the region had only recently been conquered by the Incas and marked the very limit of their domain. To secure the frontier and defend against raids by the indomitable Chiriguano tribes to the east, the Incas settled the area with different ethnic groups brought from elsewhere in the empire. All these indigenous communities speak **Quechua**, the lingua franca of the Inca empire, and at some point after the Spanish conquest they also adopted the distinctive costumes that give a semblance of unity today, but they have no collective name for themselves nor any tradition of collective political organization that suggests a common origin.

#### TRADITIONAL COSTUMES

These distinctive **traditional costumes** make the Tarabuceños difficult to miss: the men wear leather hats, known as *monteros* and shaped like the steel helmets worn by the Spanish conquistadors, along with woollen ponchos woven with bright, horizontal stripes of red, yellow, orange and green on a brown background, and three-quarter-length white trousers. In addition, they often use finely woven accessories like *chumpi* belts and *chuspa* coca-bags. Though generally more muted in colour, the traditional costumes worn by the women, particularly the woollen shawls known as *llijlas* or *aqsus*, are also decorated with beautiful and **complex designs**, and the ceremonial hats and headdresses they wear on special occasions match the *monteros* of the men in their unusual shape and design: black pillboxes with a flap covering the neck decorated with sequins and bright woollen pom-poms, or boat-shaped sombreros embroidered with silver thread. More even than their costumes, however, it is Tarabuceño **weavings** (see box, p.196) that draw travellers to Tarabuco, and selling them has become a major source of income for the Tarabuceños, who otherwise depend on agriculture for their livelihoods and live in great poverty.

## TARABUCO'S CARNAVAL

Every year on the third Sunday of March, Tarabuco celebrates **Pujllay** (or the Carnaval de Tarabuco), one of the best-known indigenous fiestas in Bolivia. Pujllay commemorates the **battle of Jumbate** on March 12, 1816, during the Independence War, when the Tarabuceños ambushed a battalion of marauding Spanish troops, slaughtering all but the drummer boy and eating their hearts in ritual revenge for abuses committed by the Spanish. During the fiesta, all the surrounding Tarabuceño communities come to town dressed in their finest **ceremonial costumes**, joined by thousands of tourists. Following a Mass to commemorate the battle, the participants stage folkloric dances and parades while knocking back copious amounts of *chicha* (fermented maize beer), beer and pure cane alcohol. The climax of the celebration takes place around a **ritual altar** known as a *pukara*, raised in honour of the Tarabuceños who died in the battle and formed from a kind of wooden ladder decorated with fruit, vegetables, flowers, bread, bottles of *chicha* and other agricultural produce. Drinking and dancing continues through the night: if you want to sleep, you're better off returning to Sucre.

### ARRIVAL AND DEPARTURE                                        TARABUCO

**By bus/truck** Buses and trucks to Tarabuco (2hr) leave on Sunday morning (and most weekdays) from Plaza Huallpari-machi in the east of Sucre, returning in the afternoon.

**By tourist bus** It is much more convenient and only slightly more expensive to go on one of the tourist buses organized by hotels and tour agencies in Sucre, which will pick you up outside the Mercado Central on Calle Ravelo in the morning and bring you back in the afternoon – *Hostal Charcas* organizes a service every Sunday around 8.30am (Bs40 return).

### ACCOMMODATION AND EATING

Several restaurants on the plaza serve basic meals and drinks, though on Sundays it's more fun to do as the locals do and eat soup or *chicharrón* (deep-fried pork) from the market stalls.

**HI Cej-Tarabuco** One block back from the central plaza ☏ 04 6440471, ⓦ hihostels.com. Housed in a converted colonial-era mansion, this small Hostelling International-affiliated hostel has clean and simple dorms and private rooms (the latter have attached bathrooms), a simple café and a TV lounge. No wi-fi. Dorms Bs32, doubles Bs120

# Cochabamba

At the geographic heart of Bolivia, midway between the Altiplano and the eastern lowlands, **COCHABAMBA** is the commercial hub of the country's richest agricultural region, the Cochabamba Valley, a modern, unpretentious and outward-looking city. Named the "City of Eternal Spring", it enjoys a year-round sunny climate that is matched by the warmth and openness of its population. Although most travellers who visit are just passing through, those who spend time here find Cochabamba to be Bolivia's most welcoming city. It is also a good base for exploring the attractions of the surrounding valley – chief among these, in the eyes of the locals at least, is **chicha**, a thick, lightly alcoholic maize beer.

For all its charm, rapidly expanding Cochabamba has few conventional tourist attractions, and little remains of the original colonial city centre. The **Museo Archeológico** is worth a visit, as is the **Cristo de la Concordia**, the Christ statue that overlooks Cochabamba from the east. Otherwise, the most interesting areas are the massive, rambling **street markets** that stretch to the south of the centre, the commercial heart of this market city.

### Brief history

The **Incas** were quick to spot the region's agricultural potential when they conquered it in the mid-fifteenth century, moving Quechua-speakers here to cultivate maize. Inca control of the area was ended by the **Spanish**, who founded the city of Cochabamba on

January 1, 1574, naming it La Villa de Oropeza in honour of the Conde de Oropeza, father of the Viceroy Francisco Toledo, who ordered its settlement. Locals soon reverted to calling it by the indigenous place name Cochabamba, a combination of the Quechua words for lake and plain, though all but one of the shallow, swampy **lakes** that once stood here have been filled in.

The Spanish established **haciendas** to produce grain for Potosí's silver mines, and so important was their agricultural work to the colonial economy that the valley's indigenous population was exempted from having to work in the mines under the *mita* system. When the mines went into decline towards the end of the colonial period and the early republican era, much of the hacienda land was rented out, and the region saw the emergence of a class of small but independent Quechua-speaking **peasant farmers**, very different in culture and outlook from the rather closed Aymara *ayllus* of the Altiplano. These peasant farmers played a central role in the emergence of Bolivia's radical peasant political organizations in the 1950s and 1960s and, as migrants to the Chapare, assumed a key role in the coca-growers' movement.

# Plaza 14 de Septiembre

The centre of Cochabamba is **Plaza 14 de Septiembre**, a peaceful and pleasant square with flower-filled ornamental gardens, a colonial stone fountain and benches shaded by tall palm trees. It is named after the date in 1810 when Cochabamba's citizens rose up against Spain in reaction to news of Pedro Domingo Murillo's execution in La Paz (see p.56). At its centre stands an obelisk topped by the statue of a condor – a monument to the Cochabambinos who died during the Independence War. The plaza is flanked by nineteenth-century buildings that extend over the pavement and are supported by pillars, forming arched arcades.

**4**

### La Catedral Metropolitana

Plaza 14 de Septiembre • Mon–Fri 8am–noon & 5–7pm, Sat & Sun 8am–noon • Free

Sideways on to the south side of the plaza stands the **Catedral Metropolitana**, founded in 1571 and the city's oldest church, though little of the original structure remains. The main entrance, facing out onto Calle Arze, is a fairly straightforward mestizo-Baroque portico decorated with spiralled columns, carvings of flowers and squat angels that look rather like pre-Columbian idols. The airy but unexceptional Neoclassical interior is brightly painted with floral designs and images of saints.

---

### COCHABAMBA AND THE WATER WAR

Referred to by its inhabitants as "La Llacta", the Quechua equivalent of the Spanish word *pueblo*, meaning at once city and people or nation, Cochabamba is the focus of a vigorous **regional identity**, and throughout Bolivian history has enjoyed a reputation for political independence and rebelliousness, a tradition that continues to this day. In 2000 the city's water system was privatized and sold to a consortium of international companies, which immediately doubled or even tripled water rates. In response, Cochabamba erupted in a series of spontaneous protests that became known as **La Guerra del Agua** – "the Water War". Thousands of citizens from all social classes took to the streets to demand that rates be lowered, blocking roads in and out of the city. The Banzer government responded in familiar fashion: a state of siege was declared, protest organizers were arrested, **armed troops** were sent in and plain-clothes snipers opened fire on protesters, killing one and injuring many others. Despite this oppression, the demonstrations continued, and the water consortium eventually backed down – a popular victory that was welcomed by anti-globalization campaigners around the world. The excellent film *Tambien la lluvia (Even the Rain)*, starring Gael Garcia Bernal, is set during the Water War.

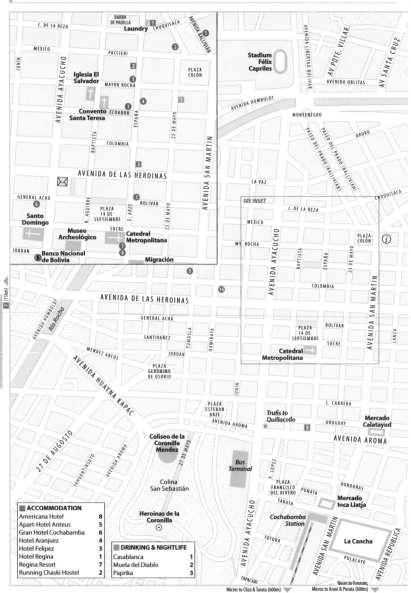

# Museo Archeológico

Aguirre and Jordán • Mon–Fri 8am–6pm, Sat 8.30am–12.30pm • Bs25 • ☎ 04 4250010

A block south of the plaza sits the interesting and extensive **Museo Archeológico**. The displays are poorly explained, but the collection does convey the evolution of **pre-Hispanic culture** in the Cochabamba region, stretching from the Tiwanaku culture, through a number of regional groups to the Incas. Among the most interesting exhibits are small **stone idols** (thought to represent Pachamama), along with bronze Inca

**COCHABAMBA**

| EATING | |
| --- | --- |
| Café Paris | 5 |
| Cafétería Ideal | 6 |
| La Cantonata | 3 |
| Casa de Campo | 11 |
| La Estancia | 12 |
| Goss Sushi Cafe | 2 |
| Menta Restobar | 4 |
| Sole Mio | 9 |
| Sucremanta | 1/7/14 |
| Terra | 10 |
| Vainilla | 13 |
| Wist'upiku | 8 |

| SHOPPING | |
| --- | --- |
| The Spitting Llama | 1 |

| TOUR OPERATOR | |
| --- | --- |
| Fremen Tours | 1 |

axeheads, ceremonial knives, star-shaped stone maces and well-preserved Tiwanaku woven skull caps made to fit skulls deformed by ritual trepanation. Also intriguing are items used by early Catholic missionaries in their efforts to convert the indigenous peoples – these include sheepskins painted with bizarre hieroglyph-like ideographs, and clay discs encrusted with fragments of stone and pottery which were used like rosaries to remember sequences of prayer and other mysteries of the faith. There's also a small display of ethnographic material from the peoples of the **Amazon lowlands**.

## Convento Santa Teresa

Baptista N-344 • Guided tours Mon–Fri 9am, 10am, 11am, 2.30pm, 3.30pm & 4.30pm, Sat 2.30pm, 3.30pm & 4.30pm • Bs20; cameras Bs5 • ☎ 04 4525765

The **Convento Santa Teresa** has the imposing feel of a fortress. There has been a convent on this site since 1760, though the original was destroyed by an earthquake. The current Baroque structure dates to 1790, and is still home to a small community of Carmelite nuns, though they now live in more modern, comfortable quarters next door (off-limits to visitors). Visits are by guided tour (in Spanish) only, and feel like a step back in time to a different age. Highlights include some fine mestizo-Baroque (see p.157) artworks and altarpieces. The convent is periodically closed for restoration work.

## Colina San Sebastián

West of the bus terminal on Av Aroma, about 600m south of Plaza 14 de Septiembre

A tree-lined pedestrian avenue leads up to the summit of the **Colina San Sebastián**, a low hill with views over the city, which was the scene of one of the most dramatic events in Cochabamba's history. During the Independence War, the city was quick to join the rebellion against Spanish rule, but in 1812, after its menfolk had gone off to fight elsewhere, the women of Cochabamba found themselves virtually defenceless against an advancing royalist army. Refusing calls to surrender, the women fortified the hill where, on May 27, they fought heroically until finally overwhelmed. Known as Las Heroínas de la Coronilla, these women are commemorated with a **monument** at the top of the hill, a cast-iron statue of Christ surrounded by images of women fighting or sheltering their children. In Bolivia, Mothers' Day is celebrated on May 27 in memory of the Heroínas de la Coronilla.

This area has a decidedly dodgy reputation, so if you visit, go during the day, in a group, and take a taxi (and ask the driver to wait for you).

## La Cancha

Nine blocks south of Plaza 14 de Septiembre

In the south of the city, an entire block between calles Tarata and Pulucayo on the east side of Avenida San Martín is occupied by the massive covered street market known as **La Cancha** ("walled enclosure" in Quechua), where campesinos and merchants from throughout the region come to buy and sell their produce. Wandering through the market's sprawling labyrinth of stalls is the best way to get a feel for the vibrant commercial culture of the city and the surrounding area: the buzz of Quechua fills the air and the **traditional costumes** of different campesino groups are very much in evidence, in particular the straw sombreros and brightly coloured *pollera* skirts of the women of the Cochabamba Valley. This is effectively one massive clearing house for **agricultural produce**, and the range of foodstuffs on sale reflects the full diversity of Bolivia's different ecological zones. You'll also find pretty much anything else poor Bolivians might need: sacks, rope, ironmongery, medicinal herbs, ritual items for making offerings to Pachamama and the mountain gods, and cheap manufactured goods. La Cancha has overflowed its original bounds, and now spreads across Avenida San Martín on to the disused railway, and northwest to occupy another entire block between Tarata and Punata, an area now known as the **Mercado Inca Llajta** ("Inca Town" in Quechua).

## Palacio de los Portales

Av Potosí, around 1km north of the centre • **Palace** Guided tours Tues–Fri 3pm, 3.30pm, 4.30pm, 5.30pm & 6pm (Spanish), 4pm, 5pm & 6.30pm (English/French), Sat & Sun 10am, 11am & noon (Spanish), 10.30am & 11.30am (English/French) • Bs20 • **Garden** Tues–Fri 3–6.30pm, Sat & Sun 9am–noon • Free • ☎ 04 4489666, ⊛ centropatino.fundacionpatino.org

The **Palacio de los Portales** is the luxurious former house of the Cochabamba-born "King of Tin", **Simón Patiño** (see box, p.146). Built between 1915 and 1922 in a bizarre mix of architectural styles including **French Neoclassical** and *mudéjar*, the palace shows that the mining magnate possessed rather more money than artistic sense. The interior is decorated with astonishing opulence: marble fireplaces and statues of Roman emperors and St Bernard dogs; walls covered in rich damask or panelled in fine wood; Venetian crystal chandeliers and Louis XV furniture. If anything, though, it's the magnificent **garden** that really impresses, laid out in perfect proportion by Japanese specialists and featuring a beautiful and rare ginkgo tree. Patiño never actually lived here, as by the time the palace was complete he was based permanently overseas, and the building now houses the Instituto Cultural Simón I. Patiño, an education and literacy charity. There are also regular (often free) art exhibitions and concerts.

## Cristo de la Concordia

Above Av Ruben Dario, 1.5km east of the city centre • **Cristo de la Concordia** Statue interior Sat & Sun 10am–6pm • Bs2 • **Cable car** Tues–Sat 10am–6pm, Sun 9am–6pm • Bs10.50 return

On the summit of the Serranía de San Pedro stands the **Cristo de la Concordia**, a monumental statue of Christ with arms outstretched overlooking the city. The statue was modelled on the more famous Christ figure that looms over Río de Janeiro but, as locals proudly tell you, it's a little bit taller, measuring over 34m (40m, if you include the pedestal), and thus the tallest statue in South America. Towering high above the city and weighing over two thousand tonnes, by Bolivian standards it's a truly massive monument.

From a station at the eastern end of Avenida Las Heroínas, a **cable car** (*teleférico*) makes the five-minute journey up the Serranía de San Pedro to the statue (a taxi costs Bs40–50). The **views** from the base of the statue are splendid, and on weekends you can climb up the spiral staircase inside the hollow steel figure for an even better panorama. There's also a small **café**, and several stalls rent binoculars and telescopes.

Note that muggings have taken place on the summit, so it is best not to visit on your own. The walk up to the summit from Avenida Las Heroínas is unsafe and should not be attempted.

### ARRIVAL AND GETTING AROUND                    COCHABAMBA

**By plane** Jorge Wilsterman airport (☎ 04 4222846) is a few kilometres southwest of the city; a taxi into the centre costs Bs30–40; alternatively, take micro B, which goes up Av Ayacucho to Plaza 14 de Septiembre. In addition to domestic flights there are also a few services to neighbouring countries. The flights below are all direct; for most destinations, there are several more connecting flights.

Destinations Cobija (1 weekly; 1hr 20min); La Paz (11–13 daily; 30min); Santa Cruz (10–12 daily; 45min); Sucre (2 daily; 30min); Tarija (2–3 daily; 1hr); Trinidad (1–2 daily; 50min).

**By bus** Most long-distance buses arrive at and depart from Cochabamba's bus terminal, in the south of the city on Av Ayacucho just south of Av Aroma. The terminal has an information kiosk, post office, phone booths, a left-luggage store, a restaurant and several ATMs. The surrounding area is rough, especially at night, so be very careful. A taxi to the city centre costs about Bs10–20, and is a far better bet than walking. Buses and trufis to the Chapare region (including Villa Tunari; 3hr–3hr 30min) depart when full from close to the junction of Av Oquendo and Av 9 de Abril, southeast of the city centre.

Destinations La Paz (roughly hourly; 7–8hr); Oruro (6–7 daily; 5–8hr); Santa Cruz (10–12 daily, most leaving in the morning or eve; 10–12hr); Sucre (3 daily, departing early eve; 10–12hr).

### INFORMATION AND TOURS

#### TOURIST INFORMATION

The tourist office, on the eastern side of Plaza Colon (Mon–Fri 8am–noon & 2.30–6.30pm, Sat 8.30am–noon; ☎ 04 4662277, ⓦ www.cochabamba.bo/turismo/), has free city maps and leaflets, but is unable to provide much else in the way of information. There is also an information kiosk at the bus station (officially same hours, though they are not always kept to; ☎ 04 4220550), and on Blvd de la Recoleta (officially same hours, though it's rarely staffed).

#### TOUR OPERATORS

**Fremen Tours** Tumulsa N-245 ☎ 04 4259392, ⓦ andes-amazonia.com; map p.210. Respected operator offering a wide range of tailor-made tours throughout Bolivia. In

## COCHABAMBA'S STREET NUMBERS

Cochabamba's **street numbers** are prefixed N, S, E or O – north, south, east or west – depending on whether they run north or south from Avenida Heroínas, or east or west from Avenida Ayacucho. The first two digits in the street number refer to the block in terms of how far it is from these two major intersections, the second two to the number of the building: thus España N-349 is on España at no. 49, three blocks north of the intersection with Avenida Heroínas.

the Cochabamba region, it runs trips into the Chapare, where it owns *Hotel El Puente* in Villa Tunari (see p.226), as well as city tours and visits to the market towns of the Valle Alto, Parque Nacional Torotoro, and the ruins at Incarakay and Incallajta. It also organizes adventurous camping trips in the Parque Nacional Isiboro-Sécure (see box, p.286).

**Tusoco Viajes** Sagarnaga 227, La Paz ☎02 2140653, ⓦtusoco.com. Tusoco is an umbrella organization representing community-based tourism projects across the country. In the Cochabamba region, the Chocaya group offers camping in the Chocaya forest, north of Quillacollo. The Kawsay Wasi group, meanwhile, has a range of tours in the Chapare region (see p.226). Tusoco's office is in La Paz, so contact via the website or by phone.

**Villa Etelvina** Torotoro ☎7073 7807, ⓦvillaetelvina .com. Based at the lodge of the same name (see p.224), this agency offers hiking, mountain biking, rappelling, and tours of Parque Nacional Torotoro.

## ACCOMMODATION

Apart from a couple of top-end options, accommodation in Cochabamba is unexceptional. The better mid-range places tend to be rather dull **business hotels**, though there are some decent budget options; the flophouses around the bus station are best avoided. There are also some decent options in the town of **Tiquipaya**, around 10km northwest of the city centre (20min or so by taxi). The only time accommodation can be difficult to find is in mid-August during the **Fiesta de la Virgen de Urkupiña** in nearby Quillacollo (see box, p.220) when it's best to book in advance. All include breakfast unless mentioned otherwise.

**Americana Hotel** Arze S-788 ☎04 4250552, ⓦamericanahotel.com.bo; map p.210. A good-value high-rise hotel with attentive staff and comfortable, well-equipped en-suite rooms with TVs and city views (from rooms on the higher floors). The area isn't the safest, however, so take care at night. $55 (Bs374)

**Apart-Hotel Anteus** Potosí N-1365 ☎04 4245067, ⓦhotelanteus.com; map p.210. Small, modern hotel located across the street from the Palacio de los Portales in a smart residential neighbourhood, a short walk from Blvd Recoleta. The bright rooms have private bathrooms, TVs and kitchenettes. Bs480

**Gran Hotel Cochabamba** Plaza Ubaldo Anze E-415 ☎04 4282551, ⓦgranhotelcochabamba.com; map p.210. This luxurious Art Deco country club-style hotel is the flashiest joint in town, with spacious en suites over a swimming pool and a palm-filled garden, a spa and a fine restaurant-bar. It lacks the character of *Hotel Aranjuez*, though. $132 (Bs898)

★ **Hotel Aranjuez** Buenos Aires E-563 ☎04 4240158, ⓦaranjuezhotel.com; map p.210. Located in the upmarket Recoleta neighbourhood, close to the Palacio de los Portales, *Hotel Aranjuez* is a stately place, with professional staff, classy and well-equipped en suites, a bird-filled garden and a good restaurant-bar. If you have the budget, this is the place to stay. $100 (Bs680)

**Hotel Felipez** España N-172 ☎04 4506393, ⓦfelipezhotel.com; map p.210. The orange-and-cream colour scheme may not be to everyone's taste, but this no-nonsense hotel does the basics well: clean and comfortable en-suite rooms, and a friendly welcome. While the doubles are a decent size, the singles are decidedly cramped. Bs220

**Hotel Regina** Reza and España ☎04 4257382; map p.210. Good-value, mid-range hotel in a central location, with efficient staff, plus a bar and restaurant. Although they're not the most stylish, a recent redesign has freshened up the large, bright en suites (all have TVs; some also have kitchenettes). Bs400

**Regina Resort** Tiquipaya, a 20min drive west of the centre ☎04 4316555; map p.210. If you don't fancy staying in the city, this appealing resort in leafy Tiquipaya is a good choice, especially for families; there are two pools, two restaurants, a playground, games rooms, several sports pitches and a spa. The en suites themselves are spacious and comfortable. A taxi into the centre costs around Bs40. Bs550

**Running Chaski Hostel** España N-449 ☎04 4250559, ⓦrunningchaski.com; map p.210. Cochabamba's top hostel has mixed and female-only dorms, with eight to ten beds in each, plus simple singles and doubles (with private bathrooms) and flashier suites sleeping up to four people (Bs250 for double occupancy). Dorms Bs49, doubles Bs195

## EATING

The most affordable places to eat are Cochabamba's many **markets**, in particular the Mercado Calatayud, on San Martín and Aroma, which offers **local specialities** like *picante de pollo* (chicken in a spicy sauce), *silpancho* (a breaded beef schnitzel), and delicious empanadas and *salteñas*, which seem twice as big as elsewhere in Bolivia and are served with a choice of different sauces. Cochabambinos are adventurous eaters, and the choice of **restaurants** here is broad.

★**Café Paris** España and Bolívar ☎04 4503561; map p.210. Sophisticated French-style café with Parisian posters on the walls, wrought-iron chairs and a stained-glass-covered bar. There's an extensive range of coffees (Bs6–25), plus sweet and savoury crêpes (Bs13–28), ice-cream sundaes, and daily quiche and gateau specials. Mon–Sat 8am–10pm.

**Caféteria Ideal** General Acha and Ayacucho ☎04 4251016; map p.210. Tucked away on a side street and lacking a sign, this tiny café would be easy to miss if it weren't for the enticing smell of fresh coffee. This lost-in-time place serves great *cortados*, cappuccinos, espressos and *cafés con leche* at rock-bottom prices (Bs5–15). Mon–Sat 9am–6/7pm.

**La Cantonata** España and Venezuela ☎04 4259222, ⓦlacantonata.com.bo; map p.210. One of the smartest restaurants in the city centre, *La Cantonata* serves up tasty, though slightly overpriced, Italian food (mains Bs50–100). Mon–Sat noon–2.30pm & 6.30–11.30pm, Sun noon–3pm & 7–10.30pm.

**Casa de Campo** Blvd Recoleta ☎04 4243937; map p.210. An attractive, if tourist-orientated restaurant, *Casa de Campo* offers classy (and rather pricey) versions of traditional local dishes like *piques*, *silpancho* and *picante de pollo* (mains Bs60–85) around a pleasing central courtyard. There are often *peña*-style programmes at the weekends. Daily noon–midnight.

**La Estancia** Blvd Recoleta ☎04 4249262, ⓦlaestancia.com.bo; map p.210. This excellent Argentine *parrilla* (steakhouse) is the best of the barbecue restaurants in this area, serving generous portions of delicious grilled beef (the more expensive Argentine cuts, from Bs95, are well worth splashing out on), chicken or fish accompanied by a massive salad bar. Daily noon–10/11pm.

**Goss Sushi Café** Ballivián and Mexico ☎04 4524050, ⓦgossbolivia.com; map p.210. Bolivia's landlocked status means sushi is rare and pricey, but *Goss* is well worth a look. In addition to salmon, prawn and octopus sushi (Bs35–50), there are noodle dishes, *yakitori* and sliders (Bs45–85), and generally a lunch special (main and a drink) for around Bs40. Daily 24hr.

★**Menta Restobar** España N-356 ☎04 452 0113; map p.210. The best vegetarian restaurant in the city, *Menta* has a cool, modern design, with exposed brickwork and plenty of pale-wood furnishings. For lunch, go for the set meal (Bs21) or choose from one of the stacked bean, quinoa, chickpea or lentil burgers. The dinner menu expands to cover pizzas and mains (Bs25–55) including lasagne and tacos. Great juices too. Mon–Sat noon–3pm & 6.30–10pm.

**Sole Mio** América E-826 ☎04 4283379, ⓦsole-mio.net; map p.210. This family-run Italian restaurant in the Recoleta neighbourhood has decent, fairly thin-crust pizzas (Bs55–100), as well as a range of pastas, risottos and salads. Set lunch Bs35. Mon–Fri 6–10pm, Sat & Sun noon–2pm & 6–10/11pm.

**Sucremanta** Arze S-348 ☎04 4222839; map p.210. Popular restaurant specializing in traditional pork-based dishes from the Chuquisaca department (Sucre) including delicious chorizo sausages, *fritanga* (a thick, spicy stew), *salteñas* and empanadas. There are other branches at Av Ballivián N-510 and Hamiriya N-126. Mains Bs22–50. Daily 9am–2pm.

**Terra** Pando 1140 ☎04 4418912; map p.210. Slick restaurant with a globe-trotting menu that has influences from Italy, France, Peru, Mexico, China, the US and even Finland. There are plenty of fusion options, but the Latin American options are the best bets, most notably the ceviche. Prices are on the high side (Bs60–90), but there's an economical set lunch for Bs42. Mon–Sat noon–midnight, Sun noon–10pm.

**Vainilla** Salamanca and Antezana ☎04 4522104; map p.210. Aping the style of an international coffee chain, popular with middle-class Cochabambinos, expats and tourists alike, *Vainilla* is a good breakfast spot, with eggs Benedict, waffles and French toast among the options (Bs22–34), plus sandwiches, wraps, salads, bagels, cakes and pastries, as well as a short selection of mains. The coffee's not bad, and the wine and beer list is surprisingly extensive. Mon–Sat 8am–10.30pm, Sun 8am–9pm.

**Wist'upiku** Arze S-370 ☎04 4503920, ⓦwistupiku.com; map p.210. Dating back to 1939, this local chain has branches throughout the city (and beyond), though this is the most conveniently central. It specializes in delicious and inexpensive baked and fried empanadas and *salteñas* (Bs5–8) to eat in or take away. Daily 11am–7/8pm.

## DRINKING AND NIGHTLIFE

Nightlife in Cochabamba is centred on three different districts, each catering to a distinct crowd. Wealthy Cochabambinos head to the **Recoleta** neighbourhood, just east of Plaza Quintanilla, north of the Río Rocha at the top of Avenida Oquendo, about 1km from Plaza 14 de Septiembre. More straightforward entertainment – inexpensive steakhouses, beer palaces with football on big-screen TVs, and sound systems pumping out Latin pop – can be found along **Avenida Ballivián** (also known as El Prado), just north of the city centre. Centred on the intersection of **España and Ecuador**, in the city centre, meanwhile, is a laidback bohemian scene of bars and cafés popular with Cochabamba's large student population. Many restaurants stay open late at weekends and double as bars, and in all three areas places go in and out of fashion very quickly.

★**Casablanca** 25 de Mayo and Ecuador ☎04 4521048; map p.210. A bohemian joint, decorated with classic film posters and photos of jazz legends, drawing students, young foreign volunteers, and (during the day at least) a few old timers. Although coffee and food are on offer, the beer (including a few craft options; from Bs18), wines from Bolivia, Argentina, Chile and Italy (glass Bs15), and cocktails (around Bs35) are the best bet. The first-floor balcony is great for people-watching, and there are often film screenings. Daily 9am–1/2am.

**Muela del Diablo** Potosí 1329 ☎7622 0409, ⓦfacebook.com/mueladeldiablo; map p.210. Next door to the Palacio de los Portales, this atmospheric restaurant-bar-music venue is a great place to spend the night. Live bands (generally of the rock variety), a good range of beer (from Bs20) and cocktails, and thin-crust pizzas to sate hunger pangs are all on offer. Mon–Sat 5.30pm–2am.

**Paprika** Chuquisaca N-688 ☎04 4662400, ⓦfacebook .com/Paprika.Cbba; map p.210. This trendy café-restaurant-bar boasts fancy lighting, a wide-ranging (though overpriced) menu that features everything from sandwiches and wraps (Bs25–40) to pizza and pasta (Bs50–72), and an extensive beer and cocktail list (from Bs18). Daily 11.30am–2am.

### SHOPPING

**The Spitting Llama** España and Ecuador ☎04 4894540; map p.210. This excellent multilingual bookshop and exchange also stocks camping and hiking gear, as well as other travel supplies, and even a selection of craft beers. Mon–Fri 9am–1pm & 3–8pm, Sat 9am–1pm.

### DIRECTORY

**Banks and exchange** There are plenty of ATMs, including at the Banco Nacional de Bolivia, Jordán and Aguirre, which also changes US dollars.

**Hospitals** Clínica Belga, Antezana N-0457 ☎04 4231403.

**Language lessons** Escuela Runawasi, Maurice Lefebvre N-0470, Villa Juan XXIII (☎04 4248923, ⓦrunawasi.org),

offers Spanish and Quechua lessons (from Bs1340/week), plus homestays (from Bs665/week).

**Laundry** Limpieza Superior, España N-616 (Mon–Sat 9am–6pm; Bs12/kg; ☎04 4521307).

**Post office** Correo Central, Ayacucho and Heroínas (Mon–Fri 8am–9pm, Sat 8am–noon).

# Around Cochabamba

East of Cochabamba stretches the densely populated upper Cochabamba Valley, or **Valle Alto**. Set at an altitude of about 2600m, it is blessed with rich alluvial soils and a warm, spring-like climate. The valley's fields of maize and wheat are among the most fertile and productive in the country – not for nothing is it known as the breadbasket of Bolivia. This region is dominated by peasant farmers: though still Quechua-speaking, they're much more outward-looking than the communities of the Altiplano, and played a key role in the emergence of radical peasant federations in Bolivia in the 1960s and 1970s.

## Cliza, Punata and Arani

Cliza market: Sun; Punata market: Tues; Arani market: Thurs

The rural centres of **CLIZA** (40km from Cochabamba), **PUNATA** (45km) and **ARANI** (55km) all make interesting excursions, especially during their bustling weekly **agricultural markets**, when peasants from the surrounding districts come to buy supplies, sell produce, meet friends and drink *chicha*. The women wear the characteristic brightly coloured *pollera* skirts and white straw boaters of the Cochabamba Valley, and carry their goods on their backs in luridly striped shawls. The markets are rather prosaic compared to the more tourist-orientated market at Tarabuco (see p.207), and there's almost nothing in the way of handicrafts on sale, but it's still

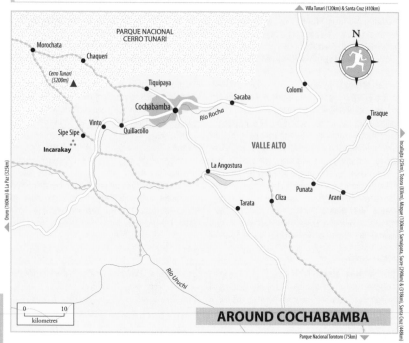

interesting to watch the energetic scenes, as people haggle over great piles of fruit and vegetables, live sheep and cattle, and cheap manufactured clothes. The liveliest markets are in Arani and in Cliza; the market in Punata, 45km from Cochabamba, is smaller, but the town is famed as home to Bolivia's best *chicha*, the fermented maize beer that was sacred to the Incas and which is still produced and consumed in large quantities in the Cochabamba Valley. With a tart, yeasty flavour, *chicha* is definitely an acquired taste, and can play havoc with the digestion, but drinking a few glasses is the best way to get talking with the local campesinos. It is served from huge earthenware pots and drunk from gourds – you'll find it on sale in a number of private houses, marked by a white flag or bunch of flowers raised on a pole outside.

### ARRIVAL AND DEPARTURE                 CLIZA, PUNATA AND ARANI

**Micros and trufis** To Arani (every 15–20min; 45min) and Punata (every 30min; 40min) they leave from the corner of Av Republica and Manuripi in the south of Cochabamba; those for Cliza (every 15–20min; 25min) leave from the corner of avenidas Barrientos and Manuripi.

## Parque Nacional Cerro Tunari

Gate around 7km north of Cochabamba • No fixed opening times • Free

Some three thousand square kilometres of the Cordillera Tunari – the mountain range that forms the northern boundary of the Cochabamba Valley – is protected by **Parque Nacional Cerro Tunari**. Named after the region's tallest peak, the 5200m Cerro Tunari, the park was set up primarily to protect the forested watershed that provides the irrigation water that is vital to the agriculture of the Cochabamba Valley, and to conserve rare high-altitude queñua forests, home to the Cochabamba mountain finch, which is found nowhere else in the world. Given its proximity to the city, the park's ecosystems are far from pristine; the lower slopes closest to Cochabamba in particular are affected by illegal building. It's easy to visit from the city, however, and is popular amongst Cochabambinos at weekends.

From the gate, a track climbs steeply up into the park; roughly an hour's walk (or a short drive) will bring you to a series of picnic sites and playgrounds amid eucalyptus groves where Cochabambinos like to relax around a barbecue, enjoy the views and stroll or ride mountain bikes along the various tracks and trails. If you continue walking uphill for two to three hours you'll reach a series of small **lakes** from which the views are even more spectacular. If you make an early start and travel via Quillacollo (see below), it is also possible to visit the higher reaches of the park and the peak of Cerro Tunari itself, from where you can gaze down at Cochabamba and the valley and – on clear days – across to the shimmering peaks of the Cordillera Real far to the west. Condors are also a frequent sight.

### ARRIVAL AND DEPARTURE               PARQUE NACIONAL CERRO TUNARI

Although you can get there by public transport, the most hassle-free way to visit the park is on an organized trip with a Cochabamba-based tour agency (see p.213), which will provide transport, a guide and accommodation.

**By trufi** To reach the most accessible section of the park, immediately above Cochabamba, flag down trufi #103, which heads along Av Ayacucho to the park gate, about 7km north of the city centre.

**By micro to Cerro Tunari** To get into the higher reaches of the park and climb the peak of Cerro Tunari itself, you'll need to take a micro very early in the morning to Quillacollo

(see below) and then catch another micro from there towards the rural town of Morochata (1 daily at about 7am), which lies north of Quillacollo on the other side of the Tunari range and the national park. You alight from the micro at the hamlet of Chaqueri, about 25km from Quillacollo at an altitude of 4200m, from where a path leads to the summit; it's a fairly straightforward ascent (4–5hr), though you may need to ask locals for directions. Transport back to Quillacollo passes by Chaqueri in the afternoon, but given the timing you'll need to camp overnight if you're doing the ascent independently.

### ACCOMMODATION

If you want to scale Cerro Tunari independently, you will need to take your own camping gear, food and water supplies, as public transport timings do not allow you to do the ascent in one day.

**Berghotel Carolina** Cerro Tunari ☎ 7213 0003, ⓦ berghotelcarolina.com. Located in a eucalyptus forest at the base of Cerro Tunari, this charming lodge has a cosy, appealingly alpine feel, with comfortable en-suite rooms, a sauna, and a range of activities on offer, including bird-watching, hiking, mountain biking, paragliding, and wine tasting. Rates are per person and include full board. Bs651

## Quillacollo

About 15km west of Cochabamba, and all but engulfed by the city's urban sprawl, is the bustling market town of **QUILLACOLLO**, the Cochabamba Valley's second-biggest settlement. It's a lively commercial centre and transport hub famous for its **Fiesta de la Virgen de Urkupiña** (see box, p.220), staged annually in August. Outside fiesta time, however, there's little to see other than the reputedly miraculous but rather ordinary-looking image of the Virgen de Urkupiña herself, inside the modest Neoclassical Iglesia de San Idelfonsino a few blocks south of the main plaza. The town is also well known for the spicy food and heady brews available in its raucous *chicherías* (traditional restaurants serving *chicha*).

### ARRIVAL AND DEPARTURE           QUILLACOLLO

**By micro** Frequent micros run from Av Aroma in Cochabamba (every 10–15min; 25min).

### ACCOMMODATION

**Eco Hotel Spa Planeta de Luz** 5km north of Quillacollo ☎ 04 4261234, ⓦ hihostels.com. This Hostelling International-affiliated lodge, set amid expansive gardens, has a hippy vibe. There are options for most budgets – including clean dorms, private rooms and cabins – as well as a pool, sauna, spa treatments and a vegetarian restaurant. Dorms Bs55, doubles Bs280, cabins Bs550

## THE FIESTA DE LA VIRGEN DE URKUPIÑA

Every year for three days around August 15, Quillacollo hosts the **Fiesta de la Virgen de Urkupiña**, which attracts up to half a million visitors and involves a massive parade of costumed dancers from all over Bolivia, as well as copious eating and drinking intertwined with sincere expressions of spiritual faith – many pilgrims walk to Quillacollo by night from Cochabamba. The fiesta dates back to the early nineteenth century, when a local Quechua-speaking shepherdess had repeated visions of the Virgin Mary on the nearby **Cerro Cota hill**. When the villagers of Quillacollo investigated, they saw a brief glimpse of the Virgin ascending to heaven, and later found a carved image of her hidden among the rocks. This was carried to the parish church of San Idelfonsino, and soon credited with numerous miracles. The name Urkupiña is derived from the Quechua for "on the mountain" – the shepherdess's cry when she pointed out the Virgin to the villagers.

As with most major Bolivian religious fiestas, however, its true origins lie deep in the pre-Christian past. Significant pre-Hispanic burial sites have been uncovered in the centre of Quillacollo, and the town's name means "**mountain of the moon**" in Quechua – the Incas considered the moon to be a major female deity, and following the Spanish conquest it was often conflated with the Virgin Mary. As well as the procession and dances, a central feature of the fiesta is a visit to the rocky outcrop where the Virgin appeared, during which tourists and pilgrims alike hack lumps of rock from the **sacred mountain** to take home with them in the belief that this will ensure health and material prosperity. They also make libations of coca and alcohol and burn candles, offerings associated with **Pachamama**. As in the fiesta of Alasitas in La Paz (see box, p.57), pilgrims buy miniature replicas of objects they wish to possess in the belief that by doing so the real thing will be theirs before the year is out.

The best way to visit the fiesta is as a **day-trip** from Cochabamba, though you'll need to get to Quillacollo early in the morning to ensure a good spot from which to watch the dances. Accommodation in Cochabamba is hard to find during the fiesta.

# Incarakay

Set high on the mountainside overlooking the Cochabamba Valley about 25km west of the city, the ruins of the Inca outpost of **Incarakay** make an excellent if rather strenuous day-trip from Cochabamba. The site itself is fairly small, a collection of a dozen or so buildings of rough-cut stones with the trapezoidal internal niches and doorways and **earthquake-resistant** inward-leaning walls characteristic of Inca architecture. What really impresses, however, is the setting: perched on the mountainside at an altitude of 3200m, Incarakay enjoys fantastic views over Cochabamba to Cerro Tunari. From up here, the flat expanse of the Cochabamba Valley with its neatly irrigated green fields of maize seems a vision of order and fertility in contrast to the harsh, arid mountain ranges on either side.

It's not certain quite what purpose Incarakay served, but it seems likely it was some kind of **imperial administration centre**. The Incas invested great energy in the Cochabamba Valley after they conquered the region in the mid-fifteenth century, bringing in agricultural settlers from other parts of the empire to cultivate the **maize** which fed the Inca armies, and this would seem a perfect site from which to calculate how much the imperial share of the harvest should amount to each year. On the return journey it's well worth stopping off in the town of Sipe Sipe to sample some **chicha**.

### ARRIVAL AND DEPARTURE · INCARAKAY

To reach the ruins, take a micro from Av Aroma in Cochabamba to Quillacollo (every 10–15min; 25min), then another from Plaza Bolívar in Quillacollo to Sipe Sipe (every 15–20min; 20min), a peaceful agricultural town about 8km west of Quillacollo. From Sipe Sipe it's a steep 2–3hr climb up to Incarakay; the route is fairly easy to find on your own, though you can always ask directions from the locals. From the southwest corner of the plaza in Sipe Sipe, follow the road that heads out of town towards the mountainside. About 1km from the plaza, the road crosses a stream and turns sharply to the left; about 160m further on, just past a gully, a path climbs from the right-hand side of the road up to the ruins. The path is indistinct, but if you keep climbing towards the southwest the ruins will eventually become visible above you.

# Tarata

The pretty town of **TARATA**, 30km southeast of Cochabamba, makes for a pleasant half-day excursion from the city. It was the birthplace of notorious president Mariano Melgarejo (see p.309), who briefly declared Tarata the country's capital in the 1870s, and whose remains now lie in the town's church. Tarata has several other significant colonial buildings, including the former constitutional palace and a Franciscan convent. Nearby Huayculi village, 8km southeast of Tarata, is famous for its pottery.

### ARRIVAL AND DEPARTURE                                                TARATA

Trufis (30min) leave when full from the junction of avs Magdalena and Barrientos in Cochabamba, and can drop you off anywhere in the centre of Tarata. A taxi from Tarata to Huayculi costs around Bs30.

# Incallajta

The other major Inca site in the Cochabamba region is **Incallajta**, a far more substantial complex about 143km east of the city, which was built as a military outpost to protect the valley from raids by the unconquered Chiriguano tribes of the eastern lowlands. There are good camping spots at the ruins and water is available, but you'll have to take all the food you need with you. Incallajta is 15km off the road to Sucre, just south of the point where it joins the old highland road between Cochabamba and Santa Cruz.

### ARRIVAL AND DEPARTURE                                            INCALLAJTA

Unless you rent a 4WD, the easiest way to visit Incallajta is with a Cochabamba-based tour agency – a day-trip costs about $100–120 (Bs680–816) per person for a group of four people. Reaching Incallajta by public transport is very difficult.

**4**

# Totora

The road from Cochabamba to Sucre, 366km to the southeast, passes through a scenic region of rugged mountains and fertile valleys, but unfortunately all public transport between the two travels overnight, so unless you've got your own transport, you're unlikely to see much. The road also passes through what was once one of the prettiest colonial villages in Bolivia – **TOTORA**. Sadly, the village was devastated by a powerful earthquake that shook the region in 1998, but after a lengthy corruption-plagued reconstruction effort it has finally regained much of its original charm. The entirely, and generally faithfully, rebuilt central plaza offers a unique opportunity to experience the plaza much the way it would have looked at the height of Spanish rule.

### ARRIVAL AND DEPARTURE                                                TOTORA

While it is possible to get off one of the through buses in the middle of the night, it is much better to visit Totora on a day-trip from Cochabamba. Micros leave from the corner of Av 6 de Agosto and República between 1pm and 4pm (3hr). Shared taxis, which depart when full, shave an hour from the journey, and only cost a little more.

# Mizque

The charming small town of **MIZQUE**, some 152km southeast of Cochabamba, offers a slice of traditional rural life, largely untouched by tourism. There's an attractive church, local history museum, colourful market (Monday), and several hiking routes in the surrounding countryside. There are a handful of simple guesthouses and restaurants – and make sure you try the tasty local cheese.

### ARRIVAL AND DEPARTURE                                                MIZQUE

**By bus of trufi** Daily buses run between the junction of avenidas Barrientos and 6 de Agosto in Cochabamba and Mizque (2–3 daily; around 4hr); trufis also serve this route.

# Parque Nacional Torotoro

Some 130km south of Cochabamba, **PARQUE NACIONAL TOROTORO** protects a remote and sparsely inhabited stretch of the arid, scrubby landscape that is characteristic of the eastern foothills and valleys of the Andes. Covering just 164 square kilometres around the village of the same name, Torotoro is Bolivia's smallest national park, but what it lacks in size it makes up for with its powerful scenery and varied attractions. The park encompasses a high **hanging valley** and deep eroded **canyons**, ringed by low mountains whose twisted geological formations are strewn with fossils, dinosaur footprints and labyrinthine limestone cave complexes. In addition, the park's woodland supports considerable wildlife – including parakeets and the rare and beautiful red-fronted macaw, found only in this particular region of Bolivia – while ancient rock paintings and pre-Inca ruins reveal a long-standing human presence. The main attractions are the limestone caves of **Umajallanta**, the scenic, waterfall-filled **Torotoro Canyon**, and hiking expeditions to the pre-Inca ruined fortress of **Llama Chaqui**. Two days are generally enough to see the main attractions, though it's worth taking longer if you want to explore more fully.

### Brief history

Though reached from Cochabamba, Parque Nacional Torotoro actually lies within Northern Potosí department. Before the Spanish conquest this was the core territory of the **Charcas Confederation**, a powerful collection of ethnic groups subject to Inca rule. Following the conquest, the different Quechua- and Aymara-speaking groups that made up the confederation retained their identities as separate *ayllus* (extended kinship groups). The *ayllus* of Northern Potosí mostly live in the higher-altitude lands to the west, where they grow potatoes and raise livestock, but they maintain islands of territory in the dry valleys such as Torotoro, where they cultivate maize, wheat and other lower-altitude crops. This system ensures each group has access to the produce of different altitudes, and represents a distinctly Andean form of organization that has long fascinated anthropologists.

Throughout the colonial era and long after independence, Northern Potosí was the focus of frequent **indigenous uprisings**. As recently as 1958, during the upheaval following the 1952 revolution, Torotoro village – which was formed in the late colonial period by mestizo migrants from Cochabamba – was ransacked by armed *ayllu* members, who seized the lands of the haciendas that had been established on their traditional valley territories.

## Torotoro

The administrative centre of the park and the only base from which to explore it is the sleepy village of **TOROTORO**. Home to just a few hundred people, it stands beside the river of the same name at the top of a broad hanging valley at an altitude of about 2600m. Torotoro's main annual celebration is the **Fiesta de Tata Santiago**, held on July 25 each year, when the *ayllus* descend on the village to drink, dance and stage ritual *Tinku* fights (see box, p.164).

## The dinosaur tracks of Cerro Huayllas

The park's clearest **dinosaur tracks** are on the lower slopes of Cerro Huayllas, the mountain just east of the village across the Río Torotoro (generally only a stream in the May–Sept dry season). To reach them, walk back along the road to Cochabamba and cross at the ford, turn right and walk upstream about 100m, then climb about 20m up the rocky slope to your left. The tracks were made by a quadruped herbivore that roamed the region in the Cretaceous period more than sixty million years ago – they comprise a trail of deep circular prints about 50cm in diameter imprinted in a sloping plane of grey rock and set about 1m apart. A little further upstream there's another trail of smaller (and much less distinct) prints left by a three-toed carnivore.

## Along the Río Torotoro

Follow the Río Torotoro downstream from the Cerro Huayllas dinosaur tracks for about twenty minutes and you'll reach a stretch where the rushing rainy-season waters have carved great stone basins out of the soft bedrock – locals refer to this stretch as **Batea Cocha** (Beating Pool), as they look a bit like basins for pounding laundry. About 7m up the rock face on the left bank, protected by a low adobe wall, is a collection of ancient **rock paintings** (*pinturas rupestres*). Mostly abstract designs painted in red ochre, with several zigzags – including one that looks like a serpent and another that could be the sun or a star – the paintings are all less than 1m long and have been partly defaced, but they provide a focus for what is anyway a pleasant stroll down the river. A little further downstream there's a pretty **waterfall** that forms a good swimming hole; beyond that, the river plunges down into the deep Torotoro Canyon and you can walk no further, though you can access the canyon from further downstream.

## Torotoro Canyon

Just north of Torotoro village the Río Torotoro plunges through the deep **Torotoro Canyon**, probably the park's most beautiful section. Enclosed on either side by sheer, 200m-high cliffs covered with stunted trees and spiky bromeliads, the river creates a series of waterfalls as it tumbles over a jumble of massive boulders, forming pools that are ideal for swimming. The route down to the rock-strewn canyon floor is easy to find without a guide (though you shouldn't go alone in case you hurt yourself and can't get back).

To get down into the canyon, follow the road out of town towards Cochabamba for about 200m. Where the road turns sharply to the right, follow the track heading off to the left, and walk for about twenty minutes until you see some well-made stone steps dropping steeply down the side of the canyon to your left. The most picturesque stretch of the canyon is a few hundred metres downstream from where the steps reach the bottom, where a 10m-high waterfall known as **El Vergel** emerges from the side of the canyon on the right in several streams which cover the rock face in slimy-green water weeds.

## Caverna de Umajallanta

The most extensive and easiest to visit of the park's many limestone cave systems is the **Caverna de Umajallanta**, where nearly 5km of underground passages have been explored. The cave makes a great day-trip from Torotoro and is one of the park's most popular attractions; on no account attempt to visit without a guide as it is easy to get lost once inside. Its entrance is about 8km northwest of Torotoro, a walk of ninety minutes to two hours across the rolling landscape with good views of the dramatic geology of the mountain ridges that surround the Torotoro valley – about halfway you'll pass a trail of **dinosaur footprints**.

The cave complex was formed by the waters of the **Río Umajallanta**, which disappears below the surface here and re-emerges as a waterfall high above the Torotoro Canyon, 6km away to the east. It consists of a series of interconnected limestone caverns of varying sizes, one of which contains a lake fed by the river that is home to some blind white fish. Sadly, most of the stalactites and stalagmites have been broken off by visitors in the years before protective measures were established, but a visit to the cave is still very enjoyable, unless you're claustrophobic – trips involve clambering and crawling for a couple of hours through some very tight places up to 800m underground. Take a torch and drinking water and expect to get dirty. For serious cavers and speleologists there are a number of other caves in the area to explore – talk to staff at the park office.

## Llama Chaqui

About 16km east of Torotoro stands **Llama Chaqui**, a ruined pre-Inca fortress that energetic hikers can visit (with a guide) in a long day-trip from the village. The walk to the ruins takes you over the mountains to the east of the Río Torotoro, with spectacular views across the deep valley of the Río Caine and the rugged brown mountains that march away to Cerro Tunari, the peak that rises above Cochabamba. The scenery is very beautiful, with steep rocky slopes and narrow hanging valleys patchworked with maize and barley fields set around the occasional isolated hamlet.

Set on a knife-edge ridge high above the **Río Caine**, Llama Chaqui itself is an excellent observation point and natural fortress, though other than the walled enclosure little remains of the ancient settlement and the entire complex is heavily overgrown. Even so, you can still make out the foundations of individual houses, and the ground is scattered with pottery fragments and rough-cut stones.

## Museo Pachamama Wasi

Charcas s/n • No fixed opening hours • Bs5

The **Museo Pachamama Wasi**, in the home of a Torotoro resident and amateur geologist, contains hundreds of prehistoric objects that have been found over the years in the national park. You need a bit of luck to visit, as the museum is only open when the owner or his family are home.

### ARRIVAL AND DEPARTURE     PARQUE NACIONAL TOROTORO

**By bus** Buses to Torotoro leave Cochabamba from the corner of avenidas 6 de Agosto and Republica (Mon–Wed & Fri to Sat 6pm; Thurs & Sun 6am; they return from Torotoro Mon–Thurs & Sat 6am, Fri 6pm, Sun noon, 1pm & 3pm).

The bus ride takes about 7hr in the dry season (May–Sept), a rough and dusty trip along unpaved roads and dry riverbeds – in the rainy season (Nov–March) it takes much longer and the route is sometimes impassable.

### INFORMATION

**Tourist information** The tourist office on the village main square (officially daily 8am–noon & 2–5pm, though opening hours are erratic; ☎7227 0968, ⓦvisitatorotoro .com.bo) is where you pay the Bs30 park admission fee. It has basic information about the park and can find you a local guide for around Bs100 a day – forming a group with other travellers to share the costs is rarely a problem.

### ACCOMMODATION AND EATING

Eating options are decidedly limited: the best restaurant is at *Villa Etelvina*, and you can also get a reasonable meal at *Las Hermanas*. Otherwise, there are a few basic shops where you can buy simple provisions, though it's worth bringing some supplies with you from Cochabamba to supplement this rather meagre fare.

**Hostal Las Hermanas** Cochabamba s/n ☎04 4135736. This simple, welcoming lodge is the best of the village's low-budget *alojamientos*. The rooms – with either shared or private bathrooms – are clean, basic and fine for a night or two. There's also good home cooking available. Bs100

**Villa Etelvina** Sucre s/n ☎7073 7807, ⓦvillaetelvina .com. Easily the best place to stay in Torotoro, the well-run *Villa Etelvina* has comfortable en-suite bungalows sleeping up to six people, rooms with shared bathrooms, and camping facilities. There's a restaurant, and staff can organize hikes, mountain biking and rappelling. Advance bookings essential. Doubles Bs360, bungalows Bs830, camping Bs50

# The Chapare

Northeast of Cochabamba, the main road to Santa Cruz crosses the last ridge of the Andes and drops down into the **CHAPARE**, a broad, rainforest-covered plain in the Upper Amazon Basin heavily settled by peasant migrants from the highlands, who turned the region into the main source in Bolivia of coca grown for the **cocaine** trade. Conflicts between government drug-enforcement officers and local peasant farmers have decreased in recent years, and there have been attempts to limit the amount of coca grown here. Nevertheless, the Chapare is not the place for exploring far off the beaten track.

For all the region's troubles, however, the towns along the main Cochabamba–Santa Cruz road are safe, though most are fairly unattractive. **Villa Tunari**, a former narco-traffickers' playground, is now at the centre of efforts to promote the Chapare as a tourist destination: the rainforests of the **Parque Nacional Carrasco** are nearby, and the town enjoys a beautiful setting and is a good place to relax. Otherwise, the main point of stopping in the Chapare is to make the exciting river trip from **Puerto Villarroel**, the region's main port, north to Trinidad in the Beni.

# Villa Tunari

About 160km from Cochabamba, **VILLA TUNARI** is the biggest settlement in the Chapare and the centre of efforts to develop the region as a tourist destination. Set beside a broad sweep of the Río San Mateo, with the last forested foothills of the Andes rising behind, Villa Tunari has a picturesque setting, and at an altitude of just 300m enjoys a warm, tropical climate. Its odds of becoming a successful ecotourism destination, however, seem long, and independent travel in the surrounding area remains inadvisable. This is a shame, as from **Puerto San Francisco**, an hour's drive north of Villa Tunari, you could rent a motorized canoe and boatman to take you down the ríos Chipiriri and Isiboro into the rainforests of the **Parque Nacional Isiboro-Sécure** (see box, p.286); though Fremen Tours (see p.213) runs trips along this route, doing so independently is not advisable.

The main Cochabamba–Santa Cruz road, which runs through the town, is lined with restaurants and hotels where in better days the movers and shakers of the **cocaine trade** would come to blow some of their massive earnings, but which now depend on weekenders from Cochabamba and a few tourists. The main plaza is two blocks north of the road.

### Parque Machia

250m east along the main road in Villa Tunari and across the bridge over the Río Espírito Santo • Tues–Sun 9.30am–4pm, closed rainy days • Bs6, cameras Bs30 • 15-day volunteer programmes Bs1770 • ☎ 04 4136572, ⌨ intiwarayassi.org

**Parque Machia** is a small, private ecological reserve that also serves as a refuge for Amazonian animals rescued from captivity. It has 4km of trails and lookout points with beautiful views across the Río Chapare and the forest-covered mountains rising to the high peaks of the Andes behind. You'll meet most of the semi-tame animal residents, which include several species of monkey, macaws and a puma, many of which roam free. After heavy rains, the trails are sometimes closed for safety reasons.

The reserve is managed by the **Inti Wara Yassi** organization, which relies largely on volunteers, many of them young foreign travellers.

### Parque La Hormiga

12km east of Villa Tunari • Daily 8am–5pm • Bs25, including a guided tour • ☎ 6768 0760

Also known as Las Hormiguitas, **Parque La Hormiga** is a small nature park run by Fremen Tours (see p.213), which is home to a range of Amazonian flora and fauna, including monkeys, turtles and snakes. A taxi there and back from Villa Tunari, with waiting time, costs around Bs100.

| ARRIVAL AND DEPARTURE | VILLA TUNARI |

**By bus** Buses (every 1–2hr; 3hr 30min) and trufis (leave when full; 3hr) to Villa Tunari leave from the intersection of avenidas Oquendo and 9 de Abril in Cochabamba. Heading back to Cochabamba from Villa Tunari, you can catch a bus or trufi from the office of Trans Tours 7 de Junio on the main road; alternatively, flag down one of the services passing through town on their way to Cochabamba from elsewhere in the Chapare. Buses from Santa Cruz will drop you off at the police control *tranca* at the west end of town, and buses heading to Santa Cruz sometimes pick up passengers here if they have room, though most pass through in the middle of the night.

## TOUR OPERATORS

**Fremen Tours** Cochabamba (see p.213) and Hotel de Selva El Puente (see below) ⓦandes-amazonia.com. Excellent operator offering a range of activities, including zip-lining (from Bs150), white-water rafting (from Bs150), and a wildlife park (see p.225).

**Tusoco Viajes** Sagarnaga 227, La Paz ⓣ02 2140653,

ⓦtusoco.com. An umbrella organization representing community-based tourism projects across the country. In the Chapare region, the Kawsay Wasi group offers white-water rafting, visits to local villages, and tours of Parque Nacional Carrasco. Tusoco's office is in La Paz, so contact via the website, or phone them up.

## ACCOMMODATION

**Hostal Habana Las Cocas** A block north of the main road, opposite the church ⓣ04 413 6597. Probably the best budget option in town (not that there's a lot of competition), with a range of clean rooms with shared or private bathrooms, fan or a/c, plus a small pool. **Bs180**

★**Hotel de Selva El Puente** About 4km east of town ⓣ04 4580085, ⓦhotelelpuente.com.bo. Villa Tunari's best option is *Hotel El Puente*, operated by Fremen Tours (see above), which has simple en-suite *cabañas* with fans (ones with a/c cost Bs430) set amid a patch of rainforest. There's a swimming pool, fourteen delightful natural river pools (open to non-guests for Bs10) and a restaurant. Various activities are available (see above), but no wi-fi. A

taxi from town costs around Bs20. **Bs365**

**Hotel Las Palmas** On the south side of the main road ⓣ04 4136501. A rather overpriced mid-range hotel offering a pool and comfortable but run-down en-suite rooms with a/c, fridges and TVs; some also have river views. There's a decent restaurant, and *San Silvestre* (see below) is next door. A taxi from town costs around Bs20. **Bs400**

**Los Tucanes** Around 2km east of town ⓣ04 4136506, ⓦlostucaneshotel.com. A good place to get away from it all, this self-contained resort has en-suite, a/c rooms with private patios (nos. 1–6 have at least partial river views), plus a pool, volleyball court, and restaurant-bar. A taxi from town costs Bs10. **Bs400**

## EATING

Most hotels have restaurants, and inexpensive food is available from stalls along the main road, though hygiene is not necessarily the top priority at the latter. Sadly, many places offer wild game – armadillo, peccary and so on – which should be avoided.

**San Silvestre** On the main road, next to Hotel Las Palmas. The town's best restaurant is a huge open-walled place with coconut trees, manicured laws, huge plastic macaws and toucans, and outdoor seating overlooking the

river (a good spot for a sundowner). Big portions of *comida típica* (mains Bs45–90) like *pique a lo macho* and *milanesas*, as well as local river fish, notably the delicious *surubí*. Daily 10am–10/11pm.

# Parque Nacional Carrasco

Around 10km south of Villa Tunari • Daily 8.30am–3.30pm • Bs40–90, depending on the size of your group, including a 2hr guided tour in Spanish • ⓣ7275 1669

South of Villa Tunari on the other side of the Río San Mateo, 6226 square kilometres of the forested northern slopes of the Andes are protected by **Parque Nacional Carrasco**, which adjoins the Parque Nacional Amboró (see p.240) to the east. Plunging steeply down from high mountain peaks, the park encompasses a variety of ecosystems from high Andean grasslands and cloudforest to dense tropical rainforest, ranging in altitude from 4000m to just 300m. It also supports a great range of wildlife, including jaguars, tapirs and peccaries, and over seven hundred species of bird, several of which are endemic. The park is seriously threatened by illegal logging, hunting and forest clearance for agriculture by settlers along both its northern and southern margins, but the mountainous forest-covered landscape is so impenetrable that the inner regions remain pristine.

## Cavernas del Repechón

The most popular excursion into the park is to see the **Cavernas del Repechón**, caves that are home to a large population of *guacharós*, or **oil birds**. These large nocturnal fruit-eating birds are found in only a few other places in South America. Visits are by guided tour only (included in the park entry fee), so arrive early to ensure you don't miss the guards when they set off. From the park entrance, you will be taken across the tumultuous Río San Mateo in a primitive cable car. It's a thirty-minute walk through the rainforest to the caves, where you'll be able to see the oil birds nesting (except in May and June, when they migrate to Venezuela). The birds only leave the caves at night to eat fruit, and navigate by echolocation, emitting a strange clicking sound. For longer park trips, contact Fremen Tours or Tusoco (see opposite).

### ARRIVAL AND DEPARTURE             PARQUE NACIONAL CARRASCO

**By taxi** To visit the park you'll need to reach the settlement of Paractito, about 9km from Villa Tunari on a side road heading south off the main road just east of town – a taxi should cost about Bs50–70, and twice that if you want the driver to wait around for a few hours and take you back after your visit.

## Ivirgarzama

About 65km east of Villa Tunari, the unappealing market centre of **IVIRGARZAMA** has little to distinguish it from other Chapare towns apart from the fact that it's from here that a side road leads north to Puerto Villarroel, from where you can travel by boat to Trinidad (see p.284) in the Beni. There are a couple of very basic *alojamientos*, but no reason to spend the night here.

From Ivirgarzama the main road continues east to Santa Cruz, 247km away, passing through **Buena Vista** (141km), an entrance point to Parque Nacional Amboró (see p.240).

### ARRIVAL AND DEPARTURE             IVIRGARZAMA

**By bus and trufi** Buses to Ivirgarzama (every 2–3hr; 5–6hr) depart from the intersection of Av Oquendo and Av 9 de Abril in Cochabamba. If you are travelling from Villa Tunari, you need to take a trufi to Shinaota (every 20–30min; 20min), then another one from Shinaota to Chimoré, and finally a third from Chimoré to Ivirgarzama. Trufis to Shinaota and buses to Cochabamba leave from one end of the main street, trufis to Puerto Villarroel (every 20–30min; 30min) from the other.

## Puerto Villarroel

Some 26km north of Ivirgarzama is **PUERTO VILLARROEL**, a small port on the **Río Ichilo** from where cargo boats travel north to Trinidad (see p.288). This route is an important transport link between Cochabamba department and the **Beni**. Puerto Villarroel is an untidy collection of tin-roofed houses, many of them raised above the muddy, unpaved streets to protect them from flooding when the river bursts its banks (not uncommon in the November-to-March rainy season). Most activity takes place on the riverbank, where there's a **rudimentary port**.

### ARRIVAL AND DEPARTURE             PUERTO VILLARROEL

**By trufi** Trufis to Ivirgarzama (every 20–30min; 30min) arrive at and depart from the small central plaza.

**By boat** To find a boat to take you downstream, ask around among the captains or in the Capitanía del Puerto (the naval port authority office). The journey through the rainforest to Trinidad (see p.288) takes 5–7 days, depending on the level of the river, the type of boat, and how many stops it makes to load and unload cargo. In the dry season (May–Sept) low river levels can make the trip downstream impossible. During the rest of the year there are usually several departures to Trinidad each week, though you may have to wait around a day or two – boat captains generally let passengers sleep on board while waiting to load. Bring your own hammock and mosquito nets (you can buy these in the markets in Cochabamba or Ivirgarzama), insect repellent and drinking water, and snacks to supplement the basic food supplied on board.

### ACCOMMODATION

**Alojamiento Richard** Near the river ☎ 04 4133522, 🌐 alojamientorichard.com. Puerto Villarroel's accommodation options are decidedly underwhelming, but this is the best of the bunch. The bare-brick rooms, with TVs, fans and private bathrooms, are acceptable for a night. It has a simple restaurant. **Bs120**

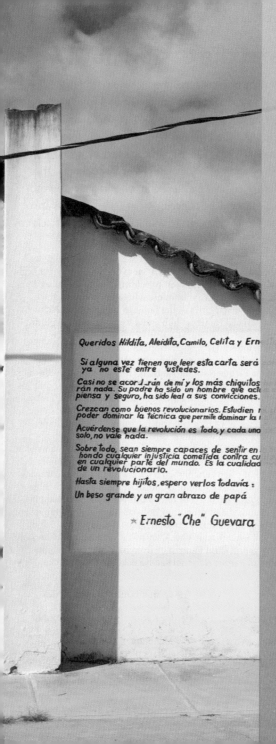

# Santa Cruz and the eastern lowlands

HOSPITAL SEÑOR DE MALTA, VALLEGRANDE

**5**

# Santa Cruz and the eastern lowlands

Stretching from the last Andean foothills to Brazil, Paraguay and Argentina, Bolivia's eastern lowlands (llanos orientales) form a vast and sparsely populated plain. The area's varied ecosystems range from Amazonian rainforest in the north, through broad savanna and tropical dry forest in the centre, to the immense wetlands of the Pantanal in the far east and the arid Chaco to the south. Rich in natural resources, the region's economy is the most important in the country, fuelled by significant oil and gas reserves, cattle-ranching and massive agricultural development. Its attractions are diverse, from the modern city of Santa Cruz to wildlife-filled Parque Nacional Amboró and the fascinating former Jesuit missions of Chiquitos.

At the centre of the eastern lowlands' economic boom is **Santa Cruz**, the lively tropical regional capital, which in just a few decades has been transformed from an isolated provincial backwater into a booming modern metropolis with a brash commercial outlook utterly distinct from the reserved cities of the Bolivian highlands. The city lacks tourist attractions, but is a crucial transport hub and a handy base for exploring the surrounding area, where much of the beautiful natural environment survives, despite the ravages of ongoing deforestation and development.

About 40km west, the exceptionally biodiverse rainforests of the easternmost foothills of the Andes are protected by the **Parque Nacional Amboró**. The beautiful cloudforest that covers the upper regions of Amboró can be visited from **Samaipata**, a tranquil resort town and home to the fascinating pre-Inca archeological site El Fuerte. From Samaipata, you can also head further southwest through the Andean foothills to the town of **Vallegrande** and the hamlet of **La Higuera**, which witnessed the last desperate guerrilla campaign of Che Guevara, who was killed here in 1967.

East of Santa Cruz the railway to Brazil passes through the broad forested plains of **Chiquitos**, whose beautiful Jesuit mission churches played a crucial role in Spanish colonial history, when a handful of priests established a semi-autonomous theocratic state in the midst of the wilderness. In the remote far north of the region, accessible only by air or an extremely arduous overland journey, **Parque Nacional Noel Kempff Mercado** is perhaps the most beautiful and pristine of Bolivia's protected rainforest areas, though sadly now extremely difficult (and expensive) to visit. Finally, south of Santa Cruz stretches the vast and inhospitable **Chaco**, an arid wilderness of dense thorn and scrub, reaching south to Argentina and Paraguay. Here you'll find the dramatic, though little visited, landscapes of **Parque Nacional Kaa-Iya del Gran Chaco**.

EL FUERTE, NEAR SAMAIPATA

# Highlights

**❶ Santa Cruz** Although lacking traditional tourist attractions, Bolivia's eastern capital comes to life at night, with an excellent range of places to eat and drink. **See p.232**

**❷ Parque Nacional Amboró** The country's most accessible stretch of rainforest boasts a spectacular abundance of birdlife, with more species than any other protected area in the world. **See p.240**

**❸ Samaipata** Gorgeous town set in an idyllic valley with excellent hiking nearby, as well as the mysterious pre-Hispanic ceremonial site of El Fuerte. **See p.242**

**❹ The Che Guevara trail** Retrace the final steps of the iconic Argentine revolutionary through the town of Vallegrande and the hamlet of La Higuera, where his ill-fated guerrilla campaign ended in capture and execution. **See p.247 & p.249**

**❺ The Jesuit missions of Chiquitos** Scattered across the sparsely populated forest region east of Santa Cruz, the immaculately restored mission churches of Chiquitos are a reminder of one of the most unusual episodes in Bolivia's colonial history. **See p.251**

HIGHLIGHTS ARE MARKED ON THE MAP ON P.232

# 5  Santa Cruz and around

Set among the steamy, tropical lowlands just beyond the last Andean foothills, **SANTA CRUZ** is Bolivia's economic powerhouse. An isolated frontier town until the middle of the twentieth century, the city has since become the biggest in the country, a sprawling metropolis with a booming oil, gas, timber, cattle and agro-industry economy. This rapid growth – and the availability of land – has attracted a diverse range of immigrants

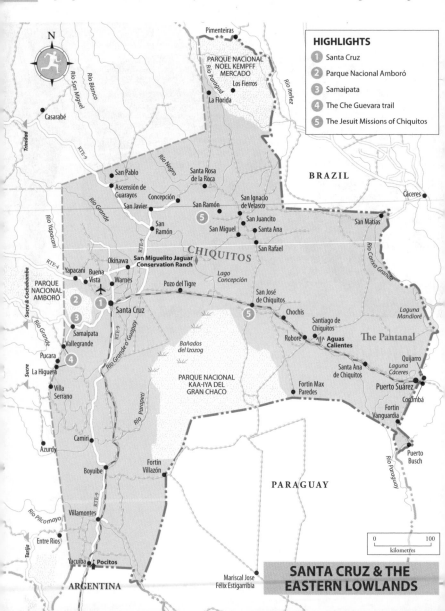

**HIGHLIGHTS**

1. Santa Cruz
2. Parque Nacional Amboró
3. Samaipata
4. The Che Guevara trail
5. The Jesuit Missions of Chiquitos

**SANTA CRUZ & THE EASTERN LOWLANDS**

to Santa Cruz, including Japanese rice farmers, Low German-speaking Mennonites and, far poorer, indigenous migrants from the Andes.

Native **cruceños**, however, still dominate the city. Known as **cambas**, they are culturally a world apart from the rest of Bolivia (they in turn refer with mild contempt to the highland immigrants as **collas** – the two terms being old Inca words for lowland and highland peoples respectively). Generally loud, brash and happy-go-lucky, their language, music and outlook are infused with a tropical ease and sensuality, which feels closer in spirit to Brazil or Colombia. Santa Cruz has few conventional tourist attractions, and some find its brash commercialism and pseudo-Americanism unappealing. Others, however, enjoy its dynamism and lively eating, drinking and nightlife scenes.

The city continues to grow at a phenomenal rate, spreading inexorably in a mixture of ragged shantytowns, commercial developments and exclusive residential districts where oil executives, businessmen and made-good drug-traffickers relax in opulent mansions and drive around in imported 4WDs (known as "narcocruisers"). The old colonial **city centre**, however, is still dominated by whitewashed houses with tiled roofs that extend over the pavements, and when everything closes up in the middle of the day for an extended lunch break the city is suffused with a languid tropical indolence.

### Brief history

Santa Cruz de la Sierra was founded in April 1561 by the conquistador **Nuflo de Chávez**, who had arrived in the region at the head of a large military expedition accompanied by thousands of indigenous Guaraní. The original city stood 260km east of its present location, close to the town of San José de Chiquitos (see p.259). The new settlement proved precarious, however, surrounded by a hostile indigenous population and far from any other outpost of Spanish power. In 1594 it was moved to its present location, a more easily defended site on the west of the **Río Grande**, close to the last foothills of the **Andes**. For the next three and a half centuries Santa Cruz remained an isolated frontier outpost. Things began to change in the 1950s with the construction of a railway link to Brazil and a road to Cochabamba. Subsequently Santa Cruz became the main supplier of cotton, rice, sugar, soy and other tropical agricultural produce to the rest of Bolivia (as well as exporting to other countries in South America and beyond).

---

**TENSION IN THE EAST**

Santa Cruz has long been a **flashpoint** for tension between the country's eastern and western halves. The Chaco area in the south of the region is rich in natural gas and oil and, when combined with other resources like huge iron ore deposits, this means that Santa Cruz's economic output represents a disproportionately large slice of the country's GDP. However, significant wealth is filtered off to La Paz and elsewhere, which has caused resentment, and many in Santa Cruz have called for greater autonomy and even independence.

In 2006, President Evo Morales put the **national gas industry** under state control in an effort to share the proceeds with the impoverished, indigenous majority, rather than continue to line the pockets of a privileged few. The terms of nationalization, however, seriously jeopardized agreements with the area's foreign investors. Morales' dramatic **land reform** policy, which also started in 2006, was bitterly opposed by Santa Cruz landowners too. Huge swathes of state-owned land were redistributed to help the nation's poor recover from historical injustices, and the government seized tracts of privately owned land that was unproductive, or obtained illegally, and distributed that as well. In Santa Cruz, the **autonomia** movement became very evident, with T-shirts, graffiti and green-and-white regional flags all bearing witness to the anti-government feeling.

Tensions remain today, though in recent years Morales has – partially, at least – managed to co-opt many of his opponents in the region.

**5**

The cocaine, oil and gas economy

Santa Cruz's economic boom really took off in the 1970s, when the city emerged as the centre of the Bolivian **cocaine industry**. Cocaine brought enormous wealth – as well as corruption – to the city, much of which was reinvested in land, agriculture, construction and other legitimate businesses. Growth was further fuelled by oil and gas revenues from the Chaco, and generous government subsidies to large landowners and agro-industrialists. The population of Santa Cruz leapt from around 42,000 in 1950 to

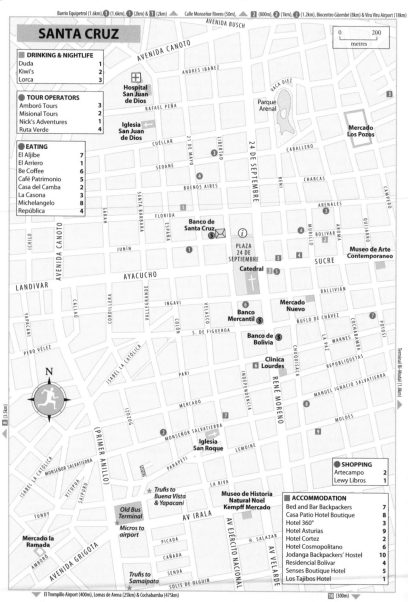

# SANTA CRUZ

### ■ DRINKING & NIGHTLIFE
| | |
|---|---|
| Duda | 1 |
| Kiwi's | 2 |
| Lorca | 3 |

### ● TOUR OPERATORS
| | |
|---|---|
| Amboró Tours | 3 |
| Misional Tours | 2 |
| Nick's Adventures | 1 |
| Ruta Verde | 4 |

### ● EATING
| | |
|---|---|
| El Aljibe | 7 |
| El Arriero | 1 |
| Be Coffee | 6 |
| Café Patrimonio | 5 |
| Casa del Camba | 2 |
| La Casona | 3 |
| Michelangelo | 8 |
| República | 4 |

### ● SHOPPING
| | |
|---|---|
| Artecampo | 2 |
| Lewy Libros | 1 |

### ■ ACCOMMODATION
| | |
|---|---|
| Bed and Bar Backpackers | 7 |
| Casa Patio Hotel Boutique | 8 |
| Hotel 360° | 3 |
| Hotel Asturias | 9 |
| Hotel Cortez | 2 |
| Hotel Cosmopolitano | 6 |
| Jodanga Backpackers' Hostel | 10 |
| Residencial Bolívar | 4 |
| Senses Boutique Hotel | 5 |
| Los Tajibos Hotel | 1 |

Barrio Equipetrol (1.6km), ❶ (1.6km), ❶ (2km) & ▮ (2km) Calle Monseñor Rivero (50m), ▲ ❷ (800m), ❷ (1km), ❷ (1.2km), Biocentro Güembé (8km) & Viru Viru Airport (18km)

El Trompillo Airport (400m), Lomas de Arena (25km) & Cochabamba (475km)

Terminal Bi-Modal (1.8km)

10 (300m)

over 1.6 million today, making it the country's biggest city. Tensions, however, remain with the Morales government (see box, p.233).

# Plaza 24 de Septiembre

Santa Cruz's spacious leafy central square **Plaza 24 de Septiembre** is named after the day in 1810 when Santa Cruz declared independence and joined the struggle against Spanish rule. At its centre stands a statue of **Colonel Ignacio Warnes**, a pro-independence Argentine guerrilla leader who was military governor of Santa Cruz from 1813 to 1816. He massacred over a thousand indigenous Chiquitano prisoners captured fighting on the Spanish side, before being executed himself along with nine hundred others when a Spanish army recaptured Santa Cruz.

## La Catedral

Plaza 24 de Septiembre • **Catedral** Daily 7am–7pm • Free • **Mirador** Daily 8am–noon & 3–6pm • Bs3

On the south side of the plaza stands the salmon-pink **Catedral** (or Basílica Mayor de San Lorenzo), a hulking brick structure with twin bell towers. The cathedral was built between 1845 and 1915 on the site of an original church dating back to 1605. The interior boasts some fine silverwork around the altar. Just to the right of the main entrance, you can climb up to a **mirador** in the bell tower with good city views.

### Museo de Arte Sacro

La Catedral, Plaza 24 de Septiembre • Mon–Fri 3–6pm • Bs10

The city's best religious art, sculpture and silverware is tucked away in the **Museo de Arte Sacro**, whose entrance is just to the right of the altar in the cathedral. There are some beautiful eighteenth-century mestizo-Baroque woodcarvings of saints, including a magnificent **Santiago Matamoros** (St James the Moor-slayer), representing the patron saint of Spain. Other exhibits include some exquisite silverwork and a 7mm book – one of the world's smallest – in which the Lord's Prayer is written in various languages.

# Museo de Arte Contemporáneo

Sucre and Potosí • Mon–Fri 9am–noon & 3–7pm, Sat 3–8pm, Sat 3–8pm • Free • ☎ 03 3369581

A former public school has been converted into the pleasant courtyard setting of the **Museo de Arte Contemporáneo**. Various peculiar and eccentric art displays can be found throughout the maze of small rooms, and there is usually someone at the door who is more than happy to help you try and make sense of them.

# Museo de Historia Natural Noel Kempff Mercado

Av Irala 555, near the corner with Av Ejército Nacional, eight blocks south of the plaza • Mon–Fri 8am–noon & 3–6.30pm • Bs1 • ☎ 03 3371216, ⓦ museonoelkempff.org

The **Museo de Historia Natural Noel Kempff Mercado** has an extensive collection of dead insects, stuffed birds and pickled snakes from Bolivia. Of particular interest is the display of dangerous insects, such as the *vinchuca* or **assassin bug** (see p.39). Look out also for the *vibora cuco*, a moth that bears a passing resemblance to a snake's head and which is widely (but incorrectly) considered extremely dangerous.

# Biocentro Güembé

Km 7, Camino a Porongo/Zona Los Batos, 8km north of the city centre • Daily 8.30am–6pm • Adults Bs180, children Bs60, with a basic day package • ☎ 03 3700700, ⓦ biocentroguembe.com • 30min taxi ride (around Bs70) from the city centre

**Biocentro Güembé** is a luxurious resort with an array of attractions including a huge **butterfly dome**, an **orchid park** and a series of **pools**. You can trek, horse ride and swim;

**5**

there are also various accommodation options. Though it may be too artificial for some, it is popular with wealthy *cruceño* families.

# Lomas de Arena

25km southwest of Santa Cruz • No public transport so best to visit on a tour; try those run by Nick's Adventures (see opposite); from Bs245

A short drive outside the city is **Lomas de Arena**, a protected area of desert and tropical forest spanning around 130 square kilometres and containing a series of dramatic sand dunes, some of them 12m in height. As well as sandboarding, there's the chance to spot sloths, capybaras, caymans, and over 250 species of birds (including toucans).

## ARRIVAL AND DEPARTURE

### SANTA CRUZ AND AROUND

Santa Cruz is divided into concentric rings by successive ring roads – **anillos** – beginning with the Primer Anillo, which encompasses the colonial city centre, and extending outwards to the ninth ring. Other than the main airport, most places of use and interest are within the first two *anillos*.

**By plane** The Aeropuerto El Trompillo, just south of the centre in the Segundo Anillo, is sometimes used by military airline TAM and some smaller carriers. But the vast majority of airlines use the modern Aeropuerto Viru-Viru (☎ 03 3852400), 17km north of the city centre and currently undergoing an expansion. It is a Bs70 taxi ride from the city centre; alternatively, catch a micro (every 20min; 30min) to the old bus terminal, seven blocks southwest of the city centre. In addition to the domestic flights listed here, there are also international connections to Miami, Madrid and several cities in neighbouring countries. The flights below are all direct; for most destinations, there are several more connecting flights.

Destinations Cobija (2 weekly; 1hr 40min); Cochabamba (13–17 daily; 45min); La Paz (13–17 daily; 1hr); Rurrenabaque (3 weekly; 1hr); Sucre (5–7 daily; 40min); Tarija (1–2 daily; 50min); Trinidad (7 weekly; 50min).

**By train** The Terminal Bi-Modal – the bus and train terminal (☎ 03 3488482, ⊛ www.fo.com.bo) – is 2km east of the city centre at the end of Av Brasil. A taxi into the centre costs around Bs20; alternatively, take any micro heading east along Av Brasil and marked "Plaza 24 de Septiembre". Trains from here travel east to the Brazilian border at Quijarro, via San José de Chiquitos. There are currently two different trains: the *Expreso Oriental* and the *Ferrobus* (the quickest, most comfortable and priciest); getting a seat at intermediate stations can be a problem. There is also a weekly service (Thurs) south to the Argentine border at Yacuiba via Villamontes. Unless you're taking the *Ferrobus*, you can expect delays. Buy tickets for all services

in advance from the Terminal Bi-Modal; note that there's a small departure tax for train passengers.

Destinations Quijarro (6 weekly; 13hr–16hr 40min); San José de Chiquitos (6 weekly; 5hr 10min–6hr 10min); Villamontes (1 weekly; 13hr 45min); Yacuiba (1 weekly; 16hr 35min).

**By bus** Services arrive at and depart from the Terminal Bi-Modal (see above). For the major routes there's generally no need to buy tickets in advance, but for all other destinations try to get one the day before. Note that most long-distance buses travel overnight.

Destinations Cochabamba (10–12 daily; 10–12hr); Concepción (around 8 daily; 6–7hr); La Paz (10 daily; 16–18hr); Oruro (1 daily; 12–14hr; or via Cochabamba); San Ignacio (around 3 daily, eves; 10–12hr); San Javier (around 7 daily, with departures in the morning and early eve; 4–5hr); Sucre (5 daily; 14–16hr); Tarija (6 daily; 16hr); Trinidad (18–22 daily; 9–10hr); Vallegrande (2–3 daily; 6–7hr).

**By trufi and micro** The quickest, most comfortable way to reach Buena Vista and Samaipata is by trufi, collective taxis/minivans that depart when full (most people travel in the morning). For Buena Vista (1hr 30min–2hr), catch a trufi to the town of Yapacani from Calle Izozog La Riva, just north of the old bus terminal. Trufis to Samaipata (2hr 30min–3hr) depart from two stops: two blocks south of the old bus terminal on Av Omar Chávez and Solis de Olguín; and from the corner of Av Grigotá and Arumá in the second *anillo*. Trufis to Vallegrande (around 5hr) run from Plazuela Oruro, also in the second *anillo*.

## INFORMATION AND TOURS

### TOURIST INFORMATION

There are several tourist offices in Santa Cruz: staff can answer simple questions (in Spanish) and provide you with a free map. The most central one is in the Prefectura building on the north side of Plaza 24 de Septiembre (Mon–Fri 8am–noon & 2.30–6.30pm; ☎ 03 3368900). Other locations include the Terminal Bi-Modal (Mon–Fri

8am–noon & 3–7pm; ☎ 03 3218316) and the Museo de Arte Contemporáneo (Mon–Fri 8am–noon & 3–7pm; ☎ 03 3369581).

### SECURITY

Be careful walking around the city centre at night as muggings do sometimes take place.

## TOUR AGENCIES

Many agencies run trips to Parque Nacional Amboró, the Jesuit Mission towns, the Pantanal and other destinations; day-trips cost from Bs350/day.

**Amboró Tours** Libertad 417, 2nd floor 161 ☎7261 2515, ⓦamborotours.com; map p.234. A well-established agency with friendly staff and a range of tours across the region, including to the national park from which it takes its name.

**Misional Tours** Top Center building, Av Beni, second anillo ☎03 3300898, ⓦmisionaltours.com; map p.234. As the name suggests, tours (lasting from one to five days) of the Jesuit missions are the focus here. Pantanal and Kaa-lya tours are also available.

**Nick's Adventures** La Plata 8 este 11, Barrio Equipetrol ☎03 3441820, ⓦnicksadventuresbolivia .com; map p.234. Another professional agency specializing in mid- and top-end wildlife tours, including to Amboró (see p.240), Kaa-Iya (see p.258) and the San Miguelito Jaguar Conservation Reserve (see p.250), plus trips to see the spectacular Espejillos and Jardín de los Delicias waterfalls.

**Ruta Verde** 21 de Mayo 318 ☎03 3396470, ⓦrutaverdebolivia.com; map p.234. A well-run agency run by a very helpful Dutch-Bolivian couple, Gijs and Maria, who have excellent local knowledge and speak Spanish, Dutch and English. A superb choice for the Pantanal and Amboró, in particular.

## ACCOMMODATION

There's an oversupply of **top-end accommodation** in Santa Cruz. However, most of it is located on the outskirts in the wealthy Barrio Equipetrol, about 5km northwest of the city centre. Most **mid-range** and **budget accommodation** by contrast is conveniently located in or around the old city centre. A fan or a/c is pretty much essential in the warmer months – all but the cheapest rooms have one or the other. Hotels in all classes in Santa Cruz tend to be a bit more expensive than elsewhere in the country.

### CITY CENTRE

**Bed and Bar Backpackers** Velasco 480 ☎03 3536090, ⓦfacebook.com/bedbarbackpackers; map p.234. The name of this hostel neatly sums up its sociable ethos. There are colourful six- to ten-bed dorms and private rooms, a roof terrace, friendly staff and – of course – a well-stocked bar, though no breakfast. Dorms Bs45, doubles Bs150

**Hotel 360°** Abaroa 548 ☎03 3264920; map p.234. In the heart of the Los Pozos market (see box, p.238), this sparkling hostel has super-clean dorms and private rooms (the latter have their own bathrooms, TVs, and fan or a/c; note, though, that some of them only have internal windows), a sun-trap roof terrace, communal kitchen, a hearty DIY breakfast and a helpful owner. It's a 10–15min walk from the main square. Dorms Bs65, doubles Bs215

**Hotel Asturias** Moldes 154 ☎03 3339611, ⓦhotelasturias.com.bo; map p.234. Reminiscent of a 1970s-era US motel, this whitewashed mid-range hotel has dated but comfortable en suites with a/c, minibars and TVs, as well as a decent-sized pool, and a restaurant. It's a 15min walk from the plaza. $75 (Bs510)

★**Hotel Cosmopolitano** Pari 70 ☎03 3323118, ⓦcosmopolitano.com.bo; map p.234. The coolest place to stay in the city centre, this boutique hotel blends vintage furnishings with a modern vibe. Alongside minimalist en suites, some of which boast balconies and bathtubs, there's a small outdoor pool and deck, and a restaurant-bar. Given the quality, it's extremely good value. $60 (Bs408)

**Residencial Bolívar** Sucre 131 ☎03 3342500, ⓦresidencialbolivar.com; map p.234. Based in an appealing colonial-era building, this long-standing backpackers' haunt has helpful staff and small but clean rooms with fans or shared or private bathrooms around a cool, leafy patio with hammocks and several resident toucans. It's very popular, so reserve in advance. Dorms $18 (Bs122), doubles $35 (Bs238)

**Senses Boutique Hotel** Av San Martín 6 ☎03 3396666, ⓦsensescorp.com; map p.234. In a hard-to-beat location just off the Plaza 24 de Septiembre, this smart hotel is bang in the centre of the action. The over-the-top decor in the lobby (which includes mannequins with lamps for heads) is fortunately in sharp contrast to the minimalist en suites (which can be noisy at weekends). There are three restaurants/bars, pool, gym and great roof terrace. It has a sister hotel in Barrio Equipetrol. $75 (Bs510)

### OUTSIDE THE CITY CENTRE

★**Casa Patio Hotel Boutique** Av Ibérica and C 5, Las Palmas, between the third and fourth anillos ☎03 3511814, ⓦcasapatio-hotelboutique.com; map. p.234. Delightful, intimate guesthouse in a middle-class residential neighbourhood. Inside it feels more like a museum, with an array of paintings, prints, antiques and knick-knacks – keep an eye out for the signed works by Picasso, Miró and Dalí. The owners are equally charming, and the rooms full of character. $66 (Bs449)

**Hotel Cortez** Cristobal Mendoza 280 ☎03 3331234, ⓦhotelcortez.com; map p.234. This upper-mid-range hotel in the Segundo Anillo, near lively Calle Monseñor

**5**

Rivero, has very comfortable – if not particularly stylish – en suites with TVs, phones, a/c and plenty of space; those at the front, however, suffer from road noise. There's also a pool, sauna, gym, and a pair of restaurant-bars. Bs880

★ **Jodanga Backpackers' Hostel** El Fuerte 1380 ☎ 03 3396542, ⓦ jodanga.com; map p.234. This excellent Hostelling International-affiliated hostel is just a 20min walk from the plaza. It has private rooms (with shared or en-suite bathrooms) and six- to ten-bed dorms, plus a swimming pool, jacuzzi, TV/DVD room, communal kitchen,

laundry service and Spanish classes. Dorms Bs57, doubles Bs180

**Los Tajibos Hotel** Av San Martín 455 ☎ 03 3421000, ⓦ lostajiboshotel.com; map p.234. This large hotel in Barrio Equipetrol is the city's best. The contemporary en suites are a little lacking in character, but have all the facilities you'd expect; the suites (from $180/Bs1224) even have jacuzzi baths. There are lovely gardens, a pool, spa, health centre and several excellent restaurants (notably *Jardin de Asia*) and bars. $150 (Bs1020)

## EATING

Santa Cruz has a wide range of restaurants, catering to all budgets. **International cuisine** and **vegetarian food** are widely available, though local *camba* (lowland) food can also be found, mostly good beef accompanied by rice and *yuca* or plantain. Most restaurants open Monday to Saturday for lunch and dinner, though on Sundays many only serve lunch. On Friday and Saturday nights, many stay open late and turn into bars. Cafés are generally the best bet for breakfast. With a few exceptions, the places listed here are in the **city centre**, though many popular restaurants are further afield on the **Segundo Anillo** ring road (Av Cristóbal de Mendoza) between calles Alemania and Beni, 1.5km to the north. Particularly popular are the massive, open-air places serving huge plates of barbecued meat at weekends. European-style bars and restaurants are strung along **Calle Monseñor Rivero**, about seven blocks directly north of the plaza. As elsewhere in Bolivia, the markets are the best bets for cheap eats (see box, below).

### CITY CENTRE

**El Aljibe** Potosí and Ñuflo de Chávez ☎ 03 3352277, ⓦ elaljibecomidatipica.com; map p.234. Based in an atmospheric colonial-era home, with a garden patio frequented by hummingbirds, this charming family-run restaurant specializes in traditional, home-style *cruceño* cooking. Expect dishes (Bs25–50) like *sopa de mani* and *picante de pollo*. Mon 11.30am–3pm, Tues–Sat 11.30am–11pm, Sun 11.30am–4pm.

**Be Coffee** Ingavi and Independencia ☎ 03 3329232; map p.234. A hip café that takes its coffee very seriously indeed, turning out excellent – though pricey – flat whites and the like (Bs14–30) using an array of gadgets, including AreoPresses and Chemex filters. Daily 8.30am–10pm.

**Café Patrimonio** Sucre 50 ☎ 03 3323082, ⓦ facebook.com/cafepatrimoniobolivia; map p.234. Inside the Casa de Melchor Pinto art gallery, and with a beautiful patio, this classy coffee shop serves up everything from cappuccinos to *cortados*, lattes to cold

brews (Bs14–30), as well as a few simple snacks. Daily 7.30am–10.30pm.

**La Casona** Arenales 222 ☎ 03 3378495, ⓦ bistrolacasona.com; map p.234. German-run restaurant-bar in a nineteenth-century building with a lovely patio, mellow music (live bands on Thursday nights, and sometimes at the weekend) and a relaxed ambience. There's a strong German influence on the menu (schnitzel, *wursts*; mains Bs62–150; two-course set lunch around Bs40), and especially on the excellent range of beers (Bs19–50). There's also a small deli. Mon–Sat 11.30am–late.

**Michelangelo** Chuquisaca 502 ☎ 03 3348403; map p.234. Perhaps the finest Italian restaurant in Santa Cruz, offering superb cuisine and immaculate service in an intimate atmosphere. Prices are steep (mains Bs80–160), but it is an excellent place for a treat; the pasta and fish dishes are among the highlights. Mon 7–11.30pm, Tues–Thurs noon–2.30pm & 7–11.30pm, Fri & Sat noon–2.30pm & 7pm–midnight, Sun noon–3pm.

---

## MERCADO LOS POZOS

In the northeast corner of the city centre, the **Mercado Los Pozos** is arguably the best food market in Bolivia, with row upon row of stalls serving inexpensive and delicious local dishes like *locro de gallina* (chicken stew) and *sopa de maní* (peanut soup), while others sell an astonishing variety of tropical fruit juices and excellent *empanadas* and *salteñas*. There's also a whole subsection of Chinese food stalls where you can get a tasty meal for around Bs20. You might also like to spend a few hours at the **Mercado La Ramada**, Avenida Grigota and Calle Sutos, where pretty much everything you can think of is on sale across a sprawling mass of stalls. **Mercado Nuevo** is smaller but has the same hectic market bustle and is a conveniently short walk from the central plaza.

**República** Bolívar 175 ☎03 3347050, ⓦrepublica .com.bo; map p.234. Contemporary photography and paper sculpture on the walls, well-chosen music, and just-so cooking, with excellent pasta and salads, plus pizzas, panini and steaks (mains Bs45–80). The exterior courtyard has a bar. Mon–Wed & Sun 10am–midnight, Thurs–Sat 10am–1am.

### OUTSIDE THE CITY CENTRE

**El Arriero** Av San Martín and Storni ☎03 331694, ⓦelarrierosantacruz.com; map p.234. This Barrio Equipetrol restaurant is the best steak joint in the city, with

prime Bolivian and pricier, and even tastier, Argentine cuts. Prices are steep – expect to pay around Bs150 for three courses and drinks – but it's worth it to splash out. Mon–Sat noon–3pm & 7–11.30pm, Sun noon–3.30pm.

**Casa del Camba** Av Cristóbal de Mendoza 1365 ☎03 3427864, ⓦcasadecamba.com; map p.234. The best of the many large, traditional *cruceño* restaurants on this stretch of the Segundo Anillo, and a great place to enjoy a reasonably priced *parillada* (mixed grill) or *pacumutu* (a kind of massive shish kebab), often to the accompaniment of live traditional *camba* music. Mains Bs35–120. Daily 11.30am–midnight.

## DRINKING AND NIGHTLIFE

Whether it's because of the humid climate (as visiting *collas* from the highlands assert), the beauty and hot-bloodedness of the *cruceñas* (as locals insist), or the combination of large disposable incomes and abundant cocaine (as one may suspect), many *cruceños* love nothing better than to stay up late, eating, drinking and dancing the night away. This comes to the fore during **Carnaval** (late Feb or early March). The celebrations here have more in common with those in Brazil than with Oruro (see p.143): the city stages a series of wild masked balls, street processions and beauty pageants. Most of the flashier clubs are in the brashly exclusive **Barrio Equipetrol**, about 5km northwest of the centre, on a stretch of Avenida San Martín between the second and third *anillos*. Cover charges (from around Bs50) are standard, and doormen aren't afraid of turning away scruffy gringos. In addition to those listed below, many of the restaurants are good spots for a drink, notably *La Casona* (see opposite).

### CITY CENTRE

Nightlife within the city centre is relatively low-key and dispersed, but there's still a good range of bars, many with live music on the weekends.

**Duda** Florida 228 ☎7760 0655, ⓦfacebook.com/ dudapub; map p.234. This cool, idiosyncratic bar, decked out with old photos, toys and other knick-knacks, is one of the best nightspots in the city. The playlist is as varied as the decor, and there's a good range of *tragos* (alcoholic drinks; from Bs20). Tues–Thurs 9pm–2am, Fri & Sat 9.30pm–3am.

**Kiwi's** Bolívar 208 ☎03 3301410; map p.234. The narrow front leads into a big, airy space with a slightly New

Age vibe, offering good drinks, shisha pipes, and a menu ranging from salads to burgers, crêpes to fajitas (Bs30–60). There are tango dances and classes every Saturday night. Mon–Fri noon–11.30pm, Sat 2.30pm–1.30am.

★**Lorca** René Moreno 20, first floor ☎03 3340562; map p.234. This bohemian cafe-bar, just off the plaza, has a balcony perfect for people-watching and an interior patio filled with arty displays. There are regular live jazz, blues and folk performances (Thurs–Sun nights), a strong list of drinks (beer Bs25–40, glasses of wine Bs25–33, cocktails Bs30–60), and a creative menu (dishes include *moqueca*, a Brazilian fish stew). Mon–Thurs 9am–11.45pm, Fri & Sat 9am–3am, Sun 6–11.45pm.

## SHOPPING

**Artecampo** Salvatierra and Vallegrande ☎03 3341843; map p.234. Showcasing the work of artisans in the region surrounding Santa Cruz, Artecampo features quality textiles, clothes, home furnishings and other crafts. It's run as a cooperative, and seventy percent of the price of each product goes directly to the artisan responsible.

Mon–Sat 9.30am–12.30pm & 3.30–7pm.

**Lewy Libros** Junín 229 ☎03 3360865; map p.234. This small bookshop has a limited (and rather pricey) selection of English-language fiction and non-fiction, as well as a much wider range of Spanish-language titles. Mon–Sat 9am–noon & 2–6pm.

## DIRECTORY

**Banks and exchange** You can change foreign currency at any of the string of *casas de cambio* on the east side of Plaza 24 de Septiembre. ATMs are very common.

**Hospital** Clinica Lourdes, Moreno 352 (☎03 3325518), is a good place to go if you need a doctor. For emergencies, head to Hospital Municipal San Juan de Dios, Cuéllar and España (☎03 3332222), or Hospital Japonés, third *anillo*,

close to the junction with Conavi (☎03 3462031 or ☎03 3462031).

**Language lessons** Jodanga Backpackers' Hostel (see opposite) offers good-value language classes (Bs80/hr guests, Bs100 non-guests), as does *Residencial Bolívar* (see p.237).

**Post office** Correo Central, just northwest of Plaza 24 de Septiembre on Junín.

5

# Buena Vista

Some 100km northwest of Santa Cruz lies the peaceful little town of **BUENA VISTA**, the northern gateway to **Parque Nacional Amboró**. Raised slightly above the plains, the town is aptly named, enjoying good views of the densely forested mountain slopes of Amboró. Buena Vista is a popular summer retreat for weekenders from Santa Cruz, though during the week it remains a sleepy place. The town was founded in 1694 as a **Jesuit mission**, though, sadly, the eighteenth-century Jesuit church was demolished in the 1960s and replaced by the unattractive modern brick structure that stands today.

## ARRIVAL AND INFORMATION

BUENA VISTA

**By trufi/micro** Regular trufis and micros (1hr 30min–2hr) to and from Santa Cruz arrive at and depart from the plaza.

**By moto-taxi** Moto-taxis are the easiest way to get to some of the more far-flung hotels; they congregate on the plaza.

**Tourist information** There is no tourist office, but tour agencies on the plaza, as well as operators in Santa Cruz and Samaipata, can organize excursions into Parque Nacional Amboró. There's a SERNAP office two blocks southwest of the plaza where you can buy an entry permit, though beyond that it is of limited help.

**Money** There is a Banco Fassil ATM in town, but it's not especially reliable, so bring some cash with you.

## ACCOMMODATION AND EATING

Accommodation options are fairly limited. There are also a number of **luxury** country-club-style places with a/c and swimming pools, several kilometres from town on the main Cochabamba–Santa Cruz road, but these are expensive and inconvenient if you want to visit Amboró. There are several restaurants and cafés on the **plaza**, though the cheapest place to eat is the **market**, a block back from the plaza; this is also the place to buy food and supplies if you're heading into the Parque Nacional Amboró.

**Amboró Eco Resort** 7km along the Carretera Nacional to Santa Cruz ☎ 03 3422372, ⓦ amboroecoresort.com; map opposite. Set in beautiful forest surroundings with a network of private trails, this resort has comfortable and spacious a/c rooms, as well as a swimming pool with accompanying bar. Rates include full-board. <u>Bs450</u>

**La Casona** On the plaza ☎ 03 9322083. This whitewashed building ("the Big House"), bang in the heart of town, is popular with backpackers for its clean, no-frills rooms with fans and either shared or private bathrooms. <u>Bs100</u>

**Hotel Flora and Fauna** 4km from town on the road south towards Huaytú, then another 1km up the marked drive off to the left ☎ 7104 3706, ⓔ hotelfandf@hotmail.com; map opposite. Owned by British ornithologist Robin Clarke, this delightful place is ideal for nature lovers. The simple en-suite cabins with fans are set amid well-preserved, wildlife-rich rainforest (featuring 450 bird species) – there's an observation tower, and expert guides are available. Good food is on offer too; full-board available. Minimum two-night stay. Rates include full board. <u>$70 (Bs476)</u>

**Residencial Nadia** Just off the north corner of the plaza ☎ 03 9322049. Another reasonable budget choice, right in the town centre, the family-run *Residencial Nadia* offers large but scruffy single and doubles, all of which come with fans. <u>Bs120</u>

# Parque Nacional Amboró

Forty kilometres west of Santa Cruz, **PARQUE NACIONAL AMBORÓ** spans 4300 square kilometres of a great forest-covered spur of the Andes. Situated at the confluence of the Andes, the Amazon rainforest and the Northern Chaco, and ranging in altitude from 3300m to just 300m above sea level, Amboró's steep, densely forested slopes support an astonishing biodiversity. Over 830 different types of **bird** have been recorded here – the highest confirmed bird count for any protected area in the world – including rarities such as the cock-of-the-rock, red-fronted and military macaws and the blue-horned curassow or unicorn bird, which was once thought to have been extinct. There are also jaguars, giant anteaters, tapirs and several species of monkey. Its enormous array of plant and insect species, meanwhile, is still largely unexplored. This biological wealth is all the more amazing given that Amboró is so close to Santa Cruz. You must be

**5**

accompanied by a **guide** – best organized through a travel agency or hotel in Buena Vista or Samaipata before setting out – to enter the park.

### Brief history

The national park, established in 1984, was expanded in 1990 to encompass some 6300 square kilometres. However, by this time the park's fringes were already under huge pressure from poor **peasant farmers**, who began clearing the forest for agriculture, as well as hunting and logging inside the park boundaries. In 1995, amid rising tension, the Bolivian government gave in to political pressure and reduced the park by two thousand square kilometres, creating a "Multiple-Use Zone" around its borders. This buffer zone is now largely deforested, and the peasant farmers are beginning to encroach on the remaining park area. The easiest parts of the park to reach are also the most likely to have been affected by this **encroachment**, though the pristine interior regions of the park are deliberately kept relatively inaccessible. Nonetheless, the park refuges are set amid splendid, largely intact rainforest, and the chances of spotting wildlife are fairly high. The park's higher-altitude southern section, which includes beautiful **cloudforests**, can only be visited from Samaipata.

## The Buena Vista section

From Buena Vista, a rough road runs southeast along the borders of the Multiple-Use Zone (marked by the Río Surutú), passing through a series of settlements, the landscape around which is heavily deforested. However, on the west side of the river the steep, densely forested mountains of Amboró loom inviolate.

Some 20km from Buena Vista, the road reaches **Huaytú**, from where a rough track crosses the river and enters the park. It then leads 14km to **La Chonta**, a park guards' station. There are plenty of trails through the surrounding forest from here, and you can swim in the nearby **Río Saguayo**. About four hours' walk from here in the interior of the park is a site where the extremely rare blue-horned currasow can be seen, while a tough day's walk downstream along the Río Saguayo brings you to another park guards' station, **Saguayo**, from where it's another day or so on foot back to Buena Vista.

Continuing along the main track beyond Huaytú for a further 15km brings you to the settlement of **Santa Rosa**. From here, a rough 10km track crosses the river and

**5**

### COMMUNITY-BASED TOURISM PROJECTS

The Santa Cruz-based NGO **PROBIOMA** (Cordobá 7 este 29, Barrio Equipetrol; ☎03 3431332, ⓦprobioma.org.bo) links tourists to communities without taking a cut of the money, unlike tour operators offering similar deals. The projects it promotes are managed and run locally, ensuring the money goes to help the community as a whole. The surrounding environment is also protected as tourism provides an economic alternative to damaging practices such as logging, or exhaustive farming techniques. One of the most successful of these sites is **Ecoalbergue de Volcanes** on the south side of Amboró. It is reached by an 8km trek along the Río Colorado from Bermejo, about 40km east of Samaipata on the Santa Cruz road. Situated to the north of Amboró, **Villa Amboró** and **Isama** are both great centres for hiking and observing wildlife. There is also a project in **Chochis** (see p.261). A stay at one of these sites will cost about $60 (Bs408) a day, including food and guides.

heads to the park guards' refuge at **Macuñuco**, inside the Multiple-Use Zone. There are plenty of trails here, one of which leads to a delightful waterfall. A few kilometres before you reach Macuñuco on this track, you pass the village of **Villa Amboró**, where there's another basic **refuge** and a series of forest trails.

### The Samaipata section

The southern border of the park lies just a dozen kilometres from Samaipata (see below) on the other side of the **mountain ridge** that rises to the north, and is easy to visit with one of the town's tour agencies (see p.245). This section is much higher in altitude than the areas close to Buena Vista, and is therefore ecologically very different, comprising beautiful cloudforest with gnarled trees covered in lichen and epiphytes. Most one-day trips to Amboró head to the hamlet of **La Yunga** from where a short walk takes you into the **cloudforest**. Although you'll see large numbers of rare and strangely prehistoric-looking tree ferns up to 10m high, this region lies in the Multiple-Use Zone close to areas of human settlement, so the chances of seeing much in the way of wildlife are slim. To reach pristine cloudforest you'll need to trek further into the park and camp overnight.

#### ARRIVAL AND TOURS

**By micro** A micro from the plaza in Buena Vista runs daily along the boundary of the park via Huaytú and Santa Rosa, returning the next day – times vary, so ask around in Buena Vista. Also check the return time with the driver so you don't get stuck on the way out. From the road you'll still have to cross the Río Saguayo (often impassable in the Nov–April rainy season) and walk over 10km to reach either La Chonta or Macuñuco.

#### PARQUE NACIONAL AMBORÓ

**By jeep** A good alternative is to hire a jeep and driver to take you into the park and return later to collect you – you can arrange this through one of the tour operators.

**Tour operators** You can only visit the park with a guide or official tour operator. Agencies in Buena Vista, Samaipata and Santa Cruz offer tours ranging from day-trips (from US$55) to twenty days.

#### ACCOMMODATION

**Refuges** Overnight trips in the park involve stays at one of several very basic (and not always well-maintained) refuges, or camping; the cost of this (and food) is generally included in the price of your tour. The Santa Cruz-based NGO PROBIOMA also has a trio of significantly more comfortable community-run lodges around the park (see box, above).

# Samaipata and around

Some 120km west of Santa Cruz on the old mountain road to Cochabamba, the tranquil little town of **SAMAIPATA** is a popular destination for Bolivians and foreigners alike. Nestled in an idyllic valley surrounded by rugged, forest-covered mountains, the town enjoys a cool, fresh climate compared to the sweltering eastern plains. All this makes Samaipata the kind of place many travellers end up staying longer than they expected, and some of them settle permanently – there are residents from over thirty countries here – often setting up hotels, restaurants and tour agencies.

The town's heart is the **Plaza Principal**, which lies at the centre of a small grid of tranquil, often unpaved streets, lined with pretty whitewashed houses. Although generally peaceful, things can get busy with visiting *cruceños* at weekends. Just outside town stands one of Bolivia's most intriguing archeological sites, **El Fuerte**, and the opportunities to explore the surrounding countryside are immense in this beautiful region of rugged, forested mountains, divided by lush valleys whose lower slopes are covered by rich farmland, where hummingbirds, condors and flocks of green parakeets are a frequent sight. The low mountains surrounding Samaipata make for excellent hiking – just follow any of the paths or tracks leading out of town. You can also access the Samaipata section of nearby **Parque Nacional Amboró** (see opposite).

## Museo Arqueológico

Bolívar • Mon–Fri 8am–noon & 2–6pm, Sat & Sun 8am–4pm • Bs5 or free with an El Fuerte entry ticket

The **Museo Arqueológico** has a small collection of archeological finds from across Bolivia, including some beautiful Inca ceremonial *chicha*-drinking cups known as *kerus*; Inca stone axes and mace heads; and a range of pottery from various different cultures. Sadly, there's relatively little on display related to El Fuerte.

## Refugio de Fauna Silvestre Jacha-Inti

2km southeast of town on the road to San Juan • Daily 8am–6pm • Bs20 • ☎ 7661 8454, ⓦ jachainti.com

A pleasant fifteen-minute or so walk from the plaza, the **Refugio de Fauna Silvestre Jacha-Inti** is a Swiss-run refuge for rescued animals, and has everything from cats and dogs to some very playful monkeys. You can also ride horses, and there's a small café, souvenir shop, guest rooms, and plenty of volunteering opportunities.

## El Fuerte

About 9km east of Samaipata • Daily 9am–4.30pm • Bs50 • Guides Bs75/hr for a group of up to six people

The archeological complex known as **El Fuerte** is among the most striking and enigmatic ancient sites in the Andes. At its centre lies a great sandstone rock carved with a fantastic

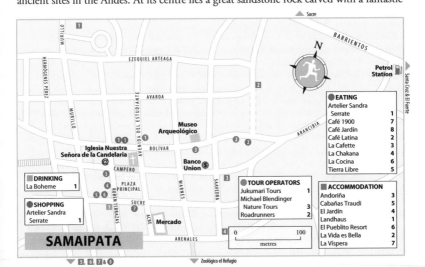

**5**

variety of **abstract and figurative designs**, including animals and geometric shapes. The rock is surrounded by the remains of dozens of **Inca buildings**, but the carvings predate Inca occupation of the region by over two thousand years. The site's original indigenous name has been lost – the Spanish name El Fuerte, meaning "the fort", reveals more about the military obsession of the Spanish conquistadors than it does about the primary purpose of the site, which was clearly religious and ceremonial.

The easiest way to reach El Fuerte is by taking a taxi from Samaipata (Bs100 return with waiting time; a moto-taxi costs around half that) or going on a guided tour (see opposite), many of which involve beautiful treks. You can walk to the ruins in about two hours – follow the road out of Samaipata towards Santa Cruz for a few kilometres, then turn right up the marked side road that climbs to the site; note that it's an uphill slog on the way there, and there is little shade.

### Brief history

It's thought the first carvings at El Fuerte were made before 1000 BC by an ancient lowland people who were perhaps driven from the region by **Chiriguanos** – a collective name given to those from the eastern Chaco. Chiriguano groups arrived here in force in the fifteenth century after migrating across the Chaco from the lands east of the Río Paraguay. It is believed that they might also have considered this an important ceremonial centre. The **Incas** arrived here around the same time and occupied the site, which served as an administrative and military outpost at the easternmost fringes of their empire. They altered and embellished the rock itself, suggesting that they too considered it a sacred site – though, like the Spanish, they had a habit of appropriating the religious centres of conquered peoples as a means of reinforcing their domination. Archeological evidence shows the Inca occupation occurred in two distinct periods, suggesting the outpost may have been overrun and destroyed by Chiriguano raiders before being re-established. The site was then occupied by the **Spanish** and their indigenous allies in the 1570s during their border war with the Chiriguanos, and eventually abandoned when the town of Samaipata was founded in the early seventeenth century.

### The site

On a hilltop at just under 2000m above sea level, with commanding views of the surrounding mountains and the valley below, **the rock** itself is a huge lump of reddish sandstone measuring 160m long and up to 40m wide. Its entire surface has been sculpted and carved with all manner of figurative and abstract designs, including pumas, serpents, birds, lines, steps and niches.

On the **western end** of the rock you can still make out two circular carvings, 2m in diameter, of pumas or jaguars, and one of a coiled serpent. Beyond this is a series of square indentations and a low Inca wall with numerous niches, behind which are two long, parallel slots running exactly west to east with zigzags down either side and in the centre: it's likely to have been used for ritual libations of *chicha* or blood.

A path runs along the **south side** of the rock, which is carved with stone steps, platforms, seats and niches of all shapes and sizes, including classic Inca trapezoids 2m high, all facing due south: these probably once held idols and the mummified bodies of long-dead Inca priests and officials. On your right as you walk round are the foundations of several Inca stone buildings that may have housed priests and other attendants, and the remains of a small sixteenth-century Spanish building. Walking round to the **north face** of the rock, you'll find a low Inca wall, five massive north-facing niches cut out of the rock face and a good view of the surface of the rock, here carved with recesses and channels. **East of the rock** a path leads down to the ruins of a building with commanding views of the valley below, then on to the foundations of a classic Inca *cancha* (living compound), where archeologists have also found post holes from wooden houses and ceramic fragments suggesting an earlier, possibly Chiriguano, occupation of the site.

**5**

From the rock's east end, a path runs downhill to the south, reaching a broad terrace. From here, the path continues 200m to **La Chinkana**, a deep well that has inspired improbable myths of underground tunnels leading to faraway Inca sites. Returning to the terrace and turning right brings you to the site's main complex of Inca buildings. Passing the foundations of several ruined buildings, you emerge on a broad plaza measuring about 100m by 150m and flanked on three sides by partially overgrown Inca ruins of which only low walls or foundations now remain.

Every year, on June 21–22, El Fuerte is the site of colourful ceremonies and celebrations to mark the winter solstice and the **Aymara New Year** – Evo Morales has attended in the past.

## ARRIVAL AND DEPARTURE

**By bus** Services to Vallegrande (3hr 30min) or Sucre (around 12hr) can be flagged down on the main road opposite the petrol station. Those for Vallegrande pass through 11.30am–12.30pm and 3.30–4.30pm, and always stop for passengers. For Sucre, it's best to buy a ticket in advance from a travel agency in town; buses pass through 6.30–9pm. For Cochabamba (2 daily; around 10hr), head to the town of Mairana, 16km west of Samaipata (a taxi costs around Bs60). Alternatively, you can travel via Santa Cruz.

## SAMAIPATA AND AROUND

**By micro or trufi** Micros from Santa Cruz (3hr) arrive at and depart from the plaza, but trufis (2hr 30min) are quicker, more comfortable and only a little more expensive. Coming from Santa Cruz, they stop at the plaza and can normally be persuaded to drop you at your hotel; heading back, they leave when full from both the plaza and the petrol station.

**By taxi** For trips around town and to surrounding attractions, taxis can be found at the office on the plaza. Moto-taxis congregate near the market.

## INFORMATION AND TOURS

### TOURIST INFORMATION
The best places to go for information are the tour agencies. There's also a useful website: ⓦ samaipata.info.

### TOUR AGENCIES
Samaipata's tour agencies make it easy to visit the surrounding area's less accessible attractions; most offer English-speaking guides. One of the most popular excursions is along the Ruta del Che, a two-day, one-night trip that traces the last steps of iconic revolutionary Che Guevara (see box, p.248).
**Don Gilberto Aguilera** Sucre ☎03 9446050 or ☎7261 5523. Samaipata's most experienced trekking guide, Don Gilberto is the man to go with if you want an off-the-beaten-track adventure in the cloudforest north of Samaipata, or a trip on the Ruta del Che. If you speak Spanish, go with him. He doesn't have an office, so give him a call.

**Jukumari Tours** Av del Estudiante ☎7576 0013, ⓦfacebook.com/jukumaritours; map p.243. Friendly agency with multilingual guides offering tours of (among others) Amboró, El Fuerte, the "Elbow of the Andes" (see box, p.247) and the Ruta del Che.

**Michael Blendinger Nature Tours** Bolívar, diagonally opposite the museum ☎03 9446227, ⓦdiscoveringbolivia.com; map p.243. As well as local tours, the biologist and ornithologist who owns this agency can organize multi-day bird-watching trips in Bolivia (and in neighbouring countries).

**Roadrunners** Bolívar ☎03 9446193, ⓔtheroadrunners @hotmail.com; map p.243. This very friendly, enthusiastic and efficient German-run agency is a great source of information about Samaipata and Bolivia as a whole, and can arrange tailor-made tours of Bolivia (and beyond). It specializes in tours of El Fuerte, and also offers the "Elbow of the Andes" hike. It also has a great café.

## ACCOMMODATION

You are spoilt for choice for accommodation in Samaipata, from **hostels** in the town centre to more expensive chalet-style **cabañas** on the outskirts of town. Everything fills up (and prices rise) at weekends and on public holidays, particularly between October and April. In addition to those listed below, Michael Blendinger Nature Tours (see above) also has a wide range of cabins to rent across the region.

### IN TOWN
★ **Andoriña** Campero, east of the plaza ☎03 9446333, ⓦandorinasamaipata.com; map p.243. Top-class hostel with a vaguely New Age vibe. It has comfortable and excellent-value private rooms and two- or three-bed dorms, a communal terrace and balcony with hammocks,

guest kitchen, book exchange and plenty of information for travellers. The breakfast (included in rates) is among the best in Samaipata. No wi-fi. Dorms $\overline{Bs60}$, doubles $\overline{Bs130}$

**Cabañas Traudi** Outside town, 800m south of the plaza ☎03 9446094, ⓦfacebook.com/cabanas detraudisamaipata; map p.243. A wide range of quirky

**5**

en-suite rooms (shared or private bathrooms) and *cabañas* (sleeping two to eight people, and featuring kitchens and fireplaces). They are set amid spacious grounds with a large pool, sauna and a talkative pet parrot. Doubles Bs120, cabins Bs160

**El Jardín** Arenales, two blocks east of the market ☏7310 1440, ⓦeljardinsamaipata.blogspot.co.uk; map p.243. This Belgian-Bolivian-run campsite and lodge is one of the best budget options in town. As well as sites to pitch your tent, there are simple three-bed dorms and private rooms, and more comfortable cabins. Breakfast costs extra. Camping Bs20, dorms Bs35, doubles Bs80, cabins Bs130

**Landhaus** Murillo, 200m north of the plaza ☏03 9446033, ⓦsamaipata-landhaus.com; map p.243. Spick-and-span rooms come with private bathrooms and TV at this well-run hotel, which also has cabins that sleep larger groups. There's also a small pool and garden area, book exchange and a good restaurant. Doubles Bs190

**El Pueblito Resort** Around 2km southwest of the plaza ☏7739 4757, ⓦelpueblitoresort.com; map p.243. On a hilltop overlooking town, this charming resort is set out to look like a quaint village (there's even a central plaza). The attractive, colourful rooms and *casitas* are come with minibars and heaters. There's a pool and restaurant. Doubles Bs560, *casitas* Bs700

**La Vida es Bella** Avaroa and Cespedes, a 10min walk from the plaza ☏03 9446447, ⓦla-vida-es-bella-bolivia.com; map p.243. This charming hotel, run by the owners of cafés *Latina* and *1900*, is in a secluded location that's still close to the centre. The spacious en suites have been thoughtfully decorated, and feature wood-beamed ceilings and private balconies. There's a nice garden, and the breakfast (included in rates) is top class. $50 (Bs340)

★**La Víspera** Outside town, 1km south of the plaza ☏03 9446082, ⓦlavispera.org; map p.243. Sublime rural idyll with fantastic views, a beautiful herb garden and fields with horses, dogs and cats. There's a wide range of rooms and cabins, each thoughtfully decorated, as well as a campsite (gear is available to rent). Staff provide a wealth of information. They also have a superb café-restaurant (see below). Breakfast costs extra. Camping Bs50, doubles/cabins Bs230

## AROUND SAMAIPATA

**Ginger's Paradise** Around 35km east of Samaipata ☏6777 4772, ⓦgingersparadise.com; map p.241. A working organic farm where owners Cristobal and Sol offer hearty meals and a host of activities, including handicraft sessions, horseriding, swimming in nearby rivers and Quechua lessons, as well as a recording studio (Cristobal was in the band American Flag). To find it, ask the bus driver to stop at Bermejo (76km from Santa Cruz on the road to Samaipata), cross the bridge and walk about 250m up the path where you will see their multicoloured house. The rates here are for accommodation only; there are also half-board options, and several accommodation-food-volunteering combinations. Camping Bs40, doubles Bs160, cabins Bs250

**Refugio Los Volcanes** Around 75km east of Samaipata ☏03 3372042, ⓦrefugiolosvolcanes.com; map p.241. *Los Volcanes* is an attractive lodge situated in a deep valley with spectacular views of lush forests and sandstone cliffs. The comfortable double rooms have private bathrooms and solar power. It's a great place for observing wildlife – over two hundred bird species have been spotted from the lodge. Rates include full-board and guided walks. $170 (Bs1156)

## EATING

There is a varied range of restaurants and cafés in town, though some only open at weekends. At the **market**, a block south of the Plaza Principal, you can get inexpensive meals and picnic provisions.

**Artelier Sandra Serrate** Bolívar 89 ☏7739 4757, ⓦfacebook.com/arteliersandraserrate; map p.243. A delightful café and craft shop with an array of cakes (including carrot, banana and marmalade sponges, plus brownies and Swiss rolls; around Bs12), plus great coffees, teas, fresh juices and smoothies. Opening hours are rather vague, with a sign stating: "We open when we arrive and close when we go." Tues–Sun 9/10am–5/6pm.

**Café 1900** Sucre, on the main plaza ☏03 9446023; map p.243. Under the same management as *Café Latina*, *Café 1900* is a good spot at any time of the day with breakfasts, coffee, main meals (Bs33–50) such as *coq au vin*, cakes and ice-cream sundaes. There's an inviting terrace out back, as well as tables in front overlooking the plaza. Daily 8am–10pm.

**Café Jardín** La Víspera ☏03 9446082, ⓦlavispera.org; map p.243. Don't miss out on a meal at this excellent outdoor café, where the focus is on slow food and many of the ingredients (much of them organic) are grown on-site. Alongside breakfast options, there are huge omelettes and fresh bread, pasta dishes, tortillas, salads, and a few Southeast Asian stir-fries and curries (mains Bs45–60). There is an extensive range of herbal teas, the perfect accompaniment for a slice of rhubarb tart (Bs25). Mon–Wed & Sun 8am–3pm, Thurs–Sat 8am–9pm.

★**Café Latina** Bolívar 3, a block north and three blocks east of the plaza ☏03 9446153; map p.243. Charming owners Lenny and Sylvain have created a sophisticated atmosphere with romantic lighting, modern artwork and an appealing wooden bar. The concise menu features delicious

**5**

## EXCURSIONS FROM SAMAIPATA

There are numerous interesting places to explore around Samaipata. About 40km south of town on the road towards the village of Postrer Valle, a path leads 6km or so to **La Pajcha**, a beautiful triple-tiered waterfall that plunges 30m into a cool pool that is excellent for swimming. There's no public transport, so you'll either have to come by taxi (around Bs300 return with waiting time), or go on an organized trip. About 20km east of Samaipata, a set of three waterfalls, **Cascadas las Cuevas**, is a very accessible option for seeing a little more of the countryside when you're pushed for time (a taxi costs about Bs100 return, with waiting time). You can swim in the pools, which makes it very popular with local families. One of the best treks in the region is the **Codo de los Andes** (Elbow of the Andes), offering spectacular scenery, waterfalls, and the chance to spot condors. Roadrunners and Jukumari (see p.245) both offer guided hikes.

steaks, salads, pasta dishes, and *antipasti* (mains Bs45–70), plus a good choice of beers and wines. Mon & Wed–Fri 6–10pm, Sat & Sun noon–2.30pm & 6–10pm.

**La Cafette** Plaza Principal ☎ 7857 5470, ⓦ facebook .com/lacafettesamaipata; map p.243. Cute little café serving Illy coffee (a cappuccino costs Bs12) and a hard-to-resist range of quiches, sandwiches, panini, pastries and cakes: try the passion fruit tart or the lemon meringue pie. Wed–Sat 9am–1pm & 4–8/9pm, Sun 9am–1pm & 4–6pm.

**La Chakana** Plaza Principal ☎ 7260 6331; map p.243. This café-restaurant, right on the plaza, serves decent coffees, juices, breakfasts, snacks, more substantial meals (Bs28–58) and a good-value two-course menu of the day (Bs34). It also has a small book exchange. Daily 8am–10/11pm.

**La Cocina** Sucre ☎ 6878 2105; map p.243. Snazzy, super-popular joint with a handful of tables and seats at the counter, and a selection of high-quality burgers, burritos, falafel wraps and more, plus great chips (Bs30 or so will get you a good feed). An added bonus: you can also order *La Cocina*'s dishes at *La Boheme* (see below) at no extra cost. Tues–Sat 6–10pm.

**Tierra Libre** Sucre ☎ 7315 1955; map p.243. A versatile restaurant-bar, good for a meal from a menu that features spaghetti, lasagne, stir-fries, salads, and some unusual options like veal goulash and chicken tikka masala (mains Bs35–65) and an evening drink on the patio. Mon & Wed–Sun 11am–10pm.

### DRINKING

Several places in Samaipata sell wines from local vineyard Uvairenda (ⓦ uvairenda.com); the Tannat and the Syrah rosé, in particular, are well worth a try.

★ **La Boheme** Rubén Terrazas and Sucre ☎ 6091 1243, ⓦ labohemebar.net; map p.243. Easily the best bar in town, with a welcoming vibe, regular live music (cover charge around Bs20), shisha pipes, book exchange and a

fine range of draught and bottled beer (from Bs20) and cocktails. If you get peckish, you can order food (at no extra cost) from *La Cocina* (see above). Tues–Thurs 5pm–midnight, Fri & Sat 5pm–3am, Sun 5pm–1am.

### SHOPPING

**Artelier Sandra Serrate** Bolívar 89 ☎ 7739 4757, ⓦ facebook.com/arteliersandraserrate; map p.243. Inside the café of the same name, this little art and craft shop

is ideal for a spot of souvenir shopping, with beautifully decorated mugs, flower pots, textiles and wooden boxes among the items on offer. Tues–Sun 9/10am–5/6pm.

### DIRECTORY

**Banks** There's a Banco Union (and a not especially reliable Visa-only ATM) on Campero, just east of the plaza; it's worth bringing some cash with you.

**Laundry** The nameless house (no fixed opening hours) opposite *Andoriña* offers a laundry service.

# Vallegrande

Some 68km southwest of Samaipata on the old road from Santa Cruz to Cochabamba, a side road leads 53km south to **VALLEGRANDE**, a pleasant market town set in a broad valley at an altitude of just over 2000m. The town's main attraction is its association with **Ernesto "Che" Guevara**.

**5**

## Brief history

A peaceful backwater founded as a Spanish outpost in 1612, Vallegrande leapt briefly to the world's attention in 1967, when the arid region of low mountains and broken hills to the south of the town became the scene of a doomed guerrilla campaign led by the hero of the Cuban revolution (see box, below). Vallegrande served as the headquarters of the Bolivian army's successful counter-insurgency campaign; after Che was captured and executed on October 9 in the hamlet of La Higuera, about 50km to the south, his body was flown here strapped to the skids of a helicopter and put on display in the town hospital.

What happened next remained a closely guarded secret for the next 28 years, until the Bolivian general Mario Vargas Salinas revealed that **Che's body** – minus his hands, which were amputated for identification purposes – had been buried by night in an unmarked pit near the **airstrip** on the edge of town, to prevent his grave from becoming a place of pilgrimage. After a year and a half of investigation, in 1997 his remains, along with those of several of his guerrilla comrades, were found by a team of Cuban and Argentine forensic scientists and flown to Cuba, where they were

---

### THE LIFE AND DEATH OF CHE GUEVARA

Of all the adventurers to pass through Bolivia, none has matched **Che Guevara**. Born in the Argentine city of Rosario on May 14, 1928, Ernesto Guevara de la Serna studied **medicine**, but preferred life on the road, travelling throughout Latin America both during and after his studies.

In 1954 he witnessed the CIA-backed overthrow of the progressive Arbenz regime in **Guatemala**, which confirmed his commitment to revolutionary Marxism and fervent opposition to the US. It was here he was nicknamed **Che**, a Guaraní-derived word meaning "hey you" or "mate" in Argentina. He headed to Mexico City, where he met exiled Cuban rebel **Fidel Castro**, who was planning to overthrow the dictator Fulgencio Batista. Che signed up as the expedition's doctor, but over the next two years proved himself a ruthless, determined, fearless, radical and tactically astute guerrilla commander. When Castro took power in 1959, Che was one of his closest associates. For several years he served **Cuba** as president of the National Bank, roving ambassador and Minister of Industry.

Che saw the Cuban revolution as the first step in a continent-wide revolution against **US imperial control**. In 1965 he resigned his Cuban citizenship, ministerial position and rank of *commandante*, and set off to spread revolution. After an unsuccessful stint supporting rebels in the **Congo**, he turned to Bolivia, where he hoped to start a guerrilla conflagration that would spread into neighbouring countries and draw the US into a "second Vietnam", culminating in a continent-wide revolution. Bolivia's rugged terrain and strategic position seemed attractive, but the choice was a fatal mistake – Bolivia was the only country in South America where **radical land reform** had been carried out, and the revolutionary potential of the peasantry was low.

#### CHE IN BOLIVIA

In 1966, Che set off to Bolivia with a small band and set up a base at Ñancahuasu, a farm on the fringes of the Chaco in the Andean foothills, 260km southwest of Santa Cruz. But the **Bolivian Communist Party** quickly withdrew its support, the few Bolivian recruits Che managed to enlist were unreliable, and the guerrillas' presence was quickly betrayed by deserters. Unable to attract a single recruit from the local peasantry, Che's small band (never numbering more than fifty) found itself on the run in harsh terrain, while the Bolivian army, backed by US military trainers and CIA advisers, closed in. On September 26, 1967, the fighters marched into an ambush in the hamlet of **La Higuera**: three guerrillas were killed, and Che and the sixteen other survivors retreated into the **Quebrada del Churo** canyon, where they were surrounded.

On October 8 they were captured: Che was shot in the calf, taken to La Higuera and interrogated in the schoolhouse. The next day, the order to execute him came through, and a sergeant volunteered for the task. According to legend, Che's last words were: "Shoot, coward, you are only going to kill a man." His body was flown to **Vallegrande** and displayed to the press before being secretly buried, as if his enemies feared him more in death than in life. Perhaps they were right to do so, as Che went on to inspire thousands across Latin America – and beyond.

re-interred in a specially built mausoleum on the outskirts of the city of **Santa Clara**, the scene of his greatest victory in the Cuban revolutionary war.

## Centro Cultural Ernesto Che Guevara

10–15min walk northeast of Plaza 26 de Enero or a short taxi ride • The centre and the graves of his comrades can only be visited on a Spanish-language guided tour (Bs40), daily at 8.30am, 11.30am, 2.30pm & 4.30pm; book at the office opposite the Plaza 26 de Enero; they last 1hr 30min–2hr 30min, depending on whether you do it on foot on in a car/taxi

To mark the fiftieth anniversary of Che's death, the new **Centro Cultural Ernesto Che Guevara** has been set up, featuring his mausoleum, a small museum, library, room for film screenings, snack bar and souvenir shop. The mausoleum is located on the edge of the airstrip on the outskirts of town: 100m away behind the cemetery (and thus not on consecrated ground) you'll find the grave from which his remains and those of six other guerrillas were exhumed in 1997. The pit has been left open and is now covered with a red-tiled brick and concrete mausoleum filled with photos of Che. The museum, meanwhile, tells the story of the revolutionary's time in Bolivia, with plenty of photos, witness testimonies, and some choice quotes from Che himself, including the apt: "In a revolution you triumph or you die."

A five-minute walk away is a house with a swimming pool, along which a path leads to the four pits where the bodies of many of Che's mostly Cuban and Bolivian guerrilla comrades were buried after being killed in combat or executed after capture.

## Hospital Señor de Malta

Three blocks south of Plaza 26 de Enero on Señor de Malta • The hospital features in the Che tours of the Che Guevara centre (see above)

At this working hospital you can visit the **laundry room** where Che's body was put on gruesome display to the world's press, though there's little to see here today. At the time, word that he bore a striking resemblance to Jesus Christ spread quickly, and local women cut locks from his hair as good-luck charms.

### ARRIVAL AND TOURS
### VALLEGRANDE

**By bus** A couple of daily buses from Santa Cruz (6–7hr) via Samaipata (3hr 30min) arrive at and depart from the offices of two different bus companies: Trans Vallegrande on Santa Cruz and Florida, two blocks southeast of Plaza 26 de Enero, and Trans Señor de los Milagros, a block further southeast on Florida. Taking a trufi, however, is quicker and

generally more comfortable.

**By micro/trufi** There are also more frequent micros and irregular trufis to Santa Cruz and Samaipata; they generally pass through the main square looking for passengers.

**Tours** Two-day, one-night Che tours taking in Vallegrande and La Higuera cost around $200–250.

### ACCOMMODATION AND EATING

In addition to *Plaza Pueblo Hotel*, there are plenty of inexpensive, though not particularly exciting, places to eat on Calle Chaco near the covered market.

**Hostal Juanita** Caballero 123 ☎ 03 9422231, ✉ hostaljuanita@cotas.net. A friendly place with a central courtyard and a (non-functioning) fountain, *Hostal Juanita* has reasonable rooms, though housekeeping standards aren't always as high as they should be. No breakfast. Bs160

**Plaza Pueblo Hotel** Virrey Mendoza 132 ☎ 03 9422630, ✉ plazapueblo.hotel.vallegrande@hotmail.com. Located just up from the covered market, *Plaza Pueblo Hotel* has the feel of a motel, offering neat, clean and relatively modern en-suite rooms, as well as a restaurant. Bs200

# La Higuera and around

**LA HIGUERA**, the isolated hamlet where Che's dreams of leading a continent-wide revolution ended in defeat and death, lies about 50km south of Vallegrande, a three-hour drive along a very rough dirt road via the slightly larger village of Pucará.

**5**

Set in a region of low, crumpled mountains covered in scrubby vegetation broken by occasional maize and potato fields, La Higuera is a tiny collection of simple adobe houses with tiled roofs. A handful of **monuments** commemorate the fallen guerrilla leader. The most recent is a large, well-made bronze bust of Che, erected in 1997 on the thirtieth anniversary of his death. The other is a small, roughly fashioned plaster bust that was destroyed three times by the Bolivian army over the years, and replaced each time by local sympathizers. The schoolhouse where Che was executed has been turned into a small museum. Many of Che's admirers visit, but unless you share their veneration of the charismatic revolutionary icon, there's little reason to come here.

If you ask around you'll probably find someone willing to guide you to the **Quebrada del Churo**, the ravine a few kilometres away where Che was captured. It is a beautiful, and poignant, two-hour hike. You may have to pay a small (around Bs10) fee to pass through private land en route; if the owner of the land is around, he can give you a guided tour (Bs100).

## Museo Comunal La Higuera

No fixed opening times; if you ask around, you can normally find someone with a key • Bs10

This one-room **museum**, in the schoolroom in which Che was killed, has the atmosphere of a shrine. It features relics like Che's machete; the wooden chair where he sat for the last time; bullets, ammo clips and a rifle used by the other guerrillas or their military pursuers. There's also a map of the campaign; plenty of photos and newspaper cuttings; and lots of leaflets and pamphlets donated by Che sympathizers. A local guide is generally available at the museum and will know a great deal about the failed guerrilla campaign. On October 8–9 each year there's a small gathering of revolutionaries and other sympathizers who come to commemorate Che's death.

### ARRIVAL AND TOURS

### LA HIGUERA AND AROUND

**By bus** Buses (3–5 daily; 7–8hr) from Plazuela Oruro in Santa Cruz travel via Vallegrande to Pucará, from where you arrange a pick-up from one of the La Higuera lodges (see below) or a taxi (around Bs80). Moving on, it's also possible to reach Sucre from Pucará via the town of Villa Serrano; it's a roundabout route and schedules vary, so check the latest

with the La Higuera lodges.

**Tours** Two-day, one-night Che tours taking in Vallegrande and La Higuera cost around $200–250 (Bs1360–1700). The owners of *La Casa del Telegrafista* (see opposite) offer adventurous multi-day hikes to the site of Che's camp near the Rio Grande.

### ACCOMMODATION AND EATING

There are a couple of accommodation options in La Higuera. Those listed here can also both provide meals. There's also a small **shop** selling basic provisions, though if you're self-catering it's best to pick up supplies in **Pucará** en route.

**Albergue Los Amigos** 5min walk from the museum, near the entrance to the hamlet ☏ 7108 8433, ✉ barlosamigoslahiguera@gmail.com. This French-run

guesthouse has charming rooms (with artful shared bathrooms) set around a small garden (a plunge pool is apparently in the pipeline). There's a well-stocked bar, and

---

### SAN MIGUELITO JAGUAR CONSERVATION RANCH

Located around 180km northeast of Santa Cruz (a 3hr drive), the **San Miguelito Jaguar Conservation Reserve** (☏ 7845 8046, 🌐 wildlifeconservationtour.com) is surrounded by wetlands that boast one of the highest concentrations of jaguars in South America (approximately eleven per square kilometre), as well as significant numbers of five other big cats: pumas, ocelots, margays, Geoffroy's cats and jaguarundis. As a result you have a far better than average chance at this working cattle ranch of spotting these incredible creatures in the wild. Hiking, 4WD tours, canoeing, fishing and horseriding are among the activities on offer, while accommodation is provided in a comfortable lodge. Nick's Adventures in Santa Cruz (see p.237) can arrange tours, and there are also opportunities to volunteer.

plenty of Che memorabilia. Breakfast costs an additional Bs35; a three-course dinner costs Bs60. Camping Bs35, doubles Bs160

★ **La Casa del Telegrafista** Near the museum ☎ 7160 7893, ✉ casadeltelegrafista@gmail.com. In an old telegraph building used at different times by both Che and his comrades and the soldiers who killed him, this lodge (also French-run) has atmospheric stone-walled rooms

with high ceilings (and a shared bathroom) set around a patio filled with cacti and plants. The dining room features a Che photo display, there's a site to camp, and, a short walk away, a cabin (Bs90/person). The owners can provide a wealth of information, and offer hikes (see opposite). Breakfast costs an additional Bs35; a three-course dinner costs Bs60. Camping Bs30, doubles Bs180

# Chiquitos: the Jesuit missions

East and northeast of Santa Cruz stretches a vast, sparsely populated plain covered in scrub and fast-disappearing dry tropical forest, which gradually gives way to swamp as it approaches the border with Brazil. Named **Chiquitos** by the Spanish (apparently because the original indigenous inhabitants lived in houses with low doorways – *chiquito* means small), in the eighteenth century this region was the scene of one of the most extraordinary episodes in Spanish colonial history, as a handful of Jesuit priests established flourishing **mission towns** where the region's previously hostile indigenous inhabitants converted to Catholicism and settled in their thousands, adopting European agricultural techniques and building some of South America's most magnificent colonial churches. This theocratic socialist utopia ended in 1767, when the Spanish crown expelled the **Jesuits**, allowing their indigenous charges to be exploited by settlers from Santa Cruz, who seized the Chiquitanos' lands and took many of them into forced servitude. Six of the ten Jesuit **mission churches** still survive, however, and have been restored and declared UNESCO World Heritage Sites – their incongruous splendour in the midst of the wilderness is one of Bolivia's most remarkable sights.

## ARRIVAL AND INFORMATION

## CHIQUITOS: THE JESUIT MISSIONS

**By bus and train** The missions can be visited in a five- to seven-day loop by road and rail from Santa Cruz. From the city a rough road runs northeast to San Javier and Concepción, then continues to San Ignacio de Velasco (from where the churches of San Miguel, San Rafael and Santa Ana can all be visited by taxi in a day). From San Ignacio, the road heads south to San José de Chiquitos, the easternmost of the surviving missions and on the railway line between Santa Cruz and the Brazilian border at Quijarro. Buses connect all these mission towns as far as

San José, from where you can get the train back to Santa Cruz or continue east to the Brazilian border. Alternatively, you could travel the loop anticlockwise, starting from San José and returning to Santa Cruz by road via the other mission towns – indeed, transport links are slightly more convenient going in this direction.

**Money** Currently only Concepción, San Ignacio de Velasco and San José de Chiquitos have ATMs (all on or around the plazas); none is particularly reliable, though, so it's wise to bring some cash with you.

## San Javier

Some 220km northeast of Santa Cruz, **SAN JAVIER** (also known as San Xavier) is the westernmost of the Chiquitos Jesuit mission towns and was the first to be established in the region, having been founded in 1691. The town is now a quiet cattle-ranching centre with no real attractions other than the mission church itself.

### Iglesia de San Javier

Main plaza • Daily 8am–7pm • Free

Completed in 1752 under the direction of **Martin Schmidt**, the formidable Swiss Jesuit priest, musician and architect who was responsible for several Chiquitos mission churches (which were immaculately restored between 1987 and 1993 under the guidance of the equally dedicated Swiss Jesuit architect Hans Roth), the huge church

**5**

has a squat, sloping roof supported by huge spiralled wooden pillars, with a simple Baroque plaster facade. Above the doorway a **Latin inscription** common to most Jesuit mission churches in Bolivia reads *Domus Dei et Porta Coeli* (House of God and Gateway to Heaven).

On the right side of the church as you face it a doorway leads into a cloistered **courtyard**, which features a freestanding bell tower. Inside the church the exquisite modern wooden **retablo** behind the altar features beautiful carved scenes from the Bible and of the Jesuit missionaries at work in Chiquitos. The initials IHS inside the flaming sun at the top of the retablo stands for "Jesus Saviour of Man" in Latin: combined with three nails and a crucifix, this is the symbol of the Jesuit order, and you'll see it painted and engraved on mission buildings throughout Chiquitos.

---

## THE UTOPIAN KINGDOM OF THE JESUITS IN CHIQUITOS

When the Spanish first arrived in what is now eastern Bolivia, the vast, forest-covered plains between the Río Grande and the Río Paraguay were densely populated by up to fifty different **indigenous groups**. To the Spaniards this was a strategically vital region, providing a link between the silver of the Andes, their settlements in Paraguay and the Río de la Plata. However, a century of constant military expeditions failed to subdue the indigenous population – known collectively as the **Chiquitanos**.

In exasperation, at the end of the seventeenth century the colonial authorities in Santa Cruz turned to the **Jesuits** to pacify the region and secure the empire's frontier. By this time the Jesuits had more than a century of experience in South America, and were quick to implement the missionary strategy that had proved successful elsewhere. Small groups of dedicated priests set out to convert the indigenous peoples and persuade them to settle in missions known as **reducciones**, places where they could be brought together and "reduced" to European "civilization", which included being converted to Catholicism. Though many missionaries met gruesome deaths at the hands of those they sought to convert, the different tribal groups of Chiquitania quickly flocked to join the new settlements, which offered them many advantages. After a century of war, many had anyway been seeking a peaceful accommodation with the colonial regime, and under the aegis of the Jesuits they were protected from the rapacious slave raids of the Spaniards in Santa Cruz and the Portuguese in Brazil, as well as from their own tribal enemies.

### "CIVILIZING" THE CHIQUITANOS

Ten **missions** flourished under the Jesuit regime: European livestock and crops were successfully introduced; the Chiquitanos had limited autonomy under their own councils or *cabildos*, and were taught in their own languages (one of these, Chiquitano, was eventually adopted as the main language in all the missions); indigenous craftsmen were trained in European techniques and built magnificent churches; European musical instruments were introduced and quickly mastered by the Chiquitanos, establishing a **musical tradition** (see box, p.255) that survives to this day. The missions were not quite the autonomous socialist utopia Jesuit sympathizers have since tried to make out – many indigenous people were brought in by force, and the political and ideological control exercised by the fathers was pretty much absolute – but in general the missions provided a far more benign regime than anything else on offer under Spanish rule.

### SPANISH DOMINANCE

In the end, though, for all their self-sufficiency and autonomy, the Jesuit missions were utterly dependent on the Spanish colonial authorities. When in 1767 political developments in far-off Europe led the **Spanish king** to order the Jesuits out of the Americas, the fathers meekly concurred, and the Chiquitanos were quickly subjected to **forced labour** and the seizure of their best lands by the settlers of Santa Cruz. Within a few decades the missions were a shadow of their former selves, and this decline has continued pretty much ever since, leaving only the beautiful mission **churches**, now restored to their full glory with European aid money, to testify to the missions' former prosperity.

**FROM TOP** IGLESIA DE SAN MIGUEL (P.257); TREE FROG, THE CHACO (P.263) >

**5**

## ARRIVAL AND DEPARTURE                                    SAN JAVIER

**By bus** There are several daily buses (around 7 daily; 4–5hr) between Santa Cruz and San Javier; in addition, all services between Santa Cruz and Concepción (1hr from San Javier) also stop off in San Javier to pick up or drop off passengers. If you just want to visit the church you could easily come here on the first bus in the morning from Concepción or Santa Cruz, spend an hour or two looking around, and then catch another bus onwards (or back).

## ACCOMMODATION AND EATING

**Hotel Momoqui** Av Santa Cruz, close to the main plaza ☎ 03 9635121. This mid-range hotel has pleasant if not especially stylish en-suite rooms with a/c and fridges. There's also a pool, neatly tended garden and a restaurant. Tours can be arranged here. **Bs300**

**El Ganadero** On the main plaza. This centrally located restaurant serves the best steaks in town, as well as a few *milanesas* (thin breaded steaks, served with chips, salad and usually rice) and chicken dishes, plus an economical set lunch. Mains Bs30–60. Mon–Sat noon–2pm & 6–9/10pm.

# Concepción

About 68km to the east, the former mission town of **CONCEPCIÓN** is slightly larger than San Javier, but otherwise very similar. The mission was founded in 1709 by **Father Lucas Caballero**, who was killed two years later by the Puyzocas tribe, which later settled here. At the town's centre is a broad **plaza** lined with single-storey whitewashed adobe houses with tiled roofs that extend over the pavement, a colonial architectural style introduced after the expulsion of the Jesuits. In the middle of the square stands a simple **wooden cross**, surrounded by four palm trees – originally a feature of all the mission compounds.

Concepción is the centre for efforts to reconstruct the Jesuit mission churches of Chiquitos, and the main **workshops** for woodcarving and painting are behind the church a block east of the plaza. The staff here are usually happy to show visitors around for free at 10.30am and 3.30pm from Monday to Friday.

## Catedral de Concepción

On the east side of the plaza • Daily 8am–6pm • Free **Museum** (same times) Bs25 (combined entry for all the town's museums)

The town's mission church, now the **Catedral de Concepción**, is a massive barn-like structure with an overhanging roof supported by 121 colossal tree-trunk columns, and with a separate, similarly supported bell tower. Designed by **Father Martin Schmidt** and completed in 1756, it was the first Jesuit church in Chiquitos to be restored, and is the most extravagantly decorated of them all, with a lavishly painted facade decorated with golden Baroque floral designs, angels and two images of the Virgin Mary on either side of the door. The interior is smothered with **gold leaf**, a powerful reminder of the vast wealth the missions once possessed. Amid the beautifully carved altarpieces, confessionals and statues of saints, the most interesting detail is the modern **Via Crucis**, a depiction of the Easter story that runs around the top of the walls. Christ is shown living in present-day Chiquitos, surrounded by lush tropical forest inhabited by parrots and tortoises, and his betrayal and death are imbued with contemporary political and ecological metaphor. There's also a small museum.

## Museo Misional

On the south side of the plaza • Mon–Sat 8am–noon & 2.30–6.30pm, Sun 10am–12.30pm • Bs25 (combined entry for all the town's museums)

An old colonial house that was the childhood home of the former military dictator and later elected president Hugo Banzer now houses the **Museo Misional**, dedicated to the restoration of the mission churches of Chiquitos. On display are some good pictures of the different churches before, during and after reconstruction; examples

**5**

## THE CHIQUITOS MUSICAL RENAISSANCE

Of all the European arts and crafts introduced to Chiquitos by the Jesuits in the eighteenth century, the one that gained most rapid acceptance among the indigenous tribes was **music**. Imported organs, trumpets, violins and other instruments were enthusiastically adopted by the Chiquitanos, who quickly learned to manufacture their own instruments, while the choirs and orchestras of the mission settlements were said by contemporaries to have matched anything in Spanish America at the time. **Father Martin Schmidt**, the Swiss Jesuit who designed the churches of San Javier, San Raphael and Concepción, was a keen composer who taught music and brought the first church organs to the region, while the missions also benefited from the presence of an Italian named **Domenico Zipoli**, who had been a well-known composer in Rome before coming to South America.

### AFTER THE EXPULSION OF THE JESUITS

Like all the cultural accomplishments of the missions, their musical tradition all but disappeared in the centuries following the expulsion of the Jesuits, though its influence remained in the **folk music** of the Chiquitanos themselves. When the restoration of the mission churches began in the 1970s, however, researchers in Concepción discovered a substantial archive of liturgical and orchestral Renaissance Baroque musical scores, including works by Schmidt and other Jesuit composers. The rediscovery of this lost music inspired a musical revival in Chiquitos, and throughout the mission towns and outlying settlements you'll come across children and young adults playing violins and other instruments.

### CHIQUITOS MISSIONS MUSIC FESTIVAL

In 1996 this revival inspired a group of music lovers to organize the first **Chiquitos Missions Music Festival**, featuring performances of the music recovered from the lost archives. Since then, the festival has grown into a major biennial event (in even-numbered years), attracting dozens of orchestras and musical groups from around the world, and involving performances in all the mission towns of Chiquitos as well as in Santa Cruz. For further information, visit ⓦ festivalesapac.com.

of the crumbling original wooden pillars and statues which were replaced; and a **small workshop** where a local craftsman demonstrates the laborious task of restoring the original statues. There are also **photographs** of letters written and musical scores composed by Father Martin Schmidt, which were discovered in the 1970s, and an irreverent totem-pole-like statue of Hans Roth, the architect who led the reconstruction effort for 27 years until his death in 1999. The museum **shop** sells beautiful miniature carved wooden angels and other souvenirs made by local craftsmen, as well as Baroque music CDs; there are several other handicrafts shops around the plaza.

### ARRIVAL AND INFORMATION

### CONCEPCIÓN

**By bus** Most buses arrive a block north of the plaza; Flota Jenecherú services arrive two blocks south of the plaza on Lucas Cabellero, where you can also buy tickets in advance. There are several buses to Santa Cruz (around 8 daily; 6–7hr) that travel via San Javier (1hr). To reach San Ignacio de Velasco, you need to catch a through bus (around 3 daily; 6–7hr) from Santa Cruz, which passes through Concepción

roughly between 11.30pm and 3am. Buses from San Ignacio de Velasco often arrive in the early hours of the morning – if you are coming from there, consider booking a room in advance.

**Tourist information** There is an intermittently open tourist office just north of the plaza on Lucas Caballero (officially Mon–Fri 8am–noon & 2–6pm; ☎ 03 9643057).

### ACCOMMODATION

**Alojamiento Tarija** A block north of the plaza, opposite the Linea 131 del Este office ☎ 03 9643020. One of the better options for budget travellers, *Alojamiento*

*Tarija* offers fairly clean, sparsely furnished rooms with either shared or private bathrooms. No breakfast. Bs60
**Gran Hotel Concepción** On the west side of the

**5**

plaza ⊕03 9643031, ⊛granhotelconcepcion
.com.bo. The best hotel in town, though not quite as
"gran" as its name might suggest. The spick-and-span
rooms are set around a beautiful courtyard garden,
which also has a small swimming pool, hammocks, sun
loungers and a restaurant. Bs500

**Hotel Chiquitos** Av Killian Final ⊕03 9643253. A
solid mid-range option, *Hotel Chiquitos* has spacious a/c
en suites, a lush garden strung with hammocks and easy
chairs, a small kidney-shaped swimming pool – and a
talkative pet parrot. It's a 10–15min walk from the
centre. Bs400

### EATING

**Buen Gusto** On the north side of the plaza. *Buen Gusto*
specializes in traditional Bolivian cuisine, serving hearty if
not particularly exciting soups, stews and meat-heavy
main courses (Bs25–50) in a shaded courtyard filled with
plants, local crafts and a pair of squawking parrots. Daily
11am–9pm.

**Heladería Alpina** On the north side of the plaza. Near
*Buen Gusto*, this low-key ice-cream parlour is a good place
to cool off, with decent cones, cups and sundaes (Bs6–30),
plus coffee, cold drinks and simple snacks. Theoretically
Mon–Sat 3/4–9/10pm.

## San Ignacio de Velasco

Some 178km east of Concepción, **SAN IGNACIO DE VELASCO** was founded in 1748,
just nineteen years before the expulsion of the Jesuits from South America, but
quickly grew to become one of the largest and most developed of the mission towns.
Now the largest settlement in Chiquitos, it acts as a bustling **market centre** for an
extensive frontier hinterland of large cattle ranches and isolated indigenous
Chiquitano communities. At its centre lies the broad **Plaza 31 de Julio**, which is
graced by numerous massive swollen-bellied toboroche trees, whose tangled
branches blossom into brilliant pink and white in June and July. The town's wide,
unpaved streets fan out from the plaza, and are lined with low houses whose tiled
roofs extend over the pavement,
supported by wooden beams.

SAN IGNACIO DE VELASCO

### Catedral de San Ignacio

Main plaza • Daily 8am–7pm • Free

The **Catedral de San Ignacio** stands on
the north side of the plaza. The town's
magnificent original church collapsed in
1948 – the attempt to rebuild it in the
style of the original is spoiled by the
ugly modern concrete bell tower but
otherwise well executed, though the
painted facade decorated with statues of
saints, each accompanied by an animal,
is if anything too neat and symmetrical.
The **interior** still houses many of the
original statues of saints and
magnificent carved Baroque altarpieces
that graced the old mission church.

### Laguna Guapamó

On the outskirts of town the streets run
down to **Laguna Guapamó**, an artificial
lake created by the Jesuits to provide
water and fish for the mission, where
locals like to come swimming and fishing
on sultry afternoons; note that the lake is
home to piranhas.

### ARRIVAL AND INFORMATION

**By bus** San Ignacio has no terminal, so buses arrive and depart from the offices of the various different companies, most of which are located in the market area, three blocks southwest of the plaza. Services to Santa Cruz (3 daily; 10–12hr) via Concepción (6–7hr) or San Javier (9–11hr) generally travel by night. There is generally a daily bus to San José de Chiquitos (5–6hr) too; schedules tend to change frequently, so check the departure times when you arrive. Several buses leave daily for San Matías (10–12hr) on the Brazilian border. For Parque Nacional Noel Kempff Mercado, there is usually a weekly bus (12–14hr) to La Florida; check departure days at the SERNAP office at Bolívar 87 (☎ 03 3932747).

### SAN IGNACIO DE VELASCO

**By micro and taxi** A couple of micros travel each day between San Ignacio and San Miguel (1hr), San Rafael (1hr 30min) and Santa Ana (1hr), but hiring a taxi (around Bs400 for a day-trip visiting all three missions) saves you a great deal of time; you can find them on San Ignacio's main plaza.

**Tourist information** There's an intermittently open tourist office in the Casa de Cultura, just off the main plaza (officially Mon–Fri 8am–noon & 2.30–6.30pm; ☎ 03 9622056). SERNAP also has an office at Bolívar 87 (Mon–Fri 9am–noon & 2.30–4pm; ☎ 03 3932747); call in here if you're planning to visit Parque Nacional Noel Kempff Mercado.

### ACCOMMODATION

**Apart Hotel San Ignacio** Cochabamba and 24 de Septiembre ☎ 03 9622157, ⓦ aparthotel-sanignacio .com; map opposite. A smart hotel with a beautifully kept garden strung with hammocks and boasting a swimming pool. The en suites are some of the best in the region, with TVs, a/c and plenty of space. $49 (Bs333)

★ **Hotel La Misión** Plaza 31 de Julio ☎ 03 9622333, ⓦ hotel-lamision.com; map opposite Attractive hotel, in the neo-colonial style, with modern en suites (all with a/c, TVs and phones), and a breezy courtyard with a fountain

and small swimming pool. There's a similarly good (if rather pricey) restaurant, plus a small gym and a rather superfluous business centre. $60 (Bs408)

**Hotel Tierra Linda** Comercio and Chiquitos ☎ 03 9622889, ⓦ hoteltierralinda.com; map opposite. This hotel has modern a/c, en-suite rooms with distinctive orange-and-white colour schemes, as well as a sizeable outdoor swimming pool. Although it lacks the character of some of its rivals, it does represent good value. $40 (Bs272)

### EATING

**Restaurante Venecia** On the southwest side of the plaza ☎ 03 9622590; map opposite. Ideally located for looking out onto the attractive plaza, *Venecia* serves set

almuerzos and mains (around Bs50) like steak, chicken and *pique a lo macho*. Mon–Sat noon–2pm & 6–9/10pm.

# San Miguel

Set amid scrubby forest broken by patches of cattle pasture, **SAN MIGUEL** is a sleepy collection of whitewashed houses about 40km south of San Ignacio on the main road to San José de Chiquitos. Its humble structures make the first sight of the splendid **Iglesia de San Miguel** (no fixed opening times; free) even more astounding: set on a small rise overlooking the central plaza and dominating the town, the restored church is perhaps the most beautiful of the mission churches. Founded in 1721 and built in the same barn-like style as most of the others, the church facade is beautifully painted with Baroque floral designs, with pictures of St Peter and St Paul on either side of the main door.

To get inside, enter the walled **cloister** to the right – part of the original mission compound or Jesuit college, which is now used by the parish priest: go under the freestanding white adobe bell tower and ask in the parish offices for someone to let you in – you are likely to have to ask around for someone with a key. Inside, the soaring roof is supported by massive tree trunks carved in spirals, while the walls are lined with metre-high wooden statues of angels. The main **altarpiece** is smothered in gold leaf, with alcoves filled by statues of angels and saints including (in the centre) the Archangel Michael, in a golden helmet and shield, holding a three-pronged sword aloft as he tramples the Devil underfoot.

**5**

## San Rafael

The second Jesuit mission in Chiquitos when it was founded in 1696, the town of **SAN RAFAEL** sits 35km southeast of San Miguel, and boasts the biggest of all the region's Jesuit churches, the **Iglesia de San Rafael** (no fixed opening times; free). A cavernous structure with a freestanding bell tower supported by four spiralled wooden pillars, it was built under the direction of Martin Schmidt between 1747 and 1749. The magnificent interior features beautiful frescoes of angels, and some beautifully carved statues of saints in the alcoves of the golden altarpiece.

## Santa Ana

About 20km north of San Rafael on a different road back to San Ignacio, the village of **SANTA ANA** is home to perhaps the least architecturally imposing of the mission churches of Chiquitos. Occupying one side of a large grassy plaza where donkeys graze and schoolchildren play football, the **Iglesia de Santa Ana** (no fixed opening times; free) has not yet been fully restored and as such retains an intimate, rustic charm more in keeping with the sleepy atmosphere of its surroundings than the grandiose edifices of San Rafael or Concepción. There's some speculation as to whether this is the original Jesuit church at all – built entirely of wood, it has none of the usual IHS signs and may have been rebuilt shortly after the order was expelled in 1767.

## San José de Chiquitos and around

About 130km south of San Rafael, the dusty town of **SAN JOSÉ DE CHIQUITOS** is home to a distinctive mission church, and also stands on the railway line that runs east from Santa Cruz to Puerto Suárez, Quijarro and the Brazilian border. Despite this (for Chiquitos) abundance of **transport connections**, like the other mission towns San José has a torpid feel and is now nothing more than a dreary frontier market town and supply centre for the surrounding cattle ranches and Mennonite colonies.

### The mission complex

Main plaza • Mon–Sat 8am–noon & 2–6pm, Sun 10am–noon • Free

The mission of San José was founded in 1696, close to the original site of the city of Santa Cruz de la Sierra. Its **mission complex** was built in the last decades before the Jesuits' expulsion in 1767. Occupying one side of the central plaza, it's utterly distinct from the other churches of Chiquitos, being closer in design to those of the Paraguayan missions, with an elegant Baroque stone facade. The complex consists of four buildings linked by a 3m-high wall that forms a defensive compound. From right to left, these four buildings are the **Casa de los Muertos**, were bodies where once stored before being buried; the **church** itself; the four-tiered stone **bell tower**

---

### PARQUE NACIONAL KAA-IYA DEL GRAN CHACO

While most of the vast **Parque Nacional Kaa-Iya del Gran Chaco** lies in the Chaco (see p.263), the main access route is via San José de Chiquitos (see above). The reserve covers over 34,000 square kilometres southeast of Santa Cruz and stretching down to the Paraguayan border. This rugged landscape is home to a diverse range of wildlife species, including jaguars, pumas, tapirs, wolves and armadillos (and the chance of sightings is pretty high). The park has little in the way of tourist facilities and is only really accessible on an organized tour; try Nick's Adventures in Santa Cruz (see p.237) or Tucandera Tours in Samaipata (☎7316 7735, ⓦ facebook.com/tucandera.tours).

**5**

## THE MENNONITES

The region's most unlikely sight is the bizarre spectacle of tall white people with flaxen hair and ruddy cheeks – the men dressed in denim dungarees and straw hats, the women in full-length dresses and headscarves – walking around town or driving horse-drawn buggies. These are the **Mennonites**, members of a radical Protestant sect founded in the Netherlands by Menno Simmons in the sixteenth century. For the next four centuries the Mennonites found themselves driven from country to country as they attempted to escape religious persecution and conscription, and to find land on which to pursue their dreams of an agrarian utopia. After migrating to Germany, they moved in succession to Russia, the US and Canada, Mexico and Belize, until finally arriving in Bolivia and Paraguay in the twentieth century, attracted by the availability of cheap land and guarantees of religious freedom. Around fifteen to twenty thousand Mennonites now live in communities across the **eastern lowlands**, farming and raising cattle in self-contained agricultural communities.

### CENTRAL TENETS

The central tenets of the Mennonites are the refusal to take oaths or bear arms (they are exempt from military service in Bolivia); the baptism only of believers (that is, only of people who willingly adopt the faith, which excludes infants); simplicity of dress and personal habits; and an unwillingness to marry outside the faith. They also to varying degrees reject most **modern technology**, including cars and computers, though faced with the difficult agricultural conditions of Chiquitos, many Bolivian Mennonites allow the use of tractors – though not, bizarrely, of rubber tyres, so their wheels are covered with steel spikes. Though some speak Spanish, and a few of the older ones who grew up in North America also have some English, among themselves they speak **Plattdeutsch**, an archaic German dialect. If you can bridge the language barrier, many Mennonite men are happy to talk about their lives.

### DISTRUST

However, there seems to be some level of distrust between the Mennonites and the locals, possibly based on the Mennonite buying up of land in the area. The irony is that, two and a half centuries after the **Jesuits** were expelled, religiously inspired utopian dreams are still being pursued in the plains of Chiquitos, albeit by white Protestants instead of indigenous Catholics. This isn't, however, an irony that would have been appreciated by the Jesuits themselves – their order was set up precisely to combat Protestant sects like the Mennonites.

that would also have served as a lookout post; and the **Jesuit college**. That these elegant structures have survived for over two and a half centuries is all the more impressive, given the fact that they were built by indigenous masons with no previous experience of stonework. Behind this facade, however, the main body of the church is built of wood, with a roof supported by tree-trunk pillars: this may have been completed by the Chiquitanos after the Jesuits had departed. The interior itself has been restored, and there are some beautiful religious statues and other ornaments.

## Santa Cruz La Vieja

Other than the church there's nothing to see in San José, though if you've got an afternoon to kill you could walk down to the site of **Santa Cruz La Vieja**, the original site of the city of Santa Cruz, founded by conquistador Nuflo de Chávez in 1561 but abandoned in 1594 in the face of persistent indigenous attack and moved to its current site 260km to the west. From the plaza, turn right as you face the church and head south out of town for about 4km and you'll reach a sign to the **Parque Nacional Histórico Santa Cruz La Vieja**, a grandiose title for what is in fact simply a series of overgrown mounds set amid dense scrub and giant cactus trees.

**5**

### ARRIVAL AND DEPARTURE

**By train** The train station (☎03 3488482, ⓦwww.fo
.com.bo) is two blocks north and four blocks east of the
plaza. Trains to Santa Cruz pass through late at night; trains
heading towards Quijarro near the Brazilian border call in
slightly earlier. The *Ferrobus* is quicker and more comfortable
than the *Expreso Oriental*. Buy tickets in advance.
Destinations Quijarro (6 weekly; 7hr 50min–10hr 5min);
Santa Cruz (6 weekly; 5hr 10min–6hr 10min).
**By bus** Buses along the bumpy – but passable, even in

### SAN JOSÉ DE CHIQUITOS AND AROUND

rainy season – road to San Ignacio arrive and depart from
the offices of the two bus companies that serve the route:
Trans Carreton, a block east of the plaza; and Trans
Universal, four blocks north of the plaza beyond the petrol
station on the road out of town. The daily bus to San
Ignacio (5–6hr) tends to leave early in the morning, but
check the latest timetables when you arrive. There is also
usually a service or two to Santa Cruz (16–17hr), though
the train is a far better option.

### ACCOMMODATION

**Hotel La Casona** Ñuflo de Chávez ☎03 9722285,
ⓦlacasonachiquitana.com. A slightly cheaper
alternative to *Villa Chiquitana*, *La Casona* has a small
collection of bright, a/c en-suite rooms, set around a
patio, and located a few steps away from the main
square. Bs350
**Hotel Turubo** On the west side of the plaza opposite
the church ☎03 9722037. The clean and comfortable
*Hotel Turubo* is the best low-cost bet in town, offering
simple rooms with fans and TVs, as well as more expensive

options with private bathrooms and a/c. No breakfast or
wi-fi. Bs120
**Villa Chiquitana** C 9 de Abril ☎7315 5803,
ⓦhotellavillachiquitana.com. The smartest act in town,
with thoughtfully decorated rooms – all have a/c and TVs;
the more expensive options also have minibars – and
spacious grounds, including a pleasant garden, pool,
volleyball court and children's play area. There's also a good
restaurant-bar, with a menu that reflects the heritage of
the French owners. Bs400

### EATING

**Sabor Chiquitano** Main plaza ☎7864 5095. One of the
better of San José's restaurants, though the menu holds
few surprises. Expect mains (Bs30–60) like *milanesas*,

steaks and fried chicken. Mon–Sat 9am–10pm, Sun
noon–4pm.

# Parque Nacional Noel Kempff Mercado

Occupying 16,000 square kilometres of the far northeast on the Brazil border,
**PARQUE NACIONAL NOEL KEMPFF MERCADO** is the country's most isolated,
pristine and spectacular national park, and one of the most remote wilderness
regions in South America. Encompassing several different ecosystems including
Amazon rainforest, savanna, and scrubby Brazilian *cerrado*, the UNESCO World
Heritage Site supports an astonishing range of **wildlife**, including over 630
species of bird, eleven species of monkey, all the major Amazonian mammals,
pink freshwater dolphins and the highly endangered giant river otter.
Moreover, your chances of seeing these animals are much higher here than elsewhere
in Bolivia.

---

### HUANCHACA PLATEAU

The park's most remarkable natural feature is the **Huanchaca Plateau** (or the Caparú Plateau),
a vast sandstone *meseta* (plateau) rising 500m above the surrounding rainforest to an elevated
plain of grasslands and dry *cerrado* woodlands, from where spectacular waterfalls plunge
down the sheer escarpment into the park's rivers. This isolated plateau covers over seven
thousand square kilometres, just under half the park, and inspired Arthur Conan Doyle's novel
*The Lost World* – at least according to Colonel Percy Harrison Fawcett, the legendary British
explorer who was the first European to see the plateau when he came here in 1910 while
demarcating Bolivia's borders, and who later described the landscape to Conan Doyle in
London. Fawcett's story is told in the excellent book *The Lost City of Z* (see p.435) and the rather
less excellent 2017 film of the same name.

Established in 1979 as the **Parque Nacional Huanchaca**, the park was renamed (and expanded) in 1988 in honour of the pioneering Bolivian biologist and conservationist Noel Kempff Mercado, who was murdered by drug traffickers after stumbling across a secret cocaine laboratory on the Huanchaca plateau. The park was expanded again in 1997 under a pioneering "carbon credit" scheme, whereby two US energy corporations and the oil giant BP paid around $10 million to buy out loggers operating in an adjacent forest area of 6340 square kilometres, which was then added to the park (though in recent years loggers have moved back into the area).

The park's remote location, however, means it is extremely expensive and difficult to visit: even the organized tours are very tough going, and most travel agencies have stopped running tours because of the lack of maintenance and infrastructure. The park's southern border is over 200km from the nearest town, **San Ignacio de Velasco**, itself another 400km from Santa Cruz. It is also extremely difficult – and often impossible – to visit the park during the rainy season (Nov–May), when the mosquitoes and other insects are also particularly ferocious.

### ARRIVAL AND INFORMATION PARQUE NACIONAL NOEL KEMPFF MERCADO

#### ORGANIZED TOURS

Very few travellers visit the park, and almost all of those arrive by chartered light aircraft from Santa Cruz (around $250; 1hr) organized by a Santa Cruz-based tour agency. At the time of writing, Nick's Adventures (see p.237) was planning to trial trips to the park. Theoretically, it's possible to travel there independently via San Ignacio de Velasco, but given the difficulty of the journey and the lack of basic infrastructure, this is not recommended.

#### INFORMATION

**Tourist information** If you want to visit the park, you must inform SERNAP in San Ignacio de Velasco (Bolivar 87; ☎ 03 3932747) first. The Santa Cruz-based tour operators, however, are a much better source of information. There's no official entry fee, but local communities have charged around Bs100/vehicle in the past.

# East of Santa Cruz

From **Santa Cruz**, the railway line runs some 680km east to the **Brazilian border** across a seemingly endless expanse of forest and tangled scrub, gradually giving way to the vast swamplands of the **Pantanal** as the border draws near. Settlements along the line remain few and far between, and the region's main towns are both close to the Brazilian border: **Puerto Suárez**, a half-forgotten lakeside outpost that was once the focus of Bolivian dreams of access to the Atlantic via the Río Paraguay, and the dismal border trading settlement of **Quijarro**, the train's last stop before the frontier.

## Chochis

Between San José de Chiquitos and the town of Roboré, an immense mass of red rock marks the community of **CHOCHIS**, about 360km east of Santa Cruz. At the foot of this spectacular rock tower is the **Santuario de Chochis** – a beautifully quaint church established by the survivors of a disaster that rocked the area in 1979. After twenty days of torrential rain, on January 15, 1979 a volcanic eruption caused the railway bridge to collapse, killing many passengers on a passing train. It is well worth the climb to take the path that goes some way up the *cerro*, as the views stretch right across the strange moon-like landscape.

### ARRIVAL AND ACCOMMODATION CHOCHIS

**By bus** A couple of daily buses from San José (4–5hr) stop off in Chochis en route to the Brazilian border.
**Accommodation** NGO PROBIOMA (see box, p.247) supports a community project that has cabins and camping facilities, provides excellent food and offers guide services. Book in advance.

**5**

## THE PANTANAL

Much of Bolivia's far east along the Brazilian border is covered by the **Pantanal**, the vast flood plain on either side of the Río Paraguay that forms the world's biggest freshwater wetland system. Stretching over two hundred thousand square kilometres is a mosaic of ecosystems, including swamps, lakes, seasonally flooded grasslands and different kinds of forest, most of which is turned into an immense inland freshwater sea during the rainy season (Nov–March). This largely pristine wilderness supports possibly the densest concentration of **wildlife** in the Americas, including a vast array of birds, reptiles like anacondas and caymans, and mammals including swamp deer, giant otters, jaguars, capybaras and tapirs, all of which can be seen with greater frequency here than anywhere in the Amazon.

About eighty percent of the Pantanal lies in Brazil, but the fifteen or so percent within Bolivia's borders (the rest is in **Paraguay**) is arguably more pristine and virtually uninhabited. In theory it is also better protected – north and south of Puerto Suárez, huge areas of the Pantanal are covered by the **Area Natural San Matías** and the **Parque Nacional Otuquis**, which together cover almost forty thousand square kilometres. The flipside is that it can be difficult to visit: facilities are few and far between, and it's generally cheaper to organize expeditions into the Pantanal from Corumbá in Brazil.

Several Bolivian **tour operators** offer a Pantanal package, however, including Ruta Verde and Nick's Adventures in Santa Cruz (see p.237). Hotels in Puerto Suárez and Quijarro also arrange excursions. Alternatively, more simply, you can hire a fisherman in Puerto Suárez to take you out across **Lago Cáceres**.

## Puerto Suárez

Just before reaching the Brazilian border at Quijarro (see box, opposite), the railway line passes through the older and more agreeable **PUERTO SUÁREZ**, situated on the shores of Lago Cáceres, which is linked to the mighty Río Paraguay. Founded in 1875, the town has long been the focus of Bolivia's ambitions to gain access to the Atlantic Ocean via the ríos Paraguay and Paraná, but Lago Cáceres has always been too shallow to take anything other than small boats. Puerto Suárez receives very few tourists, but is a peaceful and dignified place, beautifully set on a bluff overlooking the calm blue waters of the lake, and with the city of Corumbá in Brazil visible in the distance.

### ARRIVAL AND DEPARTURE                                    PUERTO SUÁREZ

**By plane** The airport is 6km outside town; military-run airline TAM (ⓦtam.bo) periodically has flights to/from Santa Cruz.

**By train** The train station is a couple of kilometres outside town; you can walk into the centre or take a taxi (Bs20). There are regular trains (ⓣ03 3488482, ⓦwww.fo.com.bo) to Santa Cruz, San José de Chiquitos and Quijarro. The *Ferrobus* is quicker and more comfortable than the *Expreso Oriental*. Buy tickets as far in advance as possible.

**Destinations** San José de Chiquitos (6 weekly; 7hr 35min–10hr 15min); Santa Cruz (6 weekly; 12hr 45min–14hr 30min); Quijarro (6 weekly; around 15min).

**By bus** Several daily buses from Quijarro to Santa Cruz (15–24hr) pass through Puerto Suárez, though the journey is quicker and much more comfortable by train. There are other frequent services between Quijarro and Puerto Suárez; the journey takes around 20min.

### ACCOMMODATION AND EATING

**Hotel Casa Real** Vanguardia 39 ⓣ03 9763335. A block away from the main plaza, this tired hotel is just about acceptable for a night. Rooms all have private bathrooms, TVs and a/c (though there's a small fee for wi-fi access), and there's a so-so restaurant too. **Bs250**

## Quijarro

The last stop on the railway line in Bolivia, around 10km east of Puerto Suárez, is **QUIJARRO**, a fairly dismal collection of shacks and dosshouses surrounding the station – if you're heading on to Brazil, you're better off pushing on to the border

**5**

## CROSSING THE BRAZILIAN BORDER

Trufis run when full to the Brazilian border at **Arroyo Concepción** from the train stations in **Quijarro** (around 2km) and **Puerto Suárez** (around 10km). To cross the border at Arroyo Concepción, get your passport stamped at the Bolivian *migración* office (daily 8–11am & 2–5pm), then walk across into Brazil, where taxis, moto-taxis and regular buses wait to take passengers across the bridge over the Río Paraguay and on into the city of **Corumbá**, where you'll need to get an entry stamp from the Federal Police office at the bus station. If you need a visa, head to the **Brazilian consulate** (Mon–Fri 8am–2pm) two blocks southeast of the plaza on the waterfront in Puerto Suárez. You will also need a yellow fever certificate to enter Brazil. If you're arriving from Brazil, you should go straight to the train station to buy a ticket for a train heading west, as these can sell out quickly.

at Arroyo Concepción, 2km away. However, hotels in town can also organize Pantanal trips.

**ARRIVAL AND DEPARTURE**                                                        **QUIJARRO**

**By train** There are regular weekly trains (☎03 3488482, ⓦwww.fo.com.bo) to Santa Cruz and San José de Chiquitos. The *Ferrobus* is quicker and more comfortable than the *Expreso Oriental*. Buy tickets as far in advance as possible from the train station, by the main square.

**Destinations** San José de Chiquitos (6 weekly; 7hr 50min–10hr 30min); Santa Cruz (6 weekly; 13hr–14hr 45min).

**By bus** Several daily buses travel from Quijarro to Santa Cruz (15–24hr), but the train is a far better option.

**ACCOMMODATION AND EATING**

**Hotel Jardin del Bibosi** Luis Salazar 495 ☎03 9782044, ⓦhotelbibosi.com. The best place to stay in Quijarro, *Hotel Bibosi* has comfortable rooms (with shared or private bathrooms and fans or a/c), pleasant gardens, a pool and a decent restaurant. <u>**Bs200**</u>

# The Chaco

South of the Santa Cruz–Quijarro railway line, the tropical dry forest gradually gives way to **the Chaco**, a vast and arid landscape of dense scrub and virtually impenetrable thornbrush stretching south to the Paraguayan border and far beyond. Inhabited only by isolated cattle ranchers and occasional communities of Guaraní and semi-nomadic Ayoreo, the Chaco is one of South America's last great wildernesses and supports plenty of wildlife – much of it now protected by the **Parque Nacional Kaa-Iya del Gran Chaco** (see box, p.258).

The region's main towns are **Villamontes**, the Bolivian Chaco's biggest settlement, and **Yacuiba**, on the Argentine border. Adventurous travellers can also take the strenuous trans-Chaco road, which heads east to the Paraguayan border at Fortín Villazón, and then on to the Paraguayan capital, **Asunción**.

## Villamontes

A hot and dusty but welcoming frontier town with a mostly Guaraní population, **VILLAMONTES** was the scene of one of Bolivia's few military victories during the disastrous **Chaco War** (see p.311) with Paraguay. Today the town remains very much dominated by the Bolivian army.

### Museo Historico Militar Heroes del Chaco

Plaza 15 de Abril • Tues–Sun 8am–noon & 2–6pm • Bs5

The **Museo Historico Militar Heroes del Chaco** is full of military paraphernalia and the garden is filled with trenches, dugouts, bunkers and artillery pieces. Inside, there

**5**

---

### THE GUARANÍS

The western Bolivian Chaco is home to around 75,000 **Guaranís** – known historically as Chiriguanos – the largest indigenous group in the Bolivian lowlands. Guaranís originally migrated across the Chaco from east of the Río Paraguay in search of a mythical "Land Without Evil", occupying the southwestern fringes of the **Andes** in the fifteenth and sixteenth centuries just as the Inca empire was expanding into the same region. Despite this, Guaranís successfully resisted conquest by the Incas, and subsequently proved among the fiercest and most tenacious indigenous opponents of the **Spanish**. Not until well into the Republican era were they completely subjugated, when the last great Guaraní uprising was brutally crushed in 1892, after which their remaining lands were seized by the Bolivian state and divided into large private ranches defended by **army forts**. In recent decades, the Guaraní people have been struggling to regain control of their ancestral territories using **land reform** and indigenous rights legislation, and in spite of obstructive bureaucracy have now recovered large areas, where they farm maize, cotton, peanuts and other crops. Despite this, hundreds if not thousands of Guaranís still work on large **cattle ranches** under conditions of debt servitude that are little different from slavery.

---

are photos of the terrible conditions endured by troops on both sides in the Chaco War, in which around 65,000 Bolivian soldiers were killed (out of a population of roughly two million).

#### ARRIVAL AND DEPARTURE VILLAMONTES

**By train** The train station is two blocks north of the bus terminal on the same street. There are weekly trains (☎03 3488482, ⓦ www.fo.com.bo) to and from Yacuiba (2hr 50min) and Santa Cruz (15hr 45min).

**By bus** From the central Plaza 6 de Agosto the town's main street, Av Mendez, runs north eight blocks to the small bus terminal, where there are several daily buses to/from Tarija (10–12hr) and Santa Cruz (8–12hr).

**By micro/trufi** Micros and trufis to Yacuiba (1hr 30min) arrive at and depart from Av Mendez, three blocks north of the plaza.

#### ACCOMMODATION AND EATING

Inexpensive meals can be found in the covered public market, a short walk north of the plaza on Av Mendez. On the road out of town towards Yacuiba a series of stalls serves delicious fried *surubí* fish from the nearby Río Pilcomayo, one of the finest fishing rivers in Bolivia.

**Hotel Raldes** A block east of the plaza ☎04 6722088. A welcoming, family-run hotel with mediocre though inexpensive rooms set around a courtyard: choose from ones with a/c and private bathrooms or cheaper options with fans and shared bathrooms. $\overline{\text{Bs60}}$

**Rancho Olivo Hotel** Av Mendez Arcos, opposite the train station ☎04 6722059, ⓦ elranchoolivo.com. The mid-range *Rancho Olivo* is the best place to stay in Villamontes. Its cosy (though rather beige) en-suite rooms come with TVs, fridges and a/c, and there's a restaurant and a pool. $\overline{\text{Bs500}}$

## Yacuiba

The more modern border town of **YACUIBA** lies about 90km south of Villamontes by road and rail, and most travellers just pass through en route to or from Argentina. Yacuiba sprang up following the construction of the railway and oil pipeline to **Argentina** in the 1960s, and retains an Argentine flavour, dominated by restaurants and duty-free shops. There's no reason to linger unless you arrive at night and have to wait for transport out.

#### ARRIVAL AND DEPARTURE YACUIBA

**By train** The train station is two blocks south and a block west of the main plaza. There are weekly trains (☎03 3488482, ⓦ www.fo.com.bo) to/from Villamontes (2hr 50min) and Santa Cruz (18hr 35min).

**By bus** The bus terminal, from where there are morning and evening departures to Tarija (10–12hr) and Santa Cruz (10–14hr), lies about 1km south of the plaza. There are also buses (15hr) for the Paraguayan capital Asunción.

**By micro/trufi** Micros and trufis (1hr 30min) to and from Villamontes arrive at and depart from the offices just off the plaza on the road to the bus terminal.

**CROSSING THE ARGENTINE BORDER**

**By taxi** The border crossing with Argentina is at Pocitos, 4km south of Yacuiba: to get there, take a collective taxi from the main plaza.

## ACCOMMODATION AND EATING

There are several good places to eat around the plaza; most serve tasty Argentine beef, as well as the usual mix of Bolivian standards, chicken and pizza. Most restaurants open daily for lunch and dinner, though most close early on Sunday.

**Hotel Paris** Comercio ☎04 6822182, ⓦhotelparis .com.bo. One of the more comfortable of Yacuiba's hotels, with modern rooms (with a/c, TVs and private bathrooms), though the gaudy colour schemes won't win any awards for style. The restaurant, meanwhile, does a good line in steak and grilled chicken. **Bs400**

**Residencial Grand Victoria** Near the bus station ☎04 6822320. If money is tight, head to *Residencial Grand Victoria*, which offers basic, rather musty rooms with aged a/c units and a choice of shared or private bathrooms. **Bs70**

# The Amazon

AMAZONIAN RAINFOREST

# The Amazon

Although the classic image of Bolivia seems forever tied to the Andes and the Altiplano, around a third of the country lies within the vast and often impenetrable wilderness of the Amazon basin, the same mind-bending expanse of swamp, savanna and tropical rainforest that first set Colonel Fawcett (see p.299) on his fatal quest to find El Dorado. Deforestation has accelerated to a worrying degree in the region, but it remains one of the most biodiverse places in the world, with large areas virtually unexplored. Here, jaguars, tapirs and giant anteaters roam beneath the towering forest canopy; monstrous anacondas slither through the swamps; playful pink dolphins swim through the rivers; and the skies are filled by a kaleidoscopic variety of birds.

Often referred to as the **Beni**, after one of the rivers that are its dominant geographical feature, the Bolivian Amazon lies more than a thousand kilometres from the mighty Río Amazon itself, and contrary to what you might expect, not all of the region is covered by rainforest. While the last foothills of the Andes are fringed with dense and humid **premontane forest**, the great watery plains that open up beyond are partially covered by a seemingly endless sea of savanna, dotted with islands of forest. Known as the **Llanos de Moxos**, these plains are flooded each year when the mighty rivers that meander slowly across them – the Beni, Mamoré, Guaporé and their tributaries – are swollen by innumerable Andean streams. Unsurprisingly, then, this entire region (which is roughly the size of Great Britain) remains sparsely populated, apart from the great herds of semi-wild cattle that were first introduced by the Jesuit missionaries in the sixteenth century.

Sweltering quietly on the eastern edge of this area is **Trinidad**, the capital of the Beni and a bustling frontier outpost with few obvious attractions, though nearby are remnants of a fascinating pre-Columbian civilization. For the adventurous, the town is also the starting point for slow boat journeys down the Río Mamoré to the Brazilian border. The vast majority of travellers in the Bolivian Amazon, however, head solely to the ecotourist centre of **Rurrenabaque**, set on the banks of the Río Beni. Given its proximity to the stunningly pristine forests of **Parque Nacional Madidi**, and its focus on sustainable, community-focused tourism, it's an obvious destination for anyone wanting to experience the Amazon's flora, fauna and indigenous peoples up close.

Further north, around the towns of Riberalta and Cobija towards the Brazilian border, the savanna gradually gives way to the high-canopied **Amazonian rainforest**

FIESTA PATRONAL, SAN IGNACIO DE MOXOS

# Highlights

❶ **Parque Nacional Madidi** One of the most biodiverse protected areas in South America – and, for that matter, the world – Madidi is the region's premier national park and home to numerous excellent ecolodges, notably Chalalán. **See p.274**

❷ **Flying from La Paz to Rurrenabaque** This short, low-altitude hop from the Andes to the Amazon has to be one of the best-value in the world; feel your chin hit the floor as savage pinnacles and blinding icefields loom within touching distance, falling away to a seemingly infinite expanse of green. **See p.276**

❸ **San Ignacio de Moxos** Quite possibly the friendliest village in all South America, with unique flute and drum music, a famous July fiesta (the Fiesta Patronal), and a historic, candlelit Jesuit church. **See p.282**

❹ **Lomas** A mysterious pre-Columbian culture built thousands of earthworks across the Bolivian Amazon, including raised mounds known as lomas, several of which lie within striking distance of Trinidad, notably the Chuchini complex. **See p.284**

❺ **Río Mamoré** Sling your hammock up and relax on a slow boat down this mighty wilderness river between the town of Trinidad and the Brazilian frontier. **See p.290**

**HIGHLIGHTS ARE MARKED ON THE MAP ON P.270**

(known locally as *selva*) more characteristic of the Amazon region as a whole, where logging and the collection of wild rubber and Brazil nuts are the only industries of any size. Roads in the whole region are poor in the best of conditions and in the rainy season between November and April are often completely impassable.

## Brief history

Recent archeological evidence (see box, p.284) suggests that the pre-Columbian Bolivian Amazon supported a populous and sophisticated society of between five and six million people, 95 percent of whom were decimated through the sixteenth century by smallpox and flu introduced by Europeans.

### The Jesuit missions

Failing to find the fabled El Dorado (see box, p.284), the Spanish turned the region over to the religious orders, above all the Jesuits, in the hope that they might have more success in subjugating the forest tribes and securing the northeastern border with Brazil. In the late seventeenth century, a handful of **Jesuit missionaries** did just that, accomplishing in 25 years what the civil and military authorities had been unable to do

THE AMAZON

BRAZIL

**HIGHLIGHTS**

1. Parque Nacional Madidi
2. Flying from La Paz to Rurrenabaque
3. San Ignacio de Moxos
4. Lomas
5. Río Mamoré

in over a century. In a precursor of the theocratic society they established in Chiquitos (see box, p.252), the Jesuits founded a series of mission communities where the various indigenous tribes adopted Christianity and a settled, agricultural existence, raising cattle and growing crops. These missions flourished, and by the mid-eighteenth century were home to over 31,000 converts, supervised by just 45 European priests. With the expulsion of the Jesuits from the **Spanish Empire** in 1767, the mission inhabitants were left at the mercy of Spanish landowners, with many being forced into slavery.

### The rubber boom

Worse was to come in the nineteenth century as a result of the growing international demand for rubber, a material derived from trees which were particularly abundant in the Bolivian Amazon. An unprecedented economic boom ensued, and the industry was quickly dominated by a small group of ruthless **rubber barons** who made overnight fortunes and subjected the indigenous population to a brutal regime of forced labour. The most famous – or, rather, notorious – of these was **Nicolás Suárez** (see box, p.296), who ruled over a vast rainforest empire and remains a legendary figure in the Beni.

The richest rubber-producing area, the Acre, was largely settled by rubber collectors from Brazil. When the Bolivian government sought to tax rubber exports, the Brazilians rebelled and declared independence. A short conflict – **the Acre War** – ensued, ending with Bolivian defeat, and in 1903 the Acre was annexed by Brazil. In the early twentieth century, the rubber boom collapsed after the British smuggled rubber seedlings out of the Amazon and established plantations in Asia, rendering wild rubber collection uncompetitive.

### The twentieth century

By the middle of the twentieth century the economy began to recover as large landowners began exporting **cattle**, transporting them by river to the growing markets in Brazil and in military surplus aircraft to the Altiplano. Some landowners also made great fortunes during the **cocaine** boom of the 1980s and 1990s. Strategically positioned between the coca-growing Chapare and the markets to the north, the isolated ranches of the Beni provided the perfect location for clandestine drug laboratories, and their private airstrips were ideal bases for the small planes that used to smuggle the cocaine north, leapfrogging through the Amazon to Colombia and beyond.

### The twenty-first century

With ongoing road construction having opened up the Amazon's natural resources for exploitation to an unprecedented degree, and with attendant settlement from the highlands continuing apace, the consequences for the environment have become ever more obvious over the past fifteen years or so: during the record-breaking **drought** of 2005, slash-and-burn fires flared out of control, with the resultant incineration of around five thousand square kilometres. The **floods** of 2011, meanwhile, were the worst for decades; those of **2014** were even more devastating for the Bolivian Amazon and the Beni region in particular. Unusually heavy rainfall, climate change, deforestation and two dams across the border in Brazil were all variously blamed. More than 68,000 families were displaced, with 59 people reported dead, crops destroyed and up to 50,000 cattle lost.

There are even darker clouds on the horizon. The government has plans for some major **hydroelectric dams** (see p.274) in the region, road-building continues (the one between Rurrenabaque and Trinidad was nearly complete at the time of research) and oil exploration is ongoing. The implications of these developments for the environment and the region's indigenous communities are huge, and potentially devastating.

**6**

# Rurrenabaque and around

Set on the banks of the Río Beni, some 430km by road north of La Paz, the town of **RURRENABAQUE** is easily the most popular ecotourism destination in the Bolivian Amazon. If you've just arrived from bustling La Paz, its appeal won't be long in beguiling you, as residents are some of the friendliest and most laidback people in the Beni. Picturesquely located on a broad sweep of the river, between the last forest-covered foothills of the Andes and the great lowland plains, Rurrenabaque – or "Rurre", as it's commonly known – is close to some of the best-preserved and most accessible wilderness areas in the region, including the spectacular rainforests of **Parque Nacional Madidi** and the **Reserva de Biosfera y Territorio Indígena Pilon Lajas**, as well as the wildlife-rich pampas along the **Río Yacuma**. These are easily visited with one of Rurrenabaque's wide range of tour agencies (see p.277).

However, having been a fixture on the backpacker trail for many years, Rurrenabaque has an **uncertain future**. Between 2013 and 2016, tourist numbers fell by as much as fifty percent, which has had a devastating impact on the local economy. This has been blamed on the introduction of visa restrictions on Israeli and American travellers (the former previously made up a third of tourists in the town), a hike in the Madidi entry fee, the devastating 2014 floods, and the plans for a major hydroelectric project nearby (see p.274).

### Brief history

Rurrenabaque was founded in 1844 as a centre for the extraction of quinine (used to treat malaria), but first came to prominence during the **rubber boom** of the late nineteenth century, serving as the gateway to the Amazon region from the highlands.

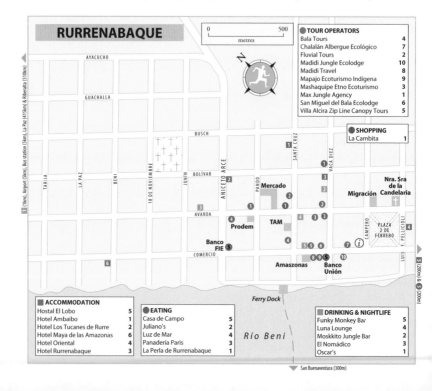

**RURRENABAQUE**

0   500
metres

● **TOUR OPERATORS**
| Bala Tours | 4 |
| Chalalán Albergue Ecológico | 7 |
| Fluvial Tours | 2 |
| Madidi Jungle Ecolodge | 10 |
| Madidi Travel | 8 |
| Mapajo Ecoturismo Indigena | 9 |
| Mashaquipe Etno Ecoturismo | 3 |
| Max Jungle Agency | 1 |
| San Miguel del Bala Ecolodge | 6 |
| Villa Alcira Zip Line Canopy Tours | 5 |

● **SHOPPING**
| La Cambita | 1 |

■ **ACCOMMODATION**
| Hostal El Lobo | 5 |
| Hotel Ambaibo | 1 |
| Hotel Los Tucanes de Rurre | 2 |
| Hotel Maya de las Amazonas | 6 |
| Hotel Oriental | 4 |
| Hotel Rurrenabaque | 3 |

● **EATING**
| Casa de Campo | 5 |
| Juliano's | 2 |
| Luz de Mar | 4 |
| Panadería Paris | 3 |
| La Perla de Rurrenabaque | 1 |

■ **DRINKING & NIGHTLIFE**
| Funky Monkey Bar | 5 |
| Luna Lounge | 4 |
| Moskkito Jungle Bar | 2 |
| El Nomádico | 3 |
| Oscar's | 1 |

Río Beni

Ferry Dock

San Buenaventura (300m)

Until fairly recently, the extraction and processing of **timber** from the surrounding rainforest was Rurrenabaque's main industry, but this has been curtailed somewhat by the exhaustion of valuable timber species and the establishment of Parque Nacional Madidi and other protected areas. The **ecotourism industry** emerged as one of the few economic alternatives to this highly destructive and largely illegal activity, though that is now under severe threat.

## Plaza 2 de Febrero

**6**

Though many modern brick and concrete structures have sprung up in recent years, Rurrenabaque's streets are still largely lined with traditional palm-thatched wooden houses. Official buildings are clustered around the pleasant **Plaza 2 de Febrero** at the south end of town, but most commercial activity is concentrated along the first few blocks of **calles Avaroa** and **Comercio**, which run north from the plaza parallel to the river, lined with ramshackle stores selling hammocks, rubber boots, machetes, chainsaws, tinned food and other supplies for people living in the surrounding area.

## The riverside market

Sun early morning–early afternoon

The riverside is an interesting place to while away the time watching canoes arriving along the Beni and unloading cargoes of bananas or freshly caught fish. It's particularly lively during the small Sunday-morning **market**, when indigenous people from the hinterlands of the surrounding rainforest come to town to pick up supplies and sell fish, agricultural produce and (for tourists) handicrafts like woven baskets and wooden bows.

## The miradors

To escape the jungle heat and humidity, head up to one of the swimming pool *miradors* (viewpoints), either **Oscar's Swimming Pool** (Bs40), or the nameless, quieter one (Bs20) a minute further up the same road. Both have great views of the town and river, while *Oscar's* is also a popular bar (see p.280). Ask a moto-taxi to take you (around Bs10).

## San Buenaventura

If you've got some time on your hands you can take the ferry (daily 6am–midnight; every 20min or so) across the river to the small village of **SAN BUENAVENTURA** on the opposite bank. Controversial plans for a proposed bridge are still rumbling on amid argument and counter-argument over its potential impact on both the tourist trade and

---

### YOSSI GHINSBERG AND RURRE'S TOURIST YEAR ZERO

Rurrenabaque's tourist boom was in part inspired by the adventures of **Yossi Ghinsberg**, an Israeli traveller who in 1981 tried to reach Rurrenabaque independently from the highlands with his two companions, trekking down through what's now Parque Nacional Madidi. Lost in the forest and running out of food, the group split up. Ghinsberg continued and eventually reached the Río Tuichi, where he was rescued and taken to Rurrenabaque. His two companions were never seen again. Ghinsberg's account of the ill-fated expedition, **Back from Tuichi** (later republished as *Jungle*; a 2017 film adaptation of the book stars Daniel Radcliffe), became a bestseller in Israel, inspiring many Israeli backpackers to visit the region, with travellers from around the world following swiftly in their wake. Ghinsberg was also involved in the foundation of the *Chalalán* ecolodge (see p.277), while his rescuer founded Rurrenabaque's first rainforest tour company (see p.277). Visit ⓦ ghinsberg.com for more information.

Parque Nacional Madidi. They are complicated by the fact that San Buenaventura is actually within the political remit of La Paz Department. For that same reason, several public buildings are located here rather than in Rurrenabaque, including the park's SERNAP administration office (see below).

## Parque Nacional Madidi

SERNAP office: Calle Libertad, San Buenaventura • ☏ 03 8922540, ⓦ sernap.gob.bo • Bs200

**6**

On Rurrenabaque's doorstep, and spanning nearly nineteen thousand square kilometres, **PARQUE NACIONAL MADIDI** is home to some of the most diverse plant and animal life in the world. It ranges in altitude from less than 300m to over 5500m above sea level, encompassing a variety of Andean and Amazonian ecosystems – from dense tropical rainforests and seasonally flooded savanna to pristine cloudforest and glacial mountain peaks. The park's wildlife is astonishing: more than seven hundred species of animal have been recorded, along with over a thousand species of bird (this represents a staggering eleven percent of the world's total bird species). There are also around a thousand butterfly species and also more than five thousand species of flowering plant. Madidi was recognized as a national park in 1995 and, together with the neighbouring **Pilon Lajas** reserve and **Parque Nacional Tambopata-Candamo** across the border in Peru, forms a corridor of biodiversity that is generally considered to be one of the 25 most critical conservation areas in the world.

The real wonder of the park is its spectacular scenery and the bewildering complexity of the rainforest ecosystem, and you should treat viewing **wildlife** as a bonus rather than the main purpose of a visit to the park. Having said that, on a standard three- or four-day trip you should see a fair amount of the local fauna, including several species of monkey, capybaras, caymans and a veritable cornucopia of birds, including brightly coloured toucans, macaws and parrots. If you're lucky you may also see larger animals like the mighty jaguar or the lumbering tapir. Be warned, though, that many species are rare, nocturnal and shy, and the areas of the park most easily accessible by river were logged and hunted until relatively recently.

However, dark clouds lie on the horizon. The Bolivian government continues to push ahead with a major **hydroelectric project** in the region, with proposed dams in the El Bala and El Beu canyons. Ministers claim only two percent of the park will be affected by the project – one of the biggest of its kind in South America – but this is contested by conservation groups and local people. If the dams go ahead, around two thousand square kilometres of land would be flooded, threatening the lives and livelihoods of thousands of indigenous people and the fragile ecosystem of one of the world's most significant protected areas.

All in all, you should visit while you can. If you want to get into the park's really pristine areas you'll need to go on a trip of about a week, travelling on foot or horseback into the more remote regions of the forest around the headwaters of the **Río Madidi**. The upper regions of the park can only be reached from the highlands north of La Paz, and even from there they are pretty much inaccessible unless you organize a serious expedition with a La Paz tour operator (see p.76).

## Pampas del Yacuma

SERNAP office: Calle Libertad, San Buenaventura • ☏ 03 8922540, ⓦ sernap.gob.bo • Bs150

Northeast of Rurrenabaque, the dense forests of the Andean foothills quickly give way to the **Pampas del Yacuma**, vast, swampy grasslands that dominate much of the Beni. Though they have been grazed by cattle for hundreds of years, the pampas still support a great deal of wildlife, particularly along the forested banks of the great rivers that meander across them. The pampas themselves are not that impressive: a great expanse of swamp and tangled cattle pasture with the occasional lake. Tours with the agencies

## THE THREAT TO THE FOREST

Although the **forests** of the Beni can appear endless when you fly over them by plane or pass through by boat, in fact, they're disappearing at an alarming rate. Because it is such a vast area no one can tell exactly how fast the forests are disappearing, even with satellite monitoring, but estimates suggest Bolivia is losing about three and a half thousand square kilometres of forest a year, one of the highest rates worldwide (and much higher than in neighbouring Brazil, the primary focus of "Save the Rainforest" campaigns since the 1970s). Moreover, rates have increased significantly in recent years. Much of the damage is being done in the Beni, with catastrophic consequences for the region's unique ecosystems.

The causes of this deforestation are various. The most obvious culprits are **timber companies**, ranging from small gangs with chainsaws to major commercial operations. Rather than clear-cutting the forest, they concentrate on valuable hardwood species such as mahogany and Spanish cedar. But for every tree they extract several others are damaged, and the trails they cut into even the most remote areas open the way for **colonists** who are responsible for even greater destruction.

Successive Bolivian governments have seen the comparatively empty lands of the Amazon as a solution to poverty and land shortage in the highlands, encouraging the migration of poor farmers from the Andes, who have moved down into the lowlands, clearing the forest to plant food and cash crops. Every year towards the end of the dry season the skies above Bolivia are obscured by thick smoke from thousands of fires set to clear the forest for **agriculture** and **cattle pasture**, a process known as *chaqueo*. Yet when the forest cover is slashed and burned on a wide scale, nutrients are quickly leached away by rain, and within a few years soil fertility declines so much that the land becomes useless for agriculture.

When it finally recognized the potential biological value of the country's rainforests, the government established extensive **national parks** and other protected areas in the Amazon, as well as recognizing large areas as indigenous territory (arguably the most effective way of protecting the rainforest) and introducing laws to limit logging and forest clearance. Yet the immense scale and remoteness of the region makes enforcing legislation almost impossible, and many of the protected areas exist only on paper.

Moreover, the government has also pushed ahead with controversial road-building and major hydroelectric projects (see opposite), despite fierce local opposition.

listed here (many of which have lodges in the pampas) are nevertheless worth it for the amount of wildlife you'll see along the Río Yacuma.

### The Río Yacuma

In the rainy season (roughly Nov–April), the **Río Yacuma** river bursts its banks and floods great expanses of the surrounding grasslands, causing wildlife to become more dispersed and breeding ferocious mosquitoes. In the dry season, however, it's reduced to a narrow river that attracts an amazing abundance of fauna. Sinister-looking black-and-white **caymans** – some over 2m long – lounge on the muddy banks, slipping quietly into the water as you pass; **turtles** queue up to sun themselves on logs protruding from the water; groups of **capybara**, the world's largest rodent, watch with apparent indifference as canoes pass right in front of their noses. Most spectacular of all, though, are the **pink freshwater dolphins**, known as *bufeos*, that fish and play in the wide bends of the river. In addition, all manner of **birds** live on the banks, including herons, three different species of kingfisher, elegant roseate spoonbills, massive storks and the clumsy hoatzin.

## Reserva de Biosfera y Territorio Indígena Pilon Lajas

Just south of Rurrenabaque, some four thousand square kilometres of rainforest between the Río Beni and the road south to La Paz are protected by the **Reserva de Biosfera y Territorio Indígena Pilon Lajas**. Though threatened by loggers and migrant

6

## ECOTOURISM IN RURRENABAQUE

The term **ecotourism** has, in the past, often been used in Rurre in connection with practices that are rather dubiously ecofriendly, and with tours where prices have been driven down to unhealthy and unsustainable levels. Yet things have improved in recent years, with **strict guidelines** now developed for standards in safety, environmental awareness, sustainable tourism and socio-cultural sensitivity, which agencies must adhere to in order to be certified.

One of Rurre's great successes has been its community-run projects, with the internationally renowned **Chalalán** (see opposite) leading the way. Established with support from international conservation groups in a bid to demonstrate how rainforest conservation can provide sustainable livelihoods for local people who might otherwise turn to logging or other destructive activities, it's owned and managed by the 116 families that make up the Quechua-Tacana community of San José de Uchupiamonas, located 25km further up the Río Tuichi, and the only settlement of any real size inside Parque Nacional Madidi. Other respected community operators include **Mapajo Ecoturismo Indígena** (see p.278), whose *Albergue Ecológico Mapajo* is wholly owned by the indigenous communities of the Río Quiquibey, and was established at a fraction of the cost of *Chalalán* and with a greater degree of community autonomy; and **San Miguel del Bala** (see p.278), co-owned by 35 families and founded with help from both the United Nations Development Programme and USAID.

Parque Nacional Madidi itself wouldn't exist, however, without the efforts of the remarkable Rosa Maria Ruiz, manager of **Madidi Travel** (see p.278). The company emerged from Eco Bolivia, the foundation Ruiz created in the early 1990s and with which she convinced the government – with support from the World Bank and Conservation International – to create the national park. After a series of setbacks that could fill a book in their own right – it's covered briefly in Gaia Vince's *Adventures in the Anthropocene* (see p.326) – she went on to create the Reserva de Serere, a pristine, privately owned, forty-square-kilometre protected area, which forms part of the Madidi Mosaic, a 150,000-square-kilometre network of protected areas stretching to the Peruvian border.

settlers along the road that marks its eastern boundary, the rainforests of Pilon Lajas, like those of Parque Nacional Madidi, are exceptionally biodiverse and survive in a largely pristine state. Declared a Biosphere Reserve by UNESCO in 1977, the reserve protects some 642 species of flora, 499 species of bird and 170 species of fish. Pilon Lajas is also home to a small population of indigenous Mosetén, T'simane and Tacana communities, spread out along the length of the **Río Quiquibey**, which runs through the centre of the reserve.

Unfortunately, like Madidi, Pilon Lajas is also threatened by the government's plans for hydroelectric power stations in the region, so visit while you can.

### ARRIVAL AND GETTING AROUND

### RURRENABAQUE AND AROUND

**By plane** Of all Bolivia's flight paths, the busy route between La Paz and Rurrenabaque is by far the most spectacular, and if you're going to splash out on any internal flights, this is the one to go for (not least because the bus journey is probably the most arduous in the country). The majority are operated by Amaszonas (Comercio and Santa Cruz; ☎ 03 8922472, ⓦ amaszonas.com), whose nineteen-seat, twin-prop planes ensure a condor's-eye view of the Cordillera Real, swooping down through the scree and snow to the emerald hills of the Yungas and the endless, sweltering acres of jungle beyond, or vice versa if you're flying the other way. Planes arrive at the tiny airport a short distance north of the town, and are met by a shuttle bus (Bs10; 10min) that will take you to the Amaszonas office (this is also where you catch a bus back to the airport). Military airline TAM (3 weekly flights;

☎ 02 268111, ⓦ tam.bo) also has flights to/from La Paz, and small-scale operator Alas (☎ 6938 6507) has three weekly flights to/from Trinidad. Note that flight cancellations during the rainy season are not uncommon.

Destinations La Paz (4–6 daily; 30–40min); Trinidad (3 weekly; 30min).

**By bus/micro** Buses arrive at, and depart from, the new Terminal Terrestre, close to the airport; a taxi to/from the town centre costs Bs10. Note that the times given below are for optimum dry season conditions – even a short cloudburst can extend them considerably. A new road now connects Rurrenabaque and Trinidad, though it's still an arduous journey.

Destinations Cobija (1 daily; 24hr); La Paz (3 daily; 20–24hr); Riberalta (1–2 daily; 20–30hr); San Ignacio de

Moxos (en route to Trinidad; 1–3 daily; 12–16hr); Trinidad (1–3 daily; 20–30hr); Yolosa (for connections to Coroico; 3 daily; 14–20hr).

**By boat** When the road is closed in the rainy season, motorized canoes occasionally carry passengers between Rurrenabaque and Guanay, a small town about 230km northwest of La Paz (6–8hr), and Riberalta (8–10 days). Book in advance with one of the tour agencies.

**By moto-taxi** Motorbikes pretty much rule the road in Rurre; they are easy to flag down in town and standard local journeys cost around Bs5.

## INFORMATION

**Tourist information** The tourist office (Comercio, near the corner with Campero; Mon–Sat 8am–noon & 2.30–6pm) has maps, limited materials on the national parks, and a list of authorized and certified tour agencies. The most useful feature, however, is the volumes of detailed questionnaires filled in by tour-returning travellers.

## TOURS

Rurrenabaque is the best place in the Bolivian Amazon to organize a trip into the wilderness, either to the rainforests of **Parque Nacional Madidi** (see p.274) or the **Reserva de Biosfera y Territorio Indígena Pilon Lajas** (see p.275), or into the **Pampas del Yacuma** along the Río Yacuma to the north (see p.274). There are a huge number of travel agencies in the town, and it's not always clear as to which companies are community-owned concerns and which are private. Note that prices do not normally include the Parque Nacional Madidi or Pampas del Yacuma **entry fees** (Bs200 and Bs150, respectively). Be suspicious of super-cheap tours – corners, in your comfort and from a conservation point of view, will have been cut – and check the size of the group (the smaller the better) before booking. If you're going on a tour, it's a good idea to book a room for your return (all places will store luggage when you're away).

### PRIVATE TOUR OPERATORS

Generally cheaper than community-run operators and hence more popular with backpackers, private agencies offer trips to the rainforest (*selva*) and the pampas, generally lasting three nights, and with varying standards of rustic accommodation – this is long enough to see the pampas properly, though to really appreciate the rainforest it's well worth taking a longer trip.

**Bala Tours** Santa Cruz and Comercio ☎03 8922527, ⓦbalatours.com; map p.272. Professional, well-regarded operator offering three-day pampas and *selva* tours for around $240 (Bs1632), with jungle accommodation in their solar-powered, Río Tuichi-sited lodge, plus a five-day combined pampas and *selva* option for around $440 (Bs2992) and specialist three- or five-day bird-watching tours from $330 (Bs2244).

**Fluvial Tours** Avaroa, between Santa Cruz and Vaca Díez ☎03 8922351, ⓦfluvialtoursbolivia.com; map p.272. The tour operator that started it all in 1985, with experienced guides and frequent departures to the pampas and *selva*, as well as longer jungle trips. The owner, Tico Tudela, "the original Bolivian Tarzan", apparently, was the man who helped find Yossi Ghinsberg (see box, p.273).

**Max Jungle Agency** Avaroa and Pando ☎7251 9548, ⓦmaxjungle.com; map p.272. Run by the formidable Tereza Hodkova de Nava (originally from the Czech Republic), with the motto "no chairs, no tables, no beds", Max offers ascetic one- to 25-day expeditions, ranging from standard jungle and *selva* tours (three-day tours Bs1350/person) to back-to-basics expeditions with indigenous guides, no home comforts whatsoever and various levels of extremity. The latter includes a three-day "hardcore survival" option; all you get is a machete, a mosquito net and a guide (from Bs1750/person).

### COMMUNITY TOUR OPERATORS

The alternative to a standard agency tour is to stay at one of the community-based projects established in the mould of the internationally renowned *Chalalán* lodge, the first such venture in the area. While you'll pay considerably more for a tour with most of the community projects (rates typically include transport, tours, food and accommodation), your money will help ensure that sustainable tourism continues to triumph over logging and hunting as a way of preserving community life.

★**Chalalán Albergue Ecológico** Comercio, near the plaza ☎03 8922419, ⓦchalalan.com; map p.272. A beautiful, multi-award-winning ecolodge, deep in Madidi beside the Río Tuichi, 5hr by boat upriver fom Rurrenabaque. The lodge overlooks a large lagoon, teeming with cayman and all manner of water birds, and the surrounding forest is covered by a 25km network of trails. Accommodation is in thatched wooden cabins built in a traditional Tacana style, with mosquito netting, comfortable beds and solar-powered lighting and shared or private bathrooms. Tours cost from $399 (Bs2713)/person; combined pampas trips are also available.

**Madidi Jungle Ecolodge** Comercio, between Vaca Díez and Campero ☎7128 2697, ⓦmadidijungle.com; map p.272. This project was started by four families from San José de Uchupiamonas, the same community that founded *Chalalán*. With more basic, shared accommodation and capacity for eighteen people maximum, this is a relatively cheaper, more intimate alternative (from $260 (Bs1768)/person for an all-inclusive three-day/two-night

**6**

trip); longer and shorter trips are also available. The ecolodge itself is around 3hr from Rurre by boat.

★**Madidi Travel** Comercio, between Santa Cruz and Vaca Díez ☎03 8922153, ⓦmadidi-travel.com; map p.272. This might not be a community-run project per se, but one hundred percent of the profits are ploughed back into the communities it works with. Accommodation (three-day tours Bs1899/person) at its private reserve, Serere, around 3hr by boat from Rurre (see box, p.276), is in spartan yet stylish, two-storey *cabañas*, located by Lago San Fernando, with a top deck for hammock lounging; they serve food prepared from almost wholly organic ingredients sourced from local communities. A healthy population of big cats such as pumas, jaguars and ocelots attests to the health of the area's ecosystem, and with daily walks led by excellent guides, as well as various viewing platforms, there's ample opportunity to experience it all. Volunteering opportunities are available.

**Mapajo Ecoturismo Indígena** Comercio ☎6801 0508, ⓔmapajo.ecoturismo.indigena@gmail.com; map p.272. The *Albergue Ecológico Mapajo*, on the Río Quiquibey in the Reserva de Biosfera y Territorio Indígena Pilon Lajas, is 3hr upstream by motorized canoe from Rurre. A two- to six-day visit to the lodge – from $180(Bs1224)/person – offers excellent opportunities for exploring the rainforest and spotting wildlife, as well as the chance to visit the local indigenous communities. Benefiting from a lovely setting on a high bluff overlooking the river, the lodge has comfortable cabins built in traditional indigenous style, and there are over 20km of trails.

**Mashaquipe Etno Ecoturismo** Avaroa, between Santa Cruz and Vaca Díez ☎03 8922704, ⓦmashaquipeecotours.com; map p.272. Run by indigenous Tacana, T'simane and Mosetene families, this highly respected, community-oriented organization runs the *Mashaquipe Ecolodge* inside Parque Nacional Madidi, and offers customized tours at competitive prices (from $210 (Bs1428)/person for a three-day tour), with accommodation in dorms or simple private rooms.

**San Miguel del Bala Ecolodge** Comercio, between Vaca Díez and Santa Cruz ☎03 8922394, ⓦsanmigueldelbala.com; map p.272. Only half an hour down the river from Rurre, this is the perfect place to experience a taste of a traditional Tacana community, particularly if you're short on time (one- to five-day tours are available). The project comprises two distinctive lodges, the handsome *San Miguel del Bala* with en-suite rooms (on the Río Beni), and the smaller, partly shared *Caquiahuara* (deep within Parque Nacional Madidi). It goes without saying that the guides are all local, and full of forest folklore.

**Villa Alcira Zip Line Canopy Tours** Comercio, between Santa Cruz and Vaca Díez ☎03 8923875, ⓦtusoco.com/villa-alcira; map p.272. Run by the nearby Tacana community of Villa Alcira (15min from Rurre by boat) and offering two daily tours (8am & 2pm; Bs300, plus Bs35 "community entry fee") on a series of zip lines, trips allow you to whizz through the upper canopy of the trees along 1200m of cable and across nine platforms. You can also stay overnight with the locals (doubles around $100/Bs680).

## ACCOMMODATION

With a couple of exceptions, accommodation in Rurrenabaque itself is generally underwhelming and overpriced.

**Hostal El Lobo** Comercio and Ballivián ☎7012 5362, ⓦwww.ellobohostel.com; map p.272. Around 500m south of Plaza 2 de Febrero, this solid budget choice has tidy dorms and rooms (with shared or private bathrooms, TVs, and shared balconies overlooking the river), a swimming pool, a restaurant and a games room. The mozzies, however, can be ferocious. Dorms Bs100, doubles Bs180

**Hotel Ambaibo** Santa Cruz and Bolívar ☎03 8922686; map p.272. An ample garden and the biggest pool in the centre of town is the main draw here, though en-suite rooms – clean, spacious and with TVs and fans or a/c – are good in their own right. Bs350

**Hotel Los Tucanes de Rurre** Aniceto Arce and Bolívar ☎03 8922039, ⓦhotel-tucanes.com; map p.272. Though the thatched-roof reception suggests the rooms may be slightly smarter than they are, this is nevertheless one of the nicer budget options, and even if the rooms (with private or shared bathrooms) need a fresh lick of

paint, they're clean and cool enough, and are grouped around a small bar. Bs100

**Hotel Maya de las Amazonas** Comercio and Beni ☎03 8922380, ⓦhotelmayarurre.com; map p.272. The smartest hotel in Rurre itself, overlooking the river and a 10min walk from the centre. Its a/c, en-suite rooms have plenty of space, there's a breezy raised deck, and the flower-filled garden features a small swimming pool. The breakfast is above average too. Bs410

**Hotel Oriental** Plaza 2 de Febrero ☎03 8922401; map p.272. This ever-reputable, family-run hotel remains one of Rurre's better budget options, with cool, comfortable rooms (some with private bathrooms) set around a peaceful courtyard garden with hammocks. Save for the occasional brass band parping away in the plaza of an evening, it's also one of the most tranquil; stern in-room notices make clear that neither alcohol nor noiseniks will be tolerated. Bs150

**Hotel Rurrenabaque** Vaca Díez and Bolívar ☎03 8922481, ✉hotelrurrenabaque@hotmail.com; map p.272. As the oldest two-storey house in town, this is the place to stay if you want some character in your lodgings, though the faded yellow-and-red sign indicates that it has seen better days. Most of the floors and some of the walls still bear the original wooden boards, while the carved doors add a touch of class. The rooms themselves are clean and – owing to the thickness of the old walls – slightly cooler than you'll find elsewhere, and some are en suite. There's a communal balcony overlooking the street strung with a couple of hammocks, as well as a sizeable garden, restaurant and laundry service. Bs130

**6**

## EATING

Note that time is a conspicuously elastic concept when it comes to **restaurants** in Rurre; don't be surprised to find somewhere closed when it should be open, or, occasionally in the middle of the afternoon for the whole town to be minus any eating options at all (if you're wise – and indeed, up in time – you'll eat a decent breakfast). Most restaurants double up as bars (and vice versa).

★**Casa de Campo** Comercio and Ballivián, by Hotel Lobo ☎7921 5612; map p.272. One of the best restaurants in Rurre, in a tranquil location around 500m south of Plaza 2 de Febrero, is perfect if you're lusting after something more healthy and wholesome than standard backpacker food, with a menu of natural fruit juices, quinoa and pumpkin soups, salads and the most delicious homemade croissants (mains Bs30–60). Keep an eye out for the exquisitely patterned little bowls fashioned from orange peel (smell it to believe it); they make for great-value souvenirs. Daily 8am–2pm & 6–10pm.

**Juliano's** Santa Cruz and Bolívar ☎7392 0088; map p.272. A sophisticated spot (by Rurre standards at least) for a night out, *Juliano's* has a cosmopolitan menu and an easy-going atmosphere. As well as the usual fish, meat and pasta dishes (Bs30–60), they also do thin-crust pizzas, North African-style chicken and crispy calamari. Make sure you save room for the crème brûlée. Daily 5–11pm.

**Luz de Mar** Avaroa ☎7320 2501; map p.272. Rightly popular café-restaurant, this is one of the few in town that is (fairly) reliably open during the day. The menu ranges from pastries, cakes and sandwiches (try the cheese-and-chive empanadas; Bs10) to standard mains (around Bs40), with drinks including juices, shakes, beer and cocktails. Tues–Sun 7.30am–10.30pm.

**Panadería Paris** Avaroa, between Santa Cruz and Vaca Díez; map p.272. It might be a bit scruffy but this is a honeypot for tourists in the morning, who come for wonderful pastries (the *pain au chocolat* is particularly good) and bread rolls. Add a coffee, orange juice or *licuado* (smoothie) for an excellent breakfast (Bs12–20 in total). Mon–Fri 6.30am–12.30pm & 3.30–6.30pm, Sat 6.30am–12.30pm (or when they run out of goods).

**La Perla de Rurrenabaque** Bolívar and Vaca Díez ☎7102 2388; map p.272. Set in a lush garden, shaded by a pair of venerable mango trees, the *Perla* is inconsistent, though the good nights outnumber the bad. The focus of the menu is on fish – dishes include the house speciality, garlic *surubí* (a local freshwater fish). Most mains Bs40–50. Daily 7am–9pm.

## DRINKING AND NIGHTLIFE

**Funky Monkey Bar** Comercio, diagonally opposite the Amaszonas office ☎7255 9023; map p.272. As distinctive in its own way as *Moskkito*, the *Funky Monkey* is better as a bar than a restaurant, with friendly staff, a cache of provocatively named cocktails (around Bs30–50), and a raucous, rock-heavy soundtrack. Daily 5pm–midnight.

**Luna Lounge** Avaroa, near Santa Cruz ☎03 8922719; map p.272. Open during the day for decent thin-crust pizza and a variety of omelettes (mains Bs40–60), this is more of a bar than a restaurant, with bamboo walls and shell drapes. Forget the cocktails and sample one of the heavenly papaya, strawberry, milk and yoghurt concoctions instead. There's also a pool table and book exchange. Happy hour 7–11pm daily. Mon–Sat 9am–3am, Sun 6pm–3am.

**Moskkito Jungle Bar** Vaca Díez ☎03 8922267, 🌐moskkito.com; map p.272. Dating back to 1999, and something of a local legend, this convivial bar is popular with locals and travellers alike, with cold beer and suggestively named cocktails (from Bs20; happy hour daily 7–9pm), a booming rock soundtrack, pool table and dartboard. Skip the mediocre food, though. Daily 4pm–3am.

★**El Nomádico** Avaroa ☎7284 3850; map p.272. Although it describes itself as the "best kept secret in Rurre", this bar-restaurant is far from in the shadows. As well as a fine selection of drinks (beer from Bs20; daily happy hour 7–9pm), there's live sport on the TV, and a good range of food (try the fish curry). Mon–Thurs 6pm–12.30am, Fri 6pm–2.30am, Sat 4pm–2.30am, Sun noon–12.30am.

**Oscar's** In the hills to the north of town ☎03 8922710; map p.272. Rurrenabaque's equivalent of a beach bar, this swimming pool eyrie is routinely packed out with people who've either returned from a tour, or are killing time till a tour leaves – and what a spot to do it in, with a glorious view back down over the Beni, not least at sunset when the heavens blush a roaring orange-red. Free entry after 6pm (otherwise Bs40). Daily 10.30am–1am.

## SHOPPING

**La Cambita** Avaroa, between Santa Cruz and Pando ☎ 7157 8493; map p.272. This small yet perfectly formed *artesanía* store is run by Natsumi Kawata, who buys jewellery and other crafts from surrounding communities and sells them in her professionally laid-out shop. Each piece of work is initialled with the name of the artist, and a corresponding board provides a name and photograph. Daily 8am–9pm.

## DIRECTORY

**Banks and exchange** Banco FIE (Comercio and Aniceto Arce) and Banco Unión (Comercio and Vaca Díez) both have ATMs, but make sure you withdraw enough cash in La Paz before flying down in case they don't accept your card. You can obtain a cash advance on both Visa and Mastercard at Prodem on the corner of Pando and Avaroa.

**6**

# The Llanos de Moxos

Between Rurrenabaque and Trinidad stretch the vast, watery plains known as the **Llanos de Moxos** (or Mojos). Spanning the area between the ríos Mamoré and Beni, the region is largely covered by seasonally flooded savanna or natural grassland interspersed with swamp and patches of forest. During the November to April rainy season, the whole area is flooded for months at a time and the road (which is currently being upgraded) between Rurrenabaque and Trinidad becomes impassable, while during the dry season between May and September the grasslands become very dry, resembling the savannas of Africa much more than the lush greenery usually associated with the Amazon basin. This is **cowboy country**, and the economy of the plains is dominated by enormous ranches, stocked with the semi-wild descendants of the cattle first introduced by the Jesuits in the seventeenth century. The Llanos are also home to semi-nomadic indigenous groups such as T'simanes (or Chimanes), for whom hunting is still an important source of food, though shotguns have largely replaced bows and arrows as the weapon of choice.

Away from the former mission towns of **San Ignacio de Moxos** and San Borja, the Llanos remain a sparsely populated wilderness where most of the wild animal species of the Amazon still thrive, and because of the open vegetation they can be easier to spot than in the forest. Even from the road, the **birdlife** you'll see here is spectacular and abundant, with water species like storks and herons being particularly evident. Jaguars abound, and you may also spot species not found in the forest, like the maned wolf, a long-legged, solitary hunter that moves through the high grasses with a loping stride, or the rhea, a large flightless bird similar to the ostrich. A few hours west of San Ignacio de Moxos, a large area of this distinctive environment is protected by the **Reserva de la Biosfera del Beni**, Bolivia's oldest protected area.

---

### WHEN SAN IGNACIO IGNITES: THE FIESTA PATRONAL

For most of the year San Ignacio is a sleepy backwater, except in late July, when the **Fiesta Patronal** or Ichapekenepiesta rouses the town from its tropical torpor in celebration of its titular patron saint. Considered the greatest **folkloric festival** in the Bolivian Amazon, it reaches its zenith on the 31st in a riot of noise, colour, dancing and wonderful music, performed on flute, drums, violin and metre-long palm-leaf *bajones* – a kind of giant tropical equivalent to the highland quena (a type of traditional flute). The most iconic dance, the *Machetero*, is both a salutation to the sun and a thinly veiled portrayal of the struggles against Spanish rule, hypnotically performed by indigenous Moxeños dressed in brilliant feather headdresses and long cotton robes. The austere-looking *achus*, by contrast, represent the spirits of the ancestors, their dark suits topped off with carved wooden masks and raw-leather hats. Needless to say, it's all accompanied by copious quantities of alcohol and the familiar whiff of cordite; just don't expect much sleep.

## San Ignacio de Moxos

About 100km west of Trinidad lies the singular town of **SAN IGNACIO DE MOXOS**, the so-called "Spiritual Capital of the Jesuit Missions", founded by the Jesuits in 1689. It's a humble yet incredibly welcoming place with a unique and unforgettable atmosphere, where horse- or ox-drawn carts are as common as motor vehicles, and where the largely indigenous population retain more of the traditions of the Jesuit era than any other town in the Beni. While there's not much to do outside fiesta times, it's enough to simply marinate in San Ignacio's lost-in-time aura; don't be surprised if complete strangers stop you in the plaza simply to say "hello", ask where you're from and how long you'll be staying.

### Plaza Principal 31 de Julio

Many of the village houses are simple, palm-thatched cane structures, but the **Plaza Principal 31 de Julio** is lined with stone houses whose tiled roofs extend over the pavement to provide shelter from the harsh tropical sun and frequent rain. In its centre stands a **statue** of an indigenous warrior in the same costume as that worn by the *Machetero* dancers during the July fiesta.

#### Iglesia de San Ignacio

Plaza Principal 31 de Julio • Daily 8am–7pm • Free

On the east side of the Plaza Principal is **Iglesia de San Ignacio**, the town's physical and spiritual centre. Built in the barn-like style favoured by the Jesuits, its interior is brightly painted in a beautiful naïve style with scenes from the life of Ignacio Loyola, the mercenary soldier turned saint who founded the Jesuit order. The church is still run by Spanish Jesuit priests, who are once again heavily involved in defending the rights of the indigenous population against logging companies and large landowners, and who continue to inspire a deep faith in their congregation. Hundreds of people attend Mass on Sundays, and it's even more atmospheric in the not so unlikely event of a power cut, when services are held by flickering candlelight.

#### Museo de Moxos

Ballivián, on Plaza Principal • Mon–Sat 8.30am–12.30pm & 2.30–6pm, Sun 9am–1pm • Music archive Mon–Fri only • Bs15

The small, church-run **Museo de Moxos** is housed around the Iglesia de San Ignacio's peaceful cloisters and gardens, with illustrated displays on the history of both the Moxos people and the mission itself. The real reason to come here, though, is the famous archive of **Moxeña music**, containing over seven thousand antique pages. Many of its more recent acquisitions were retrieved from the scattered communities of the **Parque Nacional y Reserva Indígena Isiboro-Sécure**: polyphonic and antiphonic pieces, devotional songs and sacred operas of European origin, hybridized over time with indigenous music and dance, and, given the area's geographical isolation, all but immune from the tides of cultural change. Many of the scores have now been restored, catalogued and digitized, and the music revived in the performances of the local Baroque music school (see box, below).

---

### SCHOOL OF BAROQUE

In a kind of magic-realist reversal of the Manaus opera house bringing highbrow European culture to the Brazilian Amazon, the **San Ignacio de Moxos music school** on Ayacucho (☏ 03 4822347) has taken its singular brand of indigenous Baroque from the Bolivian Amazon to Europe. Founded by a Navarrese nun and counting between two and three hundred students, the school has been teaching violin, cello and flute to the town's youth since the mid-1990s, creating a unique ensemble whose performances have brought acclaim from Buenos Aires to Barcelona. The school also has a concert hall; if you're in town it's worth checking to see if there are any upcoming recitals.

## Laguna Isirere

A twenty-minute walk or five-minute moto-taxi ride north of Plaza Principal brings you to the attractive **Laguna Isirere**, where you can relax, swim and observe the abundant birdlife. Legend has it that anyone who drinks from the lagoon will never leave San Ignacio – not such a terrible fate all in all. Lake transport is via either muscle- or motor-powered canoe (Bs5–10).

### ARRIVAL AND DEPARTURE                      SAN IGNACIO DE MOXOS

**By plane** Though not for the faint-hearted, the antiquated, two-passenger *avionetas* (air taxi) which fly between San Ignacio and Trinidad (30min; around Bs400/return, though you can sometimes secure a seat for far less – locals in need of a fellow passenger sometimes search out people waiting for buses) can make for a cheap and unforgettable way to experience the Llanos de Moxos. To hire one yourself, phone Captain

Emilio Arios Díez (☎7114 9435) or ask at one of the tour agencies in Trinidad (see p.288).
**By bus** Buses to and from Trinidad (3–4 daily; 4hr) and en route from Trinidad to Rurrenabaque (1–3 daily; 12–16hr) arrive and depart from the far end of Santiesteban, the road that heads out of town to the east; trufis are a quicker and more comfortable option for Trinidad. During the rainy season (Nov–Feb) the roads are often impassable.

### ACCOMMODATION

**Plaza Hotel** Plaza Principal and Santiesteban ☎03 4822032. This hotel has rudimentary rooms, leading off a sociable reception often bustling with locals. They also have their own generator so at least some of the rooms (which have shared or private bathrooms) have power during blackouts. <u>Bs100</u>

**Residencial Don Joaquín** Plaza Principal and Montes ☎03 4828012. Delightfully antiquated, family-run clutch of spartan yet atmospheric, whitewashed rooms (shared or private bathrooms) with ceiling fans, original beams and heavy furniture, all grouped around a courtyard garden with hammocks. <u>Bs100</u>

### EATING AND DRINKING

There are several basic restaurants on Santiesteban, all of which open late and close early, and most of which offer good-value **almuerzos**. If you're after an early breakfast, head for the small **covered market** on the same street.

★**Restaurante Ecoturistico** Antonio de Orellana, three blocks from Plaza Principal ☎03 4822709. This modern, NGO-funded restaurant, with its plate glass and hardwood columns, is the unlikeliest edifice in San Ignacio, perhaps the

whole Beni. Service couldn't be friendlier and the great-value food (Bs30–50) is excellent, ranging from fried fish with *yuca* and plantain to a macaroni cheese. It's a good spot for a drink in the evening, too. Daily 6.30–11.30pm.

# Reserva de la Biosfera Estación Biológica del Beni

Arrange entry in advance with the reserve office in the village of San Borja, at the junction of Trinidad and 18 de Noviembre • Admission Bs35 • ☎03 8953898 • Micros for San Borja (frequent; 3–4hr) depart throughout the day from the bus terminal in Rurrenabaque; the reserve office can advise on transport to and within the reserve; alternatively, arrange a tour through one of the agencies in Rurrenabaque or Trinidad

Covering some 1350 square kilometres of savanna and rainforest to the east of San Borja, the **Reserva de la Biosfera Estación Biológica del Beni** (Beni Biosphere Reserve) was one of the first protected areas to be established in Bolivia. Standing at the intersection of two important biogeographical zones, the reserve is exceptionally biodiverse, hosting some five hundred species of birds and one hundred species of mammals – these include almost half the protected species in Bolivia, among them many that are in danger of extinction. Illegal hunting, unfortunately, still poses a major threat. The most popular excursion here is to the **Laguna Normandía**, populated with rare **black cayman** easily observed from rowing boats or the 11m tower on the shore. The lake is about a one-hour hike from the reserve headquarters at **El Porvenir**, a former ranch about 100km west of San Ignacio on the road to San Borja. You should be able to arrange guides, horses (if required) and accommodation here, but it's best to contact SERNAP in La Paz (see p.36 ) for the current situation if you don't have time to visit the office in San Borja. Alternatively, arrange a tour through one of the travel agencies in Rurrenabaque (see p.277) or Trinidad (see p.288).

# Trinidad and around

Close to the Río Mamoré, some 500km northwest of Santa Cruz, the city of **TRINIDAD** is the capital of the Beni and the commercial and administrative centre of a vast wilderness hinterland of swamp, forest and savanna where rivers remain the main means of transport and cattle-ranching is the biggest industry. Like most towns in the region, Trinidad was originally a Jesuit mission, but few signs of that past remain, and

**6**

## THE REAL EL DORADO?

Long before the Spaniards first arrived in the Americas, the Incas told stories of a mighty civilization in the watery plains to the east of the Andes. In the fifteenth century, the Inca **Yupanqui** sent a great army down one of the rivers of the Upper Amazon in search of this kingdom. Ravaged by the exigencies of the jungle, the depleted army finally met its match in the warlike Musu, or Moxos peoples, among whom the surviving Incas settled. Hearing tales of this mythical realm, known, variously, as **El Dorado** and **Paitití**, Spanish conquistador Gonzalo Pizarro led a huge expedition down into the Amazon in 1541. Though the gold dust of their fevered imaginings was nowhere to be found and the expedition ended – like so many others after it – in despair and death, Dominican friar **Gaspar de Carvajal** chronicled sightings of roads, riverbanks thronged with people, exquisite ceramics and, famously, "cities that glistened in white". While his reports were initially shelved and later disparaged, recent archeological discoveries look, centuries later, to be finally proving him right.

### THE ARCHEOLOGICAL EVIDENCE

Until about forty years ago archeologists doubted that any large, settled population could ever have survived in the Amazon Basin. The accepted wisdom was that the region's thin, **acidic soils** made intensive agriculture impossible, and that the area could support only small, scattered communities practising slash-and-burn agriculture along with hunting and gathering. But subsequent research has suggested that the forests and savannas of the **Llanos de Moxos** were in fact once densely populated by well-organized societies who, sometime between 3000 BC and 1000 BC, modified the environment on a massive scale to allow intensive agriculture and large urban settlements. The region is dotted with hundreds of raised earth mounds or hills, known as **lomas**, most of which are covered by forest. Seen from the ground, these mounds are hardly impressive, and were long thought to be merely the remnants of natural levees left by rivers as they meandered across the plain. But when archeologists looked at these mounds from the air, they realized they were far too extensive and regular to be natural.

Instead, they concluded that they were the remnants of a massive system of **earthworks** – including raised fields, canals, causeways, reservoirs, dykes and mounds stretching over hundreds of square kilometres – that could only have been built by a large and well-organized society. Excavations on some of the mounds revealed that they had been built up over many centuries. By cultivating these raised mounds, researchers believe the ancient inhabitants of the Moxos were able to overcome the problems of poor soil and seasonal flooding and drought, producing enough food to support a population density much greater than was previously believed possible in the Amazon. Moreover, further north in the Brazilian, once-Bolivian, territory of Acre, deforestation – together with the wonders of Google Earth – has revealed hundreds of **geoglyphs** of similar magnitude, while excavations of *terra preta*, or ultra-fertile soil cultivated by humans, seem to coincide with the locations of the riverside cities described by Carvajal.

These discoveries have enormous implications for both conservation and development in the Amazon. They suggest that, far from being a fragile natural environment, large areas of the Amazon are in fact **anthropogenic**, or man-made, ecosystems, modified by centuries of human activity and even now capable of supporting far larger populations than is currently the case.

### VISITING THE EARTHWORKS

Trinidad's Kenneth Lee museum (see p.287) is dedicated to this culture, and several earthworks lie within easy reach of the town, including at the Chuchini reserve (see p.287). For some background reading, pick up a copy of Charles C Mann's excellent book *1491: The Americas before Columbus*.

it's now a modern commercial city that's dominated by a vigorous cowboy culture and economy. Though you can organize excursions into the surrounding rainforest, Trinidad is a world removed from Rurrenabaque, with a distinct difference in atmosphere and much more conspicuous wealth. In addition, the streets are lined with open sewers which, while they may be necessary for drainage, emit a horrible stench (particularly at night), provide an ideal breeding ground for the mosquitoes that plague the town, and represent a dangerous obstacle for unwary pedestrians. The place is, however, the jumping-off point for an adventurous trip by cargo boat down the **Río Mamoré** to Guayaramerín on the Brazilian border, as well as to the smaller cattle-ranching town of **Santa Ana de Yacuma** and the bird-watching haven of the **Barba Azul Nature Reserve**. Trinidad also comes alive every June during the raucous **Santísima** (or Chope Piesta) celebrations.

**6**

## Brief history

Trinidad was founded in 1686 by **Father Cipriano Barace**, a pioneering Jesuit missionary who introduced the first cattle herds to the region. The town prospered under the Jesuits, but fell into rapid decline after their expulsion in 1767, with many of its indigenous inhabitants – drawn from several different tribes from the surrounding area but known collectively as the **Mojeños** – being dragged off to work as virtual slaves on plantations near Santa Cruz. The Mojeños were still strong enough to play an important role in the Independence War, when an indigenous government led by Pedro Ignacio Muiba was briefly established in Trinidad in 1810, before being ruthlessly crushed by a royalist army, which also stripped the town of its last valuable Jesuit ornaments.

### The rubber boom

With the advent of the **rubber boom** the town's population fell dramatically as thousands were forcibly recruited to work as rubber collectors in the forests to the north, while many others fled rather than face the same fate. In 1887, at the height of the rubber boom, the Mojeños launched their last uprising, a non-violent religious movement led by a messianic chief called Andrés Guayocho, who was said to be a great sorcerer and excellent ventriloquist. But the rebellion was swiftly and brutally put down by the Bolivian authorities, many of the survivors fled, and the town was left in the hands of non-indigenous merchants and landowners.

### The modern era

The region's **cattle economy** really developed in the second half of the twentieth century, when enterprising ranchers began cross-breeding the semi-wild cattle descended from the herds brought in by the Jesuits with sleek Xebu cattle brought in from Brazil. Until the road down from Santa Cruz was built in the 1970s, Trinidad was effectively cut off from the rest of Bolivia, and it remains an

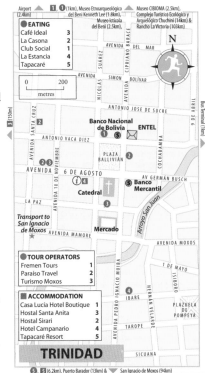

EATING
| Café Ideal | 3 |
| La Casona | 2 |
| Club Social | 1 |
| La Estancia | 4 |
| Tapacaré | 5 |

TOUR OPERATORS
| Fremen Tours | 1 |
| Paraíso Travel | 2 |
| Turismo Moxos | 3 |

ACCOMMODATION
| Casa Lucía Hotel Boutique | 1 |
| Hostal Santa Anita | 3 |
| Hostal Sirari | 2 |
| Hotel Campanario | 4 |
| Tapacaré Resort | 5 |

**TRINIDAD**

**6**

## INDIGENOUS PEOPLES OF THE BOLIVIAN AMAZON

The Bolivian Amazon is home to 29 indigenous peoples, each with their own distinct language and culture, ranging in size from the **Moxeños**, who number around 43,000, to groups like the **Araonas**, now reduced to no more than about a hundred people. While the combined population of these indigenous peoples is in the region of one million, this is a mere fraction of the population that lived here before the arrival of European diseases and the near-genocidal impact of the rubber boom, when huge numbers were enslaved and forced to work in appalling conditions. After centuries of external contact – with conquistadors, missionaries, rubber barons, soldiers, drug traffickers, anthropologists and now tourists – many of the indigenous people of the Amazon now speak Spanish and have adopted a fairly conventional Bolivian lifestyle, engaging in the market economy as workers and consumers and preferring rubber boots and football shirts to their traditional handmade costumes. However, many others still survive by hunting, fishing and cultivating manioc and other crops in small clearings in the forest, much as they have done for thousands of years, and rely for medicine on the powers of traditional healers and their encyclopedic knowledge of thousands of different rainforest plants. The most traditional indigenous groups are the uncontacted tribes – known as the **Nahuas** and **Toromonas** – small nomadic bands thought to be living deep in the rainforest who eschew all contact with Bolivian society.

### THE STRUGGLE FOR AUTONOMY

Largely dependent on the rainforest for their livelihoods, the indigenous peoples of the Bolivian Amazon were among the first to recognize the danger posed by the gathering pace of deforestation. In 1990 they staged the first of several "**Marches for Territory and Dignity**", walking 650km from Trinidad to La Paz to demand the recognition of their right to land and self-determination. This campaign drew international attention to their plight and led to new legislation and the recognition of large areas of the Beni as indigenous territorial reserves. While the 2005 election of Evo Morales brought further legislative successes, with the ratifying of indigenous rights to self-determination, self-government and financial management, the situation on the ground remains precarious, with Morales facing the uneasy contradictions of bolstering the rights of native people while developing the country's newly nationalized oil, gas and mineral reserves.

In May 2010, the region's indigenous groups declared themselves in a "state of emergency", demanding that the government protect them from oil, logging and mining companies, and speaking out against ongoing delays in the titling of indigenous lands. They also denounced corruption in governmental consultations with the Moxeño, Yuyucare and T'simane peoples of the **Parque Nacional y Reserva Indígena Isiboro-Sécure**, a beautiful wilderness region between the ríos Isiboro and Sécure, through which the Morales administration had approved the construction of a major road. After several indigenous protest marches on La Paz (violently suppressed by the government), in 2011 the movement scored a major victory when an act was passed effectively blocking any road construction (and the exploitation of forests for timber) in the national park without first consulting indigenous communities (the planned route has now changed, but as of 2017 remains a contentious issue).

More controversy arose when Evo Morales approved a Supreme Decree extending oil exploration into both **Parque Nacional Madidi** (see p.274) and the **Reserva de Biosfera y Territorio Indígena Pilon Lajas** (see p.275) in 2010. In response, the Bolivian Environmental Forum (aka FOBOMADE) launched the "Amazon Without Oil" campaign (ⓦ fobomade.org.bo). The government's plans for a major hydroelectric project (see p.274) in the region are equally controversial, and at the time of writing it showed little sign of backtracking.

isolated and somewhat inward-looking place, voluble in its right-wing opposition to the La Paz administration (the walls are plastered with anti-Evo Morales graffiti) and fiercely defensive of its *camba* (lowland) identity, though increasing numbers of migrants from the highlands have arrived in recent years. The ranchers – known as *ganaderos* – see themselves as rugged, self-reliant pioneers who have tamed a wild region and created prosperity with almost no help from central government (something particularly evident in the lack of support after the devastating floods of 2014).

## Plaza Ballivián

Though most of its buildings are modern, Trinidad maintains the classic layout of a Spanish colonial town, its streets set out in a neat grid pattern around a shady, well-maintained central square, the **Plaza Ballivián**, which the locals proudly insist is the biggest in Bolivia. On the south side of the plaza, the **Catedral de la Santísima Trinidad** is an unexceptional modern structure built between 1916 and 1931 on the site of the earlier Jesuit church. The buildings around the plaza, meanwhile, are all built with eaves overhanging the raised pavements.

**6**

## Museo Etnoarqueológico del Beni Kenneth Lee

Av Ganadera • Mon–Fri 9am–12.30pm & 2.30–6pm, Sat & Sun by appointment • Bs10 • ☎ 03 4624519

North along Avenida Cipriano Barace, some 1.8km from the centre of town, the illuminating **Museo Etnoarqueológico del Beni Kenneth Lee** focuses on the emerging research that suggests a mighty and sophisticated civilization existed in the Amazon basin between 3000 and 1000 BC (see box, p.284). The museum was the fruit of the labour of Kenneth Lee, a Texan engineer who visited the area for work and became impassioned by the Moxos peoples and their highly advanced hydro-agricultural systems of raised fields and earth mounds. Housed in a yellow, circular building, two rooms of ceramics, photos and storyboards outline the basic facts and findings, along with an impressive range of pottery, musical instruments and striking masks – the latter are elegant, stylized human faces rather than the supernatural extravagances favoured in the highlands. Although the museum hasn't been particularly well maintained in recent years, it remains an essential visit, especially if you're planning on heading out to visit some of the *lomas*.

## Museo Ictícola del Beni

Universidad Autónoma del Beni • Mon–Fri 7.30am–3pm • Free • ☎ 03 4621705

Around 2.5km north of the town centre, on the university's Dr Hernán Melgar Justiniano campus, the eerily atmospheric **Museo Ictícola del Beni** is a large room of basic design that houses one of South America's most important collections of aquatic life, preserved in a series of tanks and jars. Well worth a visit, it contains over four hundred samples of the weird and wonderful fish and snakes captured in rivers in Beni and Pando. At the head of the collection is the imposing piraiba – a huge specimen with numerous, sharp-looking teeth. The director of the museum is a font of knowledge, and is happy to show you round.

## Museo CIBIOMA

Universidad Autónoma del Beni • Mon–Fri 8am–noon & 2–6pm • Free, but donations welcome

On the university campus, a couple of minutes' walk from the Museo Ictícola del Beni, the newer **Museo CIBIOMA** has interesting displays on the plants, trees, birds and mammals you might encounter in the surrounding countryside, as well as the conservation efforts to protect them.

## Complejo Turístico Ecológico y Arquelógico Chuchini

14km northwest of Trinidad • Daily 8am–6pm • Bs20 • Guided half-day tours Bs100 (excluding transfers), one-day tours with accommodation, and board Bs600 (including transfers) • Transfers between Trinidad and Chuchini Bs100 one-way • ☎ 7284 2200, ⓦ chuchini.org

The highly recommended Bolivian–Swiss-run **Complejo Turístico Ecológico y Arqueológico Chuchini** is based on one of the 20,000 Moxos-built *lomas* (see box, p.284) that dot the Bolivian Amazon, just off the Río Ibare. Set on the edge of a glorious

**6**

lagoon, the reserve has a range of trails through the surrounding rainforest, which is home to toucans, monkeys, coatis and many other species. There's also a fascinating **museum** filled with exhibits from the Moxos culture and dinosaur fossils that have been found locally. Activities include cayman-spotting boat trips, guided walks, swimming and fishing. Although you can visit for the day, it's well worth staying overnight (or longer) to make the most of the place; accommodation is in clean and spacious en-suite rooms, while meals are tasty and copious. Volunteering opportunities are available too.

During the dry season, the reserve is accessible by road; in the rainy season, you can travel by boat via the port at Loma Suárez, a Moxos-built mound that was once the transport hub of the Suárez rubber empire (see box, p.296).

## Rancho La Victoria

103km northwest of Trinidad, a 2hr journey by car or a 15min flight • All-inclusive two-night trips Bs2000 • ☎ 7114 7183, Ⓦ rancholavictoria.net

For a taste of gaucho life, head north to **Rancho La Victoria**, a working cattle ranch run by the charming Gonzalez family. As well as the chance to ride horses and help milk the cows, guests can go canoeing, fishing and bird-watching. Jaguars also frequent the ranch, and you have a good chance of spotting them here.

### ARRIVAL AND DEPARTURE
### TRINIDAD AND AROUND

**By plane** The airport is 2km northwest of town and the busiest in the Bolivian Amazon; a moto-taxi into the centre costs around Bs10–12; regular taxis charge at least Bs25. Destinations Cobija (1 weekly; 1hr); Cochabamba (1–2 daily; 50min); Guayaramerín (5 weekly; 50min); La Paz (1–2 daily; 55min); Riberalta (1–2 daily; 50min); Rurrenabaque (3 weekly; 30min); Santa Cruz (6 weekly; 50min).

**By bus** Buses arrive at, and depart from, the Terminal Terrestre on Av Mendoza between Viador Pinto Saucedo and Beni, eight blocks east from the centre of town. Services from San Borja arrive just behind the terminal on Av Beni.

Destinations Guayaramerín (1–2 daily; 25–28hr); Rurrenabaque (1–3 daily; 20–30hr); San Ignacio de Moxos (3–4 daily; around 4hr); Santa Cruz (18–22 daily; 9–10hr).

**By truck** Trucks (*camionetas*) for San Ignacio de Moxos (1–2 daily; 3–4hr) arrive at, and depart from, 1 de Mayo near Velarde.

**By boat** Along the Río Mamoré arriving from, or departing for, Guayaramerín (2–3 weekly; 3–7 days) or Puerto Villarroel (2–3 weekly; 7 days), boats usually dock at Puerto Almacén, 9km southwest of Plaza Ballivián on the Río Ibare (a Mamoré tributary). Moto-taxis ply the 15min route back into town (around Bs25).

### GETTING AROUND

**By taxi** The easiest way to get around is by moto-taxi: they charge about Bs5 for journeys in the town centre, about Bs10–12 to or from the airport and around Bs25 to the river port. Regular (car) taxis are rare and charge at least Bs25 to/from the airport.

**Motorbike/bicycle rental** Motorbikes are available for rent on the plaza, and cost from around Bs15/hr or Bs120/ day, though you'll need to leave your passport as a deposit. Paraíso Travel (see below) rents out bicycles for Bs100/day.

### INFORMATION AND TOURS

#### TOURIST INFORMATION
The main municipal tourist office is at Felix Pinto Saucedo and Nicolás Suárez (Mon–Fri 8.30am–12.30pm, 2.30–6pm; ☎ 03 4621322, ✉ direccion.turismo@gmail .com). The local hotel association has a small, helpful office on Av 6 de Agosto, by *Hotel Campanario* (Mon–Fri 8.30am–12.30pm, 2.30–6pm; ☎ 03 4621141).

#### TOUR OPERATORS
**Fremen Tours** Av Ciprian Barace 332 ☎ 03 462 2276, Ⓦ andes-amazonia.com; map p.285. This agency

specializes in four-day/three-night cruises on the Mamoré aboard its floating hotel (or "floatel"), the *Reina de Enín*. Cruises (from $450/Bs3060 per person) feature visits to indigenous villages and Moxos-built *lomas* (see box, p.284), cayman spotting and more.

**Paraíso Travel** Av 6 de Agosto 138 ☎ 03 4620692, ✉ lyliamgonzalez@hotmail.com; map p.285. Well-run agency with excellent guides offering an array of trips in and around Trinidad, including bicycle tours (full-day tours Bs250) and rental (Bs100/day), and excursions to explore the nearby man-made *lomas* and waterways (see box, p.284).

**Turismo Moxos** Av 6 de Agosto 114 ☎ 03 4621141, ✉ moxosibc@hotmail.com; map p.285. Offers a variety of one- to three-day trips into the rainforest by motorized canoe along the Río Ibare, a tributary of the Mamoré, with plenty of opportunity for seeing wildlife (including pink dolphins) and visiting indigenous communities. Horseriding trips are also available.

## ACCOMMODATION

**Casa Lucía Hotel Boutique** El Palmar 32 ☎ 03 4620339, ⓦ facebook.com/CasaLuciaHotelBoutique; map p.285. Tranquil hotel a little out of the action to the north of the centre, with rooms furnished in a slightly quirky blend of Baroque antiques (wood beds, red-tile floors, rugs) and contemporary design (stripy painted walls, arty bedspreads). There's an appealing pool and the friendly owners also cook up great meals. Bs350

**Hostal Santa Anita** Antonio Vaca Díez 354 ☎ 03 4622257; map p.285. This family-run hostel has bright, capacious and spotlessly clean rooms, complete with private hammock and either fans or a/c, giving onto a slender, leafy patio, while masks and painted plant pots add some pizzazz. Bs180

**Hostal Sirari** Santa Cruz 526 ☎ 03 4624472, ✉ hsirari@hotmail.com; map p.285. Though they could do with a little sprucing up, the *Sirari*'s ageing, beamed-ceiling rooms complement what has to be the most verdant courtyard in Trinidad, with a trio of gorgeous toucans pottering about amid the foliage. The lower rooms also come with lovely white-painted, glass-panelled doors, while the upper rooms are more modern; a/c rooms cost around Bs40 extra. Bs170

**Hotel Campanario** Av 6 de Agosto 80 ☎ 03 4626501,

---

## TRAVELLING DOWN THE RÍO MAMORÉ

From Puerto Almacén, 9km southwest of Plaza Ballivián (a moto-taxi will take you for around Bs25), you can get a ride on the regular cargo boats that ply the waters of the **Río Mamoré**, either downstream to **Guayaramerín** on the Brazilian border or upstream as far as **Puerto Villarroel** in the Chapare (see p.227). In parts more than 3km wide, the mighty Mamoré – its name means "Great Mother" in Moxeño – was once one of the great waterways of the Bolivian Amazon and still sees a good deal of traffic. Canoes, barges and double-decker river boats ply its silt-laden waters, carrying supplies to the isolated communities along the riverbank, collecting cargoes of timber or bananas, and carrying cattle downstream to markets in Brazil.

Travelling this way is one of the classic Amazon experiences, and an excellent way to get a feel for the immense scale of the forest and the lifestyle of its inhabitants. The river boats glide through the forest at a languid pace, with plenty of opportunities for spotting **wildlife** along the way, particularly cayman, pink river dolphins and innumerable birds. Every so often the dense vegetation of the riverbank breaks to reveal a riverside settlement, usually no more than a cluster of thatched houses on stilts. For the villagers, isolated in the midst of this immense wilderness, the arrival of a boat can be the main event of the day, and if yours stops to load or unload cargo it's likely to be besieged by locals selling bananas or fish, or simply seeking the latest news and gossip from upriver.

### PRACTICALITIES

Boats depart up and down river two or three times a week, though when river levels fall in the **dry season** (May–Sept) the route south to Puerto Villarroel can be impassable. The trip downstream to Guayaramerín takes between three days and a week, depending on the level of the river, the size and power of the boat, whether it's equipped to travel by night, and how many stops it makes to load and unload cargo; upstream to Puerto Villarroel takes five to seven days. The trip downstream should cost Bs300–400 including basic meals, but be prepared to bargain; the longer trip upstream will probably cost slightly more. The **food** served on board the boats is usually pretty bland, consisting mainly of rice, plantains and *charque*, so it's worth taking along fresh fruit, snacks and maybe some tinned food. It's also essential to take your own drinking **water** or at least some purifiers. **Accommodation** on board is pretty basic; you'll need your own hammock to string up on deck as well as a mosquito net if the boat is likely to moor at night.

To check departure dates and arrange passage, you really have to take a **moto-taxi** to either port and speak directly with the boat captains. You may have to wait around a few days before getting a ride; some captains will let you sleep on board while awaiting departure.

ⓦhotel-campanario.com; map p.285. One of the smartest options – certainly the best hotel in the town centre – with spacious, modern a/c rooms and tiled floors, friendly staff, a small pool and an attached restaurant. Bs450

**Tapacaré Resort** 5km southeast of town ☎6936 9293,

ⓦtapacare.com; map p.285. On the banks of Laguna Suárez, in lush grounds, this resort is a peaceful place to stay, with spacious en suites, an outdoor pool, sauna, and a pair of restaurants (see below). A taxi to/from town costs around Bs40. $67 (Bs456)

## EATING

Try the **market**, two blocks south of the plaza, for *masaco*, a deep-fried mixture of mashed plantain or *yuca* and dried meat. Another local speciality is *pacumutu*, great chunks of meat and chicken marinated and grilled on a skewer. In addition to the options below, several of the hotels have good restaurants, including the *Campanario* (see opposite).

**Café Ideal** La Paz 93 ☎03 4621103, ⓦcafeideal.com .bo; map p.285. This coffee shop has a low-key charm, and as well as top *cortados* and *café con leches* (Bs5–15), there is an array of refreshing fresh juices, plus a selection of snacks. Mon–Fri 8am–noon & 2.30–7.30pm.

**La Casona** Plaza Ballivián ☎03 4622437; map p.285. As one of the few places on the plaza to offer outdoor seating, and to open right through the day, every day, this Trini institution is always busy, and a life-saver on Sunday evenings when everyone else has shut up shop. Along with the obligatory almuerzos, they also serve up relatively pricey (Bs50–90) steak, fried river fish and kebabs. Daily 8am–11pm/midnight.

**Club Social** Plaza Ballivián and Suárez; map p.285. A vast, elegant dining hall with a rather old-fashioned feel, serving up good-value, filling almuerzos and standard Bolivian dishes like *milanesa* (beef or chicken escalopes) and *pique macho* (mains Bs30–60). Daily 11am–2.30pm & 6–10pm.

**La Estancia** Ibare and Av Pedro Ignacio Muiba ☎03 4620022, ⓦfacebook.com/ChurrasqueriaLaEstancia; map p.285. The premier steakhouse in Trinidad, *La Estancia* offers prime cuts of barbecued meats in gut-busting portions. If there's two or more of you, go for the *parrillada*, a mixed grill accompanied by an array of sides (from Bs140). Mon & Wed–Sun 11am–3pm & 7–11.45pm.

**Tapacaré** 5km southeast of town ☎6936 9293, ⓦtapacare.com; map p.285. Based at the resort of the same name (see above), right on the banks of Laguna Suárez, a popular weekend destination for Trinidad residents, this restaurant is an atmospheric place for a meal. The menu focuses firmly on steak – try the succulent *bife de chorizo*. Expect to pay around Bs75 for a hearty meal. A taxi from town costs about Bs20. Mon–Sat 12.30–2.30pm & 6–10pm.

## DIRECTORY

**Banks and exchange** There are ATMs all over town, particularly around the plaza and Av 6 de Agosto. You'll find *cambios* on Av 6 de Agosto between Suárez and Av

18 de Noviembre.
**Post office** Just off the plaza on Av Cipriano Barace (Mon–Fri 8am–7.30pm, Sat 8am–6pm).

# Santa Ana de Yacuma

Few travellers make it to the small town of **SANTA ANA DE YACUMA**, 180km north of Trinidad, but those who do get a real slice of the cowboy lifestyle. Founded by the Jesuits in 1708, and later the birthplace of the notorious "king of cocaine" Roberto Suárez (see box, p.296), the town's focus is now firmly on cattle ranching. North of Santa Ana de Yacuma are scores of beautiful lakes, many of them linked by man-made canals (see box, p.284).

## ARRIVAL AND DEPARTURE
### SANTA ANA DE YACUMA

**By trufi** During the dry season, regular trufis (4hr) run between Trinidad and Santa Ana; it is also possible to charter a trufi to take you to the lakes north of town, though it will be far easier to organize a trip with a travel

agency in Trinidad (see p.288). Note that in the rainy season the town often floods and is only accessible by charter plane.

## ACCOMMODATION

**Hotel Mamoré** Av Roca Suárez ☎03 3378294. The pick of the town's handful of hotels, with comfortable a/c en suites, plenty of hammocks to lounge in, and a curvy

swimming pool to cool off in. It's around 600m southwest of the central Plaza Baltazar Espinoza, not far from the airstrip. Bs350

## Reserva Barba Azul

The **RESERVA BARBA AZUL** was established by conservation NGO Armonía in 2008 to protect the critically endangered blue-throated macaw. There are only 200 to 250 of the birds left in the wild, with around a hundred of these frequenting the reserve, alongside some 287 other avian species (the current record for the number of birds spotted in a single day in the reserve is an impressive 132). Spanning 110 square kilometres of savanna, palm-forested islands, marshes and rivers, the reserve is also home to jaguars, ocelots, wolves, giant anteaters and howler monkeys. The best time to visit is the May–September period, when the macaws are easiest to spot.

**6**

### ARRIVAL AND DEPARTURE                                      RESERVA BARBA AZUL

**By plane** The Barba Azul Nature Reserve is currently only accessible by plane, which sadly makes visits extremely expensive: an air taxi from Rurrenabaque or Trinidad (approximately 45min from either destination) costs around $1400 (Bs9520) return, with space for up to five people; return flights from Santa Ana de Yacuma (around 15min) costs about $600 (Bs4080), again for up to five people. Staff at the reserve can help to arrange this for you.

### ACCOMMODATION

**Barba Azul cabins** Inside the reserve ☎ 03 3568808, ⓦ armoniabolivia.org. There are four simple en-suite cabins, overlooking the Río Omi, in the reserve. The rates here are for a three-night package (the minimum stay), including full-board and daily boat rides/horseriding (but not transport to/from the reserve, which bumps the cost up significantly). Per person **$450 (Bs3060)**

# The northern Amazon

Now a remote economic backwater, just over a hundred years ago Bolivia's **northern Amazon** frontier was one of the most commercially desirable stretches of territory on earth. The region supports some of the richest natural rubber forests in the whole of the Amazon, and in the late nineteenth century a surge in international demand for rubber generated an unprecedented economic boom. Great fortunes were made by the so-called "rubber barons" who controlled production, but for the indigenous peoples of the Amazon the **rubber boom** was an unmitigated disaster. They were recruited by force to work collecting wild rubber under conditions of appalling brutality, and their population declined catastrophically. Little of the money made was reinvested, and when the boom ended in the early twentieth century with the establishment of rubber plantations in Asia, the region – and its main towns, agreeable **Riberalta** and Brazilian-flavoured **Guayaramerín** – slipped back into the economic torpor which characterizes it today, with collections of wild **Brazil nuts** (known as *castañas*) the main export industry. To the north of Guayaramerín, the small and sleepy town of **Cachuela Esperanza** provides an atmospheric insight into the days of the rubber boom.

## Riberalta

Set on a bluff above a great sweep of the Río Madre de Dios, just after its silt-laden waters are joined by those of the Río Beni, **RIBERALTA** is the second-biggest town in the Amazon lowlands (after Trinidad), with a population of around 80,000, largely employed in the processing and export of Brazil nuts. Riberalta's economic fortunes never really recovered from the collapse of the rubber boom; while its valuable rubber exports once circumnavigated the globe, it is now a net importer. Though there's little reason to stop here, there's a certain low-key charm about the place that makes it perhaps the most likeable of the Northern Amazon outposts.

## Plaza de Armas 3 de Febrero

At the heart of Riberalta lies **Plaza de Armas 3 de Febrero**, or just Plaza Principal, a huge swathe of greenery that attracts hundreds of locals every evening – this modern version of *el paseo* mostly takes place on the backs of motorcycles, which whole families ride around the plaza again and again (it's been dubbed the "Kawasaki derby"). The plaza recalls the official foundation of the city on February 3, 1894, with a statue of pioneer **Dr Antonio Vaca Díez** (1849–97) in the northeast corner (the province is named in his honour). The impressive **Catedral Nuestra Señora del Carmen** on the plaza is the largest church in the Bolivian Amazon, but though it has an attractive Spanish Missionary-style design, it's a relatively recent construction.

**6**

## Parque Mirador La Costanera

While the optimistically named **Parque Mirador La Costanera**, a couple of blocks north of the Plaza Principal, is really just a few square metres of weeds and broken rubble overlooking the Río Beni, it's worth sauntering down to its plank-less benches to witness the wholly surreal sight of an 1899 Scottish-built steamboat, the **Tahuamanu**, mounted in concrete; the first and last such craft to navigate the Bolivian Amazon, it served in both the Acre and Chaco wars (it looks a bit like the *African Queen*). The park also offers a magnificent sunset view: a molten-glass ferment best accompanied by a cold beer, if you can find one. At the weekend, you might have some luck at the adjacent **Club Náutico**, a curiously dated, lido-esque pool ringed by thatched shades and a bar, where you can also take a dip.

## Tumi Chucua

23km south of town (Rte-8), towards the Cobija road junction • A taxi costs around Bs180 return

A short drive south of town lies the lush, sinuous oxbow lake of **Tumi Chucua** (formed from the Río Beni), its centre filled by an oblong forested island and its shore lined with large, if increasingly dilapidated, timber houses home to controversial US evangelist group the **Summer Institute of Linguistics** between 1955 and 1985. There's a small jetty from which you can dive in, though the turbid waters are supposedly home to an anaconda; you may also be able to rent canoes from the locals. Sadly, if typically, the area around the jetty is littered with rubbish.

### ARRIVAL AND DEPARTURE                                                    RIBERALTA

**By plane** The tiny airport is about 1km south of town (around Bs5 on a moto-taxi, or 20min walk from Plaza Principal). At the time of writing the only direct scheduled flights were with Ecojet to Trinidad (1–2 daily; 50min), from where you can connect to destinations throughout Bolivia. An alternative is one of the daily *avionetas* (air taxis) that leave when they are full, which fly direct to Guayaramerín as well as Cobija; enquire at the airport.
**By bus** Buses arrive at, and depart from, the potholed terminal at the eastern edge of town, 2km from Plaza Principal

on the road to Guayaramerín (around Bs5 on a moto-taxi).
Destinations Cobija (2–4 daily; 12–16hr); Guayaramerín (5–6 daily; 2hr 30min–3hr); La Paz (1–2 daily; 35–40hr); Rurrenabaque (1–2 daily; 20–30hr); Trinidad (1 daily; 28hr).
**By boat** You can still find occasional boats heading up the Madre de Dios to Puerto Maldonado in Peru: departures are posted on a notice board outside the Capitanía del Puerto office at Puerto El Pila 1km east of town. Boats also occasionally travel up the Beni to Rurrenabaque when the road is closed during the rainy season (Nov–March).

### GETTING AROUND

**By moto-taxi** The principal mode of transport here; standard journeys in town cost around Bs5.
**Motorbike rental** Motorbikes are also available for rent a

block south of the plaza at Av Nicolás Suárez and Moreno (around Bs120/24hr), though you'll need to leave your passport as a deposit.

### INFORMATION AND TOURS

**Tourist information** There's no tourist information office, though the owners of *Hotel Jomali* (see p.294) are a good source of information, as is Riberalta Tours (Av Beni Mamoré 850; ☎ 03 8523475, ⓦ riberaltatours.com),

which offers trips to local Brazil nut factories as well as Tumi Chucua (see above) and, further afield, Cachuela Esperanza (see p.296) and the Reserva Manuripi (see p.299).

**6**

## ACCOMMODATION

★**Hotel Colonial** Plácido Méndez 745, just off the plaza ☎03 8523018, ⓦhotelcolonialriberalta .boliviafull.com. One of the nicest surprises in this part of the Bolivian Amazon, this tranquil hotel has whitewashed rooms hidden behind a curtain of tropical fronds. There's an elegant common area with a chess set and a library-calm hush, and an overflowing patio garden. **Bs280**

**Hotel Jomali** Av Nicolás Suárez, just off the plaza near Banco Ganadero ☎03 8522398, ⓦhoteljomali.com.

Homely, comfortable hotel run by a hospitable brother and sister team, with brightly painted, sprucely furnished and immaculately tidy pastel rooms (with fans or a/c) above a prepossessing courtyard scored with window boxes. **Bs270**

**Residencial Los Reyes** Sucre 781, between Oruro and Chuquisaca ☎03 8522628. If bolivianos are tight, try the pleasant *Residencial Los Reyes*, located near the airport. As well as simple rooms, there are hammocks in the garden courtyard, and free coffee and chilled drinking water. **Bs80**

## EATING AND DRINKING

**Club Social Progreso** Plaza Principal ☎03 8523024. Of all Beni's Clubes Sociales, this one – nearly a hundred years old – has by far the most ramshackle charm. Under ancient ceiling fans, amid rickety chairs and huge window shutters, the charming owners serve up inexpensive meals (Bs20–40), refreshing fruit juices and decent coffee. Daily 9am–10/11pm.

★**Restaurante Tropical** Oruro 632, eight blocks south of the plaza ☎7293 0188. If you can get past the trophy skins and armadillo shells, this is one of the region's most enjoyable restaurants, with a gregariously endearing owner and huge portions (easily enough for two; Bs50–110) of *pique a lo macho*, chicken curry and fried river fish. Mon–Sat noon–3pm & 7pm–midnight, Sun noon–3pm.

## DIRECTORY

**Banks and exchange** There are several ATMs around the plaza, most of which accept foreign credit/debit cards.

**Post office** The post office (Mon–Fri 8am–noon & 3–6.30pm, Sat 9am–noon) is on the Plaza Principal.

# Guayaramerín

Set on the banks of the Río Mamoré some 86km east of Riberalta, **GUAYARAMERÍN** is the main crossing point on Bolivia's northern border with Brazil, a modern and prosperous frontier town with a distinctly Brazilian flavour and a thriving economy based on duty-free sales. Many of the streets are lined with shops and boutiques selling perfume, electronic

---

### THE RAILWAY TO NOWHERE

Guayaramerín is the last navigable point on the **Río Mamoré**, the most important waterway in the Bolivian Amazon. Downstream from Guayaramerín a series of nineteen cataracts and **rapids**, stretching for over 400km down the ríos Mamoré and Madeira, cuts off the Bolivian river network from Brazil and access to the Atlantic Ocean. During the rubber boom, Bolivians and foreign speculators dreamed of bypassing these rapids and opening up the Bolivian Amazon to trade with the world. In 1872 the US journalist and speculator **George Church** formed a company to build a railway circumventing the rapids. Yet the crews sent to begin the work met with immediate disaster: their boats sank, and, ravaged by fever and Indian attacks, the workforce abandoned their equipment and fled through the forest. Church's company went bankrupt and the contractors concluded that the region was "a welter of putrefaction where men die like flies. Even with all the money in the world and half its population in it is impossible to finish this railway."

Church himself was undeterred, and by 1878 had raised enough financial support to launch another attempt, with equally disastrous consequences. By the time the project was abandoned three years later, five hundred workers had died but only 6km of track had been laid. But the dream of a railway around the rapids would not die. In 1903 **Brazil** promised to complete the project in compensation for the annexation of the Acre territory from Bolivia. Work began again in 1908, and three years later the Madeira–Mamoré Railway – or the **Devil's Railway**, as it had become known – was finally completed. More than six thousand workers are thought to have died in its construction, a sacrifice that was quickly shown to have been made in vain, since the railway opened for business just as the Amazon rubber boom collapsed. The Brazilian government kept it running until 1972, when it was finally abandoned, its rusting rails, swallowed by encroaching jungle, providing an eloquent testimony to a failed dream of progress in the Amazon.

**6**

## CROSSING THE BRAZILIAN BORDER

From the port at the bottom of Av Federico Román, regular passenger boats (daily 6am–6pm; every 30min; additional services 6pm–6am at irregular times; Bs10) make the 5min **crossing** to Guajará-Mirim in Brazil. The Bolivian *migración* (Mon–Fri 8am–8pm, Sat & Sun 8am–noon) is to the right of the port as you face the river: you should get an exit stamp here if you're continuing into Brazil but it's not necessary if you're just making a day-trip. **From Guajará-Mirim** there are frequent buses to Porto Velho, from where there are onward connections.

If you need a **visa**, go to the Brazilian Consulate (Mon–Fri 9am–noon & 3–5pm; ☏03 8553766) on the corner of calles Beni and 24 de Septiembre, four blocks south of the port. Note that to enter Brazil you need to have an international certificate of **yellow fever vaccination**; if you don't, there's a clinic beside the immigration office in Guajará-Mirim where you can get vaccinated.

goods and designer clothes to the thousands of Brazilian bargain-hunters who flock over the border on shopping trips. If you want more choice or a higher standard of accommodation and food, however, go to **Guajará-Mirim** across the river in Brazil.

### ARRIVAL AND DEPARTURE | GUAYARAMERÍN

**By plane** The primitive airport is just four blocks east of the plaza along 25 de Mayo. At the time of writing the only direct scheduled flights were with Ecojet to Trinidad (5 weekly; 50min). *Avionetas* (air taxis) serve other destinations on an ad-hoc basis; enquire at the airport.

**By bus** Buses arrive at, and depart from, the Terminal de Buses about 3km from the centre of town along Beni; a moto-taxi from here should cost about Bs5. Buses to Riberalta leave throughout the day; only in the dry season do services attempt the long journeys to Trinidad, Rurrenabaque and Cobija – the length of the journeys varies significantly due to road conditions.

Destinations Cobija (1–2 daily; 15–16hr); La Paz (1–2 daily; 32hr); Riberalta (5–6 daily; 2hr 30min–3hr); Rurrenabaque (1 daily; 26–48hr); Trinidad (1–2 daily; 25–28hr).

**By boat** Trinidad (2–3 weekly; 5–6 days); enquire at the Capitanía del Puerto office opposite the *migración* office (see box above) for forthcoming departures.

### GETTING AROUND

**By moto-taxi** The principal mode of transport; standard journeys in town cost Bs5; there's also a fleet of rickshaw taxis charging around Bs15.

**Motorbike rental** You can rent motorbikes on the southeast side of the plaza for Bs15/hr or Bs120/24hr, though you'll have to leave your passport as a deposit.

### INFORMATION AND TOURS

**Tourist information** There's no tourist office, but Mary Tours, on the north side of the main plaza (Oruro; ☏03 8553883, ✉mary-tours@hotmail.com), is a good source of information, and also runs trips to Cachuela Esperanza (see p.296).

### ACCOMMODATION

**Hotel Balneario San Carlos** Av 6 de Agosto 347, a block north and east from the plaza ☏03 8553555. The entrance is under a misplaced, nightclub-like awning yet minus a sign. This hotel boasts a/c rooms, an appealing swimming pool and some pretty *azulejo* tiles, though the garish pink and purple colour scheme may give you a headache. Bs350

**Hotel Santa Ana** Av 25 de Mayo 611 ☏03 8553900. As the sole salubrious option on this street, *Hotel Santa Ana*'s spotless, timber-ceilinged rooms are best booked in advance, thus avoiding the gaggle of hopefuls that routinely fill up reception after a flight. Relax in the cool courtyard garden instead, and look forward to some real granny-quality hospitality. Bs160

### EATING

**Antonella** Plaza Principal (northwest corner). Cute little snack bar and *heladería* with a green and yellow colour scheme, a cluster of alfresco tin tables, and a menu ranging from lasagne and empanadas (Bs10–30) to ice-cream sundaes and fruit salads. Daily 8am–11pm.

**Los Cocos** Huacaraje and Oruro ☏03 8554150. Inside a lavish, brick-walled compound, under robust hardwood beams, *Los Cocos* serves up what is widely regarded as the best food in town, with service to match. Prices are high (mains around Bs80), but portions are huge: dishes include the usual Amazonian standards – steaks, *surubí*, *chicharrón*. Don't miss the flagons of fresh peach juice. Daily noon–3pm & 6.30–11pm.

## DIRECTORY

**Banks and exchange** Cooperativa Jesús Nazareno (Mon–Fri 8.30am–12.30pm & 2.30–6pm, Sat 9am–12.30pm; ☎ 03 8553039), Mariscal Santa Cruz at Av 24 de Septiembre, on the northeast corner of the main plaza, has an ATM that should accept foreign cards, and you can also obtain a cash advance on a credit card and change both dollars and Brazilian reais. Prodem on Plaza Principal can also give cash advances on Visa and Mastercard.

**Post office** The post office (Mon–Fri 8am–noon & 2.30–6pm) is on Oruro, two blocks south of Plaza Principal.

## Cachuela Esperanza

From Guayaramerín a rough dirt road runs 42km northwest to the small town of **CACHUELA ESPERANZA**. Founded on the rapids of the Río Beni in the heart of the wilderness in 1882, this was once the headquarters of **Nicolás Suárez** (see box, below) and the most advanced town in the Bolivian Amazon, with modern offices and homes, state-of-the-art medical facilities, a theatre that attracted international stars and its own narrow-gauge railway. Though the long-decimated population has grown a little over the last decade, and a controversial $2.5 billion hydroelectric project has put it back in the media spotlight, Cachuela Esperanza remains a sleepy little backwater, for now at least.

Tragically, a major fire broke out here in September 2016, destroying many of the Canadian pine and brick houses, which had hitherto survived in remarkably good condition given their age and the ravages of heat and humidity. One of the few historic buildings to escape the blaze was the small, wooden clapboard **Capilla de Cachuela Esperanza**, built in 1909, that would look more at home in the American West than here in the Amazon. Close by stands the modest stone **tomb of Suárez**, with an inscription praising him as a "heroic patriot and eminent industrial progressive".

### ARRIVAL AND DEPARTURE                                 CACHUELA ESPERANZA

**By truck/car** Trucks and *autos* run between Guayaramerín and Cachuela Esperanza most of the day, leaving when full – ask a moto-taxi to take you to the *paradero* (truck stop) opposite the Palacio de la Cultura in Guayaramerín.

**By moto-taxi** Most moto-taxis in Guayeramerín will charge around Bs200 for a full day-trip; it takes around 1hr to reach Cachuela Esperanza.

# Pando

The northwestern-most tip of Bolivia is covered by the department of **Pando**, a remote and sparsely populated rainforest region where logging and the collection of wild rubber

### NICOLÁS SUÁREZ: RUBBER BARON

At the peak of his powers, **Nicolás Suárez Callaú** (1851–1940) was the absolute ruler over more than 60,000 square kilometres of rainforest where rubber was collected by a massive workforce of Caripuña Indians who were slaves in all but name. He also controlled the Beni rapids that separated the Bolivian river system from the Amazon proper (charging huge tolls for the transport of cargo around them) and even raised a private army to fight the separatist rebellion of Brazilian settlers in the northern territory of Acre in 1899. With the annexation of Acre by Brazil, however, he lost many of his rubber holdings, and after the collapse of the rubber boom in the 1920s his empire gradually disintegrated. He died in Cachuela Esperanza in 1940, and though virtually forgotten elsewhere in Bolivia, in the Beni and Pando he is still revered by some as a heroic pioneer who brought progress and civilization to the wilderness, the dire conditions of his workers who toiled in conditions little better than (and sometimes actual) slavery conveniently overlooked.

Ironically, decades later his great-nephew, **Roberto Suárez** (1932–2000), came to control a similarly powerful empire based on the export of another Amazonian product for which the industrialized world had developed an insatiable appetite: cocaine. Nicknamed the "King of Cocaine", he amassed a personal fortune so vast that in the 1980s he reputedly offered to pay off Bolivia's entire national debt of $3 billion.

**THE PANDO MASSACRE**

The events of September 11, 2008 proved just how dangerous standing up for your rights can be in the remote communities of Pando. In a now infamous incident near the settlement of Porvenir, described by the Union of South American Nations (UNASUR) as a crime against humanity, nineteen indigenous protestors were shot dead – and many more injured – by right-wing paramilitaries organized by the authorities of Pando prefect Leopoldo Fernández. After spending years under house arrest, Fernández was convicted and sentenced to fifteen years in prison in 2017. Many of his henchmen, however, have yet to be brought to justice; Amnesty International has reported that some of them are still walking around Cobija. One of the accused, ex-Pando senator Róger Pinto, lives in exile in Brazil after being allowed to escape via the Brazilian embassy in La Paz in 2013 – the Brazilian foreign minister resigned in the aftermath. In 2017 a Bolivian court convicted Pinto in absentia and sentenced him to five years in prison.

**6**

and Brazil nuts are the main economic activities. At one time Pando was accessible only by boat along the ríos Madre de Dios, Tahuamanu and Orthon, which flow into the region from Peru, but now a rough road cut through the rainforest runs from just south of Riberalta to **Cobija**, the departmental capital, on the Brazilian border. While the bus journey along this route is an adventure in itself, involving a short and somewhat surreal cruise along a tributary of the Madre de Dios, large swathes of land on both sides of the road have already been deforested, with blackened stumps of trees protruding like broken teeth from pale green pasture and scrubby secondary growth.

Though the southwest corner of Pando is covered by the **Reserva Nacional Amazónica Manuripi** (see p.299), the forests of much of this wild frontier region remain hotly disputed. The businessmen who control the collection of rubber and Brazil nuts, some of whom are descended from the nineteenth-century rubber barons, claim ownership rights over some thirty thousand square kilometres of forest – nearly half the department. But these claims are contested by the indigenous and campesino communities who collect the nuts and rubber – often working under a system of permanent debt so severe it amounts to a disguised form of slavery. While these communities have used land-rights legislation to demand that the forest be recognized as theirs, the political situation in the region remains volatile (see box, above).

# Cobija

Though its population of almost 60,000 is expanding rapidly, **COBIJA** remains an isolated yet thriving border town with a distinctly Brazilian flavour. Founded on the Río Acre in 1906 as a rubber collection centre, the town's economic fortunes now depend more on **duty-free** sales to Brazil and central government investment in infrastructure, part of a Pando-wide policy aimed at attracting settlers and establishing a human frontier to prevent a repeat of what happened across the border in the Brazilian state of Acre (see box p.310).

Most of the streets are well paved and the town boasts a modern airport out of all proportion to its needs, though with few obvious attractions and the highest rainfall in Bolivia, it's no surprise that few travellers make it here. Cobija does, however, offer an adventurous back route into Brazil and even Peru, and the chance to explore a rainforest region where tourism has yet to make an impact.

## ARRIVAL AND GETTING AROUND | COBIJA

**By plane** The modern Aeropuerto Capitán Aníbal Arab lies 5km from the centre, at the far end of Av 9 de Febrero; a moto-taxi costs around Bs10. For direct flights to Guayaramerín and Riberalta you'll need to take *avionetas* (air taxis); these can usually be arranged via your hotel. The flights below are all direct; for most destinations, there are several more connecting flights.

Destinations Cochabamba (1 weekly; 1hr 20min); La Paz (1–2 daily; 1hr 5min); Santa Cruz (2 weekly; 1hr 40min); Trinidad (1 weekly; 1hr).

**6**

## CROSSING TO BRAZIL AND PERU

### TO BRAZIL

The Bolivian immigration office (daily 8.30am–8.30pm) is on the main **border crossing**, the international bridge over the Río Acre at the end of Av Internacional. A taxi from the town centre across the bridge to the federal police office (where you'll need to clear immigration) in the Brazilian town of **Brasiléia** should cost about Bs40; otherwise it's a 20min walk. Note that you need an **international yellow-fever vaccination certificate** to enter Brazil. If you require a **visa**, go to the Brazilian Consulate (Av Rene Barrientos s/n; Mon–Fri 8.30am–1.30pm & 2–5pm; ☏ 03 8422110), just off the plaza in Cobija. From Brasiléia there are regular buses to Río Branco (4hr), from where you can get onward connections into the Brazilian Amazon, though note that Porto Velho is another 7–8hr.

### TO PERU

There's also an adventurous route into the Peruvian department of Madre de Dios from here. **From Brasiléia** you can get a bus to **Asis Brazil** (2hr), 95km west on the border with Peru, and cross over to the Peruvian settlement of **Iñapari**, from where a paved road (part of the Carretera Interoceánica) heads south to Puerto Maldonado, a route plied by frequent *colectivo* cars. Puerto Maldonado is linked by road and daily flights to Cuzco and Lima.

**By bus** Buses from Riberalta and beyond arrive at offices strung out along Av 9 de Febrero; the times below are the minimum – delays are not uncommon.
Destinations La Paz (1 daily; 48hr); Riberalta (2–4 daily; 12–16hr); Rurrenabaque (1 daily; 24hr).

**By moto-taxi** Though moto-taxis aren't as common in Cobija as elsewhere, they're still the cheapest and most convenient way to get around; most journeys cost around Bs5.

### ACCOMMODATION

**★El Dorado Suites Hotel** Av Internacional 583 ☏ 03 8422967, ⊛ dorado-hotel.com. One of the newer hotels in town is also the most comfortable choice, offering bright, stylish rooms (with a/c, fridges and TVs), a small pool, and a tranquil location right next to the border with Brazil. Bs300

**Hotel Asai** Saucedo 605, Km 3, Barrio Paz Zamora ☏ 03 8423903. Although it's a little way out of town, near the airport, this tempting knot of palm-thatched, hardwood, a/c *cabañas* will at least serve to remind you that you're in the tropics, with an orange-dirt path running between hammock-strung balconies and palms swaying at every corner. There's also a swimming pool and a restaurant. Bs350

### EATING

**Esquina de la Abuela** Av Fernández Molina 49, at Sucre ☏ 03 8422364. One of the most popular restaurants in Cobija, with friendly service and a cluster of pavement tables sheltered by palm-thatched eaves. Fish and steaks are in the Bs60 range, and don't miss the tropical-raspberry taste sensation that is their *acerola* juice. Daily noon–3pm & 6.30–10pm.

### DIRECTORY

**Banks and exchange** Banco Unión, at La Paz 42 on central Plaza Germán Busch (Mon–Fri 9am–5pm, Sat 9am–1pm), has an ATM, will change dollars and reais, and offers cash advances on credit cards.
**Post office** Plaza Germán Busch (Mon–Fri 8am–8pm & Sat till 3pm).

## Reserva Nacional de Vida Silvestre Amazónica Manuripi

Around 120km south of Cobija between the ríos Tahuamanu and Madre de Dios, almost 7500 square kilometres of some of Bolivia's most pristine lowland Amazon rainforest are protected, at least on paper, as the **Reserva Nacional de Vida Silvestre Amazónica Manuripi**. With financial help from Germany, the park's SERNAP-administered staff have, for several years, been working with the reserve's scattered campesino communities to promote the sustainable extraction of rubber and Brazil nuts, while improving social and working conditions. While there are long-standing aspirations to develop ecotourism, there's currently no real infrastructure in the reserve save for some very basic *cabañas* (Bs50) in the small village of **San Silvestre**, 120km

## THE MYSTERY OF COLONEL FAWCETT

The forests of the Bolivian Amazon have long attracted adventurers, eccentrics and explorers, but few have matched the exploits of **Colonel Percy Harrison Fawcett**. An officer in the British Indian Army, Fawcett first came to Bolivia in 1906 to survey the unmarked and largely unexplored wilderness frontiers between Bolivia and Peru and Brazil. Over the next nineteen years, he travelled the length and breadth of the Beni, keeping a diary which his brother Brian would later use as the basis for the iconic **Exploration Fawcett** (see p.325). First published in 1953, the book painted a vivid if, as some have speculated, somewhat embellished picture of life in the Amazon at the peak of the rubber boom. This was a time when "slavery, vice and bloodshed ruled supreme on the rivers", and during which the indigenous inhabitants – considered "wild and hostile savages" – were "as a rule…either shot on sight like dangerous animals or ruthlessly hunted down to be sent as slaves to rubber estates". Fawcett's own adventures involved frequent close encounters with 20m-long anacondas, ferocious cannibal tribes, virulent tropical diseases and brutal and corrupt officials. On one occasion he and a small exploration party found their canoe marooned on a sandbar in the **Río Heath** and surrounded by heavily armed Guarayos warriors. Realizing that to fight would be hopeless, Fawcett says he ordered his companions to sing, accompanied by an accordion. After a few verses of *A Bicycle Made for Two*, the previously hostile tribesmen were completely pacified.

### FROM MAN TO MYTH

In other respects a typical product of the British Empire, the longer Fawcett spent in the Amazon, the more he came to love the wilderness and sympathize with its inhabitants. Over the years he became convinced that somewhere hidden deep in the forest stood a magnificent city inhabited by an ancient and highly advanced race of white Indians. Condemned by many of his contemporaries as a mystic and a dreamer, in 1925 he set off to find this **mythical city** in the wilds of the Brazilian Amazon, and was never seen again. Since then, countless expeditions have gone in search of the colonel, while rumours concerning his possible end abound; according to David Grann's definitive book *Lost City of Z* (see p.325), the most likely scenario is that Fawcett – along with his son Jack – was murdered by one of the warlike tribes in the **Xingu region** of Brazil. The truth behind his disappearance has never been established conclusively, however, and his own fate has now become the kind of mystery that so entranced him when he was alive. As the archeological evidence continues to mount up, moreover, his core theory of an advanced Amazonian civilization looks more and more like the work of a visionary rather than a dreamer.

south of Cobija; you'll need to take all your own food and bedding. There are plenty of trails used by the *castañeros* during the Brazil nut-collecting season (Nov–Feb), however, and at least one specific walking route, a two-hour-plus trek from the tiny community of Curichon to Lago Bay, from where you can continue to Arroyo Malecón, near the Peruvian border. Lago Bay is also accessible via the motorized canoes (around $50) with which the guards patrol the river in search of illegal loggers. Before setting off, you'll need to give advance notice – ideally a couple of days – to the park office in Cobija.

### ARRIVAL AND INFORMATION
### RESERVA MANURIPI

**By truck/boat** Trucks depart for the small settlement (and main guard post) of San Silvestre (1–2 daily; 3–4hr) from the offices of Transbioceánica on Av 9 de Febrero in Cobija.

**Park office** James Horto 54, Cobija (Mon–Fri 8.30am–12.30pm & 2.30–6.30pm; ☎03 8423399). The staff will tell the park guards you're coming, and can arrange basic accommodation in the cabins.

### CROSSING THE PERUVIAN BORDER

From **San Silvestre**, irregular trucks continue south along the road through the reserve to Chivé on the Río Madre de Dios, where you may be able to catch a lift on a boat for an even more adventurous backdoor route upstream into Peru, or downstream to Riberalta. An exit stamp can usually be obtained from the Bolivian border post of Puerto Heath, though you'll probably have to go as far as Puerto Maldonado to sort out your entry into Peru.

BOLIVIAN PRESIDENT EVO MORALES

# Contexts

# History

Bolivia's first inhabitants were descendants of the nomadic hunting groups that migrated into the Americas from Asia during the last Ice Age (20,000 to 40,000 years ago). Having crossed the Bering Strait between Siberia and Alaska, when a bridge of land and ice linked the two continents, successive generations gradually migrated throughout the Americas, reaching the Andes at least 20,000 years ago, where they lived in semi-nomadic tribes, hunting prehistoric animals like mastodons and giant sloths.

At the end of the Ice Age (around 10,000 years ago) these species became extinct. During the same period, humans began the long, slow transition to an **agricultural society**. By about 2500 BC, agriculture and herding had become the main form of subsistence in the highlands and along the Pacific coast, though in the forested lowlands a semi-nomadic lifestyle combining hunting and fishing with limited cultivation remained the norm. As population density increased and agricultural techniques developed, social organizations grew more complex and governments and ceremonial religious centres began to emerge. By about 1800 BC, **pottery** was in widespread use, and primitive metal smelting developed soon after.

## Tiwanaku

The first major civilization to develop on the Bolivian Altiplano was the **Tiwanaku** (or Tiahuanaco) culture, centred on the city of the same name, which was located on the southern shores of Lake Titicaca. First founded around 1200 BC, by 100 BC Tiwanaku had become an important religious and urban centre with distinct classes of peasants, priests, warriors, artisans and aristocrats.

From around 700 AD Tiwanaku's influence dominated an area comprising much of modern Bolivia, southern Peru, northeast Argentina and northern Chile. At its height, Tiwanaku city was a sophisticated **urban ceremonial complex** with a population of over fifty thousand, lying at the centre of a vast empire of colonies and religious centres. Some time after 1000 AD, however, the Tiwanaku empire dramatically collapsed, its population dispersed and its great cities were abandoned. The reasons for this remain unclear: possible explanations include a cataclysmic earthquake or foreign invasion, though the most likely is **climate change** – from about 1000 AD, the region suffered a long-term decline in rainfall, suggesting that a prolonged drought may have wiped out the intensive agriculture on which Tiwanaku depended.

## The Aymaras

The Tiwanaku empire was succeeded by numerous much smaller regional states. The Altiplano around the shores of Lake Titicaca fell under the control of the **Aymaras**,

| Around 18000 BC | 1000 BC | 1000 AD |
|---|---|---|
| Bolivia's first inhabitants – descendants of Asian migrants who crossed the Bering Strait – appear. | The Tiwanaku culture becomes the first major civilization to develop on the Bolivian Altiplano. | The Tiwanaku empire collapses, and is replaced by many regional states, including the Aymara kingdoms. |

who probably migrated to the region from the highlands to the east sometime after the empire's collapse. Aymara society was radically different from that of Tiwanaku: Aymaras lived in fortified settlements (*pucaras*), relied on large-scale llama and alpaca herding rather than intensive cultivation, and followed a more localized religion, building few ceremonial sites other than the stone tombs (**chulpas**) where important individuals were buried. The basic unit of Aymara society was the **ayllu** – an extended kinship group – above which were powerful regional nobles, or *kurakas*, who held land independently from the *ayllus* over which they ruled; the *kurakas* were in turn subject to a warrior chief or king. Aymara territory was subdivided into at least seven militaristic kingdoms, of which the **Lupaca** and **Colla** were probably the largest and most powerful. Though centred overwhelmingly on the Altiplano, the Aymaras maintained colonies in different ecological regions to ensure access to a wide range of produce. As well as major livestock herders, the Aymaras were also important producers of gold and silver, which were found in abundance on the Altiplano, making it one of the wealthiest Andean regions.

## The Incas

By the mid-fifteenth century the Aymara kingdoms found themselves in growing competition with the **Incas**, an expansionist, Quechua-speaking people with their capital at Cusco in southern Peru. Despite their military power, the Aymara kingdoms proved incapable of uniting against this common threat and were gradually incorporated into the Inca empire. Initially, the Incas did little to alter Aymara society, contenting themselves with extracting tribute. In 1470, however, the main Aymara kingdoms around Lake Titicaca rose in revolt, prompting the Incas to dispatch a great army from Cusco to crush the rebellion.

Thereafter, the Incas reinforced their control of the Altiplano, building roads, storehouses and fortresses, and incorporating the region into their domains as the **Collasuyo**, one of the richest and most populous of the empire's four quarters, or **suyus**. Aymara rulers were permitted to remain in place, though with limited autonomy; they were also required to send their young nobles to Cusco both to serve as hostages and be indoctrinated. A different system of government was used in the fertile inter-Andean valleys east of the Altiplano, where the Incas established military-agricultural colonies of loyal Quechua-speakers, known as **mitamaqs**. These guaranteed Inca control of this rich, temperate region and protected the southeastern frontier of the empire against raids by semi-nomadic peoples from the Eastern Lowlands.

With the conquest of the Collasuyo the Incas confirmed their status as the most powerful Andean empire since Tiwanaku, with which they consciously sought to associate themselves, claiming their founding ancestor, Manco Capac, had been brought into being on the Isla del Sol in Lake Titicaca, the Andean world's sacred centre where it was believed the sun itself had been created. Within a century, the Incas had become masters of the greatest empire yet seen in the Americas – an empire stretching over 5000km from southern Colombia to northern Chile, boasting a population of perhaps twenty million.

Quite how this great empire would have developed, however, will never be known. Within eighty years of their conquest of the Altiplano, the Inca empire was brought

| **Mid-1400s** | **1470** | **1532** |
| --- | --- | --- |
| The Aymara kingdoms are gradually incorporated into the expansionist Inca empire. | An Aymara revolt around Lake Titicaca is crushed. The Incas become the most powerful Andean empire. | A small band of Spanish conquistadors defeat Atahualpa's army at Cajamarca, Peru. |

## THE POWER OF INCA RULE IN THE ANDES

The Inca empire combined authoritarian government with rational and egalitarian social and economic organizations, a unique system that has been described as "**theocratic communism**". Though the powerful Inca armies played a key role in the empire's expansion, many regional groups submitted voluntarily. Conquered peoples were required to accept the official state religion – which saw the Inca ruler as the direct representative of the sun god Inti – but beyond that they were also allowed to maintain their own religious and cultural practices.

Local rulers who surrendered voluntarily were often allowed to remain in place, while the Andean peasantry was left to work the land in return for supplying tribute either in the form of produce or labour service (**mita**). The enormous food surplus created by this system was used to feed standing armies and the ruling Inca elite of priests, administrators and nobles, as well as providing insurance against crop failure and famine for the peasantry themselves. The labour service was used to construct a massive network of roads, monumental palaces and temples, and sophisticated agricultural terracing and irrigation systems.

As well as this civil engineering, the genius of the Incas lay in their **administrative bureaucracy**, which succeeded in controlling the movements of goods and people to an astonishing degree, despite having no written language, creating a level of prosperity, wellbeing and security that the people of the Andes have probably never seen matched before or since.

to a catastrophic end by a small band of Spaniards led by **Francisco Pizarro**, who landed on the coast of northern Peru.

# The Spanish conquest

From the Incas' point of view, the arrival of the first conquistadors in 1532 could not have come at a worse time. Just five years before, the empire had been swept by a devastating epidemic – probably smallpox, introduced to the Americas by Spanish conquistadors. Almost a third of the population are thought to have died, including the ruling Inca, **Huayna Capac**, who left his empire divided between two of his sons: his favourite, **Atahualpa**, who had established himself at Quito in what is now Ecuador, and **Huascar**, the legitimate heir to the throne, who was based in Cusco. A bloody civil war broke out, from which Atahualpa emerged victorious.

Atahualpa retired to Cajamarca in northern Peru to savour his victory. It was here that he heard of the arrival of strange bearded foreigners on the coast nearby. At the first decisive encounter between the two, Pizarro and his 170 followers kidnapped Atahualpa and massacred thousands of his men, demonstrating their overwhelming military superiority: mounted on horseback (an animal never previously seen in South America), with **steel weapons and armour**, and backed by terrifying cannons, the conquistadors were virtually invincible, and even small bands proved capable of defeating massive indigenous armies. Atahualpa was ransomed for a fabulous hoard of gold and silver and then treacherously killed, though not before sending orders for Huascar to be **executed**. Huascar's faction in Cusco initially welcomed the Spaniards, if not quite as liberators then at least as useful mercenaries who had defeated their enemy just as all seemed lost. With large areas of the Inca empire only recently conquered and not yet fully assimilated, the Spaniards also found indigenous allies among the subject tribes. They occupied Cusco without a fight and installed **Manco Inca** as a puppet emperor.

| 1533 | 1537 | 1538–40 |
| --- | --- | --- |
| Atahualpa is killed. The Spanish install Manco Inca as a puppet emperor. | An Inca rebellion is brutally put down as the Spanish conquer the whole of Alto Peru. | La Plata (now Sucre) is the first Spanish city founded in Alto Peru. |

### Manco Inca rebels

Following this military success, **Diego de Almagro** led the first Spanish expedition south into the Altiplano, reaching as far as present-day Chile. However, in 1537, Spanish abuses in Cusco and the realization that they were bent on permanent conquest prompted a massive Inca rebellion led by Manco Inca himself. After a series of bloody battles, the Spanish military conquest of the **Collasuyo** – which they referred to variously as Charcas, the Collao or, most commonly, **Alto Peru** – was swiftly completed.

With its dense indigenous population and rich mineral wealth, Alto Peru offered a rich prize, though initial efforts to consolidate control of the region were delayed by an outbreak of fighting between rival Spanish factions, an episode in which more Spaniards were killed than in all the fighting with the Incas. The full extent of the region's potential became apparent in 1545, when South America's richest silver deposit was discovered southwest of La Plata at what became known as Cerro Rico (see p.162).

### Spanish settlement

The first Spanish city founded in Alto Peru was **La Plata** (now Sucre), strategically located in a temperate valley southeast of the Altiplano. A second city, **La Paz**, was founded in 1548 just east of Lake Titicaca to reinforce control of the densely populated northern Altiplano and secure the route between the Potosí mines and Lima, the centre of Spanish power on the Pacific coast of Peru. Further cities at **Cochabamba** and **Tarija** followed (both in 1574), strategically located in the well-populated, fertile and temperate inter-Andean valleys, where maize and crops introduced from Europe could be grown to supply food to Potosí. La Plata was confirmed as the **capital** of Alto Peru in 1558, when it was made the seat of an independent royal court and administration – the Audiencia de Charcas – with judicial and executive power over the entire region.

Like the Incas, the Spanish were initially only able to establish control over the highlands; the semi-nomadic peoples of the Amazon lowlands and eastern plains remained unconquered despite numerous military expeditions. In 1561 the city of **Santa Cruz de la Sierra** was founded in the midst of the eastern lowlands by a group of conquistadors who had marched across from Paraguay, the centre of Spanish power on the Atlantic side of South America. Their aim was to reach the silver of the Andes and establish a strategic link across the continent, but the new settlement remained isolated, precarious and surrounded by hostile indigenous groups.

## Colonial society

Initially, the Spanish sought to continue the Inca system of control through indirect rule. Colonial society was conceived of as consisting of two separate communities, the Spanish and the **Republica de Indios**. A class of indigenous nobles – **kurakas** or **caciques** – was left in place to act as intermediaries between the Spanish and the mass of Aymara- and Quechua-speaking peasants, who were permitted to remain in control of their land in return for tribute in the form of produce and labour service. These peasants were administered through the exploitative **encomienda** system, whereby individual conquistadors were granted control of the tribute paid by large indigenous

| 1545 | 1548 | 1558 |
|---|---|---|
| The world's largest silver deposits are discovered near Potosí. | The city of La Paz is founded. | La Plata becomes the capital of Alto Peru. |

groups in return for taking charge of converting them to **Catholicism** and generally "civilizing" them – the standard moral justification for the Spanish conquest.

In the highlands, the strict boundaries the Spaniards had erected between themselves and the indigenous majority quickly broke down. The conquistadors were overwhelmingly men, and most took indigenous wives and concubines: soon they were surrounded by an ever-increasing number of mixed-race children – known as **mestizos** (or *cholos*). A complex system of class and caste developed, with Spanish-born *peninsulares* on top, followed by Spaniards born in the Americas – criollos. The middle orders comprised several different mestizo classes, while at the bottom was the indigenous majority.

The initial colonial settlement was undermined by the catastrophic decline in the indigenous population caused by **European epidemics** and diseases, as well as by the harsh burden of the *encomienda* system. With the indigenous tribute base falling each year and the supply of labour for the mines in decline, and fearing that the *encomenderos* were becoming over-powerful, in the 1570s the representative of the Spanish king in Peru, the Viceroy **Francisco Toledo**, launched a major reform of the empire's social and economic structures (see box, p.306).

## The Great Rebellion

Indigenous resistance to Spanish rule continued throughout the colonial period. Generally revolts were local in nature, and usually easily crushed. In 1780–82, however, the Andes were swept by a massive indigenous rebellion that shook the Spanish colonial regime to its foundations. This so-called **Great Rebellion** encompassed the southern Peruvian highlands

### THE SPIRITUAL CONQUEST OF ALTO PERU

The need for a **spiritual conquest** to reinforce its successful military conquest of Alto Peru was taken seriously by the Spanish Crown, which sponsored all the major religious orders to undertake the conversion of the Aymara and Quechua masses. Inca religious ceremonies, pilgrimages and public rituals were banned, idols and ceremonial sites destroyed. Beneath the surface, however, their mystical and magical appeal endured and, while publicly accepting **Christianity**, the indigenous population preserved its own deep-rooted **pre-Inca cults**. In time, elements of Catholicism and traditional beliefs intermingled, as the Aymaras and Quechuas appropriated the symbolism of the Christian faith, turning it into a vehicle for their own religious expression.

The religious orders were also employed as a cheap means of pacifying the **tribes** of the northern and eastern lowlands, who had resisted conquest. Small groups of missionaries had considerable success in drawing semi-nomadic groups into settled agricultural communities, where they were converted to Catholicism and enjoyed the mixed benefits of Spanish civilization – as well as, most importantly, being protected from the ravages of the conquistadors. However, the regime of forced labour and the constant epidemics that swept the settlements meant many groups later abandoned or rebelled against the mission regimes, and many missionary priests met violent deaths. Missionary efforts reached their apogee in the seventeenth and eighteenth centuries in the **Jesuit missions** of Moxos and Chiquitos, where a handful of priests established a utopian, semi-autonomous society. Here thousands of indigenous people successfully adopted European agricultural techniques and built flourishing communities graced by some of the finest churches in all the Americas.

| **1561** | **1570s** | **1572** |
|---|---|---|
| The city of Santa Cruz de la Sierra is founded. | Viceroy Toledo launches a major reform programme of the empire's economic and social structures. | The last ruling Inca, Túpac Amaru, is executed by the Spanish. |

## THE HUMAN TOLL OF TOLEDO'S REFORMS

During the 1570s the reforms of **Viceroy Francisco Toledo**, the Spanish king's representative in Peru, had a dramatic impact on what is now Bolivia. The **encomiendas** were gradually phased out, and the indigenous population moved into large communities (**reducciones**), where tribute payments could be more easily collected. To address the labour shortages in the Potosí mines, Toledo revived the Inca system of labour service, the **mita**. Under this regime, an area stretching from Cusco to northern Argentina was divided into sixteen districts, each of which had to send one-seventh of its male population to the mines each year. Among Toledo's other reforms was the establishment of a royal mint to ensure the Crown received its share of mining revenues. These reforms launched a century-long boom that turned Potosí into the most important source of wealth in the Spanish empire. For the indigenous population, however, the *mita* labour system was a catastrophe. Of the thousands of **mitayos** who went to the mines each year, only a few ever returned to their home communities: up to nine million indigenous workers and African slaves died in the mines.

and Alto Peru. It was in part provoked by the **Bourbon reforms**, a tightening of the tribute system aimed at centralizing administration and boosting royal revenues, which had declined substantially during a long period of economic depression (caused by a decline in silver production) in the late seventeenth and early eighteenth centuries.

### The revival of the Inca kings

Above all, though, the rebellion was inspired by the Andean belief that a **reincarnated Inca king** would return to drive out the Spanish. The uprising's leading figure was José Gabriel Condorcanqui, an indigenous *kuraka* who in November 1780 declared himself the direct descendant of the last ruling Inca (Túpac Amaru, who had been executed in 1572) and rightful Inca king of Peru, adopting the name **Túpac Amaru II**. Raising a large indigenous army and slaughtering a Spanish force, he seized control of most of the southern Peruvian highlands and laid siege to Cusco for several months. Though Túpac Amaru himself was subsequently captured and killed, his nephews continued the rebellion around Lake Titicaca. Here, they formed an uneasy alliance with Aymara forces led by the radical Julian Apaza, who adopted the name **Túpac Katari**.

Though they joined forces to lay siege to La Paz, however, the two movements were fatally divided by ideology and **factionalism**. While the moderate Túpac Amarus sought to form a broad-based, rebel coalition – including mestizos and even white criollos – Túpac Katari and his followers were extreme Aymara nationalists intent on killing all whites and completely erasing Spanish rule. Several powerful indigenous **kurakas** rejected the revolutionary message altogether and sided against the rebels, leading large indigenous forces to fight on the Spanish side. The war was characterized throughout by great brutality on both sides: in two years, about one hundred thousand people were killed.

In October 1781, La Paz was relieved by a royalist army from Argentina. The Túpac Amaru leaders surrendered in return for pardons or exile, while Túpac Katari was captured and executed. By early 1782, the rebellion had been comprehensively crushed, and the indigenous nobility destroyed. Thus ended the last major **indigenous uprising** against Spanish rule in the Andes.

| 1780–82 | 1808 | 1809 |
| --- | --- | --- |
| The Great Rebellion against Spanish rule takes place and is eventually crushed. | After Napoleon's invasion, the Spanish government collapses, which inspires independence movements across the Spanish empire. | Open revolt by the criollos and mestizos. La Paz declares independence. The Spanish thwart revolts but still lose control of several rural areas. |

# The Independence War

By the early nineteenth century, growing discontent with **Spanish rule** had spread among the white criollo and mestizo population of Alto Peru, the result of severe economic depression, their exclusion from high-level administrative jobs (which were reserved for Spanish-born immigrants), and regulations preventing trade with any country other than Spain. At the same time the powerful ideas of the French Revolution and the Enlightenment, as well as the successful revolt in North America, made independence from Spain seem more realistic. However, the **Great Rebellion** had left the white criollo and mestizo population with an abiding fear of disorder and indigenous revolt, so it wasn't until the sudden collapse of the government in Spain, following Napoleon's invasion in 1808, that the impetus for revolutionary change arrived.

With Napoleon's brother **Joseph** crowned king of Spain, a radical "Junta Central" claiming authority in the name of the abdicated Fernando VII, and supporters of Fernando's sister Carlota's claim to the throne, the elite classes throughout the **Spanish empire** were confronted with conflicting loyalties. Surprisingly, it was in Alto Peru that the first moves towards open revolt against Spanish rule took place. On May 25, 1809, the judges of the **Audiencia de Charcas** refused to recognize the authority of the Junta Central, arguing that the colonies owed loyalty to the person of the king (now abdicated) rather than to Spain. This effective declaration of independence, known as the **Primer Grito Libertario**, was the first in Latin America. In July, the citizens of **La Paz** declared an independent government. These revolts were put down, but this only fuelled the growing criollo enthusiasm for independence. Though Spain controlled the main cities, pro-independence guerrilla forces quickly established control of six rural areas that became known as **Republiquetas**.

## Argentina attacks

In May 1810, the citizens of Buenos Aires successfully rebelled against Spain, and the same year sent an army to drive the Spanish from Alto Peru. Supported by the Republiquetas and revolts in several cities, the **Argentine army** liberated the whole region before being routed by a Spanish force from Cusco. Over the next seven years three further Argentine armies were sent to Alto Peru, but each failed to permanently drive out the Spanish forces. Most major cities changed hands and were sacked several times, with the retreating Argentine armies showing the same contempt for local citizens as the Spanish. The forces unleashed by the independence struggle proved difficult to control, as both sides came to rely more and more on arming the **indigenous population** to provide troops, which led to growing violence and social conflict.

Though it was the first South American region to declare independence from Spain, Alto Peru was the last to achieve it. In 1817 the Argentine **General José de San Martín** liberated Chile, and by 1821 the great Venezuelan independence leader **Simón Bolívar** – **El Libertador** – was advancing south through Ecuador, having finally freed Venezuela and Colombia. The two forces converged on Peru: Lima was occupied and, in 1824, Bolívar's general, **General Antonio José de Sucre**, destroyed the last Spanish army at Ayacucho in the southern Peruvian Andes, securing Alto Peru's freedom early the following year.

Despite its new freedom, **Alto Peru**'s fate remained uncertain. Bolívar initially opposed the creation of an independent state there, and handed control of the region to General Sucre. In 1825, Sucre called a constituent assembly in the city

**1810**

Buenos Aires rebels against Spain, and repeatedly sends in the army to fight the Spanish in Alto Peru.

**1825**

Bolivia becomes the final South American country to win independence. General Sucre is made first president.

that would later be renamed in his honour. The delegates unanimously rejected union with Peru or Argentina, and on August 6 adopted a **declaration of independence**. Five days later they resolved to name the new republic **Bolivia**, rightly guessing Bolívar would be less likely to obstruct the independence of a country named in his honour.

## The early republic

The new Republic of Bolivia faced enormous problems from the outset. Sixteen years of **war** had devastated the country's infrastructure and economy: the mining industry in particular was in sharp decline, thanks to a scarcity of labour and the damage to the mines that had taken place during the conflict. Nor did independence change much for the vast majority of the population – the indigenous Aymara and Quechua campesinos – who remained excluded from power, which was exercised by a narrow ruling elite of mostly white **criollos**. Though the **mita** system had been abolished by Bolívar, a head tax levied on indigenous community members was maintained, generating over half of all government income.

The country's first president, **General Sucre**, sought to organize the state along classic liberal lines, but his efforts to introduce a modern tax system were frustrated by the lack of a trained bureaucracy, and he struggled to attract foreign capital to revitalize the mining sector. His one major success was confiscating most of the **Catholic Church's wealth** and property, a revolutionary act from which it never really recovered. After surviving a coup and assassination attempt, he left office in 1829 and went into voluntary exile (only to be killed a year later in Ecuador).

Sucre's liberal and reformist policies were maintained by his successor, **General Andrés de Santa Cruz**. During his ten-year rule Santa Cruz created a relatively stable political and economic order. Though he ruled as a dictator he kept bloodshed to a minimum by contemporary standards, but was also unable to revitalize the economy. His downfall followed his involvement in politics in neighbouring Peru, where he had served briefly as president in 1826–27. In 1835 he intervened decisively in Peru's civil war, defeating arch rival Peruvian **General Agustín Gamarra**. He then sought to join Bolivia and Peru together in a confederation, a move seen as a threat by Chile, which sent forces into Peru. In 1839, Santa Cruz was finally defeated by Chile, and the Peru–Bolivia confederation was dissolved.

### The rise of the *caudillos*

For the next forty years Bolivia was characterized by political chaos, presided over by a series of *caudillos* (military strongmen). **General José Ballivián** (1841–47) defeated **General Gamarra** at the battle of Ingavi, ending the entanglement of Peru and Bolivia's affairs. He also reduced the size of the army and established the department of the Beni, sending military colonies to the Amazon lowlands where Cinchona bark – from which quinine is extracted – emerged as a major export. **General Manuel Isidoro Belzu** (1848–55), who took power a year after Ballivián was overthrown, was a populist demagogue. After surviving over forty coup attempts in just seven years, he handed over power peacefully in 1855 in Bolivia's **first legal elections** (although only 13,000 people were allowed to vote) and went into exile.

| 1829 | 1835 | 1855 |
|------|------|------|
| After surviving an assassination attempt and a coup, Sucre leaves office and goes into voluntary exile. He is replaced by General Andrés de Santa Cruz. | Moves to form a confederation with Peru are thwarted by Chile. | The country's first civilian president, José María Linares, is elected. |

Bolivia's first civilian president was **José María Linares** (1857–61), though even he assumed dictatorial powers. Linares opened the country to free trade and foreign investment, but was unable to control the military and was ousted within four years and replaced by **General José María Achá** (1861–64). Achá's regime was the most violent of Bolivia's nineteenth-century governments, but even his notoriety was exceeded by that of his successor, **General Mariano Melgarejo** (1864–71), the archetypal Bolivian *caudillo*, famous for his violence, drunkenness, womanizing and corruption – as well as for signing away a vast area of the Amazon lowlands and Pacific coast to Brazil and Chile. Though his hold on power proved resilient, he was overthrown in 1871 and killed a year later in Lima.

Surprisingly, the endless succession of military coups, plots and revolts that characterized the early decades of the republic caused relatively little social and economic disruption. During the middle of the century, the nation's economy actually began to improve, thanks to the silver-mining industry's revival. From 1870 the growth of **silver production** was phenomenal, and an influential new class of mine owners emerged.

## The War of the Pacific and the age of silver

As well as silver exports, economic growth in the second half of the nineteenth century was also spurred by the export of **guano** and **nitrates** (both used as fertilizer) found on Bolivia's coastal strip. In 1878, President Hilarión Daza, the latest military *caudillo*, increased export taxes, ignoring protests by Chilean and British companies – who controlled the nitrates industry – and offering Chile the excuse to pursue its long-standing expansionist aims. Early the next year Chilean forces began the **War of the Pacific**, occupying the entire Bolivian coastline and then invading Peru, which was allied to Bolivia. Bolivian forces sent to fight alongside the Peruvians were easily defeated, and Bolivia watched helplessly as its coastline was annexed and its ally Peru defeated and occupied. Though Bolivia officially ceded the territory to Chile in 1904, the loss of the coast was seen as a **national tragedy**. Ever since, Bolivian politicians have invoked this loss as a means of cementing national identity.

Having witnessed an incompetent military regime stumble into a conflict that disrupted their exports and damaged relations with Chilean investors, Bolivia's new silver-mining elite realized that a stable, financially sound government was vital to their interests. The mining entrepreneurs formed a new party, the **Partido Conservador**, which ruled Bolivia for the next nineteen years. They were opposed by the **Partido Liberal**, initially formed by those against an early settlement with Chile, but otherwise differing little in ideology. Between 1880 and 1936, the parliamentary system worked fairly well, despite the limited nature of the electorate (a tiny handful of men) and the fact that neither party was ever prepared to relinquish the presidency when voted out of office, ensuring that limited violence remained a feature of Bolivian political life.

The high point of conservative rule came during the presidency of **Aniceto Arce** (1888–92), a major silver-mine owner who completed the railway from La Paz to the Chilean port of Antofagasta, Bolivia's first rail link to the sea and a vital route for mining exports. The expansion of the mining industry and transport infrastructure had a strong impact on rural Bolivia. The growing demand for food in the mining centres of Potosí and Oruro stimulated the expansion of the **hacienda system**, with

| 1870 | 1879 | Late 1800s |
|---|---|---|
| Silver mining starts to grow phenomenally, creating a wealthy new elite. | Bolivia loses its entire coastline to Chile in the War of the Pacific. | As silver prices plunge, a tin boom begins. Powerful tin barons emerge. |

## THE RUBBER BOOM

The late nineteenth century saw the explosion of the **rubber boom** in Bolivia's Amazon lowlands. The massive increase in the international demand for rubber transformed the remote rainforests of northern Bolivia into some of the most valuable real estate in the world, and the region was quickly overrun by **rubber barons**, who made immense fortunes and forced the region's previously unconquered tribes to work as virtual slaves. The **indigenous population** declined catastrophically and was saved from total destruction only by the end of the rubber boom in the early twentieth century, after rubber plantations had been successfully established by the British and Dutch in their **Asian colonies**, where production costs were much lower. One consequence of the boom was the occupation of the richest rubber-producing area along the **Río Acre** by Brazilian rubber-tappers. When the Bolivian government sought to tax their production they rebelled, declaring the Acre an independent state in 1900. After three years of sporadic fighting – the **Acre War** – the region was annexed by Brazil, an act later recognized by Bolivia in return for compensation.

hacienda-owners acquiring indigenous land through purchase, fraud or outright force. Though some communities maintained their traditional social and political structures, many others broke down, and migration to the cities and mining centres increased.

## The Federal Revolution and the rise of tin

Its dependence on mining exports made Bolivia increasingly subject to international economic forces, and towards the end of the nineteenth century the international price of silver collapsed, breaking the power of the silver-mining oligarchy. Fortunately for Bolivia, this collapse coincided with a growing global demand for **tin**, a formerly unimportant by-product of the country's silver mines. A tin boom ensued, centred on the Oruro mines and led by a new class of Bolivian entrepreneurs who replaced the traditional silver-mining barons.

The new tin-mining elite and the growing urban professional classes of La Paz (the main service centre for the tin mines) increasingly backed the **Partido Liberal**. Frustrated by the impossibility of taking power through peaceful means – election results were always rigged – they moved to overthrow the conservative regime. In 1898 a revolt broke out after the conservative government in Sucre rejected the demands of liberals in La Paz for local federalist rule, while a major Aymara uprising erupted simultaneously in the Altiplano. Breaking the traditional rules of elite politics, the liberal leader **José Manuel Pando** sought an alliance with the Aymara rebel leader **Pablo Zárate Willka**, promising to protect indigenous lands in exchange for support against the conservatives. With the help of thousands of Aymaras, Pando defeated the conservatives in bloody fighting in 1899 and took power in what became known as the **Federal Revolution**. No sooner was this achieved, however, than Pando reneged on his promises and turned against his Aymara allies, crushing the uprising and executing or imprisoning its leaders. Nor did Pando's federalism last: once in power, the liberals simply made La Paz the seat of an equally centralized government (though Sucre remained the capital in name).

The Federal Revolution ensured the political supremacy of the new tin-mining elite, who chose to rule indirectly through a class of professional politicians, a

| **1899** | **1904** | **1922** |
|---|---|---|
| La Paz becomes the capital city following the Federal Revolution. | Bolivia officially cedes the coastline it lost during the War of the Pacific to Chile. | Trade unions launch a general strike as workers – especially miners – demand better conditions. |

system known as **La Rosca** (The Screw). Their dominance was such that, between 1899 and 1920, there was not a single coup attempt. In other respects, however, politics remained much the same: voting was restricted to a small elite, with the indigenous majority completely excluded; a liberal economic policy with low taxes was maintained; and the assault on indigenous landholdings continued.

Perhaps surprisingly, given that there were no restrictions on foreign investment in the mines, tin mining in the Altiplano during the late 1800s and early 1900s came to be dominated by home-grown capitalists, above all by three tin barons – **Simón I. Patiño**, **Mauricio Hochschild** and **Carlos Aramayo** – who between them owned most of Bolivia's mines. But when world demand for tin slumped in 1913–14, opposition within the Partido Liberal grew, leading to the formation of a splinter **Partido Republicano**. In 1920 the Republicans, led by **Daniel Salamanca** and **Bautista Saavedra**, seized power. Their new government quickly found itself under pressure, however: a major Aymara uprising erupted on the Altiplano, while the mostly indigenous miners had begun to organize trade unions to push for better conditions. The first **general strike** was staged in 1922, and a year later the army carried out the first of many massacres of striking miners at the Uncía mine near Oruro.

As the 1920s progressed, the increasingly factional Republicans faced economic decline and growing social unrest. The international price of tin fell, and the government found it difficult to make payments on its huge foreign loans. Tin production peaked in 1929, and then plummeted as the **Great Depression** struck Bolivia's economy with a vengeance. Massive job losses further fuelled labour unrest, while strikes and military intervention at the mines became ever more frequent.

## The Chaco War

By 1931 the government, led by Daniel Salamanca, was confronted by widespread opposition and deepening **economic crisis**; it responded by stepping up its oppression of trade unions and the opposition and increasing its military spending. At the same time, the Bolivian army began aggressively probing the disputed frontier with Paraguay in the Chaco: by July 1932, the **Chaco War** had broken out. Though many Bolivians afterwards came to believe the conflict had been provoked by foreign oil companies anxious to exploit deposits in the Chaco (which later turned out not to exist), it's now clear Salamanca himself deliberately started the war, perhaps thinking that a quick victory would improve his political standing.

Over the next two years the Bolivian army was smashed and driven out of all the disputed territory with terrible loss of life. Late in 1934 the army forced Salamanca to resign; early the next year **Major Germán Busch** ended the Paraguayan advance, and both sides sued for peace. Some 65,000 Bolivian soldiers had died out of a population of around two million. Known as the "**Chaco Generation**", many Bolivians emerged from the war deeply critical of the traditional political system. The country became increasingly open to radical left-wing ideas, and the old political parties faded in importance.

In 1936 a group of young officers, led by David Toro and Germán Busch, seized power, establishing a radical "**military socialist**" regime influenced by European fascism. In an unprecedented step, the next year the government nationalized the holdings of **US Standard Oil**, which had illegally sold Bolivian oil to Paraguay during the war while

**1929**

**1932–35**

Tin production peaks, and then collapses as Bolivia's economy is hit by the Great Recession.

Bolivia fights the disastrous Chaco War and loses to Paraguay, at the cost of some 65,000 soldiers.

claiming it couldn't produce enough for Bolivia. In alliance with a range of left-wing parties, the military regime drew up a new constitution, but its radical initiatives ended in 1939 when Busch committed suicide. A more conservative military regime close to the tin barons followed, but the growth of radical ideas in the postwar period meant that any return to the prewar consensus was impossible.

## The road to revolution

The most important of the many new political parties that emerged in the period following the Chaco War was the **Movimiento Nacionalista Revolucionario** (MNR), which had a pro-Nazi stance and advocated nationalization of the mines. Together with several left-wing groups, it quickly came to dominate the national congress. Meanwhile, the union movement was also growing more extreme, and began to stage frequent strikes – many of which were brutally put down.

In 1943, in alliance with a cabal of radical army officers, the MNR seized power. The new regime, with **Major Gualberto Villaroel** as president, supported the labour movement and sought to involve the indigenous masses in national politics. In 1944 mineworkers formed the **Federación Sindical de Trabajadores Mineros de Bolivia** (FSTMB; Federated Union of Mineworkers of Bolivia), which took over leadership of the labour movement and gave important support to the MNR: over the following decades it proved one of the most powerful political forces in the country. In 1945 the government sponsored the first **National Indigenous Congress** and banned the hated labour service obligation required of indigenous communities on hacienda lands (though this decree was never enforced). These populist measures, however, were accompanied by the vicious suppression of any opposition – when the Marxist **Partido de la Izquierda Revolucionaria** did well in elections in 1944, the government assassinated its leaders; the same happened to the traditional parties in 1945. The use of violence against politicians outraged public opinion, and in 1946 Villaroel was hanged by a civilian mob, while the army stood by.

For the next six years Bolivia was ruled by an **alliance** of the traditional parties, which struggled to cope with growing popular unrest and an economic downturn. During this period the MNR re-created itself as a radical populist party linked to the labour movement. In 1949, it launched a major civilian revolt; though crushed by the army, this revolt moved the MNR closer to the FSTMB, which had adopted communism. Though its leaders remained in exile, in 1951 the MNR won the general elections outright, only for the army to intervene, making the party believe that a **popular armed uprising** was the only way it would return to power.

## The National Revolution

The uprising that the MNR had been hoping for – the **National Revolution** – began in La Paz on April 9, 1952. MNR activists distributed arms to civilians, and miners marched on the city and stopped army reinforcements from reaching it. After three days of fighting in which over six hundred people died, the army surrendered, and the MNR's leader, **Víctor Paz Estenssoro**, took power. However, by arming the general population and involving the workers, the MNR effectively found itself committed to a massive social

| 1935–51 | 1952 | 1964 |
| --- | --- | --- |
| New political parties – including the radical MNR – and a powerful mining union emerge. | The National Revolution ushers the MNR into power. A massive social and economic reform programme follows. | A coup ends civilian rule and results in successive repressive military governments. |

change far beyond its original programme. The first step was the introduction of **universal suffrage**. This was followed by a drastic reduction in the size of the army. In addition, the government supported the organization of a powerful national workers' confederation, the **Central Obrera Boliviana** (COB), which was controlled by the influential miners' union. The COB, which represented the MNR's most important support base, immediately pressed for further revolutionary measures. In October, the government nationalized the holdings of the three big mining companies of Patiño, Aramayo and Hochschild, bringing two-thirds of the tin-mining industry under state control. The mines were managed by a new state mining company, **COMIBOL**, which, like the mines, was to be partly administered by the workers themselves. Despite these measures, the MNR was wary of offending the US by appearing communist, and so promised compensation to the tin barons and left medium-sized mines in private hands.

In the countryside, events quickly spiralled out of the government's control. With no army or police to restrain them, the indigenous campesinos began violently taking over haciendas. Though it had never been part of their policy, the MNR was forced to issue a radical **Reforma Agraria** (agrarian reform), under which hacienda lands were given back to indigenous peasants to be managed collectively – the resulting federations emerged as a powerful force, and have played a major political role ever since.

With the support of the newly enfranchised peasants and workers, the MNR easily won subsequent elections in 1956, with **Hernán Siles** taking over as president from **Paz Estenssoro**. But with the economy in crisis, the MNR leadership shied away from further revolutionary measures and turned to the US for financial aid, which was given – in return demanding open access for US oil corporations, an end to workers' control of the mines, a wage freeze, and limits on government expenditure and action.

These harsh measures stabilized the economy to a degree and helped attract foreign investment, while **US loans** were used to build an extensive road system, invest in health and education and drive development in the Santa Cruz region – all key aims of moderates within the MNR. Despite this, a bitter factional rift opened within the party, with Siles and the trade unions eventually driven into opposition. To counterbalance this, Paz Estenssoro began rebuilding and rearming the army in an attempt to shift the balance of military power away from the workers' militias. This quickly proved a terrible mistake. In 1964, Paz Estenssoro was elected for a third term with an army officer, **General René Barrientos**, as vice-president. Within a month, a military junta led by Barrientos had turned on Paz Estenssoro and ousted him from power.

## Military rule

At first it was thought that the **coup** would be only a temporary break from civilian rule, but the army remained in government for the next eighteen years. Barrientos immediately moved against the left: the leaders of workers' organizations were sent into exile, wages were slashed and thousands of miners sacked; the army also occupied the mining camps to crush strike action, resulting in a major massacre at the Siglo XX-Catavi mine in 1967. A charismatic orator and fluent Quechua-speaker, Barrientos simultaneously maintained the support of the **peasant federations** (who, having secured their rights to land, had become relatively conservative) by promising not to reverse the Agrarian Reform in return for their continuing loyalty. This relationship

| 1967 | 1974 | 1983 |
|------|------|------|
| Che Guevara is killed by US-trained Bolivian soldiers in La Higuera. | The army slaughters protesting peasants in the Cochabamba Valley, an event that becomes known as the "Massacre del Valle". | Hernán Siles is elected as president, marking a return to civilian rule. |

underlay the failure of **Che Guevara**'s attempt to launch a continent-wide guerrilla war in Bolivia, which was crushed in 1967.

Barrientos remained in control until his death in a helicopter crash three years later. After a brief civilian interregnum he was replaced by **General Alfredo Ovando**, who was ousted just over a year later by **General Juan José Torres**. Torres sought to move military government to the left, but was ousted within a year by right-wing army colleagues backed by the US. This brought to power **Colonel Hugo Banzer**, whose regime lasted for the next seven years. Initially, Banzer ruled in coalition, before seizing absolute power, after which he banned all political parties and established an entirely military regime. In this he was clearly influenced by similar events in Chile and Brazil. Banzer employed ruthless violence to enforce his rule, including torture, mass detention without trial and the murder of hundreds of political opponents.

## Banzer and the boom times

Banzer's regime coincided with unprecedented economic growth, fuelled by a long-term rise in mining production and mineral prices. Foreign investment poured into the privately owned mining sector and also into the **Santa Cruz region**, where vast areas of land remained concentrated in private hands. The region's subsequent agricultural boom, plus the exploitation of local oil and gas deposits, produced massive economic growth in the eastern lowlands, transforming Santa Cruz itself into the country's second-biggest city.

Despite the economic success and the regime's brutality, Banzer was unable to prevent opposition to his rule. Although he maintained land grants under the Agrarian Reform, Banzer alienated the peasant federations by ignoring their demands for price controls, credit and government assistance. In 1974 the army machine-gunned protesting peasants in the Cochabamba Valley, the **Massacre del Valle**. Meanwhile, the labour movement regained its strength and launched a series of strikes. Even Banzer's traditional middle-class nationalist support was eroded by his failure to negotiate a Bolivian outlet to the sea with his Chilean counterpart General Pinochet. Under pressure from the US, Banzer promised to hold democratic elections, but popular discontent was by now boiling over, and in 1977, amid widening protests and strikes, Banzer prepared to step down.

## Coups and corruption

The next four years saw dramatic political turmoil. In 1978 elections were held then annulled after massive fraud by Banzer's chosen successor, **General Juan Pereda**, who was set to lose to a left–centre alliance led by Hernán Siles. Pereda seized power, but was then overthrown by younger officers who promised fresh elections with no military candidate. Two elections, two brief presidencies (including that of **Lidia Gueiler**, the first woman president) and a further bloody coup followed, as new political groupings formed and attempted to gain electoral majorities. Finally, in elections in 1980, the centre-left coalition led by Hernán Siles emerged victorious.

Before Siles could take office, however, hardline officers launched yet another military coup, bringing to power **General Luis Garcia Meza**. Backed by a fearsome conspiracy involving the Argentine military, the Italian fascist lodge P-2, drug barons and Nazi war criminals (including Klaus Barbie, the "Butcher of Lyon"), Garcia Meza presided over the most brutal and **corrupt** military regime in modern Bolivian history, enforced by paramilitary death squads and funded by his government's direct involvement in the

| 1985 | Mid-1980s | 1993 |
|---|---|---|
| The New Economic Plan, a series of neo-liberal shock policies, is introduced. | The cocaine trade helps to ease Bolivia out of recession, as well as fuelling massive corruption. | The government starts a broad wave of privatization of key industries, including oil and gas. |

emerging international cocaine trade. But, despite its repressive measures, the extent of popular hatred against the military government, together with growing economic chaos and international disapproval, was such that it could not survive long.

## The return to democracy

Garcia Meza was deposed in an army revolt in 1981 and two years later the last military junta was forced to resign following massive protests. The recalled congress elected **Hernán Siles** as president, marking a return to **democratic rule** that has lasted ever since. Siles, however, was unable to control the economy, which had entered a sharp decline after years of mismanagement. With **hyperinflation** rampant, he stepped down in 1985. The largest share of the vote in the subsequent election was won by **Hugo Banzer**, standing as head of a new right-wing party, the ADN (Alianza Democratic Nacional). This wasn't enough to secure him the presidency, however: instead, 77-year-old **Víctor Paz Estenssoro**, the central figure of the National Revolution 33 years before, was elected for his fourth presidential term.

To great surprise, Paz Estenssoro turned his back on the traditional MNR approach and adopted the **New Economic Plan** – a raft of orthodox liberal shock policies designed to combat hyperinflation. The currency was devalued, price and wage controls scrapped, and government expenditure slashed, while steps were taken to dismantle the state mining corporation **COMIBOL**. Strikes and protests by the miners' union followed, until in 1985 the international price of tin crashed completely and the state-run industry effectively collapsed. The government sacked most of the miners and the power of their union was broken irrevocably.

The New Economic Plan was maintained by subsequent governments. Although it succeeded in ending hyperinflation, it also plunged Bolivia into a recession that was eased only by a growing trade in **cocaine**. The huge wealth generated by the cocaine industry created enormous corruption at every level of Bolivian society, with all the major political parties forging links with drug traffickers.

Elections in 1989 saw the MNR win a majority of votes, but horse trading in the congress led to the third-placed candidate, MIR leader **Jaime Paz Zamora**, becoming president with the backing of the ADN. Dubbed the Patriotic Accord, this cynical alliance between two former enemies shocked many Bolivians, although it also highlighted the growing consensus between the main parties. In 1993 the MNR returned to power under **Gonzalo Sánchez de Lozada**, known popularly as Goni. He oversaw a programme of privatization, which saw oil, gas, mining, railways and utilities sold to foreign companies – a reversal of the MNR's revolution in the 1950s. Goni was followed as president in 1997 by **Hugo Banzer** – the former military dictator returning to power through electoral means – who pursued the same neo-liberal agenda. But while the leaders of Bolivia's main political parties were agreed on the direction of the country's development, new political forces were making themselves heard.

## A new revolution

Under pressure from the US, Banzer made the **eradication of coca production** a key policy – a particular irony, given the known links of most of his government to drug

| 1997 | 2000 | 2003 |
|---|---|---|
| Coca eradication programme provokes resistance from campesino movements led by Evo Morales. | The sale of Cochabamba's water company into foreign ownership provokes a spontaneous non-violent popular uprising, the Guerra del Agua (Water War). | The country is paralyzed by public protests, forcing de Lozada to flee the country. |

## THE COCAINE ECONOMY

Starting in the 1970s in response to rising demand for **cocaine** in the US, highland migrants in the Yungas and in the Chapare had begun growing **coca**, which was then processed in secret laboratories in the Beni and flown to Colombia and on to the US. By the 1980s, coca was a boom industry, generating good incomes for the peasant growers (whose numbers were swelled by thousands of laid-off miners after 1985) and huge fortunes for the traffickers. Much of the money made was reinvested in legitimate businesses in **Santa Cruz**, fuelling economic growth in the eastern lowlands – at the peak of the boom, cocaine exports were estimated to exceed all Bolivia's legal exports combined, and at one stage the leading Bolivian cocaine baron, **Roberto Suárez**, even offered to pay off the entire national debt in return for immunity from prosecution.

traffickers. However, sending the army in to destroy coca crops in the Chapare provoked massive resistance from well-organized campesino syndicates, led by the radical indigenous activist **Evo Morales**. Meanwhile, on the Altiplano, a new generation of radical leaders was using the powerful national peasants' union, the **CSUTCB**, to press for the complete transformation of Bolivian society to meet the needs of the indigenous majority. And in Cochabamba in 2000, the sale of the city's water company into foreign ownership provoked a spontaneous non-violent popular uprising that became known as the **Guerra del Agua** – "the Water War".

Banzer responded to this rising tide of popular discontent by sending in the troops. Unrest continued to escalate when Goni returned as president in 2002, after a narrow election victory over Morales. Peasants, miners and civic groups united around the demand for the re-nationalization of Bolivia's massive **natural gas** reserves, by now the mainstay of the economy. The widespread belief was that, as with silver and tin, Bolivia's richest natural resource was being exported unrefined with little benefit to the majority population. Tumultuous protests paralyzed the country, with the people of El Alto playing a key role in cutting off La Paz. After armed forces failed to quell the unrest, Goni fled into exile in 2003, leaving his vice-president, **Carlos Mesa**, to manage the crisis. Mesa held a referendum on the gas issue but refused to implement full nationalization and was himself forced to resign after mass demonstrations in 2005.

### Bolivia's first indigenous president

In the 2005 elections Bolivia's indigenous population finally asserted its political weight. **Evo Morales** – head of the coca growers' union and leader of the Movement towards Socialism (MAS) – was elected president, becoming the first indigenous head of state since the Spanish conquest. Brought up in a humble adobe home by Aymara parents in Oruro province, Morales worked as a llama herder and sugar-cane cutter before moving to farm coca in the Chapare, where his career as an activist began.

As president, he immediately pursued what he called a **revolutionary agenda**, inspired by both socialism and indigenous dreams of a return to a more egalitarian society that existed before the Spanish conquest. The gas industry was nationalized, and a massive programme of agrarian reform was launched to redistribute land. **Indigenous languages** were taught at schools, and made obligatory for civil servants, and a new assembly was elected to rewrite Bolivia's constitution to better reflect the aspirations of the indigenous majority. Determined to end the US influence in the region, Morales

| **2005** | **2008** | **2009** |
|---|---|---|
| Morales is elected as South America's first indigenous president. | After winning two referendums, Morales continues his radical programme designed to benefit the indigenous majority. | Morales is re-elected for a second term. |

cultivated links with Fidel Castro in Cuba and Hugo Chávez in Venezuela. But despite the excitement, Evo – as everyone calls him – still faced huge challenges in governing Bolivia, not least bitter opposition to his **nationalization programme** among the powerful business elite in Santa Cruz.

Despite this, he retained widespread support among indigenous and working-class Bolivians. In 2008 he won two **referendums** – one over whether he should stay in power, another over constitutional reform – and the following year was re-elected as president (with 64 percent of the vote). He later nationalized energy-generating firms and extended the state pension to millions of poor Bolivians. But **coca** – and the crop's link to the international drug trade – remained a contentious issue. The government scrapped legislation in 2010 that would have aimed to cut cocaine production following protests from coca growers, and in 2011 renounced the UN Convention on Narcotic Drugs because it classified coca as an illegal drug. However, in 2013, after a successful bout of international lobbying, Bolivia was readmitted to the convention, which gave a special dispensation recognizing that the chewing of coca leaves was legal in the country.

In 2013 the Constitutional Court ruled that Morales could run for a third term in office. With the country posting some of the highest economic growth rates in the region, it was little surprise that the incumbent won the **October 2014 election**, with sixty percent of the vote. However, after decades of growth, falling global commodity prices soon ended Bolivia's mini economic boom. This was compounded by controversy over the president's private life, allegations of corruptions and cronyism, and unease about the increasing reliance on Chinese investment. In February 2016 Morales lost a **referendum** – by just 160,000 votes – that would have allowed him to stand for a fourth term as president. Later in the year there were widespread strikes, protests and blockades by miners over industry reforms. These resulted in violent clashes with the police, and several miners were killed.

A bad situation deteriorated further in August, when deputy interior minister **Rodolfo Illanes** was beaten to death after travelling to the town of Panduro to mediate with miners. Morales accused Carlos Mamani, president of the National Federation of Mining Cooperatives, of the murder, which he described as a "conspiracy" to overthrow him. As the year drew to a close, with the country suffering its **worst drought in 25 years**, MAS unanimously approved Morales as the party's candidate for the 2019 presidential elections, studiously ignoring the February referendum result. Early 2017 brought further controversy over the opening of a state-of-the-art US$7 million museum – officially the Museum of the Democratic and Cultural Revolution, unofficially the "Evo Museum" – in the president's birthplace, the small town of Orinoca.

With old problems of poverty and underdevelopment, a precarious global economy, and the growing impact of climate change, protests and political instability seem likely to remain a fixture of life in Bolivia for some time to come.

| 2010 | 2013 | 2016 |
| --- | --- | --- |
| Four major electricity companies are nationalized. | The Constitutional Court rules Morales can run for a third term in 2014, which he wins. | Amid widespread protests, Morales announces he will run for a fourth term, despite having lost a referendum on the issue earlier in the year. |

# Wildlife and ecology

From the high peaks of the Andes to the tropical rainforests of the Amazon, the Pantanal wetlands and the arid scrub of the Gran Chaco, Bolivia's extraordinary range of geography and climates supports an astonishing array of plant and animal life. This is one of the most biodiverse countries on earth, home to more than 17,000 known plant species, around 1400 different birds, including many species found nowhere else, and around three hundred species of mammals. Moreover, large areas are still relatively undisturbed by human activity, and around twenty percent of the total land area is now covered by national parks and other protected areas.

## The Andes

The Bolivian Andes are home to a huge range of ecological zones, from cactus-strewn semi-desert to swampy moorland and lush cloudforest. Much of the region has been settled for over two thousand years, and the original woodland has largely been replaced by eucalyptus imported from Australia. But patches of native Andean forest remain, including **queñua (polylepis) woods** that survive at over 5000m – the highest forests in the world. The most visible animals in the Andes are domesticated, in particular the herds of **llama** and **alpaca** which graze the arid grasslands of the Altiplano, but in more remote regions their wild relative, the diminutive **vicuña**, can also be seen.

Large predators are rare, but the **puma** is still present at most altitudes. Its preferred prey includes Andean deer and **viscacha**, a rabbit-like animal. The more humid eastern slopes of the Andes are also home to the elusive **spectacled bear**, the only bear in South America. Though difficult to view close up, the revered **Andean condor** – with a 3m wingspan, the largest bird that can fly – can often be seen soaring at high altitudes (at the opposite end of the scale, there are also 83 species of **hummingbird**). The margins of Lake Titicaca and other high-altitude lakes and marshes attract a great variety of swimming and wading birds, including ibis, grebes, geese, herons and – particularly in the far south of the Altiplano – three different species of **flamingo**, the Andean, Chilean and James.

## The Amazon

The greatest biodiversity in Bolivia – and indeed pretty much anywhere on earth – is found on the well-watered eastern slopes of the Andes, where the mountains plunge down into the Amazon basin through a succession of different ecological zones, from the high **cloudforest** or *ceja de selva* – whose gnarled trees are festooned with hundreds of different kinds of **orchid** – to the lowland tropical rainforest. With mighty trees soaring to create a canopy over 30m above the ground, the rich and luxuriant vegetation of the **Amazon rainforest** is in fact extremely fragile. The soils beneath the forest are generally very poor, and the forest ecosystem flourishes only through a complex system of nutrient cycling involving plants, insects and fungi, so if the forest is cleared, the quality of the land deteriorates rapidly.

The rainforest ecosystem supports an incredible variety of plant and animal life: over six thousand species of plant have been recorded in one small tract of forest, and the Amazon's unidentified species of insect alone are thought to outnumber all earth's known animal species. Seeing wildlife in the Amazon is not easy; nevertheless, on any rainforest trip you're likely to spot innumerable **birds** including brightly coloured toucans, parrots, tanagers, kingfishers, trogons and macaws of various kinds. Several of Bolivia's more than thirty **monkey** species are also easy to see, including long-limbed spider monkeys, howler monkeys, chattering squirrel monkeys and diminutive tamarinds and titis. Larger mammals include the **capybara**, the world's largest **rodent**; the **tapir**, a lumbering beast the size of a cow with an elephant-like nose; herds of **peccary**, a kind of wild boar; as well as **giant armadillos** and **sloths**. All of these are potential prey for a range of wild cats, the largest of which is the **jaguar**. The rivers of the Bolivian Amazon teem with fish, from giant catfish to the **piranha**. You'll also see **turtles** and **cayman crocodiles** of various kinds, as well as **giant anacondas** and **pink freshwater dolphins**.

Many of the larger animals are easier to see as you head east through the Bolivian Amazon, where the dense rainforest gives way to the more open vegetation of the **Llanos de Moxos**, where seasonally flooded grasslands are interspersed with islands of forest and patches of swamp. Here, you're more likely to spot creatures such as **giant anteaters** and **rheas** (large flightless birds similar to ostriches), or even **maned wolves**.

## The eastern lowlands

To the south of the Bolivian Amazon the forest ecology gradually changes as it adapts to lower and more seasonally varied rainfall. The **Chiquitania** region east of Santa Cruz has some of the world's largest remaining tracts of **tropical dry forest**, home to many of the same animal species, plus a great variety of bird life. Heading further south, this forest gets drier still as it merges into the Gran Chaco. This vast, arid wilderness also supports abundant wildlife, including **jaguar**, **puma**, **deer**, at least ten different kinds of **armadillo**, and even an endemic species of wild boar, the **Chacoan peccary**.

The contrast between the Chaco and the far east of Bolivia could not be greater. Here, the plains and rainforests of Amazonia gradually give way to the immense watery wilderness of the **Pantanal**, the world's largest wetland ecosystem, which stretches far across the border with Brazil and is home to many Amazonian species. Though it does not match the overall biodiversity of the rainforest, the Pantanal is unique in terms of the sheer abundance of wildlife. Concentrations of fauna here are thought to be the highest in all the Americas, comparable to the densest wild animal populations in Africa – one estimate puts the number of **caymans** in the region at ten million. It's also one of the best places to see **jaguars** and the highly endangered **giant river otter**. Bird life too is extraordinarily abundant, including innumerable water birds such as **roseate spoonbills**, **herons**, **egrets** and the massive **jaburu stork**, the symbol of the Pantanal, and at least fifteen species of parrot, including the highly endangered **hyacinth macaw**.

# Music and dance

Bolivia's music is vibrant and varied. Much of it has a similar flavour to that of neighbouring Andean countries, evidence of the continuity of musical traditions among the indigenous peoples of the Andes, and there's a wealth of popular music connected with the various festivals that dot the year, or to key events in the agricultural calendar. Inevitably, much of this music is inextricably involved with dance: if you're lucky you might see the unforgettable sight of a squad of young women *comparsas* swirling their *pollera* skirts, with *manta* shawls around their shoulders and bowler hats on their heads.

## Andean instruments and traditions

The persistence of Bolivia's **agricultural traditions** means that musical life in most rural areas has enjoyed enormous continuity, and traditional music, bearing a direct relationship to that played in pre-Inca times, still thrives today at every kind of **celebration** and **ritual**. Because all the country's musical traditions are oral and bound to local events, music varies from one village to another – all over the Andes, villages have different ways of making and tuning instruments and composing tunes.

Many of Bolivia's distinctive **musical instruments** date back to pre-Hispanic times. Perhaps the most haunting and memorable are the breathy-sounding handmade sets of bamboo panpipes and quena flutes that are played across the Altiplano. In addition, other pre-conquest Andean instruments – conch shell trumpets, shakers, ocarinas, wind instruments and drums -- are still used by groups all over the country.

### Panpipes and quenas

**Panpipes** (*siku* in Aymara, *antara* in Quechua and *zampoña* in Spanish) are ancient instruments. While modern panpipes – played in the city or in groups with other instruments – may offer a complete scale, allowing solo performance, traditional models are played in pairs, as described by sixteenth-century Spanish chroniclers. The pipes share the melody, each playing alternate notes of the scale, so that two or more players are needed to pick out a single tune using a **hocket technique**. Usually one player leads and the other follows. Symbolically this demonstrates reciprocity and exchange within the community; in practice it enables players to play for a long time without getting too dizzy from over-breathing.

Played by blowing (or breathing out hard) across the top of a tube, panpipes come in various sizes. Several tubes made of **bamboo reed** of different lengths are bound together to produce a sound that can be jaunty, but also has a melancholic edge depending on tune and playing style. Many tunes have a minor, descending shape to them, and panpipe players traditionally favour dense overlapping textures and **syncopated rhythms**. Playing is often described as "breathy", as overblowing to produce harmonics is popular (modern city-based groups often evoke this breathiness using special microphone techniques).

Simple **notched-end flutes**, or **quenas** (which do not have a proper mouthpiece to blow through, just a cut in the open bamboo end), are another characteristic Andean instrument found in both rural and urban areas. The most important pre-Hispanic instrument, quenas were traditionally made of fragile bamboo and played in the dry season, with **tarkas** (stocky vertical flutes, like a shrill recorder made from the wood of a taco tree) taking over in the wet season. Another small Andean flute with a span of three octaves is called the **pinquillo**, also made of bamboo. The **moseño** is a long thin bamboo flute probably modelled on the European transverse flute and played from the side.

## Charangos

The **charango** is another characteristic Andean instrument. This small, indigenous variant of the lute or mandolin was created in Bolivia in imitation of early string instruments brought by the Spanish colonizers, which indigenous musicians were taught to play in the churches. Its characteristically zingy sound was the result of the natural Andean preference for high pitches, and because its size was restricted by the fact that it was traditionally made from the shell of an **armadillo** (although modern charangos are now generally made of wood). There are many varieties of charango: from flat-backed instruments with strident metal strings to larger instruments with round backs that are capable of deeper and richer sounds. The charango usually has five pairs of strings, though tunings vary from place to place and from musician to musician. The charango may have acquired its name from the Quechua word *ch'ajranku*, from the verb *ch'ajray*, meaning to scratch, since in early colonial times indigenous Bolivians used to refer to the way Spanish musicians played their plucked instruments as *sumaj ch'ajranku*, meaning "rich scratch".

The charango is used to play a host of different types of music and dances. In many rural areas different instruments are played in different seasons: the charango is usually played during the **winter** months of June and July, when its shrill sound is thought to attract the frosts essential for freezing potatoes to make *chuño*; those in small towns and urban areas often play it all year round. In some areas, different tunings and melodies are used for different seasons.

## Fiestas

Major fiestas and other significant social events call for musical performance on a more extended scale, including large **marching bands** of brass instruments, drums or panpipes. The drums are deep-sounding, double-headed instruments known as *bombos* or *wankaras*, originally made out of the hollowed-out trunk of a tree with the skins of a llama or goat. These marching bands exist for parades at fiestas, weddings and dances in the Altiplano and around Lake Titicaca. It is perfectly normal for a whole village to come together to play as an orchestra for important events and fiestas – music is an integral part of all communal celebrations and symbolically represents the sharing and interdependence of Andean rural life.

---

### CHARANGOS, COURTSHIP AND MERMAIDS

In rural areas, particularly around Lake Titicaca, the charango is used by young, **single men** to woo the female of their choice. They are helped, at least according to local beliefs, by **mermaids** (*las sirenas*). Ethnomusicologist Tom Turino records that most towns and villages around Titicaca claim that a mermaid lives in a nearby spring, river, lake or waterfall, and notes that new charangos are often left overnight in such places to be tuned and played by the mermaid. Some villagers even construct the **sound box** in the shape of a mermaid to invest their charango with supernatural power.

When young men go courting at the weekly markets in larger villages they not only dress in their finest clothes, but also decorate their charangos in elaborate **coloured ribbons** – these represent the number of women their charango has supposedly conquered. At times a group of young people will get together for the ancient **circle dance** called the *Punchay kashwa* where the men form a semicircle playing their charangos, facing a semicircle of young women. Both groups dance and sing in bantering fashion, participants using a set syllabic and rhyming pattern so that they can quickly improvise.

## Andean fusion music

The political events of the 1950s and 1960s are crucial to an understanding of recent Bolivian folk music and the development of Andean fusion music. The **1952 Revolution** led to a period of social and economic reform that accorded more rights to Bolivia's indigenous inhabitants; such reforms conferred new respect on Andean traditions, and were enthusiastically supported by many Latin American intellectuals. At the same time, rural people migrated to urban areas, bringing their languages and traditions with them. The new Bolivian administration created a folklore division in the **Ministry of Education**, one of whose functions was the organization and sponsorship of traditional music festivals. Radio stations started to broadcast in **Aymara** and **Quechua** and play the music of these communities.

### Los Jairas

Around 1965, an influential new form of Andean music emerged with **Los Jairas**, founded by Edgar "Yayo" Jofré. Jofré established the group to play at the Peña Naira in La Paz – one of a string of new urban venues where people could hear what became known as *música folklorica*. The idea was to form a **quartet** of charango, guitar, quena and *bombo*, instruments that had never been played together before. The quartet adapted Aymara and Quechua tunes and restructured Andean melodies to suit an urban and European aesthetic. In addition, the group's quena player, the Swiss–French flautist **Gilbert Favre**, brought to his playing approaches learnt for the European flute, including the use of vibrato, dynamics and swooping glissandi, all of which were completely novel to the traditional Amerindian aesthetics. It was this style that became standard for urban folk music groups.

Numerous groups have followed the Los Jairas model. While some continue to deliver inspired arrangements of traditional tunes, others play **foreign music** on traditional instruments. There are also those who use both instruments and music as the basis for new compositions. As a result, the same tune can appear in different guises under different titles in various styles.

### Los K'jarkas

**Los K'jarkas**, from Cochabamba, are one of the country's most influential and successful groups. In common with other Bolivian bands, they retain a strong sense of national identity: "K'jarkas" refers to a pre-Spanish fortress, while the group's **logo** – a stylized anthropomorphic condor and carving from the archeological site of Tiwanaku – appeals to a pre-Columbian past and millenary culture at the heart of the Andes. Astute composition and arrangements, which take into account the multiple audiences within Bolivia itself, earned Los K'jarkas an enormous following in the late 1960s, which has carried through to the present day.

Los K'jarkas songs are largely sentimental, conjuring up a bucolic vision of beautiful maidens, alongside evocations of **Pachamama** (Mother Earth). Where they score at home is in large part due to their incorporation of traditional urban dance forms. They mainly use the **huayño** dance, but also employ the hugely popular **sayas**, which originated with African slaves brought to Bolivia. *Sayas* are especially popular during fiestas, when they're usually played by the brass bands, as well as *música folklorica* groups.

### Canto nuevo

The sound of Andean panpipes and quenas was also at the heart of early Chilean **nueva canción** through groups like Los Curacas, Inti Illimani and Quilapayún. Influenced by Los Jairas and the work of Chilean folklorist and composer Violeta Parra, they adopted Andean instruments and music in the 1960s and 1970s, adding extra Latin percussion, guitars and other instruments. The move neatly combined music and politics: the Andean roots asserting collective values and an unmistakable ancient indigenous identity. Their styles fed back to Bolivia, where they were adapted into an even richer

## CLASSIC ALBUMS

**Emma Junaro** *Canta a Matilde Casazola "Mi corazón en la ciudad".* Junaro's beautiful voice here brings to life the mestizo songs of the great poetess, singer, guitarist and painter, Matilde Casazola.

**Los K'jarkas** *Canto a la mujer de mi pueblo.* This classic K'jarkas album, an idealistic tribute to Bolivian women, contains the song *Llorando se fue* ("In tears, she left"), which later become the Brazilian *lambada*.

**Los K'jarkas** *El Amor y La Libertad.* Another set of beautiful songs sung in the rich style of this group who epitomize modern folkloric styles.

**Kallawaya** *Shaman (Medicine Man).* A magnificent album with superb ensemble performances of the group's own compositions, which draw on styles and traditions from the whole of the Americas.

**Mallku de los Andes** *On the Wings of the Condor.* One of the most popular Andean albums ever, with the engaging sound of its panpipes and charangos smoothly arranged.

**Rumillajta** *Hoja de coca.* Beautifully produced and arranged album of Bolivian music displaying a full range of styles and delivered by a fine group of musicians.

**Various** *Bolivia Calendar Music of the Central Valley.* Contemporary recordings of music dating back to pre-Columbian times, including music for panpipes, flutes and drums used for Quechua rituals and ceremonies.

**Various** *Charangos et guitarillas du Norte Portosí.* Spirited local recordings from north Potosí department of songs in Quechua.

**Various** *Peru and Bolivia, The Sounds of Evolving Traditions: Central Andean Music and Festivals.* Lively and accessible introduction to more modern sounds from both Peru and Bolivia.

**Various** *The Rough Guide to the Music of the Andes.* A vigorous and broad range of Andean music, including tracks by Los K'jarkas and Emma Junaro.

blend of harmonized singing, with alternating solo and chorus patterns. In Bolivia, *nueva canción* was subsequently reinterpreted as **canto nuevo**: top exponents include **Emma Junaro** and **Matilde Casazola**.

# Modern music and dance

**Salsa**, **cumbia**, **merengue** and **reggaeton** have come down from Central America and the Caribbean to enjoy great popularity among young Bolivians, who are now making tropical hybrids with their own dance genres. Likewise, **samba** has come over from Brazil. **Hip-hop** is increasingly popular too, and a vibrant scene has sprung up in El Alto in particular, where groups like Ukamau y Ké, Wayna Rap and Nueva Flavah rap in a mix of Aymara, Spanish, Quechua and English.

Many older dances still remain popular, including the **huayño**, which involves swirling partners and can be done processionally, like European country dances. Other dances include *taquiraris, tarqueada, sayas, chovena* and *machetero*, all of which come from ancient rituals influenced by Spanish tradition. Spanish and European folk and ballroom traditions spawned popular couple dances that still endure, including the **waltz** and the **cueca**, which imitates the amorous adventures and conquest of a farmyard cock and hen, with complex choreographic figures and footwork.

Jan Fairley

With thanks to Gilka Wara Céspedes in Bolivia and Henry Stobart in the UK

# Books

There are few books published exclusively about Bolivia, and even fewer Bolivian writers ever make it into English. That said, the works listed below offer a good range of background material on Bolivian history, culture, society and the natural world. If you read Spanish, Bolivian novelists to look out for include Alcides Arguedas, Oscar Cerruto, Renato Prada Oropeza and Juan Recacochea. Titles marked ★ are especially recommended.

## HISTORY AND SOCIETY

★**Jon Lee Anderson** *Che Guevara: a Revolutionary Life*. Absorbing and exhaustively researched account of Latin America's most famous guerrilla, by the journalist whose investigations led to the discovery of Che's secret grave in Vallegrande.

**Domitila Barrios de Chungara** *Let Me Speak*. Harrowing autobiographical testimony of one of the miners' wives who took part in the hunger strikes that brought an end to the Banzer regime.

**Brian S. Bauer and Charles Stanish** *Ritual and Pilgrimage in the Ancient Andes: The Islands of the Sun and the Moon*. Richly detailed description of the archeology of Lake Titicaca's two sacred islands and their roles as major pilgrimage centres in the Inca and pre-Inca worlds.

**John Crabtree** *Patterns of Protest: Politics and Social Movements in Bolivia*. A concise description of the tumultuous political movements that helped to bring Evo Morales to power.

**James Dunkerley** *Rebellion in the Veins: Political Struggle in Bolivia 1952–82*. Dense but readable academic account of the 1952 National Revolution, and of the bitter cycles of dictatorship, repression and popular resistance that followed.

★**Eduardo Galeano** *Open Veins of Latin America: Five Centuries of the Pillage of a Continent*. A stunning history of the continent by the esteemed Uruguayan author, which offers, in particular, an excellent insight into the colonial exploitation of the Potosí mines.

**Pete Good** *Bolivia: Between a Rock and a Hard Place*. Readable account of Bolivian history that is particularly good on the rise of Evo Morales and the impact of globalization.

**Claire Hargreaves** *Snowfields: The War on Cocaine in the Andes*. Detailed journalistic account from the front line of the war on drugs during the coca boom of the 1980s.

**Olivia Harris** *To Make the Earth Bear Fruit: Ethnographic Essays on Fertility, Work and Gender in Highland Bolivia*. Collection of ethnographic essays exploring the culture and everyday lives of the deeply traditional *ayllus* of the northern Potosí department.

**Kevin Healy** *Llamas, Weavings and Organic Chocolate: Multicultural Grassroots Development in the Andes and Amazon of Bolivia*. Intriguing portrait of nine different rural development projects – including one that led to the renaissance of traditional weaving techniques in Sucre – that have used imaginative and culturally appropriate approaches to tackle poverty in Bolivia.

**John Hemming** *The Conquest of the Incas*. The authoritative account of the Spanish conquest, combining academic attention to detail and excellent use of contemporary sources with a compelling narrative style.

★**Herbert S. Klein** *Bolivia, the Evolution of a Multi-Ethnic Society*. The best English-language history of Bolivia from the arrival of early man to the present day: concise, detailed and clearly written, if a little dry.

**Alan Kolata** *Valley of the Spirits: a Journey into the Lost Realm of the Aymara*. Lively account of the rise and fall of Tiwanaku by the archeologist who has done most to reveal its secrets.

**Charles C. Mann** *1491: The Americas Before Columbus*. Groundbreaking exploration of pre-Columbian Latin America that reveals the sophistication and influence of the Tiwanaku and Moxos cultures. His follow-up, *1493: How Europe's Discovery of the Americas Revolutionized Trade, Ecology and Life on Earth*, is equally good, with an eye-opening account of Potosí during the silver rush among the highlights.

**Anne Meadows** *Digging Up Butch and Sundance*. Engaging tale of an adventurous quest to solve the mystery of what really happened to the infamous North American outlaws – were they really killed by police in Bolivia and buried in the bleak mining camp of San Vicente?

**June Nash** *We Eat the Mines and the Mines Eat Us*. Fascinating and sensitive anthropological study of the daily lives of the miners of Potosí and the deeply rooted customs and beliefs that help them survive tremendous hardships.

**Leo Spitzer** *Hotel Bolivia: The Culture of Memory in a Refuge from Nazism*. Thoughtful account of the little-known history of the thousands of Jews who fled to Bolivia with the rise of the Nazis in Europe, forming a refugee community that never felt quite at home, and which has since largely migrated to Israel.

★**Steve J. Stern (ed)** *Resistance, Rebellion, and Consciousness in the Andean Peasant World*. Absorbing collection of richly detailed historical essays on Quechua and Aymara insurrections and uprisings, ranging from the Great Rebellion of the late eighteenth century to the radical peasant politics of today.

**Chris Taylor** *The Beautiful Game: A Journey through Latin American Football*. Entertaining account of the history of the continent's sporting obsession. The chapter on Bolivia focuses on the country's struggle to defend its right to play international fixtures at high altitude, and a Santa Cruz football academy that turns street kids into major stars.

## TRAVEL

**Yossi Brain** *Trekking in Bolivia: A Traveller's Guide*. Specialist trekking guide covering a good range of routes throughout Bolivia, with clear descriptions, sketch maps and useful background information and advice.

**Yossi Brain** *Bolivia: A Climbing Guide*. A must for all serious climbers visiting Bolivia, with expert route descriptions and excellent logistical advice and information by the man who was the leading climbing guide in the country.

**Mark Cramer** *Culture Shock! Bolivia*. Light-hearted and sometimes witty introduction to Bolivian culture, customs and etiquette from a US expatriate living in La Paz.

**Percy Harrison Fawcett** *Exploration Fawcett*. Rip-roaring account of the adventures of the eccentric British explorer who surveyed the borders of Bolivia at the height of the rubber boom in the early twentieth century. The book was published posthumously after the author disappeared looking for the mysterious civilization that he believed lay hidden somewhere deep in the Amazon.

**Yossi Ginsberg** *Jungle: A Harrowing True Story of Survival*. First-hand account by the only survivor of a disastrous expedition by three young travellers who tried to reach Rurrenabaque overland through the forests of the Alto Madidi – this is the book that launched Rurrenabaque as a backpacker destination. A Hollywood film adaption is in the pipeline.

★**Richard Gott** *Land Without Evil: Utopian Journeys in the South American Watershed*. Wonderful account of a journey through the former Jesuit mission towns of Brazil and eastern Bolivia, interspersed with finely researched histories of the many fruitless journeys and forgotten expeditions across the same region made by travellers through the centuries.

**David Grann** *The Lost City of Z: A Tale of Deadly Obsession in the Amazon*. A fascinating account of gentleman explorer Percy Fawcett, who set off in the 1920s in search of the mythical kingdom of Z; although set mainly in Brazil, Bolivia also features.

**Ernesto "Che" Guevara** *Bolivian Diary*. Published posthumously, the iconic Argentine revolutionary's description of his disastrous attempt to launch a continent-wide guerrilla war from the backwoods of Bolivia reads like the chronicle of a death foretold.

**Ernesto "Che" Guevara** *The Motorcycle Diaries*. Amusing account of Che's motorcycle trip through South America in the 1950s, providing an intimate portrait of a young beatnik traveller and romantic idealist undergoing some of the experiences – particularly in revolutionary Bolivia – that would later transform him into a ruthless guerrilla leader.

**Michael Jacobs** *Ghost Train through the Andes: On My Grandfather's Trail in Chile and Bolivia*. This book retraces the steps of the author's father as a British railway engineer in Bolivia in the nineteenth century, uncovering an extra-ordinary love story.

**Vivien Lougheed** *Understanding Bolivia: A Traveller's History*. An entertaining and wide-ranging account of Bolivia's history and culture, with vignettes on some of the colourful characters who have passed through the country, including Butch Cassidy and Che Guevara.

**Rusty Young** *Marching Powder*. Hilarious and terrifying account of a small-time English cocaine smuggler's experiences locked up in La Paz's notorious San Pedro prison.

## WILDLIFE AND THE ENVIRONMENT

**Michael Bright** *Andes to Amazon: A Guide to Wild South America*. Good general introduction to the astonishing range of ecosystems and wildlife in South America, lavishly illustrated with colour photographs.

**L. H. Emmons** *Neotropical Rainforest Mammals: A Field Guide*. Authoritative descriptions and beautiful illustrations of over two hundred species, ideal for identifying animals in the wild.

**Susannah Hecht and Alexander Cockburn** *The Fate of the Forest: Developers, Destroyers and Defenders of the Amazon*. Comprehensive, highly readable account of the threat to the Amazon rainforest, with detailed description of the political and social conflicts that underlie the destruction of the rainforest.

**Sebastian Herzog (ed)** *Birds of Bolivia Field Guide*. Comprehensive guide to the 1425 bird species in the country (the sixth-highest tally in the world), compiled by researchers at Louisiana State University and Bolivian ornithologists.

**John Kricher** *A Neotropical Companion*. Enjoyable general introduction to the flora, fauna and ecology of the tropical lowlands of South and Central America, well written and packed with detail.

**Norman Myers** *The Primary Source: Tropical Forests and our Future*. Compelling account by a leading expert of the world's most diverse and complex ecosystem, the manifold ways in which humans benefit from it, and the dangers arising from its destruction.

**Martin de la Pena** *Illustrated Checklist: Birds of Southern South America and Antarctica*. Comprehensive field guide with over a thousand bird species. This is the serious birdwatcher's best bet, given the lack of a Bolivia-specific bird book.

**Gaia Vince** *Adventures in the Anthropocene*. An award-winning look at humanity's impact on the natural world, blending science, reportage and travel writing. Although the focus is global, there are some fascinating sections on Bolivia, notably on the foundation of and ongoing challenges to Parque Nacional Madidi.

## FICTION

**Rosario Santos (ed)** *The Fat Man from La Paz*. A rare English-language collection of Bolivian short stories, featuring some of the country's best-known authors. The title tale, by Gonzalo Lema, is about a Raymond Chandler-esque detective.

# Spanish

Although Spanish is the main language of government and commerce, nearly sixty percent of Bolivians speak one or more of the country's thirty or so indigenous languages as their mother tongue, and over ten percent speak no Spanish at all. English and some other European languages are spoken in tourist centres and well-to-do hotels and agencies, but otherwise you'll need to know a bit of Spanish to get around and conduct day-to-day business.

The most widely spoken indigenous language is **Quechua**, the language of the Inca Empire, spoken above all in the highlands of Cochabamba, Potosí and Chuquisaca, followed by **Aymara**, which is spoken mainly in the Altiplano. Most of the country's other thirty languages are spoken by minority groups in the Amazon and the Eastern Lowlands, ranging in size from tens of thousands to just a few hundred speakers. As well as Spanish, Quechua, A22ymara and **Guaraní** (the most commonly spoken lowland language) are all official languages, and since Evo Morales became Bolivia's first indigenous president in 2006, they are used much more frequently in the corridors of power, with all civil servants required to speak at least one indigenous language. Unless you're trekking in particularly remote regions, you're unlikely to come across communities where you can't get by with Spanish, although learning just a few phrases of Quechua or Aymara is a good way of making a favourable impression.

If you already speak Spanish you'll have little trouble adjusting to the way the language is spoken in Bolivia, which pretty much conforms to standard textbook **Castellano**, spoken without the lisped "c" and "z". That said, it does, of course, have its own idiomatic peculiarities, one of which is the tendency to add the ending *-ito* or *-cito* to words. Technically this is a diminutive, but in fact asking for a **cervezita** won't get you a smaller beer; it's more often used to express familiarity and affection, and failing to add it onto the ends of words can seem abrupt or impolite among the indigenous peoples of the highlands. Bolivian Spanish is also peppered with indigenous expressions, particularly **Quechua** and **Aymara** words such as *wawa* (baby), *pampa* (plain) and *soroche* (altitude sickness); the indigenous languages also influence the somewhat unorthodox grammar and sentence structure used by many highland Bolivians when speaking Spanish. Bolivian Spanish also readily borrows from **English**, resulting in a slew of words which are regarded with horror by the Spanish themselves, such as *chequear* (to check), *parquear* (to park), *rentar* (to rent), *mitín* (meeting) and *líder* (leader); this tendency is particularly evident in mining regions where a host of nineteenth-century English technical terms is still in use.

The fact that Spanish is a second language for most Bolivians means that they're generally patient with foreigners' attempts to speak the language and not too precious about the finer points of grammar. The slow, clear pronunciation of Bolivian Spanish (in the highlands, at least) also makes it a good place to learn Spanish, and a number of Spanish (and Quechua and Aymara) language schools catering to foreign travellers have now opened in La Paz, Cochabamba and Sucre. In the Eastern Lowlands around Santa Cruz, Spanish is spoken with a much more relaxed, tropical drawl in which consonants often disappear at the end of words: thus "*arroz con pescado*", for example, becomes "*arro' con pe'ca'o*". Here, the diminutive *-ingo* is used instead of *-ito*.

On the following pages we've listed a few essential words and phrases, though if you're travelling for any length of time a dictionary or phrasebook is obviously a worthwhile investment. If you're using a **dictionary**, bear in mind that in Spanish CH, LL, and Ñ count as separate letters and are listed after the Cs, Ls, and Ns respectively.

## PRONUNCIATION

The rules of Spanish **pronunciation** are pretty straightforward and, once you get to know them, strictly observed. Unless there's an accent, words ending in d, l, r and z are **stressed** on the last syllable, all others on the second last. All **vowels** are pure and short.

**a** somewhere between the "a" sound of back and that of father.

**e** as in get.

**i** as in police.

**o** as in hot.

**u** as in rule.

**c** is soft before E and I, hard otherwise: cerca is pronounced "serka".

**g** works the same way, a guttural "h" sound (like the ch in loch) before E or I, a hard G elsewhere: gigante becomes "higante".

**h** is always silent.

**j** is the same sound as a guttural G: jamón is pronounced "hamon".

**ll** sounds like an English Y: llama is pronounced "yama".

**n** is as in English unless it has a tilde over it, as with mañana, when it's pronounced like the "n" in onion or menu.

**qu** is pronounced like an English "K".

**r** is rolled, RR doubly so.

**v** sounds more like B, vino becoming "beano".

**x** is slightly softer than in English, sometimes almost SH except between vowels in place names where it has an "H" sound: for example México (Meh-hee-ko).

**z** is the same as a soft "C", so cerveza becomes "servesa".

## WORDS AND PHRASES

### BASICS

| | |
|---|---|
| **Yes, No** | Sí, No |
| **Please, Thank you** | Por favor, Gracias |
| **Where, When** | Dónde, Cuando |
| **What, How much/many** | Qué, Cuanto |
| **Here, There** | Aquí, Allí |
| **This, That** | Este, Eso |
| **Now, Later** | Ahora, Más tarde |
| **Open, Closed** | Abierto/a, Cerrado/a |
| **With, Without** | Con, Sin |
| **Good, Bad** | Buen o/a, Mal o/a |
| **Big** | Gran(de) |
| **Small** | Pequeño/a, Chico/a |
| **More, Less** | Más, Menos |
| **Today, Tomorrow** | Hoy, Mañana |
| **Yesterday** | Ayer |

### GREETINGS AND RESPONSES

| | |
|---|---|
| **Hello, Goodbye** | Hola, Adiós |
| **Good morning** | Buenos dias |
| **Good afternoon/night** | Buenas tardes/noches |
| **See you later** | Hasta luego |
| **Sorry** | Lo siento/discúlpeme |
| **Excuse me** | Con permiso/perdón |
| **How are you?** | ¿Como está (usted)? |
| **I (don't) understand** | (No) Entiendo |
| **Not at all/You're welcome** | De nada |
| **Do you speak English?** | ¿Habla (usted) inglés? |
| **I don't speak Spanish** | (No) Hablo español |
| **My name is ...** | Me llamo ... |
| **What's your name?** | ¿Como se llama usted? |
| **I am English** | Soy inglés/a |
| **...American** | ...americano/a |
| **...Australian** | ...australiano/a |
| **...Canadian** | ...canadiense/a |
| **...Irish** | ...irlandés/a |
| **...Scottish** | ...escosés/a |
| **...Welsh** | ...galés/a |
| **...New Zealander** | ...neozelandés/a |

### HOTELS AND RESTAURANTS

| | |
|---|---|
| **Twin room** | Una habitación doble |
| **Room with double bed** | Una habitación matrimonial |
| **Single room** | Una habitación sencilla/ simple |
| **Private bathroom** | Baño privado |
| **Shared bathroom** | Baño compartido |
| **Hot water (all day)** | Agua caliente (todo el día) |
| **Cold water** | Agua fría |
| **Fan** | Ventilador |
| **Air-conditioned** | Aire-acondicionado |
| **Tax** | Impuesto |
| **Mosquito net** | mosquitero |
| **Key** | Llave |
| **Check-out time** | Hora de salida |
| **Do you know...?** | ¿Sabe...? |
| **I don't know** | No sé |
| **There is (is there)?** | (¿)Hay(?) |
| **Give me...** | Deme... |
| **(one like that)** | (uno así) |
| **Do you have...?** | ¿Tiene ...? |
| **...a room** | ...una habitación |
| **...with two beds/ double bed** | ...con dos camas/ cama matrimonial |
| **It's for one person (two people)** | es para una persona (dos personas) |
| **...for one night** | ...para una noche |

| (one week) | (una semana) |
| --- | --- |
| It's fine, how much is it? | ¿Está bien, cuánto es? |
| It's too expensive | Es demasiado caro |
| Don't you have anything cheaper? | ¿No tiene algo más barato? |
| Can one…? | ¿Se puede…? |
| …camp (near) here? | ¿…acampar aqui (cerca)? |
| Is there a hotel nearby? | ¿Hay un hotel aquí cerca? |
| I want | Quiero |
| I'd like | Querría |
| What is there to eat? | ¿Qué hay para comer? |
| What's that? | ¿Qué es eso? |
| What's this called in Spanish? | ¿Como se llama este en español? |

## DIRECTIONS AND TRANSPORT

| Bus terminal | Terminal terrestre, Terminal de buses |
| --- | --- |
| Bus | Bus, flota, movilidad |
| Ticket | Pasaje |
| Seat | Asiento |
| Luggage | Equipaje |
| How do I get to…? | ¿Como se llega a…? |
| Left, right, straight on | Izquierda, derecha, derecho |
| Where is…? | ¿Dondé está…? |
| …the bus station | …el terminal de buses |
| …the train station | …la estación de ferrocarriles |
| …the nearest bank | …el banco más-cercano |
| …the post office | …el correo |
| …the toilet | …el baño |
| Where does the bus to …leave from? | ¿De dónde sale el bus para…? |
| What time does the bus leave? | ¿A qué hora sale el bus? |
| What time does the bus arrive? | ¿A qué hora llega el bus? |
| How long does the journey take? | ¿Cuánto tiempo demora el viaje? |
| Is this the train for …? | ¿Es éste el tren para …? |
| I'd like a (return) ticket to… | Querría pasaje (de ida y vuelta) para… |

## NUMBERS AND DAYS

| | |
| --- | --- |
| 1 | un/uno/una |
| 2 | dos |
| 3 | tres |
| 4 | cuatro |
| 5 | cinco |
| 6 | seis |
| 7 | siete |
| 8 | ocho |
| 9 | nueve |
| 10 | diez |
| 11 | once |
| 12 | doce |
| 13 | trece |
| 14 | catorce |
| 15 | quince |
| 16 | dieciséis |
| 20 | veinte |
| 21 | veitiuno |
| 30 | treinta |
| 40 | cuarenta |
| 50 | cincuenta |
| 60 | sesenta |
| 70 | setenta |
| 80 | ochenta |
| 90 | noventa |
| 100 | cien(to) |
| 101 | ciento uno |
| 200 | doscientos |
| 500 | quinientos |
| 1000 | mil |
| 2000 | dos mil |
| first | primero/a |
| second | segundo/a |
| third | tercero/a |
| Monday | lunes |
| Tuesday | martes |
| Wednesday | miércoles |
| Thursday | jueves |
| Friday | viernes |
| Saturday | sábado |
| Sunday | domingo |

## FOOD AND DRINK

### BASICS

| Aceite | Oil | Comida típica | Traditional food |
| --- | --- | --- | --- |
| Ají | Chilli | Cuchara | Spoon |
| Ajo | Garlic | Cuchillo | Knife |
| Almuerzo | (Set) lunch | La cuenta | The bill |
| Arroz | Rice | Desayuno | Breakfast |
| Azúcar | Sugar | Ensalada | Salad |
| La carta | Menu | Galletas | Biscuits |
| Cena | (Set) dinner | Harina | Flour |
| | | Hielo | Ice |

| | | | |
|---|---|---|---|
| Huevos | Eggs | Majadito | Fried rice with charque, eggs and plantain |
| Llajua | Chilli sauce | | |
| Mantequilla | Butter | Milanesa | Breaded escalope |
| Mermelada | Jam | Parillada | Barbecued meat |
| Miel de Abeja | Honey | Pato | Duck |
| Mostaza | Mustard | Pavo | Turkey |
| Pan (integral) | (Wholemeal) bread | Pique a lo macho | Bite-sized pieces of beef with potatoes in a spicy sauce |
| Pimienta negra | Black pepper | | |
| Plato | Dish | | |
| Queso | Cheese | Plato paceño | A plate of corn, beans, potato and fried cheese, usually with meat too |
| Sal | Salt | | |
| Salsa | Sauce | | |
| Tenedor | Fork | Pejerrey | Kingfish |
| Vegetariano | Vegetarian | Pollo (a la brasa) | (Spit-roasted) chicken |
| | | Riñon | Kidney |

### COOKING TERMS

| | | | |
|---|---|---|---|
| A la parilla | Barbecued | Sopa de maní | Meat, bean and peanut soup |
| A la plancha | Griddled | | |
| Ahumado | Smoked | Surubí | Catfish |
| Al ajillo | In garlic | Tocino | Bacon |
| Al horno | Oven baked | Trucha | Trout |
| Asado | Roast | | |
| Crudo | Raw | | |

### VEGETABLES (*VERDURAS*)

| | | | |
|---|---|---|---|
| Duro | Hard boiled | Arvejas | Peas |
| Frío | Cold | Camote | Sweet potato |
| Frito | Fried | Castaña | Brazil nut |
| Picante | Spicy | Cebolla | Onion |
| Relleno | Stuffed | Champiñon | Mushroom |
| Revuelto | Scrambled | Choclo | Corn on the cob |
| Sancochado | Boiled | Espinaca | Spinach |
| | | Frijoles | Beans |
| | | Habas | Broad beans |

### SOUP (*SOPA*), MEAT (*CARNE*), POULTRY (*AVES*) AND FISH (*PESCADO*)

| | | | |
|---|---|---|---|
| | | Lechuga | Lettuce |
| | | Locoto | Chilli pepper |
| Anticuchos | Skewered heart | Maíz | Maize/corn |
| Atún | Tuna (tinned) | Maní | Peanut |
| Bistec | Steak | Palmito | Palm heart |
| Cangrejo | Crab | Palta | Avocado |
| Carne de cerdo/chanco | Pork | Papa | Potato |
| Carne de res | Beef | Tomate | Tomato |
| Chairo | Hearty meat soup | Yuca | Cassava/manioc |
| Charque | Dried meat (usually llama) | Zanahoria | Carrot |
| Chicharron | Deep-fried pork | Zapallo | Pumpkin |
| Chicharron de Pollo | Deep-fried chicken | | |

### FRUIT (*FRUTAS*)

| | | | |
|---|---|---|---|
| Chuleta | T-bone steak | Banano/Guineo/Plátano | Banana (the latter is also plantain) |
| Chuleta de Cerdo | Pork chop | | |
| Churrasco | Minute steak | Carambola | Star fruit |
| Conejo | Rabbit | Chirimoya | Custard apple |
| Cordero | Mutton | Durazno | Peach |
| Hamburguesa | Hamburger | Frutilla | Strawberry |
| Higado | Liver | Limón | Lemon |
| Jamón | Ham | Mandarina | Mandarin |
| Lechón | Roast pork | Mango | Mango |
| Lomo | Filet steak | | |

| | |
|---|---|
| Manzana | Apple |
| Maracuyá | Passionfruit |
| Naranja | Orange |
| Papaya | Papaya |
| Piña | Pineapple |
| Toronja/pomelo | Grapefruit |
| Tuna | Prickly pear |
| Uvas | Grapes |

## SNACKS

| | |
|---|---|
| Choripán | Hot dog |
| Cuñapes | Cassava and cheese pastry |
| Empanada | Cheese or meat pasty |
| Humitas | Maize, cheese and raisin porridge wrapped in leaves |
| Papas fritas | Potato chips/French fries |
| Salchipapa | Sliced-up sausage and French fries |
| Salteña | Juicy meat, chicken and vegetable pasty |
| Tostados | Toast |
| Tucumana | Fried meat and vegetable pasty |

## DESSERTS (*POSTRES*)

| | |
|---|---|
| Arroz con leche | Rice pudding |
| Ensalada de frutas | Fruit salad |
| Flan | Crème caramel |
| Gelatina | Jelly |
| Helado | Ice cream |
| Torta | Cake |

## DRINKS (*BEBIDAS*)

| | |
|---|---|
| Agua | Water |
| Agua hervida | Boiled water |
| Agua mineral (con gas/sin gas) | Mineral water (fizzy/still) |
| Api | Hot, thick, sweet maize drink |
| Café | Coffee |
| Café con leche | White coffee |
| Cerveza | Beer |
| Chicha | Fermented maize beer |
| Chocolate | Hot chocolate |
| Chopp | Draught beer |
| Chufflay | Singani and Sprite |
| Jugo (de naranja) | Orange juice |
| Limonada | (Real) lemonade |
| Leche | Milk |
| Mate | Herbal tea |
| Mate de coca | Coca tea |
| Mate de manzanilla | Camomile tea |
| Refresco | Soft drink |
| Té | Tea |

## GLOSSARY

**Achachila/Apu** Powerful mountain gods or spirits believed to inhabit high Andean peaks

**Aguas termales** Thermal baths, hot springs

**Apacheta** Stone cairn marking mountain passes, created by travellers carrying stones on the climb up as penance and as an offering to the mountain gods

**Artesanía** Traditional handicrafts

**Ayllu** Andean extended kinship group, roughly equivalent to a clan or tribe

**Barrio** Neighbourhood, quarter or suburb

**Cabaña** Cabin

**Calle** Street

**Camba** Old Inca term for lowland tribes, now used as slang term for people from the Eastern Lowlands

**Camion** Lorry

**Camioneta** Pick-up truck

**Campesino** Peasant: literally, from the countryside

**Canoa** Dugout canoe

**Caudillo** Chief, military strongman

**Chaco** Cultivated clearing in the forest, also the verb for creating such clearings through slash and burn

**Challa** Ritual offering of alcohol and sweets to the mountain spirits, often carried out as a blessing for a new house or car

**cholet** A colourful mansion, decorated in bright "Neo-Andean" style

**Cholo** Mixed race or urbanized indigenous person

**Colla** Ancient Aymara nation, now a slang term for people from the Altiplano

**Cordillera** Mountain range

**Criollo** "Creole": used historically to refer to a person of Spanish blood born in the American colonies

**Curandero** Healer

**ENTEL** Bolivia's national telephone company

**Gringo** Originally someone from the United States, now a non-derogatory term used for all white foreigners

**Guardaparque** Park guard

**Hacienda** Large private farm or estate

**Huaca** Sacred place or object

**Indígena** Used adjectivally to mean "indigenous", or as a noun to refer to an indigenous person

**Junta** A ruling council; usually used to describe small groups who've staged a coup d'état

**Kuraka** Indigenous nobleman in the colonial era

**Lejía** Alkaline reagent used when chewing coca

**Mestizo** Person of mixed Spanish and indigenous blood

**Mirador** Viewpoint

**Nevado** Snowcapped mountain

**Pampa** Plain

**Peña** Nightclub where live folk music is performed

**Plata** Silver; slang for money

**Puna** High-altitude grassland, starting around 3000m

**Quebrada** Ravine, dried-out stream

**Salar** Saltpan or lake

**Selva** Jungle or tropical rainforest

**S/n** Used in addresses to indicate "sin número", or without a number

**Soroche** Altitude sickness

**Tinku** Andean ritual combat

**Tranca** Police roadblock

**Wiphala** Rainbow-chequered flag used as a symbol of indigenous Andean identity

# Small print and index

## A ROUGH GUIDE TO ROUGH GUIDES

Published in 1982, the first Rough Guide – to Greece – was a student scheme that became a publishing phenomenon. Mark Ellingham, a recent graduate in English from Bristol University, had been travelling in Greece the previous summer and couldn't find the right guidebook. With a small group of friends he wrote his own guide, combining a contemporary, journalistic style with a thoroughly practical approach to travellers' needs.

The immediate success of the book spawned a series that rapidly covered dozens of destinations. And, in addition to impecunious backpackers, Rough Guides soon acquired a much broader readership that relished the guides' wit and inquisitiveness as much as their enthusiastic, critical approach and value-for-money ethos. These days, Rough Guides include recommendations from budget to luxury and cover more than 120 destinations around the globe, from Amsterdam to Zanzibar, all regularly updated by our team of roaming writers.

Browse all our latest guides, read inspirational features and book your trip at **roughguides.com**.

## Rough Guide credits

**Editors**: Alice Park and Claire Saunders
**Layout**: Ankur Guha
**Cartography**: Animesh Pathak
**Picture editor**: Michelle Bhatia
**Proofreader**: Jan McCann
**Managing editor**: Edward Aves
**Assistant editor**: Payal Sharotri

**Production**: Jimmy Lao
**Cover photo research**: Nicole Newman
**Editorial assistant**: Aimee White
**Senior DTP coordinator**: Dan May
**Programme manager**: Gareth Lowe
**Publishing director**: Georgina Dee

## Publishing information

This fifth edition published February 2018 by
**Rough Guides Ltd**,
80 Strand, London WC2R 0RL
11, Community Centre, Panchsheel Park,
New Delhi 110017, India
**Distributed by Penguin Random House**
Penguin Books Ltd, 80 Strand, London WC2R 0RL
Penguin Group (USA), 345 Hudson Street, NY 10014, USA
Penguin Group (Australia), 250 Camberwell Road,
Camberwell, Victoria 3124, Australia
Penguin Group (NZ), 67 Apollo Drive, Mairangi Bay,
Auckland 1310, New Zealand
Penguin Group (South Africa), Block D, Rosebank Office
Park, 181 Jan Smuts Avenue, Parktown North, Gauteng,
South Africa 2193
Rough Guides is represented in Canada by DK Canada, 320
Front Street West, Suite 1400, Toronto, Ontario M5V 3B6
Printed in Singapore
© Rough Guides 2018
Maps © Rough Guides

## Help us update

We've gone to a lot of effort to ensure that the fifth edition
of **The Rough Guide to Bolivia** is accurate and up-to-date.
However, things change – places get "discovered", opening
hours are notoriously fickle, restaurants and rooms raise
prices or lower standards. If you feel we've got it wrong
or left something out, we'd like to know, and if you can
remember the address, the price, the hours, the phone
number, so much the better.

Please send your comments with the subject line
"**Rough Guide Bolivia Update**" to mail@uk.roughguides.
com. We'll credit all contributions and send a copy of the
next edition (or any other Rough Guide if you prefer) for
the very best emails.

## Acknowledgements

**Daniel Jacobs**: My colleagues Shafik Meghji, Claire
Saunders and Alice Park (who are always a pleasure to
work with); Eduardo Zeballos, Claudio Vera Loza and
Mauricio Vera Loza at Grupo Rosario; Derren Patterson
at Gravity Bolivia and Jeff Sandifort at Climbing South
America; Remo Baptista and Claudia Arteaga and Leticia
Sandi at Adventure Brew; Jasmin Caballero and Teresa
Flores at America Tours Bolivia; Ani at the *Green House*
in Oruro; Koala Tours & Koala Café in Potosí; Alex Cruz
Mamani and David Mamani Chambi at Vertical Bolivia
in Uyuni; Fabiola Mitru at the *Hotel Mitru* in Tupiza; Ana
Gabriela Sánchez in Villazón; Fatima Belmonte at *Café
Bistrot* in Copacabana.

**Shafik Meghji**: Many thanks to all the travellers and locals
who helped out along the way. A special *muchas gracias*
to: Alice Park for her sterling editing work; co-author
Daniel Jacobs; Edward Aves at RG HQ; Kati Taylor; Janette
Simbron; everyone at Chalalán Ecolodge; Lyliam Gonzalez;
Miriam and Efrem Hinojosa; Gabriela Aranibar and
Stephen Taranto; Frank Reinkens; Daniela Röthlisberger;
Sylvain Truchot; Jean, Nizar and Nina Meghji; and Sioned
Jones.

## ABOUT THE AUTHORS

**Daniel Jacobs**, from London, has co-authored Rough Guides to Morocco, Egypt, India, Mexico, Kenya, Brazil and Colombia.

**Shafik Meghji** An award-winning travel writer, journalist and broadcaster, Shafik Meghji first visited Bolivia in 2004 and has returned regularly ever since. He has co-authored/updated over 30 Rough Guides, and writes for print and digital publications around the world, including *The Guardian* and BBC Travel. Shafik is a member of the British Guild of Travel Writers and a fellow of the Royal Geographical Society. ⓦshafikmeghji.com. Twitter: @ShafikMeghji.

## Readers' updates

Thanks to all the readers who have taken the time to write in with comments and suggestions (and apologies if we've inadvertently omitted or misspelt anyone's name):

Dave Bain; Eric Dafoe; Charlotte De Beule; Ken Burton; Nikki Frick; Ery and Makka Hughes; Bryan Kingsfield; Marine Ladner; Tim Laslevic; Marc and Mich; Erika Massoud; Nicholas Mcphee (Nick's Adventures Bolivia);

Emma Maev O'Connell; Koos Reitsma;  Matthias Rempel; Monique Robillard; Olivier Schalbetter; Adam Scherling; Tiffany Woods-Shepherd.

## Photo credits

All photos © Rough Guides, except the following:
(Key: t-top; c-centre; b-bottom; l-left; r-right)

**1 Alamy Stock Photo**: Lucas Vallecillos
**2 4Corners**: Ben Pipe
**4 Getty Images**: Art Wolfe
**5 Alamy Stock Photo**: Pep Roig
**9 AWL Images**: Peter Adams (b). **Corbis**: Carlos Cazalis (tl).
**Robert Harding Picture Library**: Pete Oxford (tr)
**11 Getty Images**: Jamie Marshall / Tribaleye Images (t); Aizar Raldes (b)
**12 Photolibrary** : M&G Therin-Weise
**13 Corbis**: Ocean (b). **SuperStock**: Photononstop (t)
**14 Corbis**: Nico Tondini / Robert Harding (c).
**Getty Images**: Neil Emmerson / Robert Harding World Imagery (b); Hemis.fr (t)
**15 AWL Images**: Ian Trower (b). **Corbis**: Theo Stroomer / Demotix (t)
**16 Corbis**: Patrick Escudero / Hemis (t); Anders Ryman (b)
**17 Alamy Stock Photo**: Jennika Argent (bl). **Alamy Stock Photo**: James Brunker (br). **Getty Images**: Aurora Creative (t)
**18 Alamy Stock Photo**: Travelscape Images (c). **Corbis**: Patrick Escudero / Hemis (b). **Getty Images**: Gallo Images (t)
**19 Axiom Photographic Agency**: Greg Von Doersten (b). **SuperStock**: Escudero Patrick (t)
**20 Fotolia**: Briseida (tl). **NHPA/Photoshot**: Nick Garbutt (tr)
**22 Alamy Stock Photo**: Age Fotostock
**50–51 AWL Images**: Hemis
**53 AWL Images**: John Coletti
**65 SuperStock**: LatitudeStock (t). **Alamy Stock Photo**: Lucas Vallecillos (b)
**73 Robert Harding Picture Library**: Cem Canbay
**96–97 Alamy Stock Photo**: Mariusz Prusaczyk
**99 Alamy Stock Photo**: Luke Peters

**107 Corbis**: Paule Seux / Hemis (t). **Getty Images**: Steve Allen (b)
**119 Alamy Stock Photo**: Joris Roulleau (t). **Dreamstime.com**: Elifranssens (bl). **Getty Images**: Carlos Sanchez Pereyra (br)
**136–137** Nicole Newman
**139 Alamy Stock Photo**: Chris Howarth / Bolivia
**153 AWL Images:** Christian Kober (b)
**155 Alamy Stock Photo**: imageBROKER (t)
**163 Corbis**: Eitan Simanor / Robert Harding World Imagery
**183 Getty Images** Gafapasta Photography (t). **Corbis**: Theo Allofs (b)
**189–190 Getty Images**: Win Initiative
**191 FLPA**: Jurgen and Christine Sohns
**197 Alamy Stock Photo**: Michael Boyny (t). **Alamy Stock Photo**: Design Pics Inc (b)
**215 Alamy Stock Photo**: David Litschel (br); Maxime Dube (bl). **SuperStock**: Hemis.fr (t)
**228–229 Corbis**: Ira Block / National Geographic Society
**231 Alamy Stock Photo**: Juergen Ritterbach
**253 AWL Images:** DanitaDelimont (t). **FLPA**: ImageBroker (bl)
**266–267 Alamy Stock Photo**: Dirk Ercken
**269 Alamy Stock Photo**: Leonid Plotkin
**279 Alamy Stock Photo**: John Warburton-Lee Photography (t). **NHPA/Photoshot:** Andre Baertschi (b)
**289 Alamy Stock Photo:** Maxime Dube
**300 Getty Images**: Aizar Raldes / AFP

**Cover:** *Yareta*, the typical fungus of Bolivian deserts
**4Corners:** Massimo Borchi

# Index

Maps are marked in grey

# Map symbols

The symbols below are used on maps throughout the book

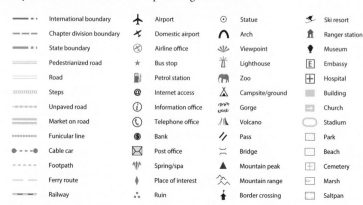

| | | | | | |
|---|---|---|---|---|---|
| International boundary | Airport | Statue | Ski resort |
| Chapter division boundary | Domestic airport | Arch | Ranger station |
| State boundary | Airline office | Viewpoint | Museum |
| Pedestrianized road | Bus stop | Lighthouse | Embassy |
| Road | Petrol station | Zoo | Hospital |
| Steps | Internet access | Campsite/ground | Building |
| Unpaved road | Information office | Gorge | Church |
| Market on road | Telephone office | Volcano | Stadium |
| Funicular line | Bank | Pass | Park |
| Cable car | Post office | Bridge | Beach |
| Footpath | Spring/spa | Mountain peak | Cemetery |
| Ferry route | Place of interest | Mountain range | Marsh |
| Railway | Ruin | Border crossing | Saltpan |

## Listings key

Accommodation

Eating

Drinking & nightlife

Shopping

Tour operator